BUYING A HOUSE

ON THE
MEDITERRANEAN

BUYING A HOUSE

ON THE

MEDITERRANEAN

Victoria Pybus

Distributed in the USA by
The Globe Pequot Press, Guilford, Connecticut

Published by Vacation Work, 9 Park End Street, Oxford
www.vacationwork.co.uk

BUYING A HOUSE ON THE MEDITERRANEAN

Editor: Victoria Pybus

First edition 2004

Copyright © 2004

ISBN 1-85458-319-0

Publicity by Charles Cutting and Roger Musker

Cover design and chapter headings by mccdesign ltd

Drawings by Mick Siddens

Typeset by Brendan Cole

Printed and bound in Italy by Legoprint SpA, Trento

CONTENTS

GIBRALTAR

GREECE

ITALY

SPAIN

TURKEY

FOREWORD

Most people are aware by now, if only from the vast media coverage given to the subject, that owning a property abroad is an option for more people than ever. The huge rises in house values in most parts of the UK have given Britons a particular advantage in being able to fund a home abroad as they can raise equity on their current home, or downsize their UK residence and use the difference to buy a home abroad in cash. The proliferation of cheap airfares to regions all over Europe has also helped to fuel the frantic rate of foreign property purchases. It has recently been estimated that by 2020, one in five members of the population aged 55+ will be foreign residents somewhere, and of these many have already bought their 'retirement home'.

Many people want to be on, or near the Mediterranean. So far the overwhelmingly popular place for coastal property is Spain, but the search for seaside property at affordable prices has led buyers to Croatia, Greece, Cyprus and Turkey as well as islands great and small including Malta and the French and Italian outposts of Corsica and Sardinia; who knows, the next edition of this book may include the littorals of the North African countries such as Libya and Tunisia. There is no exact figure for the number of Britons living abroad but one estimate puts it in the region of four million.

And it is not just Britons who are buying abroad. People from the United States, Canada and Australia are looking to Europe for a different style of living, while Germans, Dutch, Russians and Scandinavians from Northern Europe look with envy to the warmer Mediterranean climate and for property to buy there.

Of course, not everyone buys a property abroad to live in it permanently. Some might live there for the UK's or US's dismal winter months, some might use it just for family holidays, while others will buy with rental incomes and their investment portfolios in mind. Whatever your reasons for dreaming of a property on the crystal coasts of Mediterranean, this is the first book to give you the whole buying picture from around the rim of the world's most historic and beautiful sea.

Victoria Pybus
June 2004

ACKNOWLEDGMENTS

Individual country chapters in Buying a House on the Mediterranean were written by: **André de Vries** (France), **Pat Yale** (Cyprus and Turkey) and **Gordon Neale** (Italy). In addition, Guy Hobbs and Dan Boothby, were co-writers of the chapter on Spain. The remainder of the book was written by Victoria Pybus.

Grateful thanks are also due to the following: Peter Ellis of Croatia Property Services who answered countless questions on Croatia, Tara Hawkins of Croatian Villas for advice on renting out property in Croatia, David Watrous of Greek Islands Club for advice on the Greek islands, Aileen French of Thassos Property Services for her contribution on Greek conveyancing and advice on Greece, and Colleene Almeida for her contribution on conveyancing in Gibraltar.

GENERAL
INTRODUCTION

WHERE TO BUY ON THE MEDITERRANEAN

Those who bought their houses abroad twenty or thirty years ago, pre-European Union and pre the end of the communist eastern bloc, would not have had the choice of countries that anyone buying property has today. Europe has opened up in the wake of the founding of the Common Market. Even countries not yet part of the EU including Croatia and Turkey, want to be members, and are waving their friendly credentials. Croatia is due to join in 1997; Turkey's accession looks more doubtful.

Although Spain is the number one country for Mediterranean coastal properties by sheer scale of building developments, real estate on most of the Mediterranean is now accessible to foreigners and the local markets are either in the process of adapting or have adapted to their requirements. To the tried and tested real estate markets of Spain, France and Italy have been added ex-communist Croatia, and the eastern Mediterranean areas of Greece, Cyprus and Turkey. The Anglophile island of Malta also has a well developed market for foreign buyers. Turkey, has the cheapest property on the Mediterranean with prices for an apartment starting at £14,000. The most expensive area is the luxurious French Riviera including Monaco, with the trendier parts of the Italian coast running a close second. Somewhere around mid-price are Greece and its Islands, Malta and Cyprus where two-bedroomed apartments can be bought for £55,000 and ruined buildings for slightly less. Even the tiny sovereign state of Gibraltar is experiencing a property boom. Croatia, which most people expect to be cheaper than it actually is, has its own expanding millionaire's row around Dubrovnik and has experienced a big leap in property values since the end of the 1992 war, which caused the break-up of Yugoslavia and freed Croatia to build on its successful pre-war economy in tourism, which has led to a boom in prime real estate development.

The Factors Influencing Where to Buy

Budget. How much can you afford? If you are scraping the money together to buy, then you will probably choose a ruin that you can do up mostly yourself, probably in the Greek islands or in Turkey where the prices for this type of property are cheapest. Note that cheap does not mean convenient; usually it means quite the opposite: bad roads, far from the nearest airport, no mains water or electricity etc. The art of buying cheap is to see where the property market is heading and have the imagination to see how it will improve and develop and enhance the value of your property as it does so. Even if your budget is small, choose the best location you can, allowing for your circumstances.

If your income is modest but solid then Malta makes those who apply for residency very welcome and offers them generous fiscal advantages. Property on Malta is good value too and the island has many historical connections with Britain that make it simultaneously international and comfortingly familiar.

Investment Potential. If this is your primary reason in choosing where to buy, you will be looking at places where the values are rising the fastest. Currently these include Gibraltar's high-rise penthouses, and the Spanish costas del Sol and de Almeria. If you choose the location well, you will get both a sound investment and a regular income from letting out. For this you will need to look at areas with good airport and road connections, and which are by the sea, or just inland, and at properties with a swimming- pool if possible. This would rule out for instance Northern Cyprus, where property may be cheap, but title is uncertain as it is occupied territory, and its international pariah status means there are no direct flights. Gibraltar, on the other hand has an airport you can walk from to the town centre, and has access, just over the Spanish border, to fabulous golfing. Croatia and Turkey do not have many airports, but this will probably change as the countries develop.

Personal Preferences and Motivation. Many people who buy a property say that they are looking for somewhere, which has a quality of life that has all but disappeared from daily life in Britain and the US. In short they are looking for somewhere with 'old values', picturesque views and unstressed lifestyle away from clogged roads, long commutes and overcrowded urban dwelling, not to mention the dreary winter climate. These are people with a vision and they will most likely realise it on a Greek island, in a Turkish fishing village, or in any Mediterranean country, slightly inland from the coast. Most Mediterranean countries have old buildings of character waiting to be found in villages and small towns, or they have farmhouses and even cave houses waiting to be refurbished. Such people will tend to shun the areas where Britons and other northern Europeans and Americans buy and prefer instead to integrate themselves into the local population. This ultimately, is the key to making a success of where you buy, especially if your property is going to become your second, and later on, your main home.

GETTING THERE – CHEAP FLIGHTS ETC

Cheap flights are good news: for foreign homeowners wanting to let to holiday tenants all year round as well as for getting there themselves. Owners of a holiday home abroad, make an average of six visits a year to their home and some even try to fly out most weekends. There is no denying the fact that Britons buying second homes abroad have fuelled a demand for cheap flights to Europe and that they form a considerable and growing part of the clientele for Ryanair, British European, MyTravelLite, EasyJet and other no frills, bargain basement airlines in this ever changing and highly competitive bargain aviation market. British Airways has muscled in on the no frills market through its franchised operation GB Airways, which competes favourably with budget airlines on some routes. Furthermore GB Airways covers most destinations on the Mediterranean. Ryanair is likely to remain the market leader in Europe as it already has the greatest number of destinations throughout France, and some coastal destinations in Italy and Spain. The former charter airline Monarch Air has a good reputation and its scheduled European operation focuses mainly on Spain and the Balearics. For more on flights and airlines relating to individual countries see *Getting There* sections in the introductory chapter for each country.

The competitiveness, which makes budget airline prices so irresistible to the consumer, means these airlines operate on a tight margin of profitability, which causes some instability in the budget airline scene. The huge demand means that there will probably always be budget airlines and cheap fares, but the companies offering them will come and go and the destinations change frequently. The worst aspect of this for foreign property owners is that the no frills airline may withdraw its flights suddenly for a variety of reasons. In early 2004, Ryanair caused a missed heartbeat amongst the population of expats in France when it mentioned it might cut back on routes to France if they were unprofitable. This followed a ruling by the EU that the company had to pay back £2.7 million of the subsidies it received from Belgium for creating a base with lots of local jobs at Charleroi airport. Ryanair could even decide to pull out of France completely, and look for routes elsewhere in the expanding EU. Of course, this may not happen, but it shows how vulnerable the owner of a foreign home can be if the reliability of cheap flights to their area cannot be predicted. On the bright side, it seems that hardly a week goes by without one or other budget airline offering new destinations from a range of UK airports.

Apart from the main no frills and budget airlines listed below, for individual countries it is also worth contacting holiday tour operators specialising in your chosen country as they often sell flights only, and these may well be at charter prices. In any case tour operators, particularly the ones that deal with a single country or area are the experts on getting there and can at least offer advice. Just ask any travel agent to give you details of flights that go to your chosen country and then call the tour operators direct. Alternatively, search the internet and if you are comfortable enough with the net to book online, this can also reduce your flight costs (flights cost £6 to £10 more if booked by telephone). British Airways, (www.ba.com) scheduled flights may also be competitive if booked in advance or at less popular times and are also worth checking.

Below, are some useful airline contacts. For detailed information on airlines and airports serving a particular country and contact details of national carriers, see individual countries' *Getting There* sections.

Useful Contacts – No Frills/Charter Airlines

Avro plc: Wren Court, 17 London Road, Bromley, Kent BR1 1DE; ☎ 0870 458 2841; fax 020 8695 4004; www.avro-flights.co.u; e-mail reservations@avro.co.uk. Leading charter airline with flights to the Spanish costas and Balearics, Gibraltar, Greece and Turkey from most UK airports.

Bmibaby: (☎ 0870 264 2229; www.bmibaby.com no frills, tiny fares operates out of four UK regional airports to Nice in France and the Spanish Costas and the Balearics. Also operates flights between the USA and the UK.

easyJet: www.easyJet.com. France, Greece (Athens), Italy, Spain (incl Balearics). Flies from Gatwick, Stansted and several regional airports in the UK.

Excelairways.com: bills itself as a 'low cost airline with all the frills'. Flies from Gatwick, Manchester & Glasgow to 30 destinations including the Spanish costas and Balearics, Athens, Bodrum (Turkey) and various islands in Greece including Crete, Samos and Santorini. You can also book by phone on 08709 98 98 98.

First Choice Airways (formerly air2000): www.firstchoiceairways.com, the charter airline arm of The First Choice group. Has charter flights from various UK airports to Mediterranean destinations including: Antalya (Turkey), Barcelona, Cyprus, Malta and Paphos.

GB Airways: The Beehive, Beehive Ring Road, Gatwick Airport, West Sussex RH6

OLA; ☎01293-664239; fax 01293-664218; www.gbairways.com; bookings via British Airways at www.ba.com). GB Airways, the franchised subsidiary of British Airways operates scheduled flights out of Gatwick on routes that are not profitable to BA at competitive prices (e.g. from £89 return to Marseille) and covers destinations: France, Gibraltar and Spain (incl Balearics).

Ryanair: www.Ryanair.com. France, Italy (including Sardinia) and Spain.

Thomsonfly: www.thomsonfly.com. The newest budget airline launched in December 2003 and operating flights from Coventry to: Marseille and Nice (France); Ibiza, Malaga, Palma and Valencia (Spain); Naples, Pisa, Rome, Venice (Italy). Thomsonfly intends to operate from other UK airports in the future.

Useful Websites

There is a small but growing number of websites which check dozens of air travel websites including those of bargain airlines, ticket discounters and scheduled airlines to come up with the cheapest fare to your chosen destination. Some of the ones currently offering this service are:

www.lastminute.com
www.skyscanner.com
www.traveljungle.co.uk - (launched also in Germany and the USA)
www.travelsupermarket.com
www.whichbudget.com
www.openjet.com (deals only with a limited number of airlines)

Alternatively, check the sites of ticket discounters (the e-version of bucket shops) such as www.cheaptickets.com, www.cheapflights.com, www.dialaflight.com, www.majortravel.co.uk, www.opodo.co.uk and www.travelocity.com, to name but a few.

Nerds can check the punctuality statistics of every scheduled departure out of the UK at the Civil Aviation Website www.caa.co.uk.

ESTATE AGENTS

Is an Estate Agent Essential?

For most people buying a property abroad, an estate agent is the first person they are likely to deal with as they embark on a search for their ideal home. All the countries in this book have estate agents, but the main problem is finding one who speaks English. Areas where there are established numbers of foreigners such as the Greek islands of Corfu and Crete, or Malta, or Cyprus are not likely to be a problem, but if you want to go off the beaten track to look for property, you will need to find an alternative such as a local person who can make enquiries on your behalf, or interpret for you.

Finding a property without using an estate agent may seem like a good idea. Not using an estate agent means you could find a more interesting property, and you will also avoid paying an agent's commission for finding you a property. This varies from 3.5%-7%, sometimes within the same country.

There are also primarily internet estate agents, such as UK based www.property-abroad.com and www.medpropertyshop.com and the US-based www.escapeartist.com, which are useful as an introduction to what kinds of property are on offer in various countries.

Estate agents are listed in the individual countries' *Where to Find Your Ideal Home* sections.

Using Estate Agents

Discuss your property requirements with estate agents; sound them out to see if what you want is available in the area you want, or whether your ideas are unrealistic. Although the agents will want to sell properties already on their books, if they are bona fide they may well tell you honestly that you might do better by going to see their sister company or another estate agency which will be more likely to offer what you want. Giving an agency a clear idea of what you are looking for will hopefully save both you and them time and money. You don't want to end up being shown totally unsuitable properties.

Alternatively, you may engage an agent to act on your behalf and search for suitable properties for you. In these circumstances you will pay a fee for their services but they will not be tied to the propositions on offer from any one particular agent.

On the other hand discussing your requirements with an agency will also allow you to find out about what alternatives there are. You may think you want a particular kind of property but the agency may come up with other types of property or localities that you hadn't considered previously.

If an agent is showing you the wrong kind of properties let them know so that you, and they, can get back on to the right track.. Even so, Murphy's Law often dictates that the right property will turn up on the last day of your trip ('Well, there is this other property, but we didn't think it would suit you!') necessitating an extension of your trip, or a return to Spain, Cyprus etc. as rapidly as possible.

Large international companies mainly deal with the grander developments (which they may own and manage) in resort areas, rather than selling individual properties.

It is also worth bearing in mind that in some countries estate agents are not regulated, or only partly regulated. For instance to be an estate agent in France you have to have to be both qualified and licensed. In Spain, anyone can call themselves an estate agent, likewise in Croatia and Greece. Some countries have voluntary associations for estate agents and these include Spain. Greece has just recently set up its first Estate Agents Association and Turkey also has a licensing system, yet many agents are still operating independently and others have other jobs such as architect or tourist worker and being an estate agent is just a sideline.

This lack of regulation in some countries means that standards of practice vary widely. Whether you buy through a foreign or UK estate agent it is essential that the company is either licensed or if that is not applicable that you find out as much about them as possible and check satisfaction with previous clients. Any official status will be indicated on their stationery and their official licence, if they have one, should be displayed on the premises.

Estate agent's websites and advertisements can give you a rough idea of the types and prices of property dealt with by a certain agent but they will probably show only a proportion of the properties on the books. Also look in estate agents' shop windows, check out price ranges and property on offer in different parts of the country through property magazines, local English-language newspapers, the internet, but don't tie yourself immediately to one or several estate agencies before you are sure about where you are hoping to buy. It will also be far more productive for those looking for an individual property (rather than a newly-built one) to research properties (and estate agents) on the ground, in the country they have decided upon.

Inspection Trips

Some agents will arrange inspection trips where you pay for your flights and the agent shows you around properties, the local amenities and provides free or very cheap accommodation. If you are sure of the area where you wish to buy a three- or four-day visit is often adequate, though a longer trip leaves room for the unexpected to turn up

There are several caveats to heed over inspection trips laid on by estate agencies including a certain amount of pressure being bought to bear by not giving you time away from their consultants to reflect on what you intuitively feel about the properties you have been shown. Avoid mass inspections at all costs. They are a waste of time. Remember, the agent is investing time and money in you as a client and they will want a return on their investment.

UK Estate Agents

Contacting UK agents is a good starting point if they deal with the region/s where you are interested in buying. Prospective buyers should make sure that they are aware of and very clear about everything that is taking place 'on their behalf' during negotiations and to be in control of proceedings. Before entering into a contract through one of these agents check to see what charges for services are going to be levied and ask for a breakdown of costs and commission. It may work out to be far more expensive going through an agent back home than dealing with a foreign-based estate agent direct.

Internet

Another good resource, for both prospective property buyers and service companies is the internet. Although you won't be able (and would not want) to buy properties over the Internet there is a growing number of websites that deal with property – from estate agents' home pages, to those of property developers, mortgage lenders, letting agencies, and websites aimed at the expat, and the house-hunter. Estate agents and property developers are increasingly using the web as a marketing tool – as a relatively cheap way to get their name out there. There are internet portals (websites dedicated to one area of information and/or commerce), which deal exclusively with properties for sale from thousands of leading agents and developers. Using a search engine such as www.google.com or a web directory such as www.yahoo.com will lead you into a selection of websites dealing solely with Spanish, Italian, French etc. property for sale.

Because of the vast amount of information (as well as misinformation and downright junk) that is posted on the Internet you will need to narrow down any search that you make using a web directory or search engine. Rather than just typing in for example, 'property, Turkey' or 'villas for sale, Costa del Sol' name the specific area or town you are looking to buy in. If you have a name of a property developer or estate agent that you are thinking of doing business with, then use the web as a research tool. Find out as much as you can about their company. You can make initial contact with vendors of property which interests you by using email (you can get a free email address at www.hotmail.com, or yahoo.co.uk) but be very wary of any company or individual who asks for payment of any kind over the internet. Although e-commerce has come a long way and although those who have the money to invest in internet security have made it virtually impossible for a 'hacker' to get hold of clients' credit card details that are given over the web, smaller operators may not have this security. If you decide to continue with negotiations after initial contact over the internet it will be better to set up a face to face meeting as soon as possible. Anyone can be anybody they want in cyberspace.

The Internet can be a great marketing tool
The Hamptons website for example has reported getting 150,000 hits (visitors to its website) in one month alone. A few sites worth looking at, especially for those looking to buy at the top end of the property market, are Knight Frank (www.knightfranks.com), Hamptons (www.hamptons.co.uk), www.primelocation.com (which includes property from 250 estate agents), www.propertyfinder.com (property from 900 agencies), www.altea.com, and newskys.co.uk. Brokers such as Lacey & Co cover several countries on the Med, in their case Spain (including the Balearics), Greece and Malta. The best of these websites will allow you to search for suitable properties by specifying search criteria such as whether you want a villa with or without a swimming pool, its proximity to the beach, hospitals etc., as well as your desired region, and of course purchase price. Increasingly, agencies are linking up to property portals; www.eured.com has details of properties for sale in every European country.

Useful Contacts

Names of other agents dealing in property abroad can be obtained from the *National Association of Estate Agents*, Arbon House, 21 Jury Street, Warwick CV34 4EH; ☎01926-496 800; www.naea.co.uk (select the international section). They can send a list (ask for their 'Homelink' department) of members specialising in various countries: for example there are 15 on their list that deal with Spain, four for Greece, half a dozen for France etc. Altenatively, contact the *Royal Institute of Chartered Surveyors*, 12 Great George Street, Parliament Square, London SW1 3AD; ☎020-7222 7000; www.rics.org.

The CEI (Confédération Européenne de l'Immobilier: European Confederation of Real Estate Agents) is one of Europe's largest professional organisations of estate agents, now counting well over 25,000 members from hundreds of cities in thirteen European countries, Austria, France, Germany, Greece, Hungary, Ireland, Italy, the Netherlands, Portugal, Romania, Spain, the United Kingdom and the Slovak Republic, representing a total of over 60,000 operators in real estate. The CEI website (www.web-cei.com) has a search facility.

The Federation of Overseas Property Developers, Agents & Consultants (FOPDAC) is a membership organisation restricted to agents, developers and consultants active in the international property markets whose probity is beyond reasonable question. They can be contacted at Lacey House, St. Clare Business Park, Holly Road, Hampton Hill, Middlesex, TW12 1QQ; ☎020-8941 5588; fax 020-8941 0202; www.fopdac.com.

Outbound Publishing: Johnston Press Plc., 1 Commercial Road, Eastbourne, E Sussex BN21 3XQ; ☎01323-726040; fax 01323-649249; outbounduk@aol.com; www.outboundpublishing.com. Publishers of well known property magazines and newspapers including *World of Property* and *Focus on France*. Also organises *World of Property* exhibitions, held twice annually and which are useful for making contact with estate agents and developers. European countries covered usually include Cyprus, France, Greece, Italy, Malta, Portugal, Spain and Turkey.

Lawyers

While you may locate a property without using an estate agent it is extremely unwise to hand any money over without engaging a lawyer to oversee the process and ensure that everything about the transaction is legal. It is essential to check that the person selling is legally the owner and that your purchase is protected by the weight of the law. The only possible exception to this is Turkey, where it is a matter of fact, and not necessarily recommended, that foreigners are buying property without either an estate agent or the services of a lawyer. Buyers in Turkey do however have to pay property purchase tax.

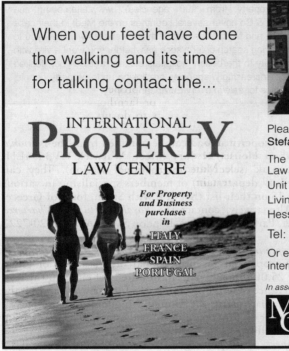

Specialist UK-Based Lawyers

Bennett & Co Solicitors: 144 Knutsford Road, Wilmslow, Cheshire SK9 6JP; ☎01625-586937; fax 01625-585362; e-mail: internationallawyers@bennett-and-co.com; www.bennett-and-co.com.

John Howell & Co: The Old Glassworks, 22 Endell Street, Covent Garden, London WC2H 9AD; ☎020 7420 0400; fax 020 7836 3626; e-mail info@europelaw.com; www.europelaw.com.

Mr Stefano Lucatello, The International Property Law Centre, Unit 2 Waterside Park, Livingstone Road, Hessle HU13 OEG; ☎01482 350-850; fax 01482 642799; e-mail internationalproperty@maxgold.com; www.internationalpropertylaw.com.

WHAT TYPE OF PROPERTY TO BUY

After where to buy, the next big decision is what type of property: old or modern, apartment or villa, marina development, town house or farmhouse etc. You have to weigh up the merits of each. A ruin can take years to do up, while a modern condominium apartment, or a villa can be purchased fully furnished and ready to move into the moment you have paid for it. Do you want to live in a village inland or on the coast, or do you want to be near a busy resort? Perhaps you prefer an apartment in an historic city such as Dubrovnik, Nice, Marseille, Trieste, Palermo or Valletta, a stone's throw from the cafés, shops and entertainment?

Old

Many people looking for their dream holiday home imagine a traditional old house a few miles inland or by the sea. However, such properties are, understandably, highly sought after and, depending on the state of disrepair, will be harder to find than more modern properties. Many estate agents prefer a good commission on a straightforward property that won't require the added hassle of getting structural surveys, finding out about boundaries, rights of way over the land etc., etc., so you may have to do some exploring on your own.

Renovation costs on such properties can be exorbitant and many old houses are without adequate sanitation, power provision, access to mains electricity, telephone lines and water etc., which is often why the former owners abandoned them. Before deciding on buying a picturesque ruin in a beautiful setting ask yourself: how much will it cost to install all the mod cons deemed necessary to 21st century living, and then double it. The British especially seem to have a reputation for buying up old piles of stones and spending vast amounts of time and money turning them into habitable dwellings once more.

Without some experience of renovating property, what may have seemed like a bargain can end up just being a burden – both financially and mentally. A relatively small initial financial outlay to buy a tumbledown property will be augmented by the need to hire builders and architects and sort out planning permissions. Time, patience, perseverance and, above all, money will be needed to create or recreate the house and grounds of your dreams and without a generous supply of all these the project may falter and the dream die.

Before buying such a property you will need to get a structural survey done to judge whether there is actually scope for renovation or whether the rot is so bad that demolition and rebuild is the only option available. If this is the case then you will need to know that changes/additions to the property are allowed by the planning authorities.

Self Build

If you are lucky, you may find an ideal plot of land and complete the bureaucratic paperchase to get building permission for it (for details of procedures in individual countries – see relevant chapters). Once building starts it is advisable to be on site as much as possible. If you can't be there to oversee the building process personally, then try and find someone who you trust to keep an eye on things, or employ a professional to supervise and troubleshoot. Builders everywhere can occasionally be unreliable, and maybe decide not to turn up for work if something more lucrative has been found for a few days.

You should also check the plans, make sure that the footings are laid correctly – it would be a great shame if your house ended up facing the wrong way for example – and check on type and costings of materials. Do you want cheap, chic, expensive, or flash? This is your house that is being built and you will want to be on hand to choose materials and fixtures and fittings. Keep in mind that things rarely go exactly to plan – for instance there may be rock where the footings should go and blasting this out of the way will increase the labour cost, or you may decide that you want changes made to the original designs. It is therefore a good idea to factor in at least 10-30% on top of the original estimate. Building costs are likely to come in at £1000 per square metre of build but remember that land is likely to increase in value before the building work is complete.

Stagger the payment schedule to the builder (for example make payments on: the signing of the contract, the completion of the exterior walls and roof, the completion of the interior, the completion of plumbing, installation of electricity etc., on completion of exterior landscaping) and negotiate to hold back a final payment until a certain period has passed once the house has been completed so that should cracks in walls appear, or there be problems with drainage, plumbing, electrics, etc., you will have some clout should you need to call the builders back in to repair defects.

Depending on the size and design of the house expect a wait of at least a year and probably more, before being able to gaze upon your dream house. Even after the completion of the house it could take an additional year or two to knock the garden and surrounding land into shape.

Off-Plan. Off-plan means you buy your property based only on the developer's plans and if you are lucky a model. This sounds dodgy, but has been working well in Spain, where off-plan was pioneered more than a decade ago, and it has now spread to other countries including France, Italy and to a lesser extent, Greece. The advantages are that you can get impressive discounts as developers like to sell off units quickly so as to be sure to cover their costs, the price is fixed and you pay in stages. There is usually a penalty clause for the developer if he does not keep to schedule. The disadvantages are that you have to wait for your property to be built which can take eight months plus, or it can be late which means waiting longer than anticipated. However, you can console yourself with the fact that the property, when you finally get to use it, is probably worth more than the price you paid for it.

Essential Enquiries

Who Owns the Land? Another check to be made: in the unlikely event of a builder building on land which he does not own – the house belongs to the owner of the land.

Who is the Developer? Be careful not to confuse two or three different actors on the scene of a development: The first is the developer, or promoter of the scheme, who should own the land. The second is the building contractor. The third could be the agency that looks after the sale of the units.

It is the developer who is by far the most important of these. He is the legal counterpart of the buyer. You need to have a lot of trust in him. It is not difficult to check out his trustworthiness: Has he been on the scene for years? Has his company a large capital fund? or is he financing himself as he goes along?

Useful Publication. There is not a lot of public information on timeshare but there is a good book with all the pros and cons written by Michael Strauss called *Timeshare Condominiums for the Beginner.*

Holiday Property Bonds and Holiday Clubs

Holiday Property Bonds. Given the bad reputation of timeshares, other similar schemes have been thought up that which claim not to be timeshares. One of these is HPBs – Holiday Property Bonds. You pay a sum of money, of which the majority (around 75%) is invested into a portfolio of properties, and the rest in management fees. In return for your investment you are allocated points. Provided you have accrued enough points you can stay in one of the properties offered by the bond company. The positive side of the HPB is that you will be staying in well-managed properties, though you will still have to pay a user's fee for cleaning and maintenance. The downside is much the same as with timeshare – the property is never yours and you may make a loss if you decide to sell your HPB. These are suitable schemes if you take several short holidays a year and are prepared to take potluck about where you go.

BEWARE THE SCAM

More downmarket are **Holiday Clubs or Travel Clubs**, which promise holidays for life for a lump sum payment, with even bigger risks than timeshare. The most common scam is to tell thousands of people that they have won a free holiday, and charge them to attend a presentation. There are endless horror stories about holiday clubs and no one should touch them with a barge pole.

BUYING FOREIGN CURRENCY FOR YOUR PROPERTY

If you're buying a property abroad for the first time, you've probably got enough to do without worrying about exchange rates. You've found your dream home and secured the price of your property, and now all you have to do is look forward to your new life abroad. Right? Well, partly. Somewhere along the line you will have to change your pounds into euros, and that's where the dream can become a nightmare if you don't plan ahead. Whether you're buying a property outright or buying from plan in installments, protecting yourself against exchange rate fluctuations can save you hundreds, if not thousands of pounds on the price of your new home.

Foreign exchange markets are by nature extremely volatile and can be subject to dramatic movements over a very short space of time. In some ways it's all too easy to leave your currency exchange to the last minute and hope that the exchange rates fall in your favour. But if you don't take steps to protect your capital, you could find yourself paying a lot more than you bargained for.

As a matter of course, many people will approach their banks to sort out their currency, without realising that there are more cost-effective alternatives in the marketplace. There are a number of independent commercial foreign exchange brokers who can offer better rates and a more personal, tailored service. Their dealers will explain the various options open to you and keep you informed of any significant changes in the market. They will also guide you through every step of the transaction so that you are ultimately in control and able to make the most of your money.

If you're still not convinced of how planning ahead can help you, take a look at the following example.

In recent history the euro stood at 1.54 and within six months had fallen to 1.38. Therefore, in just 6 months the cost of a €200,000 house would have increased by over £15,000!

Although changes in the economic climate may be beyond your control, protecting your capital against the effect of these changes isn't.

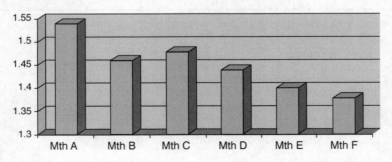

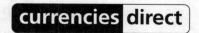

There are a number of options available to you:

- **Spot Transactions** – Buy now, pay now. These are ideal for anyone who needs their currency straight away as the currency is purchased today at the current rate. However, if you have time to spare before your payments are due, it may be wiser to consider a Forward Transaction.

- **Forward Transactions** – Buy now, pay later. These allow you to secure a rate for up to 18 months in advance to protect yourself against any movements in the market. A small deposit holds the rate until the balance becomes due when the currency contract matures. This option not only protects against possible drops in the exchange rate but also gives you the security of the currency you need at a guaranteed cost, regardless of fluctuations in the market.

- **Limit Orders** allow you to place an order in the market for a desired exchange rate. This has the advantage of protecting you against negative exchange movements whilst still allowing you to gain from a positive movement. Your request is entered into the system and an automatic currency purchase is triggered once the market hits your specified rate.

- **Regular Currency Transfers.** Currency can also be transferred overseas on a regular basis at commercial rates. This is ideal for any regular monthly payments and even foreign mortgages, pensions or salaries.

If you haven't had to deal with this kind of transaction before, it can all seem a little daunting. But that's where a reputable currency company can really come into its own. With specialists in the field ready to explain all the pitfalls and possibilities to you in layman's terms and guide you through each stage of the transaction, you can be sure that your currency solutions will be perfectly tailored to your needs.

Currencies Direct has been helping people to understand the overseas property markets since 1996. Specializing in providing foreign exchange solutions tailored to clients' individual financial situations, it offers a cost-effective and user-friendly alternative to the high-street banks.

With offices in the London, Europe and Australasia, *Currencies Direct* is always on hand to help you. For more information on how you can benefit from their commercial rates of exchange and friendly, professional service, call the *Currencies Direct* office in London on 020 7813 0332 or visit their website at www.currenciesdirect.com.

FINANCE

IMPORTING CURRENCY

Purchasing a foreign property involves sending large amounts of money abroad to cover the costs involved. When you find the right property to buy, you will be given the price in euros or the foreign currency. However, until you have bought all of the currency you will need, you won't know the total costs involved. Depending on the exchange rate fluctuations between your home currency and the foreign currency during the conveyancing procedures, the property could eventually cost you more or less than you had originally thought. Importing money into another country can take time and there are various ways of going about transferring funds. Some solicitors can transfer money between accounts held at home and abroad, and for many potential buyers this may be the quickest and easiest way of doing things.

Another method of transferring funds is to obtain a banker's draft from your UK bank. This is a cheque guaranteed by the bank, which can be deposited into your bank account anywhere in the world. When making the final payment on the purchase of a property at the notary's office it is advisable to hand over a banker's draft made payable to the vendor. Note that a banker's draft works along the lines of a cheque, and once it is paid into an account there will be a short period of waiting before it is cleared and you are able to access the money. You can also transfer money by SWIFT electronic bank transfer. This procedure can take several days and rates of exchange will vary.

Because of currency fluctuations converting currency, for example sterling to euros, will always be something of a gamble. If the pound falls against the euro you will end up paying more than you budgeted for. If, as soon as you sign the contract to begin the process of buying, you convert the total cost of the property into euros you may be happy with the conversion rate but you will lose the use of the money while further negotiations take place over the settlement of the property.

To avoid this, a specialised foreign currency provider such as *Currencies Direct* (Hanover House, 73-74 High Holborn, London WC1V 6LR; tel 020-7813 0332; fax 020-7419 7753; www.currenciesdirect.com) can help in a number of ways, by offering better exchange rates than banks, without charging commission, and giving you the possibility of 'forward buying', i.e. agreeing on the rate that you will pay at a fixed date in the future, or with a 'limit order', i.e. waiting until the rate you want is reached before making the transaction. For those who prefer to know exactly how much money they will need for their purchase, forward buying is the best solution, since you no longer have to worry about the movement of the pound against the foreign currency working against you. Payments can be made in one lump sum or on a regular basis. For example, it is usual when purchasing a new-build property to pay in four instalments, so called 'staged payments'.

There is a further possibility, which is to use the services of a law firm in the UK to transfer the money. They can hold the money for you until the exact time that you need it. However, remember that law firms will also use the services of a currency dealer themselves, so you may be better off going to a company like *Currencies Direct* yourself to avoid any excess legal fees.

Intra-EU Credit Transfers. In July 2003 a new system of transferring funds in euros between accounts within the EU was launched using an account holder's unique International Bank Account Number (IBAN) and Bank Identifier Code (BIC) which is also known as the 'SWIFT' code which is a unique code issued to every bank. Banks are obliged to provide bank statements with the IBAN and BIC printed on them. Firms issuing invoices within the EU now have to print their IBAN and BIC numbers on their invoices

UK MORTGAGES

A number of people planning to buy second homes abroad arrange loans in the UK – taking out a second mortgage on their UK property and then buying with cash. Alternatively, it is possible to approach the banks for a sterling loan secured on the property abroad. If you are considering borrowing in the UK, then the method of calculating the amount that may be borrowed is worked out at between two and a half, or three and a half, times your primary income plus any secondary income you may have, less any capital amount already borrowed on the mortgage. Sometimes the amount that may be borrowed is calculated at three times to three and a half or three times joint income, less outstanding capital. Your credit history will also be checked to assess whether you will be able to manage increased mortgage payments. It is most usual for buyers to pay for their second home with a combination of savings and equity from re-mortgaging an existing property.

Naturally, the mortgage will be subject to a valuation on any UK property, and you can expect to borrow, subject to equity, up to a maximum of 80% of the purchase price of the overseas property (compared with the availability of 100% mortgages for UK properties). If you are going to take out a second mortgage with your existing mortgage lender then a second charge would be taken by the mortgage company. Note that some lending institutions charge a higher rate for a loan to cover a second property. Also taking out a second mortgage on your existing property puts that property at risk.

MORTGAGES OVERSEAS

Opportunities for obtaining a mortgage abroad are covered in the individual country sections below, but it is also possible to arrange an overseas mortgage from the UK. Conti Financial Services (CFS) - 204 Church Road, Hove, East Sussex, BN3 2DJ; ☎01273-772811; Fax: 01273-321269; E-Mail: enquiries@contifs.com; Web Site: mortgagesoverseas.com - are the UK's leading overseas mortgage broker and 1,000s of other professions advisers and mortgage specialists worldwide refer their clients to them. CFS provide a full hand-holding service, advising on the most favourable overseas lending terms, whilst negotiating competitive loan-to-value schemes over suitable timescales.

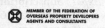

Conti's country specific in-house teams, give clients and lenders consistency while dealing with any mortgage application and ensure that clients are put in touch with other professional overseas specialists to enable clients to comply fully with any planning, valuation and legal conditions. CFS can currently negotiate loans in more than 20 countries and are introducing schemes for Eastern European states, so as to ensure they continue to offer clients more competitive products and choice.

OFFSHORE MORTGAGES

Another option open to expatriates is to take out an offshore mortgage. For convenience and tax-free interest on their savings, expatriates often utilise offshore banking and financial services. Jersey, Guernsey and the Isle of Man are the prime offshore banking centres in Europe, along with Switzerland, Liechtenstein and Luxembourg for those with a lot of money. Banks in Jersey, Guernsey and the Isle of Man operate under UK banking rules and offer reliable and efficient banking and financial services, including Euro mortgages for buying property in Europe.

Offshore mortgages work slightly differently to standard mortgages and potential mortgagees should investigate them thoroughly before taking one on. Articles on offshore mortgages and details of providers can be found in expatriate magazines such as *FT Expat, Nexus* etc. Independent mortgage brokers who advertise in the expatriate magazines should also be able to advise you on offshore financial services.

Offshore Mortgage Providers

Your local high street branch of *Abbey* should be your first port of call. Another building society offering offshore mortgages is the *Bank of Scotland International (Isle of Man) Ltd.* at PO Box 19, Prospect Hill, Douglas, Isle of Man IM99 1AT; ☎01624-612323; fax 01624-644090; www.bankofscotland-international.com. The Bank of Scotland, like most high street building societies and banks, has leaflets on offshore mortgages, and other financial matters such as international payments, which will be worth consulting. *Lloyds TSB Bank Overseas Club*, offers a range of services and is based at the Offshore Centre, PO Box 12, Peveril Buildings, Peveril Square, Douglas, Isle of Man IM99 1SS; ☎08705 301641; fax 01624 670929; www.lloydstsb-offshore.com.

Useful Addresses

Abbey National: PO BOX 824, 237 Main Street, Gibraltar; ☎010 350 76090; fax; www.abbeynationaloffshore.com.

Alliance & Leicester International Ltd.: P.O.B. 226, 10-12 Prospect Hill, Douglas, Isle of Man IM99 1RY; ☎01624 663566; fax 01624 617286.

Barclays International Personal Banking: PO Box 784, Victoria Road, Georgetown, Jersey JE4 8ZS, Channel Islands; ☎01534 880 550; fax 01534 505 077; www.inte rnationalbanking.barclays.com.

Brewin Dolphin Bell Lawrie Ltd. Stockbrokers: 5 Giltspur Street, London EC1A 9BD; ☎020-7246 1028; fax 020-7246 1093.

Bristol & West International: P.O.B. 611, High Street, St Peter Port, Guernsey, Channel Islands GY1 4NY; ☎01481-720609; fax 01481-711658; www.bristol-west.co.uk/bwi/.

FT Expat: Subscriptions, Oakfield House, 35 Perrymount Road, Haywards Heath, West Sussex RH16 3DH; England; ☎01444 445520; fax 01444 445599; www.ftexpat.com

Halifax International (Jersey Ltd): P.O.B. 664, Halifax House, 31-33 New Street, St. Helier, Jersey; ☎01534 59840; fax 01534 59280.

HSBC Bank International: P.O. Box 615, 28/34 Hill Street, St. Helier, Jersey JE4 5YD, Channel Islands; ☎01534 616111; fax 01534 616222; www1.offshore.hsbc.co.je.

Lloyds TSB Offshore Centre: P.O. Box 12, Douglas, Isle of Man, IM99 1SS; ☎01624 638104; fax 01624 638181; www.lloydstsb-offshore.com.

Nationwide Overseas Ltd: 45-51, Athol Street, Douglas, Isle of Man; ☎01624 663494.

Woolwich Guernsey Limited: P.O. Box 341, La Tonnelle House, Les Banques, St. Peter Port, Guernsey GY1 3UW; ☎01481 715735; fax 01481 715722.

THE INLAND REVENUE & OFFSHORE TAX HAVENS

The Inland Revenue is aware that offshore havens are being used as a tax dodge by property companies. Some foreign homeowners set up an offshore property company with shareholders, in order to avoid inheritance taxes and to earn income interest free. The Inland Revenue has recently been demanding names of beneficial owners, accounts and company tax payment details from offshore banking companies who are apparently obliged to reveal all if requested to do so by the Inland Revenue – confidentiality agreements notwithstanding.

Further information can be obtained from the Inland Revenue Publications IR20 *Residents and non-residents. Liability to tax in the United Kingdom,* which can be found on the website www.inlandrevenue.gov.uk. Booklets IR38, IR139 and IR140 are also useful reading.

Useful Addresses

Non-Resident Claims: Fitzroy House, P.O. Box 46, Nottingham, NG2 1BD; ☎0115-974 1919; fax 0115-974 1919; www.inlandrevenue.gov.uk.

Centre for Non-Residents (CNR), Residence Advice & Liabilities Unit 355: St John's House, Bootle, Merseyside L69 9BB; ☎0151-472 6202; fax 0151-472 6003.

Property Taxes

For taxes due on property, see individual countries for their local and national requirements.

TAX

If you have ever been faced with completing a self-assessment tax form you will be aware that sorting out one's tax affairs is a complicated matter and one that isn't made easier by the pages and pages of notes and explanations provided by the tax authorities. Unless your financial affairs are simple, and consist of one source of income and no investments or savings or interest payments you will be advised to enlist the aid of an accountant versed in international tax laws – at least for your first year as a property owner abroad. Qualified tax consultants should be members of *The Chartered Institute of Taxation – CIOT –* (12 Upper Belgrave Street, London SW1X 8BB; ☎020-7235 9381; www.tax.org.uk) or *The Association of Taxation Technicians – ATT –* (12 Upper

Belgrave Street London SW1X 8BB; ☎020-7235 2544; www.att.org.uk).

The circumstances of foreign home-owners vary as does their tax liability and the subject is too complex to cover in detail here. However, the main tax liability is in the country of residence, which will require taxes to be paid based on worldwide income. It is up to the tax authorities to decide where they consider an individual to be resident for tax purposes.

Holiday homeowners usually retain tax links (i.e. residence), in their own country, but are still liable in a foreign country for taxes connected with their property there – typically from income earned from renting out and any local taxes applicable to homeowners. The majority of countries have double taxation agreements whereby taxes paid in one country may be offset against tax due in the country of residence. This is to prevent an individual being taxed twice on the same income.

Double Taxation Agreements for UK Citizens

The UK has reciprocal tax agreements with a number of countries around the world, which avoids the possibility of someone being taxed twice on their income from renting property, pensions, gifts, inheritance, etc. – once by the foreign country where their holiday home is, and once by the tax authorities in their home country. However, there may be a slight hitch during the initial period of residency abroad because, for instance, the UK tax year runs from April to April and other countries' tax years run from January to January, therefore UK nationals in Spain for example, may be taxed by both the Spanish and UK authorities in the overlapping months of their first year in the new country. In this case, you would be able to claim a refund of UK tax by applying to the Inland Revenue through your local UK tax office. They will supply you with an SPA/Individual form (which offers relief at source for tax refunds concerning interest, royalties and pensions) or with the SPA/Individual/Credit form (which provides repayment on dividend income for anyone who has suffered double taxation on moving abroad). Once the form has been filled out, take it to the local tax office of the country you have moved to. They will stamp it and then you can return it to the British tax authorities as proof that you have paid tax abroad and are therefore no longer liable for British tax. It is a procedure that should be carried out while you are in the foreign country and not after your return to the UK. It is important to keep accounts of your income, expenditure etc., while abroad to meet any problems should these arise. Double taxation agreements will differ depending on the country involved and the circumstances of the individual. In some cases it may be more beneficial to be taxed abroad rather than in the UK and financial advice should be sought on this.

Procedure for UK Residents. The situation is reasonably straightforward if you are moving permanently abroad. You should inform the UK Inspector of Taxes at the office you usually deal with of your departure and they will send you a P85 form to complete. The UK tax office will usually require certain proof that you are leaving the UK, and hence their jurisdiction, for good. Evidence of having sold a house in the UK and having rented or bought one in another country is normally sufficient. You can continue to own property in the UK without being considered resident, but you will have to pay UK taxes on any income from the property.

For further information see the Inland Revenue publications IR20 *Residents and non-residents, Liability to tax in the United Kingdom* which can be found on the website www.inlandrevenue.gov.uk. Booklets IR138, IR139 and IR140 are also worth reading; these can be obtained from your tax office or from *The Centre for Non-Residents (CNR)*: St. John's House, Merton Road, Bootle Merseyside L69 9BB; ☎0151-472 6196; fax

0151-472 6392; www.inlandrevenue.gov.uk/cnr.

Double Taxation Agreements for US Citizens

Fortunately, the USA has a double taxation agreement with Italy, France, etc. so you should not have to pay taxes twice on the same income. In order to benefit from the double taxation agreement you need to fulfil one of two residence tests: either you have been a bona fide resident of another country for an entire tax year, which is the same as the calendar year in the case of the USA, or you have been physically present in another country for 330 days during a period of 12 months which can begin at any time of the year. Once you qualify under the bona fide residence or physical presence tests then any further time you spend working abroad can also be used to diminish you tax liability.

As regards foreign income, the main deduction for US citizens is the 'Foreign Earned Income Exclusion', by which you do not pay US taxes on the first $84,000 of money earned abroad (the amount has in recent times gone up by $2,000 every year). Investment income, capital gains etc. are unearned income. If you earn in excess of the limit, taxes paid on income in another country can still be used to reduce your liability for US taxes either in the form of an exclusion or a credit, depending on which is more advantageous. The same will apply to Italian taxes paid on US income.

The rules for US taxpayers abroad are explained very clearly in the IRS booklet: *Tax Guide for US Citizens and Resident Aliens Abroad*, known as Publication 54, which can be downloaded from the internet on www.irs.gov. The US tax return has to be sent to the IRS, Philadelphia, PA 19255-0207; ☎215-516-2000.

Procedure for US Citizens. The US Internal Revenue Service (IRS) expects US citizens and resident aliens living abroad to file tax returns every year. Such persons will continue to be liable for US taxes on worldwide income until they have become permanent residents of another country and severed their ties with the USA.

Moving to Another Country

Permanent expatriates (i.e. those who are no longer residents of the UK, USA etc.) are subject to certain procedures as regards tax links and they can utilise offshore banking to minimise tax liability.

Offshore Companies for Property

The principle of offshore companies involves turning a property into a company, the shares of which are held as collateral against a mortgage of up to 75% for a repayment term of up to 20 years by an offshore bank based in a tax haven such as Gibraltar or the Channel Islands. The property owner's name is confidential and the property company is administered on the owner's behalf by the offshore trustees. Previously, the advantage of offshore property purchase was that it reduced tax liability in the country of purchase, as, if and when the property was resold, it merely became a question of transferring the shares confidentially to a new owner, thus avoiding transfer taxes and VAT in the country in question.

INTERNATIONAL REMOVALS & PETS

Removals within the European Union

Any EU citizen intending to take up permanent residence in another EU country may import their household effects and personal possessions free of customs duty. There are now no customs duties to pay on household effects transported from one member country of the EU to another. However, a large selection of expensive, pristine equipment would undoubtedly arouse the suspicions of the customs officers. It is advisable that any new items show a few obvious signs of wear and tear in order not to attract import duty and VAT – another way to lessen the interest of customs officials is to make sure that the items are not perfectly wrapped in their factory packaging.

The most important regulation regarding the import of personal possessions is that the items must be imported within six months of taking up residence. The Excess Baggage Co lists current import regulations on their website: www.excessbaggage.co.uk.

If you decide to take a loaded van of furniture and other items for your home from one European Union country to another, you should have no problems, especially if the country is inside the Schengen area.

Using a Removals Company. If you are using a removals company they will handle most of the paperwork. Although it is obviously more economical to transport all of your possessions in one go, you are allowed to import all household goods in as many trips as are required. It is worth remembering that it may be difficult to import goods after the expiry of the one-year period; it can take up to a year to obtain a separate import licence and the duty on the import for non-EU citizens can be astronomical.

if you are buying anything to take with you, such as a fridge or stereo, it can be supplied VAT free if the goods are delivered direct to the remover as an export shipment from the dealer.

All reputable international removals firms should be fully aware of the regulations concerning the transport of personal and household items. Anyone thinking of taking their household effects out to another EU country in a private truck or van should first consult the nearest embassy of that country, or consulate for the most up to date regulations and advice. Much of the paperwork involved in importing goods will have to be in the language of the destination country. The *Association of Translation Companies* (Suite 10-11, Kent House, 87 Regent Street, London W1B 4EH; ☎020-7437 0007; fax 020-7439 7701; www.atc.org.uk) will be able to put you in touch with translation services specialising in translating documents relating to removals abroad, property purchase, residence, import/export etc. Translation service companies are also listed in the yellow pages.

When considering what to take with you to your house on the Med, and what to leave behind or sell at a car boot sale, start with a list of essential items and then try and cut this down again. Everything taken must be carefully considered to ensure that it really is practical, and necessary. Electrical items are slightly more expensive in most European countries than in the UK and it may be worth taking yours as long as they are compatible. However, there may be difficulties with electrical repairs, as some home appliances are likely to be of national origin and of a particular design and manufacture predominant in that country. Anything of substantial weight will be very expensive to ship abroad, and no matter how carefully you or the removals staff wrap an item, breakages occur. A good removals company can avoid or deal with most of the palaver, which is linked with uprooting yourself, your family and all your possessions to a foreign country. Hiring a removals firm will cost a minimum of £2,000.

Insurance
It is advisable to take out comprehensive insurance against possible damage to your possessions while in transit.

Useful Contacts
The British Association of Removers (3 Churchill Court, 58 Station Road, North Harrow, London HA2 7SA; ☎020-8861 3331; www.bar.co.uk) provides a free and useful leaflet *Now that you're ready to move...* which covers most of the issues you may face, and can also provide the names and telephone numbers of reputable removals companies throughout the country that are members of BAR and specialise in overseas operations. The website www.your-removals.co.uk allows you to tap in your country of destination and provides a list of companies that specialise in that particular country. The addresses and phone numbers of some of the companies, which deal with specific countries are also listed under individual countries' *Making the Move* sections.

Useful Websites
Household Goods Forwarders Association of America: www.hhgfaa.org
International Federation of International Movers (FIDI): www.fidi.com
Overseas Moving Network International: www.omnimoving.com

Useful Addresses – Removal Companies
A&G Removals: Unit 6, Keld Close, Barker Business Park, Melmerby, Ripon, N Yorks HG6 5NB; ☎01765-640882; fad 01765 640985. International worldwide.

Associated Moving Services: est. 1946. Tel 020-8947 1817; fax 01323-894474; www.amsmoving.co.uk; peter@amsmoves.fsnet.co.uk.

Bradshaw International: Tel 0800 389 2233; e-mail european@bradshawinternational.com.

Cotswold Carriers: Warehouse No 2, The Walk, Hook Norton Road, Chipping Norton, Oxon OX7 5TG; ☎01608-730500; fax 01608-730600; www.cotswoldc arriers.co.uk.

European Relocations: Unit 3, Beaumanor Road, Leicester LE4 5QD; ☎ 0116-261 0700; fax 0116-261 0700; www. europeanrelocations.com. Will go anywhere in Europe and worldwide.

Interdean: Worldwide removals (UK 020 8961 4141; USA Headquarters 55 Hunter Lane, Elmsford, New York 10523-1317; tel: 914-347 6600; fax: 914-347 0129; Chicago 630-752 8990, fax 630-752 9087; Dallas 817-354 6683, fax 817-354 5570; Houston 281-469 7733, fax: 281-469 9426; Los Angeles 562-921 0939, fax 562-926 0918; Raleigh/Durham 919-969 1661, fax 919-969 1663; San Francisco 510-266 5660, fax 510-266 5665; www.interdean.com). Interdean have offices in a number of European countries and the Far East, which can be found via the website. They also offer relocation services.

Monarch UK&International: North Road, South Ockendon, RM15 8SR; ☎01708-854545; fax 08700-940149; www.askmonarch.com; info@askmonarch.com. Goes anywhere in Europe.

Richman-Ring International Removers: Eurolink Way, Sittingbourne, Kent ME10 3HH; ☎01795-427151; www.richman-ring.com.

Union Jack Logistics Ltd.: Unit 4, Hill Barton Business Park, Sidmouth Road, Clyst St. Mary, Devon EX5 1DR; ☎01395-233486; fax 01395-233686; www.unionjac kremovals.com.

Importing a Car

Non-residents may freely drive back and forth between their country and the one where their holiday home is, with national car registration documents and an EU or International Driving Licence. Residents are obliged to either officially import their foreign registered vehicle or buy one in their newly adopted country. For drivers moving to another EU country, who are already resident in Europe (except UK and Irish residents who will have right hand drive cars), taking their own car with them is often a good idea. This is because you usually have to be resident before you buy a car abroad, and while you are waiting for residency you might have to manage without private transport for months, unless you can afford rental cars for that length of time. UK and Irish residents, who know far enough in advance that they are moving may want to buy a left-hand drive car in preparation for their relocation. Second hand left-hand drive cars for sale in the UK can found online on the Exchange and Mart website (www.exchangeandmart.co.uk).

Useful Contact

Automobile Association (AA): Import Section, Fanum House, Basingstoke Hants RG21 2EA; ☎01256-20123; www.automobileassociation.co.uk. Information is supplied only to members of the AA. Ask for information on the permanent importation of a vehicle into the country you are moving to. For membership details contact your nearest AA office.

Non-EU Nationals

A fact for non-EU citizens to bear in mind, is that the customs clearance charges involved in exporting and importing goods can sometimes be more expensive than the shipping charges themselves (also something which a good removal company should advise you of and deal with on your behalf).

PETS PASSPORTS

Before deciding to take your pet with you, think carefully about the implications for both yourself and the animal. Local authorities in the Mediterranean countries have different regulations regarding pets and it is a good idea to check what these are before importing your pet.

'Passports' for pets were introduced in 2002. These allow people from the UK to take their animals between the UK and over 30 countries and to return with them without enduring the compulsory six-month quarantine that was formerly in force. Canada, Cyprus, France, Gibraltar, Greece, Italy, Malta and Spain (including the Balearics), the UK and the USA are among approved countries in this scheme; Croatia and Turkey are not approved.

Under the Pet Travel Scheme (PETS) dogs and cats are allowed to visit certain countries in mainland Europe and rabies free areas such as Australia, Canada, Western Europe etc. if they are vaccinated against rabies. Additionally, they are required to have been treated against tapeworm *(Echinococcus multilocularis)* – which can pass to humans – and the tick known as *Rhipicephalus sanguineus* – which also carries a disease transferable to humans.

The latest details of import conditions for taking your pets abroad can be obtained by contacting the Pet Travel Scheme (Department for the Environment, Food and Rural Affairs, Area 201, 1a Page Street, London SW1P 4PQ; ☎0870 241 1710; fax 020-7904 6834; e-mail pets.helpline@defra.gsi.gov.uk or the constantly updated website www.defra.gov.uk/animalh/quarantine) and requesting the contact details of your nearest Animal Health Office. Although the 'Passports' scheme makes travelling with animals more straightforward, getting the necessary documentation can be a lengthy process. At the time of writing the Department for the Environment, Food and Rural Affairs (DEFRA) was understood to be working to a six-month deadline, so you need to plan ahead.

An increasing number of ferry companies and airlines including Monarch and Virgin will take accompanied pets, though by no means all, so check with your carrier. Travelling by air from the UK a pet can travel as excess baggage, however, coming the other way the animal must travel as cargo. The *Independent Pet and Animal Transportation Association International Inc*: www.ipata.com has a directory of members, as well a advice on transporting pets on their website.

Once in the country the animal's documentation will be checked before being taken to the Animal Aircare Centre and then released to the owner. Quarantine is not usually necessary, although regulations may change and you should consult the consulate in your home country for up-to-date information well before your planned travel date. Note that in some Mediterranean countries, dogs in cities have to be registered and insured, a dog licence required or a tax levied. Information on the registration formalities once in your new country will be found at the local town hall.

TAKING PETS OUT OF THE UK

The procedures involved are:
- O   Vet inserts a tiny microchip just under the animal's skin (cost £20-£30).
- O   Vet administers a rabies shot, or two, given two weeks apart. (£50 x 2; second shot possibly cheaper).
- O   Vet takes a blood sample from animal and sends it to a DEFRA-approved laboratory. (£70-£80 including vet's handling charge). Note: If the blood test is negative, your pet must be vaccinated and tested again.
- O   Vet issues a PETS 1 Certificate, which you have to show to the transport company (e.g. airline, ferry, channel tunnel, etc).
- O   When taking pets from Britain you will need a PETS 5 certificate (this replaces a separate Export Health Certificate) which is issued at the same time as PETS 1 (see above).
- O   Total cost is about £200.

Importing Pets Back into the UK

To get your pet back into the UK you will need a PETS Certificate to show the transport company when checking in your pet at the point of departure. A PETS Certificate is valid six months after the date of the blood test up to the date the animal's booster rabies shot is due (a dog has to be at least three months old before it can be vaccinated). You should obtain the PETS Certificate from a government-authorised vet and you can obtain a list of these from DEFRA's website (www.defra.gov.uk/animalh/quarantine/pets/contacts.shtml). Immediately (24-48 hours) prior to leaving, the animal must be treated against ticks and tapeworm by a vet. This has to be done *every* time your pet enters the UK. The vet will issue an official certificate bearing the vet's stamp with the microchip number, date and *time* of treatment, and the product used.

Pets Originating Outside Britain

If your pet originated from outside Britain where different systems for identifying dogs and cats are in force it will need a microchip insert for entry to the UK. Pets that have had other forms of registration (e.g. an ear tattoo) must be vaccinated; blood-tested and have a microchip inserted. To enter the UK the animal must have the PETS Certificate showing that the vet has seen the registration document.

Pet Travel Insurance

Due to the introduction of the PETS scheme a niche market in pet travel insurance has opened up. *Pet Plan* (Allianz Cornhill Insurance plc, Computer House, Great West Road, Brentford, Middlesex TW8 9DX; ☎0800-072 7000; www.petplan.co.uk), a well-known British animal health insurance company, offers cover for pets taking trips abroad. The minimum 30-day cover costs about £16 for dogs and £10 for cats; 60 days and 90 days' cover is also available; while with E&L Pet Travel Insurance (P.O. Box 100, York, Y026 9SZ; ☎08707-423710 insurance starts at under £14. *Petwise Insurance* (BDML Connect Ltd., Baltic House, Kingston Crescent, Northend, Portsmouth PO2 8QL; ☎08702-413 479; www.petwise-insurance.com), *RapidInsure* (Phoenix Park, Blakewater Road, Blackburn, Lancs. BB1 5SJ; ☎01254 266 266; www.rapidinsure.co.uk), *Pinnacle Pet Healthcare* (Pinnacle House, A1 Barnet Way, Borehamwood, Hertfordshire WD6 2XX; ☎020-8207 9000; fax 020-8953 6222; www.pinnacle.co.uk) and *MRL Insurance Direct* (☎0800-389 8505;

www.mrlinsurance.co.uk) also offer travelling pet insurance.

Useful Contacts
In the UK:
Animal Airlines: 35 Beatrice Avenue, Manchester, Lancs. M18 7JU; ☎0160-223 4035.

Airpets Oceanic: Willowslea Farm Kennels, Spout Lane North, Stanwell Moor, Staines, Middlesex TW19 6BW; ☎01753-685 571; fax 01735-681 655; www.airpets.com. Pet exports, pet travel schemes, boarding, air kennels, transportation by road/air to and from all UK destinations.

D.J. Williams: Animal Transport, Littleacre Quarantine Centre, 50 Dunscombes Road, Turves, Nr Whittlesey Cambs PE7 2DS; ☎01733-840291; fax 01733-840348. International pet collection and delivery service, will deliver overland or arrange air transport. Will collect from your home and arrange all the necessary documentation. For those people whose pet is not covered by the PETS scheme, they also provide quarantine services.

Littleacre Quarantine Centre: 50 Dunscombes Road, Turves, Nr Whittlesey Cambs. PE7 2DS; ☎01733-840 291; fax 01733-840 348; www.quarantine1.co.uk. Pet collection and overland delivery service. Will collect from your home and arrange all the necessary documentation. Also return home service from Europe provided.

Par Air Services Livestock Ltd: Warren Lane, Stanway, Colchester, Essex C03 0LN; ☎01206-330 332; fax 01206-331 277; www.parair.co.uk. Handles international transportation and quarantine arrangements. Can arrange door-to-door delivery of pets by specially equipped vans.

Passports for Pets: Flat 11, 45 Queen's Gate, London SW7 SHR; ☎020-7589 6404; www.freespace.virgin.net/passports.forpets/. Lobby group that campaigned for reform of Britain's quarantine laws and now acts as a watchdog of the Pet Travel Scheme. Useful website keeps up-to-date with pets travel news and campaigns.

Pet Travel Scheme: Department for the Environment, Food and Rural Affairs, Area 201, 1a Page Street, London SW1P 4PQ; ☎0870 241 1710; fax 020-7904 6834; e-mail pets.helpline@defra.gsi.gov.uk; www.defra.gov.uk.

Pets Will Travel: Unit 2A, 3 Newby Close, Norton, Stockton-On-Tees; www.petswilltravel.co.uk. Also have a good forum pages on their website.

Travelpets Ltd: 22 South Audley Street, London W1K 2NY; ☎020-7499 4979; www.travelpets.net.

Trans-Fur: 19, Dene Close, Sarisbury Green, Southampton, Hampshire SO31 7TT; tel/fax 01489-588 072

In the USA
Independent Pet and Animal Transport Association: **Route 5, Box 747, Highway 2869, 2-364 Winding Trail, Holly Lake Ranch, Big Sandy, Texas 75755 USA;** ☎903-769-2267; fax 903-769-2867; www.ipata.com. An International Trade Association of animal handlers, pet moving providers, kennel operators, veterinarians and others who are dedicated to the care and welfare of pets and small animals during transport locally, nationwide and worldwide. Citizens of the USA can contact this address for a list of agents dealing in the transport of pets from the USA to other countries.

SECURITY AND HOME INSURANCE
Crime and petty crime are endemic almost everywhere and even though the majority

of this occurs in the cities, it is important to make your property as secure as possible and insure it wherever it is situated. Needless to say, isolated properties are especially vulnerable.

It is usually better to insure with a large company than a small independent company that may be less amenable when it comes to paying out on a claim. Most companies will demand that any claim must be backed by a police report, which may need to be made within a specific time limit after the accident or burglary. If such an event takes place while the house is empty this may be impossible, which is one of the reasons why you should check the small print carefully on all contracts.

In areas where there are earthquakes or heavy flooding or forest fires premiums will be much higher than back home, and also may not be as comprehensive. Buying cover from a local Spanish, Italian etc company while there, may cost less than taking it out from an insurance company back home but you will have no idea what you are covered for or what the financial limits are (say for earthquake damage in Greece) if the policy is in a language you don't understand.

Earthquake insurance is compulsory in Turkey.

Insurance

When Renting Out. If you are going to let your property to holidaymakers getting good insurance cover is essential. You must inform your insurers, otherwise the policy may be void and you may find an extra premium may be payable. As well as covering the villa or apartment and its contents, you will need to cover your own liability in the event of the unforeseen occurring. It also makes sense to try and find a policy that will cover you for loss of earnings from rentals if your house becomes impossible to rent through problems arising from natural disasters such as floods. Policies will also need to be updated should your property rise substantially in value. Note that your property will not normally be covered for theft by a tenant. It may also be useful to get emergency travel cover so that if there is an emergency concerning your property your travelling costs to see to it, will be covered.

With **long-term rental** agreements either the owner or tenant should always arrange appropriate insurance for a property to cover the cost of rebuilding should it be necessary, contents insurance and third party liability. Apart from being a sensible precaution, third party insurance for property is also a legal requirement. Most insurers prefer a multi-risk policy covering theft, damage by fire, vandalism, etc. If the insurer has bought into a development, it may well turn out that the building as a whole is already covered. It is advisable to check this before taking out an individual policy. In any event, it is unlikely that the existing cover will include the private property of individual inhabitants.

Anyone who has purchased a resale property may find that the seller's insurance may be carried on by the next owner. However, the new owner will have to check whether the policy is transferable.

Holiday Homes. You should take out a policy adapted for holiday homes as normal home insurance i.e. for a permanent residence, would not cover a house that is empty for long periods. Premiums for insurance on homes abroad are likely to be correlated with the amount of time the house is empty; the longer it is unoccupied, the higher the premium.

If the property is rented out you will have to check whether the insurance covers lessees who might accidentally burn down, or criminally damage/steal from the property.

Some high street companies will ensure a second home abroad if you are already insured with them. *Norwich Union* (www.norwichunion.co.uk), for instance, place a premium on the value of a prospective client's main home, while Saga (www.saga.co.uk) has special premiums for those over 50 (£2 million liability for property, loss of rent provision, full cover of 60 days for untenanted properties, emergency accommodation cover, etc.). Other companies, such as Schofields include public liability of up to £3 million. *Towergate Holiday Homes Underwriting Agency Ltd*, Towergate House, St. Edward's Court, London Road, Romford, Essex RM7 9QD; ☎0870-242 2470 ; fax 01708-777 721; www.towergate.co.uk), and *Ketteridge Group Ltd*, 1st Floor, 130A Western Road, Brighton BN1 2LA; ☎01273-720 222; fax 01273-722 799 also offer a wide range of travel-related policies and schemes as well as dealing with general insurance, private cars, commercial insurance and homes insurance.

Useful Addresses – Insuring Holiday Homes Abroad

Andrew Copeland International: 230/234 Portland Road, London SE25 4SL; ☎020-8656 8435; fax 020-8655 1271; e-mail maxine.duffin@copeland.com. Insures domestic property in France, Spain, Portugal, Greece, Italy, Malta and Cyprus under the brand name Europlan.

Barlow Redford & Co: 71a High Street, Harpenden, Herts AL5 2SL; ☎01582-761129; fax 01582-462380. Insures holiday homes in Spain, France and Italy.

Insurance for Holiday Homes: 28 Waterloo Street, Weston-super-Mare, BS23 1LN; ☎01934-424040; fax 01934-424141; e-mail info@insuranceforholidayhomes.co.uk. Insures holiday homes in Spain, Italy, Portugal, Malta, Cyprus and Greece.

O'Halloran & Co: St James Terrace, 84 Newland, Lincoln LN1 1YA; ☎01522-537491; e-mail tpo@ohal.org; www.ohalloran.org.uk. Will arrange holiday homes insurance in Cyprus, France, Greece, Italy, Malta and Spain. Also does health/travel insurance.

Saga: The Saga Building, Middleburg Square, Folkestone, Kent CT20 1AZ; ☎020-8282 0330/0800 015 0751; www.saga.co.uk/finance/holidayhome/ offers holiday home insurance for France, Spain, Portugal and Italy and their islands in the Mediterranean. Offers buildings, contents, or a combined insurance policy.

Schofields Insurance Ltd: Trinity House, 7 Institute Street, Bolton, BL1 1PZ; ☎01204-365080; fax 01204-394346; www.schofields.ltd.uk. Covers holiday homes in France, Spain, Portugal and Italy.

Woodham Group Ltd: Plas Kenrhos, Graig, Burry Point, Carmarthenshire SA16 ODG; ☎01554-835252; fax 01554-835253; e-mail bryandigby@woodhamgroup.com; www.woodhamgroup.com. Brokers arranging holiday home insurance (underwritten by Leisure Underwriting) in Cyprus (south), France, Greece, Italy, Malta and Spain.

The brokers above do not deal with properties in Turkey or Croatia as they do not have the infrastructure of assessors etc. in those countries.

Security

Deterring burglars is usually the main concern. Clever automatic lighting that comes on intermittently and radios and televisions fitted to a time clock can help to convince an opportunistic would-be burglar that the house is occupied. Getting neighbours or locals to keep an eye on the house is also a possibility especially if it is empty for long periods. If you are a permanent resident, a dog can be useful to scare off unwanted visitors. Even a warning sign with a picture of a fierce dog may have some effect.

Any insurer, whether you take out a policy with a local company or with one of the international insurers will not cover you unless you have additional locks on external doors, internal lockable shutters, bars on all windows and doors at first floor level, or up to 10 metres above it. External grilles should be fitted to windows allowing them to be open and keep out intruders. Other ways of reducing your premiums include having a burglar alarm installed. It is also possible to have a webcam fitted so you can keep an eye on your property from outside the country, but this is very expensive.

Other important concerns adversely affecting the cost of insurance include whether the region is regularly susceptible to flooding, forest fires or earthquakes.

House-sitters. For temporary absences for a month or more, it is a good idea to employ house-sitters who, unlike a caretaker, would be expected to stay on the premises at night. For your own peace of mind you could invite friends to stay or employ trustworthy locals perhaps recommended by the local priest, builder, doctor etc.

Owners of holiday homes are often glad to have reliable people stay for free in their houses during the winter in return for some kind of useful work: chopping and stacking wood, garden clearing, looking after animals, painting and decorating etc. The owners then relax knowing their house is secure and if the climate requires it, heated.

EMPLOYING LOCAL STAFF

Caretakers

If you are intending to rent out your property abroad on a full-time basis, you could hire a caretaker/gardener to look after the property: to keep the garden orderly and lawn watered, as well as other household chores such as preparing the house for guests and tidying up once they have left, even looking after bills and taking care of any minor repairs that may need to be carried out from time to time. You will of course need to be sure that you can trust the person you employ. Ask your neighbours if they know of or have dealings with anyone suitable. It may be that if there are a number of properties in the vicinity being used solely as holiday homes then a gardener/caretaker could be employed full-time to look after all the properties, ensuring a good wage for the caretaker and a help to all the owners involved.

Paying for the services of a property management agency to look after your home while you are away is likely to cost far more than by employing a local to do ostensibly the same job.

Other Staff. It should not be difficult to find local staff, either through employment agencies, property management companies or by asking around and putting up advertisements in the vicinity.

Because the business relationship between the employer and the employee in these circumstances is often cash in hand such dealing are in theory illegal as the employee won't be paying tax on their earnings and the employer won't be making social security payments on the employee's behalf. There are pitfalls in employing on a cash in hand basis. Without a written contract between employer and employee misunderstandings, and grudges, can occur. Should you decide to dismiss someone you are employing, you will find that employees are better protected by labour legislation than you as the employer. You should keep a record of all transactions made between yourself and the employee and get a receipt for all wages paid. Another worry is if an accident occurs to an uninsured employee while on your property. You could be sued for negligence and your home insurance will not cover claims made by employees working on your property. It is as well to establish that any work on and in your property is carried out by employees who are covered by insurance and are registered as self-employed.

HEALTH

Healthcare facilities in the neighbourhood of a property overseas are usually a consideration, when it comes to deciding where to buy. This is especially true if your situation requires dealing with ongoing medical conditions, or if you are of retirement age when good health can no longer be taken for granted, or you need good maternity or children's doctors etc. In most of the European Mediterranean countries the facilities are more than adequate, and in some cases may even surpass what you could expect at home. It is perhaps obvious that France, Spain and Italy will operate a higher level of national health care than Turkey, which has no EU standard to conform to. Even within the EU, standards are not consistent. For instance, in Italy there is a north/south divide in state medical services with the northern facilities generally being much better quality, while Greek medical facilities consistently come in for criticism. In contrast, Malaga in Spain has state of the art facilities as well as an International airport (in case you need/want to be flown home). Spain however, has wide variations in standards regionally. If you were based on the smaller Greek or Croatian islands needless to say, you will be remote from a full range of emergency or other treatment facilities.

The website www.eurosurveillance.org publishes regular updates on communicable diseases in Europe. The information is peer-reviewed and linked to the European Commission.

For details of using individual countries' health systems, see the country chapters.

The E111

Reciprocal medical arrangements that exist between the UK and other EU countries to obtain mainly free medical treatment for those whose visits to another EU country will last for no more than three months at a time. This arrangement may well prove helpful for those going on a property-searching trip in the EU and those who already have holiday homes there. The E111 only covers temporary residence, not the first three months of a permanent residence and applies only to emergency medical treatment. The form *Health Advice for Travellers* contains the application form for the E111 and is available from post offices, or the Department for Work and Pensions Benefits Agency, (Overseas Division Medical Benefits, Tyneview Park, Whitley Road, Newcastle-upon-Tyne NE98 1BA; ☎0191-218 7547; www.doh.gov.uk).

Most EU health authorities have simplified the procedures necessary for foreigners to obtain medical treatment while in their country and now you have only to present your E111, and a photocopy of it, to the ambulance, doctor or practice when treatment is required. The original E111 will be returned after it has been checked, while the photocopy will be retained. Be sure to carry spare copies of the document, as they will be needed if further treatment is required. If you do not have an E111, you will be expected to pay for medical treatment, and it does not cover you for non-emergency treatment, e.g. prescribed medicines and dental treatment. Moreover, the E111 is not a substitute for travel insurance.

An E111 normally has no time limit but is not valid once you have left the UK permanently, or are employed abroad. It can sometimes be renewed and it is also possible to get an 'open-ended' E111 if you make frequent trips abroad for a period longer than three months. Explanatory leaflet SA29 gives details of social security, healthcare and pension rights within the EU and is obtainable from main post offices and from the Department of Work and Pensions, Overseas Directorate, Tyneview Park, Whitely Road, Benton, Newcastle-upon-Tyne NE98 1BA.

FORGOT YOUR E111?

If you forget to apply for the E111 before you leave, the International Services section of the Inland Revenue will send it to you: International Services, Longbenton, Newcastle upon Tyne NE98 1ZZ (☎0845-915 4811 *or* +44 191 225 4811 from abroad; *or* +44 191 225 0067 from abroad). Allow one month for International Services to process your application. Details are also available on the Inland Revenue website: www.inlandrevenue.gov.uk/cnr/index.htm.

The E101, E121, E128 & E106

The Inland Revenue, National Insurance Contributions Office, International Services in Newcastle issues an E101 to UK nationals working in another EU country to exempt them from paying social security contributions in that country because they are still paying them in their home country. E101 only gives free medical assistance for three months.

The E128 entitles you to medical treatment in another EU country where you are working, or if you are a student. You have to obtain an E101 *before* you can obtain an E128. Retirees need to fill in form E121 from the Department of Work and Pensions (www.dwp.gov.uk/overseas; ☎0191-218 7777).

The E106 is needed if you move to another European country on a permanent basis. The E106 is for 18 months or 2 years and entitles you to treatment on the national health service provided that you have paid sufficient National Insurance contributions.

Sickness and Invalidity Benefit

Anyone who claims sickness or invalidity benefit in the UK and is moving out to another EU country permanently is entitled to continue claiming this benefit once they are living abroad. Strictly speaking, to claim either benefit, you must be physically incapable of *all* work, however, the interpretation of the words 'physically incapable' is frequently stretched just a little beyond literal truth. If the claimant has been paying National Insurance contributions in the UK for two tax years (this period may be less, depending on his or her level of income) then he or she is eligible to claim sickness benefit. After receiving sickness benefit for 28 weeks, you are entitled to invalidity benefit, which is paid at a higher rate. Anyone currently receiving either form of benefit should inform the Department of Work and Pensions that they are moving to another EU country. Your forms will then be sent to the DWP International Services department (Newcastle-upon-Tyne NE98 1YC) who will then make sure that a monthly sterling cheque is sent either to your new address or direct into your bank account.

Private Health Care Insurance

If you are living in another country because you have bought a home there but are not paying into that country's national insurance scheme then you will not be eligible to use that country's free health service. Even if you have an E111 form (see above) you will only be able to have emergency medical treatment free. There is a large market for private health insurance offering a variety of products to suit the differing circumstances of expats and foreign homeowners. Many permanent expats subscribe to some kind of international private health care plan, which requires regular payments. Others who are making several trips a year to their home take out a travel insurance policy. The majority of such policies are valid for a year or longer and cover multiple journeys within the insured period. It is worth noting that in some countries such as Malta and Croatia, private clinic facilities are cheap enough that it may be better to pay as and when you use them.

Useful Addresses
Axa PPP Healthcare Ltd: Vale Road, Tunbridge Wells Kent TN1 2PL; ☎01892-505 990 8am-4pm Monday-Friday.
BUPA (British United Provident Association): 15 Bloomsbury Way, London WC1A 2BA; ☎020-7656 2000; fax 020-7656 2728. Aimed mostly at UK nationals.
BUPA International: www.bupa-international.com for non-UK Europeans and north Americans living and working around the world.
Exeter Friendly Society Ltd.: Lakeside House, Emperor Way, Exeter EX1 3FD; ☎96 646 1690 or 01392 353535; www.exeterfriendly.co.uk. Has a healthplan called Interplan Euro, that covers all euro zone countries.
Expacare Insurance Services: First Floor, Columbia Centre, Market Street, Bracknell, Berkshire RG12 1JG; ☎01344-381650; fax 01344-381690; e-mail info@expacare.net; www.expacare.net.
Innovative Benefits Consultants Ltd.: 40 Homer Street, London W1H 1HL, UK; tel/fax 0870-737 9000 ext 6129 (Paul Wolf). In New York ☎212 328 3030 ext 5854; info@ibencon.com; www.ibencon.com.
Medibroker International: Medibroker House, 17 Seatonville Road, Whitley Bay, Tyne & Wear NE25 9DA; ☎0191-251 6424; freephone 0800 980 1082; www.medibroker.com. Broker who will quote a range of premiums from quality international medical insurance providers.
O'Halloran & Co: St James Terrace, 84 Newland, Lincoln LN1 1YA; ☎01522-537491; e-mail tpo@ohal.org; www.ohalloran.org.uk. Health/travel insurance worldwide and holiday home insurance in Europe.
United Healthcare: BUPA partner providing services for North Americans.
Worldwide Travel Insurance: ASA Inc. USA; ☎1-602 968 0440.

INTERNATIONAL SCHOOLS

International schools tend to be regarded as the best option for the children of expatriates who do not expect to remain in another country in the long-term, or who want their children to have the option of attending university in their home country. Different schools within the category of International School offer UK, German, French, Japanese, Swedish, Spanish, and US curricula. Though international schools can seem to isolate children from the communities in which they live, most International Schools admit students from many nationalities, including that of the host country, and students are given the chance to study the local language in a way suitable for non-native speakers.

The liaison organisation, European Council of International Schools (ECIS) in the UK and the US, can advise you on where to find an international school in your area. Alternatively, you may buy their *Directory of International Schools* from www.johncatt.co.uk.

Information Sources

Council of British Independent Schools in the European Community (COBISEC): tel/fax 01303 260857; www.cobisec.org.

European Council of International Schools (ECIS): 21 Lavant Street, Petersfield, Hants U32 3EL; ☎01730-268244; fax 01730-267914; e-mail ecis@ecis.org; www.ecis.org.

ECIS North America: 105 Tuxford Terrace, Basking Ridge, New Jersey 07920 USA; ☎908-903 0552; fax 908-580 9381; e-mail malyecisna@aol.com; www.ecis.org.

REGISTERING WITH YOUR EMBASSY/CONSULATE

When you are resident in a country outside your own, it is advisable to register with your embassy or consulate. This enables the home country authorities to keep emigrants up to date with any information relevant to citizens resident overseas and also in the event of an emergency, helps them to trace individuals. Your embassy or consulate can also help with information regarding your status overseas and advise with any diplomatic or passport problems, and offer help in the case of an emergency, e.g. the death of a relative overseas.

Some embassies run social clubs for their nationals and the nationals of friendly countries may be allowed to join too. Apart from being a good place to meet fellow nationals and other expatriates, these social clubs can be useful places to network for employment and business opportunities. However, consulates do not really function as a source of general help and advice.

As a rule, British embassies and consulates interpret their role helping British citizens overseas more strictly than those of many other countries. As the many, who have needed their help in an emergency have found, diplomats tend to keep within the letter if not the spirit of their duties. Appeals for assistance in matters which fall outside these duties – explained in a leaflet available from embassies/consulates or the *Foreign and Commonwealth Office* (Consular Division, Old Admiralty Building, London SW1A 2PA; ☎020-7008 0232; www.fco.gov.uk) – often fall on deaf ears.

THE SCHENGEN ACCORD

The Schengen countries that signed up to an accord in 1997, have generally eliminated passport and baggage controls except for general airport and airline safety in the airports of their countries. In some cases this has meant modification of existing airports like the Malpensa 2000 airport in Milan to accommodate increased traffic. It is now possible to travel around much of Europe and only be aware that a border has been crossed when the street signs change language and car number plates change style. At the time of writing there are fifteen countries in the Schengen group: Austria, Belgium, Denmark, Finland, France, Germany, Greece, Iceland, Italy, Luxembourg, Netherlands, Norway, Portugal, Spain and Sweden. The United Kingdom and Ireland, who have limited border controls between their two countries, have declined to participate in the Accord because they (especially the UK) believe that they are the final targets of most illegal immigrants and so wish to maintain border controls.

The Schengen agreement also allows nationals of countries from outside the EU to enter a member country through the normal passport controls on a visa issued by that country and then move around the Schengen Accord countries freely without further passport checks. To counteract possible abuse by the criminal fraternity and those who have been deported from one country and try to return through another, the member countries came up with the 'Schengen Information System' (SIS). This will connect Consulates and Embassies worldwide to a centralised data bank in Strasbourg where the names and details of all known criminals will be stored. Apart from at Embassies and Consulates, the information can be accessed from terminals at first points of entry to the Schengen Area. Under the protection of personal data regulations, private citizens are allowed to check information relating to them that is stored in the system.

LEARNING THE LANGUAGE

If you don't speak the language, you may be forced to rely on the expatriate community for your survival; more in some areas than others. Even if you can get by in English, it is usually a rewarding and therapeutic experience learning another language, and most people, when they hear someone trying to speak their language will encourage them in their efforts.

Part-Time Courses. Part-time courses are ideal for those with domestic or professional commitments and are cheaper than the language courses offered by commercial organisations such as Berlitz, inlingua, etc. Local colleges of education and community or adult studies centres are the best option as they often run day and evening courses in a wide and amazing variety of subjects. The courses cater for a variety of standards, ranging from beginners who want to learn a language for next year's holiday or for general interest, to those who wish to take an exam leading to a qualification at the end of the course. Cultural organisations also offer courses and sometimes lessons can be arranged through the Embassy in countries where there is no formal cultural organisation.

Intensive Language Courses with International Organisations. One real advantage of an international organisation is that it offers language courses which, begun in your home country, can be completed on arrival in your chosen country. Each course is specifically tailored to the individual's own requirements as far as the language level and course intensity is concerned and the cost of the courses varies enormously depending on these factors. Further information is available from the addresses below:

The Berlitz School of Languages: 2nd Floor, Lincoln House, 296-302 High Holbourn, London WC1V 7JH; ☎020-7611-9640; fax 020-7611 9656: Berlitz USA – 40 West 51st Street, New York City, NY 10020, USA; ☎212 765 1001; fax 212 307 5336; www.berlitz.com for international centres.

inlingua School of Languages: Quality Cobden Hotel, 166, Hagley Road, Birmingham B16 9NZ; tel/fax 0121-455 6677; www.inlingua.com; for information about US inlingua schools visit www.inlingua.com/usa.html.

Linguarama: New London Bridge House, Floor 12a, 25 London Bridge Street, London SE1 9ST; ☎020-7939 3200; fax 020-7939 3230; www.linguarama.com.

Self-Study Courses. For those who prefer to combine reciting verb endings with cooking the dinner or repeating sentence formations while walking the dog, then self-study is the most suitable option and has the advantage of being portable so you can take it with you and continue to learn while practising total immersion in the language amongst the locals. Various well-known organisations produce whole series of workbooks, CDs, audiocassettes and videos for learning a wide range of foreign languages. Linguaphone (Carlton Plaza, 111 Upper Richmond Street, London SW15 2TJ; 020-8333 4898; fax 020-8333 4897; www.linguaphone.com) have courses for tourists at £12.99, beginner courses that aim to teach a new language in twelve weeks (from £49.99) to complete course leading to fluency at £299.90 and the BBC has various series of teach yourself languages books covering most of the main languages (www.bbcshop.com).

Online bookstores such as www.amazon.com, www.amazon.co.uk and www.bn.com have a wide range of courses at discounted prices on their North American, European and other regional sites.

Courses for specific languages are mentioned in the individual countries' sections.

KEEPING IN TOUCH

Expatriates who use international calls more than most for keeping in touch with friends and relations around the world have long used call-back services and other alternative telephone services. These are advertised in international newspapers and magazines (*International Herald Tribune, Time, Newsweek etc*), and on websites such as www.freephone.com and can be a great cost saver.

The latest innovation in reducing telephone costs is the utilisation of the internet for international phone calls. Services such as www.Net2Phone.com allow internet users whose computer is equipped with a microphone and sound card (most computers produced within the last three years allow a microphone/headphone set to be plugged into their soundcard) to log on to their local Internet Service Provider (ISP) and call a standard phone, via the internet, in most countries around the world. The cost of the call is then limited to the cost of being online.

American Users. Americans will find having to pay as you go for local calls different to the system prevalent in many US locations. Local and long distance calls do not vary much in price, though the time of day affects the cost of a call – out of business hours is cheaper than during them. International calls within Europe cost less after 10pm, though the peak rate for North America finishes earlier in the day. As peak rates and off-peak rates and their applicability vary it is worth checking with the national telecoms service to find the best time to make your calls.

Getting a mobile that works in multi countries is not a problem for Europeans but the American mobile system is different from Europe's and Americans will have to hunt down a phone agent that sells Motorola, Siemens, Nokia, Sony etc that will work both in the US and in Europe. You can buy or hire such a phone from www.cellularabroad.com.

WORLDWIDE ENGLISH-LANGUAGE MEDIA

British/USA Press Abroad

British newspapers are available in most of the larger cities and around areas popular with tourists. *The Guardian Weekly* (164 Deansgate, Manchester M60 2RR; ☎0870-

066 0510; www.guardianweekly.com) is available on subscription. Rates for Europe are currently £43 for six months (£77 for a year). *The Weekly Telegraph* (☎01622-335080) is a similar news digest with a subscription costing £108 for a year (£92 if you quote a coupon number from the *Daily Telegraph)*.

The International Herald Tribune (6 bis rue des Graviers, 92521 Neuilly, Cedex Paris; ☎+33-1 41 43 92 61; fax +33-1 41 43 92 10; subs@iht.com; www.iht.com), is published in Paris in conjunction with the *New York Times* and *Washington Post*. It is available on subscription in most countries.

TV & Video

The UK operates PAL-I, the USA and Canada operates NTSC and France operates MESECAM. TVs of one system do not correctly work with another (you can get black and white instead of colour, or have no sound). However, multi-system TVs and videos that play all system types are freely available and many TVs and videos now sold in Europe are multi-system.

Thanks to satellite and cable technology it is now possible to receive a huge variety of international channels via satellite, including BBC World (free to air), BBC Prime (subscription only), CCNI (free to air), CNBC, The Disney Channel and other good quality English-language channels throughout Europe. There are also many other channels available in the numerous European languages, plus the languages of the immigrant population – Arabic, Urdu, Hindi, etc. Local satellite suppliers can offer the best solution as not all areas are connected to cable networks and satellite dishes are not allowed in certain protected areas.

Useful Contacts

Dugdales European: ☎+44 1200 442616; www.dugdale@aol.com; dvddugdale@aol.com. For satellite television. Exports Ski Digital set boxes to anywhere in Europe within 48 hours.

BBC Worldwide Television: Woodlands, 80 Wood Lane, London W12 OTT; ☎020-8576-2555. Commercial subsidiary of the BBC that broadcasts two 24-hour channels; the non-subscription information and news channel BBC World and the entertainment channel BBC Prime for which there is an annual fee.

Solsat Satellite Co: ☎+34 616 314 068; info@solsat.com; www.solsat.com. Satellite company based in Europe that can provide Ski digibox and Sky viewing card at the same time. Can supply all over Europe and to Turkey.

The BBC World Service & VOA

BBC World Service. A monthly publication *BBC On Air,* which gives details of schedules plus advice and information about BBC World Service radio and BBC Prime and BBC World Television, is available on subscription (£12 for 6 months to £60 for 3 years) from BBC On Air Magazine, P.O. Box 326, Sittingbourne, Kent, ME9 8FA; (☎01795-414 555; fax 01795-414 555); e-mail bbconair@galleon.co.uk. The website: (www.bbc.co.uk/worldservice/) has details of the best frequencies to pick up its broadcasts in various countries.

Voice of America. For details of Voice of America programmes, contact VOA, Washington, D.C. 20547; ☎1-202 619 2358. Details of programmes and frequencies are also online at www.voa.gov.

MEDITERRANEAN ROUND-UP

Not everyone who buys a home abroad is seeking a rural idyll deep in the heart of the countryside. The preferred alternative for many, is a property, new, old or waiting to be built, by the blue shores of the Mediterranean or just inland from it. The enclosed Mediterranean Sea is arguably the most beautiful and historic sea on the planet, bordered by southern Europe, western Asia and northern Africa, and which is set *medius terra*, in the middle of these lands. It has shallow tides and mostly clear waters and represents an ideal within easy reach of northern Europe by cheap travel.

The other seas within the Mediterranean are the Tyrrhenian (between Italy and Sardinia), the Adriatic (between Italy and Croatia), the Ionian (between Sicily and Greece), and the Aegean (between Greece and Turkey).

The Mediterranean is also inseparable from the desirable lifestyle it conjures up, including all the most relaxing occupations you can think of including fishing, sailing and swimming, on your doorstep; or if you prefer, all the liveliness of a resort town like Malaga or big port city like Marseille or a UNESCO site like Split or Venice. If, on the other hand, island life is your dream, then the Mediterranean has thousands of potential choices, large and small, Italian, Croatian, Greek and Turkish where you can buy properties and be a Mediterranean islander.

Some parts of the Mediterranean coast have attracted resident foreigners for much longer than others: consider the French and Italian Rivieras, which have had a cosmopolitan European population for a century or longer. These exotic locations were once mainly for those whose lives included travel abroad, or their own holiday house on a Mediterranean as part of an annual round of amusements, which their wealth and privilege allowed them to indulge in. This elitism was superseded by the age of popular mass travel inaugurated by the first charter flights to Spain in the 1950s. Not long after this, Northern Europeans generally, and the British in particular woke up to the idea that life was better in the sun, and commercial interests, i.e. builders, developers and lawyers etc., began to focus on this new clientele and adapted to accommodate the needs of would-be foreign residents. There followed an eruption of building developments along the Spanish costas, which continues up to the present day. From the early 1970s when the first few, white-porticoed villas appeared, they have mushroomed continuously, covering acres of formerly virgin land along the Mediterranean, more often than not embedding ancient fishing villages and coastal towns in their midst, and fast joining up into one nearly continuous built-up coastal strip, particularly on the Costa del Sol and parts of the French coast before you reach the Riviera. As rapidly as they are built, developments fill with tax exiles, holiday homers and retired sun-seekers attracted by the cheap price of property and the even cheaper cost of living, which means even those of modest means can live within a restricted budget, or the limitations of a pension, and still have a lifestyle that would be out of their reach back home.

The development of the Spanish Costas, which have more foreign residents than indigenous ones and certainly more than any other Mediterranean coasts, turned out to be trail-blazing days indeed. While the Spanish costas were burgeoning with homes aimed at the foreign buyer and forming into well-established 'colonies' of British, Germans, celebrities, criminals etc., other sea and sun property seekers were turning their sights on spots like the Italian riviera, (once cheaper than the French one), the Sardinian coast (now very exclusive), various fragments of Greece, and the large island of Cyprus (north and south). Most recently, Croatia, which has a lengthy coastline (as does Italy), and the Mediterranean and Aegean coasts of Turkey have also gained

MEDITERRANEAN COUNTRIES COMPARISON CHART

	Croatia	Cyprus North	Cyprus South	France	Gibraltar	Greece	Italy	Malta	Monaco	Spain	Turkey
Political stability	7	5	7	9	7	8	8	9	9	8	6
Climate	9	9	9	9	9	8	8	8	9	9	8
Cost of living	8	10	6	7	7	9	7	8	4	8	10
Accessibility	5	2	7	10	7	6	7	7	9	10	6
Property availability	6	6	8	8	8	8	7	8	4	9	7
Property prices	7	10	7	7	7	9	7	9	2	8	10
Ease of purchase/ renovation	5	4	7	7	8	5	7	8	6	8	7
Capital investment potential	8	7	8	7	8	8	7	8	4	7	9
Quality of Workmanship	7	5	6	8	8	6	8	6	9	7	5
Cost of Renovation	9	10	8	6	7	9	8	7	5	8	10
Suitability for letting	9	5	9	9	7	8	8	9	9	9	7

Notes
a) For the purposes of the graph, no. 3 'Cost of living' is based on a UK rating of 6.
b) For no. 3 'Cost of Living' the higher the cost the lower the rating.
c) For no. 6 'Property Prices' and for no. 10 'Cost of Renovation' the higher the price the lower the rating.

popularity as prices get ever steeper on the traditionally popular Mediterranean coasts. Among the 'hotspots', Turkey currently perhaps offers the cheapest of all. This is despite Turkey's drawbacks of not being in the EU, and not having western European type legal, health and welfare and insurance regimes and of having endemic rabies and rampant inflation.

The seemingly inexhaustible supply of foreigners wanting an affordable property on the Mediterranean is perhaps not so surprising. The market for property behaves no differently from any other free market. Disillusioned with chilly northern European or US weather, and tired of a roller coaster ride with stocks and shares, many people have turned to property, especially foreign property, which is more affordable than at home, as an investment. Property consumers nose out where the best value is, and more and more of them buy in that area, and very soon there is either nothing left to purchase, or if there is, it is no longer cheap. This has happened on parts of the Costa del Sol and the French and Italian Rivieras and around Dubrovnik. Once demand has forced up prices the market moves on to seek out new bargain areas, and the process repeats itself. The commercialisation of foreign property markets geared to foreign buyers is already as well advanced in recently 'discovered' Croatia as it is in parts of Greece and Cyprus. However, whilst the French Riviera, parts of the Costas and certain Italian resorts like Portofino will probably always be very rich peoples' playgrounds, there are modestly-priced properties still in various spots along the Mediterranean littoral, and a little inland, as well as on Malta and Gozo and Cyprus. For those with an eye to the investment potential of their property on the Med, Turkey may not be the next big thing (as some pundits think) because of all the unknowns, which include rampant inflation and a very high risk of earthquake in some parts. Cyprus however, looks a better bet for speculators as well as being part of the EU while Malta's prices are very good value.

A very important point to make at the outset, is that a few miles (or up to 30km) inland of an expensive coastal area, the price of property can drop by enough to consider a short journey time to the coast acceptable in return for property you don't have to break the bank for, in an area you want to be in, and which gives you a higher measure of privacy and quiet and greater integration with the local population. You can even buy flats in the historic parts of Nice for little more than £100,000, simply because they do not have a sea view.

Some locations on the Mediterranean have a reputation for preserving a state of 'Englishness' from times gone by: The Greek island of Corfu, the independent island of Malta and the disputed Rock (Gibraltar), and the divided island of Cyprus, have built up some colonies with quintessential English traits. Their unique, preserved-in-aspic, character appeals to diehard anglophiles whose life's breath hinges on the crack of cricket ball on willow, or marmalade at breakfast. This predilection is not universal amongst the British however. The current trend is more for blending in with your locality and cultivating the indigenous locals as well as the other expats.

To summarise: the process of obtaining a house on the Mediterranean may well be a dream come true; it can also be an investment, or it can be a regular source of income if it is rented out.

BUYING A HOUSE ON THE MEDITERRANEAN

CROATIA

LIVING IN CROATIA

CHAPTER SUMMARY

- Croatia was part of former-Yugoslavia, which was split by war in 1991.
- Reciprocal agreements with Britain, Ireland and the USA mean that individual nationals of these countries are allowed to own property in Croatia. Other nationalities may have to create a company to do this.
- **Tourism.** Tourism is now almost back to pre-1991 levels with tour companies continuing to flock there. Great news for those with properties to let.
  - The Croatian coast has been popular with naturists for over 70 years.
- **Getting There.** Cheap charter flights to the Croatian coast are booming. Even in winter there are now reasonably-priced flights from the UK.
- **Smoking** is endemic in Croatia; almost everyone 15 years and older smokes.
  - There is a huge black market industry in cigarettes ('unregulated tobacco imports' is the official term).
- **Health.** The Croatian national health service is short of doctors and its facilities under funded; generally, however standards are typical of Western hospitals.
  - The average life expectancy for men and women is 73 years.
- **Housing.** There is 90% ownership of housing in Croatia; most of it private. The remaining 10% is the rental sector.
  - About 200,000 houses and apartments were damaged or demolished during the 1991 war.
- **Media.** The media is entwined with political interests and journalists are regularly subjected to threats and prosecutions.
- **Language.** The Croat language is spoken by Croats, Serbs and Bosnians.

INTRODUCTION

The Republic of Croatia *(Republica Hrvatska)* was part of former-Yugoslavia before the most recent war in the Balkans started in 1991. Croatia claimed independence in 1995, after four years of bloody fighting and Serbian insurgency in one of the nastiest wars of recent times. Before the 1991 war, the glorious coastline of what is now Croatia, was attracting nearly half a million British tourists a year. The war and its immediate aftermath understandably scuppered large-scale tourism in the area, though some loyal visitors still managed to holiday there as soon as the bullets stopped flying, and before the bulk of holiday companies returned. This trickle of tourists was welcomed with open arms by the Croatians; presumably in much the same way as the arrival of a few swallows means summer cannot be far behind. The Croatians also took it for a sign of much appreciated solidarity with the Croatian people in difficult times.

The good times are definitely set to roll again along Croatia's coast. Not only are the tourists returning in ever-increasing numbers (145,000 tourists from Britain booked a holiday there in 2003), but mainstream holiday companies have given it a resounding vote of confidence. In 2004, Crystal Holidays announced a new range of holidays offering self-catering and hotel accommodation in 14 Croatian resorts around Dubrovnik, and in the north on the Istrian and Opatijan rivieras. Along with the tourists, have come the property buyers, amongst whom Britons and the Irish have an advantage as their countries have signed a reciprocal agreement over property purchases in the run up to Croatia's membership of the EU (scheduled for 2007). The USA also has a reciprocal property agreement with Croatia.

HISTORY & POLITICS

History

Since early times, the area of Croatia has been under the domination of various empires and powers. The Roman Empire was the first to stake a claim and under the Romans the area prospered, even producing a handful of emperors; the best known is Diocletian, who ruled AD 284-385 and whose palace at Split is a UNESCO World Heritage Site.

With the disintegration of the Roman Empire, the vacuum was filled by waves of invaders, which included all the villains of the Dark Ages: Huns, Goths, Vlachs, Bulgars and others. It was around this time that the all important Slavs arrived in the region in their various ethnic groups including Croats to present day Croatia, and Serbs and Slovenes, who gravitated roughly to the areas that eventually became the countries named after them.

After roughly a hundred years of wealth and general prosperity, the Venetians bullied their way inward through Croatian territory from the coast, and Hungarians did likewise from the interior. For the next 700 years the surrounding powers including Austria-Hungary and the Ottomans ebbed and flowed into Croatian territory. The Croatians proudly claim however, that Croatia was never fully integrated into the Ottoman Empire. The Venetians left a legacy of elegant architecture, which is the enduring characteristic of the Croatian coastal and island towns which we appreciate today, but the downside of Venetian rule was the deforestation of the islands (repeated elsewhere in the Mediterranean) to feed an insatiable appetite for ships and other types of building.

The centuries of Venetian, Habsburg and Turkish powerplay in the region were considerably enlivened in the seventeenth century by the swash and buckle of some pirate kings originally Serbs, who were then augmented by a Foreign Legion like membership of disparate and desperate international characters including a handful of English noblemen.

The centuries of intriguing by the major powers in the area, was brought to a halt in the early nineteenth century with the arrival of Bonaparte, who created the administrative districts known as the Illyrian Provinces, which stretched from Trieste in the north (now in Italy) to Dubrovnik. After Waterloo in 1815 the Habsburgs returned, and a separate kingdom of Croatia and Slovenia was formed.

The Illyrian Provinces became for Croat nationalists an ideal that took unstoppable hold over their imaginations. After the First World War in 1918 Slovenia and Croatia linked up with Serbia to form the Kingdom of Serbs, Croats and Slovenes which became the basis of former-Yugoslavia, a Communist non-aligned state ruled by the dictator Tito until his death in 1980. Tito's demise left Yugoslavia without a pressure cap to keep the lid on the uneasy ethnic brew that was bubbling underneath. The catalyst that blew the lid off was the dismantling of the Berlin Wall (1989) and the domino effect it produced right across the communist states of Eastern Europe.

In the regional wars that followed, Croatians had a bitter internal struggle with the Serb minority, who declared their own autonomous zone within the newly hatching Republic of Croatia, and they were supported in their aims by the JNA (Yugoslav People's Army). All the horrors of internecine war occurred before the UN could broker a ceasefire in 1992 and the European Union recognised an independent Croatia.

Growing ever impatient with having the UN patrolling the ceasefire between Serbs and Croats, Croatians grasped matters into their own hands and terrible, fierce fighting ensued. Serbs fled Croatia in thousands back to Serbia driven by the fury of the Croats' determination to claim what they saw as their rightful territory. The last area of Serb-occupied Croatia (Slavonia) was only handed back (under the Dayton Peace Agreement) in 1998 and it is still riddled with unexploded mines and abandoned ordnance.

No-one, except those involved, will ever know the exact truth of what went on in the fighting between Serbs and Croats within Croatia, but the phrase 'ethnic cleansing' has joined 'holocaust' as a concept of so much horror that it is impossible to imagine. Some Croatian generals are being tried for war crimes. There is also some bitterness against the British for not supporting Croatia sooner in its struggle to become a stable nation.

Since the 1991 war, a vast programme of reconstruction has been taking place; even the incomparable city of Dubrovnik was very badly damaged and has had to be substantially reconstructed.

Politics

Political Parties. During the socialist era of Yugoslavia, the only party in Croatia was the communist party. In the first free elections, victory went to the right-wing Croatian Democratic Union (HDZ) who remained in power until 2000. In the 2000 elections, a complex coalition of six parties including the Social Democratic Party of Croatia (SDP) and the Croatian Social Liberal Party (HSLS) and the Croatian Peasants Party (HSS), all with their own personal interests to pursue, stood against the HDZ and took power until 2001. In 2001 and 2002 several disgruntled factions left the government and the rump held on to power until the 2003 elections were

won narrowly by the HDZ and a coalition of other right-wing parties. While the HDZ coalition remains in power it is considered by political analysts as detrimental to foreign relations. Although they have pledged to keep Croatia on course for EU membership in 2007, there are disputes with the EU which is putting pressure on Croatia to speed-up the process of the return of Serb refugees to Croatia.

Parliament. Croatia is a parliamentary democracy with an elected president. The constitution was adopted on 22 December 1990 and independence from Yugoslavia was declared in on June 25th 1991.

Parliament (*Hrvatski Sabor*) is unicameral and comprises 153 deputies (2003 total) who are elected by popular vote and sit for four-year terms. Parliament meets in public sessions twice yearly: January 15th-30 June and from 15 September to 15 December. Deputies sit in the chamber and decisions are made based on a majority vote if more than half the chamber is present, except on issues of national rights and constitutional issues when all are required to be present.

The current prime minister is Ivo Sanader and the president Stjepan (known as Stipe) Mesic. The last elections were held in December 2003 and the next due in 2005.

THE ECONOMY

The Economy

Before the 1991 war that resulted in the dissolution of old Yugoslavia, Croatia and Slovenia between them constituted the economic powerhouse of the former communist state with a per capita output over 30% higher than the Yugoslav average. The war may have provided Croatia with the potential to pursue its own economic success, but it was at a cost of great devastation from which Croatia is about to emerge. It is confirmation of the level of damage to the infrastructure and population that Croatia is not one of the nations in this year's wave of new eastern European members of the EU, but will have to wait until 2007, the projected date at which Croatia will be ready to join.

Croatia has had severe economic problems to overcome, but with the support of the EU, IMF and The World Bank it has made great strides, particularly in restoring and modernising its infrastructure. However, it still has an unemployment figure running at a very high 18.9%. (November 2003). Tourism was an important resource for the economy pre-1991 and this has resumed its important role in the economy again, now that big mainstream holiday companies have returned in growing numbers. Inflation, which was high after 1991 has now fallen to a fairly modest 4%. There is little doubt that Croatia has the potential to have a thriving economy and this should become apparent over the next decade. This means that a few years from now, for anyone buying property there, the prospects of making a good investment are excellent.

The Cost of Living. Some foreigners are under the impression that the cost of living is cheaper than elsewhere in Europe. According to Lara Vekic of Croatia-Estate.Com, one of Croatia's largest estate agencies:

> *I have friends from Australia and Austria who tell me how expensive they find it to live in Croatia. Croatians especially find it so, as the average annual wage in Croatia is now 20% less than it was in 1988, but the prices are the same as elsewhere in Europe.*

GEOGRAPHY & CLIMATE

Geography

Croatia is situated in southeastern Europe and is bordered by Hungary and Slovenia to the North and Serbia to the east, while Bosnia Herzegovina points up in a solid 'V' from the south and makes Croatia an oddly formed country, which has been compared to a wishbone, croissant, or a butterfly. The western part of the wishbone lies along the Adriatic coast while the eastern part is completely landlocked. This makes it geographically diverse; almost two separate countries, one Mediterranean, the other Central European.

Coastal Region. The Mediterranean (Adriatic) coast comprises a narrow strip, which is backed by mountains separating it from the hinterland. The area is predominantly karst (limestone with cave systems formed where underground drainage has dissolved the rock). This type of geological strata is noted for its dryness, and also characterises the Croatian islands, which are similarly mountainous. The Dinara range reaches down almost the whole length of the coast. The highest coastal mountain is Biokovo (1762m) in Dalmatia.

The length of the mainland coastline is 1,777 km and the coastline of the islands amounts to another 4,058 km.

The Croatian coast is extremely fragmented and indented with over 1,000 islands and islets of which fewer than 70 are inhabited.

Capital and Important Towns. The capital Zagreb, including the metropolitan area, has a population of about a million and lies towards the northeast of the country away from the coast. The next largest city is Split (population 190,000) which is on the coast.

Counties. Territorially Croatia is divided into 20 counties, 6 of which are on the coast. North to south these are: Istra/Istria *(Itarska)*, Goranski Coast *(Primorsko-goranska)*, Lika-Senj *(Ličko-senjska)*, Zadar *(Zadarska)*, Sibenik-Knin *(Šibensko-kninska)*, Split and Dalmatia *(Splitsko-dalmatinska)* and Dubrovnik-Neretva *(Dubrovačko)*.

Important Coastal Towns. Dubrovnik, Hvar town on Hvar Island, Korcula town on Korcula Island, Porec, Pula, Rovinj, Sibenik, Split, Ston and Zadar.

Population. The latest (July 2003 estimate) put the population at 4,422,248, or just under four and a half million. Nearly 90% are ethnically Croat. Of the minority ethnic groups, the largest is of Serbs (4.5%).

There are a further estimated three and a half million people around the world (the Croatian diaspora), claiming Croatian descent.

Religion. The Croatians adopted Christianity from the ninth century and they have been predominantly Roman Catholic ever since. Nearly 90% of Croatians claim to be Catholic and church attendance is higher than you will find in many western countries. Due respect is accorded to religious practices and modest attire is essential for entering churches and cathedrals.

Less than 5% of Croatians claim to be Orthodox Christians and Muslims account for a mere 1.3% of the population.

Climate

The coast has a Mediterranean climate, which means usually mild, moist winters and very dry summers. The air temperature varies with the area so in the north summer temperatures average 34°C while in the south they are 38°C. In the winter, the northern Adriatic can reach lows of -16°C, whereas in the south they stay above freezing and do not usually go below 6°C.

CULTURE SHOCK

There are certain aspects of Croatian attitudes and behaviour, which may constitute a cultural shock for some Westerners.

Smoking. 'Everyone smokes in Croatia' may be an overstatement, but that's how it usually seems. Furthermore, handing out foreign brand cigarettes to new Croatian acquaintances is one of the most acceptable social ice-breaking techniques since they are all hard at it buying contraband ones anyway. All this is difficult to deal with if you are vehemently anti-smoking.

Attitudes to Gays/Lesbians. Homosexuality may have been decriminalised in Croatia since 1977, and the age of sexual consent for gays, lesbians and heterosexuals was equalised in 1998 (to 14 years) but attitudes are far from tolerant; witness the jeering and abuse hurled at an attempted Gay Pride march in Zagreb in 2002. It is difficult to find the gay scene, even in sophisticated resorts, as it is still mostly underground. Sadly, gays and lesbians may find it more convenient and comfortable to conceal their inclinations, at least until they have become accepted into the local community. Young people are much more tolerant than the older generations.

Naturism. Croatia is a naturists' Mecca and has been since 1934 when the island of Rab became the first official naturist resort. This tradition was augmented during the 1960s when several beaches on the Dalmation and Istrian coasts became the first commercial nature resorts in Europe. As well as over 30 naturist resorts (new ones are being added all the time) nearly all the beaches have a naturist section, usually the furthest away from the point of access. If your holiday home includes a mooring for your boat, then be prepared to encounter naked windsurfers and even naked yacht crews, on your voyages around the islands. Even though it may be mainly the tourists who are stripping off, topless sunbathing for women was the norm in Croatia, even before communism ended.

   Croatia's wholehearted embracing of naturism and naturists may come as a shock to some, and a positive liberation to others.

Drinking. 'Everyone in Croatia drinks' is another overstatement that seems to be mainly true. Usually, business deals including buying property, are sealed with a shot (more likely
several) of the local firewater (typically a type of plum brandy, *Slijivovica)*. If you don't drink, or can't hold your liquor, then you are in for a hard time as most excuses are considered invalid. Even 'I have just had a liver transplant' won't cut it in a land where drinking is so much a part of the culture.

GETTING THERE

Until quite recently, when tour operators began expanding charters to Croatia, there has not been a wide choice of flights, or low prices to choose from. This has hampered the return of British tourists, but not other Europeans who visit Croatia in large numbers by car, often via ferries from Ancona and Venice. The following is a selection of airlines flying to the coastal airports from the UK.

Scheduled Flights

British Airways: ☎0845 779 9977; www.ba.com. Scheduled flights to **Dubrovnik** from Gatwick, Heathrow, London City, Manchester, Stansted. Also from UK regional airports and Scottish airports. Prices from £99 (London City or Gatwick) to £215 (Edinburgh).

Croatia Airlines: ☎020-8563-0222; e-mail lonto@croatiaairlines.hr; www.croatia.airlines.hr. Year round daily services from Heathrow via Zagreb to **Pula, Rijeka-Krk, Dubrovnik.** Also direct charter flights from London and Manchester to Pula, Split and Dubrovnik.

Czech Airlines: **to Split** from Birmingham, Gatwick, Heathrow, Stansted. Prices from £179 (Stansted to Split) to £192 (Heathrow to Split).

Other scheduled flights to Dubrovnik are offered by Alitalia, and Malev Hungarian Airlines. Most are priced around the £200 mark.

Charter Flights

Airtours: ☎0870 750001; www.airtours.co.uk. **Pula** from Gatwick and Manchester.

Croatia Airlines: ☎020-8563-0222; e-mail lonto@croatiaairlines.hr; www.croatia.airlines.hr. Croatia Airlines is the national carrier and in addition to year round scheduled flights to the Dalmation Coast via Zagreb, offers seasonal charters from London and Manchester to **Pula, Split** and **Dubrovnik.**

Holiday Options: Burgess Hill, West Sussex, RH15 9NJ; ☎01444-876500 and 0870 4208386; fax 01444-876501; www.holidayoptions.co.uk. **Dubrovnik** and **Split** from Gatwick and regional airports Birmingham, Bristol, Manchester and Norwich; plus Dubrovnik from Glasgow.

Hidden Croatia: 47 Fulham High Street, London SW6 3JJ; ☎020-7736 6066; 020-7384 9347; e-mail info@hiddencroatia.com; www.hiddencroatia.com. Direct flights from the UK to **Dubrovnik, Pula, Rijeka-Krk** and **Split** from £139 including taxes.

Newmarket Holidays: ☎020-8335 3030; www.newmarket-group.co.uk. Flights to **Dubrovnik** from Belfast, Cardiff, Edinburgh, Exeter, Gatwick, Glasgow, Liverpool, Manchester and Newcastle.

Palmair: ☎01202-200700. **Split** from Jersey and Bournemouth and **Dubrovnik** from Bournemouth.

Thomson Holidays: ☎0870 5550 2555; www.thomson.co.uk. **Pula** from Gatwick and Manchester from £159.

Thomas Cook: ☎0870 607 5085; www.thomascook.com. **Dubrovnik** and **Split** from Gatwick and Manchester.

Even the growth of charter flights from the UK to Croatia at reasonable prices will probably not prevent no frills airlines addicts from using **Ryanair's** services to Trieste (just over the border from Istria), or Venice from where there are ferries to Split and Dubrovnik. **Easyjet** and the Italian no frills airline **VolareWeb** also fly to Venice.

There are also charter flights from Ireland with Croatia Tours (www.croatiaturs.ie), Concorde Travel (www.concordetravel.ie), Sunway Holidays (www.sunway.ie) and Crystal Holidays (www.crystalholidays.ie) among others.

COMMUNICATIONS

Telephones

Deregulation of the telecoms industry has not yet swept through Croatia, or as Hvratski Telekom (www.tel.hr) puts it in their company profile 'HT is the leading telecommunications provider in Croatia, at the same time the only provider'. This is set to change as HT 's monopoly rights expired in 2003. Keep an eye out for the alternatives, which are sure to be up and running shortly and might provoke some price cutting.

HT provides a full range of telecommunications services including GSM digital mobiles, and DSL and ISDN internet services under the brand name Hinet. New subcribers go to the nearest HT Centre (a list of their addresses can be found on the HT website).

Mobiles. Croatia's mobile phone network was established in 1996 and there are different brands for various subscriber needs including billed (HT Cronet), pre-paid (HT Simpa). Analogue services are also still available under the Mobitel brand. More details can be found on the website www.htmobile.hr/english.

The cheapest and easiest way to use your (GSM) mobile in Croatia is with a Croatian SIM card (post offices sell them), which will work out cheaper for local calls than using your mobile from home.

Mobile phones use the prefixes 091, 098 and 099.

Telephone Numbers. The international code for Croatia is 00 385. The area codes for Zagreb and the main coastal cities and their surrounding region are:

Dubrovnik	020
Gospić	053
Pazin (Istria)	052
Rijeka	051
Šibenik	022
Split	021
Zadar	023
Zagreb	01

Public services and emergency numbers are:

Ambulance	94
Fire	93
General information	981
Police	92
Roadside assistance	987

Internet. ADSL Broadband is quite new in Croatia and most connections are still by dial-up. This will no doubt change over the next few years.

Post Offices

The Croatian postal service *(Hvratska pošta d.d.)* has more than a thousand outlets and employs over 12,000 people. The post office logo is a stylised black post horn symbol on a yellow background. Post office opening hours are from 7am to 7pm Monday to Friday and 7am-1pm Saturday. Opening times may vary slightly; for instance in resorts during the tourist season post offices usually open later in the evening.

Addressing Mail. Croatian postal addresses are written differently to UK and US ones: First line: title, then the first and last names of the addressee. Second line: street name, then house number, entrance number, floor number, flat number. Third line: area code and place name. For international letters add the country. The addresser should add his or her full name and address above left on the front of the envelope or package, or on the reverse of it.

Special Postal Services. All the usual postal services are available, Registered letter, Confirmed Delivery *(potvrdeno urucenje)*, Express Mail *(zurno)*. Post offices also offer a range of financial services including international ones such as postal cheques and post office giro cheques. Western Union quick cash transfer service is also available in Croatian post offices.

FOOD AND DRINK

Food

Croatian cooking has been subject to many influences including Turkish, Hungarian, Venetian and Austrian. Staples of the diet include smoked and dried meats, capiscums (peppers), meat roasts, an enormous variety of seafood and the wide use of olive oil and herbs. Herbs and flavourings can be plucked wild and include rosemary, basil, bay, mint, orange, lemon, parsley and rose petals. Desserts and cakes are made with honey, nuts and raisins and figs. Calorie-concentrated offerings include the Christmas speciality of oil fried doughnuts with almonds and raisins and *paprenjak* an aromatic pastry made with walnuts, honey and pepper, which is said to date from the 16th century. Croatia's most famous sweeties are made at the Kras (pronounced crash) factory in Zagreb (www.kras.si), Apparently they haven't changed the packaging since 1911, so they are very retro stylish. Kras also makes some savoury products and sweet biscuits and are now selling on the internet.

Meat is highly prized, and would once have been reserved for family occasions rather than for everyday consumption. Traditional family fare would be a pot roast using mixed meats from lamb, goat or mutton, roasted with vegetables and baked below ground with the embers and ashes on top. It is still be cooked this way in country areas. Meat with dumplings or noodles is another popular dish.

On the coast, there is every kind of seafood you can imagine and those you probably couldn't: black risotto, a legacy of Venetian times, made with rice and cuttlefish whose ink stains it; hence the name.

Wine

Croatia does not have a huge wine industry and it does not export wine (yet), but in former-Yugoslavia, Croatia and Serbia between them produced three-quarters of the country's wine so it has potential to become an export industry. Croatia has a total of 650 sq.km of viticulture. According to the Ministry of Agriculture about 375 sq.km are producing wine of a protected geographical origin *(Geografsko porijeklo)*. Over 90% of wine produced is white *(bijelo)* but in the coastal areas red *(Crno)* wines predominate. The islands produce some unique wines, which are worth trying if only because the methods of production on ancient presses, and washing the barrels out with seawater, go back to antiquity. Some of the most characterful wines are grown on the islands *Grk:* from *Korcula, Bogdanusa* from *Hvar* and *Vuguva* on *Vis.*

Recommended wines include *Posip* (dry white from Korcula), *Rukatac* also called Marastina (white) from *Smokvica* on the Dalmatian coast. *Plavac,* also from Korcula is one the island's best reds.

Many vineyards are privately-owned and quietly producing their owners' unregulated wines which you can buy locally. Local recommendation will probably be your best wine guide for this.

SCHOOLS AND EDUCATION

Croatia has both public and private schools but mostly the former. Private education has only recently been introduced and there is one private university. Education is compulsory from ages 7 to 15.

The academic year runs from September to June (two semesters).

The national body with responsibility for the administration and co-ordination of education is the Ministry of Education and Sport (Trg. Burze 6, 10000 Zagreb, Croatia; ☎+385(1) 461-0485; fax +385(1) 456 9087).

Primary

Osnovna škola (Primary school) lasts from ages seven to 15. Students cover a range of subjects including a foreign language and physical education plus elective studies. Assessment is through coursework and written and oral examinations. Upon completion of this eight-year cycle grades are awarded from one to five; five is the highest.

Secondary

Secondary education covers ages 14-18 and the cycle lasts three to four years. Secondary education is taken at comprehensive schools. Comprehensive secondary schools *(Gimnazija)* are of two types: general and the more academic stream-based; the streams are humanities/language, science and classical studies. This cycle of education influences the direction of studies for tertiary level.

Vocational secondary school *(Strukovna škola)* offers a more general programme that is geared to the workplace and practical training is a compulsory part of the programme.

Students are given annual reports grading their studies. Final examinations are held at the end of the cycle and a Certificate of Completed Examinations is given. Assessment is done continuously through coursework and examinations. Grading is awarded at five levels; the highest is five and two is the lowest pass mark. The qualification awarded at the end of the cycle is the *matura.*

It is also possible to attend an arts school *(Umjetni ka Skola)* for secondary education that offers specialist tuition in music, dance, visual art and design, and the award is the International Baccalaureat *(Medjunarodna Matura).*

Tertiary Education

At university level, basic degree programmes (Diploma) require studies of four to six years. Postgraduate studies including a Masters *(Magisterium)* require one to two years' study. Doctoral studies require three years beyond the Masters degree.

Universities. Croatia has four universities *(Sveuciliste)*. Together, these establishments have about 84,000 students. Students sit for examinations at the end of a particular unit of study, but exams can be postponed for several years. All units have to be passed and three attempts to pass a unit are allowed. After that, the student has to re-enrol in the unit. There is a comprehensive final exam or short thesis at the end of the programme. There are five bands of grading with the top grade *Odlican* (excellent) being 10.

Foreigners in Croatian Universities. Foreign students need a certified copy of their school leaving certificate and any other requested documents in the English language. They are also required to complete a two-semester course in the Croatian language.

Polytechnics. In addition to the universities there are seven polytechnics providing professional courses of study that are shorter than university ones and which offer practice-based professional knowledge and the updating and extension of existing qualifications.

TAXES

Whilst foreigners can enjoy some tax advantages in Croatia, for instance tax-free yachting, Croatian nationals and anyone permanently resident in Croatia, or earning income in Croatia, bears a heavy burden of income tax and VAT. Furthermore, Property Transfer tax (5%) paid when property is bought and sold, is one of the highest in Europe (see *The Purchasing Procedure* for details of this and other taxes on real estate). There are at last some rumblings from the Ministry of the Economy to the effect that the Property Transfer tax (also called Property Purchase Tax) could be lowered in the next few years.

The Croatian tax year for individuals usually follows the calendar year. Company tax returns have to be filed at the end of April following the tax year, and companies must make monthly advance payments of tax amounting to one 12th of the tax of the preceding year.

Personal Income Tax

Income tax on individuals, known in tax parlance as 'natural persons', is levied at the basic rate of 20% up to the amount of 3,750 kuna monthly. After that the rate is 35%. The personal allowance or tax threshold, before any tax is due is 1,250 kuna monthly.

Surtax. Surtax is also charged in some municipalities based on the amount of income tax due. The amount of the Surtax varies depending on the area. The most expensive areas are Zagreb (18%) and Dubrovnik (15%), Split is 10%, Rijecka 6.25% and Osijek 13%. The addition of surtax can therefore bring an individual's income tax burden to over 50%.

Social Security Contributions. These are salaried people's contributions towards health insurance and pensions and are a type of direct taxation on the individual for his or her ultimate benefit, rather than for funding government programmes such as road-building. In 2004 the basic contributions totalled 37.2%. Of this 20% is from the employee and the employer pays the rest (17.2%).

Taxable Income from Letting Property. Anyone who is letting out their property and receiving their income from it in Croatia is liable for tax in Croatia. The taxable income from a rental lease is the rental income minus 30% for expenses, or 50% if letting rooms or beds.

Exemptions from Income Tax

The following sources of income are exempt from income tax:

- Interest on hard currency, kuna current and savings accounts.
- Dividends on shares.
- Gains from the disposal of financial property.
- Pensions

VAT

In Croatian, VAT is PDV (*Porez Na Dodatnu Vrijednost*). The current VAT system in Croatia came into being on 1 January 1998. There is a single, very high VAT rate of 22%. Most EU countries have a lower standard rate (Italy 20%, Spain 16%, UK 17.5%) .

Zero-Rated. The following are zero-rated for VAT: banks and insurance companies. Also exempt are medical, cultural and educational goods, which include text-books for education, bread, milk, medical pharmaceuticals and some medical implants (as listed on the Health Fund List 1 November 1999).

Other Taxes

Capital Gains. Capital gains are not normally taxable. In the case of property there are no capital gains due if the property is sold three years or longer after purchase. If a property is sold within three years, 35% tax is payable. For other taxes related to property including *Property Transfer Tax*, and local taxes, see the section on *Property Purchase Procedure*.

Special Tax – Excise duty. Excise duty seems like a tax imposed primarily on those things, that pose a danger to health, or might kill you from excitement (or both). Addictive temptations on which special tax is due include tobacco products, beer, alcoholic beverages, coffee, personal cars, motorcycles, boats, aircraft and 'luxury products'. The amounts payable are fixed at various levels and payable by producer or importer, after VAT has been added.

Tax-Free Yachting

The tax-free yachting available in Croatia is likely to continue only until the country officially joins the EU in 1997/8. As Croatia is not yet in the EU, foreigners can avoid paying VAT on a yacht bought within the EU if the vessel is registered and exported out of EU territory. Non-EU and EU yacht-owners with Croatian residence permits can sail in EU waters for up to 18 months in any 24-month period without paying

VAT on the yacht, spare parts and equipment. In order to do this the yacht has to be registered in 'an internationally recognised jurisdiction (such as Gibraltar, St.Vincent or Guernsey) to provide proof of nationality and ownership.'

It is legal to exploit tax advantages and make substantial savings by registering a yacht in an appropriate jurisdiction and mooring outside the EU in Croatia. You still have easy access to the EU and your yacht is being run in a tax efficient way. You don't have to be an Aristotle Onassis (and you certainly wouldn't want to be a Robert Maxwell), but you do have to have the kind of income where sailing around for months at a time and conducting business from your yacht is a regular part of your lifestyle; though you could also be doing it for health reasons.

Residence Permits For Yacht-Owners. All foreign residents who wish to spend more than three months in Croatia, even when their 'residence' is a yacht moored in a Croatian marina, need to apply for a residence permit. The residence permit is valid for a year and is easily renewable. For information on how to apply for a residence permit see *Residence and Entry Regulations*.

Useful Contact and Websites
Henley & Partners: Kralja Zvonmira 36, 21000 Split, Croatia; ☎+385 21 489 511; fax +385 21 489 511; fax +385 21 489 505; croatia-office@henleyglobal.com. Helps arrange residence status and advises corporations about all aspects of investing and doing business in Croatia.
Ministry of the Economy: www.mingo.hr/english. English version of the website of the Ministry of the Economy for up-to-date tax information.
Www.hr: www.hr./wwwhr/business/finance/accounting/index.en.html. List of book-keepers, accountants and companies that help individuals and businesses with tax returns.

Accountancy & Tax Return Assistance
Infokorp: Zagreb, Croatia; ☎+385 13 095 694; e-mail danko@lace.hr; www.infokorp.hr/english.
KPMG: KPMG Croatia d.o.o. za reviziju, Nova Ves 11, 1000 Zagreb, Croatia; ☎+385 1 46 66 440; fax +385 1 46 68 030.
Orkis: Badaliceva 26a, 10000 Zagreb, Croatia; ☎ +385 1 3820 400; fax +385 1 38 20 096; orkis@orkis.hr; www.orkis.hr. Bookkeeping, tax consulting, income advising and more.
Tritem Ltd: Brace Domany 8, Zagreb, Croatia; ☎+385 1 38 44 025; fax +385 1 30 20 056; e-mail tritem@maddiving.com; www.tritem.hr. Firm started in 1992 as account-ing and consultancy company. Also does annual tax returns for individuals.

HEALTH
Medical facilities are the same level as westerners are used to. The main problem with the state system has been under-funding following severe economic problems after the 1991 war and Croatia still has fewer doctors per head of the population than EU countries. Massive investment from amongst others the EU has improved conditions greatly in the last few years. The state health service will continue to improve and the private sector of healthcare is booming. Medical standards are high and foreigners need have no apprehensions about Croatian hospitals beyond those they might have at home.

Social problems in Croatia that might be expected to cause health problems include poverty amongst those with a low education level, and the elderly. The Roma (gypsies) represent over 13.56% of all claimants of social assistance including health facilities in Croatia. However, levels of health in Croatia are surprisingly better than you might expect. An AIDs problem is just beginning to emerge, but known cases so far are in the hundreds rather than the thousands. The average life expectancy for men and women is 73. One health problem for the future is the alarming level of teenage smoking fuelled by cheap, black market cigarettes.

National Health Schemes

Health care is financed partly through employee contributions deducted from salaries. Health insurance is mandatory for Croatians and is conducted through the Croatian Institute for Health Insurance (CIHI). A small number of health services are paid through through additional health insurance from private health insurance companies.

Foreigners Using Croatian Health Facilities

Most foreigners will probably use private medical facilities in Croatia, except for emergencies under the UK/Croatia reciprocal agreement or if they have been paying Croatian national health insurance. Most foreigners therefore should ensure that they have adequate private insurance for medical services if they are living permanently in Croatia. Further details of worldwide health insurance providers can be found in the *General Introduction* to this book.

SHOPPING

Supermarkets

Croatia's retail sector has evolved in the last twelve years. Prior to 1991 retail outlets were largely state-run enterprises known as Socially Owned Enterprises (SOEs). SOEs were made up of small/medium size shops, small privately owned shops and green produce markets. Supermarkets existed only in small numbers and there was a sprinkling of non-food department stores only in the larger cities. In the first phase of transition to a market economy (1991-1996), SOEs were privatised. In 2001 Croatia opened up to foreign investment which resulted in foreign chains pouring in to set up business there. In 2000 the supermarket share in food retail was 25%, by 2002 it had rocketed to over 50% (in France, where supermarket retailing has had decades to evolve, the share is 70%). One of the first was the French hypermarket chain Leclerc. The Croatian chain Konzum provides stiff competition as it has recently expanded its retail outlets to 230 making it the largest supermarket chain in Croatia. However, Croatian retailing that continued to be small scale, could not compete and thousands of small businesses went under.

Croatians spend a large proportion of their income on food and the explosion of supermarkets with their mass buying and bargaining power to get the cheapest prices has changed their buying habits. Where once they would get their fresh produce from a green market or a local shop, they now buy in supermarkets showing how they have embraced the supermarket culture wholeheartedly. This has had a detrimental effect on Croatian farmers, small wholesalers, markets and food manufacturers. The big supermarket chains now have their own wholesale grower/providers, owned by their holding companies and which are geared exactly to their needs and produce consistently to a high standard delivered to schedule. No doubt Croatian agriculture will catch up, but it will be at the expense of small scale, environmentally sound farming practices and diversity.

Shopping hours are 7.30am-8pm for department and grocery stores. Some grocery stores close for lunch. On Saturdays most shops open from 7.30am to 2pm. In tourist resorts shops of all kinds usually keep longer hours during the season.

CROATIAN WINDS UP PENCIL AND FLIES

Eduard Slavoljub Penkala (1871-1922) was a prolific inventor in Zagreb who patented the 'automatic pencil', an invention he followed by one with a simple twist mechanism, that spread around the pencil-using world like wildfire. His company diversified into other types of writing instruments and accessories all patented by the remarkably successful E.S. Penkala, who later turned his creative mind to the study of aero-dynamics and built his own aircraft which he flew on its maiden flight in 1910.

His name fits his pen and pencil inventions but is sadly not the origin of the word, which is *penna*, from the Latin for feather.

Penkala pens and pencils are still available in Croatia.

Currency and Exchange Rates

Croatia still has its own currency, the *kuna* (kn). One kuna is made up of 100 *lipa*. Croatia is not yet an EU member although it is heading that way and membership is planned for 2007. In the meantime the kuna is subject to fluctuations against other currencies. For instance the kuna has gone from being 10 to the pound sterling to 11 to the pound in three months. A euro is currently worth 7.5 kunas. See the *Banks* section for information about foreign resident accounts.

MEDIA

With a right-wing government that brooks no opposition, the media in Croatia is greatly compromised in the areas of professionalism and objectivity, and political control of the media is ingrained.　Journalists and media people are regularly subjected to violence and court prosecutions. Despite the Law on Croatian Radio-Television adopted in 2003, progress towards a free press and media is lamentably slow. It is worth quoting an article published in 2003 by Stojan Obradovic (Editor in chief of STINA News Agency, Split).

Earlier this year, the Media Council of the Croatian Helsinki Board, established a year ago with the aim of fostering the development of freedom and professionalism in Croatian media, issued a public statement assessing the current situation in the Croatian media scene as rather grim.

Although the Council emphasises the advances made in the domain of media freedoms, it warns about notable difficulties in meeting the tasks assigned to media in a democratic society. What is especially stressed is the impact of the politics on media, which remains continuously strong.

One of the key conditions imposed on Croatia among the criteria of accession to the EU, remains media freedom, and in particular, the establishment of public television. OSCE (www.OSCE.org) and the European Commission regard that the new Law failed to fully provide elimination mechanisms of imposing political influence on the most powerful medium in the country. Meanwhile, the problems are piling up - from inadequate protection of journalists and their rights, through non-transparent media ownership, all the way to the lack of legislature concerning the accessibility of information.

Newspapers

Any newspaper or magazine that describes itself as independent is anything but (see above). Croatia has about a dozen newspapers and news magazines, most of them based in Zagreb. The only one with an English version (on the internet) is the rather unsavoury right wing *Nacional* (www.nacional.hr) published weekly. A digest of articles in English from the 'independent' press can be found on the website www.ex-yupress.com and www.balkanweb.com publishes articles on Croatia from the *Washington Post*, and a digest of articles about Croatia published by the American press.

National statistics show that 59% of the population read a newspaper and 39% take weeklies.

Television & Radio

Croatia has 19 television stations and 140 radio stations. The national broadcasting service is HRT, which has three channels. Croatian television is in a transition phase geared to meeting the standards of the EU for a truly independent national broadcasting company. Watching national television is most Croatians preferred way of keeping up with the news.

CRIME

Organised crime is endemic in Croatia and across the Balkans generally. Everything from money laundering and terrorism to drug and tobacco smuggling. However, foreign tourists or residents are rarely targets although conspicuous wealth is bound to attract unwanted attention. Violent crime is also fairly rare, which is surprising considering the wartime atrocities that took place in Croatia. At the time of press two Croatian generals were on trial for alleged war crimes including the massacre of Serbian civilians.

The death penalty was abolished in Croatia in 1990.

LEARNING THE LANGUAGE

The Alphabet

The Croatian language uses the Roman alphabet and employs 30 characters, some of which are universally recognisable while others have diacritics (accents and other symbols) which influence the pronunciation. Ignoring the diacritics, e.g. in e-mails, will not affect the understanding by a native speaker, but if you are serious about learning the language you will of course learn them. Most sounds in Croatian are represented by a single letter, unlike in English where one sound can be subject to many different spellings (e.g. clue, two, too etc). For details of how to pronounce the letters see the websites www.skeravec.chez.tiscali.fr.Pronounc.html and www.hr/hrvatska/language/izgovor.en.htm. (*Izgovor* means pronounciation). The latter site also has some useful words and phrases to get you started.

Croat is also understood by Bosnians and Serbs.

THE CROATIAN ALPHABET

A a	B b	C c	Č č	Ć ć
D d	DŽ dž	Đ đ	E e	F f
G g	H h	I i	J j	K k
L l	LJ lj	M m	N n	NJ nj
O o	P p	R r	S s	Š š
T t	U u	V v	Z z	Ž ž

Pronounciation

Seventeen letters of the Croatian alphabet are pronounced differently to English; these are:

'c' as 'ts' in gets
'č' as 'ch' in cheese
'ć' as in ceiling
'dž' as 'ju' in julip
'đ' as 'ja' in Janet
'g' as gay
'h' as 'ha' in ham
'j' as 'y' in yacht
'lj' as 'lu' in lurid
'nj' as the Spanish 'ñ'
'r' as 'trillion'
š as 'sh'
ž as 's' in measure
'a' as 'a' in senna
e as 'e' in bet
'i' as 'ee' in meet
'u' as 'oo' in moot

OFFICIAL PHONETIC TABLE FOR SPELLING WORDS, ABBREVIATIONS AND NUMBERS

A Adria	I Istra	T Trogir	4 Èetiri
B Biokovo	J Jadran	U Uèka	5 Petika
C Cavtat	K Karlovac	V Vukovar	6 Šest
È Èakovec	L Lika	W Duplo Ve	7 Sedam
Æ Ælipi	M Mostar	X Iks	8 Osam
D Dubrovnik	N Novska	Y Ipsilon	9 Devet
Dž Džamija	O Osijeck	Z Zagreb	**Decimal dot** Zarez
Đ Đakovo	P Pula	Ž Županja	**Period** Toèka
E Europa	K Ku	N Nula	
F Frankopan	R Rijeka	1 Jedinica	
G Gospiæ	S Sisak	2 Dva	
H Hvratska	Š Šibenik	3 Tri	

Learning the Language

Classes. As Croatian is not one of the more popular languages, you may have to hunt around for a class that you can attend in person. The very useful website www.languages-on-the-web.com/links/link-croatian.htm is a starting point as it lists hundreds of links for the Croatian language including courses run by universities in the USA, New Zealand and Australia. It also has details of Language schools, translators and much more. In the UK a good starting point would be the School of Slavonic and East European Studies (SSEES) at University College London (☎020-7862-8557; fax 020-7862 8642; e-mail s.aleksic@ssees.ucl.ac.uk; www.ssees.ac.uk.

Self-Teach Courses. It is more likely that you will have to learn at home using tapes with accompanying books, CD Roms or courses on the internet. For a wider selection look on the website www.maps2anywhere.com/languages/Croatian – language – course.htm. The top courses include the following:

Colloquial Croatian and Serbian: A Complete Course for Beginners: Celia Hawkesworth, Routledge 320 pages 1997. Book and two 1-hour cassettes. Available from Amazon.

Introduction to the Croatian and Serbian Language: Thomas Magner, Penn State University Press 1997, ISBN 9998417902; About £29.99. Out of print but second hand copies in circulation including on Amazon.co.uk.

Talk Now! Croatian CD ROM Language Course: Basic fun course for the beginner who wants to learn the language quickly. Does not aim for fluency. $59.95 + $5.50 p&p from www.maps2anywhere.com/Languages/Croatian – language – course.htm.

Teach Yourself Croatian: Mcgraw-Hill Books. Two one-hour audio cassettes and book (272 pages). £14.29 from Amazon UK or $32.95 + $6.50 postage. Excellent beginner language course using the latest learning methods. Available from Amazon and www.maps2anywhere.com/Languages.

SUMMARY OF HOUSING

The World Bank, in a recent report, estimated that 58% of the Croatian population lived in urban areas during 1994-2000. This figure reflects the exodus from rural areas a result of the dismantling of rurally-based state enterprises following the transition to a market economy. The war also caused a mass displacement of people within the country and accelerated migration to the towns and cities. At the latest count, the housing stock amounted to 1.65 million units. Of these about 380,000 were in public ownership and most of these, have now been sold off to private parties, mostly the tenants who were occupying them.

In the last few years, the development of the private banking sector has provided financial schemes including mortgages to finance private housing. However, mortgages are unaffordable for much of the population. In response to this the Croatian government has passed legislation allowing for socially supported housing, particularly for young families.

As one of the conditions of the loans from the EU and other sources, the Croatian government has to provide housing for returnees and Serbian refugees. Some of these people wish to return to specific properties that they were living in before the war. Foreign housebuyers should bear this in mind when buying older properties and it is important to establish that the seller is actually the title holder. For more details see *Finding Properties for Sale.*

Many of the estimated 200,000 houses that suffered wartime destruction are in rural areas where the cost of repair and providing an infrastructure of road, electricity and mains water is not considered cost effective. The government prefers to construct new housing instead.

PUBLIC HOLIDAYS

1 Jan	New Year's Day
11/12 Apr (Mar 27/28 2005)	Easter
1 May	Labour Day
10 June (26 June 2005)	Corpus Christi
22 June	Anti-Fascist Resistance Day
5 Aug	Victory Day & National Thanksgiving
15 Aug	Assumption
8 October	Independence Day
1 Nov	All Saints
25-26 Dec	Christmas

RESIDENCE & ENTRY REGULATIONS

ENTRY AND RESIDENCE REGULATIONS FOR FOREIGNERS

Croatia is not due to join the EU until 1997/8, so EU citizens receive no special treatment as they do throughout the European Union where neither residence nor work permits are usually required for nationals of other EU countries.

Entry Regulations. Most foreign nationals, including UK and US citizens do not require a visa to enter Croatia and can remain in the country up to 90 days without needing further documentation. A valid passport that does not have an expiry date within three months of entry date to Croatia is all that is required. If you are not staying in a hotel, then you are obliged to register your arrival at the local police station within 48 hours.

Residence Permit. For stays of longer than three months a visa should be applied for in advance at the Croatian Embassy/Consulate in your home country. This involves submitting a raft of forms and personal documents including proof of sufficient funds to support yourself. Once in Croatia a Residence Permit should be applied for at the central police station in your area and you should allow six to eight weeks for processing. The permit is valid for up to one year and is usually easily renewable.

Reasons considered valid for the granting of a residence permit include the renting or owning a property in Croatia.

You can also get a permit if you have a yacht moored at a Croatian marina. This is mainly used as a tax avoidance tactic, which is legal, but likely to change after Croatia accedes to the EU.

Residency Advantages. A foreign owner of Croatian property is considered to be resident in Croatia if their property is used exclusively by them for 183 days (need not be continuously) for a year, and if there is an obvious intention to keep and use the property. Residency in Croatia may be advantageous from a tax point of view, but only while Croatia remains outside the EU.

Work Permits. Foreigners that have applied for a residence permit, who are also intending to work there will, in most cases, require a work permit as well as a residence permit. This will normally be an 'entry visa for the purpose of employment' or a 'business visa' depending on the nature of their work and should be applied for in advance at the Croatian embassy/consulate in your home country. The work permit is not issued until you arrive in Croatia and you have to send off your application to the Ministry of Labour, Croatian Employment Agency. This overworked department will then process your application. They are required by the law on employing foreign nationals to do this in a maximum of 30 days.

Agencies

As the process of applying for a residence permit, is long, involved and complicated, it is unusual for anyone who does not speak Croatian to try to manage it on their own. Most foreigners engage an agent who will do the legwork for them. If you are buying a property in Croatia, it is usual for the estate agent to make the necessary arrangements to get your residence permit if required.

New Foreigners Act

A new law relating to residence and entry regulations came into force on January 1st 2004 (Official Gazette, no. 109/03 of 17 July 2003), that would provide all foreigners who want to work in Croatia with 'one-stop-shopping where they can obtain all the necessary information, residence permits, work permits or commercial visas.' Outline details of regulations on employment of foreigners are available on the website of the Croatian Employment Agency (www.hzz.hr) but unfortunately no details are available at the time of print of the proposed regional offices for this. Further information should be available from the organisations below, and from Croatian embassies/consulates.

Useful Addresses
Ministry of Labour: Prisavlje 14, 10000 Zagreb, Croatia; ☎+385 1 6969-111; www.mrss.hr/en (website in English).
Croatian Employment Agency: same address as above; www.hzz.hr.
Henley and Partners: Kralja Zvonmira 36, 21000 Split; ☎+38521 489 511; fax +385 21 489 505; e-mail croatia-office@henleyglobal.com. Tax planners and advisors. Can assist foreigners in obtaining residence status and acquiring real estate, and advise corporations and investors about all aspects of investing and doing business in Croatia. Specialises in buying property in a company name. Contact Dr. Nenad Saljic. Also: H&P Trust Co., Salisbury House, 1-9 Union Street, St. Helier, Jersey JE4 8RH; ☎+44 1534 514 888; fax +44 1534 514 999; e-mail Jersey-office@hen leyglobal.com.

Croatian Embassies & Consulates
Croatian Embassy in London: 21 Conway Street, London W1P 5HL; ☎020-7387 1790; fax 020-7387 0310; e-mail consular-dept@croatianembassy.co.uk.
Croatian Embassy in Washington: 2343 Massachusetts Ave. NW, Washington DC 20008; ☎+1 202 588 5899; fax +1 202 588 8936; e-mail webmaster@croatianem bassy.org; www. croatia.emb.org. Consulates general in Los Angeles, Chicago, New York and Cleveland.

British Embassy & Consulates
British Embassy, Zagreb: Vlaska 121/111 Floor, P.O. Box 454, 10000 Zagreb; ☎+385 1455 5310; fax +385 1455 1685; e-mail british-embassy@zg.tel.hr.
British Consulate, Split: Obala Hrvatskog Narodnog Preporoda 10/111, 21000 Split; ☎+385 21 341 464; fax +385 21 362 905.
British Consulate, Dubrovnik: Atlas Pile 1, 20000 Dubrovnik; ☎+385 20 412 916; fax +385 20 412 916.

United States Embassy
US Embassy, Zagreb: 2 Thomas Jefferson Street, 10010 Zagreb; ☎+385 1 661 2200; www.usembassy.hr.

WHERE TO FIND YOUR IDEAL HOME

CHAPTER SUMMARY

- The Foreign Ministry of Croatia estimates that 1,000 foreigners have bought houses or plots of land in Croatia in the last two years.
- The average price of a house is about £105,000/$191,000; however, dilapidated buildings for development go for less.
- **Most Expensive Areas – Istria and Dubrovnik.** The large peninsula in the north of Croatia that borders Slovenia, is one of the most expensive places to buy property. Prices have risen there faster than anywhere else, including Dubrovnik, which is also very expensive.
  - A lot of Europeans, especially Italians buy property in Istria, as it has a good climate all year round.
- **Hotspots:** Istria, Dubrovnik area, Hvar and Brac Islands, Peljesac Peninsula.
- **Beaches.** Most beaches in Croatia are shingle.
- All beaches are public in Croatia. It is not possible to buy a private beach with your property.
- **Most Accessible Islands – Krk** island is the most easily accessible island as it has a bridge to the mainland and an airport (Rijeka-Krk). **Brac** is the next most accessible with flights from Zagreb.
- **The Northern Dalmation Coast** is generally overlooked by property buyers yet it is a good place to hunt for less expensive property, especially in the smaller towns.
- **Dubrovnik.** In the opinion of some, Dubrovnik has been over-restored, both prior to the 1990 war, and after it.
  - Property is about twice as expensive in the old part, as it is in the new part.

OVERVIEW

Now that celebrities, business moguls and Hollywood film stars are buying up villas on the Adriatic coast you know that potentially, Croatia is a very good investment.

The rich and fabulous of today may think they are trendsetters, but in fact the eastern side of the Adriatic has been attracting celebrities for over 100 years: from the crowned heads of Europe who wintered in Istria, to the literary figures and icons of earlier generations: Bernard Shaw, Lord Byron, Edward, Prince of Wales and Wallis Simpson, James Joyce, Thomas Mann and Elizabeth Taylor to name but a few. Furthermore the beauty of the Adriatic coast does not need to be promoted by anyone; it sells itself: crystal waters, pretty Venetian architecture, walled cities, patterns of tiny rocky islands and an absence of high rise building outside the main towns and resorts, are just some of the attractions. Sandy beaches though are not. Croatia has few of these; shingle being the prevailing beach type. Hence the popularity of yachting. You can swim and snorkel off a yacht to your heart's content. In fact, yachts count as residences in Croatia (you can claim residency with one, if it has a marina mooring); more details in *Taxes,* in the General Introduction to Croatia.

Since 1995 when hostilities in Croatia officially ended, Croatia has been encouraging tourists to return in numbers that are increasing year on year. With stability, has come investment in infrastructure and foreign investment is beginning to flow in. Much of the post-war revival of prosperity is due to the superb natural attractions the coast has to offer. Not surprisingly, once visitors have soaked up the beauty of the Adriatic while on holiday, the inclination to buy property there follows. Croatia will probably never catch up with the Spanish Costas in terms of volume of property sold, but it could easily become as popular as Greece. The Foreign Ministry in Croatia says that more than 1,000 properties or building sites have been sold to foreigners in little more than two years and buyers from Germany and the post-communist countries are the most numerous. However, the really cheap prices that the earliest bargain hunters found just after the 1990s war are gone for good. Lara Vekic of Croatia-Estate.Com, one of Croatia's largest estate agencies explains the situation.

Just after the war, a few foreigners managed to pick up some bargains in real estate and since then many people have come to us under the illusion that Croatians are all rushing to sell their houses at bargain prices. This is simply not the case. Property is expensive here. Another thing that foreigners expect, is that when they buy a beachfront property, this includes a private beach. In Croatia, all beaches are public, and if you have a beach infront of your property, anyone can use it.

A few years ago you could pick up a largish property in need of refurbishment for £30,000/$54,500; today you will pay over twice that. Prices are rising especially quickly in the places everyone has heard of. You can still find complete ruins for £27,000. A small house in Dubrovnik will cost £140,000/$254,500, while 20 minutes away, a modern, three-bedroom apartment in a pretty village will cost you £83,000/$150,000. The average house price is about £105,000. Sought after places are *Dubrovnik, Istria,* The *Peljesac* peninsula and the islands of *Vis, Hvar* and *Brac*.

Croatian property buyers may find airport proximity and flight frequency not as convenient as in Spain and France, or some of the Greek Islands. Many buyers focus on the southern Dalmation coast, but Istria is just as interesting, mostly beautiful, and is better connected by direct flights from the UK to both Rijeka-Krk and Pula. It is also an easy drive from the Italian airports of Venice and Trieste where the budget airlines including Ryanair go to. Of course, the flight situation is constantly changing and as there are few no frills flights to Croatia, there are likely to be more, rather than fewer, flights there in the future.

There are several drawbacks of buying in Croatia, which potential buyers should be

Croatia

AUSTRIA

HUNGARY

Graz

Klagenfurt

Ljubljana

SLOVENIA

Trieste

Cakovec

Varazdin

Koprivnica

Zagreb

Bjelovar

Virovitica

CROATIA

Sisak

Slavonski
Brodd

Opatija

Rijeka

Porec

Krk

Karlovac

Rovinij

Senj

Pula

Cres

Rab

Banja Luka

Losinj

Pag
Peninsula

BOSNIA-
HERZEGOVINA

Zadar

Dugi Otok

Sarajevo

Ancona

Sibenik

Trogir

Split

Mostar

Brac

Hvar

Vis

Makarska

BOSNIA-
HERZEGOVINA
CORRIDOR

Peljesac
Peninsula

Korcula

Lastovo

Mljet

Dubrovnik

Pescara

Adriatic

Sea

Cavtat

ITALY

| 0 | | 50 | | 100 miles |
| 0 | 80 | | 160 km | |

✈ Airport

aware of.

○ The scarcity of property in the most sought after areas, Dubrovnik among them.
○ Buying a property is not a speedy process in Croatia. One buyer spent a year looking for a property in Dubrovnik. Two apartments came on the market and he bought one of them. It took another 6 months to get the obligatory permission to buy from the Ministry of Foreign Affairs (it can take longer).
○ Property valuations tend to be random as there is no overall formula applied to properties based on square metres, location and so on. Sellers name their price and as result you may find similar types of property going for a range of prices in the same town or village. The exception is Istria where property buying by foreigners is much more established and prices are applied systematically (and tend to be higher).

ESTATE AGENTS

Being an estate agent is an up-coming profession in Croatia and many agents are inexperienced and surprisingly, not always enthusiastic. As American Kerry Jones put it in her article for the magazine *International Living*:

> We found many beautiful and inexpensive properties listed on the internet. Unfortunately, the realtors, from Dubrovnik to Split, were unresponsive to phone calls and e-mails. My husband returned (to Croatia) in August and browbeat a realtor into showing him some villas. Despite our interest, nothing came of it. The realtor was clearly not interested in selling. We were depressed and frustrated and began to think that we should file our Croatian house idea under 'Fantasy'.

If you can find a switched on realtor (the Jones finally did in Amir Subasic of Optic Cruise World - listed below under *Southern Dalmatia*) you will have taken your first step on your way to owning a property in Croatia. If you are having difficulty finding a responsive agent then see if you can locate one by asking around on the spot, or try the useful contacts listed below.

In the regional chapter below, Estate agents that specialise in a region are listed under the description of the region that they specialise in. There are some however that cover several regions, or all of Croatia; these are listed below.

Useful Contacts/Resources

Avatar International: Suite 208, Boundary House, Boston Road, Hanwell, London W7 2QE; ☎08707-282827; www.avatar-croatia.com. All kinds of real estate in all the popular places along the Croatian coast. Has a national network of foreign partners throughout Croatia providing a property-buying service.

Croatia Holiday and Home: 7 Ashbourne Road, Bournemouth, Dorset BH5 2JS; ☎01202-259155; fax 0870 169 3701; e-mail info@croatia-holidayandhome.co.uk; www.croatia-holidayandhome.co.uk.
Not an agent, but can put you in touch with reliable agents and other contacts throughout Croatia. Very useful website with all kinds of information about buying property in Croatia, properties for sale and rent.

Estate Agents for All of Croatia

Broker Nekretnine: Osjecka 11, Sportski Centar Gripe, 21000 Split, Croatia; tel/fax +385 21 547 004. Also specialises in larger estates and small islands.

Furton Associates Realty: 48995 Gratiot, Chesterfield, MI 48051; ☎586-949-3230; fax 586-949 3232; e-mail sendadjakupovic@excite.com. Contact: Senad Jakupovic. Represents clients in the USA who wish to buy or sell property in Croatia.

Homes in Croatia: ☎020-7502 1371; contact Maria Bennett. Website www.homesincroatia.com under construction at time of press. Property search agency. All kinds of properties from whole islands to large manor houses and all types of property in between.

Croatia-Estate.com: Osjecka 11, S.C. Gripe, Split, Croatia; ☎+385 21 547 004; Agency in business for over a decade. Has agents in Crikvenica, Dubrovnik, Makarska, Osijek, Porec, Pula, Rijeka, Rovinj, Sibenik, Split, Umag, Zadar, Zagreb. Active in all aspects of real estate business including purchase, sales and rentals. Also has whole islands for sale.

Real Estate Nekretnine: Sizgoriceva 9, 21000 Split; ☎+ 385 98 748 505; fax +385 21 317 165; info@nekretnine.org; www.nekretnine.org.

COASTAL REGIONS OF CROATIA (NORTH TO SOUTH)

ISTRIA

Main Towns: *Pazin, Pula, Porec, Rovinj, Umag.*
Main Islands: *Brijuni Archipelago.*
Airports: *Pula, Rijeka-Krk,* also use *Trieste* or *Venice-Treviso* and *Venice-Marco Polo*
in Italy.

The Istrian peninsula in north-west Croatia bordering Slovenia, is variously described
as shaped like a heart, shield, navel or triangle and is the largest peninsula in the
Adriatic with an area of over 3000 sq. km. It is also variously spelt *Istra,* and in
Croatian, *Istarska.* Istria is encircled in the northeast by the *Ćićarija* and the *Učka*
(1396m) mountains. The interior is mostly comprised of undulating highlands dotted
with stunning little towns perched on hilltops, which are a feature of the interior
along with the jagged mountains and fertile valleys. Both the east and west coasts are
deeply indented with a thousand bays, lagoons and islands. It comes as no surprise
therefore that Istria is one of the most popular tourist areas of the Mediterranean.
Most of the visitors are Germans, Austrians and Italians, whose traditional holiday
spot it has been for a century or longer, and who arrive mostly by car. An increase in
foreign property buyers there has developed over the last four decades, though they
are merely augmenting what has been a tradition for considerably longer. Italians have
long had an interest, as Istria was part of Italy from 1918-43 and thousands of Italians
already live there.

Despite the hordes that pour in each summer to resorts like Umag and Porec to
utilise the many campsites, tourist facilities have not been allowed to spill out over
the Istrian countryside or into the enchanting towns and villages making Istria with
its easy access via flights to Italy and the Istrian peninsular itself, a most desirable
spot. This is reflected in the prices of property which are rising faster in Istria than
anywhere else in Croatia.

Istria's resorts attract visitors all year round, which makes for a very active rental
market should you not wish to live in your property for all of the year.

Brijuni Archipelago

These islands lie off the southwest coast of Istria, 6.5 km from Pula. The two largest
islands Veli and Mali Brijun, and there are a dozen others. They are all fertile thanks
to a covering of black soil. They have a superb climate that allows tropical species to
flourish. An industrial magnate from Austria bought the whole archipelago in 1893
and turned it into a luxury resort with a stadium, hunting grounds, even golf courses
and tennis courts. During the Tito era, the dictator kept them for himself and would
entertain world leaders and film stars there. In a neat twist of numbers, the whole
region was made a national park in 1983. Visitors can stay in the facilities (which are
in need of refurbishment) on Veli and Mali Brijun, but not the others.

Typical Properties for Sale - Istria

Location	Type	Description	Price
Kanfanar-okolica village 9 km from sea near Rovinj	Stone stable ruin	2 floors, 100 sq.m. building on 250 sq.m. in meadow. For renovation	€65,000
Near Porec, in small village 2km from sea	Brand new luxury apartments	Attractive 2-storey block of one-bedroom flats. Five flats of varying dimensions from 56.12 sq.m. to 81.48 sq. m. The largest has mezzanine floor to provide more sleeping accommodation.	from €63,000 to €84,000
Old part of Rovinj	Renovated town house	140 sq.m. Ground floor suitable for business premises. Sunny roof terrace 20 sq.m. View over town. 120 m from sea.	€190,000
Motovun hill top town about 25km inland	Restored stone house	100-year-old house on three floors with cellar. 2 bedrooms.	€98,000

Estate Agents for Istria

Astarta: Obala A, Rismondo 2, Rovinj 52210; ☎052 812 515; fax 052 812 515; e-mail astarta@pu.hinet.hr; www.astarta-rovinj.hr.

Dom Kontakt: Radiaeva 44, Pula 52100, Istria, Croatia; ☎052 393 053; fax 052 393 055; e-mail walter.hrovat@pu.hinet.hr.

Fuma: Trgovaeka 2/a, Umag 52470, Croatia; ☎ 052 72 04 437; e-mail Fuma@hinet.hr; www.fuma.hr.

Histria Biro: Bracka 55, Porec 52440 Croatia; tel/fax +385 52 452540; www.istra.com/ histria and www.histrabiro.com/. Wide selection of coastal and inland properties in and around Porec.

Istria Real Estate: ☎+385 (0)98 403 845; www.istriarealestate.net. Builds and sells apartments in western Istria (village Basaniji), between Umag and Portorose (Slovenia). Near the sea.

Izlaz: Joakima Rakovca 13, Labin 52220, Istria, Croatia; ☎+385 (0)52 85 24 50; fax +385 (0)52 88 53 38; e-mail astarta@pu.hinet.hr; www.astarta-rovinj.hr. Specialises in eastern coast of Istria.

Nel Blu: Dalmatinska 43, Vrsar 52450; Istria, Croatia; +385 52 441 383; fax +385 52 441 383; e-mail nel-blu@pu.tel.hr; www.istra.com/nelblu.

Passage: Garibaldi 3, 52210 Rovinj, Istria , Croatia; ☎+385 52 811 403; e-mail passage@pu.tel.hr; www.passage.hr.

Veliko Kliman: Pula; ☎052 508 190; e-mail jakob@hi.htnet.hr.

Villas Forum Properties and Services: Forum 10, Pula, Croatia; ☎+385 52 210 029; fax +385 52 383 824; e-mail Vedran@villasforum.com; www.villasforum.com.

KVARNER GULF

Main Towns: *Opatija, Rijeka.*
Airports: *Rijeka-Krk* (on Krk island). Also use *Trieste* in Italy.
The Kvarner Gulf, which runs roughly from just west of Opatija to just south of Senj and includes the islands of **Krk, Cres, Losinj** and **Rab** and **Pag**, is also refered to as *Hvratsko Primorje* (The Croatian Seaside) and lies between Istria and the north Dalmatian coast.

The thickly-wooded coast is backed up against the solid mass of the Velebit mountains and Mt Učka, which isolate the coast from the interior, but give it the advantage of protecting it from the coldest winter weather and winds.

The area includes one of Croatia's smartest coasts, The *Opatija Riviera*, and Croatia's third largest city and international port, *Rijeka.*

Opatija Riviera

Opatija means 'abbey' in Croatian and it is named from a Benedictine Abbey dating from the Middle Ages. There is not much sign of the monastic tradition there these days as Opatija is a hedonistic place where those who like sophisticated distractions might like to buy a holiday apartment (if they can afford it). Rich holiday home owners began to build villas in Opatija from the mid-nineteenth century, attracted by the sub-tropical climate which enabled them to show one-upmanship in their exotic gardens stocked with plants from around the world. A railway line from Vienna to Trieste and Rijeka also made it a very convenient wintering place for the Austro-Hungarian aristocracy whose elegant villas line the coast. The town's facilities include health giving spa waters, which are claimed to benefit those with cardio-vascular disorders and rheumatism. In the winter, the hotels are still busy,especially with older visitors who benefit from the milder winters of Opatija which never gets as cold as the south Dalmatian coast.

The area is also very popular with walkers, hikers and mountain climbers.

Krk Island

The largest of Croatia's islands, Krk covers an area of 409sq. km. and is about 38 km long. The resident population is approximately 16,400. It is the most easily accessed island in the area as it is linked by bridge to the mainland. It also has an international airport (Rijeka-Krk), which also serves as Rijeka's airport. Air Adriatic flights land there from the UK as well as other charter flights.

The northern larger part is generally lower, more forested and fertile than the southern part except for the wild, north-western coast which is nearly inaccessible. The southern part is largely barren but dotted with areas of thick forests and has the island's highest peak, *Obzova* (569m) and the town and port of *Baska,* the jumping off point for ferries to *Rab.*

Nearly a third of the island's surface is forested. Adequate rainfall (approx 1000 mm annually) keeps the island's fresh water supply going in the form of two small lakes in the centre of the island. Main occupations on the island include farming (mainly livestock and fruit), viticulture, fishery and hunting. Heavy industry includes petrochemicals and shipbuilding.

As a place to buy a holiday home, Krk is a good prospect as there is usually a choice of new apartments or renovated and non-renovated older properties. Krk is an interesting island particularly in ethnographic terms. There is a strong folk music tradition based in the Chakavian dialect. Chakavian is a five-hundred-year-old Croatian dialect from the Rijeka area.

Rab Island

The island of Rab has Krk to the north and a long finger of Pag island reaches up to its west coast from the south. Rab covers an area of nearly 100 square kilometres and is 22km in length. The permanent population is just over 9000. Salient points include the Lopar peninsula to the northeast. Rab's tourist literature claims it is one of the sunniest places in Europe. The island has a mild climate and is partially covered with Mediterranean oak, also cedar and mulberry trees as well as the ubiquitous pines. The interior is fertile enough to produces olives, wine and a variety of vegetables. The capital of the island is Rab town, a medieval gem of narrow winding streets perched on a peninsula. In addition to the main population centre of Rab there are seven island villages.

There are ferries from Rab to Rijeka and from Misnjak in the south of the island to the north Dalmation coast.

The main road runs straight from north to south between the ferry ports of Lopar and Misnjak.

As a place to live Rab is not hugely interesting apart from its natural beauty. Its folk traditions have largely faded and the island has given itself up almost wholly to tourism. It might be worth buying an investment property there as rental prospects would be good.

Cres Island

The long thin island of Cres (also spelled 'Kres') lies west and south west of Krk. The main town, also Cres, lies on a sheltered bay harbouring olive groves, and is on the west coast of the island. It has a permanent population of just over 2,000. Cres marina has berths for 460 craft and hosts a regular regatta week. The northern (greener) part of the island reaches up into the Kvarner Gulf towards Opatija; in contrast, the south is dry and barren. The islanders farm fruit, vegetables and livestock and have a sideline in medicinal alcoholic beverages.

UNCULTURED VULTURES

The northern part of Cres island is also home to about 70 pairs of protected Griffon vultures (*Gyps fulvus*). Less ugly than most vultures, these massive birds (2.8m wingspan, weighing up to 15 kilos) exert a peculiar fascination. For one thing they hatch their young on narrow cliff ledges a few metres above sea level. They live on carrion provided by the natural mortality of the sheep population. The *Caput Insulae Ecology Centre* (www.caput-insulae.com) on the island runs a study project and cares for injured or abandoned vultures. Volunteers interested in learning more about these birds are welcome for a week or longer and pay $150/£83 per week towards accommodation.

Losinj Island

Losinj lies west and south west of Cres and has a population of about 6,500 thousand. The traditional occupations of the islanders include agriculture, fishing, shipbuilding and seafaring. These have been superseded in importance by intensive touristic development that has spread over parts of the island including Mali Losinj, the main town, port and now the main tourist resort as well, and the slightly quieter Veli Losinj, both of which are in the southern part of the island. Mali has a sizeable marina and also hosts an annual regatta.

Historically, Losinj is not that new to tourism. In the 1880s elderly Austro-Hungarians spent the winter there for therapeutic reasons.

Scenically, Losinj has benefited from the activity of those early tourists who formed a society for the 'beautification and afforestation' of the island. They planted acres of distinctively bushy Aleppo pines, which characterise the island's landscapes today.

As a place to live Losinj might get a bit tedious, but it would have investment potential if you were buying somewhere mainly to let out to tourists.

Typical Properties for Sale on the Kvarner Gulf

Location	Type	Description	Price
Malinska, Krk island	brand new apartment in block of six	67 sq.m. 2 bedrooms. Large terrace. Comes with all mod cons incl. sat. TV.	€77,000
Moscenicka Draga, popular with tourists near Opatija	brand new apartment	2-bedrooms, 2 bathrooms. Terrace. In villa. Green setting. Five minutes walk to seaside.	€133,645
Opatija	Large custom-built villa (built. 1973)	300 sq. m. Completely renovated with Italian and German fixtures and fittings throughout. Terraces on every level. Six bedrooms. 4 bathrooms. 4 parking spaces	€900,000 (negotiable)
Punta centre, Krk island	Apartment in newly-renovated old house	59 sq m. two floors. Attractive building	€54,000
Banjol village Rab island	newly renovated apartment	100 sq. m. 2 bedrooms. Three balconies, garage and garden. 100m from sea.	€120,000

For ease of comparison prices in the table have been listed in euros. Although this is not the local currency it is commonly used for pricing purposes.

Estate Agents for the Kvarner Gulf

Atollo: F Eandeka 8, Rijeka 51000; ☎+385 (0)51 676-628; e-mail atollo@ri.htnet.hr.

HiddenCroatia.net: Properties on Krk Island. Can be approached also via Hidden Croatia, the independent, UK-based tour operator (☎020-7736 6066) who will then put you in touch with their estate agent on the island.

Imobilije Spektar: Osjeeka 61, Rijeka 51000; tel/fax +358 (0)51 22 69 88; e-mail info@imobilije-spektar.hr; www.imobbilije-spektar.hr.

Imobiro Mali Losinj: Ostromanova 24, Mali Losinj 51550; ☎+385 (0)51 23 13 20; fax +385 (0)51 23 13 20; e-mail sales@imobiro.com; www.imobiro.com.

Lider: M. Albaharija 5, Rijeka 51000; ☎+385 91 57 44 882; e-mail marin@lider.hr.

MS International: Korzo 4, Rijeka 51000; ☎+385 (0)51 320230; e-mail ms-international@ri.tel.hr. Has been in real estate business over ten years.

Sinisa Kuzman: +385 1 33 12 055 or +385 98 900 3804.

NORTHERN DALMATION COAST

Main Towns: *Zadar, Šibenik, Trogir.*
Airports: *Split* direct, or fly to *Zagreb* and get a domestic flight to Split.
Islands: *Kornati Islands, Dugi Otok, Ugljan.*

The northern Dalmation coast is generally less well known to foreigners, and less spectacular than the southern part of the coast, but it still has a great deal to offer in natural assets, architecture, and a fascinating history. It also has two stunning national parks: *The Kornati Islands* and the *Krka* waterfalls and lakes. This area has been generally overlooked by foreign property buyers who have tended to home in on the glamour spots of Istria and southern Dalmatia, consequently there is the potential for finding bargains, particularly in the smaller towns such as *Nin.* However, the region is planning to develop the local tourism industry more intensively (already, in tourist office-speak, the coast is referred to as the *Biograd Riviera*), which means it could be a good area for investment. Two of the main tourist resorts are *Biograd* and *Vodice.*

As this region is not the first place buyers think of looking for a property in Croatia the area is not much promoted by agents. Many of the properties available are sold by private owners who advertise them on the internet. Listings of properties for sale in Northern Dalmatia can be found on the websites such as www.realestatecroatia.com mentioned at the beginning of this chapter under *Useful Contacts/Resources.* Remember to get expert, qualified assistance when initiating and completing a sale.

Zadar. The largest city in the area is *Zadar,* which has 76,000 inhabitants and an historic old quarter located picturesquely on coast at the tip of a peninsula. It has city gates dating from the fifteenth century, 30 churches and a large amount of Roman architecture from the time, when it was an important Roman coastal town. Like many small towns on the northern Dalmation coast, it is not yet geared principally to tourists and so feels authentically Croatian. There is an archipelago of islands including *Ugljan,* just off the coastline and some of them are popular with Croatian holiday homeowners.

Dugi Otok Island. Dugi Otok means 'long island' in Croatian and it is one of an archipelago of island slivers off the coast around Zadar. It is possible to buy building land quite cheaply on this island, though getting a home built there could be another mattter (see *Building and Renovating*).

Sibenik. *Sibenik* is a wholly Slav town unlike many of the other towns on the Dalmatian Coast, which are of Greek or Roman origin. It was founded in the 11th century and has a famous 15th century cathedral, which is largely the work of the Dalmatian master *Juraj Dalmatinac* (George of Dalmatia). Until the 1991 war Sibenik was an industrial city that specialised in metal production. It suffered structural damage from shelling and is still struggling to find its economic confidence again. The heavy industry has probably gone for good and tourism is the most likely source of future prosperity.

Trogir. Trogir is a town with a population of about 10,000 and is approximately an hour by road from Sibenik. It owes its origins to the Greeks over four thousand years ago. It has been a UNESCO World Heritage Site since 1997, which has had a kiss of death effect on its atmosphere. Even though the whole place feels like a museum, swamped by tourists from land and sea, it is undeniably beautiful with its medieval city walls and gates and Renaissance and Venetian architecture. The old city is sited on an island in the Trogir channel and is connected by a stone bridge to the newer part, which is spread out for a kilometre or two along the coast.

Ciovo Island. Sometimes referred to as the Trogir-Ciovo Peninsula because it is connected to Trogir via a bridge, and Trogir is connected to the mainland by another bridge. Ciovo island which is about 15km long and 3.5 km wide is a sought-after and relatively convenient place to buy a holiday home. There is quite a large floating population estimated at about 6,000 owing to the number of Croatian weekend houses there.

Kornati Islands National Park. The national park includes the southern end of Dugi Otok and reaches down to about 7 nautical miles west of the island of **Murter**. Within its boundaries are 89 islands, islets and reefs, which take their name from the largest island, Kornat. Only about a quarter of the national park is comprised of land, but it is a stunning quarter owing to the artistry in the shapes of the cliffs and rock structures. The rest of the park is marine and submarine and is a sailors' and divers' paradise.

The Kornati islands have long been considered a wonderland. There is an oft used quotation from Bernard Shaw that seems to sum it up, *'On the last day of the Creation God desired to crown his work, and thus created Kornati Islands out of tears, stars and breath.'*

It is possible to buy property (but not to build it) on some of the Kornati islands.

Typical Properties for Sale in Northern Dalmatia

Location	Type	Description	Price
near Zadar	new detached villa	Beautifully designed villa comprising three apartments and five bedrooms in total. Fully furnished. Nice garden. Living space 220 sq. m. Land 350 sq.m. On coast. Mooring for boat	€280,000
Nin small town near sea	village house for renovation	110 sq. m. building. 2 floors. 2 bedrooms. 25 sq. m. balcony and garden. Option to purchase extra land.	€50,000
Vodice centre	reconstructed house	3 floors. Next to church in enclosed courtyard with gate. 70m to sea. Needs fittings.	€46,000
Trogir area	detached house	beautiful house, one row back from sea. 2 levels. 2 separate apartments. 4 bedrooms. Near airport. On a big plot of land.	€250,000

Tribunj small town west of Sibenik	detached old stone house	3 reception rooms. 3 bedrooms. 1 bathroom. View to yacht harbour	€90,000
Dugi Otok island	land	1000 sq.m. field for building on	€25,000
Ciovo Peninsula Businci	detached house	3 bedrooms, 2 bathrooms, front and rear garden. 60 m from shore	€110,000
Prvic-Sepurine island, one mile off coast from Vodice	semi-detached old stone house (ground floor ex-restaurant)	250 sq.m. building on 1000 sq. m. of land. 3 floors. 2 unfinished single storey small buildings nearby . 20m from beach	€120,000
Rogoznica (tiny island linked to mainland) Between Sibenik and Trogir	small house	130 sq.m. building on 2 levels 4 rooms. 2 bathrooms. 500 sq. m. land including big garden and back garden. Garage for one car. 50 m from sea with great view.	€200,000

Estate Agents for the North Dalmatian Coast

Adriatic Estates: Trg Franje Tudmana, br.27, Vodice 222 11, Croatia; ☎+385 989 691 567; e-mail info@adriatic-estates.com.

Adriatic: Zadar; ☎+385 (0)23 21 48 70; e-mail mara – @zd.hinet.hr.

Alfa Real Estate: Vodice 22211; ☎+385 91 521 4467; e-mail adriaticaestate@yahoo.com; www.geocities.com/adriaticaestate/croatia. Offers attractive properties on the Croatian coast and islands, all near the sea.

Damex: Jose Markova 1, Murter 22243; ☎+385 (0)22 43 58 16; fax +385 (0)22 43 58 16; e-mail damex@si.tel.hr. Properties on Murter island.

Laguna Nekretnine: K S Bribirskih 16, Zadar 23000; tel/fax +385(0)23 251 300; e-mail franka.buskulic@zd.htnet.hr.

Phoenix: J J Strossmayera 6a, Zadar 23000; ☎+385 (0)23 23 91 46; fax +385 (0)23 59 23; e-mail phoenix@globalnet.hr.

Trgostan-Split: Tolstojeva 32, 21000 Split; ☎+385 (0)21 343 105; fax +385 (0)21 362 140.

DALMATIANS NOT FROM DALMATIA

Contrary to popular belief, the Dalmatian dog did not originate in Dalmatia. In fact experts have failed to locate the exact origins of the breed, which could be anywhere in Europe (possibly Rome), Asia, or even Africa (spotted dogs have been, well, spotted, on Egyptian reliefs). What is more certain is that they have a strong connection with Romany gypsies, who helped to spread them throughout Europe. Their striking appearance combined with the ability to roam for miles untiringly, and get on with horses, made them a fashionable, decorative accessory for the nobility, who used to have them running alongside or underneath their carriages.

Dalmatians have been variously, circus dogs, hunting dogs, and yes, there *is* a connection with Dalmatia, where they were used as guard dogs for the borders between Dalmatia and Croatia in past centuries.

SOUTHERN DALMATIAN COAST (SPLIT TO DUBROVNIK)

Main Towns: *Split, Makarska, Zadari, Dubrovnik*
Islands: *Brac, Hvar, Vis, Korcula, Mljet*
Airports: *Split, Dubrovnik*
Southern Dalmatia consists of a strip of coastline, a long thin peninsula and five largish islands, and it is probably the best known region of Croatia thanks to its two great holiday destinations of Split which lies in the north, near Trogir, and Dubrovnik in the south near the border with Bosnia Herzegovina and Montenegro. In between these two tourist honeypots is the region known as the Makarska Riviera, centred on the town of that name, and which occupies a 60 km strip between the towns of Brela and Gradac, and offshore are some of the larger Croatian islands, which have been holiday spots for over a century, though never so popular as they are these days.

Split

Split is the second city of Croatia with about 200,000 inhabitants thanks to its rapid growth following World War Two, and the 1990s war, when it became first a place of refuge and then a permanent home to many people fleeing conflict. Split itself is no stranger to adversity having been heavily shelled by the Serbs in the 1990s and then struck by earthquake in 1997.

Inhabitants of Split are called *Splicani,* and they tend to be characterised by their gregariousness and their obsession with football, in particular the local team *Hadjuk* (bandit), one of the most vehemently supported teams in Croatia.

SPLIT, ANCIENT HISTORY

The tourist literature describes Split thus 'Loud, proud and open all hours', but there is much more to it than clubbing on the *Riva* (waterfront). It is undeniably fascinating, with its centrepiece of *Diocletian's Palace* built over a decade from AD 295, as a retirement home, nonpareil. The imperial palace, a complex of over 200 buildings built near the waterfront, has never fallen in, been knocked down, or looted for building materials. It has been literally incorporated into the fabric of the town and the daily life of its citizens: cafés, shops, bars, even their homes occupy almost every edifice. Of course the incorporation of Roman buildings into permanent everyday life is not unique to Split, but the scale of it there, is amazing.

Just outside Split are the remains of the Roman colony of Salona, spread over a site of more than 280 acres. The histories of Salona and Split are intertwined. When Salona, fell to marauding Avars and Slavs in the 7th century, the inhabitants fled to Split, and more particularly to the Diocletian Palace complex, where their descendants still live today.

The Makarska Riviera

The Makarska Riviera has the reputation of being one of the most beautiful areas of Dalmatia as well as one of the most popular tourist playgrounds on the whole coast thanks to its long sandy beaches and quiet bays. The main town, *Markarska* (pop. 12,000), sprawls in a large cove at the foot of the rocky slopes of the Biokovo mountain range, which is popular with hikers. Apart from tourism the local income is derived from vineyards, and olive and fig growing. It is possible to walk to *Brela*, another resort 15kms north along a coastal path. Some of the other larger tourist resorts include *Baska Voda, Tucepi and Podgora*.

The Islands

BRAC IN POETRY

Isle of vines and olive trees, you are the source of my ancient frenzy in summer days and of this unquenchable light in all the winter nights of my life. Isle of cicadas; eternal, unbroken, ever the same, resounds in you the shrill voice of the Mediterranean cicadas. It was heard by Greek colonists, by ancient Illyrians, by Roman conquerors, by Croat peasants and the merchants of Venice; it was known in your coves by the Saracen corsairs and the pirates of Omis, and by the shepherds from the Neretva up in your highlands. And to everyone in his own tongue this voice spoke of things that never alter, that always remain the same, in spite of all vicissitudes, all changes of peoples, beliefs, states and customs. And this voice is your voice: the voice of your stones, of your earth and of your vegetation.

Vladimir Nazor, 1876-1949

Brac. Sadly, the velocity of change on Brac (also called Brach) since 1940 when he wrote the above might startle the poet Nazor from his reverie: tarmac roads to most places, the buzz of charter aircraft, fast hovercraft connections and the constant rotation of tourists. Not much chance of hearing the cicadas above that lot, unless you choose your property carefully, away from the din.

Brac is the third largest (nearly 400 sq. km) Croatian island and one of the most easily accessible with hourly ferries from Split to *Supetar* on the north coast. There is also a small airport, which is used for summer charter flights. Flights from Zagreb operate all year round. Apart from tourism the locals' income is from wine, olive oil, figs and citrus fruits, but its most famous export, since ancient times, and which can be found in civic buildings from Washington to Berlin and from Liverpool to Vienna, is limestone, the enduring heart of Brac.

Brac has a steep, rocky northern coastline running down to lower slopes on the southern side. The highlands are of typical karst formation. The rains of winter (in the region of 800mm to 1,450mm annually) were once carefully conserved in cisterns by the islanders, as there is no indigenous fresh water on Brac. These days, a submarine pipeline from the mainland acts as Brac's giant fresh water tap.

The main resorts on the island include *Supetar, Bol* (fabulous beach), *Zlatni Rat, Sutivan, Milna and Sumartin.*

There is a good selection of property for sale on Brac from 32 sq. m. apartments for about €25,000 aimed at weekenders to new-built homes and upscale villas in the range of €175,000-€330,000. There are a few more modest homes around the €65,000 mark, but they get snapped up very quickly and for these you really need to be on the spot. Older properties are slightly harder to find than new ones. You will have to tell your agent what you are looking for. A popular island, Brac is a good investment and you should have no problems selling on.

Hvar. Hvar is the fourth largest island of Croatia (300 sq. km), and like Brac is a sunspot baked in over 2,800 hours of sunshine a year. Despite the torrid climate, the island is verdant thanks to its winter rainfall, although for its year round water supply it is dependent on the same seabed pipeline as Brac. Fields of herbs and vines are a local source of income, and the breezes often carry a heady waft of herb scents and lavender; a major export from Hvar is lavender oil.

The main resorts on the island are *Hvar town, Stari Grad, Vrboska, Jelsa* and *Sucuraj*. Hvar town is of particular interest architecturally, with many buildings of Renaissance and Venetian origins. It also has one of the earliest municipal theatres in Europe dating from the early seventeenth century. The island, and in particular Hvar, is very popular with Italians.

As you might expect from an island that is a gem, property is rather expensive with a lot of villas costing around a million euros; even apartments seem pricier there than elsewhere. This is despite the fact that transport connections are not that easy or cheap from the UK. The nearest charter flights land at Split; or you can fly Ryanair to Ancona in Italy and get an overnight ferry to Split, and then an onward one to Hvar.

Korcula. Korcula is Croatia's sixth largest island and is a land sliver of 276 sq. km, with 47km length and about 8 km width. It is one of the most densely forested Croatian islands with about 60% of its surface area covered in woodland and thickets. Despite this abundance of vegetation, it has little surface water with as little as 41 days of rain per year. The island boasts a rare species of jackal (*canis aureaus Dalmatica)* and a species of mongoose (*Mungus mungo).*

Korcula island's population has fluctuated over the centuries and thousands of its inhabitants emigrated in the early part of the twentieth century to the Americas and the Antipodes. The current population numbers about 20,000, and is the highest ever. Just over 3,000 Korculans live in the fascinating mediaeval main town, also called Korcula, which is one of several spots in the Mediterranean which claim to be the birthplace of Marco Polo. It is a short hop from Korcula by ferry to the Peljesac peninsula.

Vela Luka and *Lumbarda* are the other main resorts on the island. *Blato* is the other large town (4000 inhabitants) and it is situated in the middle of the western part of the island. Vela Luka is a good place to buy apartments if you are interested in the letting potential.

There are 48 islets in the Korcula archipelago. The *Skoji* islands is the name of a group of 19 islets near the eastern end of Korcula, some of which are inhabited. The biggest is about 1 sq. km. They are fascinating to visit and may cause you to dream of owning your very own small island.

Vis. Vis lies to the south west of Brac and Hvar and to the west of Korcula and has an area of 90 sq. km. It is the furthest Dalmatian island from the mainland, but is still reasonably well connected by hydrofoil from Split. Vis town is the oldest town in Dalmatia and was established by Dionysius, ruler of Sicily in 397 BC when its Latin name was *Issa*.

The two largest towns are Vis and *Komiza*.

Property prices are quite cheap on Vis compared to Hvar and Brac. There is a wide selection on offer from vacant plots to old stone houses that may need a little modernising, but are ready to move into. There are lots of properties in the price range €38,000-€72,000. A 5,000 sq. m. field with a tumbledown cottage on it was going for €26,000 in 2004.

The Peljesak Peninsula, Dubrovnik, Cavtat and Mljet

Mention this most southerly tip of Croatia's Dalmation coast to a potential property buyer and their heart may begin to beat a little faster as this is considered a most beautiful and desirable corner of Europe (with prices to match) for those who feel they want to buy a property somewhere different and interesting. For a start, the piece of Croatia that forms the Peljesak peninsula, and on which Dubrovnik and Cavtat are situated, is divided from the rest of Croatia by a narrow corridor that is Bosnia-Hercegovina's access to the Adriatic Sea, while to the south lies the border with Montenegro. This makes the area a sliver of Croatia attached to the side of Bosnia-Hercegovina, with the addition of the Peljesak peninsula and the island of Mljet.

The area, and in particular Dubrovnik was a ferocious theatre of war in the early 1990s when Dubrovnik was under constant siege from an array of forces including Bosnian Serbs and the Yugoslav army. The progress of that War in the region is well-documented for anyone who wishes to know the details. Dubrovnik appears outwardly to have moved on, repaired and refurbished itself and is playing host to tourists as numerous as they were before the hostilities began.

The Peljesak Peninsula. The Peljesak peninsula is a picturesque arm of land with an area of 358 sq. km that projects 90km into the sea from the twin towns of *Ston* and *Mali Ston* situated on the isthmus that links the peninsula to the mainland, north of Dubrovnik. It is virtually an island, but since it is connected to the mainland, touring is that much easier. It is about an hour by car from Dubrovnik and it is a tiny ferry jump from *Orebic* on Peljesak, to the island of Korcula. The Peljesak Peninsula is an area that has managed to keep its character *and* encourage the tourists who come here on walking and wine tours and to devour the legendary seafood. The latter is highly popular with locals too, especially at weekends when the restaurants of Mali Ston resound with oyster slurping and lobster claw cracking.

In 1996, the area was struck by an earthquake of which Ston/Slano were the epicentre) earthquake, measuring six points on the Richter scale. There was a lot of structural damage to both towns but thankfully no fatalities.

The Peninsula is known for its wines, especially the reds *Dingac* and *Postup*, and its scenic attractions are many: acres of family vineyards spreading over the rocky hillsides, mountains, steep sea views, beautiful beaches, coves and quaint villages.

Property for sale is varied in price, condition and age. The letting prospects are excellent as there is a high demand for holiday accommodation there.

Dubrovnik. 'The city of stone and light' changed its name from Ragusa in 1918 to avoid sounding Italian. The medieval walled city (about 3,000 people live in the old part; down from 5,000 pre-war), is surrounded on three sides by sea. The remarkably intact walls enclose huddled streets, palaces, churches, fountains and marble piazzas. With its stunning setting and architecture, it is no wonder that it has long been considered a gem of gems on the Adriatic. Its rival, Venice surpassed it in wealth and power but not in climate: Dubrovnik's slightly chilly winters are infinitely preferable to the bitterly cold, damp Venetian ones.

For about 700 years, Dubrovnik was an independent city; a merchant republic that traded with the East. By the end of the eighteenth century it had over 80 consuls overseas and a fleet of 700 ships. The arrival of Bonaparte's armies in 1808 brought the end of its independence. After being dominated by France, it became part of Austria-Hungary.

The walled old town dates from the 13th century, but following a huge earthquake in 1667, which destroyed most of the buildings the town had to be rebuilt. Most of what we see there today is in the late seventeenth century style. Southeast of the old town is Ploce, the tourist zone of beaches, bars and hotels (not to be confused with another Ploce just south of Split). It is also a smart residential area with many grand seaside villas, a legacy of long gone nobility who wintered there. These have now been replaced by their modern equivalent of sporting stars and entrepreneurs and a spate of luxury villa building, which shows no signs of abating.

The total population of Dubrovnik inside and outside the old walls, is approximately 50,000.

Dubrovnik has a city port (suitable for yachts), a commercial port (Gruz) where the ferries arrive, and a marina. Gruz is just over 2km northwest of the ancient town and the marina is at Komolac about 4km from Gruz. Dubrovnik airport is at Cilipi 20km south, near Cavtat.

DON'T TALK ABOUT THE WAR

It is hard to believe that the perfect looking Dubrovnik of today took such a battering in the war of the 1990s. Whilst being bombarded with shells from the surrounding hillsides of Mt Srd, the citizens put up a dogged resistance throughout the siege, managing without water and electricity but unable to prevent themselves being picked off by sniper fire. The beautiful city, with no real strategic value to the Serbs and their allies, was pretty much attacked just because it was there. The senseless shelling of the city made headlines around the world, thanks to its World Heritage status and the fact that tourism had made it familiar to many people.

At the cessation of hostilities international money was poured into Dubrovnik's reconstruction, at the expense of other, less high profile, (some say more needy) war damaged regions. These days, Dubrovnik's people do not want to harp on about the war. Just as all traces of it have vanished from the city's now overly pristine surfaces, a lack of visible reminders seems to have blanked this era from their minds too.

Property prices have shot up in Dubrovnik (though not as much as in Istria). In the old part of the city, bijou apartments are available but do not come cheap. At the time of press there was a pretty, two-bedroom apartment above commercial premises on sale for €230,000. A modern apartment in an apartment block costs about half that.

The *Elaphite islands* lie just to the north of Dubrovnik. They are tiny, traffic-free islands and three of them: Kolocep, Lopud and Sipan are inhabited. You can stay on them or visit all three on a day-trip from Dubrovnik.

Cavtat. Cavtat, 14km from Dubrovnik, is an attractive seaside resort of about 2,000 inhabitants, based around an old town that has its origins back in the time of the Greeks who set up a colony *(Epidaurus)* there. Cavtat straggles around two pretty, palm-lined bays and the slopes of its hills are thick with pine and cypress trees giving privacy and shade to the many villas built there. It is a desirable spot for property, and is therefore expensive. It is undoubtedly a good investment area.

Mljet. Mljet island lies to the south west of the Peljesac Peninsula and is often neglected by visitors as it not so accessible as islands further north or nearer the coast, but this is part of its charm. If you want to get away from it all, Mljet is wild and beautiful, and over half of it is designated a national park. In mythology, it is the island where the nymph Calypso kept Ulysses a prisoner for seven years.

Mljet is, as most Croatian islands are, elongated (37km by 3km). The national park, established in 1960, covers over 5,000 hectares of the northwestern part. Its main features are two salt lakes formed over 10,000 years ago and which are a unique geological and oceanographic phenomenon which has produced plants, which are only found on this island. In the larger of the two lakes is St. Mary's Island, complete with ruined Benedictine monastery. The other main features of the park are the brackish lakes (*blatine*) where local people catch eels. The seas of Mljet are phenomenally rich in sealife.

Mljet has a wonderfully varied landscape of cliffs, numerous islets, and steep hills that shelter many ancient villages. The outer coastline is wild and difficult to access; while the inner coastline is more accessible and has two ports where the ferries from Dubrovnik dock. The island has been inhabited by Illyrian tribes and the Romans built a settlement there. From the eighth century it has been inhabited by Croats from the Neretva area near Dubrovnik. The inhabitants are some of the few remaining speakers of the *Ijekavian* dialect.

It is possible to buy property on the island, almost certainly ruined and in need of renovation. It would be a rewarding place to live, but property there is not necessarily a good investment. The island is unlikely ever to be a mass holiday destination and so if peace and tranquility, ancient history, or naturalism are your bent, this would be an endlessly fascinating island.

Typical Properties for Sale on Southern Dalmatian Coast

Location	Type	Description	Price
Brac Island Village on coast	Plot of land with three ruined houses on it	land plot 430-450 sq. m. Houses for renovation. Car access.	€62,000
Brac Island	modern apartments on beach	30-34 sq. m. with terraces (ground floor), balconies (upper floor).	€22,500-€27,500
Makarska Riviera	apartment built 2002	62 sq.m. 2 bedrooms, 1 bathroom. Balcony, cable TV, seaview. Private parking space.	€75,000
Hvar island	modern house	comprising 2 separate apartments. Total indoor space 110 sq.m. on land 364 sq. m. Quiet spot. Seaview only from balcony. 150m from beach.	€110,000
Korcula Island Vela Luka	small house built 1989	50 sq. m. with 600 sq. m. land. 2 bedrooms. 500m from the sea.	€35,000
Vis Island	two old stone houses on a big plot	land plot of 8,500 sq. m. Houses for renovation. Car access. Surrounded by pine forest. Peaceful spot. 3km from sea.	€80,000
Peljesac Peninsula, in hamlet, 2kms from Viganj village	300-year-old house (ruin)	For renovation. Comes with some land and parking place. Elevated position with view to Korcula.	€25,000
Dubrovnik old town	fully restored 1st floor apartment in old stone house + ground floor suitable for commercial use.	56 sq. m. 1st floor, 2-bedrooms, kitchen, bathroom. Commercial property on ground floor 10 sq. m.	€230,000

Mljet island	old house part renovated	First floor finished. 2nd floor needs renovation. Garage 35 sq.m. 200m from sea	€160,000
Cavtat	new house	Built 2003. 115 sq.m. living space on 380 sq. m. land. 3 bedrooms. 2 bathrooms. Garden and garage.	€260,000

Estate Agents for Southern Dalmatia

AJ Investments: Split; ☎+385 (0)98 26 51 51; e-mail info@adriaticsun.com; www.ajinvestments.com. Offers houses and land for sale throughout Dalmatia.

B2B Real Estate Services: wants to be e-mailed in the first instance so that you can tell them what you are looking for. Specialists in the Peljesac Peninsula.

Croatia-Estate.Com: Osjecka 11, S.C. Gripe, Split 21000, Croatia; ☎+385 (0)21 547 004. Wide selection on the mainland and on the islands of south Dalmatia.

Croatia Holidays: Kuna, Peljesac peninsula, Croatia; fax +385 21 529 62 65(office in Split); www.peljesac.info (information on Peljesac peninsula). Contact Ivica Dajak. Ivica is also active in the tourist industry and has received so many requests for help in buying property that the business has now expanded to include real estate purchase. Can also be contacted on mobile phone (+385 9152962 65) and e-mail (ivo@peljesac.info).

Croatian House: www.croatianhouse.com. New British-run agency, specialises in Hvar Island.

Croatian Sun: Iva Vojnovica 61A, Dubrovnik, 20000, Croatia; ☎+385 203 12228; fax + 385 203 12226; info@croatiansun.co; www.croatiansun.com. Estabished 2003. Properties are mostly in Dubrovnik and the Dubrovnik area, but also covers Istria and some islands.

Dalmatian Villas: Kralja Zvonimira 8, Split 21000; ☎+385 21 340 680; e-mail dalmatian@dalmatianvilla.com; www.dalmatianvilla.com.

Dalmaville: www.dalmavilla.com; ☎(mobile) +385 987 33 408; e-mail info@dalmavilla.com. Sutivan, Bunta area of Brac island; luxury apartments in new complex.

Deranja-Konavle: Dubrovnik 2000; tel/fax +385 (0)20 412 487; e-mail ideranja@yahoo.com.

Dubrovnik Real Estate: Optic Cruise World Ltd., Put Tihe 4a, Cavtat/Dubrovnik 20210; ☎+385 (0)91 523 4806. Dubrovnik and area including the Peljesac Peninsula.

Katerina Brailo: ☎+385 20 32 45 50; e-mail stijepo.brailo@du.hinet.hr.

Libertas real estate Dubrovnik: Andrije Hebranga 53, 20000 Dubrovnik; ☎+385 (0)91 504 20 20; +385 (0)98 344 544; e-mail real-estate@post.hinet.hr.

Mandarinko: Zr. Frankopanska 21/1, Opuzen (Blace) 20355, Near Ploce; ☎+385 (0)20 671 225; e-mail sfilipovic@mandarinko.hr.

Milenka: Brizak b.b., Milna, 21405, Brac Island, Croatia; ☎+385 21 636221; e-mail ljiljana@milenkarealestate.com; www.milenkarealestate.com.

Nekretnine-hvar: Banski Dolac, Jelsa 21465, Hvar Island,; tel/fax +385 (0)21 761 538; e-mail info-nekretninehvar@net.hr. Properties on Hvar Island.

Nekretnine Urban: Ulica 44, br. 40, 20260 Korcula Island; tel/fax +385 (0)20 711-408; e-mail danko.urban@hi.htnet.hr or julije.urban@vip.hr. Specialised agency for the Korcula-Peljesac region.

Net Com: Poljana Grgura Ninskog 9, Split 21000; ☎+385 (0)21 34 76 61; +385 (0)21 32 60 25; e-mail estate@vip.hr.

Trgostan-Split: Korcula Island; fax +385 (0)21 362 140; e-mail trgostan@trgostan.i ms.hr.

Vela Luka Marketing: Ulica 68/23, Vela Luka 20270, Korcula Island, Croatia; tel/fax +385 (0)20 81 21 82; e-mail vl.marketing@inet.hr; www.velaluka.info/marketing. Collaborates with several larger agencies in the area. Specialises in Korcula island and the Peljesac peninsula.

Zlatka: M. Knezeviae 10, Dubrovnik 20000; ☎mobile +385 91 454 00 04; e-mail zlatka@zlatka.hr; www.zlatka.hr.

THE PURCHASING PROCEDURE

CHAPTER SUMMARY

- **Mortgages.** It is as yet unheard of to take out a mortgage in Croatia with a Croatian bank. Most people buying a property in Croatia re-mortgage their existing property in their home country, or take out a loan at home.

- **Croatian Bank Accounts.** It is relatively simple to open a non-resident bank account in Croatia using your passport for identification. You should do this as soon as possible if you know you are going to buy property.

- **Land Registry.** The Croatian Land Registry has neglected to keep proper records for the last 45 years making it very difficult and time consuming to trace property titles.

- **Clean Title.** With older properties it is often very difficult to establish, who the owner is as there may be dozens of names on the title deeds.

- With some properties, the building and the land it is on, may belong to separate owners so you are in effect carrying out two purchases from two sellers.

- Buying new property is easier than buying old as ownership is easier to ascertain.

- **Estate Agents.** There is no regulation of estate agents in Croatia. Most of them charge both the vendor and the buyer a commission and you may find their efficiency questionable.

- **Real Estate Purchase Tax** is at the single rate of 5%, which is payable on property as it is bought and sold. Either the seller or the new owner pays it, or they can agree to split it between them.

- Real Estate Purchase Tax is also called Property Transfer Tax and is payable within 30 days of the owner's title being registered at the Land Registry.

- **VAT** is charged at 22% on new property (built after 31 December 1997) if the seller is VAT registered. If the seller is a private individual, Real Estate Property Tax is payable.

- Some developers ask for part of the payment in cash so that they do not have to declare it and thereby reduce their tax liability.

FINANCE

BANKS

UK Banks

UK banks will not grant mortgages secured against properties in Croatia. The most usual way to raise the money to buy in Croatia is to secure a loan against your UK property, or to release equity in your UK property. The latter has been made possible by the enormous rise in value of many UK properties compared with Croatian ones.

Banks will usually grant mortgages through their subsidiaries abroad, but there are no British banks doing this in Croatia at present. There are German, Austrian and Italian banks in Croatia, which is helpful for their nationals wanting to buy property in Croatia. British banks may follow suit after Croatia joins the EU, which will probably be in 1997.

Croatian Banks

The Croatia National Bank (CNB) overseas the entire banking system of Croatia. The number of commercial banks operating in Croatia is 43. This is a reduction from 1998 when there were 60 banks. From 1994 there was a privatisation programme that swept through the banking system. Only Croatia Banka remains to be privatised. There is currently a shakeout of the Croatian banking system aimed at streamlining the system and bringing it up to date with new banking laws and technology. This has led to mergers and takovers by foreign banks such as the Austrian Hypo Alpe-Adria Bank and the Slavonska Banka, The Italian Banca Commerciala Italiana and Privredna Banka which is now known as Intesa BCI and the Austrian Erste & Steimermärkische bank and Rijiecka Banka. About half of the banks in Croatia are foreign owned. The Croatian banking system is highly concentrated. Over half of all banking assets belong to the two largest banks, Zagrebacka Banka and Privedna Banka. Together the five largest banks control about 80% of the market. The largest Croatian bank, Zagrebacka Banka is part (75%) owned by the Italian group Unicredito Italiano and the German Insurance company, Allianz.

Also part of the Croatian banking system are the Croatian Bank for Reconstruction and Development and four specialised housing savings banks.

Croatian Bank for Reconstruction and Development. The CBRD is entirely state-owned and is a state investment bank charged with the role of development of the economy and infrastructure. This includes providing incentives to small and medium-sized private enterprises, and stimulating house building.

Housing Savings Banks. The purpose of housing savings banks is to grant state-approved loans to Croatian citizens, who would otherwise have problems in affording housing. These institutions are funded by subscriptions from those who wish to utilise the service and also from legal entities and the State. At present only Croatian citizens, municipalities and towns can be depositors and the loans are for property on Croatian territory. Foreigners cannot use their services as they are not subscribers and depositors. After 1997, when Croatia is due to join the EU the service may have to be reorganised and made available to EU citizens.

Major Croatian Banks

Hrvatska Postanska Banka: Jurisiceva 4, 1000 Zagreb; ☎+385 (0)1 4804-400; www.hpb.hr. Croatian post office bank.

Hypo Alpe Adria Banka: Koturaska 47, 10000 Zagreb; ☎(0)1 6103 500; www.hypo-alpe-adria.hr.

Privredna Banka Zagreb: Rackoga 6, 10000 Zagreb; ☎01-4723 032; www.pbz.hr.

Raiffeisenbank Austria-Zagreb: Petrinjska 59, 10000 Zagreb; ☎01-4566-466; www.rba.hr. Austrian bank.

Slavonska Banka: Kapucinska 29, 31000 Osijek; ☎(0)31 231 100; www.slbo.hr.

Splitska Banka, member of the HVB Group: Rudera Boskovica 16, 21000 Split; ☎(0)21 304 304; fax (0)21 304 034; e-mail info@splitskabanka.hr; www.splitska.banka.hr/eng.

Varazdinska Banka: Kapucinski trg 5, 42000 Varazdin; (0)42 400-100; www.banka.hr.

Zagrebacka Banka: Non-resident Account Dept., Savska 62, 10000 Zagreb, Croatia; ☎+385 1 6305322; fax +385 16176272; e-mail jolanda.travoric@zaba.hr; also contact Nevenka Lipovac, Executive Manager, Non-Resident Account Dept (e-mail nevenka.lipovac@zaba.hr. Website www.zaba.hr.

Taking out a Croatian Mortgage

In theory, there is nothing to stop a foreigner taking out a mortgage on a Croatian property with a Croatian bank, but in practice they are very unwilling. In Britain or the USA, if you default on your mortgage payments the building society or bank can repossess the property. In Croatia it is legally very difficult legally for banks to evict defaulters or indeed any people from their homes. Even if you were able to take out a Croatian mortgage, it would probably have to be repaid in the Croatian currency *(kuna)* and if you were transferring the repayments from abroad, you would lose money in the conversion. For these reasons, many people tend to pay for their Croatian property directly, having taken out a loan at home, which is secured on their existing property, or an unsecured loan. The loan can then be paid off in sterling or dollars.

Having a Croatian mortgage might make sense if you were using rental income (if paid in kuna), from the Croatian property to pay off a mortgage, also in kunas. However, the interest rates offered by Croatian banks (currently around 9%) are unlikely to be as competitive as those offered by UK and US banks.

Buying Property on 'Hire Purchase'

According to Peter Ellis of Croatia Property Services (www.croatiapropertyservices), banks are responding to the increasing market for loans to foreigners to buy property and at the same time looking to protect their own interests. A Slovenian bank has just financed a housing development in Croatia. Purchasers are allowed to live in the development while paying off the loan they have taken out to buy their unit. The bank remains the owner of the property and retains the title deeds, which are only relinquished to the purchaser when the last due payment has been made. If this scheme is a success, it will probably catch on.

Opening a Bank Account

Non-residents can open a current or savings account in foreign exchange, or kuna, with banks licensed for opening non-residents accounts, which means most big banks. Opening an account is a fairly simple procedure for which you will need your passport. If you know that you will be making visits to Croatia to hunt for property to purchase, the sooner you open an account with a Croatian bank the better, as if you find something you want to buy, it will help speed things up. As most property purchases are currently being made in euros, you should open a euro account unless advised otherwise. It is recommended that you do this with one of the main Croatian banks listed above. The Splitska Banka has a website in English as does the Hypo Alpe-Adria Banka.

Importing Currency into Croatia

If you import a substantial amount of currency into Croatia by telegraphic transfer, it is important to declare the import. As already stated, the majority of property transactions in Croatia take place in euros. If you are concerned about currency fluctuations between the value of sterling and the euro, you can 'forward buy' euros at a fixed rate from a firm such as Currencies Direct. For more details of this and also the best ways of transferring money abroad, see *Importing Currency* in the *General Introduction* to this book.

CROATIAN TAXES ON REAL ESTATE

Croatian Income Tax and Foreign Residents

For Croatian citizens taxes are very high, up to 50% personal income tax and VAT at 22%, but if you do not receive a salary, consultancy fees or income from similar professional activities, the tax regime offers great advantages such as tax-free income from foreign pensions and interest payments on loans, investments, deposits with financial institutions, public loans and securities and similar incomes. The use of offshore mortgage and banking facilities are also utilisable for tax avoidance and planning, as Croatia's tax regime does not have any legal instruments against this tactic of avoidance.

However, probably one of the reasons why we are not all rushing to retire to Croatia is that it is likely that these tax advantages will be modified or cease after Croatia's entry into the EU planned for 2007/8, so if you have a mind to take advantage of the lacunae of the current Croatian tax regime, you have a maximum of four years in which to benefit. After that, you may find yourself obliged to pay the national swingeing rates of income tax and VAT. For further details of taxation in Croatia, see *Taxes* in the *General Introduction* to Croatia.

Real Estate Transfer Tax

There is a 5% tax levied on the transfer of property. The tax is based on the valuation of the property as estimated by the local tax authorities. Transfer tax is due within 30 days of the Contract of Sale being completed. The tax authority will then decide the exact amount of tax to be paid. Once notification of the amount to be paid is received, there are fifteen days to pay the tax in full. Tax paid late is subject to a daily addition of interest until the tax is discharged. Payments can be made in other currencies through a bank or post office and will be charged at the rate of exchange on the day of payment. Your agent or lawyer will normally manage this for you.

Real Estate Purchase Tax

Real Estate Purchase Tax is the same tax as Real Estate Transfer Tax. It is very important when negotiating with a seller to ascertain who is going to pay the tax, the vendor or the purchaser. More often than not, the buyer pays. If the vendor is paying the tax it will be added to the cost of purchase. Sometimes the vendor and purchaser agree to pay it between them.

If liability for the tax falls to you, the purchaser, and you are not likely to be in Croatia, when the tax falls due, it is advisable to make arrangements to pay the tax, either through your agent in Croatia, or by paying directly from your home country.

VAT on New Property

On properties built after 31 December 1997 by a VAT-registered builder or developer the buyer is liable to pay VAT at 22%. If the seller is a private individual and therefore not VAT-registered, then Real Estate Purchase Tax (see above) is paid instead.

Local Tax on Holiday Homes

There is also a tax levied locally on holiday homes and which is based on the square metreage of the building (but not the land). The tax is also based on the location, age and condition of the structure. Holiday homes are regarded as a luxury and the local municipality may impose an annual tax on them. The tax is levied at a rate of 5-15 kuna per square metre, which works out at a few hundred euros per year. The imposition of the tax is patchy; not all municipalities charge it. It is levied by billing and is paid to the local authority, which uses it to finance local projects. It is somewhat similar to the UK's Council Tax.

Inheritance and Capital Gains Taxes

Capital Gains. There is no capital gains tax to pay when you sell your property, unless you sell it within three years, in which case the rate is 35%. If you sell within three years but sell it to a spouse or an immediate family member, there is also no capital gains tax to pay.

Inheritance Tax. There is no inheritance tax for the next in succession. Otherwise there is a single rate tax of 5% on estate valued at more than 50,000 kuna (about £5,000).

FINDING PROPERTIES FOR SALE

PROBLEMS IN FINDING PROPERTIES FOR SALE

It is still not easy to find property for sale in Croatia and even more difficult to buy it. Even the film star John Malkovich (who has Croatian ancestry) with millions of dollars at his disposal to buy a luxury ex-Tito villa, has had to wait like those of lesser means for the bureaucratic tortoise race to run its ponderous course.

The Croatian house market is different from other European countries in that the property-buying infrastructure for foreigners is fairly underdeveloped. Yearly sales number a few hundred, rather than tens of thousands. There is also a housing shortage not only for Croatians, but also foreigners, especially in the most popular areas such as Dubrovnik. The Croatian government declares that it will have completed its post war reconstruction programme in 2004. It has also been running a programme aimed at providing subsidised housing, especially for young families and others who would otherwise be unable to afford to buy their own property. In consequence Croatia has a remarkably high level of owner occupancy. However, both these national projects have required enormous budgets and kept large numbers of construction workers busy. Private construction has not been as great a priority, but is likely to accelerate in the run up to Croatia's projected EU membership. Even so, Croatia is very keen to limit the amount of new building on the coast as it fears that unchecked development will ruin the beauty of the littoral and take away the beauty that makes it such a massive attraction in the first place. Already, in a few places illegal constructions have reared their carbuncular heads.

The other huge, and potentially much greater obstacle to finding a property to buy in Croatia is the problem of finding real estate whose owner has a legal right to sell. In many cases, there is multiple ownership comprising disappeared and untraceable title holders and the expense of trying to contact them will be all yours. The problem with land purchase is equally fraught as there has not been a complete land survey of Croatia since before the First World War.

THE PROBLEM OF CLEAN TITLE

This section should be called 'The Property is for Sale, but Can You Legally Buy It?' There is a particular problem with land titles throughout Croatia. This is a legacy from the communist era, when private ownership was discouraged by the imposition of extortionate inheritance tax, which meant that private owners handed properties on to their heirs without officially recording the transfer of title. Alternatively, new owners just kept adding their names to the title without ever removing any. The result of this fudging of ownership is that title deeds may be plastered with names (up to 30 or 50 is not unusual), many of them titleholders who may be dead, or who have emigrated, but whose ghostly presence on the title deed comes back to haunt the would-be purchaser.

Before a property can be legally sold, the title-holders listed have to be traced and this takes time and money. It is the proposed purchaser who pays the investigative costs of having the former owners traced and contacted, or eliminated.

Land Registry

The state of land registry in Croatia is at the heart of the problem of clean title owing to very lax practices during the Communist era. There is a massive project currently underway to update the land registry. The Minister for Environment Protection laid bare the Registry's shortcomings in a statement made in March 2002 and set out the remedies for bringing it up-to-date.

UPDATING THE LAND REGISTER

It is perfectly clear that in the past 45 years the Communist regime has not cared too much for private ownership. In most of the municipal centres, the land registers have not been updated. Probate proceedings have not been recorded and present owners have not been registered. The land register records, stored at register departments at municipal courts, are relevant for official purposes such as the purchase and sale of properties.

The ministry relevant for such matters, is aware of the negligence of the clerks in assessing ownership and of the unsatisfactory quality of data of properties in the field. Often one can find varying information. As a result, the State Geodetic Administration has begun a land registry update programme based on the act recently adopted by the Croatian government on the measurement and registration of properties. The government has also *adopted a programme to update data in the land registry of the islands and a general data check is also planned.*

As valid documents on ownership are a precondition for obtaining building permits and as they are one of the most frequent causes of dissatisfaction among the population, the minister responsible for this field has decided to simplify the procedure for obtaining building permits.

As the process of obtaining a permit includes other documents, which can only be obtained in the field, local administrations will have to be updated. Years and years of negligence cannot be resolved in a short period, however, one has to know where to go. Therefore, for property problems turn to the county court. If you encounter further problems in realising rights due to lack of understanding on part of the bureaucracy, contact the Ministry of Justice or the Ministry of Construction.

Bozo Kovacevic, Minister for Environment Protection and Planning

The Difference between the Land Register and the Cadastra

The Land Register and the Cadastra both record property and owner details. The Land Registry Records are stored in the Registry Department of municipal courts. These are the official records and the only ones that are legally valid for property sale and purchase.

The Cadastral holds property information such as the measurements, perimeters, description, classification and owners' details. These records form the basis of the information stored at the Land Registry but are not valid for legal purposes such as the buying and selling of real estate. Cadastral records are held at the local municipal Cadastral office.

Any would-be purchaser of a parcel of land has to check the records of both Cadastral and Land Register and hope they agree, which is invariably not the case. Usually this cross-checking is done through a lawyer engaged by the purchaser to act on their behalf)

Progress in Land Registry Reform

In the two years since the Minister gave his frank analysis of the Land Registry's chaotic state, some progress has been made. Computerised records are being created. Once municipalities see what a galvanising effect streamlined registry records produce on the local economy, the pace of change will quicken and the procedures become less dilatory. In the meantime, a new, private checking service is also being provided whereby some solicitors in Croatia will run an initial check on the title of any property you are interested in buying. They will produce a translated report of their findings, on the basis of which you can decide whether it would be wise to proceed or not. You can enquire about this service from your estate agent or solicitor. The service will cost you 200-300 euros. The larger estate agents such as Nenad Saljic, who works from the Split office of Henley & Partners (international tax consultancy and property agent +385 21 489 511) are making their own registry checks on properties before offering them for sale.

ESTATE AGENTS

Once you have identified the area you are interested in, you will need to find an estate agent to help you view properties and find the one you want to buy. As stated in the section *Where to Find Your Ideal Property,* the profession is fairly new and therefore unregulated. There is no official training or standard of work practices. In fact, some of those who claim to be 'leading' estate agents may just be those who speak the best English, German, Italian etc. rather than the most experienced at being an estate agent. Many of them have a background in tourism, hence the multi-lingual capability. Others may be qualified architects and lawyers who do some property dealing as a sideline, particularly on islands. As there is no official training, the standards of some may leave a lot to be desired and there are always rumours of land being sold for building that cannot be built on, extortionate commissions being demanded, and sheer lack of responsiveness. As the housing market develops and Croatia draws closer to EU membership day (1997/98) practices are likely to come more in line with the EU ones.

Whilst generally estate agents services can be found wanting, there are some with good reputations and these will include foreigners, (Britons, Germans, Austrians and Italians) who are doing a good job making the process as straightforward as they can in the circumstances.

Finding a reliable estate agent and one that is used to dealing with foreigners requires perseverance. In the end you will probably have to rely on your own judgement, backed up if possible by recommendations from satisfied clients. If you have to approach total strangers for testimonials, so be it. Do not hesitate to ask the estate agent for the contact details of other foreigners for whom they have acted and ask these ex-clients for their assessment of the agent's capabilities and services.

Alternatively, you can try to manage on your own. One buyer says:

You think you haven't got any contacts in Croatia but what about the restaurant where you eat, the bar where you drink, the hotel or guest-house where you are staying. Many Croatians speak reasonable English, once you have made a few friends ask for their advice. If you get them to enquire for you about properties for sale, the price will be much cheaper.

There is quite a wide selection of agents listed in the chapter *Where to Find Your Ideal Property.* Agents are listed at the end of the description of the region they deal with. At the beginning of the chapter a handful of agents that deal with all of Croatia are also given.

Estate agents' commission should be in the region of 2-4% of the purchase price. Most charge both the vendor and buyer commission. There are stories of agents charging 10% commission to both buyer and vendor; this is the sharper end of business practice.

Internet and Press

These days most people begin their search for a property to buy on the internet. In the case of Croatia, the internet is practically the only way that you can investigate the possibilities before going to Croatia. Unlike, France, Spain and other more popular Mediterranean countries, there is as yet no dedicated magazine on Croatia. The most useful magazine is probably the general *Homes Overseas* (www.homesoverseas.co.uk) magazine, which carries features on Croatian property. Articles about Croatian property also appear fairly regularly in national newspapers and these too, can be checked on newspapers' online archive facilities.

Useful Property Websites
www.avatar-croatia.com
www.croatia-estates.com

www.croatia-holidayandhome.co.uk
www.croatia-info.net
www.croatiapropertyservices.com
www.realestate.escapeartist.com
www.nekretnine.org
www.passage.hr
www.realestatecroatia.com
www.thisiscroatia.com
www.visit-croatia.co.uk
www.visitcroatia.proboards21.com (message board of Visit Croatia.com, unmissable
background to buying)
www.viviun.com

Property Exhibitions

Croatian developers feature regularly at Homes Overseas exhibitions, which are held
around the country in London, Birmingham, Manchester etc. and also in Ireland. A list of
exhibition dates and venues can be obtained from the website www.homesoverseas.co.uk/
Exhibition+Calendar or telephone 0207-939 9888 for further details.

WHAT TYPE OF PROPERTY TO BUY

There may not be the range of types of property easily available in Croatia that you
might find on the Mediterranean in Spain, France or Italy and there will certainly not
be the choice of modern properties that you find in Spain, but you may be able to find
something quite unique, especially in older property. On the other hand, older property
carries all the problems of establishing ownership (see *Land Registry* above). As said,
the property industry is less systemised than in most western European countries and
there are wide price variations amongst properties of equal size and condition, even
within the same area. Once sellers know that foreigners are the potential customers,
prices are liable to acquire an arbitrary foreigner's premium, so you should, from your
own researches, have formed a rough idea of what price properties of different types
and in different locations go for.

APARTMENTS

Modern Croatian apartment buildings are on the increase as building permits become
easier to obtain, now that the land register is being brought up to date. Apart from
purpose-built blocks, which can be a bit soulless, there are new apartments occupying
a floor (usually the top floor) of a (usually) modern house. Quite often, this is a way in
which, the seller can recoup money spent on building and renovating.

Buying an apartment can also be an entrée into one of the high-priced areas
such as Dubrovnik where houses are very expensive but apartments are generally
more affordable and you still get all the thrills of living in a stunning location. The
disadvantages include not having a place to park and the bureaucratic nightmare
(because of Dubrovnik's World Heritage Status) entailed when carrying out minor
repairs and renovations. If you are buying for investment, then you will have to

choose carefully and forgo living within an historic monument and buy into the more prestigious end of the new-build market in the most popular places.

BUILDING LAND

Buying a plot of land on which to build a new house, or wanting to change significantly a building that already exists on the land, exposes you to a whole new minefield of bureaucracy concerning the obtaining of building permits. This entails among other things, getting the approval of all your neighbours and of anyone whose land adjoins yours. It is often easier to buy a plot with a ruin on it that you can restore to its original dimensions and character, or to buy off-plan or new-build where the planning permission issue has already been dealt with by the developer.

'BUILDING LAND' CAVEAT EMPTOR
Caveat 1. At the time of press, there are reports circulating of estate agents selling 'building land' that has not been designated for residential development and which cannot therefore be built on. Please make sure that if you are buying building land that you obtain confirmation that you can build on it. Your lawyer should do this for you. Caveat 2. The land and the buildings on it may have two separate owners. Your agent will check the Land and Building Rights register for owner details. If land and building ownership are separate then the purchaser may have to purchase from both parties, unless a deal can be worked out where one owner pays off the other.

OFF-PLAN AND NEW-BUILD

Buying off-plan properties is not widely established in Croatia, as it is in Spain, and increasingly in France, but the developers have begun to make inroads, first in Istria and now on some islands. It is most important to choose a quality construction with adequate local infrastructure (this is just what many of the islands lack). For instance on Vir island (near Zadar and very popular with Hungarian buyers), there has been an apparently unauthorised development of 300 apartments built a few metres from the sea, where pollution with sewage is now an imminent problem. The island's population of 2,000 plays host to 70,000 visitors over the summer. Such developments, even if authorised are also noisy as they are adjacent to tourist facilities and you never know if your view is going to be spoilt by further development. Remember that all new property carries 22% VAT which is usually absorbed in the asking price. It is advisable to check that the price quoted includes the VAT (*PDV* in Croat).

WARNING
Note that it is not uncommon for developers to ask for part payment in cash, which they do not declare and which reduces the price actually declared on the contract. The advantage to the developer is that it reduces their VAT liability. For the purchaser, it can be worrying as not all their money is legally protected. Unfortunately, this seems to be the way things are often done in Croatia and so you will either have to go along with it or look for another property.

Village Houses

Sadly, many Croatian villages have been marred by a rash of new building thanks to Croatia's post war reconstruction policy but it is still possible to find a range of old stone houses and ruined buildings for renovation. Remember that you should expect to pay lower prices even a few miles inland, but locals will often raise the prices if they know foreigners are the potential buyers. There is also the problem of establishing title with older properties. But if this is what you really want, you should persevere, up to a point (see *Clean Title* below). You may be able to find something that is really good value and pay under £100,000 for a pretty village house; half that for a ruin.

A potential problem away from main towns is a consistent water supply. Some houses have both mains water and a back-up rain cistern.

VILLAS

Villas tend to be pricey as they are often architect designed, or if old, they may be elegant like the one-time nobility's seaside houses at Opatija and Dubrovnik. In most cases you are looking at well over £700,000 for a *fin de siècle,* crumbling mansion with a huge repair bill to make it habitable, or £172,000-£250,000 for a large modern house with land near the sea. Smaller villas start at £150,000. At the top end of the market a nine-bedroom villa divided into three apartments near Dubrovnik is on sale for £1.8 million and is on the verge of being purchased by Rio Ferdinand, the footballer.

There are also 'unfinished' villas for sale where the builder has reached the limit of his funds and wants to sell as is, to restore his finances. There may be problems with this type of property as the building permit may have expired. You should also make sure that the reasons for selling are genuine. Your estate agent/solicitor will carry out the necessary checks.

ISLANDS

Buying an island in the Mediterranean is probably the ultimate property fantasy, but in most cases it remains just that. Croatian islands are for sale at prices from £250,000 to between one and three million pounds, depending on size, location, character and whether or not they have habitable buildings. Whilst a million pounds may not seem a lot for a group of buyers to buy an island in company form, the maintenance costs could be heavy. Maintaining/creating buildings, installing a landing jetty and purchasing a yacht in which to reach the island are just some of the possible expenses involved. American movie stars have been looking at islands to buy but they needn't expect privacy. Croatian laws enshrine free public access to the whole shoreline making it paparazzi paradise, even on privately-owned islands. The larger estate agents such as Broker Nekretnine +385 21 547 004, Homes in Croatia (www.homesincroatia.com), and Croatia-Estate.com have islands for sale on their books. According to Lara Vekic of Croatia-Estate.com, her agency has not sold one island yet.

TYPES OF PROPERTY NOT FOR SALE TO FOREIGNERS

There are a few types of real estate that cannot be purchased by foreigners. These include the coast (defined as 8 metres above the high tide line), forests, agricultural land and anything classified as a 'cultural monument'. When it comes to cultural monuments, there may be some leeway allowed if Croatian nationals have been offered first refusal.

RENTING A HOME IN CROATIA

The accepted advice about what to do before you buy a place of your own in Croatia, is to get to know the area of your choice by renting before you buy, and especially to visit the area in the winter, as places often change their atmosphere completely out of season and the temperatures plummet. You can check the internet for winter deals renting apartments or a house, with rental companies such as the small, but widely-established Croatian Villas (020-8368 9978). Croatian Villas (www.croatianvillas.com) has a fixed winter tariff for stays up to 2 weeks, but for longer lets, it is possible to negotiate rates. All properties have been inspected and if they are let in winter they have to be centrally heated. According to Tara Hawkins of Croatia Villas:

> *The coast can seem very desolate in winter, the sea gets wilder and the mountain backdrops are covered with snow. I was there (Dubrovnik) in January and it was freezing cold. Most of our villas are on the coast because people like to be within easy reach of restaurants and a supermarket. We don't get asked for rural properties, so we don't have them on our books. We tried it once, but we couldn't rent them. The exception is Istria, where the interior is very pretty.*

Another good source of information on rental properties are the regional tourism websites listed below, the property websites listed above, or contact the national Tourist Board (www.croatia.hr).

Regional Tourism Websites
Istria - www.istra.com
Kvarner - www.kvarner.hr
Zadar - www.zadar.hr
Sibenik - www.sibenik-knin.com
Dalmatia - www.dalmacija.net
Split - www.visitsplit.com
Dubrovnik - www.tzudrovnik.hr

FEES, CONTRACTS AND CONVEYANCING

SURVEYS

Finding a Surveyor
Most Croatians do not bother to have property surveys done before they buy a property and there is no specialist profession of Property Surveyor as such. If you want to have a survey done you will have to ask a 'British' estate agent to arrange one. This will normally be carried out by an architect. Peter Ellis of www.croatiapropertys ervices.com based in Zagreb will arrange surveys.

LAWYERS

Checking for Clean Title

Once you have located a property you want to buy, if the estate agent has not already had the property checked for clean title at the Cadastra and the Land Registry (see above), the estate agent will introduce you to a lawyer, who will do this. **It is absolutely essential to check for clean title before proceeding any further. Only after the title has been legally established should the purchasing procedure be set in motion.** The period of time it takes to check title varies from an hour to several days. If there is little progress after a week then you are strongly advised to abandon your quest, and look around for another property, or better still, have a list of favourites and proceed to the next one.

Two Parties, One Lawyer?

If you use the lawyer recommended by the estate agent, you will find that he or she is also acting for the vendor. It is usual in Croatia for the vendor and the seller to have the same lawyer. This is quite startling to some foreigners who feel that their interests are not being protected. In fact, the lawyer is disinterested, and is there only to check the legality of the paperwork. If you want partial advice you will have to employ your own lawyer and this is what some foreigners do. It is not essential to have your own lawyer, and will almost certainly slow things down if you do, but if you want to be sure that the property is legally yours and that discrepancies will not come back to haunt you or your heirs in years to come, or when you try to sell, it may be the only way to put your mind at rest. In practice, many people find, that what is most important is that they feel confidence in the vendor and don't intuitively feel they are trying to pull a fast one.

SCALE OF CONVEYANCING FEES

The following fees are charged by www.croatiapropertyservices.com based in Zagreb. These fees constitute a yardstick. Many fees will be higher than these.

Legal Work

Initial consultation (up to 1 hr)	no charge
Initial search at Land Registry to verify title plus disbursements*	€250
Additional work(§), hourly rate (aggregated)	€100
Preparation of Pre-contract & Contract plus disbursements	1% of Contract price

Property Work - Purchasing

Buying residential property as agent for applicants including locating property, supplying report as to condition and negotiating with vendors	2%
In Croatia, it is usual to charge both seller and buyer on a sale. Fee to buyer on sale	2%

Property Work - Selling

Valuation and market appraisal	no charge
Selling residential property, including preparation of sales particulars with photos and internet advertising	3% of valuation
Local press advertising	at cost

*Court fees, translation, travel, gazetting, couriers etc.
(§) Removal of liens, regularisation of defective titles, etc.

DIFFERENT PURCHASE PROCEDURES

There is more than one way to purchase property in Croatia legally, and the estate agent will discuss with you which type of purchase procedure is being followed. In some cases, you may not be able to choose which procedure to follow. For instance, if you are from a country that does not have a reciprocal agreement (see *Which Nations Have Reciprocity with Croatia* below) with Croatia then you can only buy property by forming a company. For instance, this applies to Australians, but not to US or British citizens as they have reciprocity.

The main thing to note is that every property purchase by a foreigner in Croatia has to get authorisation from the Ministry of Foreign Affairs in Zagreb. This is a notoriously slow process, which mostly takes a minimum of six months; though a year or even three years is not unheard of. Recent purchasers of new property claim to have got permission through in two months. It is important to note that nationals of countries with reciprocity are pretty much assured of getting permission eventually, and many estate agents are taking advantage of this to complete the contract with full payment before the Ministry permission is issued. In many cases foreigners are now finding themselves with the keys to their house much faster than they anticipated. This is becoming so widespread it will soon be normal practice.

Pre-Contract

Once an offer has been accepted to a property with clean title, a Pre-contract can be drawn-up and a payment (usually 10%) is made by the purchaser. The Pre-contract governs the subsequent actions that must be taken to complete the purchase, and the parties' liabilities and obligations; it is binding to both parties. You will need a lawyer to draw this up. You will also have to have your passport certified by the local notary; this is arranged by the agent. The transfer and sale is only completed when the permission comes through from the Ministry in Zagreb.

The Pre-contract was the most commonly used purchasing procedure for foreigners with reciprocity until recently. However, the disadvantages of this method are plain to see. While the Ministry pushes paper around in slow motion, the vendor watches the price he has demanded fall behind the steadily rising house prices around him and tries to up the price. If the purchaser balks at this, the vendor may break off the contract because he can still make a profit selling at a higher price. He may even advertise the property while the purchaser is waiting. The buyer meanwhile suffers continuous anxiety wondering if he or she is going to lose their property. Also, depending on their circumstances, they may be frustrated that they cannot rent out the property and start paying back the mortgage, or move into it.

Payment in Full – No Waiting for Ministry Permission

This route is fast becoming the usual purchase procedure and involves no Pre-contract. While it does cut out the waiting time and the anxiety of being gazumped as house values rise, there are disadvantages. A Contract of Sale is presented by the lawyer to the buyer and the vendor on the same day that the buyer's funds to pay for the purchase arrive in the buyer's Croatian bank account. The buyer will already have been sent a copy of the Contract of Sale to read previous to the sale date, but this document is not actually signed by both parties (i.e. legally binding) until the day the money changes hands. When the Contract is signed, the parties proceed to the bank where the money is transferred to the vendor, and then the parties proceed directly to the Notary Public's office where the signature of the vendor is notarised. The keys are handed over to the buyer and the sale is complete.

The final stage of the procedure involves the buyer being accompanied to the local Land Registry with all his or her documents and the property title being registered as theirs. **Note that you should on no account hand over money to a vendor without a formal Contract of Sale and a lawyer present.**

WHICH NATIONS HAVE RECIPROCITY WITH CROATIA?

- ○ Only nationals of countries which have reciprocity can own property in Croatia as private individuals; nationals of other countries have to set up a company to buy property.
- ○ There is a reciprocal agreement with: EU countries (including the UK, but not Italy for historic reasons), the United States, the Russian Federation and Hungary.
- ○ Nationals of Italy, Switzerland and Bosnia-Hercegovina can only buy property as individuals if they are permanently resident in Croatia.

Forming a Croatian Company to Purchase Property

Estate agents and lawyers will sometimes tell a buyer that it is advantageous to buy property in Croatia through a company formed for that purpose. In fact, the only time it is absolutely necessary to do this, is if you are from a country such as Australia or Canada, which has no reciprocity with Croatia and so it is the only way nationals of such non-reciprocal countries can own Croatian real estate. The 'advantage' to which the estate agent may be referring can only be that it is quicker to form a property purchase company (takes about 4 weeks; sometimes less) than it is to obtain approval from the Ministry of Foreign Affairs which takes six months or longer. However, now that you can pay in full for your property and move in right away before the Ministry approval arrives, this advantage no longer exists. Peter Ellis of Croatia Property Services thinks that forming a company would make sense if you were thinking of acquiring a portfolio of properties and/or very expensive property. The new fast track buying procedure of paying in full before the Ministry approval arrives, means you are not protected if for some reason approval is denied. In practice, this is very rare. Peter Ellis has not heard of one case where it has happened.

The main disadvantage of setting up a company, is the expense of setting it up, maintaining it, submitting annual returns etc. If you are thinking of going down this route, you should get expert advice. Croatia Property Services (www.croatiapropertys ervices.com) based in Zagreb and Istria is a good place to start.

MONEY TO COMPLETE THE PURCHASE, OR TO BUY IN A SINGLE PROCESS

Methods of Payment

There are several options when it comes to paying for your property. These include paying in cash, transferring funds via a bank or via a currency dealer. As already mentioned, you may be asked to pay partly in cash 'under the table' because the developer wants to reduce his tax liability. Using a bank, means you will carry the cost of currency conversion, which can run into several thousands of euros on a large amount. By general consensus, the best method economically of paying is via a currency dealer in euros. Currencies Direct are such a dealer (see *Importing Currency*, in *The General Introduction* of this book.)

POST COMPLETION FORMALITIES

Applying for Ministry of Foreign Affairs Approval

Even though you have completed the purchase of a property, registered your title and moved in, your ownership has to be officially approved by the Ministry of Foreign Affairs. Applying for the all important MoFA approval involves writing to The Ministry of Foreign Affairs (Consular Department, Meduliceva 34, 10000 Zagreb, Croatia). In most cases the buyer's lawyer handles the application which involves sending a raft of documents, which your lawyer will already have accumulated during the purchase procedure. Delays are part of the process, and the Ministry may request additional information from your lawyer, who will then forward the requests to you. Some of these queries can be pre-empted by preparing as many documents as possible before you go if possible bearing in mind that the Ministry will not deal with documents more than six months old. In his book *How to Buy a Property in Croatia,* Martin Westby recommends having personal documents not only notarised but verified by the UK Foreign Office as he says the Ministry finds this very reassuring.

> *First you need a UK notary; there is a website at www.thenotariessociety.org.uk and listings in Yellow Pages. Ask if he/she is registered, and what their charges are including application to the Foreign Office. In my case, it cost £40 with £5 for certified copies. The FO charge £12 per copy to process the paperwork so it's quite easy to spend £100.*
>
> *It is best to give 2 copies of each document to your Croatian solicitor. I would recommend taking passports, contracts of employment/accountant's letter, proof of address and wedding certificate (if appropriate). Once you have them endorsed send them immediately to your Croatian solicitor because (The Ministry in) Zagreb will not deal with paperwork that is more than 6 months old.*

Registering your Title

You may have paid for your property, moved in and received a Ministry permission but until you have registered your title at the Land Registry you are not officially the owner. Registering the title is another service that your lawyer or agent will guide you through. Once you have established your legal ownership, you can then sign contracts with the water, gas and electricity suppliers and you can apply for planning permission if applicable. Some buyers are tempted not to Register their title for tax or other reasons. Beware of going down this route, as if you are not officially registered as the owner, you will have difficulties when it comes to selling or passing it on to your heirs.

USEFUL RESOURCES

Do not forget that there are some good resources you can turn to for information, assistance and practical help and services. It may seem invidious to single out a few from amongst those already mentioned and there may be others that deserve to be highlighted, but the following are indisputably helpful:

Websites

www.visit-croatia.com. Probably the best travel website for Croatia, from where you can click on to a property section 'Property in Croatia' or the invaluable property message board 'Visit Croatia Forum' where property-buyers are hard at it giving tips, advice, contacts, personal experiences and more. You can also go straight to the message board at www.visitcroatia.proboards21.com.

British-Based Lawyers

John Howell & Co: The Old Glassworks, 22 Endell Street, Covent Garden, London WC2H 9AD; ☎020 7420 0400; fax 020 7836 3626; e-mail info@europelaw.com; www.europelaw.com. –

Estate Agent

www.croatiapropertyservices.com. Anglo-Croatian agency based in Zagreb and Istria. Handles all kinds of property purchase, surveys, property management, company set-ups and a range of other services. Run by property and legal professionals including Peter Ellis who moved permanently to Croatia a year ago.

Publication

How to Buy a Property in Croatia. Martin Westby of Croatia Holiday and Home, 7 Ashbourne Road, Bournemouth, Dorset BH5 2JS; ☎01202-259155 (www.croatia-holidayandhome.co.uk). Seems to be the only publication dedicated to Croatia. Regularly updated publication, and mini updates can be sent by e-mail.

REAL ESTATE GLOSSARY	
Apartment - *apartman* (or *stan*)	Lawyer - *pravnik* (sometimes *advokat*)
Architect - *architekt*	New-built - *novo izgradeno*
Builder - *graditelj*	Olive trees - *maslina*
Estate agent - *nekretnine*	Piece of land - *parcela*
Garage - *garaza*	Price - *cijena*
Garden - *vrt*	Ruin - *rusevine*
House - *kuca*	Sea- *mora*
Land - *zemlja*	Vines - *vinova loza*

WHAT HAPPENS NEXT

BUILDING OR RENOVATING

Renovating

If you merely wish to renovate your property within the existing structure then you can do this without having to wait for the Permission from The Ministry of Foreign Affairs (see the previous section). Any extension of the property and other major alterations are subject to planning permission and this can only be granted when you have approval of purchase from MoFA and you have registered your title of ownership with the Land Registry.

If you have purchased property defined as a 'cultural monument' then there is a raft of legislation covering external building work.

If you are concerned that a long delay in starting building work is detrimental to your plans or wishes (i.e. if you don't want to wait six months or longer for Ministry approval) then you can speed things up considerably by forming a company to buy property. There are disadvantages as well as advantages in forming a company, and before you go ahead, you should discuss these with your agent or solicitor.

Considering the bureaucracy involved in building or renovating, it is hard to see why there is not a higher proportion of buyers taking on only new properties, or ones that only need refurbishment.

Hiring Workers and Professionals

There are really two approaches to the hiring of professionals and workers. The better one is almost certainly through recommendation from their former clients or from some estate agents. The estate agent or lawyer will be able to give you some contacts and you can proceed from there. Some estate agents in Croatia are foreigners themselves but have lived in Croatia for several years and are also a good source of contacts for architects and builders. In particular, the British-origin estate agents in Croatia that are listed in this book in the chapter *Where to Find Your Ideal Home* in particular can put you in touch with English-speaking builders and professionals.

The other approach is to ask around amongst the locals in the bars and restaurants. As well as being a way of finding properties for sale, it is also a way of tracking down architects and builders.

Do not underestimate the importance of having an architect or builder that speaks good English, or at the very least a bilingual intermediary. Many builders have worked in Germany and speak German, but this is not much use to most English-speaking people, unless they also speak the language.

Builders

It is not usually difficult to find local builders in Croatia except in some places where foreigners have moved in en masse and overwhelmed the supply. On the island of Hvar, there has been a spate of property-buying, resulting in new purchasers queuing up to get building work done, which has resulted in builders there demanding premium rates.

Standards of workmanship are generally impressive as Croatia still has a proper training system, which ensures a level of craftsmanship that is lacking now in the UK, where only older builders have learned their trade in a systematic way. Although many Croatian builders are used to working to a high specification, they are notoriously blasé when it comes to the safety aspect of their persons at work. As Peter Ellis of Croatia Property Services puts it:

Having had an involvement with Health & Safety in the UK, some of the local working practices came as a shock, but the end result has always been fine. Labour rates are way below UK ones.

Useful Address
Drustvo arhitekata Zagreba (Croatian Architects Association): Trg bana Josipa Jelaeia 3/1, Zagreb; ☎+385 1 4816151; fax +385 1 4816197; e-mail daz@zg.hinet.hr; www.d-a-z.hr .

MAKING MONEY FROM YOUR PROPERTY

Location, Location
Once you have bought your ideal Croatian property, you may find that there are good economic reasons for wanting to derive an income from it. Many property owners buy with the intention of letting part or all of the property for some of the year, usually during the peak summer season when rents are at their highest. For this purpose, the most important thing is the location and having efficient international access. According to Tara Hawkins of Croatian Villas (www.croatianvillas.com), by far the easiest properties to let are by the sea (unless in Istria) and near an airport. Most clients do not want to drive for miles before they arrive at their holiday destination. This narrows down the prime places for letting to within an hour's drive of an airport. In Istria this means near Pula, or on Krk or Brac (islands which have airports), or in or around Dubrovnik or Split.

Typical Weekly Rents in Prime Areas

Location	Description	Min. rental – low season	Max. Rental – Peak Season
Island of Hvar – Dalmatia	2-bedroom villa with garden	£280/$502/€420	£467/$836/€700
Istria - hill town	5-bed villa with swimming pool	£400/$716/€600	£1,000/$1,790/€1,500
Resort area of Dubrovnik	1-bedroom apartment		from £300/$535/€448

Being Your Own Agent
Depending on your circumstances you will either pay a letting agent/property management company 20% to oversee the entire business of letting and dealing with

the clients, or you will decide to manage everything yourself. If you are going to deal with the clients personally you should bear in mind the following:

Taxable Income from Letting Property. Anyone who is letting out their property and receiving their income from it in Croatia is liable for tax in Croatia. The taxable income from a rental lease is the rental income minus 30% for expenses, or 50% if letting rooms or beds. You will need to file an annual Croatian tax return. For useful contacts giving tax advice, see *Taxes*.

If you are resident in the UK and the rental income is paid to you there, then you will pay UK tax on the rental income.

Tourist Tax. There is a mandatory tourist tax, which all domestic and foreign guests have to pay at the local police station. Providers of all kinds of tourist accommodation are obliged to ensure that all commercial clients staying at their facilities pay this, either by collecting it from the guests and taking the money to the police station with the guests' passports, or accompanying them there. The charge is per day and ranges from 0.5€-0.8€, half that for children aged 12-18, and nothing for children under 12.

Letting Through Holiday Companies

There are dozens of holiday companies renting out apartments and villas in Croatia. You can obtain contacts by logging on to the website of the Croatian National Tourist Office (www.croatia.hr) or consult the excellent descriptive list at www.visit-croatia.co.uk/touroperators/. Most villa companies will probably require higher specifications than you might expect to have if you were managing the letting yourself. They will also be picky about the appearance of the villa, which is after all the window-dressing in their brochure. If your villa is divided into self-contained apartments (many are), there is no reason why you cannot be in your own part of the villa while the guests are renting another part.

Useful Contacts – Renting out your property
Adriatic Luxury Services: Grand Hotel Bonavia, Dolac 4, 51000 Rijeka, Croatia; ☎+385 51 357 900; fax +385 51 215502; e-mail booking@als.hr. www.adriaticlux urytravel.com. Contact Martina Grzeti. Will rent out villas for individuals mostly in Istria but will handle Dubrovnik area. Most, but not all villas have pools. 2 bedrooms upwards acceptable.
Croatia Property Services: Basaricekova 18, Zagreb, Croatia, 10000, AB1 2CD; ☎+385 981 826240; www.croatiapropertyservices.com. Offers letting service to property owners.
Croatian Villas: ☎020-8368 9978; e-mail sales@croatianvillas.com; www.croatianvillas.com. Quality villa and apartment rentals in choice Croatian resorts. Properties are rated from three to five stars. All properties have easy access to a beach or pool.
Dalma Holidays: 1 Thurlow Tower, Knollys Road, London SW16 2JY; ☎020-8677 2655; fax 020-8769 6450; e-mail info@dalmaholidays.co.uk; www.dalmaholidays.co.uk. Based in Zadar, north Dalmatian coast. Fairly new company. Most of its clients letting their properties are local Croatians, but Dalma Holidays is willing to take on the properties of non-resident foreigners. Would charge a fee per rental. Contact Natasha Blagojevic.
Dalmatian Villas: Kralja Zvonimira 8, Split, Croatia; ☎+385 21 340 680; fax +385

21 340 688; e-mail dalmatianvilla@dalmatianvilla.com. www.dalmationvilla.com. Contact Glorija Aljinovic. Based in Split and will help with letting in Split area including Brac island.

Hidden   Croatia: ☎020-7736   6066;   e-mail   info@hiddencroatia.com; www.hiddencroatia.com. Villas in Istria only. Must be not more than 15 minutes drive from sea.

Villas Forum: Forum 10, 52100 Pula, Croatia; ☎+385 52 210 029; fax +385 52 383 824; e-mail info@villasforum.com. Specialises in representing villas (mainly in Istria) for Villa Holiday Tour operators and real estate owners.

SPOTCHECK – CROATIA	
Political/economic stability:	Right-wing government may delay Croatia's entry into EU (2007). Economic problems caused by 1991 war. Huge investment being made in infrastructure. Very high unemployment (20%).
Sunshine/climate:	3,000 hours a year on the Dalmatian Coast. Winter can be chilly in Dubrovnik, milder in Istria.
Cost of living/taxes:	Going up. VAT very high (22.5%).
Accessibility:	Charter flights have increased to the mainland greatly in the last few years but only two of the islands have airports Krk and Brac.
Property availability:	Shortage around Dubrovnik area. Availability better on north Dalmation Coast.
Property prices:	Not as cheap as people think and rising rapidly: average price €150,000/£100,000/$178,250 or €50,000 for a ruin.
Costs of property purchase as % of property price:	About 10.5% (made up of purchase tax 5%; typical agent's fee 3.5%; solicitor's fees 2%).
Ease of purchase and ease of renovation:	often very difficult to establish title of older properties owing to 45 years of land registry neglect. Newer properties usually much easier to buy. Builders work to a high standard. Shortage of builders and higher prices in popular areas but renovation costs much lower than in the UK.
Annual property taxes:	Minimal
Investment potential:	Depends on the area. Annual historical rises are 50% in Istria and 30% in Dubrovnik, but Dubrovnik has a property scarcity, which may speed up price rise.
Suitability for letting:	For agencies: properties should be centrally heated if let outside summer months. Must be within 1 hour's drive from an airport, which means near Split, Dubrovnik or in Istria.

BUYING A HOUSE ON THE MEDITERRANEAN

CYPRUS

LIVING IN CYPRUS

CHAPTER SUMMARY

o Cyprus is **a partitioned island**, the southern part of which – the Republic of Cyprus – is in the EU, while the north is occupied by the Turks and not internationally recognised as a country.

o The **referendum** of 2004 confirmed the island's divided status.

o In Southern Cyprus **the cost of living** is comparable to (or higher than) the UK; in Northern Cyprus it is about 30% less than the UK.

o **House prices** in the north are still considerably cheaper than those in the south. If the island were reunited, prices would probably level off with those in the south falling slightly.

o Deciding how much a house is worth in the North is not easy as owners seem to pluck a sum from the air.

o **Cyprus's past affects house-buyers:** Cyprus's troubled recent history is something no would-be house-buyer can afford to ignore.

o There is a **question mark over property ownership in the north** as Greek Cypriots who fled their homes in 1974 may still have legal title to their former homes and land.

o The large **tourism industry** is largely centred on British holidaymakers.

o The island can be **extremely hot** in summer.

o Increasingly the population of Northern Cyprus is made up of **settlers from the Turkish mainland**. As a result the diet and lifestyle is increasingly similar to that of rural Turkey.

o Many people, both in the north and the south, speak English and cars are driven on the left.

o Ayia Napa in the south has a **wild nightlife**.

o **Shopping choices** are more limited than in the UK, and most people rely on TV and radio stations beamed in from abroad to top up dull local fare.

o **Public holidays** differ markedly north and south of the border.

o The Republic of Cyprus recently entered the **European Union** which means that many of its current procedures may have to change in the near future.

INTRODUCTION

The third largest island in the Mediterranean, Cyprus is squeezed in at the eastern end of it which has given it a strategic importance out of all proportion to its size. Its location also ensures that it has a hot, dry Middle Eastern climate although much of the middle of the island is mountainous and green. The island has two very different communities - the primarily Greek Orthodox Greek community of the south and the Muslim Turkish population of the north. For the last thirty years development on the island has been stymied by the events of 1974 when the Turkish army invaded northern Cyprus to ward off a perceived threat from a military junta which had seized power in Greece and was threatening to seize Cyprus too. The result of the invasion was that the island split into two separate entities, a situation which was set in stone in 1983 when the Turkish Cypriot leader Rauf Denktaş announced the creation of the Turkish Republic of Northern Cyprus (TRNC). With the exception of Turkey no other country accepted this division which has left Northern Cyprus in legal limbo.

While the Republic of Cyprus (Southern Cyprus) forged ahead with creating a booming tourist industry, the north languished in obscurity. In one of those disconcerting statements of human inability to rub along with each other, the two communities are now separated by the military paraphernalia of the Atilla Line and a buffer zone of no man's land.

In recent years the Republic of Cyprus has seen the same rush to buy second homes as other parts of the Mediterranean and prices soared as the date of EU entry neared. Some people have also chosen to buy houses in Northern Cyprus, seduced by its relative lack of development. However, unlike the situation elsewhere in the Mediterranean, precise ownership of property in Cyprus (especially in the north) is a murky business that may ultimately be decided by the courts. Certainly, when people buy seemingly abandoned properties they should bear in mind that the actual owners may have been forced to flee as refugees and may still harbour hopes of recovering their property.

Nevertheless Cyprus' past history as part of the British Empire gives it a particular appeal to many would-be second-homers. English is widely spoken both north and south of the Atilla Line, and people drive on the left as in the UK. Southern Cyprus is certainly 'Greek' in influence (everyone speaks a local dialect of Greek and the food is certainly Hellenic); however, with its sleepy pace it can sometimes feel reminiscent of the Britain of the 1950s but with guaranteed sun thrown in. The north, however, has become increasingly Turkish as more and more island-born Northern Cypriots have left the island, their place taken by settlers from Anatolia who are Turkish through and through.

Cyprus' troubled recent history is reflected in its muddled-up place names. In Northern Cyprus old Greek place names have been Turkified and people crossing the border from south to north are handed a list of the new names. Most importantly Kyrenia has been renamed Girne and Famagusta is now Gazimağusa. To further complicate matters, in 1994 place names in the Republic of Cyprus were also changed so that Nicosia became Lefkosia, Larnaca became Larnaka, Limassol became Lemesos, and Paphos became Pafos. Not everyone accepts these new names. However, in this chapter the new Turkish names have been used for northern towns and villages and the new Greek ones for places in the south. What was once Nicosia is possibly the most confusing of all: south of the Atilla (Green) Line it is now called Lefkosia, while north of the Line it is called Lefkoşa.

An estimated 50,000 expatriates live on Cyprus, the vast majority of them British.

There are also many residents from Eastern Europe, Sri Lanka and the Philippines. Despite the departure of the British in 1960, the UK still maintains two sovereign bases in Southern Cyprus; Dhekelia on the coast between Larnaka and Ayia Napa, and Akrotiri near Lemesos. The British also continue to use parts of the Akamas Peninsula as a shooting range.

At the time of writing the Republic of Cyprus had just been admitted to the European Union, leaving Northern Cyprus in limbo. Eventually this means that many systems in the Republic will have to change to comply with EU expectations. You should bear this in mind while reading this chapter.

HISTORY AND CURRENT POLITICS

History

Because of its political circumstances recent Cypriot history continues to have a direct impact on modern life on the island and on what is and isn't possible there. No would-be settler can afford to turn a blind eye to what has happened since the mid-1950s and especially to what has happened since 1974. It is impossible to understand how the modern Greeks and Turks feel about each other without understanding the long-standing grievances on both sides.

Cyprus has been inhabited since Neolithic times but from around 1200 BC Mycenaean 'sea people' settled on the island, bringing with them the cult of Aphrodite. These settlers are thought to have reached Cyprus via Anatolia, as did a second wave of Mycenaean settlers who effectively pushed the indigenous Cypriots into a corner.

From around 800 BC, the Cypriots were trading with the Greek mainland. A group of royal tombs found near Salamis in Northern Cyprus and dating back to 700 BC appear to imitate details of burial practises recorded by Homer.

From 708 to 669 BC Cyprus fell under the sway of the Assyrians and was forced to pay tribute to their kings. It then fell under the control of the Egyptians and the Persians. When the Persians tried to stamp their rule more forcefully on the island it led to a revolt which was inevitably crushed.

By the start of the 5th century Cyprus' geographical position ensured that it would become a pawn in the long struggle for supremacy between Athens and Persia. The island was also increasingly Hellenized in terms of its art and culture.

In 333 BC Alexander the Great swept round the Eastern Mediterranean. Initially welcomed by the Cypriots as an alternative to the Persians, he actually proved the conduit through which Hellenic culture gained a yet stronger grip on the island. After his death Cyprus fell under the sway first of the Ptolemies in Egypt and then of Rome. During the Roman occupation Cyprus was converted to Christianity by Sts Paul and Barnabas. When the Roman Empire split in two in 284 AD, Cyprus became part of the Byzantine Empire but by the 7th century it was attracting the attention of the newly-invigorated Arabs. Eventually it became a vassal state both of the Byzantine rulers in Constantinople and of the Arab caliphate, a situation which lasted until 963 AD.

Just as Cyprus's geographical position had sucked it into what was essentially a squabble between the Athenians and the Persians, so it now found itself trapped between the Byzantines and the Crusaders. In 1191 Richard the Lionheart drove out a precariously independent Byzantine ruler and took over the island, only to sell it on to the Knights Templar. When they quickly tired of it Richard gave it to the French Guy de Lusignan as a consolation prize for the loss of Jerusualem. The Lusignan rulers became fabulously wealthy on the back of passing Crusader trade and were traditionally crowned twice: as kings of Cyprus in Nicosia and as kings of Jerusalem in Famagusta. The Lusignans were Catholics and the descendants of the Orthodox Byzantines fared badly under their rule – although they were still able to paint the wonderful frescoes in the Troodos churches. By the 14th century the Venetians and the Genoese were asserting their influence on Cyprus and from 1489 the Venetians governed the island. They were unable to prevent the inevitable Ottoman conquest of Cyprus in 1570.

From then on Cyprus' history is much less complicated. The Ottomans brought an army of settlers from the Turkish mainland and most of the old Lusignan aristocracy quickly fled although the Church was left alone in return for the payment of taxes. Cyprus was ruled by the Turks until 1878 when it was leased to the British in return for their help in stemming the Russian advance on Turkey. In 1914 the British formally annexed Cyprus and secretly offered to give it to Greece if it joined the war on the Allied side. Greece turned the offer down but in 1923, under the terms of the Treaty of Lausanne, Turkey formally abandoned any lingering claim it had to the island. In 1925 it became a British Crown Colony.

During the 1950s there were calls for *enosis*, or union with Greece, which caused the Turkish minority – at that time scattered all over the island – to become uneasy. In 1954 Archbishop Makarios and General Georgios 'Dighenis' Grivas set up EOKA (Ethniki Organosis Kyprion Agoniston – the National Organisation of Cypriot Fighters) to try and force the British to agree to union with Greece. In the face of an IRA-style insurrection, the British exiled Makarios but couldn't stop the growing calls for independence. In 1957 they agreed in principle to the idea but shortly afterwards the Turkish Cypriots set up the TMT (Türk Mukavemet Teskilati - Turkish Resistance Organisation) to call for *taksim,* or division of the island between Greece and Turkey. Clashes between the Greek and Turkish Cypriots and attacks on the British followed, and some of the island's population fled north or south in a foretaste of what was to come.

In 1960 Cyprus won its freedom from the British, with Turkey, Greece and Britain agreeing to safeguard the new country's independence. However, by 1964 EOKA and TMT were back to fighting and Nicosia was split apart along a so-called Green Line. The British, concerned for their military bases, called for assistance in maintaining peace and the first UN Forces in Cyprus (UNFICYP) arrived to safeguard the Turkish-Cypriot enclaves. By then the US and the UN were also taking an interest in Cyprus; the US in particular regarded Makarios as too close to the then Communist eastern bloc. Increasingly alarmed, many Turkish Cypriots retreated into self-governing enclaves. Then in 1967 a military junta seized power in Athens. Unpopular in Greece itself, the Colonels sponsored the overthrow of Archbishop (now President) Makarios who fled first to Britain and then to the USA. In his place the Colonels recognised the EOKA-B gunman Nikas Sampson as president. A week later the Turks invaded the north of the island, citing their role as guarantors of Cyprus' constitution and the need to defend the Turkish Cypriot community. Three days after the invasion the Colonels ordered Greek soldiers to invade Turkish Thrace but they refused, leading to the downfall of the junta, followed immediately by the downfall of Sampson. During a short ceasefire Glafkos Clerides took over as president but when no agreement could be found fighting resumed. In the first phase the Turks had not done particularly well, but, reinforced, they brought a new vigour to the second phase of fighting; two days later the Turkish army was occupying 38% of the island right up to what is now the Atilla Line. By the end of this short war, 200,000 northern

Greeks had been killed, evacuated or fled south, while 100,000 Turks had been killed, evacuated or fled north, leaving the island divided in two with Lefkosia, the capital, straddling the divide. The new south had lost two towns (Girne and Mağusa), most of its tourism infrastructure and its citrus industry. Arguably the north had done much better, acquiring a disproportionate amount of land in relationship to its population.

In 1974 Archbishop Makarios returned to the island to start rehousing those left homeless in the south. Foreign aid flowed in, most of it for the south. In 1975 Rauf Denktaş, leader of the northern National Party, announced the creation of the Turkish Federated State of Cyprus and peace talks resumed without success. In 1983 Denktaş announced that Northern Cyprus would henceforth operate as an entirely new country – the Turkish Republic of Northern Cyprus (TRNC) - with its own flag and government. Since then the two communities have lived on opposite sides of the Atilla Line which is guarded by United Nations troops. Only in the southern village of Pyla (and to a lesser extent in Potamia) do Turkish and Greek Cypriots still live side by side, albeit using separate tea houses and with a UN watchtower mid-village to make sure they don't start shooting at each other. That this is no impossibility was indicated by events of 1996 when attempts to breach the Atilla Line, ostensibly in furtherance of the cause of peace, lead to the deaths of several Greek Cypriots and then of several Turks in retaliation.

CYPRUS AND THE EU

When the European Union agreed that Southern Cyprus should join it in 2003, new impetus was given to stalled peace talks. The Turkish prime minister Recep Tayyıp Erdoğan didn't want Cyprus standing in the way of Turkey's own chance of joining the EU. UN Secretary-General Kofi Annan drew up a plan to reunite the country so that both sides of the island could join the EU together. In April 2004 the Annan Plan was presented to Cypriots north and south of the divide in a referendum which asked them if they agreed to accept it or not. Roughly two-thirds of those in the north voted to accept it while three-quarters of those in the south rejected it. The result was that on 1 May the Republic of Cyprus entered the European Union on its own. However, the Turkish side won international kudos for agreeing to accept change and it looks as if some countries will now lift the trade embargo against it.

Politics

Government – Southern Cyprus has a system of government in which the president is both head of state and of the government (ie there is no prime minister). She or he is elected every five years, on a different date from parliamentary elections to the 56-seat House of Representatives.

Government – Northern Cyprus also has a presidential system of government and far fewer signs of real democracy. Despite five-yearly elections Rauf Denktaş has been president ever since the declaration of Northern Cypriot independence, although since the UN continues to deny legitimacy to the TRNC he is usually described as the 'representative of the north' at international forums.

The assembly of Northern Cyrus has 50 seats. In theory Northern Cyprus also has 24 seats in the House of Representatives although they have not been filled since 1963.

Economy

In **Southern Cyprus** the economy has boomed on the back of the tourism industry, with more than 2.5 million tourists holidaying there every year. Few stretches of the south coast are still free of high-rise hotels but Southern Cyprus attracts everyone from middle-aged British birdwatchers to youthful sun, sea and sex-seekers.

Tourism aside, Southern Cyprus also earns money from exporting fruit, vegetables, wine and fruit juice and from a small shipping industry. It also has a thriving industry offering health services to visitors from the Middle East.

In contrast **Northern Cyprus** has languished in economic limbo, attracting fewer than 50,000 tourists a year. Nor does it have any really successful industries; those it does have have been stymied by Greek pressure on other nations to boycott goods from the north. Not surprisingly, many of its most able young people have left in search of a better life elsewhere, leaving the country even more dependent on support from the Turkish Republic. The situation was not helped when the Turkish banking crisis of 2001 washed over into Northern Cyprus, causing the failure of seven local banks.

COST OF LIVING

There is a considerable difference in the cost of living between north and south Cyprus. In **Southern Cyprus** prices are comparable with those in the UK; indeed, they can sometimes be higher, a difference which will become more apparent once shopkeepers start using the euro. Typically a couple might need to budget about £60 a week for food but inflation has been brought under control.

In underdeveloped **Northern Cyprus** prices are about 30% lower than in the UK, although not as cheap as on the Turkish mainland. Typically a bottle of Turkish wine costs around £2.50, a bottle of beer about £0.50, a litre of milk about £0.40, a kilo of chicken £1.30 and a can of baked beans £0.55. Inflation is running at perhaps 30% a year.

In **Southern Cyprus** the currency is the Cypriot pound (C£). The rate of exchange is C£1 = £1.15/$2. In **Northern Cyprus** it is the Turkish lira (TL); exchange rate £1=TL2,650,000 inflation. Southern Cyprus is likely to convert to euro but this will not be for some years.

GEOGRAPHY AND CLIMATE

Geography

A mere 90 km south of the Turkish port of Taşucu, Cyprus resembles a sheepskin laid out flat with its neck facing towards the junction of Turkey and Syria. A vast plain – the Mesaoira – is squeezed in between the limestone Kyrenia Mountains of Northern Cyprus and the igneous Troodos Mountains of Southern Cyprus with the Cypriot capital Lefkosia/Lefkoşa in the middle of it. Most tourism development in the south has taken place along the flat land between the Troodos and the sea. The least-developed part of the island is the Kırpaşa Peninsula, the neck of the sheepskin pointing to the north-east. Mt Olympos, at 1951m, is the highest point on the island and plays host to a small skiing industry.

The island covers 9,250 sq.km in total and is divided into two with 68% of the land mass making up the Republic of Cyprus and 32% (3,355 sq. km) making up the Turkish Republic of Northern Cyprus. The island has a 648 km coastline.

Population. Although there has been no census since 1960, the Cypriot population is assumed to consist of around 800,000 people, of whom perhaps 600,000 are Greek Cypriots. Of the roughly 200,000 people living in the north, perhaps 75,000 are actually settlers from mainland Turkey who have taken the place of indigenous Turkish Cypriots as they left in search of a better life elsewhere; another 20,000 are students and 30,000 are soldiers which means that the Turkish population probably exceeds the Turkish Cypriot one. Although many Greek Cypriots who fled in 1974 have chosen to return to live in Cyprus again, hardly any Turkish Cypriots have returned to live in the north

Only around 400 Greek Cypriots remain in Northern Cyprus, mostly on the Kırpaşa Peninsula. There are also around 140 Maronite Christians still living on the Korucam Peninsula. Perhaps 3,000 Turkish Cypriots continue to live in the south.

There is also a growing ex-pat community, much of it British and most of it concentrated along the coast.

Climate

One of Cyprus' biggest selling points is that it has an average 300 sunny days in the year. The entire island has a typically Mediterranean climate, with hot, dry summers alternating with cooler, wetter winters and very little in between. The Troodos Mountains see snow in winter and temperatures can fall below freezing. Most of the rain falls in autumn and winter.

AVERAGE MAXIMUM TEMPERATURES				
Area	Jan	Apr	Aug	Nov
Girne (Kyrenia)	17C	23C	36C	23C
Lemesos	13C	23C	37C	21C
Platres	8C	20C	30C	15C

CULTURE SHOCK

Cyprus is an easy country to visit, with little risk of extreme culture shock. This is especially true of the south where long acquaintance with the British, followed by long experience with tourism, has knocked edges off the Greekness. Language is the most overt symbol of a Hellenic background, but so many people speak English that even that is rarely a problem.

The north is a harder nut to crack especially as more settlers arrive from economically-deprived parts of Turkey. But even there many people speak English and there is general familiarity with the ways of the west. The one exception, perhaps surprisingly, is Lefkoşa which feels increasingly like a slice of backwoods Turkey.

Alcohol. Alcohol is readily available all over Cyprus and even in the north you are unlikely to have problems with it – the Turks who come to live in Cyprus are not usually fundamentalists.

Relationships. As with alcohol, so with sex. The Cypriots have seen it all, and although they are tiring of the drunken antics of the British in Ayia Napa, they are not about to suggest that their visitors rush to the altar before they can stay together in a hotel room. Traditionally, though, the Cypriots have kept a close eye on the 'honour' of their own women; both communities have insisted that women be virgins on marriage while turning a blind eye to the rovings of their men.

Nightlife. Almost all the nightlife on Cyprus is currently concentrated in the south where resorts like Ayia Napa have given Ibiza and Falaraki a run for their money in the 18-30, party-crowd market. In Northern Cyprus only Girne (Kyrenia) makes even a stab at partying.

GETTING THERE

Several scheduled airlines fly to Pafos and Larnaca in Southern Cyprus although so far none of the low-cost fliers has taken the island on. Northern Cyprus' pariah status means that Lefkoşa's Ercan airport is only accessible by air via İstanbul, adding miles – and hours – to the journey. High-season fares usually apply from June through September, over Christmas and the New Year, and over Easter. Note that as a reward to Turkish Cyprus for supporting the unification of Cyprus in the 2004 referendum, the embargo may be relaxed to allow international flights to land there. The Northern Cyprus Tourism Centre (0207-631 1930; www.go-northcyprus.com) will be up-to-date on this situation.

In theory it ought to be possible to book seat-only places on one of the many charter airlines that carry package-holidaymakers to Southern Cyprus. However, the Cypriot authorities do their utmost to make this impossible; everyone travelling on a charter flight from Luton, Birmingham or Manchester must be booked on an inclusive tour, and only 15% of those flying from other airports can be travelling on a seat-only basis. However, this may change now that the Republic has entered the EU.

Poseidon Lines and Salamis Lines used to connect Southern Cyprus with Greece and Haifa in Israel or Port Said in Egypt by boat on a weekly basis. However, the troubles in the Middle East mean that both services are currently mothballed. Much more frequent car ferries and catamarans link southern Turkey (Taşucu, Mersin, Alanya) with Northern Cyprus (Girne). The journey by catamaran generally takes about two hours, that by car ferry around four hours. However, in winter the catamarans cannot always sail and the ferry crossing can triple in length while the captain waits for suitable sailing weather.

As it is almost impossible to pass from Northern Cyprus to Southern Cyprus but not vice versa, foreign residents of the north often opt to travel to and from the island via the south. Provided they do this they can then pass back and forth to the north at will; to work, use the hospitals etc.

Useful Contacts – Flights & Ferries

Air 2000: www.air2000.com; ☎0870-240 1402
Akgün Express: Taşucu İskelesi, Turkey; ☎0324-741 4385.
Akgünler Denizcilik: İskele Caddesi 86, Alanya, Turkey; ☎0242-512 8889.
Bosphorus European Airlines: IKB, IKB House, 230 Edgware Rd, London W2 1DW; ☎020-7724 8455; fax 020-7724 8655; Cumhuriyet Caddesi, 135/5, Elmadağ, İstanbul; ☎0212-230 4701. Twice-weekly flights between London Heathrow and Lefkoşa via İstanbul.
British Airways: www.britishairways.com; ☎0870-850 8850.
Cyprus Airlines: 5 The Exchange, Brent Cross, London NW4 3RJ; ☎020-8359 1333.
Fergün Express: Taşucu İskelesi, Turkey; ☎0324-741 2323.
Fergün Denizcilik: İskele Caddesi 84, Alanya, Turkey; ☎0242-511 5565.

Flyair: Bedrettin Demirel Caddesi 125, Lefkoşa; ☎228 0082.

Helios Airways; www.helios-airways.com; ☎020-8457 2690; 020-8457 2691.

Kıbrıs Türk Hava Yolları (Cyprus Turkish Airlines): 11-12 Pall Mall, London SW1Y 5LU; ☎020-7930 4851; Atatürk Meydanı, Lefkoşa; ☎227 3820; www.kthy.net. Twice weekly flights from London to Lefkoşa via İzmir.

Lufthansa: ww.lufthansa.de.

Olympic Airways: www.olympicairways.co.uk.

Onur Air: Senlikkoy Mahallesi, Catal Sokak 3, 34153 Florya, İstanbul; ☎0212-663 2300; fax 0212-663 2319. Regular flights from Paris and Frankfurt to İstanbul.

Poseidon Lines: Karamanli 32, Voula suburb, Athens; ☎010-965 8300.

Salamis Lines: Filellinon 12, Piraes, Athens; ☎010-429 4325.

Travel World International: Kyrenia Holidays Ltd, Ziya Rızkı Caddesi 95, Girne; ☎0392-815 2968.

*Turkish Airlines (THY):*125 Pall Mall, London SW1Y 5EA; ☎020-7766 9300; www.thy.com. Flights from Heathrow and Manchester to Lefkoşa via İstanbul.

Turkish Maritime Lines: Mersin İskele, Turkey; ☎0324-233 9858. Three times weekly car ferries from Mersin to Gazimağusa. The ships used are larger and so more reliable in winter than the ferries and catamarans from Taşucu and Alanya.

COMMUNICATIONS

In general communication between Cyprus and the rest of the world is good although it should be noted that Internet access in the north is infuriatingly slow and unreliable.

Post. Postal services, from both north and south Cyprus, are reasonably efficient and cost about the same as from the UK. One quirk is that if you want to write to an address in Northern Cyprus you must conclude it with 'Mersin 10, Turkey' rather than writing Northern Cyprus.

Post offices in the south are usually open from 7.30am to 1.30pm Monday to Friday, with Thursday opening from 3pm to 6pm except in July and August. In the north post offices open from 7.30am to 2 pm and 4pm to 6pm Monday to Friday, and 8.30 am to 12.30pm on Saturday. Both in the south and north you can post letters in British-style postboxes which still bear the old royal insignia although they have been repainted yellow.

Telephone. The Cyprus Telecommunciations Authority (CYTA) provides all the phones in the south; the Telekomunikasyon Dairesi in the north.

Making calls on a land-line to/from and within Southern Cyprus is straightforward, although international calls are expensive. However, if you want to call a number in Northern Cyprus you must first dial the Turkey international access code (90), then the Northern Cyprus code (392), then the actual number. In effect a call from Southern Cyprus to Northern Cyprus – even from Lefkoşa to Lefkosia – is charged as an international call.

To get round this hassle you need a mobile phone with roaming facilities and serviced by a company which has arrangements with both north and south. In the north you will be able to use either Türkcell or Telsim to connect your call; in the south it will be CYTA-GSM.

FOOD AND DRINK

The cuisine of Northern and Southern Cyprus has been diverging more and more as Turkish settlers have taken the place of indigenous Cypriots in the north. The British legacy also lies more heavily on the south where tepid chips come as an accompaniment to most meals and 'full English breakfasts' can be found on every street corner. In the north the influx of settlers from mainland Turkey has tended to 'turkify' the diet along with everything else.

Probably because of the British influence, meal-times in Southern Cyprus are roughly the same as they are in the UK. Unfortunately, however, the overwhelming importance of package tourism means that it is difficult to find really good restaurants in the south. In the Chrysaliniotissa district of Lefkosia, abutting the Green Line, a few pleasant pavement restaurants have recently opened.

In general what you eat in **Southern Cyprus** doesn't vary much from what you get in Greece (see that chapter for more details), with *kleftiko* (fatty lamb baked with vegetables) more or less the national dish. Also extremely popular are *souvlaki*, big chunks of skewered pork which you certainly won't find in the north. The inevitable *moussaka* also appears on most menus aimed at tourists. As the Mediterranean is slowly fished out, most restaurants serving fish are actually selling imported produce at inflated prices.

Both north and south of the Atilla Line a meal might consist entirely of the *mezes* that are technically just starters. You will be able to pick from a mixture of hot and cold dishes: salads, taramasalata, *borek* (filled flaky pastry tubes), olives, tahini, etc. One of the *meze* offerings may well be a Cypriot speciality: *haloumi* cheese, at its tastiest when made from sheep or goat's rather than cow's milk.

In **Northern Cyprus** Turkish cuisine rules supreme, with kebabs playing a big part in restaurant life (see the Turkey chapter for more details), although Girne's waterfront fish restaurants are also extremely popular.

In both north and south good quality fruit is easy to find at street markets; that in the south will probably have been home-grown, that in the north may well have been imported from the Turkish mainland. In August one unusual fruit to look out for in particular is the *papoutosyka* (prickly pear). You may also want to taste carob which is grown in the south and made into a toffee-like sweet.

Southern Cyprus has a flourishing wine-making industry. More surprisingly visitors to Khrsorroylatissa can also buy good red and white wines that were made in the monastery. Many of the Troodhos mountain villages also sell decent wines straight from the barrel. Most of the wine available in Northern Cyprus is imported from Turkey.

South of the Atilla Line the spirit of choice is *zivania* - virtually pure grape alcohol. You can also buy that favourite of the Greek mainland, *ouzo,* while in the north you can buy that favourite of the Turkish mainland, *raki,* both of them similar aniseed drinks. Before partition both Turkish and Greek Cypriots were particularly fond of brandy sours, (brandy mixed with lemon or lime and Angostura bitters). In 1975 the government of Northern Cyprus forbade the import of brandy from south of the Atilla Line, an edict that was simply asking to be broken. Another specialty is Kommanderia, a fortified wine made near Lemessos and said to date back to the Crusades.

North of the Atilla Line Efes Pilsen beer is imported from Turkey, although you can also buy imported Austrian ales; south of it the beers of choice are KEO and Carlsberg, both made on Cyprus.

SCHOOLS AND EDUCATION

The Structure of the Education System

In **Southern Cyprus** all children must attend primary school and then lower secondary school (*gymnasio*) until the age of fifteen after which they can continue to upper secondary school (*lykio*) or a secondary technical and vocational education establishment until they are eighteen. Until age eighteen all public education is free. Around 65% of students continue to higher education, with almost half of them going abroad to study at university.

Although educational standards at public schools are high most foreigners send their children to private schools for linguistic and cultural reasons. There are international schools in all the big towns.

In **Northern Cyprus** the education system mirrors that of the Turkish mainland; see that chapter for more details. Once again, most foreigners would want their children to attend private schools although the opportunities for them to do so are less than in the south.

University. Cyprus is not big enough to provide adequate university education for all the students wanting it so, depending on whether they come from the north or south, many choose to go on to higher education in Turkey or Greece. Some students choose to head for Britain or the United States. However, Northern Cyprus currently has eight universities, more than its population could sustain were they not seen as one way for the beleaguered state to raise money. Most of these universities have a poor reputation but the Eastern Mediterranean University in Gazimağusa has been rated as one of the ten best universities in – wait for it – Turkey!

International Schools

American International School in Cyprus: Lefkosia, ☎357-22 316345
American Academy: Larnaka, ☎351-24 664733
American Academy: Lemesos, ☎357-25 337054
International School of Paphos: Pafos, ☎357-26 932236
Girne American University: www.gau.edu.tr
University of Cyprus (Lefkosia): www.ucy.ac.cy
For further information on International Schools, see *The General Introduction.*

CYPRIOT TAXES

The Republic of Cyprus is a tax haven with about 40,000 brassplate companies registered there to take advantage of tax rates of 4.25% on offshore corporate profits.

Income Tax

In 2004 it was possible to earn C£9,000 before paying any income tax in **Southern Cyprus**. The rate charged up to C£12,000 was 20%, to C£15,000 25% and over C£15,000 30%. Southern Cyprus has a double taxation agreement with the UK but to take advantage of it you need to stay in Cyprus for at least 183 days in the year (or 91 days a year averaged over a four-year period) to avoid becoming liable to UK tax.

Avoiding tax is like a party game in **Northern Cyprus** where official rates are in any case low. However, Northern Cyprus' pariah status means that there is no double taxation agreement between it and the UK. In theory this means you could end up owing tax in both countries.

Anyone thinking of moving to either part of Cyprus should first seek advice from *The Centre for Non-Residents (CNR):* St John's House, Merton Rd, Bootle, Merseyside L69 9BB; ☎0151-472 6196; fax 0151-472 6392; www.inlandrevenue.gov.uk/cnr.

VAT

In **Southern Cyprus** most goods and services are subject to 15% VAT.

Most goods and services in **Northern Cyprus** are subject to between 3% and 30% VAT.

HEALTH

In general Cyprus is a healthy country and in the south at least doctors and nurses are so well trained that providing health care for visitors from the Middle East has become a lucrative source of income.

The Cypriot National Health Service

Hospitals north and south of the divide provide emergency hospital treatment for broken bones and cuts and bruises free of charge, although everything else must be paid for. Routine doctors' services must also be paid for. Pharmacists can often dispense medicines over the counter, which would require a prescription in the UK. This is true whether you are north or south of the Atilla Line.

Using the Cypriot NHS If You Are Living In Cyprus

Whether you live in North or South Cyprus you will need to take out private health insurance as few medical facilities are provided free to foreigners. However, the price of consultations with doctors and operations is much less than what it would cost in the UK (typically £10-15 a visit in the Republic, less in the north). Note that now Southern Cyprus is in the EU, medical facilities are likely to become more available to foreigners in line with other EU countries.

There are good hospitals in Pafos, Larnaka and Lemesos and many residents of Northern Cyprus opt to travel back and forth to the south to use those facilities.

Private Medical Insurance – Cypriot Providers

It is possible to arrange ex-pat medical insurance in the UK but this is likely to be more expensive than organising it in Cyprus where premiums are low; in Southern Cyprus private medical insurance is likely to cost you around £25 a month. Estate agents in the Republic usually have links to insurance companies, or you could look at www.legendtravelers.com or www.best-of-cyprus.com for recommendations.

In **Northern Cyprus** you can buy insurance from Turkish brokers including *Yapı Kredi Sigorta, İsviçre Sigorta, Anadolu Sigorta* and *Güneş Sigorta*. It may be hard to find international ex-pat insurance that covers Northern Cyprus until a peace settlement is agreed.

SHOPPING

Cyprus is hardly the world's raviest shopping destination. In the resorts most of the shops are geared to tourists and sell goods they will want to buy at prices they are assumed to be prepared to pay. Even in Lefkosia there is a surprising dearth of interesting shops and Northern Cyprus is yet more of a shopping vacuum.

In **Southern Cyprus** all the big towns except Larnaka have covered food markets which make excellent places to stock up on fruit and vegetables. The big towns also have plenty of simple general stores similar to those at home and with much of their labelling in English as well as Greek. A few hypermarkets have also opened in Southern Cyprus. Lefkosia also has branches of Marks & Spencer and Woolworth's.

In **Northern Cyprus** both Girne and Lefkoşa have covered markets for fresh produce. Girne also has a Lemar supermarket, although the Turkish labelling makes shopping trickier than in the south.

It is much harder to find English-language bookstores in the north of Cyprus than in the south. Good bookshops include Academic & General, Ermou 41, Larnaka; Green Jacket Bookshop, Yirmi Temmuz Caddesi, Girne; Kemal Rüstem, Girne Caddesi 26, Lefkoşa; Moufflon Books, Kinyra 30, Pafos; Terra Books, Ayiou Kendea 31, Pafos; and Travelers' Tales Internet Café Bookshop, Ayiou Andhreou 4, Lemesos.

Shop Opening Hours

In the southern resorts shops keep long hours suited to the tourist trade in summer, opening at 8.30am and staying open until 7.30pm. However, many of them close so that their owners can take a siesta from 1pm to 4 pm. In the north shopkeepers are much keener to stick to the nine-to-five pattern, with occasional breaks for prayer. Both north and south of the Atilla Line shops tend to shut at 2 pm on Saturdays (and Wednesdays) and not open again until Monday morning. On top of the predictable public holidays there are also many unexpected closing days; it doesn't pay to leave things until the last moment.

The Christian day of rest is closely observed in South Cyprus. In theory Sunday closure is also the norm in Northern Cyprus although in reality shops will stay open during high season.

MEDIA

Newspapers

Cyprus is too small to support a wide range of newspapers. However, the north receives most of the mainland Turkish newspapers (see the Turkey chapter for more details) which makes its newsstands look more crowded than they would be otherwise.

English-Language Newspapers in Cyprus

Southern Cyprus has two English-language newspapers: the daily *Cyprus Mail* and the *Cyprus Weekly*. Both can also be read on line at www.cyprus-mail.com and www.cyprusweekly.com.cy respectively. Northern Cyprus has the daily *Turkish Daily News* (www.turkishdailynews.com), imported from the Turkish mainland, plus the weekly *Cyprus Today*. The tourist authority also publishes the monthly *Kızey Turizm (North Tourism)* magazine with interesting articles about life in the north.

Television

Many people both north and south have satellite dishes to gain access to a wider range of channels than the island itself could support. In the north, in particular, the locally-produced programmes are almost laughably bad so most people watch channels beamed in from Turkey. In the south people are equally keen on programmes produced in Greece.

English-Language Television in Cyprus

Anyone with satellite television can pick up *BBC World* and *BBC Prime*, as well as *CNN, Euro News* and assorted other English-language channels.

Radio

Perhaps not surprisingly there is plenty of English-language broadcasting on the radio in the south. CyBC (the Cyprus Broadcasting Corporation) puts out English-language programmes, especially during the evenings, on its Programme 2, while the BBC World Service is easily picked up because of a transmitter on the coast between Larnaka and Limassol. It's also easy to pick up the British Forces Broadcasting Service (BFBS) from the transmitters in the two British Sovereign Bases. There are also smaller private music stations which broadcast in English.

It is also possible to pick up the BFBS services in the north. Otherwise Bayrak Radyo has some mundane English-language programming, especially in the evenings.

CRIME

Crime isn't much of a concern on Cyprus, even in the north where some notorious fugitives have taken up residence. The biggest danger for most visitors is straying over the Atilla and Green Lines that separate the north from the south. In most places it is difficult to do this because the boundaries are clearly marked with barbed wire and/or UN watchtowers. However, there are a few places where the line is not so clear (especially in the Dhekelia British Sovereign Base) and where it pays to take extra care. Demonstrations near the boundaries can turn nasty - keep well away.

However, there has been a recent increase in organised crime, especially in the south, and it pays to stay away from casinos, cabarets (where forcing men to pay exorbitant prices for drinks is common), brothels and anything associated with drug-taking.

Police

The Cypriot police, both in the north and south, had so little to do until recently that it is not perhaps surprising that some of them succumbed to the lure of easy profits from organised crime. You might need to contact the police if you have something stolen (not very likely) but they may ask a lot of questions before stumping up the requisite paperwork for insurance claims. Otherwise the most likely reason for a brush with the law would be some kind of motoring mishap or contravention of the road rules – and traditionally the police have been more lenient towards foreign motorists than towards locals.

LEARNING THE LANGUAGE

According to some estimates up to 15% of the vocabulary of both north and south Cyprus differs from that of Greece and Turkey and people intending to settle in Southern Cyprus need to be aware that the Greek Cypriot dialect is markedly different from the sort of Greek taught on most courses in Greece and the UK. Although traditionally very different, the Turkish spoken by most people in the north today is not so different from that spoken on mainland Turkey, as more and more mainland Turks take up residence there.

The good news for intending second-home owners is that the majority of people in **Southern Cyprus** have some familiarity with English. Perhaps more surprisingly the same is also true in **Northern Cyprus**; given that most work available is in tourism many of the settlers from the mainland know some English, although in Lefkoşa it's harder to find English-speakers.

Self-Study Courses. For information on learning Greek or Turkish, see the Greece and Turkey chapters respectively.

Language Courses in the UK. For details of courses on Greek or Turkish in the UK, see the Greece and Turkey chapters.

SUMMARY OF HOUSING

The property market in Cyprus both north and south of the border has been booming recently. Although prices in the north are still considerably cheaper than those in the south the expectation is that they will continue to rise. If the two parts of the country were eventually to be reunited it is likely that prices would level off, with those in the south falling slightly and those in the north rising still further.

That might suggest that buying in the north was likely to prove a good investment. However, a word of warning is necessary for anyone thinking of buying property on Cyprus. Because of the exchange of populations that occurred in the 1970s, many Cypriots are refugees either within their own country or abroad. A question mark, therefore, hangs over the precise ownership of many properties and pieces of land. It is true that some refugees have long since given up hope of returning to their original homes and have elected to sell them to foreigners. However, a situation like this leaves the field wide open for unscrupulous property speculators. Until there is a final settlement in Cyprus it **is imperative that anyone wishing to buy there takes good legal advice** before proceeding; taking the word of a 'friend' as to the precise legal ownership of a property could lead to expense and heartache somewhere down the line.

That said, property development is one of the biggest industries on the island at the moment. Everywhere you look new developments of apartment blocks or condominiums are going up, and one more thing to be wary about is the very real chance that the north will end up just as over-developed as many would argue the south already is. It says a lot for the speed of development in the south of the island that 2003 saw roughly 15% more building permits granted than 2002.

So far most foreign settlers in Cyprus have been more interested in buying new properties than in restoring old ones. However, in Lefkosia and Lefkoşa there are some fine old stone houses left over from the days of the Ottoman Empire which are crying out for owners who could afford to modernise them. In rural areas, there are still some tumbledown stone cottages and farm buildings, often with very rudimentary facilities, for sale, although few estate agents seem interested in dealing with them. In Northern Cyprus a typical ruinous village property is likely to cost around £50,000 but would-be buyers would need to budget for another £25,000 or so to cover the restoration. In the south you would probably have to pay twice those amounts.

Deciding how much a property is worth in Northern Cyprus is not especially easy since owners often seem to pluck prices from out of the air and can't be relied on not to put them up even after a sale has been provisionally agreed. Often they seem to work not so much from what the property is intrinsically worth as from what they want to buy as a result of the sale. In such circumstances it is not always easy to persuade them to accept a more realistic (ie lower) price. The same applies to some extent in the south too but there the property market is better established and generally less problematic.

During the last six months of 2003 property prices in Northern Cyprus doubled; they were expected to double again in 2004. However, it remains to be seen what will happen to house prices after the Republic enters the European Union on its own.

The village of Karaman in Northern Cyprus offers a cautionary tale for would-be buyers. All the houses there were once advertised for sale to foreigners on 25-year leases. Now of course those leases are almost up and their holders are unable to convert them into freeholds. Consequently Karaman has fallen from favour as a place to live in.

Since 2003 European residents of Southern Cyprus have been treated as Cypriots in the sense that they are allowed to own multiple properties on the island.

The Dönum/Skala

One initially confusing aspect of property-buying on Cyprus is that land size is still often advertised in old Ottoman measurements: the dönüm in Northern Cyprus and the skala in the south. In both cases this measurement is equal to around one-third of an acre. A dönüm of building land can cost anything from £7,500 to £45,000 in the south, even less in the north.

Likely Outcome of a Peace Settlement

The Kofi Annan peace plan stipulated that anyone buying a piece of land in Northern Cyprus for which a Greek had a title deed should be paid compensation provided they had started work on developing it. In theory this compensation was to consist of the value of the land in 1974 adjusted for inflation. The same process was also to apply when someone bought a piece of land in Southern Cyprus for which a Turkish Cypriot held the title deed. The assumption was that this compensation would be paid by the European Union or by the Turkish government and the result was a rush to make a start on buildings in the hopes of profiting from them. However, since the plan was rejected in 2004 there can be no guarantee that the compensation will ever be forthcoming.

Sources of Information

The English-language newspapers published in north and south Cyprus are a good source of information about estate agents, house prices and general issues to do with buying property on the island. In Northern Cyprus the tourist authorities publish the monthly *Kızey Turizm (North Tourism)* magazine which also contains advertisements for estate agents and information about property development on the island.

Another useful source is the www.living-cyprus.com website, which has stacks of information for people planning to settle in the Republic. Less useful but a good starting point is www.cyprusive.com which bills itself as the North Cyprus Webguide.

PUBLIC HOLIDAYS

North and South Cyprus observe different holidays as a result of the fact that the north is broadly-speaking Muslim and the south Christian. The Christian calendar is familiar to most residents of Western countries. However, the Muslim calendar of **Northern Cyprus** – a lunar calendar which means that the dates of the major holidays change by 11 or 12 days every year – is less so. Its most distinctive features are the holy month of Ramazan, during which Muslims are expected to fast from dawn to dusk, and Kurban Bayramı, on the first day of which every Muslim head of household who can afford to is supposed to sacrifice a cow or sheep and share the meat with the poor. This day of slaughter is followed by three days of celebration. Ramazan, too, is followed by three days of celebration (Şeker Bayramı) during which people visit their relatives and bestow sweets and loose change on children.

The festivities associated with Easter are especially colourful in **Southern Cyprus**, with huge bonfires preceding midnight mass on the Saturday evening and big firework displays on the Sunday. The Festival of the Flood is unique to Cyprus, with people crowding into the sea and sprinkling each other with saltwater, ostensibly to commemorate Noah's salvation from the Flood but probably as an echo of much earlier rites to Aphrodite.

In the south, banks close over all the main public holidays. In the north they close for Şeker Bayramı and Kurban Bayramı but not for Ramazan.

The Cyprus Tourist Office produces a Diary of Events that lists more local events like the Pafos and Ayia Napa Festivals and the Limassol Wine Festival.

PUBLIC HOLIDAYS IN SOUTH CYPRUS

1 January	New Year's Day
6 January	Epiphany
February/March	Lent
25 March	Greek Independence Day/Feast of the Annunciation
March/April	Good Friday
March/April	Orthodox Easter
1 April	Greek Cypriot Day
May	Kataklysmos (Flood Festival)
1 May	Labour Day
15 August	Feast of the Assumption
1 October	Cyprus Independence Day
28 October	Greek National Day
25 December	Christmas Day
26 December	Boxing Day/St Stephen's Day

PUBLIC HOLIDAYS IN NORTH CYPRUS

1 January	New Year's Day
23 April	Turkish National Sovereignty and Children's Day
1 May	Labour Day
19 May	Youth and Sports Day
20 July	Peace and Freedom Day
1 August	TMT Day
30 August	Victory Day
29 October	Turkish Republic Day
15 November	Proclamation of the Turkish Republic of Northern Cyprus

RESIDENCE AND ENTRY REGULATIONS

CHAPTER SUMMARY

O Most Western nationals can visit either part of Cyprus for up to three months **without a visa**.

O If you have evidence of **a visit to Northern Cyprus** in your passport you will not be allowed into Southern Cyprus and possibly not into Greece either.

O You can become a citizen of South Cyprus after seven years' residency. Few people would want to take Northern Cypriot **citizenship** at the moment.

O It is very hard to get a **work permit** for either part of the island since there are few job vacancies that can't be filled by locals.

O However, **EU nationals** now have the right to work in Southern Cyprus.

O The bureaucracy attached to acquiring paperwork is particularly slow and tiresome in Northern Cyprus.

VISA REGULATIONS

EU citizens, Canadians, Australians, New Zealanders and Americans can visit both North and South Cyprus for three months without a visa. Visitors should bear in mind, however, that if they have a stamp from Northern Cyprus in their passport they will not be admitted to Southern Cyprus and possibly not to Greece either; ask to have the stamp put on a separate piece of paper.

To renew your visa in **Southern Cyprus** is usually quite easy; you simply go to the Immigration Unit of the police in the district where you are living and show them proof that you have sufficient funds to support yourself. To renew your visa in **Northern Cyprus** usually means an overnight trip to Turkey to avoid the bureaucracy of official extension.

RESIDENCY

Acquiring residency in **Southern Cyprus** is not difficult although you will be expected to show proof that you can support yourself. Currently this is taken to mean that you have an annual income of C£5,600 for yourself plus another C£2,700 for each dependent. You should take evidence of this to the Aliens Branch of the district police who will then process your application.

In order to buy a house there you need to be a resident of **Northern Cyprus**, a process which could take up to two years to complete if you opt to do it yourself rather than paying a solicitor to help you. If you own a property in Northern Cyprus getting residency is virtually automatic, so to square this seeming circle the process of organising residency is normally carried out alongside that of buying a property. Perhaps surprisingly you do not have to proof that you can support yourself although the police and Interpol will carry out a search to ensure that you have no criminal record. Once residency has been granted it does not have to be renewed every few years as it does on the Turkish mainland.

Most applications for licences, visas, permits etc require an inordinate amount of patience.

CITIZENSHIP

Anyone who has been resident in **Southern Cyprus** for seven years can apply for citizenship. They will need to prove that they have been on the island for the entire year leading up to the application and will have to produce a birth certificate, a copy of their passport, a character reference, two photographs and a completed application form. They will also need to advertise their request for citizenship in a Cypriot newspaper for two days.

A foreign resident married to a Southern Cypriot can apply for citizenship after three years of 'harmonious cohabitation'. In addition to the paperwork listed above they will need to show their marriage certificate, their spouse's passport and a certificate from the chairman of the local communal council confirming that they have been living together for the two years preceding the application.

So long as **Northern Cyprus** goes unrecognised by the outside world no foreigner is likely to want – or would be advised – to take up citizenship there.

Cypriot Embassies and Consulates in the UK

Embassy of the Republic of Cyprus: 93 Park St, London W1Y 4ET; tel; 020-7499 8272; fax 020-7491 0691.
Representation of the Turkish Republic of Northern Cyprus: 26 Bedford Square, London WC1B 3EG; ☎020-7631 1920; fax 020-7631 1948.

British Embassies and Consulates in Cyprus

British Embassy in the Republic of Cyprus: Alexandrou Palli St, CY-1587 Lefkosia; ☎02-771 131; fax 02-777 198.
British Representation in the Turkish Republic of Northern Cyprus: Mehmet Akif Caddesi 29, Köşklüçiftlik, Lefkoşa; ☎228 3861.

Other Embassies and Consulates

United States
Embassy of the Republic of Cyprus: 2211 R St North West, Washington, DC 20008; ☎202-462 5772; fax 483 6710.
Representation of the Turkish Republic of Northern Cyprus: 821 United Nations Plaza, 6th Floor, New York, NY 10017; ☎212-687 2350; fax 949 6872.
US Embassy in the Republic of Cyprus: Corner Metohiou & Ploutarhou, CY-2406 Engomi, Lefkosia; ☎02-776 400; fax 02-780 944.
US Representation in the Turkish Republic of Northern Cyprus: Saran 6, Küçük

Kaymaklı, Lefkoşa; ☎227 8295.

Canada
Representation of the Turkish Republic of Northern Cyprus: 328 Highway 7 East, Suite 308, Richmond Hill, Ontario L4B 3P7; ☎905-731 4000.

Australia
Embassy of the Republic of Cyprus: 30 Beale Crescent, Deakin, ACT 2600; ☎02-6281 0832; fax 6281 0860.
Representation of the Turkish Republic of Northern Cyprus: 295 Clyde St, Granville South, NSW 2142; ☎02-2897 3114; fax 2682 4164.
Australian Embassy in the Republic of Cyprus: Corner Loeforos Stasinou & Annis Komninis 4, CY-1060, Lefkosia; ☎02-473 001; fax 02-366 486.
Australian Representation in the Turkish Republic of Northern Cyprus: Güner Türkmen 20, Köşkluçiftlik, Lefkoşa; ☎227 7332.

WORK PERMITS

Now that **Southern Cyprus** has joined the European Union, EU nationals no longer need a work permit. Otherwise, you can only work legally if you have found work and got your employer to arrange a permit before you leave home. In theory work permits are only given to people doing jobs a Cypriot couldn't do, although foreign tour companies usually manage to employ their own foreign representatives in the resorts. A work permit is usually granted initially for three or six months. Sometimes people wanting to work in hotels are given two-year permits straightaway but you cannot rely on this.

Most of the low-paid, low-skilled work in Southern Cyprus is done by immigrants from Eastern Europe, Russia, Egypt and Sri Lanka which means that there are few casual vacancies to be filled, other than in tourism where the 'pay' often comes in the form of bed and board rather than hard cash. As in the north, the most likely way of being able to work in the south is if you set up your own business with imported capital. The best place to look for job adverts is the *Cyprus Weekly.*

People wishing to set up businesses in the Republic no longer need to have a Cypriot partner. If they are given a work permit it will probably be for two, then three years.

Opportunities for finding paid employment in **Northern Cyprus** are almost non-existent. There are already too many settlers from mainland Turkey who take up any slack in the tourism industry, and immigrants from Pakistan take most of the other casual work in restaurants and hotels. If you want to apply for a work permit you need to approach the Immigration Department in Lefkoşa for advice.

However Northern Cyprus has been very keen to attract foreign investment so people hoping to set up a company there may find that they can obtain an annually renewable work permit fairly easily.

Sources of Information

For information on all aspects of residency and acquiring citizenship in the Republic of Cyprus contact the Migration Department, Ministry of the Interior, 1457 Lefkosia; ☎357-2280 4510; fax 357-226 76944; migration@crmd.moi.gov.cy. The government website, www.cyprus.gov.cy, is also very helpful.

Less useful but still a starting point for enquiries is the website of the government of Northern Cyprus, www.trnc.gov.com.

Useful Addresses for Jobseekers

Employers & Industrialists Federation: PO Box 1657, Lefkosia; oeb@dial.cylink.com.cy.

Cyprus Chamber of Commerce & Industry: PO Box 1455, Lefkosia; chamber@ccci.org.cy.

Cyprus Hotel Keepers Association: 12A.A Araouzos St, Lefkosia.

John Symonds of Larnaka says local contacts are everything

I was lucky that my purchase went extremely smoothly due to a good service from the agent and a developer whom I now consider a friend. Indeed, he has arranged employment for my wife as a nurse in a private clinic in Larnaka. I quote: 'It is who you know in Cyprus that dictates your employment prospects.

WHERE TO FIND YOUR IDEAL HOME

CHAPTER SUMMARY

- In Southern Cyprus most people have settled in or near the tourist areas along the coast, especially around **Pafos, Lemesos, Larnaka and Ayia Napa**.

- Younger foreign residents favour the area around Ayia Napa even though areas nearby have been called a developmental disaster.

- An estimated 6,000 British people have bought homes in or near Pafos.

- **Lefkosia,** the partitioned city, is a place most foreign housebuyers ignore even thought there are some potentially desirable areas there.

- If peace ever breaks out, the area to buy in would be the attractive **Chrysaliniotissa** quarter, which has fine stone houses and is close to the city's popular café and bar area.

- If you don't mind being **inland**, there are villages like **Dhora** and **Mousere** in the foothills of the Troodos mountains which are crying out for restoration.

- The villages of **Loufou,** 18km from Lemesos, and **Lania** are already becoming popular with foreign house buyers.

- More picturesque, and not cheap, are places west of prosperous Larnaka such as **Maroni** village, **Kalavassos** and **Tokni.** Similarly remote is **Khirokiti.** The most popular village is Lefkara where the streets are too narrow for cars, which is considered a blessing by many.

- Property **prices are lower** in Northern Cyprus but development is speeding ahead there, as in the south.

- In Northern Cyprus foreign settlement is centred on **Girne** and its surrounds.

- So far few foreigners have been buying in **Mağusa,** the former Famagusta.

- Most people are buying **new-build** properties rather than restoring old ones.

OVERVIEW

Most people who want to buy property in Cyprus are looking for places near the sea. Consequently most of the coast of Southern Cyprus has been heavily developed either for tourism or for second homes. Northern Cyprus has not been so comprehensively developed because its political isolation has made it unattractive to tourists and settlers. However, that situation is changing fast and many people worry that so much poorly-planned development is taking place in the north that it will soon be virtually indistinguishable from the south except in terms of prices.

In the south most foreigners have settled in and around the big package-holiday resorts of Pafos, Larnaka, Lemesos and Ayia Napa. Most settlement seems to be taking place near Pafos, a more appealing small town than Lemesos or Larnaka, both of which feel shabby and run-down. Relatively few have bothered with Lefkosia even though there are some potentially very desirable residential districts there.

In the north almost all the foreigners who have settled have made homes in and around Girne and the foothills of the Kyrenia Mountains. Few people have homed in on Mağusa, even though it is an attractive town with signs of a burgeoning café culture. Even fewer have opted for Lefkoşa which is not that surprising given its sleepy atmosphere. However, as in Lefkosia, Lefkoşa has some very attractive residential areas full of old stone houses that would make very pleasing homes if the political situation were ever to make it possible to dismantle the Green Line.

Most people settling in Cyprus are buying new-build properties rather than existing houses or flats. The result is that in many cases they are buying before the property is completed on the basis of architect's plans and drawings. Inevitably there is scope for things to go wrong, and anyone buying something that is not yet completed should do their best to inspect other properties that have been built by the same contractors to ensure that their workmanship is up to scratch.

Although there is the inevitable sprinkling of younger, mainly female settlers who have married Cypriots, in general the foreigners who have settled in Cyprus tend to be middle-aged or older, reflecting the general tenor of tourism to the island. According to some estimates as many as 80% of foreign residents are from Britain.

John Symons says what made him choose Larnaka

My initial preference in terms of ideal location was Protaras/Paralimni but on meeting an estate agent and discussing my requirements I was taken to several places on the island. I then felt that in terms of quality and value for money the property I saw in Oroklini, near Larnaka, was best. After further investigation I was persuaded that the Larnaka area (which I had never visited before except to use the airport) was an excellent location.

SOUTHERN CYPRUS

PAFOS (PAPHOS)

Population: approx 50,000
Airport: *Pafos International*
The most westerly of the towns on the south coast of Cyprus, Pafos has become more

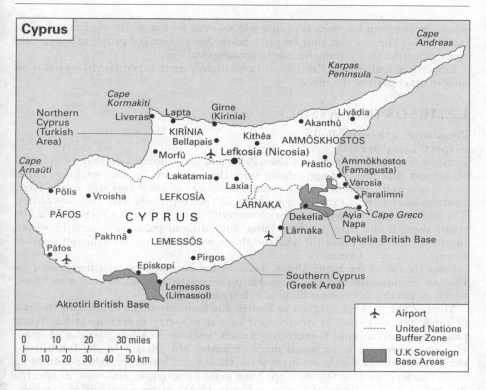

Cyprus

Cape Andreas

Karpas Peninsula

Cape Kormakiti

Northern Cyprus (Turkish Area)

Liveras • Lapta • Girne (Kirinia) Livâdia • Akanthû

KIRÎNIA Bellapais • Kithêa AMMÓSKHOSTOS

Cape Arnaûti

Morfû ✈ Lefkosia (Nicosia) Prâstio • Ammôkhostos (Famagusta)

Lakatamia Varosia

Pôlis • Vroisha Laxia Paralimni

LEFKOSÎA

PÂFOS C Y P R U S LÂRNAKA

Dekelia Ayia Napa Cape Greco

Pakhnã LEMESSÓS Lârnaka Dekelia British Base

Pâfos

Episkopi Southern Cyprus (Greek Area)

Pirgos

Lemessos (Limassol)

Akrotiri British Base

| 0 | 10 | 20 | 30 miles |
| 0 | 10 | 20 | 30 | 40 | 50 km |

✈ Airport

------- United Nations Buffer Zone

U.K Sovereign Base Areas

popular both with tourists and settlers since the opening of Pafos airport made it more readily accessible. It's a town that comes in two parts: **Ktima;** which is the older part of town at the top of a hill and **Kato Pafos** (Lower Pafos), a more ramshackle settlement of hotels and restaurants ringing the harbour and castle and opening out into an archaeological site where impressive mosaics were discovered. Ktima mostly consists of a narrow shopping street ending at a covered market which sells fruit and veg and a few tourist knick-knacks. There are some attractive old houses in this part of town but most of the incomers have opted for newly-built villas and apartments. These two sections were once quite separate. However, nowadays modern development has joined up all the gaps and both parts are rapidly vanishing anyway amid the general development of the surrounding land either for tourism or, increasingly, for second-home buyers.

Some estimates have suggested that more than 6,000 British people have bought homes in and around Pafos. There are also a large number of Eastern European residents, many of them working illegally, which means that there are not as many Greek Cypriots around as the population figure might initially suggest. All that makes for a situation in which it is easy to find other ex-pats to socialise with and where anything that someone from Britain wants to buy is likely to be available, albeit at a mark-up on the UK price.

West of Pafos foreigners have also settled at **Coral Bay** which has a good, if over-developed, beach, and in **Peyia**, which is now little more than a suburb of Pafos. Even further west is the **Akamas Peninsula,** the wildest part of southern Cyprus where development has been kept to a minimum so far but where the Laona Project (see Making Money From Your Property below) has encouraged people to convert old stone properties into sustainable tourist accommodation.

Property in and around Pafos tends to be slightly more expensive than what is on offer in other parts of the island.

LEMESOS (LIMASSOL)

Population: approx.150,000
Airport: Larnaka; Pafos

Lemesos is a much bigger town than Pafos and feels more like a long-established settlement that lives for something more than tourism (ie wine-making, citrus production and port activity). Given the proximity of the Akrotiri Sovreign Base, Lemesos has had long experience with the British, especially with their squaddies. The seafront is pleasant enough, with something of the feel of a Victorian seaside resort about it and there has been some upgrading of the town centre. However, the town is hardly beautiful and the shops would not set most people's pulses racing.

Since the fall of the Soviet Union, Lemesos has become a popular playground for Russian businessmen and the inevitable prostitutes who seem to trail after them, which means that it has some decidedly sleazy nightlife.

Most of the package tourism to Lemesos is focused on the beaches to the east of town and this, too, is where some of the property development has taken place, especially around **Governor's Beach,** a whole 30 kilometres out of town. However, there are some much more attractive old villages in the foothills of the Troodos to the north, amongst them **Dhora** and **Mousere**, where crumbling stone houses cry out for restoration. Even more picturesque, and more discovered by settlers, is the village of **Lofou,** a handy 18-kilometre drive out of Lemesos. Similarly appealing is **Lania**, where some estimates suggest that 25% of the residents are now ex-pats.

Heading east towards Larnaka, there are some properties for sale in **Kellaki** but this is not as attractive a settlement as **Akapnou** or, further east, **Pendakomo**.

LARNAKA

Population: approx.67,000
Airport: *Larnaka*

At first (and even second) sight Larnaka is a dusty, down-at-heel town with little going for it, which had to grow up abruptly and too fast when the events of 1974 brought a flood of refugees from Famagusta pouring in. However, it is extremely convenient for the airport, there are a couple of cinemas and the shops are as good as it's going to get on this side of the island. Most foreigners who have bought here have opted to live in the surrounding area rather than in the town itself.

Heading west from Larnaka a good place to start looking for a property with character is **Maroni** village which has a large British contingent already in residence. **Kalavassos** and **Tokhni** are also inviting and have some sensitive tourism developments in place. Similarly remote and inviting is **Khirokiti**. However, probably the best known and most popular of the villages in Larnaka's hinterland is **Lefkara**, which, like Pafos, comes in two parts: Pano Lefkara and Kato Lefkara. Lefkara is the biggest lace-making centre in Cyprus and lives off the proceeds of this expensive cottage industry. Pano Lefkara is extremely attractive, with old stone houses lining streets too narrow for cars to pass easily. For that reason alone prices here are steep in comparison with what you would pay elsewhere.

> **Andrew Miller of Larnaka wishes he had done more research**
> *We bought in Pafos first but did not research enough. Larnaka offers residents a less expensive and better quality of life as you don't have to pay tourist prices for everything, especially when socialising in bars and restaurants.'*

AYIA NAPA

Population: approx 3000
Airport: Larnaka

Ayia Napa is where it all happens in terms of youthful sun-and-sea tourism. It's a lurid strip of bars, hotels and restaurants which seems oddly out of keeping with the generally sleepier pace of the island. Still, this is where most of the younger foreigners who have settled in Southern Cyprus have found their home and this is where, in high summer, there is the best chance of finding casual work in tourism.

Recently the Cypriots have started to tire of the riotous goings-on and the inevitable lurid publicity overseas so it is possible that things will quieten down over the coming years. In the short-term, however, it is not a place where those in search of the 'real' Cyprus would want to settle.

People who have enjoyed holidays in Ayia Napa but don't want to live right in the town sometimes opt to buy in **Protaras** or **Paralimni** instead. However, neither of these towns is particularly attractive; indeed the Rough Guide describes Protaras as 'a developmental disaster'.

TROODOS MOUNTAINS

Centres of population: *Platres, Troodhos, Kakopetria*
Airport: *Larnaka*

For many people Cyprus' pride and joy are the Troodos Mountains where the landscape has forced the developers to rein in their ambitions. Platres, Troodos and Kakopetria are not, perhaps, the idyllic, unspoilt communities you might expect. However, there are many smaller villages which are largely deserted as young people go in search of work in the coastal towns. In these places a foreigner might be able to buy a ruined cottage and turn it into a home full of character. However, so far few have shown much interest in doing so.

Platres is the most readily accessible of the Troodos towns and stays fairly cool even in high summer. However, that is also when it becomes jam-packed with day-trippers every weekend. Quite a lot of new development has taken place in Platres, much of it to house ex-pat Russians. **Troodhos** itself is much less appealing, consisting as it does of a purpose-built resort complex which is mobbed with day-trippers. **Kakopetria** is more two-faced, with an inviting old quarter pleasingly restored rubbing shoulders with some truly out-of-place high-rise hotels. Many Cypriots here spend most of the year in London and then come back to their 'village' in summer.

Finding somewhere to buy in any of these places is probably as much to do with who you know and having an ear to the ground as relying on an estate agent to do the legwork for you.

POLIS

Airport: *Pafos*

Unlike the resorts of the south coast, Polis, on the northern side of the Akamas Peninsula, has managed to hang on to some of its old laidback atmosphere although, as elsewhere, rapid development means that that is unlikely to stay the case for much longer. This is a town where people still hang 'Rooms To Let' signs in their windows in summer, whether they have permission to do so or not, so this might be an interesting place for anyone thinking to start a small pension.

East of Polis new villa developments are going up at the usual high speed although the road east is quickly cut off by the Atilla Line, separating it from the North Cypriot town of Gözelyört (Morfou).

LEFKOSIA (NICOSIA)

Population: approx. 200,000

Airport: *Larnaka*

Lefkosia is a bustling modern city sprawling out from the old walled town at its heart which is where the limited tourism action can be found. Most people find it dusty and hot, and unfortunately the small size of the island means that even its choice of shops is pretty limited. Many tourists get by without ever setting foot in the place.

Lefkosia is more cosmopolitan than you might expect, with a large semi-resident population of Russians, Lebanese, Iranians, Turks, Syrians and Kurds, some of them working as journalists, some as spies. It was forced to grow rapidly and haphazardly in 1974 as refugees flooded in from the north but most of that growth took place to the south of the old town.

For the time being Lefkosia remains blighted by the Green Line which runs straight through it, cutting streets off so abruptly that windows actually overhang the No Man's Land beyond. This is a shame since it means that few foreigners have wanted to buy properties even in the attractive **Chrysaliniotissa** area which has some fine stone houses with lovely tiled floors and inviting courtyards. This part of town, nestling within the Venetian walls and slap up against the Green Line, was restored by UNDP and UNHCS as part of the Nicosia Master Plan. Should peace ever break out this would be the area in which to buy, especially as it is close to the Famagusta Gate area which has some of the town's most popular bars and cafés.

Typical Properties for Sale in Southern Cyprus

Southern Cyprus does not yet have the euro; the prices below are given in pounds sterling rather than Cyprus pounds.

Location	Type	Description	Price
Pafos	Apartment	One bedroom/two bedroom	£52,000/£78,403
Pafos	Villa	Three bedrooms. Swimming pool	£242,000
Polemi village near Pafos	Stone cottage	Two bedrooms	£155,000

Lemesos town	Apartment	Two bedrooms	£73,000
Lania, village near Lemesos	Cottage	One bedroom	£40,500
Kouklia large village Lemesos area	Stone house	Three bedrooms	£288,000
Larnaka town	Detached house	Four bedrooms	£140,000
Larnaka	Apartment	Two bedrooms	£55,500
Larnaka	Villa	Three bedrooms. Pool. Five minutes from sea.	£145,000

Estate Agents for Southern Cyprus

Antonis Loizou & Associates: Contact UK freephone 0800 0326203; + 357 25 871552; fax +357 25 360449; e-mail enquiries@aloizou.com.cy. www.aloizou.com.cy. Surveyors, architects, marketing and property sales throughout Cyprus. Go to www.aloizpou.com/contacts.htm for a list of offices in Cyprus or contact Halcyon Properties (see below).

Aresti Estate Agency Ltd: 7/26 Tombs of the Kings Road, P.O. Box 62371, 8063 Pafos, Cyprus; ☎+357 26 912 100; fax +357 26 912 101; e-mail sales@aresti-realestate.com. Sales and rentals, Pafos and area.

Benacon: 75 Archbishop Makarios III Avenue, P.O. Box 60560 Pafos, Cyprus; ☎+357 6 941543; fax +357 6 944110; e-mail benacon@cytanet.com.cy; www.benacon.com. Estate agents, builders, engineers and architects group. Pafos area.

Capital Growth Real Estate Agents Ltd: Shop 14, Frixos Business Centre, 33 Arch. Makarios Ave III, 6017 Larnaka, Cyprus; ☎+357 24817711; fax +357 24817784; e-mail info@cgestates.com; www.cgestates.com. Wide range of properties in Famagusta, Ayia Napa, Limassol, Lefkosia and Pafos.

Halcyon Properties: 3 Dukes Close, Seaford, East Sussex BN25 2TU; ☎01323-891639; fax 01323-892954; e-mail info@halcyonproperties.co.uk; www.halcyonpro perties.co.uk. Land and property in Cyprus. British Associate company for Anthony Loizou & Associates Cyprus estate agents. Contacts in all main towns and resorts.

Stephenson Willowby King Estate Agents: 15 Apostolou Pavlou Avenue, 8046 Pafos, Cyprus; ☎+357 26 822277; fax +357 26 822276; e-mail info@willowbyking.com; www.willowbyking.com. Properties in Pafos and Limassol (Lemesos).

NORTHERN CYPRUS

LEFKOŞA

Population: approx. 50,000
Airport: *Ercan International*
In contrast with Lefkosia, the southern half of old Nicosia, Lefkoşa is a real backwoods town and seems to be becoming even sleepier as most of the tourism and

property development action focuses on Girne. Lefkoşa could be any small town on the Turkish mainland were it not for the scattering of fine medieval buildings that pay homage to its past as the capital of the Lusignan kings. Forget exciting shopping – this may be the capital of the TRNC but so far it has little to show for that accolade.

Not surprisingly few foreigners have shown much interest in buying property in Lefkoşa. Were they to do so the most interesting area is probably **Arabahmet**. Like Chrysaliniotissa in Lefkosia, this quarter is full of fine stone houses which have been restored as part of the Nicosia Master Plan. However, as with Chrysaliniotissa, Arabahmet abuts against the Green Line and overlooks No Man's Land which means that few Westerners would want to buy there until such time as a peace plan is worked out. In the meantime many of these wonderful old houses are filled with refugees and poor settlers from the east of Turkey.

West of Lefkoşa there are few foreign settlers except in **Lefke** where some followers of the Sufi leader Kıbrıslı Şeyh Nazim have taken up residence.

GIRNE (KYRENIA)
Population: approx.15,000
Airports: *Ercan International, Lefkoşa*
In Northern Cyprus most of the foreign settlement has been concentrated around Girne (the old Kyrenia), which has a matchless setting around a fishing harbour ringed with old stone houses and dominated by the vast walls of a medieval castle. Most of the buildings around the harbour now house fish restaurants and/or hotels. Beyond the harbour Girne has a few pleasant shopping streets, a handful of small hotels, a variety of restaurants, including some serving Indian cuisine, and a terminal for shared taxis to Lefkoşa and Mağusa and that's about it. Afterwards comes the familiar sprawl of new building that can be seen all over the island.

Most of the people who have been snapping up homes in the area actually buy in the surrounding countryside and in the villages in the foothills of the Kyrenia Mountains. Decades ago Lawrence Durrell immortalised pretty little **Bellapais** with its ruined abbey by writing about his experiences as one of the first ex-pats to buy a house, restore it and settle there in his *Bitter Lemons*. Those who have come after him have been less interested in restoring old properties and more interested in buying new-built villas and apartments in the outskirts.

Villages where development is currently forging ahead include Esentepe, Edremit, Alsancak, Arapköy, Karşıkaya, Çatalköy, Ozanköy and Lapta, some of them little more than extensions of the Girne sprawl. When choosing a property in one of these settlements it is vital to think about what further developments might take place in the future, which might wreck the view for which you bought your property.

At one time **Karaman** was *the* place to buy, with the government arranging 25-year leases on all the properties there for foreign buyers only. The village was intrinsically pretty and became more so as ex-pats, most of them British and German, did up the whitewashed cottages. However, it was never a very lively place and now many of the houses are in search of new owners. Potential incomers would do well to bear in mind the essential political conservatism of most of those already settled in Karaman.

Lapta is one of the more inviting villages, with the added advantage of a reliable water supply. The government also leased houses to foreigners here but as their 25-year leases are running out, so some seem keen to sell up.

GAZİMAĞUSA (FAMAGUSTA)

Population: approx. 30,000
Airport: *Ercan International, Lefkoşa*

Mağusa (the old Famagusta) is a striking port town, much of it still enclosed within sturdy medieval walls that are said to have inspired Shakespeare's *Othello*. Few places in the world can have such a dense clustering of medieval churches and chapels, and the main square is completely dominated by a magnificent Gothic cathedral now converted into a mosque. This square is now the focus of a sustained attempt to revitalise the town, with several inviting pavement cafés gathered round the pedestrianised town.

Given how attractive Mağusa is, it is perhaps surprising that foreigners haven't been snapping up properties here as they are in Girne. However, there is a dark side to the story which is the ghost settlement of Maraş (Varosha) on the outskirts. Before 1974 this was one of Cyprus' biggest tourist centres, a Benidorm-lookalike of high-rise hotels catering to the mass market. Now, however, it stands in limbo, its hotels abandoned to the occasional UN visitor. Until a peace settlement finally sorts out what is going to happen to Maraş it is unlikely that people will feel confident enough to settle in this area.

Theoretically they could still buy north of Mağusa, around the sandy beach and Roman ruins of **Salamis**. However, so far there seem to be few takers either here or further east on the unspoilt **Kırpaşa Peninsula**, where some of the few remaining Greek-Cypriot residents of the north live.

Typical properties for sale in Northern Cyprus

Location	Type	Description	Price
Girne	penthouse apartment in new development	three bedrooms	£60,000
Çatalköy	Villa	three bedrooms	£120,000
Upper Kyrenia	new apartments	three bedrooms. 5 minutes from city centre. Sea and mountain views.	£32,000
Lapta	bungalow in a development of eight homes.	three bedrooms. Communal pool. Sea views	£61,500
Bellapais (nr Girne)	restored village house occupying third of an acre plot.	three bedrooms. Garden and fantastic views.	£69,000

Useful Contact for Northern Cyprus

North Cyprus Properties: www.northcyprusproperties.co.uk. Website of organisation that supports potential buyers looking for properties in northern Cyprus. Databases of properties for sale, lawyer list and other useful information.

Estate Agents for Northern Cyprus

Boray Estate Agency: 5 Terkan Plaza, Karaoğlanoğlu Cad., Girne, Mersin 10 North

Cyprus (also office in Lefkosia); ☎+90 392 8222919; fax +90 392 2288221; e-mail info@borayestates.com; www.borayestates.com.

Go North Cyprus.com: 23 Ecevit Ave, Girne, North Cyprus; ☎+90 542 852 1920; fax +90 392 815 5570; e-mail info@gonorthcyprus.com; www.gonorthcyprus.com.

Ian Smith Estate Agency: P.O. Box Girne, Merin 10; ☎+90 392 815 7118; fax +90 392 815 7119; www.cyprus-invest.com. Properties in Savion village.

Sunny Property Estate Agents: Peel House, 30 The Downs, Altrincham, Cheshire, WA14 2PX; ☎0161-233 0400; fax 0161-233 0400; e-mail info@SunnyProperty .co.uk; www.sunny-property.co.uk. Address in N. Cyprus: 2 Kemal Paşa Sokak, Lefkoşa, Turkey, Mersin 10; ☎+90 392 815 7791.

THE PURCHASING PROCEDURE

CHAPTER SUMMARY

- **Banks in Northern Cyprus** have not proved very reliable although those in the south are.
  - You are unlikely to be able to get a 25-year mortgage through a Cypriot bank. However, **shorter mortgages** are sometimes available, as are **finance arrangements** with developers.
- There are plenty of **estate agents** in both north and south Cyprus.
- Most people buy **villas or houses** rather than apartments.
- **Title deeds.** The particular circumstances of Cyprus mean that what is written on the title deed is more important than usual. There are four different types of title deed.
- You should be very wary where no title exists as ownership of the property is questionable and the real owners may return to claim it.
- **Rental accommodation** is in short supply, especially in the north.
- **Building standards.** The pell-mell pace of development in both north and south means shoddy workmanship is almost inevitable.
- A **retention scheme** means that most people don't need to pay all their development costs upfront.
- **Renting out.** Renting out your property using the internet is likely to be more profitable than starting a pension. Income earned on the island may be due to the island's tax authorities if paid to you there.
  - The new agrotourism movement sponsored by the Cyprus Tourism Organisation is probably the best hope for foreigners wanting to rent out their property.
  - Agrotourism is a scheme to encourage abandoned village properties to be converted to inviting rural retreats for visitors.

FINANCE

BANKS

The banks of **Southern Cyprus** are fairly reliable and efficient although they only open from 8.30am to 12.30pm Monday to Friday (on Mondays they also open from 3.15pm to 4.45pm). In tourist resorts the banks also open in late afternoon during the summer.

In **Northern Cyprus** banks only open from 8.30am to noon Monday to Friday and are nothing like as reliable as those of the south. What's more a lot of them simply collapsed in 2001, mirroring what happened on the Turkish mainland. Instead people often prefer to use foreign-exchange offices which open from 8.30am to 1pm and from 2pm to 5pm Monday to Friday and Saturday morning.

HSBC operates in both north and south Cyprus and is probably the best bet for transferring money from abroad, especially in the north. In Southern Cyprus the following banks should also be used to dealing with cash transfers from abroad: Alpha Bank, Bank of Cyprus, Co-operative Central Bank, Cyprus Popular (Laiki) Bank, Hellenic Bank and Universal Savings Bank.

In **Southern Cyprus** you are expected to set up a local disbursement account with foreign currency to pay for your day-to-day expenses. However, you are also expected to set up an external account from which to pay for your house purchase and any car purchase.

In **Northern Cyprus** it is easy to open a bank account either in Turkish lira or in sterling (unlike in Turkey itself you can open an interest-bearing foreign-currency account). However, for the time being it might be best to stick with opening accounts only at the branches of HSBC in Girne and Lefkoşa.

Useful Addresses – Banks
HSBC: Ziya Rızkı Caddesi 16, Girne; ☎0392-815 9988; fax 0392-815 9980.
HSBC: Dositheou 7, Block C, 1071 Lefkosia; ☎357 22 376116; fax 357 22 376121.

UK MORTGAGES

Few of the high-street banks are likely to want to give anyone a mortgage to buy a property in north or south Cyprus, especially while the current insecure political situation continues (although now that Southern Cyprus has joined the EU it will no doubt seem more desirable as an investment prospect). However, as long as you have adequate equity in your UK home there is no reason why you should not be able to re-mortgage it in order to raise the money to buy a property in Cyprus. Alternatively, some people have sold their UK home and used the cash to buy in Cyprus.

MORTGAGES WITH TURKISH OR CYPRIOT BANKS

You will not be able to take out a conventional 25-year mortgage with a bank in **Southern Cyprus** although you can sometimes borrow 70% of the lowest valuation on the property for between five and fifteen years (you must be borrowing at least C£25,000 to qualify). Most developers in the south can also make arrangements that work in a similar way to a mortgage, albeit on a shorter time scale. Typically, you would pay them around 30% of the purchase price upfront, with another lump payment due on completion and then monthly payments for the next 15 years.

Forget about obtaining a mortgage in **Northern Cyprus** – there is no such system as yet. Once again you may be able to make arrangements with the developers to pay in instalments. Certainly you should avoid paying all the money upfront for a property that has not yet been completed.

IMPORTING CURRENCY

You can import as much cash as you want into Cyprus, north or south. However, when buying a house in Southern Cyprus you will have to pay for it in foreign currency. Experts agree that the most economic way to do this is through a currency broker such as Currencies Direct. For more details see *Importing Currency* in the *General Introduction* to this book.

REAL ESTATE TAXES

Property Transfer Taxes

In **Southern Cyprus** house purchasers must pay a transfer fee of 3% on properties worth up to C£50,000. Between C£50,000 and C£100,000 the rate rises to 5%, and from C£100,000 upwards it becomes 8%. So on a house purchased for C£90,000 you should expect to pay C£3,500 in transfer fees.

Once a purchase has been agreed in **Northern Cyprus**, the buyer must pay 6% of the purchase price in tax; the seller pays another 3% on a first sale and 6% on any later sales. Most people understate the value of the property in order to reduce their tax liability. As long as Northern Cyprus languishes in political limbo that is unlikely to be a problem although the situation might change if it finally works its way into the EU.

VAT

VAT is not currently charged on house construction, although now that Southern Cyprus has joined the EU it may eventually follow many other EU countries and levy VAT on new build properties.

INHERITANCE AND CAPITAL GAINS TAX

At the moment Southern Cyprus has no wealth or inheritance taxes, although capital gains tax is payable at a rate of 20% on sold properties that were worth more than C£50,000.

Since anything to do with tax is in constant flux and may well change now that Southern Cyprus has joined the EU you should always get the advice of a financial expert and/or lawyer before making a decision.

Useful Contacts – Tax Consultants
Mosaic Financial Solutions Ltd: 8 Digenis Akritas Ave, Office 202, PO Box 26573, 1640 Lefkosia; ☎0357-2287 7550; fax 0357-2287 7551.
Areti Charidema: 21 Vasili Michailidi St, 3026 Lemesos; ☎357-25 746103; fax 357-25 344019; www.aretilawyers.com.
Cyprus Solicitors: 3 Alciviades St, PO Box 6055, 8011 Pafos; ☎357-26 933218; fax

357-26 44129; www.cysolicitors.com.

INSURANCE

Several international insurance companies operate in **Southern Cyprus**. One of the most reliable is likely to be HSBC Insurance (1 Michael Michaelides, Pissas Bulding, 3030 Lemesos; ☎357 25 878100, fax 357 25 355869).

Reputable insurance companies operating in **Northern Cyprus** include the main Turkey-based insurance companies such as *Güneş Sigorta* and *Anadolu Sigorta*.

FINDING PROPERTIES FOR SALE

There are plenty of estate agents in both parts of the island, and increasingly their newspapers are also full of adverts for houses.

ESTATE AGENTS

It says everything for the way that the property market is developing that whereas five years Girne had just five estate agents it now has 120. Although some people hope to save money by looking for a property to buy without using an estate agent, the vast majority do use one, and most of them in both north and south Cyprus operate in much the same way as those in the UK. Their windows are full of cards showing attractive properties, either already built or in the making, together with details of their dimensions, what they have to offer and the asking price. Sometimes it may turn out that the advertised price is as fictional as the cheap holiday offers in UK travel agency windows. However, browsing the estate agents' windows is likely to give you a good idea what to expect.

With so many new agents entering the market you would be well advised to ask other ex-pats which ones they have used in order to find someone trustworthy and knowledgeable. In Southern Cyprus many of the agents have grouped together to advertise themselves on the Internet; try www.buyrentcyprus.com/estate agents; www.cy-estates.com; or www.findaproperty.co.uk.

Andrew Miller struck gold with his estate agent
We used an estate agent in Lemesos who was brilliant and since then we have gone into business with him because of what we suffered being messed around by non-professionals, He is completely independent and has been in business since 1948. He found properties for us to look at in our price range and according to our specifications. He also introduced us to a fantastic lawyer.

Useful Addresses – Estate Agents and developers
Arch Property Development & Construction Company: 67 Ziya Rızkı Caddesi, Girne; ☎0392-815 8709; alkin@arch-cyprus-properties.com.
Beechwood Estates: Girne; 0392-815 6423; www.beechwoodestates.com.
Fraser & Beyler: Facing Astro Supermarket, Girne; ☎0392-815 8882; fax 0392-815 8682; info@fraserandbeyler.com.

Ian Smith Estate Agents: Opposite Ship Hotel, Girne-Lapta road, Girne; ☎0392-815 7118; fax 0392-815 7119; www.iansmithestate.com.

Nokta Construction & Estate Agents: Terkan Plaza 5, Girne-Lapta road, Girne; ☎0392-822 3528; www.noktaestates.com.

Useful Address; UK-Based Lawyers

Bennett & Co Solicitors: 144 Knutsford Road, Wilmslow, Cheshire SK9 6JP; ☎01625-586937; fax 01625-585362; e-mail: internationallawyers@bennett-and-co.com; www.bennett-and-co.com.

John Howell & Co: The Old Glassworks, 22 Endell Street, Covent Garden, London WC2H 9AD; ☎020 7420 0400; fax 020 7836 3626; e-mail info @europelaw.com; www.europelaw.com.

Mr Stefano Lucatello, The International Property Law Centre, Unit 2 Waterside Park, Livingstone Road, Hessle HU13 0EG; ☎01482 350-850; fax 01482 642799; e-mail internationalproperty@maxgold.com; www.internationalpropertylaw.com.

ADVERTS

Newspapers

Many estate agents advertise properties in *Cyprus Today, Cyprus Mail* and *Cyprus Weekly.* However prices advertised in Greek newspaper are often lower than those in the English-language papers so it is well worth asking a Greek-reading friend to keep an eye out for you.

Internet

An increasing number of property developers and estate agents are using the Internet to advertise their properties. Most of them are perfectly reputable. However, there can be no substitute for going to Cyprus yourself, looking at several properties and talking to locals before settling on something to buy.

Property Exhibitions

The current building frenzy on Cyprus means that more properties are being advertised at property exhibitions overseas, for example at the Homebuyers Show in London. To find out when and where the next property exhibition will be taking place check out www.tsn.co.uk, or www.internationalpropertyshow.com.

WHAT TYPE OF PROPERTY TO BUY

The current building boom has mainly seen complexes of villas and detached houses going up, even in Northern Cyprus where the mainland Turkish preference for living in high-rise apartments is much less pronounced. It's perfectly possible to buy an apartment or condo but fewer of these are being built.

At the time of writing foreigners could only buy one apartment, one villa or one plot of land no bigger than 4000 square metres in Southern Cyprus. Now that the country has joined the EU it is likely that this restriction will be lifted, probably by 2009.

VILLAS

Southern Cyprus has a lot of villas that were originally built to serve a self-catering market that is now in the doldrums. At the same time developers are racing ahead building new villa complexes. The result is that it is particularly easy to pick up a pleasant modern villa with its own pool as a second home.

HOUSES

For the time being few foreigners are buying town houses although in the future some parts of Lefkosia/Lefkoşa could become more attractive. However, alongside the villas there are also a large number of properties going up that look very similar but are marketed as detached houses.

RUINS

Unlike in Greece and Turkey, relatively few people are buying ruinous Cypriot properties to restore, perhaps because so much of the market is for comfortable, easy-to-live-in retirement homes. However, in some of the villages it is still possible to find crumbling cottages that could be converted into homes with character. Increasingly attempts are being made to market these to more affluent tourists who don't want to stay in characterless resort hotels. Consequently a ruin that might take time and money to do up might eventually turn out to be a good investment.

One Caveat – Multiple Ownership
As in Turkey, land on Cyprus is traditionally divided between all the children when someone dies. It can therefore turn out that more than one person owns the land and that not all the owners want to sell. Multiple ownership is particularly difficult to navigate where some of the owners have left Cyprus altogether. This will only be a problem if you are buying an old property to restore, rather than with one that is being built from scratch.

RENTING A HOME IN CYPRUS

DIFFERENCE BETWEEN NORTH AND SOUTH

As ever, it makes sense to spend some time on Cyprus before embarking on a house purchase. It's a good idea to find somewhere to rent for a month or so but unfortunately although there is rental accommodation in **Southern Cyprus** it is usually in purpose-built self-catering units in and around the resorts rather than in normal residential accommodation in the towns. Details of such places can usually be picked up in estate or travel agencies and also in the adverts carried by the English-language press or look for 'House/Flat for Rent' signs.

In **Northern Cyprus** even that kind of rental accommodation is hard to find. Start by asking in the local estate agents and looking for *Kiralık Ev/Dairesi* (House/Apartment to let) signs.

Rental Costs

Rents in the south average around C£140 a month for a one-bedroom flat and from C£180-230 for a two-bedroom apartment, with prices marginally lower in the north.

FINDING RENTAL ACCOMMODATION

Given the quantity of accommodation available for tourists, an alternative would be to look at the brochures of the UK travel agents and find a long-stay holiday package. These are usually offered during the winter months (from November through to Easter) and are aimed at older travellers who find the prices reasonable in comparison with the cost of heating a home through the winter; for example it might cost around £1,000 for a two-month stay in a self-catering apartment. However, there is nothing to stop anyone taking advantage of these offers.

Useful Addresses – Rental Agents
North Cyprus Rentals Ltd: ☎01420-473193; fax 01420-473643; www.northcyprusre ntals.com.
Anatolian Sky: 81 Warwick Rd, Olton, Solihull, West Midlands B92 7HP; ☎08708-504040; fax 0121-764 3559; www.anatolian-sky.co.uk.

FEES, CONTRACTS AND CONVEY-ANCING

WHY TITLE IS ESPECIALLY IMPORTANT IN THE NORTH

Because of Cyprus' complicated political situation it is important to be very sure about the exact legal situation of the property you are interested in. It is vital to see the title deed (*tapu,*) of the property and to check the number in the lower right-hand corner. If it has 'TRNC' written in front of it you should proceed with caution since it means that the property has been given to its current 'owner' by the northern Cypriot government, either as a reward for a period of military service or because they are settlers from the mainland. As many as 85% of new developments in Northern Cyprus may be TRNC-titled properties. It is unclear what will happen to these places when a final settlement is reached.

Estate agents' adverts sometimes claim that a property has an original Turkish or Greek (or even British) title deed which sounds promising. However, the Northern Cyprus government makes it difficult for such properties to be sold to foreigners, fearing that soon there will be no legally secure properties available at reasonable prices for local people to buy.

Where to Check the Title Deeds

In **Northern Cyprus** the main Land Office in Lefkoşa has a record of all *tapus* (title deeds) in the north and is the place to go to check the exact legal status of a property that interests you. This is also the place to come to check whether the property you are interested in lies on land zoned for agriculture rather than property development.

In **Southern Cyprus** you can check who owns what land at the District Land Office. The Land Registry Office in Lefkosia can usually complete all the paperwork for a property transfer inside two months.

TITLE DEEDS

The peculiar circumstances of Cyprus mean that what is written on the title deed is even more important than normal. There are four different types of title deed (*tapu* in Turkish):

- Clean freehold title deeds issued to British or other foreign owners before 1974. These are unlikely to be challenged in the future.
- Clean freehold title deeds issued to Greek or Turkish Cypriots before 1974. In the north the government restricts foreign ownership of these properties which are also relatively uncontentious.
- A foreigner can only buy one dönüm of land with this status and must apply for permission to the Council of Ministers, a process which can take up to six months to complete.
- So-called TRNC title deeds. These have been issued for properties that belonged to Greeks before 1974 and which were exchanged for land in the south in the settlement after the invasion. Some people think these deeds are legally precarious. Similar deeds exist in the south too but the trouble is that in the north the government often gave them out as rewards to Turkish soldiers and settlers whose legal entitlement to stay in the north – let alone to sell the properties is dubious.
- Untitled land which belonged to Greeks or Turks before 1974. If no title deed exists, real ownership of the land is obviously questionable, so what sounds like a real bargain may be nothing of the kind if a final settlement eventually means the real owners returning to claim it.

Unfortunately it is not always easy to get estate agents and developers to let you see the title deed at the start of the buying process. However, wherever possible you should certainly try to see it even if it means a trip to the Land Registry Office in Lefkosia or the Land Registry and Surveying Office in Lefkoşa.

THE IMPORTANCE OF GOOD ESTATE AGENTS

Although some buyers hope to save money by cutting the estate agent out of the loop, in the case of Cyprus it is particularly advisable to use a reputable agent in order to avoid the pitfall of buying a property whose ownership is questionable. A good Cypriot estate agent will help the buyer through the whole buying process, from negotiating with the seller to negotiating with builders and renovators; some of them will even help you order locally-made furniture. A solicitor recommended by an estate agent may be slightly more expensive than one found on your own. However, they will have a vested interest in recommending someone who will get everything sorted out as quickly as possible.

It is common for would-be buyers to find a suitable property with the help of an estate agent, then to leave a 10% deposit and return to the UK to arrange the transfer of the remainder of the price. Usually they must then sign a power of attorney which will permit the estate agent to act for them in their absence. In general most agents recommend that people pay for new property in instalments as the work progresses; that way they can be sure that they will not lose all their money if something goes wrong before the work is completed.

Good estate agents also undertake to oversee the building work on your property and normally build into the contract a penalty clause in case the work falls behind schedule. If you cut out the estate agent there is every chance that you will have problems with your builders.

As in the UK the agent acts primarily for the vendor so you should certainly consider taking independent legal advice.

John Symonds recommends forearming yourself with knowledge

I made contact with an agent some months before coming to Cyprus via their website. At that stage I had a multitude of questions, both practical and legal. They put me in touch with a local agent and lawyer who were very helpful in explaining the legalities and likely costs. On my arrival In Cyprus they discussed my exact requirements with me, escorted me to various plots and introduced me to several developers. Once I'd selected a plot I met their recommended lawyer in Lemesos to draw up the contract. This stipulated all the payment terms and independent survey requirements as well as the penalty clauses for failure to deliver on time.

SURVEYS

If you are buying a second-hand property and have been using a solicitor to help you they will organise a survey for you. This should identify any outstanding bills attached to the property and ensure you are indemnified against having to pay them. The surveyor should also check with the Land Office/Land Registry that the title deed is in order and that the property has proper road access. Provided there is road access, then securing planning permission for development is virtually guaranteed.

However if you are buying a new-build property there may be no reason to have a survey carried out.

FEES

A cheap lawyer in either part of the island will do your conveyancing for about £500 but a more reputable one is likely to ask closer to £1,000-1,300.

In Southern Cyprus there is a **payment retention scheme** that applies when people are buying a new-build property. Typically the buyer holds back 10% of the value of all invoices presented by the contractor until the time comes to pay the Acceptance Certificate enabling them to move in. At this moment it is usual to pay the contract or 50% of the retained money. At the end of a one-year inspection period the buyer should pay the outstanding retained money provided no faults have been discovered.

CONTRACTS

In Southern Cyprus contracts are written in English. Once both parties have signed the contract it is registered at the Land Registry in Lefkosia within two weeks and the property cannot then be resold unless the new buyer signs a new contract permitting it. It is rarely necessary to pay all the money on exchange of contracts since most people arrange to pay the contractors in instalments. Arguably this is a better and safer system than the one operating in the UK.

Even so you should beware of sales agreements that contain a clause saying that if you resell the property before the developer has issued a title deed for it you become liable for any tax that they owe.

In Northern Cyprus contracts (*tapular*) are written in Turkish and you will need a translator to make sense of them.

Useful Addresses – Property Lawyers
Hasan Balman: P.K. 552, 6 Ankara Sokak, Lefkosa Mersin 10; ☎ +90 392 227 5868; e-mail hasan@cyprusprofpertylawyer.com. Lawyer for Northern Cyprus property purchase.
Gölboy Göryel: 26-28 Cumhuriyet Cad, Girne, Mersin 10; tel: +90 392 815 2097; e-mail gulboy@cypruspropertylawyer.com. Property lawyer for Northern Cyprus.

WHAT HAPPENS NEXT

CHAPTER SUMMARY

- **Power outages** and **water shortages** are a fact of life in the north.
- Many people use **fireplaces or pot-bellied stoves** to heat their houses.
- There is no **natural gas** on Cyprus.
- **Air-conditioning** is a virtual necessity.
- **Internet access** in the north is extremely slow and unreliable.

SERVICES

While the utilities function fairly efficiently in Southern Cyprus, it is a different matter in the north where power outages and water shortages are commonplace.

Electricity

In the Republic of Cyprus you should budget around £160 a year for electricity including the cost of a television licence.

If you are using an estate agent to handle your sale in Northern Cyprus then they may be able to organise an account with Kıb-Tek for you. There is unlikely to be any problem except in remote rural areas where you need to be aware that the cost of erecting a new electricity pylon could cost you around £5,000 and could take many months.

In Northern Cyprus power outages followed by dangerous power surges are the norm and most people have rechargeable lights on their walls and surge protectors on their computers. Even in Southern Cyprus power cuts are not uncommon.

Because Cyprus is so hot in summer, air-conditioning is highly recommended whatever the expense and difficulty of running it when the electricity supply is so unreliable.

Water

In Cyprus you need budget only around £32 a year for water bills. In remote parts of the island water sometimes comes from a well rather than the mains.

If you are using an estate agent to handle your sale in Northern Cyprus then they should be able to organise a new water account for you. If not, you will need to visit the Belediye (Town Hall) and enquire about opening a new *abonelik* (account). The Belediye is also where you will go to pay your water bills.

Generally speaking in Northern Cyprus the worst water shortages are on the inland side of the Kyrenia Mountains.

Wood and Coal-Burning Stoves

Because electricity is unreliable and expensive, and natural gas non-existent, many people in Cyprus still warm their houses with pot-bellied stoves that run on a mixture of wood and coal. Typically a stove will cost around £100 and will need a couple of tons of wood to get it through the winter. Alternatively, people have built in fireplaces. Central heating is readily available in the south but not in the north where it would have to be operated off expensive, hard-to-manoeuvre industrial gas bottles.

Solar Power

Cyprus' hot summers mean that solar panels are increasingly common on roofs all over the island. If you're having a solar panel installed on yours, make sure it's facing south for the best results.

Telephone

In **Southern Cyprus** the Cyprus Telecommunications Authority (CYTA) is in charge of installing phones and is reasonably efficient. In **Northern Cyprus** it may take Netaş up to a month to install a phone line in a town but up to two years if there are no telegraph poles near the property. The cost of installation may only be around £25 but you need to be sure that you will not have to pay for poles to be erected and lines run out to your property.

In the south Internet access is rarely a problem. In the north, however, connections are so slow that most people in business pay for satellite connection. This costs around £450 initially with a further £6 or so per month in charges.

Security

In general Cyprus has such a low crime rate that most people would think a guard dog more than adequate security. However, people do take out household insurance as a matter of routine in the south and this might cost around £130 a year.

Staff/Cleaners

You will have no trouble finding cleaners in either part of the island since there is a large migrant population desperate to find work. Finding skilled workers in **Southern Cyprus** could be more problematic since the unemployment rate is currently only 4%. In **Northern Cyprus** there is a steady throughput of young Turkish males from mainland Turkey who are often willing and able workers, especially in anything to do with tourism.

MAKING THE MOVE

If you are moving to either part of Cyprus permanently you can import all your furniture and household effects from the UK either duty-free or for a negligible sum. Your best bet for a trouble-free move from the UK is to use a firm of international removal experts like Dolphin Movers. It may be harder to get an international company to move you to Northern Cyprus in which case Olaytrans Ltd (☎0090-392 366 6540) or Armen Shipping (☎0090-392 366 4086) are reputable companies.

Unfortunately it is not so easy to import your car into Northern Cyprus and the cost, once you have paid the duty, is likely to be prohibitive. Whatever you choose to bring in will arrive at the port of Mağusa (in the north) or Lemesos (in the south) and then be trucked to your home.

Useful Contact
Dolphin Movers: 2 Haslemere Business Centre, Lincoln Way, Enfield EN1 1TE;

☎020-8804 7700; www.dolphinmovers.com.

IMPORTING PETS

Before importing a cat or dog into **Southern Cyprus** you will need permission from the Veterinary Services Department and will have to show a certificate confirming that the animal was free of rabies and in good health 72 hours before shipping. Once on the island they will have to be quarantined in your home for six months under supervision by the Veterinary Services Department.

Animals imported into **Northern Cyprus** also need a certificate of good health issued by a Western vet. They will have to go into quarantine in kennels in Lefkoşa but only for two weeks.

Useful contact
Department of Veterinary Services: 1417 Lefkosia; ☎0357-2280 5235; fax 0357-2280 5174; director@vs.moa.gov.cy

Customs

In theory you can only export or import C£100 to or from **Southern Cyprus** although no one ever seems to check this. There are no legal restrictions on how much you can take in or out of **Northern Cyprus** although the fact that no one wants the Turkish lira anywhere other than in Turkey and Northern Cyprus means that you won't want to export any of them.

Cars can be brought into Northern or Southern Cyprus for three months without any problems. In the south you can then extend that permission for up to one year before having to get involved in the bureaucracy of technically importing the car. However, at Lemesos port you may have to fill out a form itemising all sorts of details supposedly to prevent the import of stolen cars; most importantly you will need to know the chassis number of the vehicle. Green card motor insurance is recognised in Southern Cyprus although you should check that your paperwork shows the CY (Republic of Cyprus) code on it. Northern Cyprus will only allow the three-month stay and doesn't recognise any insurance taken out overseas; insurers wait at all entry points for you to buy suitable cover on the spot.

Until May 2004 ex-pats could import a car into Southern Cyprus duty-free, a considerable benefit that is almost certain to vanish now that it has entered the European Union.

BUILDING OR RENOVATING

As anywhere else in the world, you need to take local advice as to which builders to employ. Ideally you should also have inspected work already done by the team to ensure it is up to scratch; your research should include looking at long-established work since faults can take time to show up. Neither in the north nor in the south are builders likely to be angels who work on unsupervised to produce a perfect end product.

Estate agents in the north and south normally work with particular teams of builders. Provided you have picked a good agent they will have a vested interest in employing good workers. However, it is still a good idea to ask to see work that has been done by their team so that you can assess its quality.

Useful Contacts – Building
Erozan Mimarlık Mühendislik Bürosu: 15 Namık Kemal Meydanı, Suriçi, Gazimağusa;
☎366 4882.
Arch Property Development & Construction Company: 67 Ziya Rızkı Caddesi, Girne,
Mersin 10; ☎0392-815 8709; alkin@arch-cyprus-properties.com.

Andrew Miller advises checking your builder's credentials
*Every man and his dog knows someone who may be selling property and will always say
they will get you the best deal. In most cases this is not true and there are many pitfalls like
not everyone in the family that owns the land wanting to sell. One ends up in the middle.
Builders promise things that do not materialise, even roads in some cases. I recommend
that you use a reputable agent and lawyer who will check the builder for credit-worthiness,
building permits and planning consents. After-sales service from some builders can also be
an issue.*

Hiring Workers

In general it is easier to find good building workers in Southern Cyprus than in
the north. In the first place there is more chance of finding workers who can speak
English and in the second since rates of pay are better in the south, the best workers
from the north tend to head south in search of work. However, the pell-mell pace
of development both north and south means that shoddy workmanship is almost
inevitable and those in the know suspect that five years down the line many of the new
developments are likely to have problems. It is therefore very important both to get
advice from locals who have had building work done recently and to get a structural
survey of any property you are thinking of buying.

The Northern Cypriot government has recently started to license building inspectors
to check the different stages of construction. You should, therefore, be able to get a
guarantee for between five and 25 years for new-build properties.

Common problems to watch for are an absence of damp-proofing, insulation or
guttering as well as inadequate drains. Some Cypriot builders also face houses with
Spritz instead of render. This is not waterprof and quickly cracks. For advice on what
else to look out for in a new building take a look at Nigel Howarth's *Buying Your
Home in Cyprus – Hints and Tips*; find it on line at www.cyprusfan.alivewww.co.uk/
housebuild/nigel-howarth-housebuild.pdf.

John Symonds on dodgy builders
*I have since heard of many people who have not been happy with the quality of the finished
product dues to a skills shortage on the island meaning that builders can't keep pace with
the demand. So non-tilers end up doing your tiling etc. Also there seem to be some less
scrupulous developers who seem much more interested in turning a quick profit than in
delivering a quality product, I feel that as the demand for property increases, so the danger
becomes more real.*

DIY

Anyone who is good at DIY is undeniably at an advantage in that not only can they
do some of the work themself, thereby saving money, but in that they are better able to

assess the quality of the workmanship around them and foresee problems before they occur. Inevitably the choice of materials for decoration is more limited than in the UK although it is getting better all the time. Now that Southern Cyprus has joined the EU it is likely to gain wider access to products from all over Europe. This may also be the case for the north if the EU decides to reward it for seeking reunion by lifting sanctions on importing and exporting materials.

Pools

Most people opt to have a swimming pool on their property despite the island's water shortages. The best pools come with an overflow that makes it possible to filter the water and then recycle it. However these do not come cheap; you should budget around £15,000 for such a pool.

Gardens

Given that so many of the Cypriot settlers are British most properties for sale come with some sort of garden attached. However, water problems, especially in the north, mean that the main flowering period tends to be very short.

MAKING MONEY FROM YOUR PROPERTY

As elsewhere in the Mediterranean, the best hope most second-homers have of turning their property into a money-making proposition is either to turn it into a pension or hotel or let it out as private self-catering accommodation.

Hotels and Pensions

Unlike on mainland Greece and Turkey, Cyprus has relatively few small pensions. That might mean that the market is wide open for the enterprising few to start up their own businesses – or it could mean that the market simply isn't there. The partition of the island has removed its obvious potential for independent travellers as a stepping stone between Greece and Turkey or between Greece and/or Turkey and Israel and/or Egypt. However, if peace talks eventually succeed and it becomes possible to cross from north to south again that could all change.

Perhaps the best hope for foreigners wanting to let out accommodation to visitors lies in the relatively new agrotourism movement. Sponsored by the Cyprus Tourism Organisation (CTO), this is a movement to convert abandoned village properties into inviting rural retreats for visitors. So far most of these properties have been restored by Greek Cypriots but in theory there is no reason why foreigners shouldn't jump on the same bandwagon.

Useful Contacts – Letting Organisations

Cyprus Agrotourism Company: 19 Leoforos Lemesou PO Box 24535, CY 1390, Lefkosia; ☎357-2-337715; fax 357-2-339723; www.agrotourism.com.cy.
Laona Project: PO Box 257, Lemesos; ☎253-69475, fax 253-52657.

Renting Out

Renting your property to other foreign visitors is likely to be more profitable than starting up a pension. Many British people do this, using the Internet to help them advertise. However, this is on the margins of legality; in theory you are supposed to declare any income from renting out your home to the tax authorities whether you settle on the island or not.

If you do want to rent out your property you should probably work on the assumption that it will only be full for around twenty weeks in the year, with the period from November to March available for you to live in it yourself. In Southern Cyprus a good three-bedroomed villa in a decent location could bring in £12,362 in the 20-week summer period.

Running a Business from Your Property

There is nothing to stop people running low-profile businesses like writing or painting from their home, although technically this is illegal without a work permit.

Selling On

For the past 27 years house prices in the Republic have moved strongly upwards; typically a three-bedroomed villa with a pool which had cost C£85,000/£96,500/$172,700 in 2001 would have cost C£150,000/£170,000/$304,750 by 2003, and it's a similar picture in the north. This might suggest that buying property as an investment to sell on later would be a good bet. However, so far it is not clear how much of a resale market will develop. For the time being there is still plenty of land available for development which means that it is usually cheaper for someone to buy a brand-new property rather than to buy from someone else who will have added a mark-up to the sale price so they can make a profit. However, now that Southern Cyprus has joined the European Union it may be that the rules for property development may have to be tightened which would mean that the pace of building work would slow down. In that case a resale market might start to develop.

Inevitably, how easy it is to sell properties to other buyers will also depend on the outcome of peace talks.

SPOT CHECK – CYPRUS

Political/economic stability:	In 2004 Greek Cyprus voted not to unite with Turkish Cyprus to join the EU. The result is that Greek Cyprus is in the EU while the northern Turkish part is not. Between the two parts is a militarised buffer zone. Tensions could rise again, or the border could be opened to allow free movement between the two. The economy of the south is stable. The north, which is under-developed and linked to the Turkish economy has rampant inflation of more than 30%.
Sunshine/climate:	Average of 300 sunny days a year.
Cost of living/taxes:	The south is comparable to the UK and in some cases higher. The north is typically about 30% cheaper but inflation is high. Income tax rates in the south are from 15%-30%. VAT 15%. In the North VAT is 3% - 30%.
Accessibility:	Lots of charter flights to the two international airports in the south but difficult to purchase flight only. Low cost airlines may start flying there now that Cyprus is in the EU. No direct flights to the north. Flights go via Istanbul in Turkey adding hours to the journey. This embargo on direct flights may change.
Property availability:	Predominantly new build detached properties. In the north new and older property is available. Old properties are not secure as pre-1974 Greek Cypriots may still have a valid legal claim to their former real estate there.
Property prices:	Typically, a new three-bedroom villa with a swimming pool costs about £150,000.
Costs of property purchase as a % of property price:	Stamp duty 3-8%. Legal fees £500-£2,500.
Ease of purchase/ ease of renovation:	There are estate agents in the north and south geared up to selling to foreigners. It is absolutely essential to check the title before buying as legal ownership is not assured in some areas. New build property is paid for by instalment as work progresses. Estate agents tend to work with a regular team of builders. Standards are very variable.
Annual property taxes:	None.
Investment potential:	Property prices have doubled in the most popular areas, but mostly 8-10% per annum. May accelerate in southern Cyprus following EU membership.
Letting potential:	Many properties fail to let if they are not within easy distance of airports and tourist nightlife.

BUYING A HOUSE ON THE MEDITERRANEAN

FRANCE

LIVING IN FRANCE

CHAPTER SUMMARY

- France is for many a promised land, the home of culture and civilisation.
- **Buying property.** There are no restrictions on owning property for EU citizens. Most non-EU citizens are also allowed to buy without restriction.
- **Tourism.** France is the world's number one tourist destination, but slightly less popular than Spain with the British.
- **Getting there.** It has never been easier or cheaper to get to France from the UK. It is safe to assume that budget airlines will continue to fly to most of their current destinations in France.
- **Health service.** France has the world's most efficient health service, financed by a system of sickness funds and private healthcare plans.
- **Public transport.** France has a superb railway system, and is developing more of its famed TGV or high-speed train lines.
- **Housing.** More and more French own their properties, with prices still quite reasonable by British standards, although rising fast in the south of France.
- **Media.** French TV is well behind the UK in quality, nor are the French great newspaper readers.
- **Language.** The key to settling down in France is knowing French.
  - Catalan may be useful in Pyrénées Orientales.

INTRODUCTION

For many years the rest of the world has believed that life is better in France than in other countries. The German poet Schiller coined the phrase 'to live like God in France' 200 years ago. France means hedonism, uninhibited people, a great climate, superb food and wines, and culture on every street corner. There are also objective reasons for believing that life is better in France; UNESCO's quality of life index puts France in second place after Canada, another country with a strong French influence, and this is to a large extent on France's healthcare and social security system, as well as the general *art de vivre*.

Northern Europeans generally cite France's climate as its main attraction, something one cannot dispute, at least as far as the south coast is concerned. The present prosperity of France's Mediterranean coast owes everything to its dry and sunny climate and in the case of the Riviera it has been largely made fashionable by wealthy foreigners moving here starting from the 19th century. The low price of property and the excellent public services are further attractions. On the other hand, while the towns of the South of France rate as the best places to live in France, they also have the highest rates of crime in the country.

HISTORY & POLITICS

The modern-day French have come from all over the place and are even more of a mixed bunch than the British. The first distinct group of immigrants that one can distinguish are the Celts, who came from much further east starting from 1000 BC. The ancient Greeks colonised the Mediterranean coast starting from 800 BC; some place names, such as Nice and Antibes (or Antipolis) are originally Greek. The Greeks came to trade, but when their power declined the Romans arrived with ambitions to expand their territory northwards. The first Roman province, Gallia Narbonensis was set up in 121 BC, then in 52 BC, the wily Julius Caesar managed to conquer the rest of Gaul.

France's Mediterranean regions, have experienced a history of their own. Southern France was part of the Frankish kingdom from 535; in 855 a Frankish prince, Charles the Bald, founded the Kingdom of Provence, which passed through various hands until 1481 when it joined France. The English armies under Simon de Montfort laid waste to southwest France in the early part of the 13th century on behalf of the French king, with the pretext of eradicating the Cathar heretics. The Popes also controlled part of Provence during the Middle Ages and based themselves in Avignon from 1309 to 1377 after the Great Schism.

The modern département of Pyrénées-Orientales was not part of France until 1659, prior to which it had been the seat of an independent Catalan kingdom (946-1492) and then part of Spain. Nice officially became part of France in 1860, while Menton and Roquebrune were bought from Monaco in 1861.

MODERN HISTORY

The rebellious-minded south of France naturally leaned towards the Protestant side in the Wars of Religion between Protestants and Catholics. While there was a period of tolerance from 1589, once Louis XIV decided that he wanted to win favour with Rome by revoking the Edict on Nantes in 1685, the Protestants had to go abroad or reconvert to Catholicism.

The biggest event in French history, the French Revolution, had its effects on the Mediterranean coastal region. It was volunteers from Marseille who gave France its modern-day national anthem, *La Marseillaise.* The population was divided between monarchists and revolutionaries, and there were massacres in Marseille and Tarascon in 1795. The Corsican general, Napoléon Bonaparte, made his reputation by laying siege to Toulon in 1793. After a short-lived empire and exile on the island of Elba, Napoleon landed at Juan-les-Pins for a last throw of the dice at Waterloo. The South of France, which was essentially an impoverished region, benefited from the expansion of France's empire during the 1850s, with Marseille becoming the gateway to French Algeria and Tunisia. The same period also saw the start of the long-term decline of agriculture in the South, which is still going on, and severe depopulation. After the Napoleonic wars the Riviera became popular with wealthy British retirees, who found the climate conducive to their health.

The end of the 19th century also saw an increasing influx of painters and other artists to Provence and the Riviera, brought here by the dry climate, the intense sunlight and the colours of the landscape. The great era of the Impressionists gave way to the mass slaughter of the First World War, greatly speeding up the depopulation of the countryside everywhere in the south.

In May 1940 France was invaded again and half the country occupied, but the southern half was initially left under the control of a French puppet regime under Marshal Pétain. The French fleet was scuttled in Toulon harbour in 1942. Allied landings at St Tropez started a new front against the Germans and led to the rapid liberation of Provence in 1944.

France reconstructed quickly after World War II, but was still plagued with political instability. The Fourth Republic was declared in 1945, but was unable to deal with the problem of decolonisation. The humiliating defeat in Vietnam in 1954 was followed by the start of the Algerian War of Independence. Algeria had the same status as mainland France, and a large European population. When the French government appeared ready to consider independence for Algeria in 1958, the European settlers and French army in Algeria threatened to carry out a military coup in Paris. General de Gaulle was granted dictatorial powers for six months and extricated the country from its Algerian nightmare.

Algeria finally got its independence in 1962, and France had to absorb 1 million *pieds noirs*, European settlers, as well as pro-French Muslim troops, the *harkis*, with many of them moving to Marseille and other coastal cities in the south. Decolonisation resulted in a drastic change in the ethnic make-up of much of southern France. Large numbers of Greeks, Sicilians, Spanish and Italians who had been moving into the southern French cities since time immemorial, have now been joined by Arabs (mainly Algerians) and Africans from old French colonies. The cultural upheaval has been exploited by the extreme right-wing Front National; some town councils are now controlled by neo-fascists.

Administration

Régions. The regions were a new layer of government between Paris and the départements initiated in 1972. From 1982 each *région* was given an elected assembly and an executive. This is not really devolution as we would see it in the UK. The regions have powers in the area of culture, education and business. The main purpose was to reduce the power of the departments, and to restore some feeling of regional identity, which had been deliberately negated by the organisation into departments after 1789.

Départements. France is logically, and conveniently, divided into 100 *départements* or departments, four of which are overseas. The rest make up what is called *La Métropole,* or *La France Métropolitaine.* Each department has a two-digit number which is, again very logically, used for postcodes and licence plates. Until 1982 there was a prefect in charge of every département, directly appointed by the President. The prefect has been replaced by the President of the General Council. The General Council is elected for a period of six years by local councillors. The chairman is elected for three years by the General Council.

GEOGRAPHY & CLIMATE

Physical Features

France is popularly called *l'Hexagone* on account of its (roughly) six-sided shape, with the Mediterranean coast taking up one side. The coastal strip from Marseille to the Italian border is very densely populated, and lack of space is a major problem where the mountains come down to the sea, especially on the Riviera. Most of Languedoc-Roussillon and Provence-Alpes Côtes d'Azur (PACA) region is only two hours from the nearest ski fields, with two mountain ranges easily accessible by car: the Pyrenees in the west, and the French Alps, including Europe's highest mountain, Mont Blanc, to the east. From October to March it is quite possible to swim in the sea in the morning, and go skiing in the afternoon. France's other main mountain range, the Massif Central, is relatively inaccessible from the south, and not sufficiently high to offer skiing.

Provence's two main rivers are the Rhône and the Durance. The Rhône has the only river delta in France, the Camargue, a rice-growing region. Much of the south coast from the Hérault to the Italian border is subject to flash floods.

Climate

The south and southeast experience a **Mediterranean** climate, with regularly hot summer and mild winters, and unpredictable low rainfall. The south is subject to strong winds from the north and sudden storms. The mountainous regions of the Pyrenees and Alps generally have heavy snowfall in winter, and cool, sunny summers with frequent rain.

EXTREMES OF CLIMATE

During 2004, temperatures remained at 40°C and over for several weeks, leading to 1000s of deaths, and huge bushfires in Provence. Some 17 square kilometres of land was destroyed in the South of France. It would be unusual for such conditions to become the norm, but France is as subject to global warming as anywhere. Fortunately, the extreme dry temperatures did not lead to problems with subsidence in the South, as most houses are built on bedrock rather than on clay.

Home insurance premiums in southeast France are about double those in other parts of France because of the high risk of fires. Flooding is a greater hazard than fire in a number of places in the south; towns such as Avignon and Arles on the Rhône are particularly at risk. Nice also experiences flash floods. If your property is built onto a slope, make sure that the water has somewhere to run off, otherwise it could come straight into your property.

Nice and the nearby coast has France's best climate: there are few heatwaves, more moderate summers and temperate winters than further west, and hardly any days of frost. Further inland, depending on altitude, winters are colder and summers hotter. All of Provence (but not the Riviera) is affected by the notorious *mistral,* an icy cold wind that blows on 150 days of the year from the north. The worst months are January and February. The effect of the *mistral* is such that it makes the inhabitants of towns such as Arles or Aix-en-Provence more irritable than those of Nice or Cannes. The *mistral* can be used as a defence if one is accused of violent crime.

Languedoc-Roussillon's climate is less ideal than that of the Côte d'Azur, the eastern side being affected by the cold wind from the north known as the *mistral* while the west has a similar wind, the *tramontane*. Inland areas have short, cold winters lasting for about six weeks.

Corsica has a hotter climate than the Riviera. Rainfall is more than adequate. The west coast of Corsica enjoys a milder climate than the east; summer temperatures can be unpleasantly hot on the eastern side of the island. For this reason tourism is concentrated on the western side of the island.

CLIMATE IN MAIN CITIES

	Sunshine Hours	Days of Rain	Days of Frost
Aix	2,801	56	35
Ajaccio	2,726	72	12
Arles	2,801	56	20
Antibes/Nice	2,693	63	3
Bastia	2,533	68	3
Cannes	2,693	63	15
Carcassonne	2,106	92	25
Fréjus	2,710	66	25
Montpellier	2,618	60	32
Nîmes	2,588	68	24
Perpignan	2,392	56	14
Sète	2,618	60	9
Toulon	2,786	61	3

Average Temperatures and Monthly Rainfall

Carpentras	Jan	Feb	Mar	Apr	May	Jun	Jul	Aug	Sep	Oct	Nov	Dec
Max	12	14	16	20	24	28	31	31	27	22	16	13
Min	1	3	4	7	11	14	16	16	13	10	6	3
rainfall	43	40	46	63	60	43	29	47	80	96	52	43

Marseille	Jan	Feb	Mar	Apr	May	Jun	Jul	Aug	Sep	Oct	Nov	Dec
Max	11	12	14	17	21	26	29	28	25	20	14	12
Min	3	3	6	8	12	16	19	18	16	11	7	3
rainfall	48	41	46	46	46	25	15	25	64	94	76	58

Nice	Jan	Feb	Mar	Apr	May	Jun	Jul	Aug	Sep	Oct	Nov	Dec
Max	13	13	15	17	20	24	26	27	25	21	16	14
Min	5	6	7	10	13	17	19	19	17	13	9	6
rainfall	83	76	70	62	49	36	16	31	54	108	104	77

Carcassonne	Jan	Feb	Mar	Apr	May	Jun	Jul	Aug	Sep	Oct	Nov	Dec
Max	9	11	14	16	20	25	28	27	24	19	13	10
Min	3	4	5	8	11	14	16	16	14	11	6	4
rainfall	67	68	65	72	62	43	29	43	46	74	57	69

Montpellier	Jan	Feb	Mar	Apr	May	Jun	Jul	Aug	Sep	Oct	Nov	Dec
Max	11	12	15	18	21	25	28	28	25	20	15	12
Min	2	3	5	8	11	15	17	17	14	11	6	3
rainfall	72	72	55	55	52	33	20	42	62	110	63	63

Perpignan	Jan	Feb	Mar	Apr	May	Jun	Jul	Aug	Sep	Oct	Nov	Dec
Max	12	13	15	18	21	26	29	28	29	21	16	13
Min	4	5	7	9	12	16	19	18	16	12	8	5
rainfall	51	45	43	56	50	28	17	32	48	90	59	54

Ajaccio	Jan	Feb	Mar	Apr	May	Jun	Jul	Aug	Sep	Oct	Nov	Dec
Max	13	14	15	17	21	28	28	28	24	22	17	14
Min	4	4	5	7	10	16	17	17	14	11	8	5
rainfall	74	70	58	52	40	19	11	20	44	87	96	75

Bastia	Jan	Feb	Mar	Apr	May	Jun	Jul	Aug	Sep	Oct	Nov	Dec
Max	13	14	15	17	21	25	28	28	25	21	17	14
Min	5	5	6	8	12	15	18	18	16	13	9	6
rainfall	62	88	75	66	43	32	15	34	51	107	88	89

CULTURE SHOCK

France is a very varied country, but one can characterise it as having a Latin culture; which generally means a more extreme, volatile, and impulsive approach to life than one would find in northern European cultures. Typically, the French value human relations more highly than making money or achieving great success. The further south one goes the more relaxed life becomes. While France is generally a very competitive society on a social level, southerners are on the whole less formal (and one might add less confrontational) than those in the north. Northern Europeans can become frustrated with the slow pace of life in the south of France. It can take months to get an answer to e-mail letters.

The darker side of the Mediterranean is the high level of corruption and Mafia activity. The British are shocked to find that the French can characterise criminal activities as just being mischievous or fun and games.

GETTING THERE

One can reasonably choose one of three methods of getting to the Mediterranean, of which the most popular has now become flying. There is a direct high-speed train from London to Avignon once a week or you can change at Lille and go directly to a number of destinations, such as Marseille, Montpellier and Nîmes. See: www.eurostar.com or www.raileurope.co.uk from the UK.

By Car. Although you cannot actually drive through the Channel Tunnel, you can put your car onto a train, and drive off the other end. If you want to take a car through the tunnel, you need the Eurotunnel/Le Shuttle service, which starts from Cheriton, Folkestone (0870 535 3535; www.eurotunnel.com). You can buy your ticket at Folkestone. The journey is short (35 minutes) and spartan.

By Air. The real revolution in travel to France has come about with Ryanair (and other airlines) flying to small airports all over France from the UK, and also now from Ireland and Belgium. It is important to bear in mind that routes can be axed and fares can rise. Direct flights from the UK only run in summer. The quickest way to see what fares are on offer on non-budget airlines is to look on the website www.ebookers.com. Flights listed below are direct from the UK. More destinations are available by changing in Paris.

Scheduled Flights

Air France: 08453-591000; www.airfrance.co.uk. Flights to Nice.
British Airways: 08708-509850; www.ba.com. Flights to Bastia, Marseille, Montpellier, Nice and Toulon.
bmibaby: 08706-070555; www.bmibaby.co.uk. Flies to Nice.
easyJet: 08717-500100; www.easyjet.com. Flights to Marseille and Nice.
GB Airways: 08708-509850; www.gbairways.com. Flies to Montpellier and Toulon.
Jet2: 08707-378282; www.jet2.com. Flies to Nice.
Ryanair: 08712-460000; www.ryanair.com. Flights to Montpellier, Nîmes and Perpignan.
Thomsonfly: 08701-90737; www.thomsonfly.com. Flights to Marseille and Nice.

EDUCATION

There is much debate about whether France's education system is any better than anyone else's. The main emphasis is on intellectual achievement, in particular in French grammar, science and mathematics. Education is compulsory from 6 to 16. Most schools are state schools (*les écoles publiques*), but there are also private schools (*les écoles privées*), which are partly subsidised by the state or by the church. Most of them are religiously based. You should in the first instance go to the *service des écoles* at your local *mairie*, who will give you a list of the schools in your area.

Structure of Education. French children go into nursery schools as early as possible. Every child from the age of 3 is entitled to a place in a nursery school (*école maternelle*). There is also the infants' school (*jardin d'enfants*) for 2-3 year-olds (not free).

From the age of 6 all children go into the primary system – *école primaire* or *élémentaire* – which comprises grades 11 to 7. From age 11 to 15 children go into the *collège d'enseignement secondaire* (CES), the same as a British comprehensive. Depending on their aptitudes, students go on to a *lycée* or a specialised *lycée technique,* where they prepare for one of a number of possible leaving qualifications. The more academic stream will take the General or Technical Baccalaureate, which qualifies them automatically to go on to university.

For more information on the education system, ask the French Embassy to send you their leaflet *Primary and Secondary Education in France* (see www.ambafrance.org.uk or www.ambafrance.org.us) or look at the government website: www.education.gouv.fr. Most of the English-medium schools in France belong to the ELSA organisation (see below) and are listed on their website.

International Schools. For those who can afford it, an international school, or a school offering the same curriculum as in your country may be the best or only solution. Most of these schools offer the International Baccalaureate which is accepted for university entrance in many countries. Some offer a mixture of instruction in

English and French. Some have nursery sections. There are liaison organisations in the UK and US who can advise you on where to find an international school in your area. See the *International Schools* in the *General Introduction* for these.

English-Medium Schools in the South of France

CIV International School of Sophia Antipolis (Nice):   ☎04 92 96 52 24; www.civissa.org.
Mougins School: ☎04 93 90 15 47; www.mougins-school.com.

Information Sources
Centre National de Documentation sur l'Enseignement Priv : ☎01 47 05 32 68; www.fabert.com.
English Language Schools Association France (ELSA): ☎01 45 04 48 52; http: //perso.wanadoo.fr/elsa.france.

FRENCH INCOME TAX

If you become French tax resident, that is, you spend more than 183 days a year in France, then you are taxed on your worldwide income in France, and you have to fill in a French tax return. If you only own a second home in France, you will still have some taxes to pay, but you should not have to pay French income tax.

MOVING TO FRANCE

British citizens should inform the UK Inspector of Taxes at the office you usually deal with of your departure and they will send you a P85 form to complete. The UK tax office will usually require certain proof that you are leaving the UK, and hence their jurisdiction, for good. Evidence of having sold a house in the UK and having rented or bought one in France is usually sufficient. France has a double taxation agreement with the UK, which makes it possible to offset tax paid in one country against tax paid in another. For further information see the Inland Revenue publications IR20 Residents and non-residents. Liability to tax in the United Kingdom which can be found on the website www.inlandrevenue.gov.uk.

FRENCH TAXATION SYSTEM

Income tax is levied on households rather than on individuals. There are generous deductions if you are married with children, or have disabled dependants. These are applied using a complex system of parts or quotients.

The system works on the basis that you pay tax in instalments on your income for the previous year, calculated on the basis of your income in the year before that. There is, therefore, a delay before a foreign resident starting work in France for the first time pays any tax. No tax is paid in advance (except for those withheld at source on savings etc.). Salaried workers can choose to pay 10 monthly instalments from January calculated on the basis of your previous tax return – the last two months are used to adjust the total tax paid; or you pay in three instalments in February, May and September. The self-employed pay in three instalments.

It is up to you to register with your local Centre des Impôts (tax office) once you become a French resident. You are liable for tax on your worldwide income from the day you arrive in France. You must request a tax return (*déclaration fiscale*) before the end of the year if you do not receive one automatically. If your lifestyle is inconsistent with your declared income you may be investigated by the tax inspectors. If you possess a yacht, an expensive car, and so on, then these will be valued and taken into account.

Pensions. Most pensions are treated as taxable income; pension income benefits from an additional abatement of 10% on top of the usual deductions granted to payers of income tax.

If tax is or will be deducted at source in the UK from your pension, you need to contact the Inland Revenue's *Centre for Non-Residents* and ask for Form FRA2/INDIVIDUAL. Once the French tax office has stamped it and you have returned it, the Centre will instruct your pension provider not to deduct tax at source. You will then pay French tax on your pension. Contact the *Centre for Non-Residents*, St John's House, Merton Rd, Bootle, Merseyside L69 9BB; ☎00 44 151-472 6196 (from France); fax 00 44 151-472 6392; e-mail non-residents@inlandrevenue.gov.uk; www.inlandrevenue.gov.uk/cnr.

HEALTH

As acknowledged by the World Health Organisation, France has the best, or at least, the most cost-effective health care system in the world. In spite of this, there are still shortages of doctors and everyone fears that the situation is going to deteriorate in the future. France spends 9.8% of its GDP on health, as opposed to 7% in the UK, and 16% in the US. French employees pay a specific 8% of their wages for healthcare insurance, but health care is still not free. You pay as you go and reclaim most of the cost afterwards. You will be treated in case of emergencies; the bills come afterwards.

British Non-Residents

If you are just going on holiday to France, or planning to stay for less than three months, don't forget to have your E111 form stamped at the post office. The leaflet T6, available from post offices, contains both an application form for the E111 (for the post office's records), and the E111 itself, a standard form for the whole European Union. Not having the E111 can be disastrous if you fall ill in France. If you do need treatment, show the E111 to the doctor or clinic, who should be *conventionné*, i.e. part of the French state system. You will then be able to reclaim up to 75% of the costs of treatment. The E111 runs out after three months, by which time you should be paying into the French social security system. If you make several trips a year to France, you can keep the same E111. It is advisable to take out health insurance anyway for trips abroad: a stay in a French hospital can cost up to £2,000 a day in the case of major surgery.

Once you are a permanent resident in France, you are no longer entitled to use the National Health Service free of charge in the UK. In practice, the French authorities allow Brits to go on relying on the NHS and the E111 for about 18 months after their arrival. Pensioners may continue to use the NHS in the UK longer than those who are working in France; contact the Department of Work and Pensions for further details (www.dwp.gov.uk).

French Healthcare System

Paying into the social security system in France entitles you and your dependants to medical treatment, and other expenses, free of charge up to a statutory limit for each type of treatment. The contributions are collected by a departmental organisation called CPAM, which then distributes the money to different *caisses*, or sickness funds, depending on your profession. Once you pay in you will receive the all-important *Carte Vitale*, a green smart card that stores all your administrative details on a microchip. You can read the information on it by inserting it into a terminal known as a *borne vitale* at any surgery or hospital.

Social security generally pays 75-90% of the cost of treatment, and 35-70% of the cost of medicines. The full cost will be paid for serious illnesses or in specific hospital practices. Hospitals and general practices can charge as much as they want for their services, but in every area groups of doctors agree to charge fees within the limits set by social security. Doctors who follow these agreements are known as *conventionné*.

To cover the shortfall in the cost of treatment, it is advisable to have additional private health insurance. Different professions have special plans – known as *complémentaires* or *mutuelles* – or your employer may pay for this. You can use a British-based health insurer, such as BUPA or one based in France (see below). You need to verify that the insurer has an existing link with French social security and that they offer adequate cover. Once you are resident in France you have to have a social security number. Private health cover does not exempt you from paying social security contributions. The health insurers below are based in France; for other private healthcare providers see *Private Health Insurance* in the *General Introduction*.

Health Insurers
Eric Blair Network: ☎04 93 12 36 10; e-mail insurance@riviera.fr; www.ericblairnet.com.
International Health Insurance Denmark: ☎04 92 17 42 42 ; e-mail france@ihi.com; www.ihi.com.

Chemists. Pharmacists (*pharmaciens*) are highly trained and can give basic healthcare advice. As a basic principle, medicines for life-threatening conditions are free, even where the condition is chronic, which is good news for the retired. For run-of-the-mill problems the refund rate may be as low as 35%; some items will not be refunded at all. There are schemes in operation allowing you to obtain prescription medicines out of hours. There will be a hole in the wall where you can insert your *Carte Vitale*.

SHOPPING

The retail scene in France is very different from the UK. While there are supermarkets (*supermarchés*) – smaller than in the UK – and hypermarkets (*hypermarchés*), there are few shopping malls. Most French like to keep a personal relationship with their local shopkeepers. Opening hours are not ideal. Smaller shops can only open five days a week, so many opt to close on Monday and stay open on Saturday, which gives rural towns a strangely dead atmosphere on a Monday.

Relative Prices. Comparisons of retail prices in different countries are notoriously unreliable. Most Britons find that the cost of living in France is about 20-25% lower than in the UK, outside of the very expensive areas of Paris and the Côte d'Azur. Local products such as wine and olive oil are very cheap. Meat is relatively expensive but better quality than in the UK. Fruit and vegetables are generally sold ripe and are more variable in quality than the standardised produce one finds in the UK.

If you are moving over to France you will have to consider whether to bring electrical equipment with you or not. The general opinion is that French electrical goods are not that cheap and are of worse quality than British ones. It is easier now to find imported electrical equipment; you should consider whether you can find spare parts.

Furniture is best bought in France; there are amazing bargains to be found if you are willing to travel around and look in at *brocanteurs* (junk merchants). Brand-new furniture is also cheaper than in England and fits in better with your French surroundings.

MEDIA

Newspapers

The newspaper scene in France bears no comparison with that in the UK. The national newspapers have a small circulation; regional newspapers are often more popular. At the weekend you will have to make do with one paper for two days. The highbrow *Le Monde* is dry, mainly consisting of long essays on current topics of interest. *Libération* is a more colourful leftwing offering; then there is *L'Humanité* founded by Jean-Paul Sartre. The daily *Le Figaro* represents conservative opinion. Regional newspapers concentrate on local news and sport; they are very popular but of little interest to foreigners.

It is impossible to get hold of a British newspaper on the day of publication anywhere south of Paris. The US *International Herald Tribune* is available all over France on the day of publication.

There are some very good English magazines for expats in France, the best being the monthly *French News* which has useful analyses of French happenings.

English-Language Publications

The Connexion: monthly published from Antibes; www.englishyellowpages.fr.
English Yellow Pages – Book 04: Directory for southeast France with services; www.englishyellowpages.fr.
French Times: Quarterly published from Dordogne; www.french-times.com.
French News: Monthly. www.french-news.fr; essential reading.
New Riviera-Côte d'Azur. Glossy magazine published every 3 months; e-mail newriviera@smc-france.fr.
Riviera Reporter: Monthly. www.riviera-reporter.com.
Riviera Times: Monthly. www.mediterra.com.

Local Media

Corsica: *Corse Matin* (www.corse.info); *Journal de Corse* (www.jdcorse.com).
Languedoc-Roussillon: *Midi Libre* (www.midilibre.fr); *Dépêche du Midi* (www.ladepeche.com); *L'Indépendant* (www/lindependant.com).
Provence-Alpes-Côte d'Azur: *La Provence* (www.laprovence-presse.fr); *Nice Matin* (www.nicematin.fr); *Var Matin* (www.varmatin.com); *La Marseillaise* (www.lamarseillaise.tm.fr).

Television and Radio

If you come from the UK, you will quickly be struck by the poor quality of French television. The main terrestrial channel is the formerly state-owned TF1. FR2 and FR3 are still owned by the state. The fourth channel is Canal Plus, a private subscription channel. Channel 5 shows La Cinq – a state-run cultural channel – in the daytime, and the highbrow Franco-German Arte after 7 pm. Channel 6 is a light entertainment channel.

If you want to have access to the BBC and other English-language stations, then you could have cable, but satellite is a far more satisfactory option. Cable TV is only available in certain areas. The cable channel Noos offers BBC World and BBC Prime, along with CNN as part of its 'bouquet' of channels. TPS and CanalSat are satellite subscription stations which offer English-language channels.

To get the maximum number of English-language channels you need to subscribe to Sky in the UK. As long as you have a UK address, Sky will supply a decoder which may or may not continue to work in France. Depending on what you pay, you can get a range of UK terrestrial and news channels. The BBC supplies its channels free of charge to Sky in a bid to persuade subscribers to switch to digital TV. You need a parabola dish – 50cm is adequate for all of France – installed somewhere on the outside of your house.

CRIME

Taken as a whole, there is less crime in France than in the UK, but the worst areas are Paris and the south coast. There is a widespread feeling that *l'insécurité* is rising, based on the idea that crime is increasing along with immigration and asylum seekers.

Avignon is officially the crime capital of France, with 173 crimes per 1000 inhabitants in 2003. Marseille, Béziers, Antibes, Cannes, Perpignan all have very high crime rates, as do other towns in the area. Muggings are a particular problem in Nice and on trains between Marseille and Nice. Foreign-registered cars are a magnet for criminals. Avoid looking like a tourist or displaying your wealth. Crime rates are publicised by the magazine *Le Point* in its annual survey of French towns: see www.lepoint.fr.

LEARNING THE LANGUAGE

The 20th century saw French lose the race to become the international language to English. The younger generation of French are much keener to speak English than older people. There are other people who have a phobia of speaking English and will be grateful if you can speak French. It is usually best to let them speak English if they want to.

It cannot be emphasised too much how important learning French is: people who have given up and gone back to the UK often cite not speaking the language as one of the main reasons for their disenchantment. If one can learn to speak French grammatically, then so much the better.

Where to Learn French

The French state expends vast sums on trying to promote French abroad; if you are lucky, there may be an Alliance Française near you offering evening classes (they also exist in the USA). Your local College of Further Education, or Community Education Centre will certainly offer courses in French. If you are in France, it is worth asking at the local *mairie* to see if there are any low-priced courses available.

A good dictionary is a must: Collins Robert is by far the best. You can more or less dispense with printed dictionaries if you have the internet: the website www.yourdictionary.com has several excellent online dictionaries which cover all sorts of specialised topics. The best one is the Canadian www.granddictionnaire.com.

Useful Addresses

Alliance Française de Londres: French Courses, 6 Porter St, London W1U 6DD; ☎020-7224 1865; www.alliancefrancaise.org.uk.
The French Institute: Studies in France, 17 Queensberry Place, London SW7 2DT; 020-7073 1350; www.institut.ambafrance.org.uk.

SUMMARY OF HOUSING

Until recently it would have been true to say that the French were less concerned about spending money on their homes than the northern Europeans. This is no longer true, and the French spend a greater percentage of their household income on housing than the British. There has been a strong shift from renting to owning in recent year. Some 62% of dwellings are owner-occupied. The state promotes house building with all kinds of subsidised loans and incentives to buy-to-let, but coupled with strict rental controls.

On the face of it, France has plentiful housing, and builds nearly twice as many new housing units than the UK per annum, simply because there is a vast amount of space to build on. There are 2 million empty or abandoned housing units: some 6.9% of the housing stock. The high costs associated with buying and selling property discourage people from moving too often. When the TGV is extended, there are big rises in property prices (Avignon is a case in point). Provence and the Riviera have been experiencing a boom lately, with some places showing a 25% rise. The Hérault and Corsica are also booming. Migration of the population and the trend for more people to live alone will support house prices in the South, even with plentiful new construction.

PUBLIC HOLIDAYS

France does not have an inordinate number of public holidays; they all commemorate something, rather than being just bank holidays.

PUBLIC HOLIDAYS	
1 January	Year's Day
Easter Monday (*Pâques*)	UK
1 May	Labour Day (*Fête du Travail*)
8 May	Victory in Europe Day
May	Ascension Day
May/June	Whitsun (*Pentecôte*)
14 July	Bastille Day
15 August	Assumption
1 November	All Saints Day
11 November	Remembrance Day
25 December	Christmas Day

Festivals

France has a large number of festivals each year. Many of them are put on to promote tourism. See: www.francefestivals.com or www.culture.fr.

RESIDENCE AND ENTRY

CHAPTER SUMMARY

- **Residence permit.** It is no longer necessary to have a residence permit if you are from the EU and wish to remain in France for an extended period without working.
  - The first residence permit is usually issued for one year and renewable every five to ten years after that.
  - There are still certain public services, which you will be unable to access without a residence permit, so people will probably still apply for them voluntarily.
- **Financial resources.** It is still possible (and does happen) that the French authorities will deport people who have no means of financial support, whether or not they are from the EU.

While France is part of the European Union, there are still formalities to be gone through if a citizen of another EU country wants to settle down here. British citizens are entitled to live in France on the same terms as French citizens. If they want to work here then they need a *carte de séjour*, or a residence permit. The status of citizens of the new EU member states, i.e. Cyprus, Czech Republic, Estonia, Hungary, Latvia, Lithuania, Malta, Poland, Slovakia and Slovenia as regards longer-term residence is yet to be decided. Non-EU citizens require visas to enter France.

OBTAINING A RESIDENCE PERMIT

EU Nationals

Travelling to France is easy enough for British and other EU citizens. The French immigration authorities may not even look at your passport. The law passed on 26 November 2003 (no.2003-1119) states that EU citizens no longer need to apply for a residence permit (i.e. *carte de séjour*) if they wish to remain in France without working; even if you work in France you may not need a *carte de séjour* (the situation is fluid at the moment). You can apply at your local *mairie* (or *préfecture de police* in Paris) for a *carte de séjour* if you wish, which will be granted if you do not represent a threat to public order. The precise implications of this law are still not entirely clear, but it is self-evident that until you make yourself known to the authorities you can remain as a tourist for as long as you like. There still remains the fact that you may not be able to obtain certain public services without a *carte de séjour*. You will also have to inform the French authorities that you are tax-resident in the UK, which means in theory spending at least 3 months of the year in the UK; otherwise you will have to pay

French taxes. It is up to you to prove where you have spent your time.

The requirement to show that you have an income equivalent to the French minimum wage becomes relevant if you apply for a *carte de séjour;* it is still possible for the French authorities to deport EU nationals who are likely to become a public charge (i.e. those without any means of supporting themselves).

Nationals of EU countries and Switzerland have the right to settle permanently in France under certain conditions. In the case of the UK, your passport must state that you are a 'British Citizen', meaning you have the right of abode in the UK. If you have another type of British passport, contact a French consulate in your home country to find out whether you can move to France.

APPLYING FOR THE CARTE DE SÉJOUR

Once you decide that you want to remain in France for more than nine months, or start working, then you need to register with the nearest *préfecture de police* (police station), or *mairie* (town hall or municipal office). You will be given a receipt (*récépissé*) which will enable you to legally take up a profession, while you wait for the *carte de séjour* to come through.

Documents. A number of documents are required to apply for a *carte de séjour:* a valid passport, four passport photographs, a birth certificate, and a marriage certificate, if you have one. If you are a single parent with dependent children, you will need proof that your children can leave the UK. The authorities may require you to have your birth and marriage certificate officially translated and legalised, although this seems to be happening less and less. Original British documents are not necessarily considered legally valid; translations have to be legalised. If you use a translator in France, they must be sworn in, or *assermenté,* all of which adds to the cost, of course. You are best advised to find a translator through a British consulate in France. If you are in the south of France your nearest consulate is in Marseille. Documents can be legalised by a French vice-consul, i.e. stamped and signed, in the UK. In France, documents are legalised by a notaire. It is advisable to have several copies made of documents and have them all legalised, as you will need them in the future. At some point you are also likely to be asked for copies of your parents' birth certificates: these can be easily obtained from the Family Records Centre in London (☎0870-243 7788; e-mail certificate.services@ons.gov.uk; www.familyrecords.gov.uk).

Financial Resources. As well as all the above, you need proof of financial resources. If you already have work, or have been offered a job, you can use your contract of employment; you can also ask your employer to make out a *certificat d'emploi* on headed paper, confirming your passport number, the date you started work, and your salary. If you plan to be self-employed, you will need some proof that you are a member of a professional body and that you have registered with a French Chamber of Commerce. Should you intend to stay in France without working, you need bank statements, again witnessed by a notaire. If your income is less than the French minimum wage or SMIC – about £8,700 a year – you may be refused a *carte de séjour.* The authorities seem to accept that two people can live together on this amount. If you show that you have a certain amount of capital (how much is not precisely clear) then this rule is waived.

Proof of Residence. If you have bought a property, your notary can supply a *certificat* giving proof of residence. If you rent, then rent receipts will be adequate proof. If you are staying with friends, and not paying rent, then your friend will need to supply an *attestation d'hébergement* and proof of their identity. Further proof of residence includes phone or electricity bills (from EDF/GDF) with your name and address.

DOCUMENTS REQUIRED FOR THE CARTE DE SÉJOUR

- ○ Passport, with copies of the main pages, stamped as *copie certifiée conforme* by the *préfecture* or *town hall*.
- ○ Four passport photographs of each member of your family.
- ○ Birth certificate, with an official translation if requested, notarised by a French Consulate or French lawyer.
- ○ Marriage certificate/divorce papers/custody papers (officially translated and notarised only if requested).
- ○ Certificate from the town hall stating that you are living in *concubinage notoire* if you live with a common-law partner.
- ○ Proof of residence: *certificat* from the notary who handled your house purchase, or rent receipts, or *attestation d'hébergement* from the person you are staying with.
- ○ Proof of entry. Your travel ticket may be sufficient; or ask the immigration police when you enter the country.
- ○ Proof of employment.
- ○ Proof of financial resources.
- ○ You may be asked for proof that you have no criminal record.
- ○ Medical certificate (for non-EU citizens).

Renewing your residence permit. The first *carte de séjour* is for one year. You need to apply for a renewal before it runs out. EU citizens will usually receive a 10-year residence permit as long as they are in regular employment in France. You will have to prove that you have paid all your taxes. The permit is then renewed again for five or 10 years at a time. The same documents as above are required, except that you will not need to produce your children's or parents' birth certificates.

VISAS FOR NON-EU NATIONALS

Non-EU citizens require a Schengen visa to enter France: normally this allows you to stay for 90 days (*visa de court séjour*). Citizens from some countries – in particular, the USA, Canada, Australia and New Zealand are automatically allowed to stay for 90 days in the Schengen area (which includes France). If you come from one of these countries and you want to stay more than 90 days, you will need to apply for a *visa de long séjour* well before you leave. The application form for the *visa de long séjour* can be found at: www.service-public.fr/formulaires/index.htm. The requirements are similar to those for the *carte de séjour*, but you will also need a certificate of good conduct from the state police, health insurance and proof of financial resources. Family connections with France, or a statement from a French citizen promising to support you financially, will also help.

Useful Addresses
French Embassy in London: 58 Knightsbridge, London SW1X 7JT; ☎020-7201 1000; www.ambafrance-uk.org.

Visa enquiries should be sent to the French Consulate:

French Consulate: Service des Visas (Long Stay Visas), 6A Cromwell Place, PO Box 57, London SW7 2EW; ☎020-7838 2048. Open 9-10am for long-stay visa applications only. Closed on UK bank holidays and French public holidays.

French Consulate General: General Inquiries, 21 Cromwell Rd, London SW7 2EN; ☎020-7838 2000; fax 020-7838 2118; www.ambafrance-uk.org. Open 9am to midday Monday to Friday; also 1.30-3.30pm Tuesday to Thursday.

French Consulate at Edinburgh & Glasgow: 11 Randolph Crescent, Edinburgh, EH3 7TT; ☎0131-225 7954. Open daily 9.30-11.30am for visas.

French Embassy & Consulate General: 4101 Reservoir Rd NW, Washington DC 20007; ☎202-944-6195; www.ambafrance-us.org; www.consulfrance-washington.org.

British Embassy and Consulates in France. Documents are issued from Paris. Consulates-General can issue forms, which you then send to the British Embassy in Paris.

British Embassy: 35 rue du Faubourg St Honoré, 75008 Paris Cedex 08; ☎01 44 51 31 00; fax 01 44 51 32 34; www.amb-grandebretagne.fr.

British Consulate: 24 ave du Prado, 13006 Marseille; ☎04 91 15 72 10; fax 04 91 37 47 06; e-mail MarseilleConsular.marseille@fco.gov.uk.

US Embassy

United States Embassy: 2 ave Gabriel, 75008 Paris; ☎01 43 12 22 22; fax 01 42 66 97 83; www.amb-usa.fr.

M.S.

WHERE TO FIND YOUR IDEAL HOME

CHAPTER SUMMARY

○ 450,000 properties are owned by British citizens in France.

○ The average price of a property in PACA now exceeds £100,000 or €150,000; the further inland you go the cheaper the properties. Languedoc-Roussillon remains relatively cheap.

○ **Most expensive: Antibes, Nice, Cannes.** Small apartments are still affordable, but anything grander is beyond most people's purses.

○ **Hot spots.** Montpellier has seen huge price rises in some areas in recent years, driven by its popularity with young people. Parts of Antibes and Nice saw 20% rises between 2002 and 2003. The western Hérault had the largest rises in 2003: up to 30%.

○ **Beaches.** There are sandy beaches along much of the Mediterranean coast. Other areas have spectacular cliffs, plain pebbles or saltwater lagoons.

○ **Accessibility.** Direct flights to Perpignan, Carcassonne, Nîmes, Marseille and Nice from the UK make getting here a doddle.

○ **Pyrenées Orientales** has been neglected by foreign buyers, even though it has both good beaches and skiing.

○ **Béziers** will soon have direct cheap flights from the UK. High crime is a disincentive to buying in the town itself.

OVERVIEW

Buying property in the South of France was for a long time the prerogative of the wealthy, but in recent years any UK owner-occupier with a decent income could reasonably consider buying a second home in France. For some it is a matter of moving permanently for the better climate, or to set up a business. The South of France includes a vast range of prices and styles of property. In the early years it was the Riviera or Côte d'Azur that was the main draw, which is no longer really the case.

The forerunner of the entire phenomenon of going to the South of France for one's health was Henry Lord Brougham (1778-1868) who was on his way to Naples in 1834 when he found himself forced to spend a night in Cannes because of a cholera epidemic. He found the climate so pleasant that he returned annually and advised his friends to do the same, leading to an influx of wealthy Britons and an explosion in hotel building. The Riviera caught on, with even Queen Victoria spending her summer holidays there. A host of great artists worked around St Tropez; Picasso is identified with a number of places around the Riviera, and is buried near Mont St Victoire. Van Gogh had a more difficult time living in down-market Arles, which the French writer Stendhal described as 'a hole where you only go to see the antiquities'.

Until the reorganisation of the regions, the whole of PACA, except for the Hautes Alpes was defined as Provence. These days the Riviera has acquired a rather separate identity, taking up the département of Alpes Maritimes.

A second wave of foreign second home-owners started with Peter Mayle's *A Year in Provence* and *Toujours Provence*, idealised views of life in the Luberon (a hilly area north of Aix-en-Provence). The result was a stampede to find similar places to those described by Mayle.

There are great variations in price in PACA. Some people want to be in the fashionable spots like St Tropez and Ste Maxime. The media has built up certain places so they have become very expensive, such as St Rémy de Provence. To some extent there is a factual basis for some places being better than others, but not always. Others see the property as an investment; they assume that it will go up in price in the future. Rich people want to congregate together. While some areas have endless ribbon developments of boxy holiday apartments, others are unsuitable for large developments, and are not at all popular with the French. Areas next to saltwater lagoons, which extend west of Marseille up to and beyond Perpignan, for example, have few holiday homes because of the lack of good beaches. Proximity to the sea is a crucial factor in the price of property everywhere in France.

The vogue for second homes in Languedoc-Roussillon is quite recent. While the Gard and Hérault have always had their fans, interest in the Aude has increased hugely since 2000, and reasonable-priced properties are very hard to find now. A nice 1-bedroom house with a good view will set you back £60,000 anywhere in the Aude. Foreigners evidently find the 'Cathar country' appealing for its dramatic landscapes and sense of history. Direct flights from London to Carcassonne have completely altered views about the Aude's remoteness.

Pyrénées Orientales, or Roussillon, is still a rather neglected part of France, even with flights to Perpignan from London, although it has the cheapest properties in the South of France. This is French Catalonia, even if not many actually speak Catalan. If you are interested in skiing then there are chalets in the Pyrenees at much more reasonable prices than in the Alps. The perception that Roussillon is remote or unfashionable seems likely to keep property prices reasonable.

The clear message is to be imaginative about where to look for property and look beyond the more obvious and over-developed coastal resorts. There is a downside to living further inland, namely the colder winters, but this is less of an issue than avoiding the *mistral* or *tramontane* – the cold winds from the north. It is vital to look at holiday resorts out of season if possible; the best time to house-hunt is the winter, when you may also get a lower price. You will then have a realistic idea of what life is like in your area when the tourists are not around and the seasonal facilities are closed. You may also find the tourist resorts unbearably crowded during August, the month the French rush like lemmings to the sea.

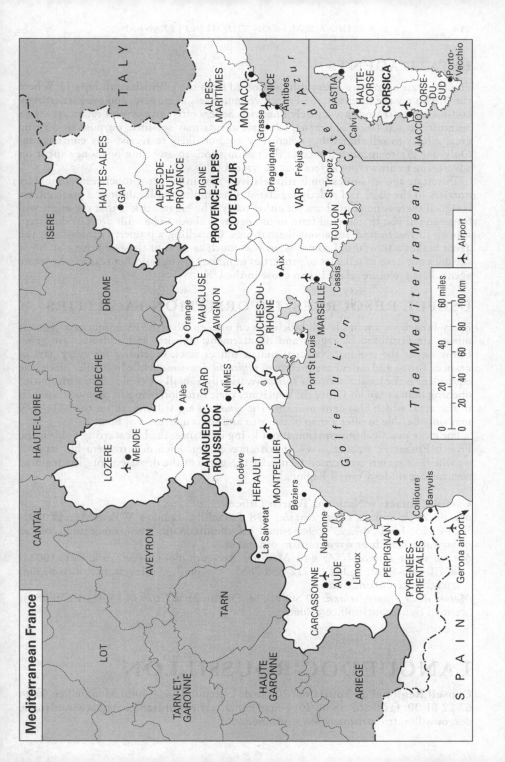

Mediterranean France

ITALY

HAUTES-ALPES

ALPES-MARITIMES

ALPES-DE-HAUTE-PROVENCE

PROVENCE-ALPES-COTE D'AZUR

● GAP

● DIGNE

MONACO
NICE
Grasse
Antibes
Draguignan
Fréjus
St Tropez

Côte d'Azur

ISERE

DROME

VAUCLUSE

● Orange

AVIGNON

VAR

TOULON

CORSICA

BASTIA

HAUTE-CORSE

Calvi

AJACCIO

CORSE-DU-SUD

Porto-Vecchio

CORSICA

HAUTE-LOIRE

ARDECHE

GARD

NIMES

BOUCHES-DU-RHONE

● Aix

Cassis

MARSEILLE

Port St Louis

Golfe Du Lion

CANTAL

LOZERE

MENDE

Alès ●

LANGUEDOC-ROUSSILLON

● Lodève

HERAULT

MONTPELLIER

La Salvetat

Béziers

The Mediterranean

AVEYRON

TARN

HAUTE GARONNE

ARIEGE

CARCASSONNE

AUDE

Limoux

Narbonne

PERPIGNAN

PYRENEES-ORIENTALES

Collioure

Banyuls

Gerona airport

LOT

TARN-ET-GARONNE

SPAIN

✈ Airport

0   20   40   60 miles
0   20   40   60   80   100 km

ESTATE AGENTS

French estate agents are a very different breed from their British counterparts. Where the British try the hard sell, the French are much less aggressive, and even irritatingly laid-back. The reasons are entirely financial. Sellers often give several estate agents an authority to sell (*mandat simple*), so estate agents may see little purpose in making great efforts to sell something when they are not likely to receive any commission. Only one estate agent will receive the commission, so any time or money spent on advertising or answering letters may be wasted.

The estate agency profession is still relatively new in France (properties were sold by notaires in the past) and strictly regulated. Gazumping is illegal; once a pre-contract is signed there is no going back for either party. The biggest risk is that the agent will forget to tell you that a wind farm or motorway is about to be built on your doorstep; it is up to you to find out about these things. On selling a property successfully, the agent makes a substantial commission – as much as 10% of the sale price – so he or she does not have to sell a lot of properties to make a living, another reason why estate agents here are more relaxed than those in the UK.

USEFUL RESOURCES/INFORMATION FACILITIES

Every French region has lavish brochures on offer to advertise its uniqueness. Tourist offices are organised by region and département; websites and addresses are given below under the regions. National tourist offices stock brochures for every part of France. Towns and cities have their own *Office du Tourisme,* while in smaller places the equivalent is the local *Syndicat d'Initiative,* usually a small welcome office with shorter opening hours than an Office du Tourisme, their function being to promote business in the area, which also eans tourism. The *syndicats* are still not all on the web; they may only be able to offer a map of the area and some addresses of hotels.

For more practical information about living in France, the best starting point is the French Embassy's website: www.ambafrance-uk.org. Each département has its own website: just search on Conseil Général + the name of the département. The regional websites are under Conseil Régional.

Useful Contacts – National Tourist Offices
Maison de la France Great Britain: 178 Piccadilly, London W1V OA1; ☎0891-244 123; fax 020-7493 6594; e-mail info@mdlf.co.uk; www.franceguide.com *or* www.tourisme.fr *or* www.tourism-office.com.
Maison de la France USA: 444 Madison Ave-16th floor, New York, NY 10022; ☎410-286-8310; fax 212-838-7855; e-mail info@francetourism.com; www.francetourism.com.
Maison de la France Ireland: 10 Suffolk St, Dublin 2; ☎1 679 0813; fax 1 679 0814; e-mail frenchtouristoffice@tinet.ie.

LANGUEDOC-ROUSSILLON

Conseil Régional de Tourisme: 20 rue de la République, 34000 Montpellier; ☎04 67 22 81 00; fax 04 67 58 06 10; e-mail contactcrtlr@sunfrance.com; www.crlangue docroussillon.fr/tourisme; www.sunfrance.com.

Population: 2,300,000; **percentage of second homes:** 30%.

The region consists of the départements: Lozère (48), Gard (30), Hérault (34), Aude (11), and Pyrénées-Orientales (66). Lozère is not considered here, as it is far from the coast. The name Languedoc derives from 'langue d'oc', that is the language – Occitan – in which the word for 'yes' is *oc,* or southern France, as opposed to 'langue d'oïl' or northern France, while Roussillon is another word for French Catalonia. While the idea of Occitan identity is very strong here, few people can speak the language, which was effectively obliterated by French with the introduction of universal education. Languedoc-Roussillon has more a stark authenticity than Provence. The atmosphere is just as Mediterranean, perhaps even more so, but without the feeling of having to keep up with the Duponts, as it were. For that reason alone the region is attracting more and more interest from foreign buyers who are turned off by the vulgarity of much of the Riviera.

Languedoc-Roussillon has traditionally been one of France's poorest regions, and at this time has the lowest per capita GDP in the country. Much of the land is only suitable for grazing goats and growing cork-oaks. The wine industry, on the other hand, has emerged from its decline to specialise in prestigious AOC wines such as Minervois and Corbières. Montpellier, the capital, is one of France's most dynamic and fastest-growing cities, but even here there is high unemployment. A great deal of investment has gone into new industries along the coastal strip, attracting jobseekers from the rest of France. The region has plenty of sunshine – anywhere up to 300 days a year – and has preserved more local traditions than most parts of France. One of these is the *transhumance,* the practice of moving herds of sheep from the Alps across to the Languedoc every year.

TYPES OF PROPERTY

Languedoc-Roussillon generally has few trees in low-lying areas, so few traditional properties are built around wooden frames; termites are also a problem. Wooden rafters are used for supporting roofs, and some wood may be used for decoration on the exterior of houses. The main building material is granite, or limestone, where it is available (e.g. Corbières). Baked brick is generally only used for internal walls.

Substantial houses are traditionally known as *mas* and some of them stand on the sites of Roman villas. The *mas* is a large farmhouse, also known as a *campanha* or *boria* in Occitan, with storehouses and cottages for the workers built on to it. These days a new *mas* is a substantial villa, usually with arched terrace and swimming pool. The wealthier wine-growers also used to build castle-like structures with stone towers. The farm-workers lived in *masets,* stone-built cottages with two storeys and a chimney; these can be substantial houses, or they can be extended. Another type of village structure is the wine-grower's house – *maison vigneronne* – typically with a large archway for wagons to pass through. Some have *celliers* or storerooms for the wine, attached.

At higher elevations, one may come across *bergeries* (rough stone shepherd cottages) that have been improved to make holiday homes. Another type of home that is advertised is the *bastide* (or *bastidon*), a bigger complex of various buildings forming a large villa.

Near the Pyrenees typical older buildings are of Pyrenean granite with one- or two-pitch roofs and arched shutters. Basic village houses in the mountains are of rough-hewn granite, sometimes with crude stepped gables, or *pignons à redents.*

The coastline has the usual uniform ochre-washed boxy holiday homes. On the whole the Languedoc uses mission tiles (*tuiles canal*). Schist slates or *lauzes* are only found at higher elevations. Additional protection from the rain is afforded by several layers of half-tiles – *génoises* – set in mortar in a cornice along the edge of the roof. Roofs can be leaky, and may need a waterproof lining. Sudden storms can blow rain horizontally into the roof space.

Languedoc-Roussillon has a distinctly extreme climate: although rainfall is adequate – around 25 inches per year – it tends to be infrequent and falls mostly in October and November. The Gard is particularly prone to flash flooding, caused by cold fronts from the Massif Central colliding with warm fronts from the south. They even talk here about 'horizontal rain', which can do serious damage. In September 2002, 27 people were killed and a large area between Nîmes and Alès was cut off from civilisation after several days of torrential downpours. Flooding is a real risk in the area and should be taken into account when buying a property. During the winter and spring a strong cold wind, the *tramontane*, comes down from the northwest, blowing away the clouds, but also freezing everything in its path. In summer a pleasant breeze from the south, the *garbi*, brings rain and cools the land.

PYRENEES-ORIENTALES

Main Tourist Office: Office du Tourisme et des Congrès, Palais des Congrès, Place Armand Lanoux, 66002 Perpignan; ☎04 68 66 30 30; 04 68 66 30 26; email contact-office@little-france.com; www.perpignantourisme.com.
Main Towns: *Perpignan, Banyuls-sur-Mer, Céret, Amélie-les-Bains, Collioure, Ille-sur-Têt, Prades.*
Airports: *Perpignan-Rivesaltes*; also *Gerona* in Spain.
The history of what is locally known as 'Roussillon' is inextricably linked with Catalonia and Spain. Catalan identity is still strong here, and more defined than the less substantial idea of Occitanie. Catalan is spoken by the older generation and taught in schools. Pyrénées-Orientales (www.cg66.fr), formerly known as Pyrénées d'Or, includes part of the grape-growing region of Corbières in the north, and the former Catalan county of Cerdagne in the west, around Font-Romeu. The coast from Etang de Leucate to the frontier of the Aude is known as La Côte Radieuse (the Radiant Coast), from the intense light.
Catalonia first came into its own when the Counts of Barcelona became Kings of Aragon in 1137, and then joined up with the Counts of Toulouse to form a united front against the French. The Occitans and Catalans suffered a setback when Toulouse fell to the French in 1229; the Catalan kingdom split into two in the next century, with the Kings of Majorca ruling from Perpignan over the French area. After centuries of disputes, Louis XIV finally managed to gain control over Roussillon with the Treaty of the Pyrenees in 1659, thus making the mountain range the border with Spain.
The heart of Catalonia is the Pic du Canigou (9180 ft), where a Catalan flag perpetually flutters from a wrought-iron cross; every true Catalan is expected to climb this mountain once in their lives. On the night of June 23-24, fires known as *feux de Saint-Jean* are lit and then carried to every village and town in Catalonia. This is the occasion for traditional Catalan *ferias* or festivals.

Côte Vermeille
The coast between the capital, Perpignan, and the Spanish border is known as the Côte Vermeille (Vermillion Coast). The King of Majorca, and then the Kings of Aragon had their summer residence at Collioure – the Palais Royal – which divides the town into two. Collioure was a favourite with the painters Matisse and Derain who started

off the movement known as *fauvisme* here in 1905, the brightly-coloured houses and Catalan architecture inspiring them to try what were, for the time, outrageous colour experimentations which earned them the name of *fauves* or 'wild animals'. Braque and Picasso also liked to paint here. Collioure has become a bit of a Fauvist theme park, but when the tourists are gone it is an attractive place to stay.

Nearby is Banyuls-sur-Mer, a fairly average coastal resort, with a busy promenade. If one heads inland, the views become increasingly spectacular and you find yourself in vineyard country.

Perpignan

The city of Perpignan's most impressive building is the Palace of the Kings of Majorca, a redbrick and stone construction somewhat resembling a lighthouse. In other respects, Perpignan is a typical French prefectural city; a lot of imposing 19th century architecture, but mixed in with Catalan tradition. The city is bisected by La Basse, a canal lined with lawns and trees. This is a place to sit out of doors at the many fine restaurants, and enjoy the Catalan cuisine. The rugby team isn't bad either.

Céret

Named after the cherry trees that grow round about, Céret is one of Roussillon's treasures, with medieval buildings, authentic Catalan architecture, and strong links to the art world. Chagall, Matisse, Picasso and Dali all stayed here at one time, and there is a Modern Art Museum (opened in 1993 by President Mitterand), displaying their works. Céret's main attractions are the views towards the Pyrenees (especially Mt Canigou) and to the sea.

Kim and Gill Bethell run La Châtaignerie (www.ceret.net), a luxury bed and breakfast in Céret, located 900 metres up in Roussillon or French Catalonia

I was looking to retire with my husband, and we found this place in a chestnut grove – which is why it's called La Châtaignerie – with superb views of Mont Canigou and over the plains of Roussillon to the sea from all the rooms. Subsequently two of my daughters decided to come and live here as well. The location is ideal; you can be on the Costa Brava, or go ski-ing in the Pyrenees, or go the French coast, all within an hour's drive The nearest airport is in Spain at Girona, and Perpignan is also close by.

We set up a Société Civile Immobilière to own the house. A SCI exists to buy and run property, so if we sell the house the money has to be reinvested in a similar business. It was very complicated actually going through the process of buying it and setting up the company; I had to sign my name 34 times. When we set up the company we were not aware of the potential difficulties caused by French inheritance laws. My husband was in the process of switching the business from the UK to France when he passed away, and things became very complicated. I could not have the whole property, even if the rest of the family wanted me to, so now I have 50% and I can remain here as long as I want. I strongly recommend all women coming to France to go to a lawyer and sort out the best way to own the property to avoid the kind of problems that we have had to deal with.

The first owner built the place as a hotel, and then retired. When we acquired it in 1996 we intended to run it as a bed and breakfast, because it's too small to be a hotel. We did a conversion job, and used the best local builder's co-operative with the best electrician, the best plumber, etc. I believe strongly that one should use local craftsmen, and not import them from other countries. They did a superb job.

We are only allowed to extend the house by 20% even though we have one hectare of land around it. There is a lot of semi-abandoned agricultural land around here – the name Céret means cherries – and there are vineyards as well. In the spring you have all the cherry blossom, and almonds and peaches in bloom too. While the owners of the land may have died a long time ago, it is still impossible to build on it (for the moment at least). Since we only did internal work we didn't require a permis de construire anyway.

Mont Canigou is a magical mountain and is more or less sacred to the Catalans (even if it is also the name of a kind of dog food!). The locals consider themselves Catalan, not French. We are in the middle of Catalan, French and Spanish culture. The area is very popular with northern Europeans. This is a wonderful spot, with great walking, riding, swimming, ski-ing and much else to do. You couldn't find a better place to live.

Pyrenees

The main selling point of Roussillon is the proximity of both ski fields and beaches. There are also the thermal spas such as Amélie-les-Bains, on the River Tech, where the water comes out of the ground at between 44-63ºC. The jumping-off point for ski bums is Font-Romeu. Snowfall is unpredictable so there are fewer package tourists than in the Alps, adding to the charm. At 1800 metres Font-Romeu also boasts 300 days of sunshine a year, so it's perfect all the year around. Villas are pricy in the ski station: reckon on €250,000 minimum for two bedrooms, but nowhere near the prices in the Alps.

Typical Properties for Sale

Location	Type	Description	Price
Perpignan	1-bed apartment, 64 sq.m.	1 bedroom, living room + kitchen, bathroom. 9th floor with view to Canigou and coast.	€107,000
Banyuls-sur-Mer	Recently constructed 2-storey villa	3 bedrooms, living and dining rooms; 2 garages, terrace. 500 m from sea.	€355,000
Palau del Vidre, nr Argelès	Village house.	2 floors, 100 sq.m. with 3 bedrooms,	€105,000
Font-Romeu (centre)	Chalet, 155 sq.m. + lofts	2 floors; 2 separate apartments entirely furnished. Loft conversion possible.	€375,000
Argelès-sur-Mer	Holiday home	2 bedrooms, dining/living. Fully equipped.	€65,000

Estate Agents in Pyrénées-Orientales

Action Immo Internationale: 32 ave Julien Panchot, 66000 Perpignan; ☎04 68 68 00 00; e-mail perpignan@a2i-immo.com; www.a2i-immo.com. Seven agencies.
Agence Littoral Soleil: 7 Route Nationale, 66700 Argelès Village; ☎04 68 95 72 22; fax 04 68 95 76 28; e-mail littoral.soleil@free.fr; www.fnaim.fr/als.
Cabinet Immobilier Etienne Roca: 25 bd Clémenceau, 66000 Perpignan ; tel04 68 34 44 02; fax 04 68 34 48 45; e-mail info@roca-immobilier.com; www.roca-immobilier.com.
Canigou Immobilier: Résidence Hôtel du Port, 66755 St-Cyprien-Plage; ☎04 68 21 56 56; fax 04 68 21 56 52; e-mail contact@canigou-immobilier.com; www.canigou-immobilier.com. Coastal.
France Méditerranée: 52 ave Jean Moulin, 66700 Argelès-sur-Mer; ☎04 68 81 68 81; fax 04 68 81 57 84; e-mail francis@lemel.fr.

Immobilière de la Loge: 51 Quai Vauban, 66000 Perpignan; ☎04 68 35 01 29; fax 04 68 34 81 29; www.immobilieredelaloge.com.

Immo Conseil 6 Rivesaltes: 18 bd Arago; ☎04 68 64 97 96; fax 04 68 38 02 90; e-mail conseili@wanadoo.fr.

AUDE

Main Tourist Office: CDT de l'Aude, 15 bvd Camille Pelletan, Carcassonne; ☎04 68 11 66 00; fax 04 68 11 66 01; e-mail cdt.aude.Pays.cathare@wanadoo.fr; www.audetourisme.com.

Main Towns: *Carcassonne, Narbonne, Castelnaudary, Limoux, Quillan, Lezignan-Corbières.*

Airports: *Carcassonne.*

The Aude has become immensely popular with second home-buyers, to the extent that one can hardly go anywhere without bumping into Brits, Dutch and Belgians. There is talk of the area becoming another Dordogne, and some resentment amongst the locals that house prices are being driven up by the outsiders. The word 'outsider' could also be applied to the French. One old gentleman in Carcassonne was recently heard to lament that 'things haven't been the same since the occupation', meaning the French invasions of the early 13th century rather than World War II.

Carcassonne

The Aude extends a long way inland, and has one of France's most popular tourist destinations with the prefectural town, Carcassonne, about one hour's drive from the sea. The huge citadel, with its lists where knights jousted long ago, evokes the Middle Ages better than anywhere in Europe. The restoration by Viollet-Leduc turned the castle into a fairy-tale version of the real thing, and was intentionally meant to improve on the original. Carcassonne can boast two UNESCO World Heritage Sites: the castle, and the Canal du Midi, a waterway running 240km from Toulouse to the sea at Agde in the Hérault, conceived by a wealthy nobleman, Pierre-Paul Riquet, who spent every last penny he had on financing it. The canal was built between 1667 and 1681, and involved constructing 99 locks and 130 bridges, as well as diverting water from the mountains. The canal had the desired effect of revitalising the local economy but fell into decline with the advent of the steam train. Commercial traffic is now banned, and the canal has become one of France's great tourist attractions. The plane tree-lined canal with its classical buildings is a wonder of elegance and ingenuity.

The Aude was a frontier province until the Treaty of the Pyrenees in 1659 moved the border with Spain to the Pyrenees. Many fortresses suddenly became redundant overnight and the region became a sleepy backwater mostly famed for its excellent wines, such as Limoux, Corbières and Fitou, now household names in England.

Cabardès-Montagne Noire

A southern continuation of the Cévennes reaching 1210 metres with the Pic de Nore, located to the northwest of Carcassonne, the Montagne Noire or Black Mountain lives up to its name, with small villages sunk into steep valleys, and a menacing redolence of the Albigensian Crusades. To understand the legacy of the cruelty of the English crusaders under Simon de Montfort, sent here in the early 1200s to eradicate the Cathar heresy, visit the hauntingly beautiful ruins at Lastours; four small and apparently impregnable castles perched on hilltops with cypress trees dotted around them. Another extraordinary attraction is the huge caves at Cabrespine. Attractive village properties are available from around €120,000, but you may not have much (or any) garden at this price.

Minervois

A more undulating region, just north of Carcassonne, rich with vineyards, and a great wealth of ancient chapels, Romanesque abbeys, prehistoric remains and menhirs. There are Neolithic remains going back 200,000 years. The landscape is broken up by limestone outcrops, but is somewhat lusher landscape than the stark Montagne Noire. Prices, are naturally, rather steeper, and good properties scarce. This has become a prosperous area since the Minervois became highly sought-after *appellation contrôlée* wine-producing country in the 1980s. The Minervois extends east over into the Hérault; the town of Minerve – after which it is named – is in the Hérault.

Corbières

Another name evoking full-blooded red wines. The region extends south of the River Aude into the Pyrénées-Orientales, and westwards to where it meets the Limouxin (the home of one of France's finest sparkling wines, Blanquette de Limoux). The landscape becomes progressively wilder as you go inland, culminating with the remarkable ruined Cathar castles of Quéribus and Peyrepertuse, the former was the last stronghold of the Cathars to fall in 1255. Corbières not only has castles on impregnable mountain peaks, but also some fine churches and Benedictine abbeys. The unofficial capital, Lézignan, has an excellent wine museum celebrating the region's famous export. This is classic tourist country, with camping sites and *gîtes* in abundance. Property prices are more moderate than in the Riviera, but more than you would expect to pay further south.

Narbonnais/Littoral

Narbonne tends to be overlooked in the rush to get to Carcassonne, yet it has southern France's finest Gothic cathedral in the Cathédrale St-Just. Narbonne became the most important city in southern Gaul under the Romans but declined when the River Aude changed its course. The city is connected to the Canal du Midi by a branch canal, La Robine. Enthusiasts for Romanesque architecture will find fulfilment with the 12th century Abbaye de Fontfroide. The coastal area has a string of typically Mediterranean beach resorts: Narbonne-Plage, Leucate-Plage and the more staid Gruissan with its unusual beach huts on stilts. Holiday homes are reasonably priced, if one feels like sharing one's space with the summer hordes.

Typical Properties for Sale in the Aude

Location	Type	Description	Price
Port-Leucate	Bungalow	Recent T3 (2 bedrooms, living), holiday home, with land to build a garage.	€116,000
Vinassan	Modern villa	120 sq.m., 3 bedrooms, 300 sq.m. garden.	€181,000
Bizanet (Corbières)	*Maison de maître*	6 bedroom mansion, on 1500 sq.m.	€350,000
Peyriac-de-Mer	Villa	156 sq.m. villa on 1000 sq.m. enclosed land, near sea.	€290,000

nr Narbonne	*Chambre d'hôtes*	900 sq.m. on 4000 sq.m. land; 15 rooms + separate apartment.	€835,000
Minervois	Village house	5 bedrooms, 2 bathrooms, 2 kitchens, for *chambre d'hôtes*.	€200,000
Cabardès	Village house	4 bedrooms, view to Pyrenees.	€110,000

Estate Agents in the Aude
Agence Hamilton: 30 rue Armagnac. 11000 Carcassonnne; ☎04 68 72 48 38; fax 04 68 72 62 26; e-mail info@agence-hamilton.com; www.agence-hamilton.com.
Appy Immobilier: 14 rue de Verdun, 11000 Carcassonne; ☎04 68 25 19 76; fax 04 68 72 00 52; e-mail appy.immobilier@wanadoo.fr; www.appy-immobilier.com.
Guy Hoquet: 78 rue Albert Tomey, 11000 Carcassonne; ☎04 68 10 39 40; e-mail carcassonne@guy-hoquet com; www.guy-hoquet.com.
Europ Immobilier: 7 rue du Pont Vieux, 11000 Carcassonne; ☎04 68 25 02 02; e-mail campredon.immobilier@wanadoo.fr; www.europimmo.biz.
Henri Michaud: 32 bd Gambetta, 11000 Narbonne; ☎04 68 32 06 77; fax 04 68 32 09 21; e-mail hm@immobilier-narbonne.com; www.immobilier-narbonne.com.
Méditerranée Immobilier: Résidence Le Saint-Cloud, 17 quai victor Hugo, 11103 Narbonne; ☎04 68 90 10 10; fax 04 68 90 10 19; e-mail info@mediterranee-immobilier.com; www.mediterranee-immobilier.com. Coast.
SARL C.G. Immobilier: 58 bd du Général de Gaulle, 11105 Narbonne; ☎04 68 65 16 00; fax 04 68 65 89 19; e-mail maison-immo@wanadoo.fr. Eastern Aude.

HERAULT

Main Tourist Office: Office de Tourise de Montpellier, 30 allée Jean de Lattre de Tassigny, 34000 Montpellier; ☎04 67 60 60 60; e-mail contact@ot-montpellier.fr; www.ot-montpellier.fr; www.herault-tourisme.com; www.cdt-herault.fr.
Main Towns: *Montpellier, Béziers, Sète, Lodève, Agde, Pézenas, St Martin-de-Londres.*
Airports: *Montpellier, Béziers.*
Northeast of the Aude is the département of the Hérault (34), mostly arid vineyard and olive country at lower elevations, and deserted hills higher up. The prefectural town of Montpellier is one of France's most dynamic cities, and has become the main centre for medical research. This is also Languedoc-Roussillon's main city and focus of investment in new industries. Montpellier attracts young people, and particularly young immigrants, looking to get away from the intolerant politics of Provence. If you are looking for a lively city that never sleeps, then Montpellier could be for you; most foreigners come here to work, however, and property prices are rising at 20% per year in the better areas.

The country surrounding Montpellier is known as *garrigue,* a landscape of limestone outcrops almost devoid of trees, originally forest degraded by overgrazing and bushfires in prehistoric times. Western parts of the Hérault are greener, and ideal vine-growing country because of the short, sharp winters, and long days of sunshine. Indeed the Hérault is France's largest wine-producing region. The coastline of the Hérault, the Côte d'Améthyste, is arid. Most foreign buyers will be looking at the western end of the Hérault, away from grossly overdeveloped holiday resorts such as Cap d'Agde and La Grande Motte.

A survey conducted in 2003 found that the western Hérault is the area the French would most likely to live in, on the basis that it is unspoilt and authentic. The result has been a huge rise in property prices: up to 30% in 2003, which is rapidly pricing many buyers out of the coastal areas. This could be a good area to invest if you can buy soon enough.

Béziers and the Biterrois

Béziers is attracting more and more interest from foreign buyers; it is quite likely that there will be cut-price flights from Stansted to Béziers from 2004, something that could boost property prices. Béziers is in any case not that cheap, and many second-home buyers may have to go further inland to find something affordable. Properties on the coast are pricey, with villas costing as much as 1 million euros (£670,000). Decent apartments in Béziers start from around €125,000 (£83,000). One could also consider Capestang, an attractive village lying on the Canal du Midi.

The attraction of Béziers is clear: superb architecture and genuine Mediterranean tradition. Béziers was here before the Romans came; it suffered severely in the Albigensian crusade, but revived with the coming of the Canal du Midi in the 1660s. The economy of the surrounding area – the Biterrois – is based on wine and fishing. Béziers is also one of France's bull-fighting centres. Tourism has made the city prosperous again, but there is also a darker side, as Béziers has one of France's highest crime rates. The widespread use of CCTV cameras is having a positive effect on the problem.

Haut-Languedoc

North of Béziers, bordering on the Minervois and Montagne Noire, lies the Parc Naturel Régional du Haut-Languedoc, a national park on the southern flanks of the Massif Central, which could be called mountainous (the local term for the peaks is *caroux*). This is a wild and thinly populated region, good for climbing, canoeing, hiking and horse-riding, where you might bump into a *mouflon* (wild mountain sheep). The main towns are Olonzac on the border with Aude, St Pons in the centre, La Salvetat on the border with the Tarn, and Bédarieux in the east. This is a region of chestnut, beech and pine forests, and lush pastures in the west where it joins up with the cattle-farming country of the Tarn.

Sète

For those who wish to get away from the overdeveloped eastern coast of the Hérault, and the very expensive western end, the downmarket town of Sète should be of interest. This is a genuine unspoiled fishing port (sardines), with the vast Bassin de Thau behind it, where oysters and clams are bred in abundance. Sète also happens to be the hometown of two giants of French literature and *chanson*: Paul Valéry and Georges Brassens. A small fisherman's cottage can be as little as €90,000 (£60,000). Beware flooding risks.

There are superb villas up on the surrounding cliffs, with a steep price tag to match. Inland from the Bassin de Thau you come to a flat agricultural plain, not especially interesting for property-buyers, although the 18th century town of Pézenas has been used as a film set for many French films. Molière lived here for many years.

Côte d'Améthyste

The Hérault local government boasts that the coastline here has been carefully preserved; one might take issue with them after seeing some of the resorts. Cap d'Agde is an egregious example of a pretty resort that has been grossly overdeveloped, with miles of tacky restaurants and nightclubs that close down out of season. Cap d'Agde also boasts one of Europe's largest nudist holiday camps; leave your kit at the entrance.

Parts of the coast are – thankfully – not so heavily built up, i.e. along the Bassin de Thau, which is not suitable for building. The resort of La Grande Motte at the eastern end is a modernist fantasy, with huge apartment blocks in all kinds of geometrical shapes. The French love it, but it will not hold much appeal to foreign second-home buyers.

Typical Properties for Sale

Location	Type	Description	Price
Olonzac	Modern bungalow	130 sq.m. built on 938 sq.m. land; 3 bedrooms, garage, terrace.	€220,000
Capestang	Traditional village house	200 sq.m. habitable space, 4 bedrooms, with 100 sq.m. courtyard.	€250,000
St Pons	19th century mansion at 700 metres altitude in national park	260 sq.m. built on 3.8 hectares of forest and fields; 6 bedrooms; granite/schist construction.	€395,000
Sète	Fisherman's cottage	1-bed cottage in town, 45 sq.m. no garden.	€90,000
Béziers	Apartment	2nd floor apartment with 3 bedrooms, balcony, lift, double-glazed, garage.	€125,000
Montpellier	Modern apartment	72 sq.m., 2 bedrooms, with central heating.	€138,000

Estate Agents in Hérault

Acanthe Immobilier: 29 ave Jean Jaurès, 34170 Castelnau le Lez; ☎04 67 79 26 26; fax 04 67 79 36 40; www.openmedia.fr/acantheimmobilier2.

Agence Le Sarrail: 312 bd Lafayette, 34400 Lunel; ☎04 67 71 94 10; fax 04 67 71 39 41; e-mail agence.le.sarrail@123immo.com; http://fr.123immo.com/agence.le.sarrail.

Caroux Immo: 58 Grand Rue, 34220 Saint-Pons; ☎04 67 97 01 89; fax 04 67 97 32 68; e-mail info@caroux-immo.com; www.caroux-immo.com. 12 agencies in Hérault.

Groupe Rambier: 3 rue Maguelone, 34000 Montpellier; ☎04 67 60 55 33; fax 04 67 52 72 88; e-mail rambier@rambier.com; www.rambier.com.

Home Office Immobilier: 453 rue Léon Blum, 34000 Montpellier; ☎04 67 15 30 28; www.home-office-immobilier.com. Seaside properties.

Patrick Harlow Agency: ave Jean Mermoz, Immeuble L'Atalante, 34000 Montpellier; ☎0825 88 68 58; e-mail contact@Patrick-harlow.com; www.patrick-harlow.com.

Sogepro: Agence Centre-Port, 34305 Cap d'Agde; ☎04 67 26 77 96; fax 04 67 26 96 47; e-mail transactions.sogepro@wanadoo.fr.

GARD

Main Tourist Office: Office de Tourisme de Nîmes, 6 Rue Auguste, 30000 Nîmes; ☎04 66 58 38 00; fax 04 66 58 38 01; e-mail office@ot-nimes.fr; www.ot-nimes.fr; www.tourismegard.com.
Main Towns: *Nîmes, Alès, Uzès, Aigues-Mortes, Lédignan, Villeneuve-les-Avignon, Bagnols-sur-Cèze.*
Airport: *Nîmes.*
The Gard – at the eastern end of Languedoc-Roussillon bordering on Provence – means Roman remains to many. The prefectural city, Nîmes, alone has two of the finest Roman monuments in France: the Maison Carré and the Amphitheatre. Add on the Roman aqueduct, the Pont du Gard, and one could say that the Gard is the most Roman of all French départments.

While it extends far to the west to the Tarn and Lozère, taking in the southern part of the Cévennes national park – the Cévennes Gardoises – the Gard has only a short coastline, the Petite Camargue, covering the western end of the Rhône delta. The small town of St Gilles, on the delta, saw the incident that led to the Albigensian Crusades against the Cathars, when the papal legate was murdered on the steps of the church in 1208.

Nîmes

Nîmes is well-known for its Roman amphitheatre, which has remained in use over the centuries, and of course the blue denim cloth named after the city. Visitors may be surprised to find out that this is also the centre of bullfighting in France, one of several cities where this goes on. Nîmes is many ways one of France's most attractive cities, with a compact city centre, university, and international airport nearby, as well as being on the TGV line to Paris and Lille. Property is reasonably priced as well.

Uzège

The Gard has always been popular with British property buyers, especially the lovely hilltop town of Uzès, northeast of Nîmes. Close by is the Pont du Gard, a well-preserved section of a Roman aqueduct and canal, 50km long, which carried water from a spring near Uzès to Nîmes, crosses the River Gardon at Vers. Enthusiasts have been reconstructing the original canal, rescuing the scattered stones from the undergrowth. Uzès was founded by Celts in the 3rd century BC and has been extensively restored. The surrounding area is arid *garrigue* (eroded limestone scrubland) once given over to olive-growing. If you are looking for tradition and authenticity, then this is a good place to start.

Bagnols-sur-Cèze

Bagnols is at the centre of the Côtes-du-Rhône *appellation* wine region in the north of the Gard, not far from the River Rhône. The region along the west bank of the Rhône calls itself the Gard Provençal – or Provence in the Gard (see www.gard-provencal.com for a detailed guide). This is where the Languedoc starts. Bagnols itself is a town where wine has been traded for centuries, with a vast marketplace. The barrels were simply labelled CDR as they were sent off to destinations around the globe.

Westwards along the valley of the Cèze are more fortified villages, many with *appellation* wines, with more and more mountainous scenery. The Cèze closely follows the border with the Ardèche, and rises in the northwest corner of the Gard in the Cévennes. This is also traditionally an area of silk-breeding. In the silk region of the Gard, a specialised stone building – a *magnanerie* – was used for breeding silk-worms. These have very large ground-floor windows, but only small openings on the first floor. The *magnanerie* would be heated and the windows sealed with paper while the silkworms were incubating on a wooden framework, and then opened up to the elements once they had emerged. Some *magnaneries* were built in wood on top of existing buildings.

Typical Properties for Sale

Location	Type	Description	Price
Nîmes	town house	2-bedroom house; 140 sq.m. with 60 sq.m. patio; central heating.	€228,000
Uzès	villa	140 sq.m. on 900 sq.m. garden; 3 bedrooms, 2 bathrooms, swimming pool. Near golf course.	€565,000
Remoulins (nr Pont du Gard	provençal house	2 bedrooms; 2 bathrooms; 1000 sq.m. garden; cellar & well.	€230,000
Villeneuve-les-Avignon	modern provençal villa	120 sq.m.on 800 sq.m. garden; 4 bedrooms, garage; 10 mins from TGV.	€290,000
Alès	*magnanerie*	90 sq.m. converted stone silkworm shed; 2 bedrooms.	€66,000
Bagnols-sur-Cèze	village house	Traditional stone house; 4 bedrooms, 2 floors; 143 sq.m. terrace.	€141,000

Estate Agents in the Gard

Actif Finance Patrimoine: 5 rue Arc Dugras, 30000 Nîmes; 04 66 04 25 17; www.fnaim.fr/afp.

Agence de la Costière: 31 rue de la République, 30600 Vauvert; ☎04 66 88 70 72; e-mail ag.costiere@wanadoo.fr; www.agencecostiere.com.

Cabinet Petrykow: 25 bd Alphonse Juin, 30240 Grau-du-Roi; ☎04 66 51 58 49; fax 04 66 51 80 69; e-mail cabinetpetrykow@aol.com; www.cabinetpetrykow.com. Camargue.

Ginoux Immobilier: 27 ave du 11 Novembre, 30260 Quissac; ☎04 66 77 30 67; e-mail infos@ginoux-immobilier.com; www.ginoux-immobilier.com.

Laffont Immobilier: 6 bd Jean Jaurès, 30900 Nîmes; ☎04 66 62 16 38; fax 04 66 62 33 49; e-mail ag496@century21france.fr; www.century21france.fr.

Toi Mon Toit: 36 ave du 11 Novembre, 30260 Quissac; ☎04 66 77 45 50; e-mail info@toimontoit.com; www.toimontoit.com.

Vaunag'Immo: 9 rue de la Cave, 30420 Calvisson; ☎04 66 01 83 04; e-mail immo.vaunag@wanadoo.fr.

PROVENCE-ALPES-COTE D'AZUR (PACA)

Comité Régional du Tourisme: 10 place de la Joliette, Atrium 10.5, BP 46214, 13567 Marseille; ☎04 91 56 47 00; fax 04 91 56 47 01; e-mail information@crt-paca.fr; ww.crt-paca.fr; www.visitprovence.com.

Population: 4,600,000; **percentage of second homes:** 26%

The Provence-Alpes-Côte d'Azur region, or PACA as it is usually called, has everything that the second home owner might want in terms of sunshine and natural beauty, with sunshine up to 3000 hours per year in some places. The intense natural colours and the promise of unfettered hedonism have long been celebrated by artists and writers. There is a sharp contrast between the highly developed coast and inland Provence, where a more authentic lifestyle goes on alongside an ever-growing community of incomers. There has been a recent trend for high-tech companies to move to the southeast, creating a sort of Silicon Valley around Valbonne, at Sophia-Antipolis. The region's capital was traditionally Aix-en-Provence, but this has been taken over by Marseille nearby. The Hautes-Alpes and Alpes-de-Haute-Provence are not considered here as they are far from the Mediterranean.

The PACA attracts large numbers of outsiders from elsewhere in France, and from abroad. It is reckoned that the population will increase by 20% by 2020, because of high birth rates and immigration. This population increase will be unevenly spread; some cities are preponderantly populated by retirees (especially Nice), and hold little attraction for the young. Growth in property prices is also uneven, and very dependent on the type of area. High crime depresses property prices in certain *quartiers* and not in others.

TYPES OF PROPERTY

Provence is an area of stone building; the only exception is in the high Alps. There are numerous limestone quarries; the yellowish tint of the limestone is one of the defining features of Provence. Before the use of cement, dry-stone construction with mortar covering was common in the countryside. In the backcountry one will see many *villages perchés:* villages built up or on top of a hillside in a defensive formation with a small castle. Houses are built facing south, if possible, sometimes without windows at the rear and sides, to combat the effects of the *mistral.* You can have sunshine almost every day of the year, but you need to be sure that the prevailing wind isn't blowing through your front window.

The *maison de maître* or wealthy farmer's house here is the *mas,* sometimes with one or more defensive towers at the corners. The asymmetrical style of architecture is actually a throwback to Roman ground plans. A smaller *mas* is a *mazet.* Houses on the plains are generally surrounded by trees; higher up they may be quite exposed to the elements. Roofing is of Spanish tiles in the countryside. An original solution to combatting the sudden storms was to fix two or more rows of half-tiles (*génoises*) into mortar along the edge of the roof. You will notice that the roofs never jut out; this is to stop a strong shadow falling over the walls, which would look unattractive.

BOUCHES-DU-RHONE

Main Tourist Office: 4 La Canebière, 13001 Marseille; ☎04 91 13 89 00; fax 04 91

13 89 20; e-mail info@Marseille-tourisme.com; www.marseille-tourisme.com.
Main Towns: *Marseille, Aix-en-Provence, Arles, Salon-de-Provence, Istres, Miramas, St-Martin-de-Crau.*
Airport: *Marseille.*
Bouches-du-Rhône (Mouths of the Rhône) is the most industrialised département in the south of France, and not much frequented by second home-buyers. Marseille is not only the capital of the PACA region, but also France's oldest city. After being founded by the Greeks in the 5th century BC the Romans took it over in 49 BC when it was called Massilia. In the Middle Ages it was under the Counts or Kings of Provence; it finally became French in 1481. In the 19th century it took on more importance as the gateway to French North Africa. In recent years it has absorbed large numbers of immigrants. A sprawling, untidy city, it is regarded as not really part of France. It is certainly cosmopolitan, and a million miles removed from the expensive resorts of the Côte d'Azur. If you include its twin city, Aix-en-Provence, Marseille is France's third city with a population of 1.4 million. Property is relatively cheap in Marseille, as more people are leaving than arriving.

Aix-en-Provence

Aix-en-Provence is one of France's most dynamic cities with a young population and three universities which bring in large numbers of American and other foreign students (about one in five of the population are students). Aix is also one of France's wealthiest cities and has a sophisticated cultural scene, with France's most prestigious arts and music festival. This is the city of Cézanne, who spent his childhood roaming the hills around about, inspiring his Cubist approach to landscape painting. Cézanne grew up on the Cours Mirabeau, Aix's most prestigious town square, which now has its most desirable properties.

Arles and the Camargue

Arles is very much the real Provence; a downhome, working-class town which just happens to have a Roman theatre and amphitheatre in the middle of it. The *mistral* blows down the River Rhône for half the year and can test the nerves of even the calmest soul. Arles is also the gateway to the Camargue, a swampy delta with wild horses and France's only rice-growing region. Much of the Camargue is a nature reserve, famed for its flamingos and cowboys; there are some very attractive old towns, such as Martigues, but not that many holiday homes.

Apart from rice and cowboys, the Camargue also represents hunting, so one might be doubly cautious to make sure that no one with a gun has a right of way across your land. If you are looking for something less frequented by tourists then one could consider the Etang de Berre and the area of Miramas (see Michael Frost below).

Michael Frost runs a luxury bed and breakfast in the Bouches du Rhône, about 15km from the Etang de Berre.
I had been working in Burgundy and was looking for somewhere with more or less good weather all the year round. I deliberately looked in January to be sure. I spent 3 months looking, full-time. I bought the place because it was in a nice location, and it has 3000 hours of sunshine a year. It is a modern building, and halfway between Aix and Arles. I wanted to be reasonably close to an airport and the TGV so my children could come and visit. If you are up some country track then people are less keen to come and visit you. One great thing about the property is that it has air-conditioning; when I bought it I didn't

care about this but now it is very useful when I'm cooking for people. I didn't plan to run a B&B; in the first place I had a lot Bosnian refugees staying here. When they left, I realised that I liked having people around, and I didn't feel that I was ready to do nothing at all, so I started on B&B. The crucial thing is that you must like having people around you; you can't view them as intruders.

The area of Provence is irrigated; a huge scheme started in 1550 to divert the River Durance. The climate is too dry here to grow anything without irrigation. It's important to think about this. You only need a pump to get the water; you pay a small annual tax to collect the water. Otherwise it comes in by gravity. Everything around here – the Crau – grows by irrigation. If you want lawns and roses then you must have it. The French generally didn't care much about gardening in the past, but now all that is changing.

Cassis and Les Calanques

About the only bit of coastline that could be called fashionable in Bouches-du-Rhône, Cassis was painted by Matisse and Derain, and Churchill is supposed to have learned how to wield a brush here. The appeal lies in the authenticity of Cassis as a fishing port, the wild and rocky coastline, and the isolated inlets or *calanques* along the coast with their sandy beaches. This is a great place for diving, fishing and hiking; to reach your *calanque* you can trek over the cliffs or take a boat. While the idle rich have tended to pass it by, Cassis still has some fairly pricy villas, and is rather overcrowded in summer. La Ciotat, down the coast, is a shipbuilding town and not a place for second homes.

Typical Properties for Sale

Location	Type	Description	Price
Marseille	villa	130sq.m. on 1000 sq.m.; 3 bedrooms, swimming pool.	€375,000
Port St Louis du Rhône	traditional Camargue house	2 bedrooms, 2 storeys, 80 sq.m. with terrace, garage.	€140,000
Arles	Provençal *mas*	300 sq.m. *mas* (villa) on 2 hectares of land, in need of renovation.	€230,000
Berre-l' Etang	villa	245 sq.m. on 951 sq.m. land with 4 bedrooms, garage, swimming pool.	€512,000
Senas	modern house	190 sq.m. on 550 sq.m. with 4 bedrooms, 2 bathrooms.	€290,000
Aix-en-Provence	apartment	3 bedroom duplex, 2 bathrooms, garage; 80 sq.m.	€390,000

Estate Agents in Bouches-du-Rhône

Acanthe Immo: 11 ave de la Libération, St-Rémy de Provence; ☎04 90 92 21 69; fax 04 90 92 21 89; e-mail acanthe.immo@wanadoo.fr; www.acanthe-immo.com.

Cabinet Florens: 1 bis rue Paul Doumer, 13100 Aix-en-Provence; ☎04 42 93 20 15; fax 04 42 93 54 99; e-mail cabinetflorens@orpi.com; www.orp-aix-en-provence.com.

Delta Alpilles: 1 bd Camille Pelletan, 13140 Miramas; ☎04 90 58 10 26; e-mail deltaalpilles@libertysurf.fr; www.deltaalpilles.com.

Grimaix: 3 cours Sextius, 13100 Aix-en-Provence; ☎04 42 26 75 79; fax 04 42 26 91 76; e-mail grimaix@wanadoo.fr.

Guy Hoquet Immobilier: 43 rue des Halls, 13150 Tarascon; ☎04 90 43 59 73; fax 04 90 91 28 72; e-mail tarascon@guyhoquet.com.

Immobilière Victoria: 128 Corniche J.F. Kennedy, 13007 Marseille; ☎04 91 31 34 34; e-mail imo@victoria@wanadoo.fr.

L'Immobilière du Littoral: 32 avenue Draïo-del-Mar, 13620 Carry-le-Rouet; ☎04 42 44 69 04; e-mail immo-du-lit@wanadoo.fr; www.immodulittoral.com.

VAUCLUSE

Main Tourist Office: 41 Cours Jean Jaurès, 84000 Avignon; ☎04 32 74 32 74; fax 04 90 82 95 03; e-mail information@ot-avignon.fr; www.ot-avignon.fr; www.avignon-tourisme.com.

Main Towns: *Avignon, Carpentras, Apte, Orange, Cavaillon, Sault.*

Airport: *Nîmes.*

The Vaucluse represents one typical image of Provence: sunflowers and lavender fields, and is rich in Roman remains. Vaucluse is not on the coast, but an integral part of Provence, and well-connected to the sea.

The prefectural city of Avignon is more touristic, surrounded by its city walls, with the well-known bridge that stops halfway across the Rhône. Avignon was also the centre of Christendom for nearly 200 years. In 1309 Pope Clement V came here at the invitation of the French king to escape unrest in Rome. The Papacy returned to Rome in 1378, but another pope was elected in Avignon, starting the Western Schism; the situation was resolved in 1403 when the last Avignon pope fled town. The city only came under French rule with the Revolution in 1789. The magnificent Palace of the Popes is one of France's great tourist draws. The tourists also draw crime, and Avignon features at the top of the French crime league.

Luberon

The Parc Régional du Luberon stretches between Cavaillon in the centre of Vaucluse to Manosque in the Alpes-de-Haute-Provence, taking in the Montagne du Luberon where the mountains reach 3500 feet. This is Peter Mayle country; in the wake of his huge bestseller, *A Year in Provence,* the area has been overrun with second home seekers, who have to some degree spoiled what made the area so attractive. There has been a lot of unplanned development, but the creation of the Parc Régional has stopped the rot. Property here is, naturally, not that cheap.

It is also worth considering that the area suffers quite badly from the *mistral* in winter, and one has to have good heating to avoid frozen pipes (as Mayle discovered).

Orange and the Rhône Valley

The city of Orange gave its name to the ruling house of the Netherlands, who by some circuitous inheritance ruled it from 1530 to 1672. It served as the last refuge for Protestants in France; in the end they were allowed to emigrate or convert. It derives its name from the Latin name Arausio, rather than from the fruit.

Orange is also one of France's great Roman cities with an amphitheatre; the theatre is in use for summer festivals. There is also a fine triumphal arch. The town has also gained a bad reputation for its extreme right-wing local government, so you may want to give it a miss if you are not an Aryan. One of the area's main draws is the Route des Vins and its *dégustations* (wine-tastings), with Châteauneuf-du-Pape the main draw. It was here that wine producers first came up with the idea for *appellation controlée* wines in 1923.

Typical Properties for Sale

Location	Type	Description	Price
Avignon	apartment	1-bedroom studio, 1st floor, town centre.	€85,000
L'Isle-sur-Sorgues	bungalow	3-bedrooms, garage, on 466 sq.m.	€195,000
Cavaillon	town house	105 sq.m., 3 bedrooms, garage.	€165,000
Fontaine de Vaucluse	18th century village house	210 sq.m., 4 bedrooms, garage, flood-free zone.	€365,000
Luberon, nr Apt	villa	4-bedrooms, 120sq.m. facing south, on 1,500 sq.m.	€275,000
Uzès	Provençal *mas*	4 bedrooms, 230 sq.m., on 2.3 hectares, swimming pool.	€880,000

Estate Agents in Vaucluse

Claude & Mylène Rey: 176 ave Charles de Gaulle, 84100 Orange; ☎04 32 81 05 46; e-mail cotesudimmo84@wanadoo.fr; www.cotesudimmo84.fr.

Immobilière du Château: Le Village, 84220 Gordes; ☎04 90 72 12 16; fax 04 90 72 08 54; e-mail IDC.LUBERON@wanadoo.fr; www.immobiliere-chateau.com.

Immobilière du Luberon: rue de la Fontaine, 84560 Ménerbes; ☎04 90 72 38 40; fax 04 90 72 46 86; e-mail immobiliere-du-luberon@wanadoo.fr; www.immoluberon-properties.com.

L'Escale Immobilière En Luberon: Route des Alpes, 84440 Robion; ☎escale.immo@wanadoo.fr; www.escale-immo.com.

Maurice Garcin: 44 bd Albin Durand, 84200 Carpentras; ☎04 90 63 93 85; e-mail carpentras@maurice-garcin.fr; www.maurice-garcin.fr. Six agencies.

MH-Immobilier: 43 rue Joseph Vernet, 84000 Avignon; ☎04 90 82 98 84; www.mh-immobilier.com.

Patrimoine Conseil: Résidence Acticentre, 84800 Isle-sur-la-Sorgue; ☎04 90 21 46 46; fax 04 90 21 46 47; e-mail patrimoineconseil.islesursorgue@wanadoo.fr; www.ladresse.com.

VAR

Main Tourist Office: Place Raimu, 83000 Toulon; ☎04 94 18 53 00; fax 04 94 18 53 09; e-mail info@toulontourisme.com; www.toulontourisme.com; www.tourismevar.com

Main Towns: *Toulon, Draguignan, Fréjus, Hyères, St-Tropez, St-Raphaël, Ste-Maxime.*

Airport: *Marseille.*

The Var, east of Marseille, is perhaps the most Provençal of all départements. The Var boasts the celebrity playground of St Tropez, and the Roman town of Fréjus, amongst other things. Sailing and beaches are two major attractions here. This is also one of the sunniest regions of the south, with over 2,500 hours of sunshine a year. This is also the most rightwing département in France (according to votes cast) and a stronghold of the neo-Fascist Front National.

Toulon, the capital and the Mediterranean's best deepwater harbour, is the French navy's biggest base, and its history is inextricably linked with the military. In 1793 a young Napoleon Bonaparte captured the city from the British and massacred the inhabitants, the start to his glorious career. In 1942 the French scuttled their fleet in the harbour entrance to stop it from falling into the hands of the Germans; the city was then heavily bombarded in 1944. Tourists tend to avoid this city, even though there are some fine museums and a good nightlife.

Côte Provençal

Less crowded and cheaper than the Riviera, the coast west of Toulon is worth a look. If you are a wine lover you will know the local wine, Bandol, a favourite of Louis XV. There is the unpretentious resort of Les Lecques, and the town of St-Cyr-sur-Mer, which boasts its own version of the Statue of Liberty.

Golfe de St Tropez and Les Maures

Few would wish to buy into 'St-Trop' as the French call it (i.e. over the top) – in summer it is unbearably crowded, and in winter quite cold, as it faces north. Les Maures is the Riviera's second highest range of mountains after L'Estérel. The coastline around here is dotted with fabulous villas costing a fortune, especially on Cap Camarat. There are tiny studios at affordable prices if you feel you must live here.

St Raphaël and L'Estérel

At the eastern end of the Var, where the Riviera's highest peak – L'Estérel – bears down on the sea, St Raphaël was at one time very fashionable with the likes of F. Scott Fitzgerald; it has now become a more sedate resort for retirees, also overcrowded in summer. Nearby is the venerable Roman city of Fréjus, with its amphitheatre and some fine museums. To the north of St Raphaël is the town of Fayence on the slopes of the Alpes Maritimes, and a centre for hang-gliding.

Central Var

The Var's second city, Draguignan and the surrounding area, Le Dracenois, is another place with a strong military presence. The atmosphere of the French colonies and the Foreign Legion is married with a pleasant market town. To the west is Cotignac, the Var's prettiest town, where half the properties are owned by the British. Further north, the Haut Var Verdon is more rugged; the town of Aups is famous for its truffle market. The valley of the River Verdon has a spectacular arid gorge, known as the French Grand Canyon – the Gorges du Verdon. Some parts of the central Var are military training grounds and out of bounds (the Camp Militaire du Canjuers).

Typical Properties for Sale

Location	Type	Description	Price
Cotignac	villa	150 sq.m., 4 bedrooms, swimming pool, jacuzzi, on 1,500 sq.m.	€430,000
Bandol	apartment	2 bedrooms, 65 sq.m.; ground floor of villa.	€230,000
Cavalaire-sur-Mer	apartment	67 sq.m., 4th floor, 2 bedrooms with central heating.	€235,000
St Raphaël	apartment	2 bedrooms, 74 sq.m.	€310,000
Tourtour (in hills north of Draguinan)	villa	200 sq.m., 3 bedrooms, on 3000 sq.m.	€1,000,000
Ste Maxime	villa	157 sq.m., 4 bedrooms, swimming pool.	€765,000

Estate Agents in the Var

Agence Centrale: 5 quai Ch. de Gaulle, 83150 Bandol; ☎04 94 29 41 17; fax 04 94 29 46 18; www.agencentrale.com.

Agence Maya: 6 rue de Verdun, 83120 Sainte-Maxime; ☎04 94 49 20 48; fax 04 94 43 82 61; e-mail info@agencemaya.com; www.agencemaya.com.

Center Immobilier Méditerranée: Centre Sirius, R.D. 562, 83440 Montauroux; ☎04 94 39 43 88; e-mail centerimmo@wanadoo.fr; www.center-immo.fr.

Foncia Baies du Soleil: Place du Hameau, La Madrague, 83270 Saint-Cyr-sur-Mer; ☎04 94 26 73 30; fax 04 94 88 71 14; e-mail courbe166@foncia.fr; www.foncia.fr.

Immovar: ZAC des Pradeaux Espace Triangle, 83270 St Cyr sur Mer; ☎04 98 03 21 40; fax 04 98 03 21 41; e-mail immovar.st-cyr@wanadoo.fr; www.immovar.fr.

Terres en Provence: 22 cours Théodore Bouge, 83690 Salernes; ☎04 98 10 23 55; e-mail Vformel@wanadoo.fr; www.terresenprovence.com.

W F King Immobilier: 74 rue Jean Aicard, 83700 St Raphaël; ☎04 94 95 13 01; fax 04 94 83 07 97; www.kingimmobilier.com.

ALPES-MARITIMES

Main Tourist Office: Ave Thiers (Gare SNCF), 06000 Nice; ☎0892 707 407; fax 04 93 21 44 50; info@nicetourisme.com; www.nice-tourisme.com.

Main Towns: *Nice, Cannes, Antibes, Grasse, Menton, St-Martin-Vésubie, Vallauris, Mougins.*

Airport: *Nice.*

Alpes-Maritimes includes the main part of the Côte d'Azur, or French Riviera, stretching from Cannes to Menton on the Italian border. The region east of the River Var belonged to the kings of Sardinia who ruled over Savoie, and was incorporated into France in 1793, but then returned to Savoie after Napoleon's defeat. It became part of France in 1860, as a gift from the Italian government to France for her support in their war against the Austrians. Roquebrune and Menton once belonged to Monaco (near the Italian border), but they revolted in 1848, and were sold to the French in 1861.

The French Riviera is naturally synonymous with high living, and as far as property prices go, the coast is in a league of its own, on a par with Paris and the most exclusive ski resorts in the Alps. Even so, it still possible to buy apartments at quite reasonable prices on the coast, and they may be a good investment as well, if you rent them out. One should also consider leaseback, a highly advantageous scheme for acquiring a property without too much initial investment or risk (see box below).

Tobias Smollett first made Nice fashionable in 1763 by bathing in the sea for the sake of his health, something that no one else had thought of before. Cannes was popularised by Lord Henry Brougham from 1838. It is now famous for its film festival and its business conferences. The main attraction of the Riviera is the all-year-round mild climate, which never gets too hot or too cold. For this reason, the Riviera became popular with wealthy convalescents, and retirees.

Overall, the coastal part of the Riviera may not be that attractive to British property buyers. The area suffers from high crime levels; the rich and famous have to employ armies of security staff to feel safe here. If you can do without the sight of the sea, an inland property has many advantages. For the price of an apartment in Antibes you could have a large house inland. Many other wealthy residents are moving away to the hills as well, so this may not guarantee you a cheap house. Prices vary depending on the status of the area.

Nice and Cap Ferrat

Whether it's 'nicer in Nice' is open to debate. While there are parts that are still very attractive, the combination of muggers, mafia and rich tourists is off-putting. A further disadvantage is the very heavy traffic in the town, which is squashed in between the sea and the mountains. This is also a city with an ageing population, with an image problem as regards attracting young people.

Nice boasts a superb micro-climate; the sea temperature never goes below 13°C and reaches 25°C in August. There is hardly ever any frost here, while at the same time there are no prolonged heatwaves either.

St-Jean-Cap-Ferrat is now the most prestigious address in France; most of us would only go there to stare at the rich and famous and their yachts.

Antibes and Juan-les-Pins

Antibes has a more balanced population and is not just a tourist resort. There is a lot of new building going on. Certainly preferable to much of the Riviera, Juan-les-Pins is a more racy resort, with a world-famous jazz festival in July. It was first developed in the 1920s on the basis that it had the best sandy beach on the Riviera. Many beaches are privately owned.

Between Antibes and Valbonne there is Sophia-Antipolis, the French *vallée silicone* with 15,000 high-tech workers. This is also the location of the Nice-Antipolis University. A happening place for the young with good work prospects.

BUYING IN ANTIBES

After some years of living in rented flats, Eric Smythe bought an apartment in 2004 in Antibes, on the top floor of a *copropriété*

We found a one-bedroom flat on the market for €140,000 (Antibes is a very expensive place), and we made an offer of €125,000. The owner agreed to sell at this price as long as we made our offer (offre d'achat) *in writing on the spot. We already knew that we could raise a mortgage of €125,000, but we were surprised to find that we were not required to put down a deposit. It is becoming quite common here to receive a 100% mortgage. Property is becoming so expensive that many people can't put down a deposit. The estate agent's commission was paid by the vendor, but we still had to find around 10% in notary fees.*

Because we had been living in France for some years and were permanent residents, we could get a 100% mortgage. Non-residents cannot get that much. We signed the compromis de vente *(pre-contract) in the presence of the estate agent, i.e.* sous seing privé *(by private agreement). The* acte final *had to be signed in front of a* notaire. *The estate agent printed off a ready-made contract from his computer. Included in the pre-contract were two* conditions suspensives *(get-out clauses): firstly, the sale was dependent on our obtaining the loan offer (we were given 45 days), and secondly, on our having guaranteed good title. As soon as the offer of the loan came through the notaire did the land search at the* bureau des hypothèques *to ensure there were no problems with the title.*

We were not asked for a translation of our birth certificates; they are quite used to foreign buyers around here. We did have to pay for an official translator at the actual signing, however. The estate agent suggested using a notaire that he worked with. To start with we said we preferred to look for one ourselves, but in the end we used the one he wanted us to use.

> There is a lot of paperwork involved, of course, in buying a property, but you can deal with some of it yourself if you know French. We approached a British mortgage broker locally but this turned out to be a mistake, because it held things up. We could easily have found the loan ourselves. Our bank manager offered us one immediately; we were good customers and had never gone in the red, but we had to go through the mortgage broker.

Grasse

On the western end of Alpes-Maritimes, Grasse rightfully claims to be the perfume capital of the world; it is the setting for Patrick Süsskind's bestseller *Perfume*. The town started out with tanning leather, which led on to perfume manufacturing from the 17th century. These days most of the flowers are grown elsewhere, and the workers are North African. The town gets its name from the word *grâce* – the state the Jews found themselves in because they were allowed to live here.

In between Grasse and Nice are some high-class villages such as La-Colle-sur-Loup and St-Paul-de-Vence (where Chagall used to live), with prices to match.

Mercantour and the Ski Fields

The Parc National du Mercantour runs along the Italian border into the next département, the Alpes-de-Haute-Provence, with isolated ski stations such as St-Martin-Vésubie (907m) and Isola Village (870m) and other towns in the Tinée valley which are also attractive medieval villages. The Mercantour consists of seven valleys, with small numbers of wolves and lynx roaming wild. The area comes into its own between October and March, when you can swim in the morning at the coast and ski in the afternoon. Some small apartments are available in ski stations at reasonable prices; but there are few chalets on offer. Note that roads are blocked by snow for some of the winter.

Typical Properties for Sale

Place	Type	Description	Price
Nice	apartment	5th floor; 2 bedrooms; sea view; 60 sq.m.	€90,000
Antibes/Juan-les-Pins	apartment	2 rooms, 45 sq.m., close to beach.	€125,000
Grasse	apartment	1 bedroom, 51 sq.m., 3rd floor.	€107,000
La-Colle-sur-Loup	villa	300 sq.m. on 4000 sq.m., 7 bedrooms, swimming pool.	€686,000
St-Martin-de-Vésubie	apartment	37 sq.m., 2 rooms, on 1st floor.	€80,000
Puget-Théniers	apartment	80 sq.m., 2 rooms, 2nd floor.	€75,000

Estate Agents in Alpes-Maritimes

Agence Funel: 9 rue Guebhard, 06460 Saint-Vallier-de-Thiey; ☎04 93 42 60 61; fax 04 93 09 60 77; e-mail funnel.agence@libertysurf.fr.

Agence Internationale de Commercialisation Immobilière: Le Gray d'Albion, 32 rue des Serbes, 06413 Cannes; ☎04 93 39 20 60; fax 04 93 39 20 04; e-mail cannes@aici.fr; www.aici.fr.

Cabinet Morère: 4 ave du 24 Août, 06600 Antibes; ☎04 93 34 12 80; fax 04 93 34 07 57; e-mail agence@cabinet-morere.com; www.cabinet-morere.com.
Capital Immobilier: La Palombière, 71 ave de Tournamy, RN 85, 06250 Mougins; ☎04 93 75 30 64; fax 04 92 92 88 17; e-mail capitalimmobilier@ wanadoo.fr; www.keops.fr.
Center Immobilier Méditerranée: 217 rue Laurent Gandolphe, 06210 Mandelieu; ☎04 92 97 47 47; fax 04 92 97 47 48; e-mail centerimmobilier@wanadoo.fr; www.center-immo.fr.
Investimmo 06: 53 ave de Boutiny, 06530 Peymeinade; ☎04 93 66 51 81; fax 04 93 09 35 71; e-mail investimmo06@wanadoo.fr; www.investimmo06.com.
L'Immo 2000: 113 bd Wilson, 06160 Juan-les-Pins; ☎04 93 67 26 26; fax 04 93 61 50 15; e-mail cesare@club-internet.fr; www.immo2000.com.

CORSICA

Regional Tourist Office: 17 blvd du Roi-Jérôme, 20181 Ajaccio; ☎04 95 51 00 00; fax 04 95 51 14 40; www.visit-corsica.com.
Population: 261,500.

The island of Corsica consists of two départements: Haute-Corse and Corse-du-Sud, although the division is rather arbitrary and the locals would like the island to become one département. Corsica is a region in its own right with a Regional Assembly. There is a strong Italian influence on the language and culture here (Corsican is a dialect of Tuscan), which makes it rather odd that the island has ended up as part of France. The locals have always had a strong antipathy towards foreign rulers, although most now accept that they are going to remain part of France. In reality, Corsica has never been independent since the time of the Romans.

The French bought the island from the Genoese in 1768. The Corsicans staged a mass revolt but were defeated in 1769. Samuel Johnson's biographer, James Boswell, tried to rally support for the Corsicans by publishing his *Account of the Island of Corsica* in 1768, but to no avail. Napoleon Bonaparte, who was born in Ajaccio in 1769, made the island a lot more noticed.

Corsica is a mere 180km long and a maximum of 80km wide, is sparsely populated and very mountainous, with deep gullies and tree-covered slopes. The *laricio* pine that grows here is prized for ship's masts. The interior is covered with *maquis* (a mix of wild flowers, herbs and dense scrub). Viewed from the sea the island looks like a mountain; it is surprisingly green considering its location. The 600-mile long coastline has Europe's finest beaches, which bring in the tourist hordes to the western coast in July and August. The east coast can be uncomfortably hot in summer.

Tourism started to take off in Corsica in 1957, when the Club Méditerranée set up its first *paillottes* or straw parasols at the extreme south of the island. Improved ferries helped to stimulate industrial development, but Corsica still remains a relatively poor region. There were grandiose plans to build tens of thousands of holiday homes, which had to be shelved in the face of any outcry from nationalists and nature lovers. The insensitivity of the French government fuelled support for an independence movement, the FLNC (Front pour la Libération National de la Corse). The worst violence was in the 1980s and 1990s. In the past, the FLNC dynamited foreign-owned villas, while lately it has been more interested in shooting up government buildings. France goes to great lengths to keep the Corsicans satisfied, by pumping in huge subsidies; the island also gets some €1 billion a year from the EU.

Corsica has exceptional natural scenery. The centre of the island is a national park, with the highest peak, Monte Cinto, reaching 8943 feet (2710 metres), with snow all the year around. More interesting are the beaches, the finest in Europe in the estimation of many; the purest soft white sand you could wish for. The recent trend has been for more and more holiday homes to be bought by British and Germans; in 2003, 15% of second homes were owned by Germans, 10% by British, and 15% by Italians. In the recent past, Italians owned 30% of holiday homes; not surprisingly, Italians are better accepted by the locals than the French, since they speak a similar language (Corsican is actually a dialect of Tuscan).

All in all, it seems that the future looks good for holiday homes on Corsica, with a rise of 20% in the value of houses, and 15% in the value of constructible land in 2003, and further large rises predicted.

Getting There

Most tourists arrive here by direct charter flight from their own country. French domestic flights leave from Paris Orly, whereas international flights arrive at Charles de Gaulle, making it inconvenient to transfer. It is preferable to fly to Marseille or Lyon and change there, if necessary. Air France has flights to the main Corsican airports – Ajaccio, Bastia and Calvi – from Lyon, Paris and Marseille; there are also flights to Figari in the south from Marseille and Lyon in season. See www.airfrance.fr for details. British Airways will run direct flights from May 2004 to Bastia from London Heathrow.

Many tourists come by ferry. There are high-speed hydrofoils from Nice to Calvi and Ajaccio. Ferries from Marseille and Toulon are slower, taking from 6 to 13 hours if you go overnight. See the following:

Corsica Ferries: ☎0492 00 43 76 (FR); 020-4560 7431 (UK); www.corsicaferries.com.

SNCM Ferrytérannée: ☎08 36 67 95 00 (FR); 020-7491 4968 (UK); www.sncm.fr.

Via Mare: ☎020-4560 7431; www.viamare.com.

Another possibility is to fly to Alghero on Sardinia by Ryanair, then take the short ferry trip from S. Teresa di Gallura (see www.mobylines.com or www.saremar.it).

TYPES OF PROPERTY

Stone has always been the preferred material, as it is found everywhere on the island. The traditional Corsican village consists of tightly grouped houses without a central square which emphasises the closed nature of the society. The living room (*sala*) for entertaining guests traditionally has a rifle by the door; the bedrooms are protected by religious icons. On the coast one will find the same types of villas and apartments as one would in the rest of southern France, with the provison that planning laws are very strictly applied, and designs have to be approved to ensure they fit in with existing style.

Estate agents on Corsica do not produce statistics on average prices of property, although individual agents can give rough figures per square metre. As of 2004, the average price of recently constructed holiday homes was estimated at a maximum €4,500 per square metre, meaning that a 2-bedroom home would come out at some €260,000 (with sea view and in perfect condition). Older buildings are far cheaper.

One can still pick up a small apartment by the sea from €90,000. Houses for renovation inland can be as little as €70,000. Building land with a sea view costs some €100-150 per square metre near towns; without a sea view the cost is €25-50 per sq.m. Land that is not *constructible,* where no building permit can be obtained is worth as little as €2 per sq.m.

Some properties are advertised privately in French magazines, e.g. *Résidence Sécondaire* and *Particulier à Particulier,* or on local websites, such as www.best-of-corse.com.

HAUTE-CORSE

Main Tourist Office: 1 rue Notre Dame de Lourdes, 20200 Bastia; ☎04 95 54 20 40; fax 04 95 54 20 41; www.
Main Towns: *Bastia, Corte, Calvi, Ghisonaccia.*
Airports: *Bastia, Calvi.*
The north and west of Corsica are in the département of Haute Corse. The island is divided diagonally along the central mountain range. Roughly speaking, this is the area with the most tourism, because of a somewhat more moderate climate.

Far North

You will arrive by ferry at Bastia's new port, or in Calvi from Nice or Marseille, unless you choose to fly. Northern Corsica would exhaust the superlatives of any writer. The wonderful beaches and spectacular scenery make this quite possibly the most beautiful spot in the Mediterranean. The best scenery is found at the very northern tip, at Cap Corse, which is also a fine AOC wine. Bastia itself is also very attractive in parts, especially the Vieux Port. The Genoese founded the city in 1378 as the capital of the island.

La Balagne and the West Coast

La Balagne is the greenest part of Corsica and a major tourist draw. It is particularly noted for its many baroque churches. The town of Calvi, birthplace of Christopher Columbus, has massive well-preserved 13th century ramparts built by the Genoese, overlooking the harbour, and original Italian-style multi-storey houses. This is also a Foreign Legion base, which has been bombarded by the Saracens, Turks, Lord Nelson, and others in its long history. The Corsican nationalist, Pascal Paoli, who unsuccessfully tried to gain independence for the island in 1768 was born here.

Inland, the Haute Balagne is a mountainous area bordering on the vast national parks that take up most of the island, spanning some 3500 square kilometres in all.

Central Corsica

In a way, Corsica is one huge mountain rising out of the sea. The main mountain range stretches diagonally across the island from Calvi to Porto-Vecchio in the southeast. The highest points are Monte Cinto at 2710m and Monte Rotondo at 2622m. Monte Incudine further south comes in at 2134m. This is hiking country, with a fairly minimal infrastructure and narrow, twisty roads. There is a light train – the *trinighellu* – from Ajaccio to Bastia via Corte, with a branch line to Calvi from Ponte-Leccia, running in the summer. In all it covers some 230 km, with 32 tunnels, and is perhaps more useful as sightseeing trip than as a speedy means of transport. There are plans to refurbish the trains to make them faster.

Typical Properties for Sale

Location	Type	Description	Price
Calvi	duplex	150 sq.m.; 3 bedrooms; air-conditioning.	€430,000
Prunelli di Fiumorbo	modern house	3 bedrooms; 169 sq.m. on 2478 sq.m..	€305,000
Nessa, nr Calvi	traditional house	4 storeys; 6 bedrooms.	€83,000
Casta-St-Florent	furnished house	3 bedrooms; 1054 sq.m. wooded land.	€150,000
Piedigriggio, nr Corte	traditional terrace house	2 bedrooms; 3 storeys.	€93,000
Ile Rousse	apartment	43 sq.m.; 1 bedroom, terrace.	€115,000

CORSE-DU-SUD

Main Tourist Office: 3 bd du Roi-Jérôme, 20181 Ajaccio; ☎04 95 51 00 00; fax 04 95 51 14 40; www.ajaccio-tourisme.com
Main Towns: *Ajaccio, Sartène, Porto-Vecchio, Bonifacio, Porto, Propriano.*
Airports: *Ajaccio, Figari.*
The capital of Corsica, Ajaccio, is also one of its main tourist attractions, surrounded as it is by mountains in a spectacular *cirque,* and close to the best beaches on the island along the west coast. The offshore islands – the Iles Sanguinaires – are also a popular tourist attraction. The name derives from their colour rather than any bloody associations. Ajaccio has a great many statues of Napoleon Bonaparte, who was born here, and his numerous relatives, but he is not much respected by the locals, who even sometimes deface his image. Napoleon had the ramparts of the city demolished in 1796 to discourage the Ajacciens from trying to return to their Genoese masters. To the Corsicans he sold out to the French.

Ajaccio has mostly escaped the ravages of overdevelopment and remains an attractive and relaxed place to live. The beaches around here, are the best on the island. The west coast also has a more bearable temperature than the eastern side of the island, so that most touristic developments are located here. The town of Porto in the north of the Corse-du-Sud is something of a tourist trap, although not quite spoiled by overdevelopment.

Sartène and the Alta Rocca

The southern end of the island, known as the Alta Rocca, is only developed in parts. Propriano near Sartène, has been expanded to take ferries from Marseille and Sardinia, but has also been plagued by terrorist attacks, with the post office being bombed three times. Sartène nearby has a well-preserved medieval centre, the local communist mayor having made sure that there was only limited new building here. Sartène was at one time a refuge for bandits, and was famed for its vendettas. Porto-Vecchio on the east coast is very developed because of its pure white beach and turquoise clear sea. Bonifacio is the closest point to Sardinia and many second homes are owned by wealthy Italians. It has the only genuine Renaissance architecture on the island; being very crowded in the summer it could not be recommended for a holiday home, however attractive it may be.

Typical Properties for Sale

Location	Type	Description	Price
nr Ajaccio	villa	3 floors, 225 sq.m., 3 bedrooms, next to beach.	€420,000
Porto Vecchio	apartment	2nd floor apartment with 3 bedrooms in town centre.	€168,000
nr Propriano	studio	21 sq.m. ground-floor studio, with 50 sq.m. terrace with sea view.	€83,000
Ajaccio	apartment	55 sq.m. 1-bedroom, 3rd floor corner apartment.	€110,000
Vico	traditional Corsican village house	300 sq.m. on 1200 sq.m. land; 6 bedrooms, swimming pool.	€600,000
nr Porticcio	land	3230 sq.m. land, with planning permission for 400 sq.m.; all utilities.	€175,000

Estate Agents in Corsica

AB Immobilier: 17 Cours Paoli, 20250 Corte; ☎04 95 61 06 93; fax 04 95 61 10 79; e-mail SARL-AB-IMMOBILIER@wanadoo.fr. Central Corsica.

ABC Immobilier: Giudice di Canarca, 20137 Porto-Vecchio; ☎04 95 70 66 40; fax 04 95 72 13 87; e-mail info@abc-immobilier.fr; www.abc-immobilier.fr. Corse-du-Sud.

Calizi Immobilier: avenue Calizi, Immeuble Napoléon bâtiment D, 20200 Ile Rousse; ☎04 95 60 54 96; e-mail info@calizimmo.com; www.calizimmo.com. Balagne.

Corse Prestige Immobilier: B.P. 573, 20186; ☎04 95 25 90 41; fax 04 95 25 90 76; e-mail infos@corseprestige.com; www.corseprestige.com. All Corsica.

F-M Immobilier: rue du Gl. Graziani, 20220 Ile Rousse; ☎04 95 60 04 02; fax 04 95 60 04 07; e-mail fm.immobiler@tiscali.fr; www.agence-immobiliere-calvi-balagne-corse.com. Balagne.

F-M Immobilier: 8 bvd Wilson, 20260 Calvi; ☎04 95 65 11 40; fax 04 95 65 09 41; e-mail fm.immobiler@tiscali.fr; www.agence-immobiliere-calvi-balagne-corse.com. Calvi.

GTI Immobilier: route de Bonifacio, 20137 Porto-Vecchio; ☎04 95 70 54 45; fax 04 95 70 35 10; e-mail gti@corse-immo.fr. Corse-du-Sud.

Ile de Beauté: Résidence le Pietra, Serena, 2 rte du fort de Toga, 20200 Ville di Pietrabugno; tel/fax 04 95 31 88 76; www.iledebeauteimmobilier.com. Bastia, Cap Corse.

SECIC Immobilier: 34 cours Napoléon, 20000 Ajaccio; ☎04 95 51 00 02; fax 04 95 51 01 44; e-mail secic@secic.fr; www.secic.fr. Corse-du-Sud.

THE PURCHASING PROCEDURE

CHAPTER SUMMARY

- **Banks:** Practices are very different from in the UK, but non-residents can open an account by post.
- **Mortgages:** Only straight repayment mortgages are available; your monthly repayments cannot exceed 33% of your income, and you will probably be offered 70% or less of the value of the property.
- **Purchasing Costs:** The high costs associated with buying make it less attractive to buy property in the hope of making a quick profit, and keep the market more stable.
- **Tax:** France is a high-taxation country, and most taxes are raised through social security contributions and Valued Added Tax, which cannot be avoided.
- **Real Estate Tax:** The amount you will have to pay will probably be less than your council tax in the UK.
- **Capital Gains:** Capital gains taxes in France encourage people to stay in one house for a long time, and penalise those who resell after a few years.
- **Inheritance Tax:** It is vital to obtain professional advice about French inheritance laws before you sign a contract to buy a property.
- **Importing Currency:** You can save thousands of pounds by using the services of a currency dealer rather than going through a high street bank.
- **Insurance:** Third-party liability insurance is compulsory for homeowners and tenants.
- **Wealth Tax:** A tax that does not exist in the UK, but which you should not try to avoid in the France.

FINANCE

BANKING

There are several types of bank in France: clearing banks such as *Crédit Lyonnais*; co-operative banks such as *Crédit Agricole*; corporate banks, e.g. *BNP Paribas*, and savings banks or *Caisses d'Epargne*. The *Crédit Agricole* has an immense advantage in that it has the largest number of branches, 7,500 in France alone. The post office, *La Poste*, has 17,000 branches in France and longer opening hours than banks.

The Calvados region of Crédit Agricole has now started a service called Britline, which allows you to open a non-resident bank account in France by post (see www.britline.com). Britline sometimes has a stall at French property fairs in the UK. Banque Populaire in Nice has started a popular English-speaking service: see www.cotedazur.banquepopulaire.fr.

Below are listed the major French banks with their websites:

Barclays Bank SA: www.barclays.fr
Banque Populaire: www.banquepopulaire.fr
BNP Paribas: www.bnpparibas.fr
Britline: www.britline.com
Caixa Bank: www.caixabank.fr
Crédit Agricole: www.credit-agricole.fr; http://www.ca-name of department].fr
Crédit Commercial de France: www.ccf.com
Crédit du Nord: www.credit-du-nord.fr
Crédit Lyonnais: www.creditlyonnais.com
Lloyds Bank SA: www.lloydstsbiwm.com
Société Générale: www.socgen.com

Barclays is the best represented UK bank. Lloyds has branches in Cannes and Marseille; HSBC owns Crédit Commercial de France. NatWest has no branches in France. British banks in France have to operate under French law; they mainly target wealthy expats with a lot of money to invest (except for Crédit Commercial de France).

Credit Cards

Strictly speaking, there is no such thing as a credit card in France, rather there are charge cards with a deferred debit. Every 30 days the amount you owe is automatically debited from your bank account, meaning that you may pay for something the day after you bought it. In the UK the credit is for 30-60 days, in France for 0-30 days. If you want to defer payment you will need to open a sub-account which allows you to borrow money, at a lower interest rate than you would pay in the UK on a credit card.

The national French debit card, the *Carte Bleue* (CB) can only be used in France. If you need a credit card that functions abroad, you can ask for *Carte Bleue/Visa* or *Mastercard*. You are expected to clear your bill at the end of each month, unless you have arranged to borrow money.

Bank Accounts

Opening a bank account is not difficult. If you are resident in France then you simply take along your passport, *carte de séjour* (or equivalent) and proof of your fiscal address in France. For non-residents the bank will ask to see your last three months' salary slips. The basic bank account is the *compte de chèque,* which comes with a cheque book. When you open a bank account you will normally be offered a *Carte Bleue,* a cashpoint card, which can also function as either a debit card or credit card; you choose one of the two. CBs work with a chip rather than magnetic strip; you key in your PIN number when making transactions in shops, so you need to remember it.

As well as the bank's own number, there is one central number for reporting lost bank cards: 01 45 67 84 84.

Resident and Non-Resident Accounts. From the bank's point of view, whether you are considered resident or non-resident depends on where you where you pay your taxes. As a non-resident you can only open a *compte non-résident.* After choosing your branch in France, you need to supply a reference from your UK bank, a legalised copy of your signature, photocopies of the main pages of your passport, and a draft in euros to start you off. You can also go to the bank's London branch. It is generally far simpler to open an account in person in France after talking to local bank staff, or to use Britline (see above).

Banking Practices

Banking services are not as sophisticated or as liberal in France as in the UK or US. The main rule to remember is that you must never go into the red without prior arrangement, otherwise you risk becoming an *interdit bancaire.* It is also worth bearing in mind that if you go into the red any standing orders that you have will automatically be stopped, so your telephone and electricity could suddenly be cut off.

When you open your account you opt for monthly or fortnightly bank statements. You can authorise utility companies to debit your account automatically (*prélèvement automatique*) for bill payment, but this is not obligatory. This is not the same as a standing order (*ordre permanent/virement automatique*).

Bank opening hours are not overly convenient; there is a law that prevents banks opening more than five days a week, so your bank may close on Mondays. Very small branches (*permanences*) in country areas may only open one morning a week. The internet is making things easier.

Cheques

Cheques are used for half of all financial transactions in France; there are no cheque guarantee cards, but you can be asked for other identification. Your bank will send you your first chequebook once there are funds in your account. French cheques are not negotiable to a third person, and are treated as being equivalent to cash. The basic form of cheque is the *chèque barré,* which is only payable to the payee (*destinataire*); the bank has to inform the tax inspectors if you want to use open cheques.

Bouncing Cheques. If you write a 'wooden cheque' (*chèque de bois*) you will be given 30 days to rectify the situation. The Banque de France is informed immediately, and you are not allowed to write any further cheques until matters are resolved. You not only have to pay money into the account to cover it, but also a fine of 12%. If the money is not paid you are put on a Banque de France blacklist, and are barred from writing any cheques in France for five years.

IMPORTING CURRENCY

When buying property in France, you will, under normal circumstances, have to pay in euros. Since the UK is not part of Euroland, anyone buying property or business abroad is confronted with the painful possibility that a percentage of their money is going to disappear into the pockets of a high street bank. Fortunately, this need not be the case, since a number of specialist foreign exchange companies have now started up to lessen the pain of the transaction. A specialised company such as Currencies Direct (www.currenciesdirect.com) can help in a number of ways, by offering better exchange rates than banks, without charging commission, and giving you the possibility of 'forward buying'. For further details see *Importing Currency* in the *General Introduction*.

OFFSHORE ACCOUNTS

Bank accounts in Monaco are completely transparent as far as the French taxman goes. The French authorities can look at your accounts at any time. Even if you live in Monaco you may be treated as a French resident, so you will need some expert advice if you choose to become a tax exile there. For more information on Offshore Accounts see the *General Introduction*.

MORTGAGES

The following is a brief summary of French mortgages. For a more detailed explanation see *Buying a House in France* (published by Vacation Work, www.vacationwork.com).

It is highly advisable to have an offer of a loan before you look for a property in France, whether you are buying something new or planning to borrow money to renovate. A French mortgage lender can provide you with a statement guaranteeing you a loan (*certificat de garantie*), for which there may be a charge. You don't have to take up the offer, but you will at least be ready to sign a preliminary purchase agreement if you see a property you like.

The only type of mortgage – *hypothèque* – available in France is the repayment mortgage. Fixed-rate mortgages are by far the most common; it is also possible to mix fixed and variable rates. The mortgage lender does not hold the deeds to your property as security; these remain with the notaire. Your mortgage is registered with the local *bureau des hypothèques*, and there is a fee to have the mortgage removed once you have paid it off.

UK and French Mortgages

There are two possibilities: one is to remortgage your UK property, the other is to take out a mortgage with a French bank using a French property as security. UK-based banks will not lend money on foreign properties; the French branches of UK banks operating under French law in France will, as well as one or two other specialised UK lenders (e.g. Conti Financial Services). Remortgaging or taking out a mortgage in the UK has advantages; fewer questions will be asked, and you will be able to borrow more than you would in France. If your income is in sterling, then it makes sense to have a UK mortgage. It is equally possible to borrow a smaller sum for a short period to cover the cost of buying your French property.

The charges involved with setting up a French mortgage (*frais d'hypothèque*) are high. French banks rarely lend more than 80% of the value of a property; 70% is a realistic amount. The maximum term is normally 15 years, but with rising prices there are now more loans for 20 or 25 years becoming available.

The Loi Scrivener and Protection for Borrowers

Borrowers are generally well protected. The lending organisation must first state in writing: the lender's name and address, the type of loan, the property that is to be acquired, the rate of interest, total repayment and the time period of the loan, and the fact that the property purchase is dependent on obtaining the loan. There is a *délai de réflexion* (cooling-off period) of 10 days before the offer of the loan can be accepted and any funds transferred. The acceptance can be sent by ordinary post. The offer of credit remains open for 30 days, during which time the borrower can look at other offers.

There is a useful French mortgage calculator on www.french-property.com (in English). French regulations mean that your monthly repayments cannot exceed 33% of your net income. At the same time, the costs and taxes associated with the property purchase – 12% to 15% of the purchase price – will also be taken into account.

Charges and Procedures Involved with French Mortgages

The lender will charge approximately 1% of the loan as a fee for arranging the mortgage (*frais de dossier*). There are further fees for valuing the property, arranging insurance, and then the notaire's own fees which add up to 1-2% of the value of the mortgage. All in all you can expect to pay some 5.9% on a loan of €50,000, or 3.5% on €200,000.

The standard type of loan, the *privilège de prêteur de deniers* (PPD) – a lender's guarantee – is not subject to 0.615% registration tax. The PPD cannot be used to borrow money for construction or renovation costs, or for anything other than buying an existing property.

Mortgage Insurance

Mortgage lenders generally insist that you take out death/disability insurance – *assurance décès/invalidité*. The type of insurance is *assurance décès temporaire,* running for the lifetime of the mortgage contract. If you die or are incapitated the mortgage is paid off. These are not life insurance contracts: there is no payout at the end.

Mortgage Brokers/Advisors

Abbey National France: 70 rue Saint Sauveur, 59046 Lille Cedex; ☎03 20 18 18 89; fax 03 20 18 19 20; www.abbey-national.fr. Branches in Marseille, Montpellier, Toulouse.

Barclays France: Côte d'Azur International Centre, 2 rue Alphonse Karr, 06000 Nice; ☎04 93 82 68 02; fax 04 93 88 58 95; e-mail cotedazur.int@barclays.co.uk.

Conti Financial Services: 204 Church Rd, Hove, Sussex BN3 2DJ;freephone 0800-970 0985; ☎01273-772811; fax 01273-321269; e-mail enquiries@contifs.com; www.mortgages overseas.com. Leading UK overseas mortgage brokers.

Mortgage France: La Fraye Touarte, Rte de Gréolières CD6, 06480 La Colle sur Loup; ☎04 93 32 13 95; e-mail info@mortgagefrance.com; www.mortgagefrance.com.

Templeton Associates: French mortgage and finance experts, with offices in UK and France; ☎01225-42282; www.templeton-france.com.

LOCAL/REAL ESTATE TAXES

Most local taxes are real estate taxes. The main real estate taxes are *taxe d'habitation* and *taxe foncière*. The rates of tax are set by local municipalities up to certain limits imposed by the national government. The rate for your area can be found in the annual publication *Impôts Locaux*, published at the start of November. See www.gui deducontribuable.com.

Taxe d'Habitation

The *taxe d'habitation* is payable by anyone who has premises at their disposal subject to the tax (also tenants). This includes both principal residences as well as any secondary homes that are available for your use. If you occupy a property on 1 January you are liable for the entire year's tax. The rates vary hugely all over France: the highest rates are charged in poor inner cities, while wealthy suburbs get off lightest. The average is €700 per annum. The tax is calculated by the local authorities on the basis of the nominal rental value of the property, called *valeur cadastrale*.

Taxes Foncières

Land tax, or *taxe foncière*, is charged on un-built and built land. This is roughly similar to the *taxe d'habitation*. The owner of a property pays the *taxe foncière*, not the tenant.

Taxe Professionnelle

The *taxe professionnelle* is the equivalent of business rates and is levied on companies and the self-employed. It was temporarily suspended for 18 months during 2004 and 2005 while the government considered whether to abolish it or replace it with something else.

CAPITAL GAINS TAX (IPV)

In French CGT is known as *Impôt sur les Plus Values* or IPV; it is levied on occasional profits on the sale of buildings, shares, furniture, works of art, precious stones and precious metals. For foreigners the main issue here is the taxation of profits on the sale of property.

The basis of the calculation is the difference between the purchase price and the selling price of your property, with some deductions allowed for the purchase costs and any renovation work you have done. A distinction is made between short-term gains – *plus values à court terme* and long-term gains – *plus values à long terme*. Short-term gains on property are those made within 5 years of acquisition. The gains are treated as ordinary income and added to your taxable income. Long-term gains are taxed at 26% for residents, and 16% for non-residents. Your liability decreases by 10% every year for 10 years so that after 15 years no IPV is payable.

INHERITANCE TAX

Planning for inheritance should start before you buy a property in France. Putting your property into the wrong person's name or not looking into ways of reducing inheritance tax can have disastrous consequences later on. Taking professional advice from a lawyer qualified in both British and French legal systems can save a great deal of trouble even if seems an expensive luxury you can do without while you are going through the purchasing process.

It can be advantageous to have separate wills in the UK and France. If you were tax-resident in France, then after your decease there could be a conflict between the French and UK authorities, since the latter rarely accept that you were no longer domiciled in the UK at the time of decease, unless you gave up your British nationality. It may be advantageous to pay inheritance tax in France if the inheritance is worth more than £263,000, assuming the property is being left to reserved heirs. If the deceased was not tax-resident in France then you can, after paying inheritance tax in the UK, get your French notaire to draw up a document stating who is the new owner of the property and the French authorities do not need to be involved.

French inheritance laws mean that you cannot choose to leave your property to anyone you like. Children have first priority, followed by parents, grandchildren and grandparents. Only where there are no surviving direct descendants or ascendants does your partner become a reserved heir (*héritier réservataire*). Children receive a tax-free sum of €46,000, spouses receive €76,000; they are then taxed on a sliding scale between 5% and 40% on the remainder. Complete strangers are taxed at 60%. Lifetime gifts can be used to lessen inheritance tax liability. While gift tax and inheritance tax are basically the same thing, there are incentives for giving away your assets if you do so early enough.

Since 2002, spouses take priority over grandparents and brothers and sisters of the deceased. As a minimum, the surviving partner should receive either 25% of the full property or the *usufruit* (beneficial use) of the property for their lifetime. The surviving partner has an absolute right to remain in the marital home for one year from the decease.

MARRIAGE REGIME CHANGE

An important means to improve your partner's situation is to change your marriage regime, but this is only possible if you are a French resident.

Patrick Delas, a French *avocat* presently practising in London with Russell-Cooke Solicitors, has some advice on changing your regime:

British people are surprised to learn that they are not free to leave their French assets to their partner under French law. One solution may be to change the marriage regime to a communauté regime under French law and provide that the community assets will remain the surviving spouse's property. This inheritance through marital contract is free of tax. Otherwise under French law, most British citizens are presumed to have been married under the separate estates regime (séparation de biens), which means that the assets of the deceased spouse will go to his/her children (if any). The partner can only claim for 25% of the whole in full property or opt for its usufruit (lifetime use). In France a change of marital contract has to be witnessed by a notaire and validated by a court. However, the La Hague Convention dated 14 March 1978 allows non-French citizens to change their marriage regime so far as it applies to their immovable property in France by executing a deed which is witnessed by a notaire. We have qualified experts in my office who can assist to carry this out. It is not, however, advisable in practice to change your marriage regime if there are children from a first marriage, because they have the right to oppose the change, in so far as it would reduce their inheritance. If you change your marriage regime to a communauté regime and you then get divorced, then you will have to go through the process of valuing the assets so as to share them out between the couple.

INSURANCE

All residential properties must be insured. Holiday homes may be targeted by burglars if they are left standing empty, and there are serious risks from flooding, subsidence and fire in some areas. While you can add your French property to your UK insurance, it is more convenient to insure with a local company in France who are able to handle claims in English, in order to get a faster response. English-speaking agents advertise in French property magazines, or look for *courtiers d'assurances* in the yellow pages.

The basic house and contents insurance is the *assurance multirisques habitation,* also often called *assurance multirisques vie privée* or *la multirisque.* This will include cover against natural disasters as a matter of course. Insurance is calculated on the basis of the surface area of your property or the number of rooms. Civil liability insurance – *responsabilité civile propriétaire* – is essential, in case an event on your property affects your neighbours. It is assumed that you will take over the existing insurance from the previous owner of the property you are buying. It is generally wiser to take out a new policy, which you are required to present to the notaire before you can sign the final *acte de vente.*

FINDING PROPERTIES FOR SALE

ESTATE AGENTS

By British standards, French estate agents are still rather amateurish in the countryside. Until recently property sales were handled by notaires; the profession of estate agent is still quite new. On the positive side French estate agents are more relaxed and less cut-throat than those in Britain. This is a regulated profession, and it is illegal to operate as an estate agent without being qualified or registered. On the other hand, French *agents immobilier* rarely have good brochures or details of properties to hand. Sizes of rooms are never given. You will generally be told the total habitable surface area (compulsory in the case of apartments), but not much else. There are more professional estate agents in the bigger towns who speak English and know what foreigners want. There is little interest among local people in big houses in the countryside – they cannot afford them – so local estate agents are not the best people to approach if you are looking for a big villa. The British universally complain that they ask to see a villa, and are shown châteaux, cottages, water mills, etc., or anything but what they wanted to see.

French *immobiliers'* commissions vary from region to region, and are on a graduated scale depending on the value of the property. The minimum is around €2000. With very cheap properties the commission can be up to 20%; above about €250,000 the commission will not exceed 2.5%. A very cheap property naturally attracts a very high percentage in commission. The total commission is unlikely to be less than 3%; the normal range is 5% to 10%. It is vitally important to find out at the start who is going to pay the *immobilier's* commission. It has in the past been usual for the buyer to pay, but it is now becoming more common for the seller to pay. The asking price that is advertised must, by law, include the agent's commission if the buyer is to pay it. Some agents may try to quote you prices *net vendeur,* i.e. the price the seller will receive, so you need to be on your guard. Another dubious practice is quoting prices with all costs included, which allows the agency to slip in a few more thousand pounds unnoticed.

You should always have a precise breakdown of all the components of the price.

Property Viewing

Property hunters should observe certain formalities in relation to agents. The British have gained a bad reputation for not turning up for meetings, or not leaving enough time to go and see a property. It is not possible to pack in several viewings a day when properties are so remote that it could take half a day to see just one. It is sensible to let agents know if you are not going to be able to make it to a viewing. Having a mobile telephone so you can keep in touch will save a lot of trouble.

Search Agents

Ideally you would want to spend several months looking at properties, but not many people can afford to spend that kind of time. There are now many British intermediaries who will arrange to show you properties advertised on the internet. If necessary they will pick you up from the airport, arrange your accommodation and do everything for you, at a price. If you do deal with UK-based agents then you must be quite clear about whether they are simply acting as intermediaries, or whether they are actually estate agents themselves – usually they are not.

The English-speaking agent receives a commission from the *immobilier,* which can be as much as 50% of the total commission where there is a long-established partnership. The commission may be added on to the French *immobilier*'s commission: one might pay a further 1% or 1.5% on top. The agent's services will not be free: there is usually a signing-on fee – perhaps £250 – which is refunded in the event that you buy the property.

Search agents advertise in property magazines and their websites; a few names are given below:

1st for French Property: 1st-for-french-property.co.uk.
French Property Shop: www.frenchpropertyshop.com.
Lavender Homes: www.lavenderhomes.co.uk.
Mediterranean Property Search: mediterranean-homes.co.uk.
Simply Côte d'Azur: www.simplycotedazur.com.

ADVERTS

For many people the first point of departure is looking at French property magazines, giving adverts for expensive properties that have probably already been sold. If you answer adverts on British websites or in magazines you may well be dealing with an English-speaking property agent rather than a private seller. Ideally, one would want to contact French sellers directly through internet and magazine adverts. One starting point is to look at newspaper and magazine websites, some of which are given under 'Media' in Part One of this section. A list of some French property websites and magazines is given below:

Property Exhibitions

The French property exhibition has become an established feature of the property-buying scene. There are generally not that many actual estate agents, but there are various interesting stalls, and one can gain some idea of what is available. A more interesting feature, perhaps, are the various free talks given at some exhibitions, e.g. at Homes Overseas. The only exhibitions of note are:

Homes Overseas Exhibition: www.homesoverseas.co.uk.
Vive La France: www.vivelafrance.co.uk.
French Property Exhibition: www.french-property-news.com.

The dates and locations are publicised in French property magazines.

Property Magazines

One possible source of property adverts are the popular French property magazines. These also run adverts by search agents and estate agents. Such magazines give rather rosy-tinted view of life in France and the property scene; they are a useful source of information as long as one remembers that the articles are not necessarily objective, and that everything is slanted towars getting you to buy a property. The main magazines are:

Everything France: www.efmag.co.uk.
French Magazine: www.frenchmagazine.co.uk
French Property News: www.french-property-news.com.
Living France: www.livingfrance.com.

TYPES OF PROPERTY PURCHASE

Apart from the straightforward house purchase, there are a number of other possibly advantageous ways to acquire property in France.

Timeshare

This is misleadingly called *multipropriété* in French, even though you would never actually own the property. The idea is that you pay for the right to use a property for a certain number of weeks per year in perpetuity. Regulations in France are so strict that there is little timeshare property on the market. If you are offered timeshare in the South of France you should not sign anything on the spot, but insist that the documents are sent to you in the UK. There is a 10-day cooling-off period after you send off the contract before any money can be transferred. The best advice is not to get involved in timeshare.

Leaseback

Leaseback, or *le leaseback,* is a useful scheme, somewhat like 'buy-to-let', but within a formal structure that guarantees your investment is safe. The idea is quite ingenious: you agree to buy a new or completely rebuilt property in a tourist complex, and then lease it back to the developer for a period of between nine and 20 years. The developer's management company runs it for you, and guarantees a rental income, which goes towards paying off any mortgage that you have taken out to buy the property. You can also expect to have the use of the property during the off-season for a number of weeks each year. At the end of the fixed leaseback period, you are the owner of the property, and you can do with it what you wish; hopefully you will be sitting on a substantial profit.

The major attraction of the leaseback scheme is that no TVA is payable on the purchase, unless you end the lease and use the property yourself, in which case TVA has to be reimbursed. Companies that deal in leaseback properties can be found through the organisation FOPDAC; see www.fopdac.com.

Buying Off-Plan

It is common in France either to sign a contract to buy a property that has not yet been built, or which is being built, or to make your own plans using an architect and have the property built by a contractor. Where you buy a property on the basis of a pre-existing plan, the term used in French is *vente en état futur d'achèvement* (VEFA). The developer will have bought a piece of land and will build a number of villas or apartments on it, which will have a certain degree of uniformity, but all services will be connected.

There are strict rules about payment in stages, and the correct handover of the property. The disadvantage of buying new is that you pay 19.6% VAT on the purchase, but the transfer fees are minimal. Both the builder and the owner must take out 10-year insurance policies on handover. The precise details of buying off-plan are given in *Buying a House in France* (published by Vacation Work; www.vacationwork.co.uk).

Buying Land

Land which is *constructible* – that has planning permission guaranteed – is very valuable in the South of France; you can still save if you build your property yourself, or hand the work over to a master builder (*maître d'œuvre*). Outline planning permission – the *certificat d'urbanisme* (CU) – virtually guarantees that you will receive proper planning permission – the *permis de construire* (PC) – but CUs are only valid for one year. If you are considering buying land, be very careful that your planning permission will still be valid when you actually start building. There is no guarantee that it will be renewed, as the rules are becoming stricter all the time. For land, see these websites:

www.allobat.fr.
http://frenchland.com.
www.terrain.fr.
www.terrain-a-batir.com.
www.terrains.com.

Multipropriétés or SCIs

If you are considering buying a high-value property together with some other people, it is worth looking at setting up a company – the *Société Civile Immobilière* specifically designed to own and manage property. The SCI allows one to get around French inheritance laws, which automatically favour children over spouses. It is particularly useful where several unrelated people own shares in a property. Transfers of shares are subject to transfer rather than inheritance taxes. Directors of an SCI are taxed as individuals, rather than paying corporation tax. Owners pay for the running costs of the property in proportion to the number of weeks they use the place.

Setting up an SCI is expensive, and is only relevant to high-value properties, or high-asset individuals. You will require the services of a specialist lawyer to set one up. There is an agency in the UK that specialises in finding, and handling the purchase of property for the purpose of co-ownership: www.ownergroups.com.

RENTING A HOME IN FRANCE

It is a truism that renting before you buy is the best policy, but it is mostly only the retired who have the leisure to do so. Even if you are only staying in a holiday villa for a week or two, you will certainly have to sign a contract stating how long the rental is for, and what you can do there. You will be asked to pay a deposit – *dépôt de garantie* – colloquially referred to as *la caution*. Where the property is rented out by the month, the maximum amount is two months' rent. Where the rental is for more than a year, the maximum is three months' rent.

The basic French word for 'renting' is *location*, so this is the word to look for in newspapers and shop windows. The sign *A Louer* is often placed in the windows of properties to rent. Otherwise you can go to an estate agent. Property is either fully furnished or not at all; fully furnished means that you have absolutely everything that you could need to live. Before you move into a place you should ask for an inspection report or *état des lieux* to be carried out, giving details of the condition of all the items in the property. When you leave another *état des lieux* will be carried out (if necessary by a bailiff) to prove that you have not damaged anything. If the owner insists that no *état des lieux* is required then you can take photographs of any existing damage in the premises to safeguard yourself from false accusations. The film should be conventional rather than digital, which can be tampered with.

Eric Smythe rented apartments in Antibes

I rented several apartments in Antibes before buying my current property. There were particular problems with one apartment; it was on the top of a 5-storey building, and all charges were included. But the heating didn't work. When we moved out after a year we received a bill for €1400 for the heating. We made a mistake because we had only informed the landlady and the syndic (manager) of the copropriété verbally that there was a problem. We were then taken to court for non-payment, and eventually had to pay half. This made us realise that you absolutely must send any complaints by lettre recommandée *(registered letter), otherwise you have no recourse. Because we were on such good terms with the owner, the agent and the manager we never imagined that they would do this.*

Practices on the south coast seem to be generally rather relaxed. We gave the estate agent a cheque as a deposit, and he simply held on to it and never cashed it, so we got the cash back when we moved out and it had no bearing on the court case. Also we have never actually seen an état des lieux *(inspection report) on a rented property. We made a list ourselves of anything that looked damaged, and there were no problems when we moved out, but strictly speaking you could get into trouble without having an official report made up when you move in. Again it seems that no one bothers around here. Our contract was for one year, because it was the owner's second home.*

FEES, CONTRACTS AND CONVEYANCING

SURVEYS

Having a property surveyed before you buy it is more or less a matter of course in the UK, but not so in France. Fewer than 3% of buyers have a survey done here. The French usually assume that if a house looks solid it is not likely to fall down within their lifetime. French property sellers are not likely to accept a clause such as 'subject to survey' in the preliminary contract. Any general survey should be done before signing the preliminary contract. General surveys are done by architects or builders; there is no such profession as 'chartered surveyor'.

All properties for sale must now be surveyed for the presence of asbestos and it is entirely normal to put a clause in the pre-contract (*compromis de vente*) making the sale dependent on the survey being done. There are also large areas of France where a survey for termites (but not other wood-boring insects) is also compulsory. To see whether you should be concerned about termites, look at the website www.termites.com.

The law requires all pre-1948 properties to be checked for lead paint. Lead paint was widely used until after World War II in towns and can cause brain damage. Having it removed is extremely expensive; in some cases owners just cover it up with plastic panelling.

Only qualified persons are allowed to carry out surveys for asbestos, termites and lead. Look under *expertises* in the yellow pages.

Boundaries. When buying a property, you need to know where the boundaries lie, otherwise you may find that you have less land than you expected. It is quite common for there to be no precise boundaries between properties. It is the job of the *géomètre-expert* to establish *bornes* or boundary markers. See www.geometre-expert.fr.

NOTAIRES

The French sometimes say that you do not need a notary (French *notaire*) to buy a property. This is true in as far as you can transfer the title of a property by private treaty – *sous seing privé* – but such a transfer is only binding on the parties who enter into it and is inferior to an authentic act drawn up and witnessed by a notaire. If someone tries to sell you a property or business by private treaty, or asks you to hand over a cash deposit, you should refuse. It is illegal to give a deposit on a property to anyone other than an *immobilier* with a *carte professionnelle*, a notaire or lawyer.

A notaire is the only person who can register the sale with the land registry – the *bureau des hypothèques*. If he does nothing more than register the sale of the property he still gets his 1% or so of the sale price. A notaire is a public official, appointed by the state, whose main function is to ensure that everything is done correctly, and that all taxes have been paid. It is normal for the notaire appointed by the seller to handle the transaction. The buyer is entitled to appoint their own notaire without paying any additional costs; the two notaires share the fees between them. The buyer pays the fee in any case.

The most important thing to understand is that the notaire does not look out for your interests. If you want impartial legal advice it is best to approach a bilingual lawyer or *avocat*, most likely one based in the UK; some are listed below. If you are concerned about inheritance issues, or whose names should be on the title deeds, then the services of a UK-based lawyer can save a lot of problems. The main thing is to get an estimate of the notaire's fees in advance. You may be required to pay fees in advance; an adjustment is then made at the end. Websites of notaire organisations can be found through www.immonot.com or www.notaire.fr. There is also a convenient list on: www.day-tripper.net/propertyxnotaires.html.

Functions of a Notaire. The notaire can amongst other things:

○ Conduct a search in the land registry to see whether any third parties have any claim on the property.
○ Check on 'easements' (*servitudes*), such as rights of way.
○ Transfer your money via a blocked account to the seller, while ensuring that all fees and taxes have been paid in full.
○ Ensure that any pre-emptive rights on the property are 'purged'.
○ Check on planning permissions that could affect your property.

Specialist UK-Based Lawyers

Bennett & Co Solicitors: 144 Knutsford Road, Wilmslow, Cheshire SK9 6JP; ☎01625-586937; fax 01625-585362; e-mail: internationallawyers@bennett-and-co.com; www.bennett-and-co.com.

John Howell & Co: The Old Glassworks, 22 Endell Street, Covent Garden, London WC2H 9AD; ☎020 7420 0400; fax 020 7836 3626; e-mail info@europelaw.com; www.europelaw.com.

Mr Stefano Lucatello, The International Property Law Centre, Unit 2 Waterside Park, Livingstone Road, Hessle HU13 0EG; ☎01482 350-850; fax 01482 642799; e-mail internationalproperty@maxgold.com; www.internationalpropertylaw.com.

PRE-CONTRACTS

Once you find a property that you like, the next step is to make an offer. Sellers in areas where there are a lot foreigners looking for property may ask for rather more than the property is worth. Knowing how long a property has been on the market is a useful guide to bidding. The offer is made to the estate agent, or the vendor if it is a private sale. You can make a formal written offer, an *offre d'achat*, or *promesse d'achat* – promise to buy – which the seller can consider. It only becomes legally binding on the seller if he or she accepts it. You are not allowed to make any deposits accompanying an *offre d'achat*. The *promesse d'achat* is not particularly recommended; it is better to make a verbal offer, and then ask for a pre-contract to be drawn up.

If your offer is accepted, a pre-contract – an *avant-contrat* – will be drawn up which will be forwarded by the *agent immobilier* to the notaire handling the sale. Although there is no legal obligation to use a preliminary contract, it is universally used. There are two main types of contract commonly used: the *compromis de vente* which is binding on both parties, and the *promesse de vente* (promise to sell), which is binding on the seller. It is normal to pay 5-10% of the sale price as a deposit.

Before Signing the Pre-Sale Contract...
Because of the binding nature of pre-contracts, it is vital to go through the following points before you sign anything:

○ Are you sure that you can use the property for your intended purpose?
○ Have you obtained preliminary planning permission for any building work you want to do?
○ How long will existing planning permission be valid for?
○ Does the sale include all the outbuildings and attached land, without reservation?
○ Are the boundaries of the property clearly marked out?
○ Do any third parties have any rights relating to the property?
○ If the property is recent, have you seen the handing-over report: the *procès verbal réception des travaux*?
○ Has planning permission been obtained in the past for any work?
○ Has the contract been checked by a qualified person?

The Promesse de Vente

With the 'promise to sell' the seller commits himself to selling within at least one month, or more usually within two to three months. In return the potential buyer will pay an *indemnité d'immobilisation*, a sum that compensates the seller for temporarily taking his property off the market. The usual amount is 10% of the sale price. The *promesse de vente* should be signed in front of a notaire. The seller pays the notaire a fee of €300-400.

It is strongly recommended that the *indemnité d'immobilisation* be paid into a blocked account held by a notaire, and not directly to the seller. If you exercise your option to purchase, the *indemnité* will be deducted from the sale price. If the deal falls through the *indemnité* will be returned to you if one of the get-out clauses can be invoked within the allotted time; otherwise you will lose it outright.

The Compromis de Vente

The more common type of pre-contract also goes under the name of *promesse synallagmatique,* since it binds both seller and buyer. It is usual to pay 5-10% of the sale price as a deposit or *indemnité;* this is not the same as the *indemnité d'immobilisation* mentioned above. The deposit should be paid into a blocked account – *compte séquestre* – held by a notaire or by the estate agent.

The nature of the deposit is vitally important. If it is an *arrhes*, then the buyer can withdraw from the agreement but will forfeit the deposit. If the seller decides not to sell, then they are required to pay the buyer twice the amount of the *arrhes* as compensation. A variation on this type of deposit is a *dédit*, a specified sum that is forfeited if the buyer pulls out of the deal.

The other type of deposit, the *acompte* – which can be translated as 'down-payment' or 'instalment' – has more serious implications. In this case the sale is legally enforceable on both buyer and seller. There is no way to prevent the sale from going ahead.

The *compromis de vente* can be signed in front of a notaire, for which there is a charge. It can also be done privately – *sous seing privé* – in duplicate, and no copy has to be registered. In the first case, you have a week's cooling-off period after receiving the draft *compromis de vente* by registered post, during which you can decide not to go ahead with the deal. With the private contract, you have a week after signing during which you can withdraw without penalties.

All payments should be made by bank transfer or banker's draft through the estate agent or notaire's blocked account. Cash sales of properties will not be registered in some parts of the south of France, as a measure against money laundering. Using a banker's draft gives you greater freedom to withhold payment if you are not happy with the terms of the final contract.

The Contents of the Compromis de Vente

It is important to understand that signing the *compromis de vente* virtually makes you the owner of the property you are promising to buy. If you sign a *promesse de vente* the seller remains the owner of the property. Getting out of a *compromis de vente* will be expensive and difficult, so you must be entirely satisfied that the contract is worded the way that you want. You may be asked to sign a standard printed contract which will not contain the get-out clauses that you need. While there are no standardised requirements as to the content, the contract should at least contain the following:

- A full copy of the entry in the population register (*copie intégrale de l'état civil*) of the buyer if they are already living in France.
- Legalised copies of passports, birth certificates, marriage certificates, divorce certificates.
- Official declaration of marriage regime, or civil partnership contract (PACS) from *mairie*.
- A description of the property, including outbuildings.
- The surface area of the land.
- The habitable surface area of the property (compulsory in the case of apartments).
- Proof that the seller is the rightful owner of the property, i.e. an authentic copy of the previous *acte de vente*, along with copies of previous *actes de vente* and other significant documents relating to the property.
- The agreed selling price of the property.
- Who is to pay the notaire's fees.
- Who is to pay the estate agent's commission.
- The property's unique number in the *Plan Cadastral* – land registry.
- Any equipment or fixtures included in the sale: e.g. fitted kitchens, burglar alarms.
- Results of reports on termites, lead and asbestos.
- Date by which the *acte de vente* is to be signed.
- Date on which you will have the use of the property.
- Penalties if one of the parties withdraws from the deal.
- Get-out clauses: *conditions suspensives*.
- Guarantees against *vices cachés* or 'hidden defects'.

The last point is very important. It is necessary to determine who will pay the costs of repairs if hidden defects are later discovered. If the property is less than 10 years old, it will be covered by a *garantie décennale* – a 10-year insurance policy against major construction defects taken out by the builder. The person who bought the new property originally should also have insurance for 10 years, the *assurance dommage ouvrage*. Evidently, once a buyer agrees to take responsibility for hidden defects, then there is no further room for negotiation if any are found. Another solution is for either the seller or the buyer to take out an insurance policy against the discovery or appearance of major faults in the building.

Get-Out Clauses

The negotiation of *conditions suspensives* is an area where expert legal help can be very useful. The most usual one is that the signature of the final deed is dependent on obtaining mortgage finance. This get-out clause should not be treated lightly. If you do not make reasonable efforts to obtain mortgage finance, and you are shown to be acting in bad faith, then you could lose your deposit. Other clauses can be inserted, e.g. you can make the purchase dependent on being able to sell your existing property, or on obtaining planning permission to make alterations to the property.

The Acte Final

After a period stated in the preliminary contract the parties will proceed to signing the final deed of sale, known as the *acte authentique de vente*. The *acte de vente* is signed by the buyer, the seller and one notaire. If there are two notaires involved, one acting for the buyer and one for the seller, only one of them will witness the *acte de vente*. Which one depends on local custom. You will be sent a *projet de l'acte* – a draft of the *acte de vente* – well in advance: a month is normal. This will contain much the same information as the original *compromis de vente*. You will be asked to produce originals of your birth/marriage/divorce certificates, and they may have to be translated and notarised; enquire well in advance. At this point you should have made arrangements for payment of all the sums involved in the purchase, including the taxes and notaire's fees. The notaire will in any case require advance payments to cover his expenses. If a French mortgage is involved, the lender will send the money via the notaire.

Power of Attorney

A date will be fixed for the signing. It is highly desirable to arrange to give a trusted person a power of attorney – a *mandat* – to act on your behalf if you are unable to attend the actual signing. For practical reasons, the power of attorney is best made up in the French form. It should be witnessed by a notaire, or at a French consulate. If it is witnessed by a British notary public, it will have to be legalised by the Foreign and Commonwealth Office (www.fco.gov.uk) to make it valid in France. The document should state what powers you are giving to your representative.

The Actual Signing

Assuming that all the loose ends are tied up, you will be invited to the signing of the *acte de vente*. This will be an interesting experience, or perhaps nerve-racking if there are last-minute hitches. Apart from yourself, the seller and the notaire, and their clerk, there may be other interested parties present. The signing has to take place on French soil, but you can use an authorised representative to sign for you, a normal practice. By this point, all the necessary funds should have been transferred to your notaire's blocked bank account, or you should have your banker's draft ready. There are various taxes and fees to be paid at the last minute, and you should be prepared for this. You should also have paid the first insurance premium on the property, *before* signing the *acte de vente*.

Certain items will often be mentioned in or attached to the *acte de vente* that will not have appeared in the *compromis de vente,* such as:

○ Details of mortgage loans.
○ Full description of the property, with details of previous sales.

- Details of the insurance policy on the property.
- The amount of Capital Gains Tax payable by the seller; or exemption.

COSTS OF PROPERTY PURCHASE

The high level of costs involved with property purchase is one of the main reasons that property prices do not go up very fast in France. The fees and taxes that have to be paid to the notaire and to the state are inaccurately referred to as *frais de notaire*, when only a part of them go to the notaire. One part of the notaire's fees are based on a sliding scale between 5% and 0.825% + TVA at 19.6%, depending on the value of the property. Additional services, such as searches in the land registry, do not have fixed fees.

The stamp duty on transfers of so-called 'new' property (less than 5 years old) is much lower: basically the cost of entering the sale in the land registry. TVA at 19.6% has to be paid on the **first transfer** of a new property, which represents a large disincentive to buying new. A second transfer within 5 years (or after) only attracts 4.89% transfer tax. The notaire's fees are identical on the sale of both new and old properties; the difference is in the transfer taxes.

Notaire's Fees

up to €3,049	5%
€3,049-€6,098	3.3%
€6,098-€16,769	1.65%
€16,769 and above	0.825%

SAMPLE CALCULATIONS					
Value	€100,000 (new)	€100,000 (50% mortgage)	€100,000 (50% mortgage)	€150,000 (50% mortgage)	€200,000
Notaire's fee	1,115.78	1,115.78	1,115.78	1,528.28	1,940.78
Notaire mortgage fee	0	0	1,546.00	0	1,821.00
TVA	218.69	218.69	521.71	299.54	737.31
Transfer taxes	4,890.00	509.84	4,890.00	7,335.00	9,780.00
Tax on mortgage	0	0	307.50	0	615.00
Registration fees	304.88	304.88	304.88	304.88	304.88
Various costs	381.10	381.10	762.20	381.10	762.20
Conservateur hypothèque	100.00	100.00	125.00	150.00	250.00
TOTAL	7,010.45	2,630.28	9,573.00	9,998.80	16,211.16

It follows that the total fees for a typical property transfer without a mortgage come to an average of 7.2% of the sale price. The *droits de mutation* – add up to 4.89%.

Another substantial expense is the commission payable to the estate agent or *immobilier,* which can range from 3% to 10% or more. It is becoming more usual for the seller to pay the estate agent's fees. In many areas where Britons like to buy it is still normal for the buyer to pay the fees. Advertisements do not always make this clear, so ask first.

After the Sale

Once the *acte de vente* has been signed, the notaire has to pay all the taxes and commissions (unless you are paying the *immobilier* directly) out of the sums that you have passed over to him. The title is registered with the *bureau des hypothèques* – the register of deeds and mortgages, as well as the mortgage, if any. Eventually you will receive a certificate informing you that the title has been registered. The whole process can take a year or more. The original title deed – *la minute* – remains with the notaire. He is authorised to make authentic copies if necessary.

Special Procedures in Relation to Copropriétés

The same surveys for asbestos, termites and lead paint have to be done with *copropriétés* or co-ownership properties (normally apartments) as with other residential property. You should also ask to see the *carnet d'entretien*, or log-book of the building, to see what kind of repairs have been carried out in recent years. The manager of the *copropriété* will most likely be present at the signing of the *acte de vente*. This must contain details of what percentage of the communal areas belong to you – your *quote part* – and what percentage of the communal charges you will be required to pay.

MS.

WHAT HAPPENS NEXT

CHAPTER SUMMARY

- **Electricity.** Foreign buyers often fail to pay enough notice to the state of the wiring in their prospective property.
- **Gas.** Mains gas is a rarity outside big cities, so you will need bottled gas.
- **Heating.** Even in the South of France, reliable heating is a necessity, even more so at higher elevations, where it can be very cold in winter.
- **Renovating.** Although many foreign buyers are dissatisfied with local tradesmen, it is preferable to use locals where possible.
- **Swimming Pools.** Installing a swimming pool greatly increases the value of your property and allows you to charge a higher rental.
- **Bed & Breakfasts.** The South of France already has an over-abundance of B&Bs. This is a serious career choice rather than an easy way to make a living.

UTILITIES

Electricity

Many foreign property-buyers take little notice of the state of the wiring in the property that they are thinking of buying, something that can prove to be an expensive mistake. One survey of French housing built before 1974 estimated that 96% of units had some deficiencies in the wiring. The main problems are lack of, or insufficient earthing, corroded wiring and unsuitable circuit-breakers. Apart from any risk of electrocution, if you are taking over an older property it is essential to find out whether the wiring can handle heavy-amperage equipment such as washing machines and electric cookers. If you need to run electric heating at the same time as other heavy equipment like an electric cooker, water heater, washing machine etc., then you will require a supply of at least 12 KvA (kilovolt amperes or kilowatts), for which heavier wiring is needed to the electricity meter.

If your property has no electricity supply, the French state monopoly, Électricité de France (EDF), will connect you to the grid; the price will depend on how far you are from the nearest electricity pylon. Where the electricity has been cut off for work to be done, then you will require a *certificat de conformité* or CC from the safety organisation Consuel to certify that the system is safe before EDF will reconnect your supply.

When buying property it is in your interest to ask the seller to allow a *Diagnostic Confiance Sécurité* to be carried out. This is a 40-minute inspection resulting in an objective assessment of the state of the wiring of your house. Once it has been carried out you can call in an electrician to give an estimate (*devis*) of the cost of any work needed. If your prospective seller refuses to allow a DCS then you should be suspicious. A DCS can be arranged by calling an EDF advisor on 0801 126 126, or through the Promotelec website www.promotelec.com. Information about different tariffs can be found on EDF's websites: http://monagence.edf.fr and www.mamaison.edf.fr.

Gas

In most of France there is no mains gas (*gaz de ville*), so you have the option of installing a large *citerne* (2 cubic metre tank) and having liquefied gas delivered, or using bottled gas. In the latter case there is a choice between propane and butane gas. If the temperature goes below freezing in your area in the winter, which is not uncommon inland in the Languedoc, then you should use propane; butane can freeze in winter.

Mains gas is the monopoly of Gaz de France (GDF), which shares offices with Electricité de France. There are 4 different tariffs depending on how much gas you use; bills are sent every two months. For more information see www.gazdefrance.com.

Water

The mains water supply is safe to drink everywhere if not always tasty. The French consume a lot of bottled mineral water. Mains water is supplied by Générale des Eaux and other local companies around France. There have been water shortages in central and southern France in recent years during hot weather. The water supply is metered and can cost twice as much as in the UK. The average price is €2.8 per cubic metre. The average person on the Côte d'Azur consumes 74 cubic metres per year. To find out the local price of water, and the nearest supplier look at the website www.generale-des-eaux.com.

Septic Tanks/Fosses Septiques

The state of one's septic tank is a favourite subject of conversation with foreign residents in France. There is a trend in France to connect more properties to the main sewage system, known as *tout à l'égout*. Cesspits – *puisards* – where all the waste simply goes into a hole in the ground are being phased out, and it is no longer legal to build one. All *fosses septiques* are supposed to meet a new government standard by the year 2005. Septic tanks process the waste from toilets and other used water, through the natural action of bacteria, so that eventually only fairly harmless water is left. All the waste runs into the first settling tank, or septic tank, where the solid matter sinks to the bottom, while scum forms on the surface. The naturally present bacteria break the waste matter down, releasing methane. The remainder goes into a second settling tank, which should be half the length of the first tank, and then into a 'drain field' or system of soakaways, with a series of drain pipes or drain tiles laid on gravel. The drain pipes or tiles are perforated so that the effluent filters away into the ground. The solid matter in the septic tank has to be emptied once in a while, the so-called *vidage*. The interval depends very much on how well the tank is maintained. Septic tanks work best in hotter climates.

Telephones

For the moment France Télécom is the only company that can install your phone and you will make your calls through them. British handsets need an adaptor to work in France: the British variety have three wires, while the French ones have only two. The Yellow Pages are on www.pagesjaunes.fr and private subscribers on www.annuaire.com.

Mobile Phones

If you spend any amount of time in France you will want to rent or buy a mobile phone there, but before you sign a contract it is worth considering the small print. You can try to have the SIM card in your phone replaced with a French one, so you can carry on using the same phone. If your phone is 'SIM-locked', i.e. the card cannot be changed, then you need a French mobile. Unless you are officially resident in France, French mobile phone companies will only let you use a phone with a pre-paid card, on production of your passport. The well-known deals are Orange La Mobicarte, SFR La Carte, and Bouygues Carte Nomad. As France is relatively thinly populated in comparison to the UK, mobile phone coverage is not guaranteed, and there are areas where you will not have any reception. For a clear overview of the different deals on offer, look at the website www.comparatel.com.

Internet

France is still some years behind the UK in terms of internet use and availability. This is to some extent because of the pioneering system known as Minitel started in 1985, which provides a service similar to the internet. Once you have settled in to your new home in France, you can look at the different internet service providers' offerings, which are more limited than what you would find in the UK. For the moment you will only be able to have ADSL (high-speed connections) in certain areas. For more information about different ISP charges look at the website www.comparatel.com.

MAKING THE MOVE

In principle, you can take anything you want with you to France. If you are an EU citizen entering France with your household effects you should have a *carte de séjour* with you (although this requirement may be scrapped soon), and a notarised certificate of ownership of your French property. There are restrictions on importing firearms, drugs, alcohol, tobacco and medicines. If you have any questions contact British Customs & Excise via the website: www.hmce.gov.uk. Non-EU citizens must show that they have owned items for at least six months prior to importing them, and such items should show signs of wear and tear. Contact your nearest French embassy for details.

If you import your furniture and other goods yourself, you should try to have receipts for expensive items such as antiques, otherwise French customs and excise may claim that you are importing goods for sale. You are required to inform French customs if you are carrying more than €8000 in cash with you.

Importing Your Car. Under EU regulations, you can bring in one car for your personal use, as long as you can show that you are going to be permanently resident in France. There are few conditions attached to importing a car: you need to have the original registration papers, invoice and proof that you have paid VAT in your home country. Do not forget to inform the DVLA in the UK that you are taking your car abroad. Once you are officially resident in France, you will need to register your car with the local authorities. The local *préfecture* will send you a leaflet explaining how to obtain your French registration document, the *carte grise*. You will also need to make modifications to the headlights and the exhaust for your car to pass the required norms. Eventually you will also be required to change your number plates.

Removal Firms. Having your effects moved to the South of France is expensive. A reputable removals firm will charge at least £1000 for a basic three cubic metres. If you are flexible about times and don't mind having your effects moved in the same consignment as other people's then you can get a reduction. By and large, it is best to buy furniture and carpets in France rather than pay a fortune to bring over stuff that will look out of place in your new home. The watchword is to make a list of the bare minimum you need and then cut it by half.

For further information on removal firms see *International Removals and Pets* in the *General Introduction*.

Pets. Importing conventional pets to France has become fairly routine for UK residents. France declared itself rabies-free in 2002, although there is always the likelihood that rabies will return from neighbouring countries. All you need now is a certificate of good health from a vet in the UK, acquired five days or less before you leave for France, as long as you do not pass through a rabies-infected country on the way to France.

If you plan to bring your pet back to the UK, then you need to obtain a PETS Passport, and have your pet inoculated against rabies every year. See www.defra.gov.uk for more information and *International Removals and Pets* in the *General Introduction*.

If you bring a pet from outside the EU into France, there are more stringent regulations. The French government does not publicise the rules on the internet. It is advisable to contact a veterinary surgeon in your country, or a specialised pets carrier and double-check the information; vets can make mistakes about dates. Contact the Independent Pet and Animal Transport Association at www.ipata.com.

BUILDING OR RENOVATING

HIRING WORKERS

Expatriates are constantly debating the pros and cons of using local tradesmen. Many foreign owners have been disappointed by local French tradesmen and swear that they will never use their services again. The difficulties generally centre on the more laid-back attitude to work in the South of France compared with Britain. Two- or even three-hour lunchbreaks are quite normal; when accompanied with wine the results can be disastrous. It is also a fact that French tradesmen are less ambitious than their British counterparts; it can take months to get someone to come round to start a job. The usual advice is to obtain estimates (*devis*) from several tradesmen so you can be sure of finding someone who can start work within a reasonable time frame. Estimates can be binding or not. In any case, it is usually necessary to supervise French tradesmen, otherwise they may not do the work properly, or simply postpone the job. If you are having a substantial job done, involving several tradesmen, you may wish to appoint a *maître d'œuvre* or master builder to supervise the whole operation.

There are risks involved in employing someone just because they speak English;

many Britons have been the victims of incompetent or dishonest builders brought over from the UK, whose work carried no guarantees. Work done by builders registered in France has to be insured for ten years – the *garantie décennale*. In addition you will not qualify for grants towards doing the work, and the cost will not be taken account in reducing your Capital Gains Tax liability if you sell within 15 years.

DIY. The British are well-known for being keen on *le bricolage* or DIY, and to a degree the French are beginning to imitate them. DIY stores such as Castorama and Leroy Merlin, as well as smaller shops in local towns, carry vast stocks of materials and equipment. You are best advised to buy locally; apart from anything else, non-metric materials won't fit. Learning the names of different items is an education in itself.

Gardens. Along with the increase in DIY stores, there are more and more garden centres in France. This is related to a general demographic shift as more affluent families move out to the countryside and commute into town, and are then confronted with the need to keep up their new gardens. Traditionally, smaller houses in southern French villages and towns did not have gardens attached to them. Houses were built close together for protection from invaders and the elements. At the most there would be a small patch of land across the road where you could grow some vegetables. Farmers had small houses on their fields where they would go to live in the summer season. If you are lucky enough to have a substantial garden with your property, then you will also need to consider how to water it. In the drier parts of southeast France there are irrigation schemes, or you may be able to draw water from a well. You should not assume that just because your property comes with a bit of land that it can be turned into an oasis of lawns and flowers.

Swimming Pools. For many foreign buyers a swimming pool is a must, all the more so if you want to rent your property out to holidaymakers in the summer. There are three main possibilities: a pre-fabricated fibre-glass pool, a galvanised steel construction with a vinyl liner, or reinforced concrete. There are no problems with a high water table in the south of France, so reinforced concrete is a popular choice. The maintenance costs of a swimming pool generally come to about 10% of the purchase price per year. Since 2004 it has been compulsory to install safety measures to prevent children from drowning in your pool, a common cause of death in the South. You have a choice of a cover or fencing. The regulations are very strict now, with a €45,000 fine for non-compliance.

MAKING MONEY FROM YOUR PROPERTY

Owning property in the South of France represents a money-making opportunity. If you are entirely reliant on renting out your property to cover the cost of the mortgage, then you run the risk of not being able to pay for it. This does not, of course, cover leaseback schemes, where your rental income is guaranteed to cover the mortgage. The *chambres d'hôtes* (bed & breakfast) and *gîtes* business is becoming increasingly competitive. *Gîtes* and *chambres d'hôtes* are very different businesses. The term *gîtes* originally meant a basic dwelling, but is now applied to any kind of self-catering lodgings in the countryside. In Britain they are called 'holiday cottages'. The implication is that the owner has little contact with the guests, and may not even need to live on the premises if they employ someone to deal with changeovers. What are known as *chambres d'hôtes* are bed and breakfasts in the English sense. They often include dinner as well, which are known as *tables d'hôtes.*

If you fulfil their strict requirements, the departmentally based organisation Gîtes de France may be able to provide grants to convert your property to make it suitable for running *gîtes* or *chambres d'hôtes.* You are then listed in Gîtes de France's annual catalogue, and pay 12-15% of your takings in return. GdF's demands can be quite unreasonable, and many foreign owners give up on them. If you quit the organisation within 10 years of taking a grant via GdF then you will have to pay it back.

You can also advertise your property and get rental customers' online bookings by having an advert on a property website such as Gecko get aways (☎0870 741 2700; www.geckogetaways.com; e-mail info@geckogetaways.com).

Running a Business from your Property

Since 2003 it has become rather easier to work as a self-employed person from home. You can carry on your professional activity from home as long as:

○   You do not receive customers at home.
○   There are no deliveries of goods.
○   You are working from your principal residence..

You are also allowed to register a company at your home address. If you are in rented accommodation, you have a right to register a company from your home address for at least five years, and indefinitely if there is nothing in the lease preventing you.

When working from home part of your electricity, telephone, gas and other expenses are tax-deductible (one-third of the total is usual). There has to be a clear separation between your working and living areas. For further details see *Starting a Business in France,* pub. Vacation Work (www.vacationwork.co.uk.

Jennifer-Jane Viner, who is originally from Australia, owns 4 small one-bedroom holiday homes in the village of Villeneuve-de-Béziers in the Hérault, together with her large family home where she now offers B&B. She is also a consultant on setting up a bed & breakfast, renovation and property management. See website www.le-guide.com/anges-gardiens or contact anges-gardiens@southfrance.com.

Jennifer-Jane Viner explains how she ended up running her businesses from home in France

We bought our first holiday property at Cap d'Agde in 1981, and then a village house near Pézenas in several years later. Then in 1983 the family moved to Villeneuve-les-Béziers after buying a lovely old town house in a very run-down condition. After selling the first two smaller properties I then bought the current four houses in order rent out long term. My business is a SARL called Anges Gardiens. Originally I had a UK-registered business but found it necessary to send the French accountants reports to England, have them professionally translated and then re-done by the English accountant. This proved very expensive so I transferred everything over here. My company deals with property management and bed and breakfasts. You need to have good professional advice. I have several lawyers including an English lady solicitor who is also qualified as a French notaire.

Although I originally started to let my small properties as holiday homes I now let most of them to young French people on long-term contracts. I use the standard 3-year contract for long-term furnished lettings. Usually an agent finds tenants for me and checks their references etc. I pay half his fee of one month's rent, and the tenant the other half. Many

French owners don't want to use agents because of the fees. If you leave it to a property management agency they will charge 10% of the rent all the way through the lease. Since I used to work for a French estate agent I know the system well enough.

There are a lot of bed and breakfasts that have started up in this area. They take a couple of years to get going and publicise and they cost a lot to set up. You have to be there all the time to answer the phone and see people in and out but one meets interesting people and one is never lonely. Out of season this is not a holiday resort, but there are tourists, e.g. Americans and Australians, who will go visiting historical places out of season.

There is a great deal of renovation and house building going on in this area. Because this is a medieval gated village it is very difficult to get permission to make exterior changes. For example, it is next to impossible to get permission for a roof terrace, especially near a church. One person was told she couldn't have one, even though it wasn't visible from the road, but she could have a loggia by taking out a part of the wall. However you can usually remove some tiles and put in large Velux windows discreetly. The builders know everything that is permitted, so you ask them. You must also be very careful to check about which colours are allowed for the exterior rendering. Be aware that neighbours can complain and it is important to keep on good terms so that they can keep an eye on the property when you are away.

Renting Out

Short-Term Letting. Many foreigners rent out their second home occasionally to people they know, or privately through placing small ads in the UK. Short-term lets of holiday homes come under the *Location Libre* regime (based only on the Civil Code), which gives considerable protection to owners. It is always advisable to have a written contract – *contrat de location* – however short the let is. This should include an inventory of the contents of the property, the *état des lieux*. For the rental to come under the *Location Libre* regime the property has to be fully furnished, and the property is only to be used for holidays by tenants.

It is usual to engage a local agent to handle the rental of your property. They will take up to 20% of the rent for their services. It is a good idea to install a telephone in the property that will only take incoming calls, so you can check up if there is someone actually staying there.

The number of weeks you can expect to rent out a property depends on the climate, and the presence of a swimming pool. Except in the south of France or Paris, the letting season is not likely to cover more than 32 weeks. The core letting season is only July and August; most French take their holidays in August. This should be taken into account when you buy a property where the income is a significant factor in your decision.

There is a basic letting tax of 25% for non-resident owners. It is very risky not to declare letting income to the French tax authorities, as they could tax you on the basis that you rented out your property for 52 weeks of the year. You are also supposed to inform the UK tax authorities that you have paid your tax in France, and you will pay the difference between the French 25% tax and the higher rate in the UK, if you are in that tax bracket.

Long-Term Letting. A rental of more than 6 months is considered long-term. Most long-term lets come under the *Loi 1989* regime, which gives tenants considerable protection against eviction. The basic lease is the 3-6-9 lease; the minimum rental period is for 3 years. Rents can be reviewed every 3 years, but there is not much scope for large rises, and in theory the rent might have to be reduced if the so-called 'construction index' goes down. You are entitled to a deposit of up to 3 months' rent which can be used to pay for damage or unpaid bills. The deposit is usually referred to as *la caution*, but officially it is the *dépôt de garantie*.

It is extremely different to evict troublesome tenants; even if you get a court order the police will not want to get involved.

Selling On

The usual way to sell a property is to give one estate an exclusive authority – *mandat exclusif* – to sell the property. You have to decide whether to leave open the possibility of finding a buyer yourself or not. If the estate agent has a *mandat exclusif absolu*, then you have to pay him the commission even if you found the buyer yourself. In the case of the *mandat simple* you can give several estate agents the authority to try to sell the property, and try looking for a buyer yourself. There may be disadvantages to placing the property with a lot of agents, as it makes it appear that the property is hard to sell. In any case, the estate agent who introduces the successful buyer to you is the one who gets the commission. There are areas where the buyer pays the commission, and this must be stated in the property advert. The *mandat* is for a limited time period.

British owners may want to try to sell privately to other foreigners by advertising on a website such as www.frenchconnection.co.uk or in a magazine. Your property may appeal more to foreigners and fetch a higher price with them. A good photo is an absolute must in any case.

The seller has to pay for reports to be drawn up on the presence of asbestos, termites and lead; each of them comes to something like €500 or more. The sale cannot go ahead until the reports have been made, and the results should usually be in the pre-contract, or *compromis de vente*.

SPOT CHECK – FRANCE	
Political/economic stability	France has recently been politically stable, and will probably remain so. The economy has been in a crisis since 1974; unemployment was at over 10% nationally in 2004. Out of 22 regions, Languedoc-Roussillon is France's poorest at number 22; Provence-Alpes-Côte-d'Azur is at 6; Corsica at 20.
Sunshine/climate	The South of France has an excellent climate. The weather is best towards the Italian border close to the sea; inland can be cold in winter.
Cost of living/taxes	France's overall cost of living is rather lower than the UK's; the Riviera is France's most expensive area after Paris. Income taxes are moderate, but social security costs are high. Total tax burden is 45% of GDP.
Accessibility	The South of France has become much more accessible with budget airlines flying to small airports. The high-speed train network extends only to Marseilles.
Property availability	There are shortages along the Riviera coast exacerbated by a rapidly increasing population.
Property prices	Prices are sky-high in fashionable parts of the Riviera. Average prices: Languedoc-Roussillon: €95,000/£33,000; PACA*: €150,000/£100,000; Corsica: €140,000/£92,000.
Cost of property purchase as % of value	Total costs are 12-14%.
Ease of purchase and ease of renovation	The purchasing process is complicated and expensive. Renovation can be difficult if you rely on local tradesmen.
Annual property taxes	Vary widely; lowest taxes are in the wealthiest towns.
Investment potential	There has recently been a UK-style boom in the south. Historically, the stock market has always outperformed property in France.
Suitability for letting	The Riviera has good potential for letting; Languedoc-Roussillon is harder work. It helps if you have a swimming pool.

* Provence-Alpes-Côte-d'Azur

Buying a House on the Mediterranean

GIBRALTAR

GIBRALTAR

CHAPTER SUMMARY

- Gibraltar has been a British Sovereign Territory since 1713 and its ownership is still the cause of a major dispute with Spain.
- **Access.** Flights from the UK to Gibraltar can cost as little as £22 return.
  - When disputes with Spain flare up the Spaniards are apt to close the land border with Spain or make crossing it a very lengthy business.
- Property prices on the Rock (Gibraltar's nickname) have tripled in the last few years and have been sustained by the release of development land.
- About 47% of Gibraltarians own their own home compared with 6% twenty years ago and they have helped fuel the current property boom along with foreign buyers.
- **Tax haven.** Gibraltar has special tax rates for wealthy individuals classed as 'individuals of high net worth' who pay tax only on the first £50,000 of income.
  - Hundreds of European millionaires have bought property in Gibraltar in the last few years.
- More land for development is likely to be released from Ministry of Defence and Naval usage.
- **Price of Property.** Because of the scarcity of land (Gibraltar is 2.5 square miles) property is always going to be expensive there.
- Petty theft and violent crime have increased in Gibraltar in recent years.

INTRODUCTION

In Greek mythology, the geological formation known as Gibraltar, The Rock of Gibraltar, or sometimes just the Rock, was one of the twin pillars set up by the demi-god Hercules at the entrance to the Mediterranean sea, when performing his tenth labour. The other Pillar of Hercules is the cliff of Acha in Ceuta, the Spanish enclave in North Africa, which projects into the sea on the southern side of the Straight of

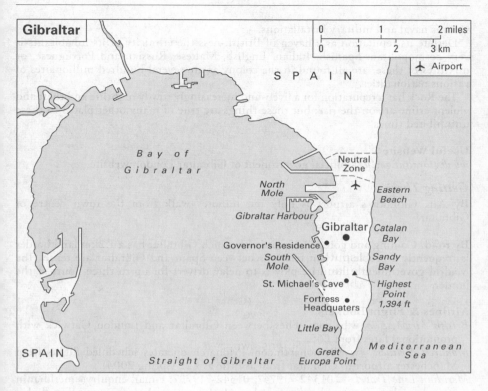

Gibraltar. In ancient times, The Pillars of Hercules marked the limits of the known world. In later times, when the known world had expanded and a nation's power was proportional to the size of its navy, Gibraltar's position guarding the ten mile span of sea between Gibraltar and Africa at the entrance to the Mediterranean Sea from the Atlantic, was one of the most strategically important in Europe.

The year 2004 will be remembered on Gibraltar as a year-long party to commemorate the de facto tri-centenary of British sovereignty and the cultural and historical links this has forged between Gibraltar and Britain. Spain lost Gibraltar in 1704 during the War of Spanish Succession and formally ceded it to Britain in the Treaty of Utrecht in 1713. In 2002 a referendum was held in Gibraltar over the British government's proposal to share sovereignty of the Rock with Spain. Gibraltarians voted overwhelmingly against this proposal and they have since tried (without success) to have Gibraltar created a Dominion with its own parliament. All this does not mean that Spain has given up attempts to repossess the Rock, far from it, they consider it a rightful part of Spain, and to indicate their displeasure at its remaining British, they periodically close the border between Spain and Gibraltar thus making life as inconvenient as possible for the Gibraltarians.

Meanwhile, Gibraltarians are experiencing a period of confidence, thanks to the referendum vote, and a buoyant economy currently showing 6% annual growth. Its 30,000 permanent inhabitants have witnessed a huge spate of residential building, particularly at the luxury end of the market and particularly on sites vacated by various naval and military installations.

Despite its reputation as a haven of British-ness the ethnicity of its inhabitants is very cosmopolitan: Spanish, Italian, English, Maltese, Russian and Portuguese, or mixtures of these, are all found in the colony as are several hundred millionaires of various nationalities.

The Rock has a reputation for a lively and increasingly rowdy nightlife and theft and violent crime are on the rise; but these things are true of many other places in these uninhibited times.

Useful Website
www.gibraltar.gov.uk - official government of Gibraltar London website.

Getting There
By Air. Gibraltar's airport is only ten minutes walk from the town centre of Gibraltar.

By road. Coming and going via Spain with which Gibraltar has a 1.2km land border is frequently a problem when relations between Spain and Gibraltar are tense. The Madrid government's favourite ploy is to delay drivers for up to three hours at the border.

Airlines & Flight Bookers
British Airways: www.ba.com. Flies between Gibraltar and London Gatwick with
   promotional fares from £65.
Monarch Airlines: www.flymonarch.com. Monarch operates scheduled flights from
   Manchester airport to Gibraltar from as little as £22 (spring 2004).
Meridian Line Travel: ☎01342-719747; 01342-719737; e-mail enquiry@meridianin
   etravel.co.uk; www.meridianlinetravel.co.uk. European charter agent offers flights
   from Luton to Gibraltar.

Taxes
Gibraltar's Special Tax Status. The Treaty of Rome allows Gibraltar exemption from the EU's common customs tariff and turnover taxes. However, the EU has an agenda to standardise and harmonise taxes throughout the EU and Gibraltar may come within its sights in the future. At present, Gibraltar does not have capital gains tax, wealth tax, or VAT. Additionally, Gibraltar has a policy of encouraging wealthy individuals to become resident in Gibraltar at very favourable tax rates.

The tax year runs from 1 July to 30 June.

High Net Worth Individuals. Special tax legislation operates as an incentive for high net worth individuals. The Gibraltar standard rate of income tax is rather high (35%), but 'high net worth' individuals benefit from having a ceiling on the amount of their income that is liable for tax in Gibraltar. This means that they pay tax only on the first £50,000 of their income and all income above that amount is tax-free. There is a minimum tax payable per annum of £14,000. The limits were last changed in July 2004.

To be accepted under this legislation an application has to be lodged with the Financial Development Secretary together with a fee of £1,000 and two references, one of which must be a financial one, usually from the individual's banker. The individual must also acquire, for his exclusive use approved residential accommodation for not less than seven months and must reside in the property for that period plus a further 30 days (which need not be consecutive) during assessment.

Special Tax Status – Companies. Up to the end of 2002 corporate entities defined as Exempt and Qualifying Companies, were allowed a zero rate tax. This category of corporation no longer exists. From January 2003, such companies are still exempt from corporation tax, but new taxes have been introduced on company personnel and property occupation, capped at 15% of profits.

Personal Taxation for Non High Worth Status Individuals. The regular income tax rates for those without special tax status are from 17%-45%.

Income band in Gibraltar £s (same value as sterling)	Rate of tax 2003/04
0-4,000	17%
4,001-10,000	30%
10,000-15,000	35%
15,001 plus	45%

Useful Addresses

Charles A Gomez & Co: P.O. Box 659, 2 Hadfield House, Library Street, Gibraltar; ☎+350 74998; fax +350 73074; e-mail carlaw@gibnet.gi. Barristers-at-law. Advice on financial services including residence and tax residence.

Cruz & Co: Suites 19 & 21, 1st floor, Watergardens 3,Waterport, PO Box 883, Gibraltar; ☎+350 76552; fax +350 76553; e-mail info@cruzlaw.gi. Tax planning, company set ups.

ECS International: P.O. Box 398, Ground Floor, Neptune House, Marina Bay, Gibraltar; ☎+350 76513; fax +350 79523; e-mail info@ecsinter.gi. Chartered accountants. Offshore, personal or corporate tax planning.

The Financial Services Commission: 943 Europort, Gibraltar; ☎+350 40283; fax +350 40282; e-mails: info@fsc.gi and fsc@gibnet.gi; www.fsc.gi.

Hassans International Law Firm: 57/63 Line Wall Road, P.O. Box 199, Gibraltar; ☎+350 79000; fax +350 71966. Largest law firm in Gibraltar specialists in offshore, commercial, financial regulation and tax.

Portland Services: Suite 1, Garrison House, 3 Library Ramp, P.O. Box 847, Gibraltar; ☎+350 43115; fax +350 40145. Tax planning, company formation.

Health

The Gibraltar Health Authority is the organisation in charge of providing health care and facilities in Gibraltar. The old St. Bernard's Hospital, that dates back to Napoleonic times has just been superseded by a brand new fully equipped general 210-bed hospital opened in 2004 and located at Europort Buildings 1-4.

Under a reciprocal health agreement with the UK, UK citizens are entitled to use the Gibraltar health facilities on the same conditions as Gibraltar citizens and they and other EU citizens are entitled to free emergency treatment. Non EU citizens have to have private insurance.

Further details of medical facilities including pharmacies and can be found at www.gibraltar.gov.uk/healthcare.asp.

Media

As English is the official language of Gibraltar there is no problem finding English-language newspapers and broadcasting services. The Gibraltar Broadcasting Corporation (www.gbc.gi) provides local radio and television services. The oldest Gibraltar newspaper is the *Gibraltar Chronicle* (www.chronicle.gi) and there are some online 24-hours news services including iberianews.gi. The news weekly *Panorama* (www.panorama.gi) is published on Mondays and lifestyle and leisure magazines include *The Gibraltar Magazine.com* (www.TheGibraltarMagazine.com).

Useful Addresses

Gibraltar Broadcasting Corporation: Broadcasting House, 18 South Barrack Road, Gibraltar; ☎+350 79760; fax +350 78673; e-mail gbc@gibraltar.gi; www.gbc.gi.
Gibraltar Chronicle: 2 Library Gardens, Gibraltar; ☎+350 78589; fax +350 79927; e-mail letters@chronicle.gi.
Iberianews.gi: for Gibraltar office fax +34 856 120 290; e-mail gisearch@gibnet.gi or gibsearch@ono.com.

Summary of Housing

Gibraltar has experienced a property boom in the last few years fuelled by masses of new development. About 47% of Gibraltarians now own their own home, compared with 6% two decades ago.

> **Janice Davies of the Norwich and Peterborough Building Society's Gibraltar branch explains the boom**
> *For many years there was little land available for building on, but in the last few years all that has changed with a lot of new land being released by the government for building purposes. Many of the Gibraltarians who bought property under the government's affordable housing schemes of past years, are now trading up and investing in the new real estate here and foreigners, including lots of British people are buying as well. Prices have trebled in the last three years; it's supply and demand and I don't know when the prices will stabilise again.*

Owing to the scarcity of land and the fact that building costs are higher, property is more expensive in Gibraltar than in Spain. Average prices have been compared to the prices in the smarter UK suburban areas, however, the cost of living is slightly cheaper than the UK.

PUBLIC HOLIDAYS	
1 January	New Year's Day
8 March	Commonwealth Day
9 April	Good Friday
12 April	Easter Monday
1 May	May Day
31 May	Spring Bank Holiday
14 June	Queen's Birthday
30 August	bank holiday
10 September	Gibraltar National Day
25 December	Christmas Day
26 December	Boxing Day

RESIDENCE & ENTRY REGULATIONS

European Union nationals have equal rights with Gibraltarians to enter the colony, work or live there. Individuals of any nationality can also apply for High Net Worth Individual status and benefit from very low tax (see *Taxes* above). The Principal Immigration Office (PIO) is responsible for handling residence permits under the guidelines set by the Immigration Control Ordinance (IPO) which holds overall responsibility for the rights of entry and residence in Gibraltar.

When it comes to regulations for staying in Gibraltar the candidates are categorised into the following groups.

British Subjects Employed by the British Government or Gibraltar Services

The above groups are entitled to residence in Gibraltar with no permits whatsoever.

Married to Gibraltarians

The remedy for sexual discrimination does not seem to have percolated the Gibraltarian body of law. A non-Gibraltarian man married to a Gibraltarian women is automatically entitled to a residence permit but not the other way around. A non-Gibraltarian woman married to a Gibraltarian man has to apply for a residence permit, which is not automatically granted by law (though in practice it generally is).

Nationals of the EU

EU nationals are entitled to automatic rights of entry and to stay in Gibraltar, but a residence permit is needed if they plan to stay. The majority of those staying in Gibraltar or buying property and living in Gibraltar will be those working in Gibraltar, or former employees of HM Government there, or retirees who have been employed there, or individuals of high net worth status (which is dealt with separately).

If the residence permit is applied for by an individual with employment in Gibraltar, then the permit is usually granted for the period of work. If the applicant is not working in Gibraltar, then a residence permit is granted for six months up to five years and is renewable.

Application for a Residence Permit. Applications for a residence permit are made to The Immigration Department (New Mole House, Rosia Road, Gibraltar; ☎+350 71543). Applicants should apply in person between 9am and 12.45pm with their passport and spare photograph and proof of residence.

WHERE TO FIND YOUR IDEAL HOME

Gibraltar lies on the southern coast of Spain and occupies 6.5sq. km (2.5 sq. miles) of land and has a 12 km coastline. The highest point of the rock is 426m (1,394 ft) but in most places, the Rock is close to sea level. There are a couple of sandy beaches, but no river water supply. Water cisterns collect some water and the rest is produced through desalination. The Ministry of Defence owns about a fifth of the land area though it has vacated several large areas over the last few years, the latest in 2004. Most of the new apartments being built are in waterside complexes, beachside complexes and on vacated MOD sites. As building land is so scarce in Gibraltar several new luxury developments are towered. Other apartments have been created through conversion of historic administrative buildings. Even the former naval hospital, which dates from the early 1900s, has had a makeover to convert it to residences.

Despite Gibraltar's reputation as a tax haven for very wealthy Europeans, hundreds of whom have bought properties there over the past few years, not all property has a millionaire price tag. The Norwich and Peterborough Estate Agents in Gibraltar have properties from £99,000.

Typical Properties for Sale in Gibraltar

As the Gibraltar £ is has parity with sterling, the following prices are given in pounds.

Location	Type	Description	Price
Gib-V Estate	Modern apartment	2 bedrooms. 1 bath. Fully furnished. Exterior parking space.	£97,000
Town centre	Modern apartment	Large. 1 bedroom decorated to very high standard including wooden floors. Spectacular views.	£155,000
Europlaza (high rise)	Apartment being built	2 bedrooms, 2 bathrooms. Spectacular new development. Will be finished 2005	£199,000,
Gowlands Ramp area	House	3 bedrooms. 2 bathrooms. 140 sq km plus 40 sq. m. loft. Air conditioning throughout. Patio. Good bay view.	£215,000

Estate Agents in Gibraltar

Ank Homes: 26 Governors Street; Gibraltar; ☎+350 44455; fax +350 44433; e-mail ankhomes@gibnynex.gi.

Ayling Property Services: 5 Casemates House, Casemates Square, Gibraltar; +350 77983.

BMI Insurance Services: BMI Property Matters Ltd., Unit 7, Portland House, Glacis Road, Gibraltar; +350 51010; fax +350 42621; e-mail info@bmigroup.gi; www.bmigroup.gi.

Bray Properties: 3 Market Lane, Gibraltar; ☎+350 47777; e-mail brayglob@gibnet.gi; www.brayproperties.com.

Brian Francis and Associates: 3rd Floor, 6A Leanse Place, 50 Town Range, Gibraltar; ☎+350 71006; also an office at 299A Main Street,Gibraltar; ☎+350 71131;e-mail info@bfagib.com; www.bfagib.com.

Cannon Real Estate: Suite 1a, 292a Main Street, Gibraltar; ☎+350 78006p; fax + 350 50877.

Fiduciary Property Services Ltd.: Unit 7 Portland House, Gracis Road, P.O. Box 469.

Hassan Raphael Estate Agents: 109 Main Street; fax +350 40471.

P&O Homes: 9/1 Cooperage Lane, Gibraltar; ☎+350 47474; fax +350 52331; e-mail info@po-homes.com. Properties in Gibraltar and on the Costa del Sol.

Norwich & Peterborough Estate Agents: 198-200 Main Street, P.O. Box 535, Gibraltar; ☎+ 350 48532; fax +350 45051; e-mail info@npea-gibraltar.co.uk; www.npea-gibraltar.co.uk.

Norwich & Peterborough Estate Agents: The Old Bank, Cannon Lane, Gibraltar; ☎+350 48532; fax +350 45051; info@npestates.com.

Prime Estate Agents: 3/1 Governor's Parade, P.O. Box 391, Gibraltar; ☎+350 48101; fax +350 43572; e-mail prime@gibnet.gi.

Queensway Quay Development Co. Ltd: Ragged Staff Wharf, Queensway 'Quay, P.O.

Box 126; ☎+350 78780; fax +350 75659; e-mail one@taywood.gi.
Richardson & Co (Estate Agents) Ltd.: 1-4 College Lane, Gibraltar; ☎+350 79285; fax +350 75659; e-mail ricco@gibnet.gi.

THE PURCHASING PROCEDURE

Banks

For a small place, Gibraltar has a lot of banks, about 30 at the current time. Most of these are branches or subsidiaries of international banks. Most Gibraltar banks offer special rates of interest to large depositors in their private banking sections. The minimum deposit is decided by the bank.

A list of banks in Gibraltar can be found at www.fsc.gi/fsclists/bnklist.asp.

Opening a Bank Account. It is fairly straightforward to open a bank account in any major currency. Property in Gibraltar is priced in pounds. The Gibraltar pound, which is the currency of the Rock, has parity with the pound and both currencies are accepted.

Useful Addresses
Barclays Bank pl: Regal House, 3 Queensway, Gibraltar; ☎+350 78565; e-mail gibraltar@barclays.co.uk.
Lloyds TSB Bank plc: 323 Main Street (PO Box 482); Gibraltar; ☎+350 77373; fax +350 70023; www.lloydstsb.gi.
NatWest: 57 Line Wall Road (PO Box 407); ☎+350 77737; fax +350 74557.
Royal Bank of Scotland (Gib) Ltd.: 1 Corral Road (PO Box 766); ☎+350 73200; fax +350 70152.

Mortgages

Banks in Gibraltar will lend against a property being bought in Gibraltar but the largest mortgages (up to 100% of the purchase price) are usually only available to Gibraltarians, or returning Gibraltarians. The Norwich and Peterborough Building Society has a niche in Gibraltar (both a branch office plus a separate Norwich and Peterborough Estate Agent's office). Norwich and Peterborough deal with applicants on an individual basis where mortgages are concerned, depending on all the circumstances. However, they usually follow the banks' line on 100% mortgages. Other British-origin building societies offering mortgages to Gibraltarians and expatriates are the Leeds and Holbeck and the Newcastle.

Useful Addresses
Leeds & Holbeck Building Society: 1st Floor, Heritage House, 235 Main Street, Gibraltar; ☎+350 50602.
Newcastle Building Society: Regal House, Queensway, Gibraltar; +350 42136/41619; nbsgibraltar@gibnynex.gi; www.newcastle.gi.
Norwich & Peterborough Building Society: P.O. Box 535, 198/200 Main Street, Gibraltar; ☎+350 45050; fax +350 45051; e-mail gibraltar@npbs.co.uk. Open 9am-5pm Mon-Thurs and 9.30am-5pm Fri.

Estate Agents

Commission. The estate agents listed above will all have properties on their books including smart town houses, penthouses, luxury apartments and studio flats. Estate agents charge a commission of about 2%. If your property buying falls through then you may find the commission is non-refundable. It is debatable if you will ever get your money back. Some estate agents will refund part of the commission if a deal falls through.

Renting/Letting. Most of the estate agents in Gibraltar have a property management department. If you need to rent before you buy or let your property after you have bought it they can provide both these services for you.

Fees, Contracts and Conveyancing

Colleene Almeida, a barrister attached to Hassans International Law Firm in Gibraltar has kindly provided the following outline of the conveyancing procedures:

Land in Gibraltar is owned by the Crown and the Government of Gibraltar through their agents, who administer the same and normally grant a 150 year lease (known as the **Headlease**) to a developer or private individual for development purposes. The developer will in turn will normally grant purchasers an **Underlease** for the term of 150/99 years less several days and then usually assign the residue of the Headlease to a Management Company, which is ultimately owned by all the purchasers.

Freehold property is also available in Gibraltar mainly in the old town areas but due to the lack of development land available ownership of freehold property is rare.

Reservation Deposit. When purchasing property through an estate agent in Gibraltar you will be required to pay the agent a reservation deposit of around 2% of the total purchase price of the property. This will reserve the property but it does not guarantee that the vendor will sell to you i.e. at this stage neither party is bound to complete on the purchase/sale of the property it is subject to contract. This reservation deposit will upon completion be retained by the estate agents as its fees.

Financing the Purchase. Once the reservation deposit has been paid, the vast majority of purchasers will finance their purchase by way of a mortgage with a bank or building society. For purchasers who will be paying tax in Gibraltar it is important to bear in mind that mortgage interest payments attract tax relief as do endowment policy payments. This should be considered and discussed with a financial adviser.

Solicitors. Building Societies in Gibraltar will generally instruct the same solicitor as the purchaser however some financial institutions have a board of solicitors who act on their behalf in any transaction and in those cases it may be cheaper to instruct a solicitor from their chosen panel rather than to pay two sets of solicitors' fees.

Once you instruct a solicitor they will arrange an initial meeting, in which they will obtain any essential documents or information required for the drafting of the necessary documentation. The purchaser will be able to raise any queries they may have and establish a date for exchange of contracts and desired completion date.

Property Search and Draft Agreement. After this initial meeting your solicitor will conduct a search of the property to ensure that title is unencumbered and they will then send a

Preliminary Enquiries Form to the vendors' solicitors to establish whether there is any planned expenditure on behalf of the lessor and/or the management company, disputes between neighbours, pending or contemplated legal action etc. The vendors' solicitor will then provide your solicitor with copies of all the title deeds for inspection together with a Draft Agreement for approval. The Agreement will contain the names and addresses of the vendor and the purchaser, the price of the property and any deposit paid, terms governing completion and payment of the purchase price, provisions concerning failure to complete by the vendor or the purchaser and lists of fixtures and fittings. Once approved, your solicitor will draft a **Deed of Assignment** (in the case of leasehold land) or a **Deed of Conveyance** (in the case of freehold property) and send the same to the vendors' solicitor and the solicitors for the lessor and/or the management company, if applicable, for their approval and consent to the sale.

Surveyor's Valuation Report. In the meantime your bank or building society will instruct a surveyor to provide a valuation report of the property in order for the bank of building society to establish your mortgage. However, it should be noted that this type of survey is not a detailed report on the actual construction of the property and a purchaser would be well advised to consider engaging their own independent surveyor to undertake a private and confidential report on their behalf.

Surveyor's Structural Report. There are various types of surveys available on residential properties ranging from a general surface inspection of the accessible parts of the property whereby the surveyor gives his/her opinion of the repairs or matters which they consider to be urgent or significant, to a more extensive report of any defects found in the property and the repairs to be undertaken together with an indication on future maintenance liability.
Whilst obtaining an additional survey will obviously involve extra expense it may be invaluable in identifying current or potential problems which could save you money in the future. This is especially important when purchasing an older property as these often require major renovation in order to modernise basic things such as wiring and plumbing.

Completion. Once satisfied with the title of the property and when your solicitor has received your mortgage offer, any necessary consent and approval of the title documentation you will be in a position to complete. At this point your solicitor will request mortgage funds from the lending institution and arrange a meeting in which you shall be required to pay the balance of the moneys required to effect the purchase together with solicitor's fees, stamp duty and registration charges and any rates (equivalent to council tax) and service charges (maintenance payments made to the management company).

Taxes and Fees. Stamp duty is payable at the rate of 1.26% of the total value of the purchase and 0.13% of the total value of the mortgage. There is also a £75 registration fee for each document to be registered. Lawyers' fees tend to be about 1% of the value of the property (up to £100,000) and an extra 0.75% of any value over and above the said £100,000. Fees on a mortgage will be 0.5% of the value of the mortgage if acting for both purchaser and financial institution.
A further £52 per document is paid to the Government's agents for the registration of the same and the production of the **Land Titles Certificate** and £20 per document (in the event that the document is less than 15 pages otherwise this cost goes up to either £40 if the document is between 15 and 40 pages or £60 if it is anything over 40 pages) is paid to the Supreme Court for registration of the same on their register.

Post Completion. Once your cheque for the balance due at completion has cleared in the solicitor's client's account your lawyer will attend a completion meeting with the vendor's solicitors in which he/she will receive all the title documentation together with the keys to the property. Your lawyer will then commence the post completion work of paying the service charges and rates till the end of the current quarter and having the records of the same amended to your name.

Registering Deeds. After all the deeds have been executed your solicitor will then attend to the stamping and registration of the same. At this point you will receive a copy of the documentation which will take around 18 months to register. Once the registration process is complete you will be entitled to keep the original title deeds unless you have mortgaged the property in which case the deeds will be forwarded to the lending institution until such time as the mortgage is redeemed (paid off).

Useful Contacts

Colleene R Almeida LL.B: Barrister-at-Law, Hassans International Law Firm, 57/63 Line Wall Road, P.O. Box 199, Gibraltar; ☎+350 79000; fax +350 71966. Largest law firm in Gibraltar specialists in offshore, commercial, financial regulation and tax.

Mr Stefano Lucatello, The International Property Law Centre, Unit 2 Waterside Park, Livingstone Road, Hessle HU13 0EG; ☎01482 350-850; fax 01482 642799; e-mail internationalproperty@maxgold.com; www.internationalpropertylaw.com.

SPOT CHECK – GIBRALTAR	
Political/economic stability:	Currently under British Sovereignty. In 2002 referendum, Gibraltar voted to remain British rather than have sovereignty split between Spain and Britain. Spain continues to dispute the Rock's right to remain British. Economy growth has been running at 6%.
Climate:	Hot and humid summers, mild winters. Average summer temperature 83°F/29C°. All year round gusty winds due to funnel effect of the Straight of Gibraltar.
Cost of living/taxes	Cost of living slightly less than the UK. Minimal tax burden for individuals with approved high net worth status. For others, income tax is high: 17%-45% income tax; average 30-35%. No VAT.
Accessibility:	Flights starting at £22 from the UK.
Property availability:	Massive spate of development as the government releases land for building. Many apartments for sale.
Property prices:	Comparable to surburban Britain. Apartments from £97,000. Many luxury new build high rise apartments from £199,000.
Costs of property purchase as a % of purchase price	Stamp duty 1.26% Lawyer fees 1%-1.75%
Ease of purchase:	Well-oiled system for selling to foreigners and Britons.
Annual property taxes:	None.
Investment potential:	Prices tripled in the last few years. Will probably rise less dramatically in the next few years.

LIVING·IN·GREECE

Buying a House on the Mediterranean

Greece

LIVING IN GREECE

CHAPTER SUMMARY

- **Classical culture.** The political and cultural legacy of classical Greece can be found throughout Western civilisation today.
- The ancient Greeks invented and practised democracy and holistic medical treatment.
- **History.** The modern Greek state emerged after winning independence from the Ottoman Empire in 1829, but was originally much smaller than today.
- Britain ruled the Ionian islands (including Corfu) from 1815-1864.
- **Geography.** Greece has the longest coastline of any Mediterranean country thanks to its 2000+ islands.
- 80% of mainland Greece is mountainous and the mountains extend into the sea as chains of islands.
- Athens is one of the most polluted capitals in Europe, but the seas around the Greek islands are some of the cleanest in the Mediterranean.
- **Climate.** Temperatures can reach 40°C in summer but are tempered by strong seasonal winds that can disrupt ferry schedules.
- **Earthquakes.** The whole of the south eastern Mediterranean is subject to sporadic seismic activity.
- In 1953, a severe earthquake caused catastrophic damage in the Ionian islands, and one in 1999 killed nearly 100 people in Athens.
- **Language.** A modern Greek can understand most of the vocabulary in an ancient Attic text of the 5th century BC.
- Thousands of words of Greek origin are used by mathematicians, scientists and technologists today.
- The Greek alphabet has 24 letters and has been in continuous use for over two and a half thousand years.
- **Crime.** Greece has one of the lowest crime rates in the EU.
- **Housing.** Over 14% of Greek households have a second home.
- There is no annual property tax in Greece on property worth less than €200,000/£140,000.

INTRODUCTION

Greece is less known these days for disseminating high classical culture, than it is for mass cheap tourism. Despite having one of the most polluted capitals in Europe, Greece has very little heavy industry (and that is confined mainly to the north), leaving the rest of Greece as a pristine playground of islands in the sun, set in some of the cleanest waters of the Mediterranean. A lack of giant industries means that outside the cities, most life revolves around small scale agriculture and local businesses, and the highly lucrative activity of helping tourists relax and enjoy themselves at the seaside; Greece has more coastline than any other Mediterranean country, thanks to its countless islands. The locals are almost as keen on relaxing at coastal resorts as the foreigners. Small wonder is it, that Greece seems ideal if what you really want is a property with a sea view.

Before 1984, only Greeks were allowed to own property in Greece so foreign residents en masse were a lot later arriving there, than in Italy, Spain and France. Accession to the European Union means that EU nationals can buy freehold property, but it is still quite difficult to find what you want in the way of individual properties. Without assistance from Greek professionals, the buying process, especially the legal issues can be a minefield for the unwary, while many new developments are aimed at the Greek market with communal pools, gardens etc. For non-EU property buyers it is even more difficult as they are not allowed to buy property as individuals (in some parts of Greece); there are legal ways around this (see *The Purchasing Procedure*). On the plus side, Greek annual real estate taxes are nil on properties valued up to €200,000 (£140,000/$184,000) and a very low 0.25% after that.

HISTORY

There is no space here to do justice to all the ancient eras of Greece – the Minoan, Mycenaean, the Classical, the Hellenistic etc. Suffice it to say that the peak of Greek civilisation was the Classical period from 500-336 BC, which bestowed a lasting legacy on the Western World, not least democratic government. This period also produced the Macedonian king and legendary conqueror, Alexander the Great, the famous buildings of the Athenian acropolis, and a flowering of Greek drama, philosophy, mathematics, medicine and art.

Modern Greece emerged in 1829 after achieving independence from the Ottoman Empire, which had occupied this part of the Balkans since 1460. By 1820 the factors needed to bring off independence were in place including the leadership of an educated elite who had been schooled at the universities of Europe, where they realised how important their ancient culture was by observing the reverence in which it was held, which in turn inspired their nationalism. Other causal factors were a starving Greek populace, and economic weakening of the Turkish Empire. The oppressed Greeks fought long and hard against the Turks from 1821 to 1832; an earlier revolution in 1788 had ended in failure. Among the fatal casualties of this war were the poet and adventurer Lord Byron, who expired from fever in north-western Greece in 1824, after taking up arms for the Greek cause. In 1827, Russian, French and British ships helped the Greeks destroy the Ottoman navy at Navarino.

The Peloponnese and a small part of Thessaly made up the orginal Greek state. The Greeks' war against the Turks was more widely significant than its immediate outcome, in that it was the first of many unequivocally nationalist revolutions in Europe, and it began the disintegration of the Ottoman Empire. The fledgling state was home to far fewer Greeks than were scattered throughout the vast Ottoman Empire. As it struggled to take shape, the Greek boundaries were under negotiation; in its first form Greece embraced few islands. The grand idea that was to inform Greek policy for most of the nineteenth and early twentieth centuries was to unite all Greeks throughout the Near East and have Constantinople as the capital. The European powers, while sympathetic to the cause of liberation were desperate to hold grandiose Greek ambition in check. Kings of Greece were appointed from the Bavarian and Danish royal families and in 1864 Britain relinquished the Ionian islands (including Corfu) (which it had ruled as a protectorate since 1815) to the Greek state. Turkey followed with the ceding (unwillingly) of Thessaly and a part of the adjacent province of Epirus – both of them on the mainland. Near bankruptcy of the Greek state in 1893 caused a wave of emigration of which the United States and Australia were the main beneficiaries. Meanwhile the Cretans were in the process of gaining their independence from the Turks and unity with the motherland.

The next stage of Greek independence revolved around the Balkan Wars (1912-1913) when Greece allied uneasily with Montenegro, Serbia and Bulgaria, who had their own territorial ambitions in the area. Greece managed to expand her territory by nearly two-thirds. She claimed a number of Aegean islands and Thessaloniki, (now Greece's second city). At the Paris Peace conference in 1919 after the First World War, Greece was given permission to occupy Smyrna (now Izmir) in Turkey plus a chunk of western Turkey but Turkey's response was to burn Smyrna to the ground and cause all Greeks who were still able, to flee back to Greece. A military coup deposed King Constantine of Greece and there was an influx of refugees who arrived from Russia and Bulgaria as well as Turkey. The total number of immigrants during this period was over 1.3 million.

Between the two World Wars there was a period of confusion of political interests and ambitions, and into the breach stepped the Communists so that by the Second World War they were the dominant political force. Greece was invaded by Germany in 1941 which together with Italy and Bulgaria set up an occupying force. There were Greek resistance movements, but often as not they ended up fighting each other. Even after Greece was liberated at the end of the War, she slid almost immediately into a fierce civil war between the communists and non-communists; this being but the newest manifestation of dissenting factions causing turmoil in Greece.

A military takeover was probably inevitable considering the instability which had resulted from a complete lack of order. The resulting 'Dictatorship of The Colonels', was a brutal and unhappy time which lasted from 1967 to 1974 until a prominent politician, Konstantinos Karamanlis was brought back from exile to oversee the seeding of genuine democracy. Karamanlis was largely instrumental in steering Greece towards membership of the European Union in 1981.

It seems ironic, that the ancient ancestors of the Greeks gave the western world democracy, yet their descendants took so long to reinstate it.

INTERNATIONAL DISPUTES

Greece has potentially serious disputes with Turkey, which are complicated and revolve around territorial claims over land and sea; and a name dispute with the Republic of Macedonia.
1. **Greek and Turkish Cypriots.** Although Cyprus is an independent republic, the Greek and Turkish Cypriots are more faithful to their respective motherlands than to Cypriot nationalism,

which is understandable considering they have different religions and cultures. It has so far proved impossible for them to see themselves as one nation. It is hoped that Cyprus's EU membership will precipitate a reintegration of the island's population and so end the north south partition.

2. **Boiling Oil.** This is complicated and involves a dispute between Greece and Turkey over the rights to the Aegean ocean floor (the point being that there could be oil under it). Turkey claims that Greece owns only the islands but not the seabed. Since neither country can agree who owns which parts of the Aegean, it could all end in tears.

3. **Aegean tea party.** Owing to some enforced understanding with the USA, whose navy needs access to Turkey for its sixth fleet, the Greeks are allowed to claim only 6 nautical miles beyond their coastline, instead of the regulation 12 nautical miles.

4. **There can be only one – Macedonia.** This is difficult to understand unless you are Greek or Macedonian. Greece wants the independent republic of Macedonia (part of former Yugoslavia), which is on the frontier of the Greek province of that name, to change its name. They both have a right to the name as both areas lie within the much larger territory of that name of ancient times. Of course it's more complicated than that – this is after all the Balkans. Incidentally, Macedonia is also a culinary term for a fruit salad (or chopped mixed vegetables) which is named from the mix of peoples in that region.

GOVERNMENT AND POLITICS

The Hellenic Republic, Republic of Greece or Ellas as it is variously called, has 13 administrative regions (9 mainland and 4 island regions) and is subdivided into 51 prefectures (*nomoi*) and the autonomous region (Ayion Oros/Mount Athos).

Parliament (*Vouli ton Ellinon*) is a single chamber with 300 members elected to serve four-year terms. In 1993 two new political parties were formed the ND (New Democracy – rightist) and PASOK (Panhellenic Socialist Movement – mainstream left). These are also the two largest parties. On March 7th 2004 voted their centre-left government out of office and voted in the centre-right and the ND is now the ruling party. Other parties typically representing around 20% of the vote, include the Communist Party of Greece (KKE), the Coalition of the Left (SYN) and the Democratic Social Movement (DIKKI). The President is the Head of State, and is elected by Parliament for a maximum of two five-year terms. Kostandinos Stephanopoulos has been President since 1995 and Prime Minister Costas Karamanlis was elected on March 7th 2004.

THE ECONOMY

The Greek economy has shown healthy expansion in recent years helped by large EU subsidies and a thriving tourist industry. Tourism earns about 20% of GDP (compared with manufacturing which contributes 12%. For 2004, expected growth is about 4%. 2004 is a special year for Greece and the Greek economy as it is the year that Greece hosts the summer Olympic games. Vast amounts have been poured into the infrastructure and organisation to ensure it all goes smoothly and it is hoped that this will produce the Olympic effect; i.e. spotlight Greece and bring benefits to the economy through increased tourism and the use of new facilities for conferences etc.

The economy has been affected by the highest unemployment rate in the EU after Spain. This has fallen recently from 10.2% in 2002 to just under 9% in 2004, which is, however, still much higher than the EU average of 7.7%.

Inflation is expected to be around 3%.
Up-to-date information on the Greek Economy can be found at the following websites:

Bank of Greece; www.bankofgreece.gr
Ministry of Economy and Finance; www.ypetho.gr
National Statistical Service; www.statistics.gr

GEOGRAPHY

Located in the south-eastern Mediterranean with the Aegean Sea to the East and the Ionian Sea to the west, Greece is a peninsular, plus an archipelago of more than 2000 islands. It lies between Albania and Turkey (Scylla and Charybdis from Greece's point of view?). It shares borders with Albania, Bulgaria, Turkey and the Former Yugoslav Republic of Macedonia. The mainland and islands of Greece have a staggering total coastline of 13,676 km. The Greek mainland is mostly mountainous; Mount Olympus (2,917m), also on the mainland is the highest point and the mountains extend into the sea as chains of islands. Some Greek islands are within two or three miles of the Turkish coast.

Demography. The population is currently just under 11 million of which 2% are non-ethnic Greeks. Excluding Athens and the second city Thessaloniki, the only other cities with more than 100,000 inhabitants are Patras, Vólos, Larisa and Iraklion (Crete). 97% of Greeks are adherents of the Greek Orthodox religion.

EARTHQUAKE ZONE

The eastern Mediterranean basin (basically the whole of Greece and its neighbour Turkey) is an area prone to seismic tremors (20,000 recorded since 1964), and periodically there are earthquakes that can cause structural damage to old houses. The reason for this is that the area lies at the point where three of the continental tectonic plates (deformations of the earth's crust) overlap and jostle each other. New houses are constructed to withstand shocks and there are minimum legal requirements that have to be followed.

As expected, the closer to the epicenter of the quake, the greater the effect felt. In 1953 a major quake centred in the Ionian region destroyed most of the buildings on the islands; the island of Zakynthos lost all of its churches but one. A quake in Athens in 1999 killed nearly 100 people and made tens of thousands homeless.

You can log on to the websites of Aristotle University of Thessaloniki Geophysical Laboratory Seismological Station (www.lemnos.auth.gr/the – seisnet/en/majorquakes.htm), or of the National Geodynamic Institute Athens (www.gein.noa.gr/services/monthly-list.html) and get a weekly seismicity report for the whole of Greece.

Climate

Greece has a hot dry Mediterranean climate and approximately 3,000 hours of sunshine a year. The heat in summer can reach a searing 40°C, but is somewhat relieved by seasonal stiff breezes, especially in the coastal regions and the north. Among them is the Meltemi, a wind that blows throughout the Aegean Sea in July and August causing disruption of ferry schedules and a poltergeist effect on beach furniture. Winters are mild in the south and cold in the north. Athens is stifling in summer and its pollution levels are notorious. The rainy season lasts from November to March.

AVERAGE TEMPERATURES				
Area	Jan	Apr	July	Nov
Athens	48.38°/9.1C	64°/15C	83.66°/28.7C	52.88°/11.6C
Corfu	49.82°/9.9C	57.56°/14.2	82°/27.8C	53/6°/12C
Heraklion	54.32°/12.4C	60.26°/15.7C	79.52°/26.4C	57.92/14.4C
Rhodes	55.22°/12.9	60.8°/16C	81.32°/27.4C	58.1°/14.5C
Thessalonika	42.26°/5.7C	58.1°/14.5C	81.5°/27.5C	48°/8.9C

AVERAGE RAINFALL		
Area	days	mm
Athens	55	404.4
Corfu	147	1083.8
Heraklion	86	288.5
Rhodes	74	536.3
Thessalonika	121	437.3

CULTURE SHOCK

- If you sit down alone in a Greek taverna, it is automatically assumed that you are waiting for someone and the waiters will ignore you, except in tourist places.
- Greeks always seem to pay in cash at restaurants.
- Greeks are very pushy and always want to be the first, which can seem very selfish to anglo-saxons.
- Greeks touch a lot as a way of communicating. This can take some getting used to.
- Honesty in Greece is almost the rule when it comes to not stealing your belongings; but cheating you, well that's probably another matter.
- You see Greek priests everywhere; they nearly always wear a long black cassock. The Greek Orthodox church does not allow women to be ordained.
- The Greek attitude towards time is very cavalier e.g. bus timetables are run to their drivers' personal ones and everything happens at a much slower pace than you are probably used to.
- The main evening meal is usually eaten from 9pm.
- Never refuse a Greek offering to treat you in a restaurant. It is a tremendous insult to seize the bill and pay it yourself. It implies that you think he does not have enough money to pay it.

GETTING THERE

Mainland

Athens – **EasyJet** from Gatwick/Luton & **Hellas Jet** from Heathrow & **Olympic Airways** (not budget) from H'row
Kavala – Charter flights from regional UK airports

Thessalonika – **Britannia Airways** (not budget) from many UK airports, **Excel Airways** (not budget) from Gatw/Manchester/Glasgow every Thursday & **Olympic Airways** (not budget) from H'row
Vólos – **Air 2000** (charter) from Gatwick

Islands

Lots of charter flights in summer; in winter scheduled flights from H'row to Athens and on to islands on local flights is possible. All the islands in the section *Where to Find Your Ideal Home* have their own airport, or the nearest one listed.

Airlines

Aegean Airlines: www.aegeanair.com. National, mainly domestic carrier (scheduled flights) which goes to 14 airports in Greece including the islands e.g. Chios, Kos and Santorini.

Air 2000: ☎0870 199 9191 (Houses of Pelion).

Britannia Airways: ☎0800 000747; www.britanniaairways.com. Charter to Thessaloniki.

Excel Airways: ☎08709 98 98 98; www.excelairways.co.uk. Corfu, Santorini, Heraklion (Crete), Rhodes, Kos and seven other Greek destinations from 8 UK airports.

Hellas Jet: ☎at H'Row: 0870 750 8202; in Greece +30 210 6244 244;www.hellas-jet.com; info@hellas-jet.com. New small Greek-based airline. Not budget.

Olympic Airways: UK Office: 11 Conduit Street, London W1R OLP; ☎0870 606 0460; www.olympicairways.co.uk or www.olympic-airways.gr. Greece's national airline.

COMMUNICATIONS

Telephones

OTE, The Hellenic Telecommunications Organisation (99 Kiffisias Avenue, 15124 Athens, Greece; www.ote.gr/oteweb/english) controls the phone system which has undergone several new numbering blitzes in recent years; the latest in November 2002. You have to dial the area code within Greece even when you are within the area you are dialing e.g. if you are in Athens, dialing an Athens number you use the local prefix 210. All area codes begin with 2. Some important area codes are:

Corfu	2661
Iraklion, (Crete)	281
Kalamata	2721
Kavala	251
Thessaloniki	231
Vólos	2428

A full list of area codes can be found at www.kropla.com/city – greece.htm.

Mobile Phones. Mobile numbers begin with 6 and calls to mobiles from abroad begin with 00306. Mobile phones and online services were late in taking off in Greece but they are catching up fast. Mobile operators in Greece include CosmOTE, Telestet and Vodaphone. CosmOTE is the largest with 3.8 million customers. All GSM mobile phones used in European and some other countries will work in Greece. Americans should note that US cell phones do not work in Greece. Americans and anyone else having problems with Greek landline telephones should consider getting a mobile.

If you are from the US and don't feel up to hiring one from a Greek, then there are agents that specialise in hiring mobiles short-term to Americans and they can be found on the internet. Try www.greecetravel.com/phones who will hire you a phone in advance for up to 45 days for a €135 (£94/$147) flat fee, or www.europe-usa-mobile-cellular-phone-rental.com (☎toll free 1888 802-9518) will hire you one for $125 per month.

Internet. Internet access numbers begin with 8.

Emergency Numbers. These include ambulance (166), Fire Service (199), Local Police (100) and Emergency Traveller Assistance 112 (for non Greek speakers).

Dialling Greece from Abroad. The code for Greece from abroad is 30. To dial from the UK it is 0030 and from the USA 011 30.

Post Office

Main Greek post offices (*tachidromio/post*) are open from 8am-1.30pm (sometimes 2.30pm) Monday to Friday and are closed on Saturdays. Smaller communities have their own arrangements and the times may be different. There are nearly always long queues and in larger offices you have to take a number from a dispenser by the door and hope there are seats provided for the wait. You can buy stamps (*grammatosimá*) in the post office or preferably at kiosks (*periptero*). Only non-urgent mail should be put in a letterbox. The letterboxes have two slots, one for internal mail and one for international. Anything time sensitive and important should be sent registered and express (an additional total charge of about €5).

Note that on small islands post is not delivered to the door but to a village centre or even the village shop.

FOOD AND DRINK

Food

Greek cuisine may not be as refined and varied as French or Italian, but it is healthy, wholesome and piquant and has a long tradition going back to ancient times. Greek food shows a strong Levantine influence, which can be seen in dishes such as tzatziki (yoghurt dip with garlic and chopped cucumber), oven baked vegetables, grilled meat in pitta bread, moussakas (vegetables with minced meat and a thick sauce). In the Ionian islands there is also a Venetian legacy of pasta and various kinds of pies. Most countries have a 'national' dish (think pizza, paella, roast beef etc.); in the case of Greece there are two: Greek salad (onion, cucumber, tomatoes, feta cheese, olives, oregano and olive oil dressing), and moussaka.

Greek meals tend to consist of a lot of small dishes (*mezedes*) all served together consisting of various types of vegetables and beans and peas, seafood, meats, a variety of cheeses including *zinomitzithra, formaella,* and *metsovone,* yoghurt and honey. Most meals are accompanied by Greek bread either pitta or leavened. Many small villages still have a village baker producing bread rolls, cheese pies, olive oil bread, and cakes made with honey, cloves, cinnamon etc. Your local baker will also bake special meals, which have been prepared by a local housewife, in his oven.

Greek desserts and sweetmeats are a decadent syrupy, backlash from the rest of the health-giving Greek diet : candied fruits, and fruits preserved whole in syrup, *loukoumi* (Turkish delight), baklava (homemade filo pastries drenched in honey and stuffed with chopped, dried nuts), sugary pastries, and the mouth-melting blocks of halva made from sesame seeds, honey and nuts.

When you buy vegetables and fruit you will find that the choice is limited to the seasonal offerings as very little of either commodity is imported. Everything tastes amazingly fresh and in late summer you can almost live on giant juicy peaches. Olives, needless to say are available in all sorts of shapes and sizes and olive oil is only sold in large volumes reflecting the Greek consumption of the stuff.

Drink

Wine is sacred in Greece where the ancient god of wine, Dionysus was worshiped upon supposedly inventing wine-making over 3,000 years ago. Thus, nowhere more than Greece is wine a gift from the gods. There are vineyards all over Greece making a variety of wines, but Greece is still best known for resined (retsina) wine, which comes from adding pine resin during fermentation. This kind of wine does not keep, yet at least half of Greek wine is made this way. Romaic red wine from Crete is a widely available non-resined wine. More than a third of vineyards are in the Peloponnese, but some quite substantial wines come from islands including Limnos, Paros, Lefkas, Rhodes, Corfu and Crete. *Mavro* is used to refer to any red wine (mavro actually means black) and *lefkos* means white wine. Rhodes and Samos produce famous sweet wines (muscat doux).

Ouzo, is the famous aniseed-flavoured aperitif, usually drunk with ice or water, either at the start of a meal with *mezedes,* or throughout the meal especially on an evening out or a meal with friends.

Mythos is a brand of Greek beer.

SCHOOLS AND EDUCATION

The Greek educational system is controlled by the Ministry of National Education and Religious Affairs. The lack of separation of education and religion (religious instruction is compulsory in state schools) goes some way to explain why the Greek Orthodox faith still holds a predominant place in Greek culture.

It is estimated that 93% of the Greek population over the age of 15 is literate.

Pre-higher Education

The Greek school system, like that of many other modern states involves three stages. Education is compulsory until the age of 15.

Primary. Primary school lasts six years from ages six to 12 and involves a type of school known as *Dimotiko Scholeio* at the end of which the student receives a certificate: *Apolytirio Dimotikou.*

Lower Secondary. This cycle lasts three years from ages 12 to 15 and is provided at a Gymnasio institution. Prior to the completion of this cycle, national examinations are held in two stages at grades 11 and 12. At the end of this cycle the award that the student gets is *Apolytirio Gymnasiou* (secondary school diploma) and success in this is essential for access to the *Lykeio* (see below).

Upper Secondary. The final phase of pre-higher education is optional and lasts from ages 15-18. Students can choose between a technical-vocational school (*Technica Epaggelmatics Ekpaideftiria TEE*) or an Eniaio Lykeio. Dependent on achieving the required grades at the end of this cycle, students can go on to tertiary education.

Private Tutors. It is quite usual for young Greeks to have private tutors, especially in maths and languages, to supplement the state school education. These classes can provide excellent employment opportunities for foreigners.

Tertiary Education

Tertiary education for graduates of the Lykeio is provided by 18 Universities (AEIs), and 14 Technological Educational Institutes (TEIs). Studies at both types last a minimum of four years except for certain faculties which require five or six years' study. Mature students of any age can gain access to Greek universities through the Hellenic Open University preparatory courses or through individual institutions' discretionary admissions policies. The academic year consists of two semesters of 13 weeks each, plus three weeks for examinations. Tuition is generally free of charge.

Useful Contact
Ministry of National Education and Religious Affairs: 15 Mitropoleos Street, 10185 Athens; ☎+30 21 0321 14 20; fax +30 21 0323 93 86; www.ypepth.gr.

Foreign Schools

There are prestigious bilingual foreign schools located in Athens and Thessaloniki. They include English, French, German, Italian and Spanish ones. Their students are drawn from the expatriate communities as well as from the Greek elite and they provide a bicultural education. A list of these is available at www.ypepth.gr.

Additionally, there are international schools, which are reserved for their respective nationalities' children based in Greece. Greek students with dual nationality are also accepted at these schools.

There is an expanding industry in foreign language schools and colleges, which teach GCSE level and final year college education in English. These are run as franchise operations of UK and occasionally US and French Universities and attract tens of thousands of Greek students annually.

TAXES

Greek Income Tax

Income tax operates on a progressive scale from 0% to a maximum of 40% with most Greek employees paying between 15% and 30%. The Greek system is somewhat different from what you may be used to in that you are taxed on either your declared income, or your estimated income, whichever is the greater. Estimated income is arrived at pretty much on your visible wealth: living expenses and any assets you may own or acquire. Taken into account are: engine size of motor vehicles, maintenance of household staff, purchase of property and maintenance costs of recreational assets such as a yacht. The system was described by one aficionado as 'very informal'.

Even the basic tax system is complicated and due for reform.

Who is obliged to file a tax return? Almost everyone has to file a tax return. Even if you don't owe any taxes (i.e. your income is derived from outside Greece) and you are non-resident, you still have to file a tax form. If you don't file a tax form, you will have problems when you try to sell, transfer or bequeath your property as you will find that large fines are imposed. Once you have a tax number, it is obligatory to complete an annual tax return even if your income (e.g. a pension) is derived from outside Greece and paid into a Greek bank account. You need to keep all Greek bank receipts for money arriving in your account to show the taxman that the money in your bank account originates from outside Greece. You will not pay tax on money derived from outside Greece.

Salaried persons receiving an income of more than £6000 derived only from one source can submit a declaration of income instead of a full tax return.

The Greek tax year ends on 31 December and tax forms are generally filed between March and May; and the date is subject to an official announcement by the Ministry of Finance. If you pay all your tax in one go a 5% discount is given. The alternative is to pay in three equal tranches.

Note that if you are a temporary resident you will not be liable for Greek income tax unless you have income earned and sourced in Greece.

You also need to have a tax number if you plan to register your car or for a telephone.

Many foreign residents use an accountant. In fact it is very advisable to do this as the laws are frequently updated and changed and the only person who will know about this is an accountant. To fill in a simple tax form you should expect to pay around €30 (£21/$32), although some have charged up to €100 for this service.

SCALES OF INCOME TAX

1. Salaried persons and pension receivers

Step	Rate	Tax for the Step	Total income	Tax
€10,000	0%	zero	€10,000	zero
€ 3,400	15%	€510	€13,400	€510
€10,000	30%	€3,000	€23,400	€3,510
Above	40%			

2. Non-salaried persons/self employed

Step	Rate	Tax for the Step	Total income	Tax
€8,400	zero	zero	€8,400	zero
€5,000	15%	€750	€13,400	€750
€10,000	30%	€3,000	€23,400	€3,750
Above	40%			

VAT (Foros Prostitthemenis Axias FPA)

The standard rate of VAT is 18% with a reduced rate of 8% on food, pharmaceuticals and a super-reduced rate of 4% on books, new building, repairs and renovations. Rates in the Dodecanese and some Aegean islands are 13% (standard) and 6% (reduced).

Annual Real Estate Taxes. These are minimal in Greece. For details of these and Real Estate transfer tax see *Real Estate Taxes* in the *Purchasing Procedure* chapter.

Inheritance and Gift Taxes. In Greece, inheritance tax is not imposed on the estate of the deceased but rather on each of the beneficiaries in proportion to their share of the inheritance and their degree of kinship to the deceased. For each category of beneficiary there is a sliding scale of rates from 0-66%.

Further Information. Detailed information on Greek taxes can be obtained from www.europa.eu.int/comm/taxation – customs/publications/info – doc/taxation/ txinventory/tax – inventory – gr.pdf

Useful Addresses

Public Economic Service (DOY) For Foreign Residents: 18 Lykourgou Street, 1052 Athens; ☎+301 52 45 308; fax +301 52 28 208.

HEALTH & SOCIAL SECURITY

National Health System

Greece was the birthplace of medicine and the Hippocratic oath, by which all doctors everywhere, still swear to be bound. From this heritage, as you might expect, Greece has many excellent doctors. In fact, there is no shortage of doctors, unlike in some other European countries. Medical talent notwithstanding, Greece has serious problems in its public health sector and many doctors would rather work in the private sector, which is very active and advanced. Greek public hospitals tend to be shockingly inefficient and often inadequately resourced.

Greece introduced a national health system, the ESY, in 1983 with the mission statement 'the state has a responsibility for providing health care to all citizens, regardless of their financial, social or professional status'. Despite pouring public money into the system, it has not lived up to its promise. In the Athens area, where nearly half the population lives, there is a chronic shortage of hospital beds. It is 'normal' to find patients being given medical treatment in corridors. In most Greek hospitals relatives are left to feed, clothe and do the laundry for their relatives being treated there. There is always a shortage of nurses. Often private payment to doctors in the form of cash or kind is the only way to ensure adequate medical treatment and this has fuelled the growth of the private sector. There has also been a boom in private health insurance by anyone who can afford it. Private hospitals unlike the public ones are highly profitable and generally efficient.

In 2001 Greece restructured the health and welfare system including dividing the ESY into 17 autonomous and independent regional branches known as PESY (Peripheral Health Systems). It is hoped this will curb some of the previous waste of resources and increase efficiency by allowing each area to run its own finances. The European Union is also due to contribute a billion dollars to Greece's public health service between 2002 and 2006, which it is hoped will bring many improvements. The private sector is also expanding a $170 million healthcare 'health park' just outside Athens, which claims be the largest of its type in Europe.

Private Health Care

As well as the international healthcare providers' details of which may be found in the *General Introduction,* Greece has many indigenous private health insurance companies. Coverage should include hospital expenses, medical practitioner fees and medication costs. As this is big business in Greece there are several large companies competing in this field including Aspis (the insurance arm of the bank of that name), Ethniki, Generali Life and La Vie. Try also Interamerican and Alico AIGlife. Most of these have branches throughout Greece and some are international.

SHOPPING

Food Shopping

Somewhere between the Syntagma and Kolonaki Squares in Athens (the Greek equivalent of Bond Street or Fifth Avenue) and the tacky souvenir shops of the tourist areas are the places for everyday shopping that you have to do for food and necessities.

Supermarkets and Fresh Food Markets. In the main centres of habitation you will find the Greek national and international supermarket chains, Marinopoulos, Alpha-Beta Vassilopoulos, Carrefour etc., and discount supermarkets Dia and Aldi. About 53% of all supermarket sales are in the grocery sector. Whilst the rise of the supermarket has seen the demise of thousands of small grocery shops, it has not affected the traditional outdoor fruit and vegetable markets where local growers sell their own produce direct to the customers. In larger markets you will also find a selection of olives, olive oil, honey, nuts, herbs and spices, while on most days, street vendors sell pistachio, almonds and walnuts etc.

Speciality Shops and Bakeries. To counteract the generic blandness of supermarket brands gourmets go shopping in speciality shops or small stores; fortunately, these are still abundant in Greece and most villages also have a bakery (*foúrnos*) with the bread made on site.

Meat and Fish. Although Greek food is based largely around fish or meat dishes, the latter is in short supply and over half the meat on sale in shops (lamb, pork, chicken and game meats) is imported. In Greek fish markets, you can buy all manner of fish (usually sold whole), shellfish and crustaceans. Frozen seafood and pre-prepared meals are not popular.

Non-Food Shopping

One of the best buys is jewellery. Greece prides itself on its tradition of craftsmanship in precious metals and gems going back to ancient times. If you want to have copies of antique jewels, or more contemporary designs, this is the place to buy them.

Pottery is another ancient craft still much in evidence and styles vary from replica antique to contemporary. Note that buying or exporting genuine antiquities without a special licence is illegal.

Leather goods are another Greek craft tradition, as are fur coats, which have not become unacceptable to wear in Greece as they have elsewhere in Europe; Athens has several famous fur shops based in Ermou Street.

Department stores like Macro, Minion, Vasilopoulos etc. have a wide presence. However, most imported clothes etc. are much more expensive in Greece than in their original country.

Shopping Hours. Shop opening hours may be subject to regional and seasonal variations but are generally: Monday, Wednesday and Saturday 8.30am to 2.30 pm and Tuesday, Thursday and Friday 8.30am-2pm and 5.30pm-8.30pm.

MEDIA

Since 1993 The Ministry of Press and Mass Media has had responsibility for overseeing media matters in Greece.

Newspapers

If your Greek is up to it you will be buying Greek newspapers, or you can read them online e.g. at www.angelfire.com. Otherwise, the newspapers listed below have English websites; more information on Greek newspapers can be found at www.world-newspapers.com/greece.

Greek Newpapers

Aegean Times: www.aegeantimes.net. Site deals with Greek and Turkish news.
Athens News: www.athensnews.gr. Weekly, which has been published for over 50 years. Was daily until 2001. Sold at news-stands throughout Greece.
Athens News Agency ANA: www.ana.gr. Official news agency.
Kathimerini: The *International Herald Tribune* produces an English-language insert translated from the Greek daily Kathimerini, or look online at www.ekathimerini.com.
The Corfiot is a monthly, English-language magazine published in Corfu by Pedestrian Publications (Afra 49100, Corfu; ☎+30 26610 52833; corfiotm@otenet.gr.) and is relevant to Greece as a whole, not just the expat community of Corfu. There is also a website of the same name (www.thecorfiot.com), though apparently they are not related.

Television

The first experimental Greek television station began broadcasting in 1961 in Thessalonika. The state broadcasting organisation is ERT SA. With the deregulation of television in 1989 the National Council of Radio-Television was founded to act as a watchdog over these media and now presides over more than 140 private television stations. In 1997 the state ERT channels were reorganised: ERT 2 became NET (mainly a news and information channel) while ERT 1 is mainly an entertainment network. There is also a range of digital channels ANT1, Mega and Alpha etc., and satellite channels such as CNN, TV5 (French) and Euronews, which are broadcast on local frequencies in Greece.

Radio

One of the biggest radio stations is Antenna 1 (northern Greece; FM 97.5). You can access live Greek radio broadcasts on the internet via the website gogreece.com/news/tv – radio.

Radio Stations Broadcasting in English. There are dozens of these around Greece and the islands broadcasting news, information and music. They include. An up-to-date list of all Greek radio stations with English output can be found at www.planetgr.com/m/m4 – 5.htm
Cool FM 106.8 – Rethymno (www.coolfm.gr)
Face FM 96.5 – Samos (www.facefm.gr)
Fly FM 9.59 – Rethymnon (Crete) (www.flyfm.com)

Radio Palama 91.4 FM – Thessaly (www.radiopalama.gr). Covers all of central Greece and broadcasts 24 hours.
Kavala FM 93.1 – Kavala (www.listen.to/kavalafm).
CRIME
There is very little violent crime in Greece, even in the capital city Athens, compared with other modern European countries and their capitals. Nonetheless, robbery and drug-related crime are on the increase in the metropolitan areas.

It is often said that in Greece your property is safe; no self respecting Greek steals your possessions, but fiddling or cheating you is OK, at least until you become a friend, or maybe a regular in his restaurant. Perhaps it is advisable to say from the outset that you are a residential tourist (ie living there some of the time), so that all your relationships get off to a good start.

Police. The Hellenic police force has two subsidiary branches, tourist police and port police. The tourist police are trained to solve minor disputes between shopkeepers etc and visitors and operate a 24/7 emergency call service (171).

The port police wear white uniforms and ensure that ferries operate safely. They supervise ferry arrivals and departures and are responsible for deciding when to cancel ferry sailings in adverse weather conditions.

LEARNING THE LANGUAGE

Most of the words (but not the grammar and syntax) of an ancient Attic (i.e. Athenian) classical Greek text of the 5th century BC are intelligible to a modern Greek. Greek schools teach the grammar, literature and history of the many centuries of their culture and such studies still play a vital role in moulding Greek nationality. Anyone learning the Greek Alphabet and a few everyday phrases will therefore be much appreciated in Greece, even though many Greeks speak English with varying degrees of accuracy. Learning a little Greek will have the added thrill of speaking some of the language of Aristotle and other seminal influencers of Western culture; Greek is the basis for thousands of terms used by scientists, mathematicians and technologists.

Learning the grammar is another matter, and is fiendishly complicated when compared to romance languages like French and Spanish. However, if you catch the learning bug there are a number of websites including www.omniglot.com/writing/greek and www.users.otenet.gr/bm-celusy/greek.html, offering encyclopaedic information on the history and development of the Greek language, while others like www.kyros.org/greek even offer online courses.

Courses
Online Courses. www.go.to/greeklessons, www.langintro.com/greek, www.greece.org/gr-english/.

THE GREEK ALPHABET

The Greek alphabet (the capital letters) has been in continuous use for over 2,700 years, has only 24 letters, and many of the letters are similar to the Roman alphabet. The lower case letters were a later arrival appearing some time after 800AD and deriving from Byzantine cursive script.

Greek Alphabet – Modern Pronunciation

Αα	Ββ	Γγ	Δδ	Εε	Ζζ	Ηη	Θθ
αλφα	βητα	γαμα	δελτα	εψιλον	ζητα	ητα	θητα
alfa	vita	gama	thelta	epsilon	zita	ita	thita
a	b	g	d	e	z	e	th

Ιι	Κχ	Λλ	Μμ	Νν	Ξξ	Οο	Ππ
γιωτα	καττα	λαμδα	μι	νι	ξι	ομικρον	πι
yioto	kapa	lamtha	mi	ni	xi	omikron	pi
i	k	l	m	n	ks, x	o	p

Ρο	Σσς	Ττ	Υυ	Φφ	Χχ	Ψψ	Ωω
ρο	σιγμα	ταυ	υψιλον	φι	χι	ψι	ωμεγα
ro	sigma	taf	ipsilon	fi	hi	psi	omega
r, rh	s	t	u, y	ph	kh, ch	ps	o

The letter sigma has a special form for use at the end of a word

There is no standard way of transliterating Greek into the roman alphabet so even island names can appear in different forms (e.g. Aegina and Eyina). The transliterated Greek words used in this book are in a form representing how they sound when spoken today.

SUMMARY OF HOUSING

The purchase of property in Greece by foreigners is a growing business, but still has a long way to go before it catches up with other Mediterranean areas. For instance Spain sold an estimated twenty to thirty thousand properties to the British in 2002; in the same year, fewer than three thousand foreigners bought properties in Greece. This is due to a number of factors including lack of cheap flights to Greece year round, and international developers being put off looking for land where they can build large developments, because Greek zoning laws restrict building in favour of the environment. No doubt attitudes are changing, not least because of the huge revenue potential of the residential tourism market for the Greek economy. Housing is an important contributor to the Greek economy. In some of the most popular areas, prices have gone up by 20%, although there is some suggestion that this is due to a combination of real price rises of about 12-15% plus inflation, rather than an sudden surge in demand.

Just over 60% of all houses in Greece are located in urban areas and over three-quarters of these are privately owned and just under 20% are rented. About 14% of Greek households own a second home and the majority of these are new housing. The average duration of mortgages is around 15 years.

PUBLIC HOLIDAYS

PUBLIC HOLIDAYS		
It is customary for commercial premises to shut on the afternoon of a public holiday until the afternoon of the following day. Easter is the equivalent of Christmas/New Year elsewhere in that it is the time that most families are reunited with their relatives from abroad etc. and there is a lot of eating and fireworks etc.		
2004	2005	
1 January		New Year's Day (Protochroniá)
6 January		Epiphany (Theofánia)
23 February	14 March	Orthodox Shrove Monday (Kathari Deftéra)
25 March		Annunciation (Evangelismós)/Independence Day
9 April	29 April	Orthodox Good Friday (Megáli Paraskevi)
12 April		Orthodox Easter Monday (Théftera tou Páscha)
1 May		Labour Day (Protomayá)
31 May	20 June	Day of the Holy Spirit
15 August		Assumption (Koimisis tis Theotóku)
28 October		'Ochi' (no to Mussolini) Day
25 Dec		Christmas (Christoúyena)
26 Dec		Boxing Day

USEFUL WEBSITES

www.gogreece.com – excellent site. One-stop shop for all kinds of information relevant to Greece and includes a Travel and Food Guide.

www.united-hellas.gr – excellent background and travel info, maps etc.

www.travelpage.gr – more excellent background information on regions of Greece etc.

RESIDENCE & ENTRY REGULATIONS

CHAPTER SUMMARY

- **EU Nationals** staying in Greece longer than 3 months but who are not employed do not need a residence permit.

- EU nationals who are employed in Greece for longer than 3 months need to apply for a residence permit.

- **Tax Reference Number.** If you are buying a car or property in Greece you will need to have a tax reference number so that all taxes that you pay in Greece will be referenced to this number.

- The tax reference number is not the same as a National Insurance Number which you get separately if you pay into the Greek Social Security System.

- **Non-EU Nationals** can apply for a short-term (3-6 months), or a one-year residence permit for which they will have to obtained a visa from the Greek embassy/consulate, before entry to Greece.

- The easiest way to get a a long-term (5-10 years) residence permit is to marry a Greek or other EU citizen.

- **Voting.** EU citizens can vote in municipal elections and stand as candidates for election locally.

- **Citizenship.** Foreigners who have lived in Greece for 15 years can apply for Greek citizenship provided that they speak Greek and own Greek property.

EU Nationals

Greece's membership of the EU means that citizens of other EU countries can reside in Greece for as long as they wish without the need to apply for a residence permit as long as they are not employed. Note that if you are working in Greece for longer than three months, you will need to have a residence permit. This can be obtained from the nearest Aliens Police Centre (*Kentro Allodapon*). You will require certain documents at the time of application:

- Two copies of a valid passport
- Three passport-size photographs
- Either: employer's declaration, stamped by the Work Inspection Authority,

or a confirmation of a declaration to open a business from the Tax Office.

Tax Reference Number (*Afimi*). You will need to have a tax reference number if you are buying a car, buying property or working in Greece. This number works somewhat like a UK national insurance number in that any taxes you pay in Greece will always be registered to your personal tax reference number. Note however, that it is not the same as a Greek national insurance number which you will also get separately if you are working in Greece and paying into the social security system IKA.

For more information on taxes see *Living in Greece* chapter.

Non EU-Citizens Entry Regulations

US citizens and other non-EU citizens can stay in Greece as a tourist for up to 3 months in any six-month period without a visa. In effect this means that if you stay for three months, you then have to leave Greece and the Schengen Zone (see *General Introduction*) for three months before returning. There are fines for overstaying in Greece, or anywhere in the Schengen zone, which can be up to €587/\$639 depending on the length of overstay.

Residence Permits for Non-EU Nationals

Short-Term Residence Permits. This is for anyone with a compelling reason to stay in Greece other than for tourist purposes. The permit is valid for 3-6 months and must be applied for 15 days prior to the expiry of the initial 90 days. Likewise the short-term residence permit may be extended to a one- year residence permit if you apply to the mayor's office or other designated local office at least two months prior to the expiry of the initial permit.

One-Year Residence Permit. Those who do not work and have funds for support and an income deriving from outside Greece and who wish to stay in Greece for one year or longer, can apply for a one-year permit. For this they will need to have obtained a visa *prior to their entry* into Greece, from the Greek Consulate or Embassy in their country of origin. The permit has to be applied for in Greece, at the local town hall, two months before the expiry of the initial legal period of entry. The fee for this permit is about €150.

You need to produce a raft of documents to support an application for the permit including:

- O Visa from the Greek Embassy or Consulate
- O Passport and copy
- O Two colour photos (passport-size)
- O A certificate of medical insurance cover
- O A health certificate from a Greek hospital certifying you are not suffering from any communicable diseases.
- O Local address
- O Evidence of financial resources to live in Greece (bank statement or similar)

If you have a one-year permit, you are free to come and go to Greece within the period of the permit.

Five to Ten Year Residence Permits. The easiest way to get a long-term permit is to marry a Greek or other EU citizen, though this is probably not a sound basis, if it is the only one, for marriage. A spouse of a Greek or other EU national can apply for a five-year residence permit, renewable for a further five years, provided that the application for extension is made two months before the original permit expires.

The permit also authorises the holder to work in Greece.

Voting

EU citizens can exercise their voting rights in municipal elections and stand as candidates. At present about 1,500 non-Greek citizens are on the electoral roll. For further information on voting and standing for election in Greece contact the Ministry of the Interior (2 Evangelistrias St., Mitropoleos Square, Thessaloniki; ☎210-322 3736 or 210 323 475823).

Citizenship

Foreign workers who have resided in Greece for fifteen years are eligible to apply for Greek citizenship subject to certain conditions such as having fluency in the Greek language and being the owner of property in Greece.

A foreigner who is married to a Greek national can apply for Greek citizenship after five years of legal residence in Greece.

EMBASSIES & CONSULATES

Greek Embassies in London & Dublin

Greek Embassy: 1A Holland Park, London W11 3TP; ☎020-7221 6467; fax 020-7229 3850; www.greekembassy.org.uk.

Greek Embassy: 1 Upper Pembroke Street, Dublin 2; ☎+3531 6767254; e-mail dubgremb@eircom.net.

Greek Embassies in North America

Greek Embassy: 80 MacLaren St., Ottawa, Ontario K2P 0K6; ☎613-2386271; fax 613-2385676; e-mail embassy@greekembassy.ca.

Greek Embassy: 2221 Massachusetts Ave NW, Washington DC 20008 USA; ☎202-939 5800; fax 202-939 5800; www.greekembassy.org. Greek consulates in Atlanta, Boston, Chicago, Houston, Los Angeles, New Orleans, New York, and San Francisco.

US Embassy and Consulate in Greece

US Embassy: 91 Vasilissis Sophias Blvd, 10160 Athens; ☎+30 210 721 2851; fax +30 210 645 6282; www.usembassy.gr; e-mail athensconsul@state.gov.

US Consulate General: Plateia Commercial Center 43, Tsimisi Street,, 7th Floor; Thessaloniki; ☎+30 2310;242905; www.usconsulate.gr and www.thessaloniki.usconsulate.gov; e-mail amcongen@compulink.gr.

British Embassy & Consulates in Greece

Embassy
British Embassy: 1 Ploutarchou Street, 10675 Athens; ☎+30 210 7272600.

Consulates
Corfu: British Consulate, 2 Alexandra Avenue & 1 Menekrates Street, 491 00 Corfu; ☎0661-30055; fax 0661-37995. Consul: Anthony Arnold.

Crete: British Consulate, 16 Papa-Alexandrou Street, 712 02 Heraklion; ☎081-224012, fax 081-243935. Consul: Mrs. Marion Tzanaki.

Kos: Honorary Vice Consulate, 8 Annetas Laoumtzi, 85300 Kos; ☎0242-21549/26203; fax 0242-5948; Honorary Vice Consul: Konstantinos Kourounis.

Patras: Honorary Vice Consul, 2 Votsi Street, 26221 Patras; ☎061-277329; fax 061-225334. Vice Consul: Marie Jeanne Murphy-Karatza.

Rhodes: British Honorary Consulate, 3 Pavlou Mela Street, P.O. Box 47, 85100 Rhodes; ☎0241-27247/27306; fax 0241-22615.

Thessaloniki: Honorary British Consul, 8 Venizelou Street, Eleftherias Square, P.O. Box 10332; 54110 Salonika; ☎031-278006/269984; fax 031-283868. Mr. George Doukas MBE.

Syros: Honorary British Vice Consul , 8 Akti Petrou Ralli Street, 84100 Ermoupolis; ☎0281-82231/88922; fax 0281-83293.

Zakynthos: Honorary British Vice Consul, 5 Foskolos Street, Zakynthos 29100; ☎0695-22906/48030; fax 0695-23769.

WHERE TO FIND YOUR IDEAL HOME

CHAPTER SUMMARY

- **Contacts.** There are sufficient agents and other contacts to give a fairly wide choice of locations to buy on the mainland, Crete or one of the smaller islands.
- **Islands.** Greece has more than 3000 islands, the vast majority of them uninhabited and uninhabitable.
- Some islands such as Crete and Corfu have a fully-functioning property-buying infrastructure for foreigners in place.
- The popularity of some regions with property buyers is often proportional to their popularity as a holiday destination.
- **Crete.** There are more estate agents and developers (dealing with foreigners) in Crete than in any other part of Greece.
- Greek government statistics show that there are more foreigners living in the prefectures of Messinia and Lakonia (the Mani peninsular) than in any other part of Greece.
- **Mainland property hotspots:** Two of the hottest spots are the Mani peninsula in the Peloponnese and the Pelion Peninsula in Thessaly.
- **Island property hotspots include:** Corfu, Crete, Naxos and Kefalonia.
- **Most beautiful island the Greeks keep to themselves:** Evia.
- **Number of foreigners a year buying property in Greece:** about 3000.

OVERVIEW

Greece is the furthest east you can go and still be in Europe. It has experienced a boom in house buying by foreigners since property laws prohibiting foreigners from buying property in Greece were relaxed in 1992 with Greece's inclusion in the EU. Property buying by foreigners is a fairly familiar occurrence in some places including certain towns in the Peloponnese and is catching on in others, so there are sufficient contacts and services in place to enable potential non-Greek buyers to have a fairly wide choice of locations on the mainland, Crete, or one of the smaller islands in the Sporades, Dodecanese, Ionian etc. groups, and also a choice of the type of property: off-plan, old, new-build etc.

Greece has been (and is) literally shaped by the Mediterranean and uniquely, almost anywhere in Greece appears ideal for a home on the Med as almost everywhere is near the sea. Even on much of the mainland, the coast is not that distant and with approximately 3000 islands (it seems there is no definitive figure), there are sea views in every direction. Of course, the majority of the islands are little more than rocky, waterless, outcrops, and not all are inhabited or indeed habitable.

Whilst there are old buildings dotted all over Greece they are usually in a very tumbledown state and expensive to restore and many people find it more practical to buy a plot of land and have a house built for them, or to buy a whole package which includes construction, or just to buy a modern house or apartment that they can move into immediately. More and more land around small towns is being made available for building and many out-of-town plots are available with planning permission already granted, so choosing a plot is a luxury you may well be able to indulge in. Land and house prices in Greece average a third less than you would expect to pay in other areas so close to the sea.

This chapter gives a fuller picture of the 'regions' of Greece, ie Athens and the mainland including the Peloponnese, the big islands of Crete (*Kríti*) and Evia (*Évvoia*) and the regional groups of islands like the Dodecanese and the Sporades. Even the least observant reader will notice that there are a relatively small number of islands with an individual mention here. For reasons of space, it is necessary to select the most popular and habitable ones, with the best communications, as these are the ones with at least the minimum (i.e. an English-speaking agent or contact) to get you started. Some islands, particularly Crete and Corfu have a fully-functioning property-buying infrastructure for foreigners already in place.

The popularity of some regions with property buyers is often linked to the fact they are well-known holiday destinations and so many foreigners get very well acquainted with them and then decide they would like to spend more and more time there. A surprising number of buyers even buy after just one visit on holiday to a particular place, although responsible agents, on the whole, caution against such impulsiveness. Other locations in Greece are historically popular with the English like the Ionian islands (once a British protectorate), Crete and areas around Athens.

If none of the areas covered in this section will do, the intrepid house or ideal plot hunter can explore the lesser known islands or mainland on their travels, and they may find their dream house, ruin, or plot of land, somewhere almost 'undiscovered' by any foreigners. If you really want to go and live remotely in an area that few outside Greece have heard of, you should be prepared for double the hassle that you would expect from a purchase in a tried and tested area and also there may be a few good reasons why no-one else wants to live there. As Debbie Taylor, who bought a Cretan ruin, puts it in her *Sunday Times* series of *Heat & Dust* articles:

> *Two bits of advice for people buying a second home: choose somewhere near a decent airport – and resign yourself to going there every year until you die.*
> *Trust me, with lesser-known Greek islands it can take days to get there, with life-threatening stopovers in the polluted hellmouth even Greeks call 'killing Athens', followed by wilting hours on a packed ferry or a nerve-shattering flight on a meccano plane.*

If you are going off the beaten track a good map is essential; you should find anything you need at www.mapsworldwide.com.

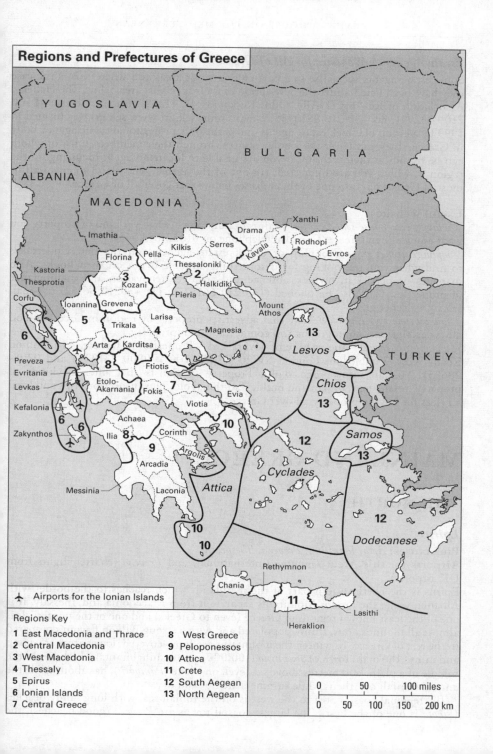

Regions and Prefectures of Greece

YUGOSLAVIA

BULGARIA

ALBANIA

MACEDONIA

Xanthi
Drama
Imathia
Kilkis
Serres
1
Rodhopi
Florina
Pella
Kavala
Evros
Kastoria
Thessaloniki
2
Thesprotia
Kozani
3
Halkidiki
Corfu
Pieria
6
Ioannina
Grevena
Mount
Athos
TURKEY
5
Larisa
13
Trikala
4
Lesvos
Arta
Karditsa
Magnesia
Preveza
8
Evritania
Ftiotis
Chios
Levkas
Etolo-
7
13
Akarnania
Fokis
Kefalonia
Evia
6
Viotia
Samos
Zakynthos
6
Achaea
12
13
8
Corinth
Ilia
9
Cyclades
Argolis
10
Arcadia
Attica
Messinia
Laconia
10
12
10
Dodecanese
Rethymnon
Chania
Lasithi
11
Heraklion

✈ Airports for the Ionian Islands

Regions Key

1	East Macedonia and Thrace	8	West Greece
2	Central Macedonia	9	Peloponessos
3	West Macedonia	10	Attica
4	Thessaly	11	Crete
5	Epirus	12	South Aegean
6	Ionian Islands	13	North Aegean
7	Central Greece		

0	50	100 miles
0 50	100 150	200 km

Estate Agents & Websites for All of Greece

Some estate agents specialise in a particular area or areas and where this is the case they have been listed under the description of their specialist area below. The Hellenic Association of Realtors (HAR), Odos Kerkyyras 47, 11362, Athens, Greece; ☎+30 210 8232931; fax +30 210 8810936; e-mail info@sek.gr; www.sek.gr) was formed in 1999 by a group of Greek estate agents and is the only professional estate agency body in Greece. They can cover the whole country through their members, a list of whom can be found on their website. If you are unable to locate an agent focussing on the region in which you are interested, try one of the agents, who claim to cover all or most of Greece or go to one of the websites below that cover all of Greece.

Useful Websites

www.greece-house-search.co.uk: Claims to hunt down whatever kind of property you want anywhere in Greece. Can also telephone on 01622-853 545.

www.realtynet.gr – Grouping of Greek estate agencies on the net. Undertakes to find what you are looking for if something suitable is not on their books. Also manages properties in owners' absence and arranges renovation and maintenance of properties. Can also be phoned (+30 210 6615278; fax +30210 6615277; e-mail sales@realtynet.gr.

www.propertygr.com – Website that advertises property by region in Greece. Good clear descriptions, photographs and contacts for each property.

www.progc.co.uk – The website of Mykra Ltd – Properties in Greece, 43 Lambton Road, West Wimbledon, London SW20 OLW; (UK ☎0800 7313254 and 0208-2869511; e-mail info@progc.co.uk). Property specialists that offer all kinds of property: resale, new, design and build, traditional old, plus inspection trips and legal services for buying property all over Greece.

MAINLAND GREECE

THE NORTH

Epirus

Prefectures: *Arta, Ioannina, Preveza, Thesprotia.*
Airports for this Area: *Ioannina* (international) and *Preveza* (charter flights from UK airports).

Epirus is the northwestern part of the mainland, which reaches to the border with Albania, while the Pindos Mountains separate it from Macedonia and Thessaly. It is one of the least known regions of Greece (even to Greeks) and one of the poorest. It is almost all mountainous, thinly populated and with a strong Balkan flavour compared to the rest of Greece. In winter, the mountains are snow-covered, lower areas are damp and rainy. The main town of *Ioannina* (100,000 approx. inhabitants) which lies in the middle of a plain, 500 metres above sea level, on a lake (*Pamvotis*), has about triple the annual rainfall of Athens while summers are hot and dry.

The regional coastal area to the west is on the Ionian sea, with long sandy beaches (*Sivota* is one of the best). The largest coastal towns are *Preveza* (good beaches), the idyllic small town of *Parga* (small islands and coves), and the port of Igoumenitsa, which is the main port for Corfu (1hr.45mins) and other Ionian islands. Ferries from there also go to Patra (12 hrs).

Finding Properties for Sale in this Area. It is difficult to find agents that specialise in this area. You could try to make contacts via the area website www.epirus.com or the town websites such as www.pargaweb.com. Alternatively, book a holiday there and have a look around yourself. Communications with the region, especially on the coast will improve in the next few years and probably the choice of realtors with it. There were apartments and maisonettes, part-built, for sale in Parga at the time of press, contact Elias Katsimitsis (☎+306937264115; elias@pargaweb.com). There is no great government drive to develop this region compared with the north-east Aegean, a fact which may appeal to some foreign buyers, but probably not to investors.

Thrace

Prefectures: *Evros, Rhodopi, Xanthi.*
Airports for this Region: *Alexandroupolis* (domestic flights) and *Kavala* (International flights).
Ferries: connect *Alexandroupolis* with Kavala, and the islands of Samothraki, Limnos and Mytilini.
This region constitutes the far northeastern corner of Greece, and it is only since 1920 that it has been part of Greece. Recent government administrative changes mean than Eastern Macedonia (i.e the prefectures of *Drama* and *Kavala*) are now part of a new region called East Macedonia and Thrace.

Geographically, Thrace is marked by large rivers and wetlands and the Rhodopi mountains. The Evros delta is an internationally protected refuge for hordes of rare indigenous and migratory species dependent on its ecological conditions. Thrace (or *Thraki*) is divided from (Greek) Macedonia to the west by the Nestos river. It shares a border with Turkey (Eastern Thrace) to the east and northwest where there is also a minority of ethnic Turks (estimated at between 80,000 and 100,000 people). The Evros river forms a natural barrier between the two countries. To the north is the Bulgarian border, which is formed from the Rhodopi mountains. The Thracian coast is to the south on the Aegean. The climate is midway between Mediterranean and Mid-European.

Prefecture of Etolo-Akarnania (West Greece)

Etolo-Akarnania, together with the Peloponnese prefectures of *Achaea* and *Ilia* form the recently designated region West Greece. Achaea and Ilia are dealt with in the *Peloponnese* section below).

Etolo-Akarnania/Aitolia-Arkanania has the almost typical Greek mainland combination of beautiful coastline and mountains. Agriculture, especially tobacco provides a large part of the local economy. The area is suffering a population decline as the younger people drift towards the cities and higher paid jobs. The capital of the prefecture is *Missolonghi/Messolongi*, with a population of about 11,000.

Messolonghi occupies a special place in the hearts of the Greeks and Lord Byron fans. Messolonghi is to the Greeks what the Alamo is to Texas, in other words, a shrine to their liberty where the cititzens held out against a Turkish seige for 4 years from 1822 before fleeing and mostly being massacred before the city was retaken once and for all from the Turks in 1928; for Byron who spent ten months there, fighting against,and helping to organise resistance to the Turks, it was his last adventure as he died there of fever in 1824 before the seige ended. Messolonghi is sited on three picturesque lagoons.

About 50 km north of Messolonghi is the summer resort of Astakos, which has several pristine beaches. Daily ferries operate between the mainland and the islands of *Kefalonia* and *Ithaki*. Further up the coast is the giant lagoon known as Lake *Amvrakia*. The large town of *Agrinio* (pop. 75,000) is at the centre of tobacco production and has excellent tourist facilities. The other large town of the prefecture is *Nafpaktos* situated on the Corinth straits between the mainland and the Peloponnese and not far from the new rail/road bridge to that region.

Macedonia

Coastal Prefectures: *Chalkdiki, Kavala, Piera, Thessaloniki*. Note that the districts of Verla and Serres only have a tiny outlet to the coast each at *Klidi* and *Nea Kerdilia* respectively.

Airports for this Area: Kavala (international airport. Many charters from UK airports); Kozani (connections to Athens and flights from Teeside Airport UK); Thessaloniki (major international airport).

Macedonia is the largest of the Greek regions at 34,177 sq. kms and has a population of 2.3 million. However the western part is worlds away from the eastern part's blue sea and sun drenched coasts and has the highest rainfall in mainland Greece. The four landlocked prefectures which make up western Macedonia are *Grevena, Florina, Kastoria and Kozani*, while Kavala and Drama prefectures in eastern Macedonia, have recently been reassigned to make a new administrative region called East Macedonia and Thrace. The large, cosmopolitan port city of *Thessaloniki* (Salonika), located in Macedonia, is Greece's second city.

Chalkidiki. Also called *Khalkidhiki* or *Chalcidice*, Chalkidiki is a peninsular that is one of the most recognisable features of Macedonia, if not of Greece. It resembles a hand with three fingers projecting down into the Aegean (the fingers or peninsulas are named *Cassandra, Sithonia/Longos*, and *Athos* – of Mt. Athos). Kassandra peninsular has long stretches of beautiful beaches and pineforests where there are tourist camping sites. There are quaint fishing villages dotted along the coast. Touristic development is expanding in the form of dozens of hotels especially at *Paliouri*, near the tip and at villages like *Fourka*. Sithonia, the middle peninsular is even more endowed with beaches and fishing villages and coves full of fishing boats. The main tourist area is around Gerakini. The third peninsular, Athos, is a self-governing monastic state which was once home to 40 monasteries and thousands of monks. It is peppered with historic Christian buildings dating from Byzantine times and about 20 are still in use. Women are still prohibited from entering Mt. Athos, as pilgrims or otherwise, as the rules of entry are unchanged since they were laid down by a papal bull of 1045. Who said Greece was behind the times!

The Chalkidiki region has been slow to encourage tourism, but this is changing with new roads being built to give access to the peninsulas and incentives for the development of the coastal areas with hotels and other tourist accommodation. The area has been heavily marketed in Germany. This is an area, which could prove a good investment for prospective land and property buyers, especially those who tend more towards the speculative end of property buying. There are hundreds of apartments and plots for sale, which could prove interesting for buyers.

Kavala. The prefecture of *Kavala* is now, along with the landlocked *Drama* prefecture, part of a new administrative region: East Macedonia and Thrace. Kavala prefecture is in the southern part of eastern Macedonia and stretches between the *Nestos* and the *Strimonas* rivers. The island of *Thassos* (see *North Eastern Aegean* below) comes under the Kavala prefectural administration. The main town of the prefecture is also called Kavala. Physically, the region is mostly mountainous but about a fifth of the territory is made up of low-lying plains.

Kavala city is a modern commercial centre housed in an ancient and historic city stacked on a hillside overlooking an attractive natural harbour. It is also the centre of Greece's tobacco industry and despite this taint of nicotine, it is regarded as Macedonia's most attractive city.

Kavala prefecture is well developed from the touristic point of view. The coast is popular with holiday makers having as it does, fine sandy beaches and many tourist resorts. Kavala airport receives regular charter flights from many UK regional airports. This area is a good prospect for investment in property on or near the coast.

Piera. *Piera* prefecture is in central Macedonia and its eastern part lies on the Gulf of Thermaiko. The region has been successful in promoting tourism in recent years thanks to a combination of spectacular mountain and coastal regions. It is the home of Mt. Olympus, which at just under 3000m, is the highest mountain in Greece and lies southwest of Thessaloniki and just west of the *Thermaik Gulf*. The coast has expanses of sandy beaches stretching from *Nei Pori* up to *Methoni*; seaside resorts include Methoni, *Aghios Panteleimonas* (complete with a castle), *Platamonas* and *Makrigialos*. The wetlands surrounding the mouth of the river *Aliamonas* are a nature reserve of outstanding natural beauty. The main town of the region is *Katerini,* about 20km inland between the plain of Piera and Mt. Olympus.

Thessaloniki. Thessaloniki city in the prefecture of that name has over a million inhabitants and is one of the oldest European cities (founded 315 BC; and figuring in the Bible) and was named for the sister of Alexander the Great. Its conurbation stretches over 12 km and overlooks the bay of *Thermaikos*. The city, especially the lower part, is largely of modern construction after a devastating fire swept through it in 1917. The city expanded when refugees arrived from Turkey in 1923 but development began in earnest from the 1950s and is continuing. The city has a busy academic, cultural and commercial life but its climate leaves something to be desired: severe winters and oppressively hot summers are the norm. From the property buying point of view, Thessaloniki has investment potential, but most foreigners living there are doing so for a purpose connected with the city, be it academic, military etc. However, it is useful base for seeking out estate agents who deal with property in the surrounding resorts and Chalkidiki.

Typical Properties for sale in Macedonia

Location	Type	Description	Price
Agia Paraskevi, Thessaloniki	Maisonette in development under construction	On 2 levels. 95 sq.m. Central heating, parking and garden	€95,000
Kalyves (Sithonia Peninsula)	Modern, 2nd floor apartment	92 sq.m. 10 years old. Excellent condition. 2-bedrooms. On sandy coast.	€85,106

Fourka, (Kassandra Peninsula)	Villa	220 sq. m. on 2 floors, 4-bedrooms, living room, 2 kitchens. Occupies plot of 1500 sq. m. with gardens, lawn and fruit trees. 30 m from sea.	€264,123
Chalkidki Island	Small Island	75,000 sq.m.	€1,173,881

Estate Agents For Macedonia

Anna Googleri Real Estate Agency: Gimnasiarhou Mikrou 22, Thessaloniki, Greece; ☎+30 2310 334302; fax +30 2310 334303; e-mail gougleri@realbase.gr. Deals in homes, commercial, land and farmland for sale and for rent.

Georgios Kouris: Amfipoleos 8, Kato Touba, 544 54 Thessaloniki; ☎2310-928333; tel/fax 2310 900390; www.kaouris.com. Building and construction company offering apartments, flats and houses mainly in the Thessaloniki area.

Halkidiki Homes: Hanioti, Halkidiki; ☎+30 6945 312 058; e-mail info@hakidikiho mes.co.uk. Deals with sales, rentals and property managment.

Kostas Mpasiakoulis Property Investments Real Estate: Gr. Labraki 38, 54638 Thessaloniki, Greece; ☎+30 2310 202632; fax +30 2310 202632; mpasiakoulis@axion.gr; www.mpasiakoulis.gr. Deals with properties in Chalkidiki and inland in Macedonia.

Malathron: 57 Voulgari Street, Corner of N. Egnatia, 54248 Thessaloniki, Greece; ☎+30 2310-315001; +30 2310-328753; e-mail melathron@axiom.gr; www.melathron.gr. Deals with the purchase, sale and rent of all types of properties in Thessaloniki and Chalkidiki. Also does engineering surveys of buildings for clients. Contact Stavros Kritikopoulos, owner.

Northland Estate Agents and Valuers: 17 Nikis Avenue, 54623 Thessaloniki, Greece; +30 2310 229 341; fax +30 2310 250 338; www.northland.gr.

Realty Greece: 25 Egeou St. Thessaloniki; ☎003231-480100; www.realty.gr. Several branch offices. Contact Grigoris Liantas. Deals with sales, apartment lettings, building plots etc. in Thessaloniki and all over Greece.

CENTRAL GREECE

Airports for Central Greece: Athens (major international airport), Kythira (domestic connecting flights from Athens)

Sterea Ellas

Prefectures: *Evia* (island), *Evtritania, Fokis, Ftiotis, Viotia.*

This region lies between the Peloponnese and Thessalia and was the first independent territory of the newly liberated Greece in the early nineteenth century. It is mountainous and dotted with small villages. There are no large towns. The surrounding mountains include to the west Helikon, the legendary home of the Muses and at 1750 metres the highest peak, and the fabled Parnassus (now a skiing base). The area may be poor in population but is so rich in classical history and legends that your entire repertoire of half-remembered classical allusions can probably be linked to its landscape: the city of Thebes, the Delphic oracle, Mount Parnassus, Dionysus, Heracles, Oedipus, Electra, Pegasus and more. Thebes, with its unique classical buildings including the Temple of Apollo, and Delphi are the two biggest tourist attractions. The main towns are Delphi, one of the most famous sites of the ancient world, *Nafpaktos, Lamia* and *Karpenissi*. The area is constantly at risk from seismic activity, which is liable to cause massive rockfalls and damage to ancient buildings.

The coastal landscape is diverse with countless bays and vertiginous coves with picturesque views to the islands. The east facing (Aegean) coast has some excellent beaches very popular with locals in summer. The coast has the added attraction of remaining cooler than the rest of the mainland. However, thanks to its many charms, coastal property is more expensive here than in many other littoral areas.

Thessalia

Prefectures: *Karditsa, Larisa, Trikala, Magnesia.*

Thessalia, also called Thessaly, lies to the north of Steréa Ellás and is the main agricultural production area of Greece thanks to its vast fertile plain, legacy of a prehistoric lake bed, which has been the basis of the area's prosperity for centuries. The low-lying interior is surrounded on three sides by mountains including the iconic Mt. Olympus, famous in Greek mythology for being the home of the gods led by Zeus, while Mt. Pelion (1550m) was the training ground for mythical centaurs (back end horse/front half man) by their leader Chiron. It is now a training ground for skiers . The region is also linked to the heroic legends of Hercules and Theseus (of defeat of the minotaur fame) and it is from the now bustling city of *Vólos* (pop. 200,000), that Jason and the Argonauts set sail in the Argo, where appropriately, many Greek sailing holidays begin these days.

The main towns of the region include *Larissa*, a bustling market centre, Vólos, the port and rapidly expanding industrial centre and airport. *Vólos* also has excellent hydrofoil and ferry links with the Sporades islands, particularly *Skiathos, Skopelos* and *Alonnisos,* and is near the popular Mt. Pelion and the peninsular of that name. *Kalambaka* is a modern town near *Meteora,* the latter a much visited site of Byzantine churches and monasteries spectacularly built on the tops of vertical cliffs.

Pelion Peninsular. Pelion is part of the Thessalia region. It is a sizeable finger of Thessalia, in the province of Magnesia, that reaches down towards the Sporades. It has acquired something of a hotspot reputation amongst foreign property buyers. The area is still unspoilt but well known to Greeks who like to weekend there and in Vólos. You can however, escape the sophistication of Vólos in a flash and immerse yourself in dense beech and oak forests, and rural sights, which are rare these days, such as home-spinning and log-gathering by donkey. The airport links to Vólos include some charter flights from Gatwick to *Nea Amcheallos* (the airport that services Vólos). There are likely to be increased connections as demand increases, but at the time of print Air 2000 (booked through Houses of Pelion) had the monopoly. There are also regular charter flights to Thessaloniki and Skiathos, the nearest island. The seas on the northeast side of the peninsular have a tendency to get rather choppy (or worse), but are perfect for swimming on calm days. The sheltered western side has a gentler sea, which is also a few degrees warmer. However, paradise comes at a price. Property is expensive in this area and a little in situ exploring might be the only hope for success if your budget is limited.

Typical Properties for Sale in Central Greece including Pelion Peninsula

Location	Type	Description	Price
Aghia Marina, Bay of Pteloy, E. of Lamia. 500m from the sea, 12km from main Athens/Thessaloniki road.	8,000 sq.m. of land	120 olive trees bordered by two roads. Electricity & telephone lines ready on land	€58,000
Village of Agios Demetrios, Pelion.	Aristocratic mansion recently featured in Greek style mag.	280 sq.m. 3 bedrooms, 2 bathrooms, separate guest house. Garden 1,300 sq.m.	Unfurnished €750,000. Furnished €1,030,000 (includes certified antiques)
Village of Katohori, 11km from Vólos	1,500 sq.m. of land with old stone building (2 floors) in non habitable condition.	Stunning village. Site has panoramic views of the sea and part-view of Vólos	€47,000
Edge of village of Milina, southern end of Pelion Peninsular	Plot of 850 sq. m. with 100 sq m. building (a former café)	10 m from the sea. Building could be converted to dwelling or additional new building created for business purposes.	€170,000
Paleo Trikeri (an island), foot of Pelion Peninsular	2 adjacent plots of 3,200 sq. m and 800 sq.m suitable for building summer houses	On tiny island with one village and sandy beaches	€62,000 and €19, 000. For sale together or separately

Useful Contacts/Websites for these Areas

Houses of Pelion: 0870 199 9191; www.pelion.co.uk. Charter flights to Vólos, and is also an estate agent.

Agents for these Areas

Domiki Thessalias AE Construction and Real Estate: 54ou Syntag. Ellas 18, Vólos, Thessaly, Greece; ☎24210 39395; fax 24210 39394; www.domiki-thessalias.com.

Houses of Pelion: Asprogia, N. Pagase, 38500 Vólos, Greece; tel/fax +30 24210 87610; e-mail info@pelionproperties.com; www.pelionproperties.com.

Immobilien-griechenland-pilion.de/english: German agent with large selection of properties.

Pelion Properties: Asprogia, N. Pagase 38500, Vólos. Greece; ☎24210 87610; fax 24210 87610; info@pelionproperties.com; www.pelionproperties.com.

Vakim Real Estate: Plateia Lakka, Arahova, Viotia, Greece; ☎22670-32549; Athens office: 3 Septembriou 84, Athens, Greece; ☎210-8256681-1; www.vakim.com/properties.html. Properties all over central Greece.

Thirty Eight Degrees: Registered address: Haraugis 33, Halandri 152 32 Athens, Greece; ☎+30 210 682 3098 and +30 697 66 44 779; e-mail info@thirtyeightdegrees.com; www.thirtyeightdegrees.com. Ask for Katerina Samaropoulou.

Vasiliki Ganidi: Iroon Politecnhiou 133, Larissa 41223, Thessaly; ☎2410-551115; 2410-552657; e-mail ganidi@panafonet.gr. Only member of Hellenic Association of Realtors in Thessaly. Deals in all types of property.

SOUTHERN GREECE

Airport for this Region: Athens. There are domestic flights from Athens to Kythera.

Attica and Athens

Prefectures: *Attica-Athens,* and the islands *Kythera, Megara, Salamis.*

Attica is a peninsular jutting into the Aegean Sea in the south-eastern part of mainland Greece. To the north lies the Boeotian plain and to the west it is bordered by Corinth. South of Attica is the Saronic Gulf and the large island of *Evia/Euboea* lies alongside the northern coast. In some ways, Attica is the heart of Greece as it contains the capital Athens and on the plain of Attica dwell nearly four million people, or about 40% of the Greek population. Less than a hundred years ago, the whole of the plain of Athens was under cultivation, a riot of olive groves and vineyards. Athens increased in size hugely in the first part of the twentieth century due to rapid repatriation of Greeks fleeing from Turkey. As the last century progressed all the old agricultural land up to the very edges of the mountains disappeared under urban sprawl. However, the inland country of Attica has some of the richest soil, best wines, most unspoilt hamlets and fantastic medieval churches in all of Greece.

The area should not be shunned by the potential house-buyer because of the fearsome reputation of Athens as the smog and congestion capital of Europe; there are leafy suburbs dotted with beautifully restored villas. Piraeus, the port of Athens is one of the busiest in the Mediterranean from where there are 'flying dolphins' (hydrofoils) and ferries to most of the islands. Attica also has its own beach playground: the Apollo coast runs for 70km from *Cape Sounion* to Piraeus and its main, rather glitzy resorts include *Glyfada, Voula, Vouliagmneni, Varkiza, Kabouri, Lagonissi, Anavissos and Sounion.* The nearest islands to the Attic coast are the Saronic Islands (see below) which provide retreats for wealthy Athenians.

Not surprisingly, house and apartment prices in Athens are some of the most expensive in the country but there is still plenty of room for price growth and the Olympics in 2004 has generated a lot improvements in city transport systems and amenities. If the rush and bustle gets too much to bear, you can always cast your eyes up to the Acropolis, visible from many points in the city, and reflect on the legacy of the progenitors of 7,000 years of European civilisation.

Typical Properties for Sale in Attica including Athens

Location	Type	Description	Price
Anavissos	Maisonnete	Set in a 4000 sq.m. plot of olive trees. Private road. Very good view	€850,000
NW Attica, Chalkoutsi, 55km from Athens airport	Apartment	175 sq.m. 3rd floor. 3 bedrooms. Sea view to Evia	€400,000 plus taxes
Varkiza about 20 km from Athens	Luxury detached house still under construction.	On three levels. 270 sq.m. on land of 400 sq.m. Has swimming pool and heating.	€763,023
Glyfada, Athens area	New apartment	4th (top) floor 115 sq.m. plus private roof garden. 3 bedrooms, exceptional mountain and sea views.	€282,000
Central Athens	Apartment	On two floors. 150 sq.m. Two bedrooms and two bathrooms on upper floor. Roof terrace with view of the Acropolis and to the sea	€450,000

Estate Agents for this Region

Anastasios-Konstantinos N. Tsiganos Real Estate Agency: Galatsiou ave. 73, 11146 Galatsi, Attica; tel/fax 010 291 7333; info@tsiganos.gr; www.tsiganos.gr.

Espresso Realty: Gounari 135, 16561 Glyfada, Athens; tel/fax 210 9642 742; e-mail info@espressorealty.com. Estate agents for Attica and Athens.

Estate 2000: Iridanou 20 & Michalakopoulou, Ilisia, TK 115-28, Athens, Greece; ☎+301 7241500; fax +301-7216963; e-mail info@estate2000.gr; www.estate2000.gr.

Christos Giannakopoulos Estate Agency: Vari-Koropi Ave 7, Vari, TK 16672, Athens, Greece; ☎8973205; fax 8975873; e-mail info@greekproperty.gr; www.greekproperty.gr.

Ecotypon Real Estate Agency: Sozopoleos 25, 10446 Athens, Greece; ☎+301 8660773-74; fax +301 8664342; e-mail oikotypon@oikotypon.ath.forthnet.gr; www.forthnet.gr/oikotypon.

Politia Real Estate: Papanikolaou Xanthi, 81, Panormou Street, Ambelokipi, Athens; ☎010 6911885; 6919320; e-mail papanikolaou@politia.com.gr; www.politia.com.gr. Situated in Athens, Ampelokipi and deals with property in Athens and the wider area of Attica.

Riviera Real Estate: Lambraki 33, Glyfada 166 75; ☎+30-210 8953634; fax +30 210 8953634; e-mail casabanka@pathfinder.gr; www.greekrivierarealestate.com. Member of Athens Realtors' Association, dealing with properties in Athens and suburbs, and Attica. Also some Greek Islands.

THE PELOPONNESE

Airport for this Region: Kalamata (international airport, many charter flights from UK airports)

Prefectures: *Achaea* (north), *Arcadia* (centre), *Argolida* (east), *Ilia* (north west),

Corinthia (north east), *Lakonia* (south east) and *Messinia* (south west). Achaea and Ilia have recently been made into a new administrative district called West Greece, which also comprises a new prefecture of *Aitolia-Acarnania* north west of the Peloponnese. The Peloponnese (also called Peleponisos and Peloponessos) region of 201,440 sq.kms is treated as mainland Greece even though it is separated (just) from the rest of the mainland by the Corinth canal, which, in 1893 was cut through the isthmus linking the two areas, in order to speed up sea traffic between the Ionian and Aegean seas. Technically therefore, it is an island and indeed was known as the Island of Pelops in ancient times. Engineering ingenuity now links the Peloponnese to the mainland via a new road and rail bridge opened in 2004.

The Peloponnese, region is mainly mountainous but there are alluvial plains towards the coast. For lovers of archaeology it is a treasure trove of palaces, cities and civilisations from Helen of Troy to Sparta and from Mycenae to Messene.

The present day population of this fascinating region is approximately a million and the largest towns are *Patras* in the north and *Kalamata* in the south west whilst the more picturesque city of *Nafplio* was the first capital of modern Greece before it was moved to Athens.

There are many people that consider the Peloponnese to be the 'real' Greece. As a quasi-island it is perceived to have remained aloof from the hordes of Albanians, Macedonians etc, who have made their presence felt through the rest of Greece. However, its complex history and ancient civilisations prove this is not strictly true as the heredity of the people of the Peloponnese is as mixed as anywhere in the complicated tribal territories of the Balkans. Today however, the invading hordes are likely to be the growing number of holiday-makers homing in to the resort areas around Kalamata (where the charter flights go to); beautiful landscapes and beaches are decidedly some of the Peloponnese's great attractions. However, the region has some flaws, which are significant enough to warrant consideration if you are thinking of buying property there. Although the maximum length and width of the region is barely over 200 km, journey times can take longer than expected owing to the tortuous terrain. There is a fast road from Corinth (the usual entry point) to *Tripolis,* which is near the centre and the new bridge linking Achaea to West Greece (see below).

Global warming seems to be affecting Peloponnese weather, which during the last quarter of a century has produced some notable heatwaves. Since the millennium, new records have been established for summer temperatures in the area: the highest recorded was in the mid-40s Celsius in 2002, and the average is around 35C.

Earth tremors are another inconvenience. Every year there are dozens of small tremors caused by the many fault lines running under the area making trees shake and rattling buildings and the western part of the Peloponnese is susceptible to more severe seismic activity.

Nonetheless, probably no area of the Peloponnese should be overlooked from the property buying point of view:

Achaea/Achaia. Almost a third (300,000) of the entire population of the Peloponnese live in Achaea province and most of them live in the *Patras* metropolitan area. Patras, the main city of the Peloponnese, is also Greece's third largest city. The region will also benefit from the completion of the 1.4 km *Rhion Antiron* bridge across the Corinth strait, linking the Peloponnese to western Greece. Other sizeable (for Greece) towns include *Aigio* (pop. 12,000) *Aigiera, Akrata, Kalavryta, Pteri, Chalandritsa* and *Diakopton.* You can ski from the *Panachaicus* east of Patras or at *Mt Chelmos,* (now called *Aroania)* near *Kalavrita.*

Buying property on the Med in this region is not very popular. The only level coastal areas are the marshes at Cape Araxos. The majority of the coast rises quite steeply to the mountains. A good investment might be to buy in Patras or one of the pretty coastal towns particularly Aigio.

Arcadia. Arcadia is the largest prefecture taking up nearly 20% of the Peloponnese. The main city of the prefecture is Tripoli. Almost enclosed by, and full of, mountains, Arcadia is a land of forests and peaks and a notable number of streams and rivers that have a tendency to disappear underground; in fact it is all you would expect of a land that gave birth to the mythical god Pan (half goat/half shepherd), and which came to embody the pastoral ideal thanks to the poetry of Virgil and his Renaissance successors. It is still remarkably unspoilt and agricultural (some might say boring) today. The only blot on the idyll is the combination nuclear/fossil fuel power station that lies south of the ancient ruins of *Megalopolis* and is visible from them.

Even though it is mainly landlocked, Arcadia has a notable coastline with some bustling tourist spots and fine beaches. The old village of *Paralio Astros* is located on a promontary, which is also the site of an ancient Greek settlement. The spot is popular with locals from Tripoli and also Athenians who have summer apartments there. 'Paralio' means coastal and distingishes Paralio Astros from plain *Astros*, situated about 4 km inland. Astros is less touristy as it is a commercial and business centre with all the facilities you might expect from a county town: shops, lawyers, doctors etc. The area of *Tsakonia* (about 10 km south) is a fascinating and still remote part of Greece where the local people speak an ancient Dorian language and keep customs that have all but vanished from most of Greece. There are several pretty coastal villages in this area. The inland ones are bound in by the mountains and rather isolated.

Argolida. The prefecture of *Argolida* is a peninsular with a most attractive coastline and many pretty inland and coastal towns and villages as well as some top notch classical sites such as the Epidavros Greek amphitheatre, still used for performances, and the town of *Mycenae*, cradle of the Mycenean civilisation.

Main coastal, and near coastal towns include *Argos* (the commercial centre), *Tolo, Asini, Methana, Poros, Porto Heli, Nea Kios* and *Agia Moni*. By far the largest and most beautiful is *Nafplio*, the former capital of liberated Greece. It is old, with very picturesque architecture, which includes wooden balconies and Turkish and neo-classical buildings. There is also a 16th century Venetian citadel accessible by climbing over 500 steps up from the main town.

Corinth/Corinthia. The prefecture of Corinthia is the second most populated of the Peloponnese after Achaia. The main city, *Corinth* (pop. 29,000) is the second largest town on the Peloponnese after Patras. The city was reconstructed after an earthquake wrought havoc in 1928. The ancient city of Corinth thrived on trade and rivalled Thebes and Athens for wealth and culture and was notable for its hedonistic lifestyle. Whether or not this trait lives on is hard to say, but there are reminders of a glittering past, such as the magnificent upright remains of the Temple of Apollo which look down on the modern city from the acropolis today. The Corinth Canal lies 2.5km east of the city.

Resorts especially *Kokoni* and *Xylocastro* and their respective beaches, on the Gulf of Corinth are extremely popular with weekending Athenians. Property prices are therefore at the high end of the Greek market.

Elia/Ilia Prefecture. About a third of *Elia* is fertile farming country producing tormatoes, peppers, potatoes, livestock, melons, oranges etc. The rest of the province is mostly mountainous and not suitable for arable farming. Ironically, there are plenty of springs providing water in the barren mountains but the fertile coastal plain relies on artificial reservoirs and dams to supply its needs. A lot of the coastal reservoir water is treated with contaminants and is not suitable for drinking. The prefecture's coastline is composed mostly of sandy beaches, nearly 300 km of them. Tourism plays a big part in the region's economy and is mainly centred on *Kyllini* with its thermal springs and easy access to the Ionian islands. The province's chief archaeological site is Olympia where the original Olympic games were held. In late summer 2002 a series of earthquakes struck the Elia area measuring 5.4-5.6 on the Richter scale.

Lakonia. *Lakonia* or *Laconia* is a stark land that occupies the south-eastern Peloponnese and includes two of its peninsulas, the western one is known as the Mani (see below). The western part of Lakonia includes the inland towns of *Vresthena, Leonido, Mystras* and the prefecture's capital, *Sparti.* The Lakonian Mani includes the coastal towns of *Kelafa, Areopoli* (nearly coastal) and *Kotronas*, while *Ageranos, Mavrovouni* and *Gythio* are on the *Lakonian Gulf.* The easternmost finger of the Peloponnese has the Lakonic Gulf on the West and the *Mirtoo Sea* on the eastern side. There are villages scattered along the coasts and perched on hilltops inland. The area is characterised by beautiful long beaches, some of them still deserted. There is a small island, *Elafonisos* or *Elafonissi,* reached from *Neapoli* near the south western end of the peninsula.

Lakonia is rich in archaeological sites, spectacular scenery, caves, historic buildings and has a wonderful coast. Coastal places of note include Gythio which has a town square and port, beautiful beaches at *Elia* and *Plitra* and the spectacular walled town of *Monevasia* with its Byzantine and Venetian buildings (including 40 churches) on the Mirtoo Sea.

PROPERTY HOTSPOT – THE MANI

Mani Peninsular. This region, usually just known as the *Mani* or *Maina,* is the most southerly, and middle peninsular of the Peloponnese. The Mani is mostly in the prefecture of Lakonia but incorporates part of Messinia in the northwest and yet is perceived, because of its isolated aspect, and the legendary courage and hardness of the Maniots, as having its own identity regardless of bureaucratic boundaries. It is also a property hotspot: Greek government statistics show there are more foreigners living in the prefectures of Messinia and Lakonia than anywhere else in Greece. This makes for better and improving services in this region in contrast with some other regions, and as a result, foreigners find life easier there.

The Mani has proved so inspirational to travellers and writers that now foreign housebuyers are increasingly flocking to the magic of the place. It is not difficult to see why the Mani has acquired such a following. It is a region of barren mountains comprised of the southern end of the *Taiyetos* Mountains, which reach down to *Cape Matapan*, which is the southernmost tip of the peninsular. The mountain area below Areopolis is called by the local name of *Kakouvounia*. The Maniots are often compared to the Cretans due to similarities in national dress (loose breeches, clamped with wide leather belts, embellished waistcoats and head-binding bandannas; and the whole effect set off with a luxuriant moustache). Their culture lives on through a unique folk poetry expressed in songs and dances. There is also a form of Greek lament known as *moirologia*, which is particularly expressed by Maniot women in poetry sung at the graveside, and which carries strong echoes of antiquity. The Greek Orthodox church does not approve, and has tried to discourage this practice.

Despite the unpromising, and harsh nature of the terrain, olive trees abound, and any fertile soil on the steeply terraced mountainsides is laboriously coaxed into agricultural productivity. The Mani is dotted with fascinating buildings including Byzantine churches, its trademark tower houses (a legacy of the Turkish occupation). Castles, villages and churches are perched precipitously amongst the peaks and on the coast. The tower houses (there are an estimated 800 of them), make characterful homes. If you want to find out what they are like to live in, you can stay in one as a tourist as many of them are guest houses run by the Greek tourist organisation. Whatever kind of property you are looking for, it is also a good idea to rent over the winter when you can see how quiet some places are without the tourists. Also to experience the weather which although usually pleasant in winter can bring torrential rain and gales.

The coast has many excellent sandy beaches and ancient and historic sites and fishing villages. This region attracts those drawn to its history and atmospheric landscapes and hardy people, rather than to the pulsating tourist resorts.

Messinia. The Messinian prefecture occupies the south-western part of the Peloponnese including the most western peninsula and the north-western area of the Mani. Coastally, it lies on the Ionian Sea (with several picturesque islets including *Schiza* and *Sapientza*, just offshore), and the Messinian Gulf on which *Kalamata,* the capital town is situated. The area is known for its agriculture, relatively cool summers and mild winters. It has abundant water supplied by many springs, and furthermore, it is a landscape layered deep with antiquity.

Kalamata is a modern commercial and manufacturing town and port of 45,000 inhabitants. In 1986 it suffered a severe earthquake which resulted in heavy casualities and structural damage in the town and the surrounding area, which has undergone major reconstruction since. Other important coastal settlements of the area include the historic town and port of *Pylos,* the villages of *Kyparissia, Koroni, Finikoudas* and *Petalidi* which are all popular with tourists. Important archaeological sites of the area include the Mycenean King Nestor's Palace, north of Pilos. Between Kalamata and Kyparissia on the western (Ionian) coast is the agricultural and fertile Lower *Plain of Messini* where crops including citrus fruits and bananas make a significant contribution to the region's economy along with the Kalamata olives, which have an international reputation. *Gargalianoi* also on the western side of Messinia is sited high on a lush hillside with olive groves stretching out as far as the sea.

Other notable seaside towns include *Methoni, Kallithea* and *Agios.*

Useful Contacts for the Peloponnese:

Homes in Greece: ☎+30 2 7210 58868; e-mail info@homesingreece.com; www.homesingreece.com. Based in Mani. A collaborative relationship of several construction professionals, including architect, builders, structural engineers and tradespeople. All partners are certified professionals in Greece. Provides project management services and also offers land for sale and building/renovating services.

Internet Forum: A very useful website and users' forum is http://groups.msn.com/ lefktromanigreece which is based in the north-western area of the Mani (village of Lefktro), but it has lots of info relevant to the Mani generally and is good for background information. You can also look in the 'property for sale' section, become a member, leave messages, find out who to contact for advice on renovation etc. The site is run for the expat foreigners living in, or moving to, this district.

KJM Properties: tel/fax 01624-677958; e-mail kjmmprops@hotmail.com. Has apartments, villas and traditional houses for retirement or holiday homes.

OffToGreece: Off To Greece (www.offtogreece.co.uk) is a marketing and consultancy business that helps visitors to Paralio Astros, (situated about half way down the eastern coast) to locate property to buy or to rent in that area.

Estate Agents for the Peloponnese:

Clare Developments International: Pen Lea, Arkell Avenue, Carterton, Oxfordshire OX18 3BS; ☎01993-842597. Has specialised in the Mani for over a decade. Land and houses.

George Maragos Real Estate; junction of V.Sofias and Danau Road, Central Square, Argos, Argolida; ☎+30 27510/67778; fax +30 27510 23180; www.greekhouses.gr/englsite.htm. Range of plots, villas, houses etc. Argos, Nafplion and around Argolida.

Greek-estate Ltd: 75 Galinou Street, 18758 Attica, Greece; ☎+30 210 4323198; info@greek-estate.net; www.greek-estate.net.

Hellenic Realty: Route de la Vigne au Chat, 01220 Sauverny, France; ☎+33 (0) 450 42 71 98; +33 (0) 450 42 76 24; info@hellenic-realty.com; www.hellenic-realty.com. Hellenic Realty is licensed by the Athens Realtors' Association and handles properties on some of the Greek islands as well as the Peloponnese. All types of property from ruins to ready-to-move-ins, and plots of land. Can help with finding architects and builders and legal and notary services.

John Goodwin International Property Consultant: Homestead Cottage, Main Road, East Boldre, Near Brockenhurst, Hampshire S042 7WT; ☎01590-626266; fax 01590 626413; e-mail info@livinginthesun.com; www.livinginthesun.com/src./greece.

Konstantinos Kopanitsanos Estate Agent: Commercial Center, Sq. Ag. Georghiou 3, Patra 26221, Achaea; ☎2610 225500; fax 2610 623923; conkopas@otenet.gr.

Kthma.Net Real Estate in Greece: 1 Mavromichali str., 24100 Kalamata, Greece; fax +30 2721096197; e-mail info@realestate-greece.com. Deals with property in the Peloponnese including the Mani. Aso other regions and islands.

Mani Props: 12, Dimosthenous St., Kalamata 21400, Greece; ☎+3 27210-22031; fax +3 27210 89543; e-mail mani1@otenet.gr; www.maniprops.com. Headed by Greek Civil Engineer Andreas Moshandreou who has lived in the region for nearly 20 years. His agency covers the Mani peninsular, Kalamata and the region as far as Koroni on the western peninsular (Messinia). The agency has a very wide choice of properties of all types and has a sound understanding of restoration. Contacts with other areas of Greece may be possible.

O'Connor Real Estate: Aristomenous and Fratzi 18, 24100 Kalamata, Greece; tel/fax +30 27210 96614. Provides a complete service from finding a property to introducing you to English-speaking lawyers, restoration experts, and guiding you through the house-buying process.

Real Estate Greece: info@realeste-greece.com; www.realestate-greece.com. Wide range of properties old and new. Also provides lawyer for property buying (lawyer@realestate-greece.com); ☎+30 2721096197; fax +30 1734 6876 649 and can arrange full renovation and restoration of old and new properties.

Susan Shimmin: e-mail Susanshimmin@yahoo.com. Susan Shimmin has been involved in selling property in Greece for over a decade. She lives in the Mani most of the time.

Trifiliaki: Meliou 5, Gr. 24500 Kyparissia, Greece; ☎+30 27610 22730; fax +30 27610 23780; www.trifiliaki.gr/english. Offers a range of possibilities around Kyparissia, south western Peloponnese. Choose from: plots, have a house built, or buy a package which includes plot, plan and construction. Properties can be supplied ready to move into.

Vitoras Agency: www.estategr.com; ☎297530/99927; fax 27530/42110. Land, farms, sale and rental of houses, apartments etc. Epidauros, Argolida.

Typical Properties/Land for Sale in the Peloponnese

Location	Type	Description	Price
Koroni area, 40km from Kalamata, 1km from village. 200m from sea.	(Unfinished) new, 2-storey house 100 sq.m.	4000 sq. m. plot with foundation for a second house. Views of Messinian Gulf.	€210,000 (finished price)
In the area of Mistras, 5km from Sparti and (approx.) 45km from coast). Set in 25,000 sq. m. of olive and fig trees and vinery.	Traditional stone house.	2-storeys. 90 sq. m. on each level. Renovated to original style. 2-bedrooms. Connected to electricity and water supply. 1km from Byzantine castle.	€140,000
Petaldi, south west peninsula (Messinia district)	Seaside plot with olive grove	2,500 sq. m. Short stroll to village (Petaldi). 40 olive trees with pebble beach boundary. Spectacular views	€103,000
Kyparissia, (coast of south western Peloponnese)	Off plan (plot and construction)	Plot 1,818 sq. m. House 85,58 sq.m. Veranda 41.77 sq. m. Set in olive grove	€148,500 basic; up to €174,000 with extras such as air conditioning
Ano Verga, near Kalamata	Abandoned stone house	2-storey house of 70 sq.m. with a courtyard of 40 sq.m. Small, but with beautiful views of the sea from a very pretty village	€25,000 (restoration cost estimated additional €44,000)
Mani peninsula village next to coast	18th century Mani tower house	125 sq. m on a 1000 sq. m. piece of land. 4-storeys. Walls in perfect condition. Interior needs reconstruction. Comes with additional land of 680 sq. m. and traditional building (ruin) of 60 sq. m.	€210,000

THE ISLANDS

The islands of Greece have long exerted a pull over the imagination of increasing numbers of people; travellers, then tourists, and now foreign homeowners. Although there are estimated to be around 3,000 Greek islands, a tiny minority of these are inhabited or habitable. Geographically, the islands are categorised by several large groups: North East Aegean, Cyclades, Dodecanese, Ionian etc. The names and rough positions of these groups are usually easier to remember than the names and positions of the individual islands within them. The two largest islands are obvious on a map: Crete, which is also the most southerly, and Evia (*Euboea*) which is strikingly similar in shape to Crete, and is one of the nearest to the Greek mainland. Other well known larger islands include *Rhodos* (Rhodes), Lesbos, Corfu and Kefalonia (*Cephalonia*) which are also the islands that many people have heard of.

When looking for island property there are important considerations such as ease of access and local amenities and communications. These days with the internet and e-mail, staying in touch has made living on an island a less isolating experience, however, even the joy of expat chat rooms, e-news and video conferencing from home via your PC, are no substitute for real human interaction and there might be little of that unless you speak some Greek and are prepared to integrate. For this reason, many holiday home owners and foreign residents tend to head for islands where there is already a community of expats. These tend to be also the places where Greek entrepreneurs have moved in to create a supply line of estate agents, plots, house construction companies, builders, lawyers and all the other services necesssary to support the foreign housebuyer achieve their dreams. This is far from widespread in the Greek islands and Crete, partly because of its size, has the edge for services. However, you shouldn't let this put you off exploring the possibilities of other, much smaller islands.

Some of the islands where expats are beginning to appear in numbers have enterprisingly begun offering classes in the Greek language.

Estate Agents

There are estate agents on individual islands, though there is obviously more choice on the islands with established colonies of expats such as Corfu, Crete etc. However, as the building boom takes off in Greece, there are likely to be English-speaking agents found increasingly on the smaller islands as well.

Agents that deal with specific areas are listed in their appropriate section below. Some websites (e.g. www.greecegreekislands.com and www.greekislandsRealEstate. com) deal with property on all the Greek islands and might be a good place to start if you haven't decided which island you want to buy property on, or if there are no details of agents for a particular island.

CRETE

Area: 260km by 50km; **Population:** 550,000 (approx); **Main Cities:** Chania, Heraklion; **Airports:** Chania and Heraklion (many charter flights from the UK to both airports from about £135). Heraklion is also the main ferry port.

Crete is the largest Greek island, and one of the world's top tourist destinations, which is at its heaving worst during the summer season. For foreign housebuyers, winter can be the best time to house hunt; the climate is mild and the prices go down a little, as Debbie Taylor, author of a *Sunday Times* column, *Heat and Dust,* which deals with her purchase and renovation of a Cretan ruin puts it 'Winter's the perfect time for househunting in Crete. Although cheap-as-chips charters won't start again until April, there are lots of scheduled flights and car rentals are at rock bottom.'

Away from the coast Crete is verdant in the north west and wild and craggy in the south. Geographically, it is long and thin and lies horizontally on the 35th parallel with its double-horned head pointing towards the Peloponnese and its tail towards Rhodes. It falls naturally into four areas which are the prefectures: *Chania* (the west), *Rethymon, Heraklion* (the middle) and *Lassithi* (east) which are divided by the spectacular mountain ranges. The 18km Gorge of Samaria in the *Lefka Ori* range in the west, is the longest European gorge, for which Crete is famous; just as it is for the remains of the Minoan city of Knossos; Greece's second most visited tourist attraction after the acropolis of Athens.

Before becoming part of an independent Greece, Crete was occupied by other empires from the Venetian in 1210 (for over 450 years), to the Ottoman. After the Venetians had been ousted, the Turks made a move during 1645, winning the island by a combination of betrayal which took the Cretans by surprise, and the siege of Heraklion that endured 21 years until its final capitulation in 1669. Greece finally obtained revenge on the Turks over two hundred years later in 1898. They were aided by the great powers of the time including Britain, and earned a foreign ruling prince until they managed to oust him in favour of an indigenous Cretan governor in 1909. Crete joined independent Greece four years later.

Cretans have an enviable longevity that is not only a matter of accumulated years but also of good health and sprightliness well into their nineties. This phenomenon is proven to be attributable to their diet of which olive oil is the main source of fat, rather than meat or milk, and to an extremely varied selection of beans and pulses, fruits and vegetables, herbs, cheeses and honey. Produce which comes from the island can be bought from local shops, and on market day stalls groan under the weight of their various cornucopias.

Until recently the eastern part of Crete has been thought of as too touristy, especially the coast. However, a little inland there are unspoilt villages from where you can still see the sea from your bedroom, and where properties can still be bought for low prices. Undoubtedly the roads inland can be pretty rough but choose carefully just a little inland from the coast and where there is a decent road to your village. South West Crete is even more wild and there the roads are slow and winding.

There are well-established communities of expats on Crete and the property buying procedures are well oiled. If you opt for renovating a ruin you might be advised to read the already mentioned weekly *Sunday Times* articles entitled *Heat and Dust* written by Debbie Taylor, editor of a women writers' magazine. She gives an incidental account of the trials, tribulations and rewards in her efforts to renovate a 'four-room farmhouse perched on a hillside in Crete' that she bought for £30,000. Her narrative will almost certainly give you a good notion of what to expect when you fall in love with and buy a 'cheap-as-chips' ruin.

Note that buyers who are not from the European Union countries have certain restrictions imposed on them in the vicinity of border areas of which Crete is one. Authorisation may be granted following an obligatory application to the Council of the local prefecture.

Useful Contacts

Greek Estate Ltd: Crete office: 38 L. Soudas Str., 73100 Chania, Crete, Greece; tel:

The Greek Islands

| 0 | 50 | 100 miles |
| 0 | 50 | 100 | 150 | 200 km |

BULGARIA

Black Sea

Edirne

TURKEY

GREECE

Thessaloniki

Amphipolis   Kavala

Alexandroupolis

Sea of Marmara

Thassos

Samothrace

Thracian Sea

Lemnos

Thermatic Gulf

Volos

Sporades Islands

Skiathos

Alonissos

Skopelos

Aegean Sea

Skiros

Lesvos

TURKEY

Eubaea

Chios

Athens

Andros

Samos

Tzia

Ikaria

Tenos

Mykonos

Kithnos

Syros

Cyclades Islands

Leros

Gulf of Argolis

Serifos

Náxos

Kalimnos

Kalamata

Sifnos

Paros

Kos

Melos

Ios

Amorgos

Astipalaia

Kythira

Santorini

Dodecanese Islands

Rhodes

Sea of Crete

Karpathos

Kassos

Chania   Heraklion

CRETE

✈ Airport

+30 28210 88102; fax +30 28210 94091; e-mail info@greek-estate.net; Large realty organisation with 20 offices in Greece is expanding its market share in Crete.

Buy the Best: A comprehensive net shopping guide with an extensive directory of Cretan property agents and links to their sites at www.best-packageholidays.co.uk/Crete-Property.html. Also flights to Crete etc.

Estate Agents for Crete

Alpha Estate Realty: 84 Kountouriotou str. 74100 Rethymo, Crete, Greece; ☎+30 28310 51341; fax +30 28310 20416; info@alphaestate.gr.

Amalia Atsalaka: ☎+30 6977640576; +30 2825032568; fax +30 28250 32568. Traditional Cretan houses – constructions. Specialises in villa developments and houses built to clients' wishes. Prices from €88,000.

Cretan Traditional Homes: UK ☎01763-849309; fax 01763-849854; Chania Crete head office: ☎+30 28210 234622; fax +30 28210 23463; www.cretantraditionalhomes.com. Specialises in western Crete has range of homes from €50,000.

Cretan Traditional Houses: 67, Venizelou Street, Sitia, Crete; ☎+ 30 28430 24215; e-mail fragaki@sit.forthnet.gr; www.cretehome.com. Contact Vassilia Fragaki. Covers eastern Crete. All types of old country properties and new stone-built, apartments etc. Run by a Greek from the area who can find village properties a few kilometres from the sea for the price of a car.

Crete Island Homes: Ayios Ionnis, Makri Gialos, Sitia 72055, Crete; ☎+30 28430 51256; e-mail creteislandhomes@yahoo.co.uk. Contacts: Judy Friedland Ramm and Ann Holdsworth. Specialises in south east Crete around Makri Gialos and mountain villages in the region. Step-by-step assistance.

Crete Property Consultants: Oonagh and Cassie Karanjia, Crete Property Consultants, 78 Gascony Avenue, London NW6 4NE; ☎020-7681 6054; fax 020 7328 8209; e-mail oonaghk@btinternet.com; www.creteproperty.co.uk; Covers all types of property all over Crete.

David Watrous: UK ☎020-8232 9780; e-mail dew@vch.co.uk) specialises in Greek properties for investment and can put prospective buyers in touch with sellers and agents on Crete.

Euroland-Crete: 304 Center, 73003 Kalives, Chania, Crete; ☎+30 28250 32557; fax +30 28250 32548; e-mail euroland@grecian.net. All kinds of properties in western Crete.

Europa Real Estate Crete: Daskaogianni Str. (Splanzia), Chania, Crete, Greece; ☎+30 28210 23111; fax +30 28210 23113; e-mail info@europa-crete.com. Variety of properties: villas, apartments (new and resale), plots of land, village houses.

Giakoumakis Real Estate Agency: P.O. Box 100, 70007 Malia, Crete, Greece; ☎+30 2810 285968; e-mail info@giakoumakis.gr. Villas, plots of land, houses, apartments – all types of properties. Office also in Heraklion.

Greek Island Property: ☎UK 0115-932 2751; e-mail info@greek-island-property.com; www.greek-island-property.com. Contact Susan Taylor LL.B(Hons), LL.M, who founded the company after living and working in Crete for many years. She has a network of agents and covers the entire island of Crete.

Kissamos Property Consultants: P O Box 68, Kissamos, Crete, Greece; ☎+30 28220 22055; fax +30 28220 83316; www.kissamos-property.com. Deals with land and property in western Crete. Has a network of contacts amongst the professions required to buy and renovate property in Crete.

Typical Properties for Sale in Crete

Location	Type	Description	Price
Palaikastro, Nr Siteia, eastern Crete	Single-storey old stone building	Complete ruin on edge of a village with sea view	€23,200 plus additional land €13,000. Cost of renovation to make 4 rooms €72,000
Russo Eklisia, eastern Crete	Corner plot of land in traditional village	1.200 sq.m. Old buildings presently on land could be renovated or permit to build 1,050 sq. m. of houses or other buildings. Sea views.	€130,000 (negotiable).
Ayios Stephanos mountain village south eastern Crete	Village house	On village square. 4 rooms plus bathroom and roof terrace. Needs some superficial refurbishing. View to Makri Gialos (coast)	€78,500 (negotiable)
10 minutes from resort of Georgopolis, Chania, western Crete	Village house	2 bedrooms. Guest accommodation. Large garden	€100,000
Village of Slavi, Sitia region inland	Village residence	Well renovated. 5 large rooms built round 3 sides of a generous courtyard	€117,000
Gouves resort area, north coast of mid-Crete in Heraklion region.	Traditional villa	Well maintained with mature gardens. Popular village, 1km from beach.	€125,000

THE CYCLADES

Islands in this Group: *Amorgos, Anafi, Andros, Antiparos, Delos* (uninhabited), *Folegandros, Ios, Kea (Tzia), Kythnos, Milos, Mykonos, Naxos, Paros, Santorini, Serifos, Sifnos, Sikinos, Syros, Tinos.*
The Cyclades are the largest group of Greek islands; there are nineteen of them located in the southern Aegean, north of Crete. They are clustered together in a sort of circle (more of a huddle really) which gave them their name which derives from *'kiklos'* which means circle. As with many Greek islands, they have some stupendous beaches and a rich history both mythical and actual. Information on some of the most important Cycladic islands is given below. A general website for property in the Cyclades is www.cycladeshouses.com.

Mykonos

Airport: Mykonos airport has international flights all year round.
Ferries: Frequent connections to Piraeus (5.35hrs or 3 hrs with highspeed ferry) and other Cyclades islands and Crete.

Despite being a rather barren island, Mykonos is well known as a cosmopolitan, hedonistic, hip haunt where posh yachts vie for space in the harbour with the fishing boats. It has a reputation for being expensive, having crowded beaches, exciting nightlife, and is known for attracting a large gay clientele, which the island's website (www.mykonos-web.com) claims only goes to show what good taste they have, and in any case, so it goes on, 'the majority of visitors are not gay'. So now you know! Mykonos is five hours from Piraeus by standard ferry service and it has an airport. It has good investment potential as it is such a popular island, but is pricey in real estate as in everything else.

Estate Agent for Mykonos

Leonardos Paleologos Real Estate Agency: Fabrika, Mykonos Town, Cyclades Islands, Greece; ☎+30 22890-28204; www.mykonos-realestate.com. Sells villas, houses, complexes etc. on Mykonos island.

Naxos

Airport: International airport. Many flights from UK airports year round.
Ferries: frequent ferry connections to Piraeus (7 hrs or 3hrs highspeed). Summertime service from port of Rafina (Rafina is an hour's drive from Athens); Rafina to Naxos takes 3hrs.

Naxos at 448 square kms is the largest of the Cyclades islands. It has a shoreline of 148 km and some very long and beautiful beaches including, *Agia Anna, Agios Yorgos, Mikri Vigla, Kastraki* and *Plaka.* The port of Piraeus is 103 nautical miles from Chora, the main town. There are regular ferries and year round flights. To the west is Paros, while Mykonos and Delos are to the north. Its abundant water supply make Naxos a very green and productive island for citrus fruits etc. The interior is mountainous, with stunning valleys and is full of classical mythological connections: Theseus and Ariadne, Dionysus, even Zeus are all linked to its landscapes and there is even a half-finished statue of Apollo which has been lying in the quarry where it was abandoned over two and half thousand years ago. Naxos is a bit of a find and once you have found it, you may want to invest in its properties.

The island has its own website, www.naxos-greece.net/ where you can link to the island webcam and get a closer peek.

Estate Agents for Naxos

Konstantinos Kapiris: Naxos Town Seafront, Naxos Island, Cyclades, Greece; ☎+30 22850 22908; fax +30 22850 23276; www.realestatenaxos.gr. Architect with his own planning and construction company. Houses and villas.
Naxos Greece Real Estate: Aghios Arsenios, 84300 Naxos Island, Cyclades Islands, Greece; ☎+30 22850 25295; fax +30 22850 25294; www.united-hellas.com/real-estate/land-naxos/index.html. Sells real estate and land on Naxos.
Stefanos Manilaras: ☎+30 (2)2850 26305; ☎+30 (2)2850 26012; ☎+30 (6)972 248651; e-mail nobody@nax.forthnet.gr. Private properties for sale on Naxos.
Takis Kontopoulos: Chora Naxos, Naxos 84300, Greece; tel/fax +30 (2) 2850 23157;

info@naxos-houses.com; www.naxos-houses.com/.

Paros

Airport: International and domestic. Flights from many UK airports. Flight from Athens takes approximately 35 minutes.

Ferries: frequent ferrries from Piraeus (about 5hrs) and other islands including Santorini and Mykonos.

Paros has marketed itself successfully as a modern tourist resort though Parikia, the popular main port and town (awash with foreigners and internet cafés) has an almost concealed ancient history. Also highly popular is the picturesque fishing village Naoussa, which is pulsating with visitors in summer. Parikia is a busy sea traffic port with criss-crossing connections to the other islands and is 6 hours by ferry from Piraeus. The island website is www.ParosWeb.com, which has the inevitable webcam and links for hunters of real estate who might find a good investment/holiday property there or at least an idea of what is on offer.

At the time of print there were still properties for sale at various stages of construction on a development 3km east of Parikia. For information visit www.leosvillage.com or contact Michael Leos, engineer, economist and developer living in the complex (☎ +30 22840-23421; e-mail info@leosvillage.com).

Estate Agents for Paros

Aegean Style.Com: ☎ 6937821957; fax 2284028754; e-mail real-ad@aegeanstyle.com; www.aegeanstyle.com/real-estate-greece/. Land, newly constructed properties, resale properties.

Kastro Real Estate Agency: 84400 Parikia, Paros; ☎ +30 22840 24964, 92035; e-mail kastro@realestate-greek-islands.com; www.realestate-greek-islands.com. Located near the sea front in Parikia. Run by Kristel Henauer, a Greek and English-speaking German/Swiss national. Who claims she can find you almost any kind of property you want anywhere on the island.

Mikes Leontis: Main Square, Parikia; ☎ +30 22840 21322 24573. General real estate, land, and houses on the island.

Santorini

Airport: has direct international charter flights in summer. In winter access is via connecting flight from Athens. Flight time 40 minutes.

Ferries: ferries from Piraeus take about 9 hours. Fast ferries from Rafina take 4-5 hours.

Santorini, also called *Thira,* is one of those Greek islands that exerts a particular pull on the imagination, and has spectacular geological phenomena and sunsets, but perhaps you wouldn't want to live there. For a start, its tourist-mobbed capital *Fira* is located at 900 feet, which translates into over 500 steps, a funicular or donkey ride, to see it. Santorini also has a geological claim to fame from a volcanic explosion, which occurred three and half thousand years ago, and produced damage, which some scholars believe included the destruction of the Minoan civilisation on Crete, 70 nautical miles south. There is some pricey real estate available on the island. Try a general site like www.hellenic-realty.com for some examples.

Typical Properties for Sale in the Cyclades

Location	Type	Description	Price
Santorini Island Thira	Beach Villa	Single-storey. Built 1985. 2 bedrooms, lounge, modern kitchen and sunken bathroom	€120,000
Paros Island Near Marpissa	Traditional style stone house built 2002	130 sq. m in landscaped grounds of 2,000 sq. me. Two bedrooms, two bathrooms large covered verandas and superb views across to Naxos. 700m to sea. All mod cons.	€320,000
Naxos Island Amitis	Plot with house under construction	120 sq.m house on plot of 2000 sq.m. 3 other houses on separate adjacent plots	€144,000 in present state
Kythnos Island	Restored village house	100 sq.m. 2-storeys, 2 bedrooms, 2 bathrooms. Upper floor terrace with superb sea view	€305,000 and possibility to buy 1000 sq.m. of land behind house separately.
Kea/Tzia Island	Small luxury estate of 7 stone houses	80 sq.m. per 2-storey house. Two bedrooms, 2 bathrooms. Communal swimming pool, gardens and private parking.	from €202,000 to €227,000
Kythnos Island Southern part of island	Modern house built 1995	70 sq m. Two-storeys. Set in grounds of 660 sq.m with spectacular sea view.	€117,000

Estate Agents for Other Cyclades Islands

Antiparos

Yannsis Maounis: ☎+30 22840 61605. Real estate broker and building and contracting services for this tiny island west of Drios.

Drios/Dryos

Miranda Tritsbida: ☎+30 (22840) 42560. Offers a variety of houses, apartments and land, both in the town and within villages around this island, which is just west of Paros.

THE DODECANESE

The Dodecanese is so named because there are twelve (the Greek for twelve is *dodeka*) main islands in this grouping of over 160 islands and islets. The majority of the Dodecanese form a line in the south Aegean Sea, off the south-western coast of Turkey. Twenty-six of the Dodecanese Islands are inhabited. The group includes *Astypalaia,*

Halki, Kalymnos, Karpathos, Kassos, Kastellorizo, Kos, Leros, Nissyros, Patmos, Rhodes, Symi and *Tilos*. The ones popular with foreign property buyers are detailed below.

Kalymnos

Nearest airport: is on Kos island, which has regular international charters and connecting flights from Athens. Then ferry from Kos to Kalymnos (45 minutes).
Ferries from Piraeus: 6-10 per week (13hrs).
Kalymnos has a population of about 14,500 tucked into its 110 square kms and prides itself on being composed of traditional communities with strong local customs. Sponge diving has been associated with the island since ancient times. Kalymnos is actually referred to as the sponge fishermens' island, and there is even a museum dedicated to sponges in the capital and port of *Pothia*.

The island has a number of language schools and links with the USA and Australia are quite developed. The island has several tourist resorts including *Myrties* pictured on the island's website (www.kalymnos-isl.gr). There is usually a small but varied selection of properties for sale and the island is probably a good bet for property as an investment. A very useful website for property on Kalymnos is (www.hellenic-realty.com/kal042.htm).

Leros

Airport: small airport takes domestic traffic. Connecting flights from Athens take 1hr. 45 mins.
Ferry: from Piraeus via Patmos (11hrs).
Leros is small, 54 square km, and 15km long and a minimum width of about 1.5 km and with a coastline of 46km. Despite its diminutive size it is quite active from the real estate point of view. Traditional island houses can be bought quiet cheaply. If you are seriously interested contact Leros Properties by e-mail (lerosproperties@yahoo.gr).

The island website is www.lerosisland.com.

Rhodes

Airports: international airport with direct flights from many countries mostly in summer but all year round. Also connecting flights from Athens which take 55 minutes.
Ferries: frequent ferrry services connect with Piraeus (13-18 hrs), also Crete and Thessaloniki, Cyprus and Turkey.
Rhodes (known as *Rhodos* or *Rodos* in Greek), is the largest island of the Dodecanese (area of 1,400 sq. km), and has been a popular tourist destination since the 1970s with all that that implies in developed tourist infrastructure. The capital is also called Rhodes and is at the northern tip of the island. It is a magnificent walled city designated by UNESCO a World Heritage Site, and has some of the most impressive fortifications you will ever see. The medieval feel is continue by its many old buildings and cobbled streets, and historic connections with Turks, Crusaders, Knights of St. John and others. The city's history goes back even further to ancient times when the acropolis of classical Rhodes, now a mile from the city, was built. Tourism has left its inevitable mark on Rhodes; witness the burgeoning resorts such as *Faliraki, Ixia, Ialissos* and the once delightful town of *Lindos* with its higgledy-piggeldy whitewashed buildings stacked up along the winding cobbled streets, which now heave with foreigners during summertime. Rhodes also has a clutch of four and five star hotels.

Those contemplating buying a property on the island should note that apartments for sale are fairly rare but there are old buildings and one or two developments specifically marketed to foreigners. While Rhodes remains popular and building restrictions remain stringent making properties not easy to find, property purchased there is likely to be a good investment. Both Aegean Homes and Savvaidis & Associates (see below) offer a rental service for properties owned on Rhodes.

Contact for Restoring Old Houses
Architektonikes Meletes: Annis Marias 83, Rhodes 85100, Greece; ☎+30 241 35100; fax +30 241 73325; e-mail info@am.rho.forthnet.dr. Architectural studio experienced in construction and restoration of old buildings. Also real estate and legal consulting and assistance. Can help with both Rhodes and neighbouring islands.

Estate Agents/Developers for Rhodes
Aegean Homes: UK representative Sunwood Travel Services Ltd., Havelock House, High Street, Bean, Kent DA2 8AS; ☎01474-707080; fax 01474-707090; sales@aegeanhomes.com. Aegean homes specialise in small developments on the island of Rhodes. Offers a complete construction package including village or countryside location, custom designs, furnishings, financing, professional property management and maintenance and renting out the property if required through sister company, Rhodes Select.
Cybarco: Cybarco House, Dollis Mews, Dollis Park, London N3 1HH; ☎020-8371 9700; fax 020-8371 3999; e-mail info@uk.cybarco.com; www.cybarco.gr. International developer offers seasonal residences and properties for new starts on Rhodes.
Kefaleo Real Estate and Consulting: Seferi 12, 85100 Rhodes, Greece; ☎+30 22410 600601; fax +30 22410 60062. Manager Antonis Tsourounakis.
Miko Invest: Alexandrou Diakou 9, Rhodes 85100 Greece; ☎+30 22410 70840; fax +30 22410 70841; e-mail info@mikoinvest.gr. Villa developer.
Savvaidis & Associates Real Estate Agency: Ethel Dodekanision 29, Rhodes 85100; ☎+30 22410 26281; fax +30 22410 34663; e-mail info@rre.gr. Member of the Hellenic Association of Realtors. All kinds of properties old and new, developments on Rhodos.

Symi
Nearest airports: Rhodes (see above) and then a ferry from Rhodes 2hrs. Alternative airport is Kos.
Although Symi is a small, some might say tiny (58 square km), island with a mountainous interior and a population of about 2,500, it has some good beaches and a gem of a port with attractive neo-classical architecture surrounding the harbour. The town rises steeply to the ruins of a castle that dates from Crusader times. There is a regular ferry service from Rhodes.

As the island is tiny, you would expect not to find a lot of choice of real estate but contrarily there seems to be quite a variety on offer, although plots larger than 200 sq.m, are very hard to find. If you are interested enough to pursue it, you may find something quite unique and old that you can rent out once it is renovated. According to estate agents on the island, most commonly for sale are bare land or completely ruined buildings. Remember that returning to Symi year after year, might get tedious as it is so small and mountainous.

A useful website that might give you some idea of the variety on offer is www.symivisitor.com/real – estate.htm

Estate Agents for Symi

Doma Estate Agents: 85600 Symi Port, (over the old coffee shop), Gialos, Greece; ☎+30 0241 72619; fax +30 0241 72458; e-mail maltos@otenet.gr. Fully licensed estate agent.

Lefteris Hatzipetrou: Symi Gialos, Symi 85600; ☎+30 (0) 241 71657; fax +30 (0) 241 71234; e-mail leftarc@otenet.gr; www.symi-island.gr. Estate Agent, Architect, Surveyor and Valuer.

Nikolaos Maltos: Symi Gialos, Symi 85600; ☎+30 (0) 241 72619; e-mail maltos@otenet.gr; www.doma.gr. Mechanical & Electrical Engineer and Property Consultant.

Typical Properties for Sale in the Dodecanese

Location	Type	Description	Price
Leros Island	Traditional island house	2-bedrooms, kitchen, bathroom roof terrace. Sea front, right on beach. Ideal for small family	€70,000
Symi Island	Ruined old house	Lot surface 53 sq.m. Potential living space on two floors 70sq.m.	€44,000
Rhodes Island Koskinou Village, 7 km from Rhodes town.	Traditional village house	House built 1913. In good condition, maintained by woman from village. Features include cosy courtyard with pomegranate tree.	€88,000
Kalymnos Island Pothia village	Traditional stone house	Fully renovated in 1998. Greek architect. 3-levels total surface 127 sq. m. on a plot of 107 sq. m. 2 bedrooms. 2 bathrooms and lovely terrace and small garden. Close to harbour.	€186,000
Kos Island 11km inland	Brand new apartments	70 sq. m. 3 bedrooms, big terrace. Sea and country views.	€97,000
Rhodes Island Edge of Kalathos Village	Off-plan new stylish development of five town houses	2 bedrooms, 2 bathrooms, patios, balconies and communal large swimming pool. Views over the Aegean Sea.	from €130,000

THE IONIAN ISLANDS

The Ionian islands lie off the west coast of Greece, Epirus and West Greece including the Peloponnese. They are sometimes called the *Heptanesos* or *Eptanissa* (Seven

Islands). The Ionian islands include Corfu (*Kerkyra*), Ithaca (*Ithaki*), Kefalonia (*Kefallonia, Cephalonia*), Kalamos, Lefkas (*Lefkada*), Paxos *(Paxi)* and Zakynthos (*Zante*). Kythera (*Kithera, Cerigo*) is sometimes included in the Ionian group even though it is miles from the others 14 nautical miles off the most south eastern tip of the Peloponnese.

A useful website for the Ionian group is www.ionian-islands.com and the agent David Watrous (020-8232 9780) has connections for buying property on Paxos, Kefalonia and Ithaca.

The islands most interesting from a property purchase point of view are detailed below.

Corfu

Airport: international airport with direct flights from many cities in Europe and several charter flights a day in summer. Relatively few flights in winter. There are also connecting flights from Athens (1hr).

Ferries: ferries from Igoumunitsa on the west coast take about an hour. You can get to Igoumounitsa by bus from Thessaloniki or Athens (500kms) which both take 7-8 hours. Corfu also has many ferry connections to places in Italy including Ancona and Bari.

Corfu (Kerkyras) is the second largest of the Ionian islands at 647 square metres. It has a particular English association as it was a British protectorate for 50 years from 1814. Before that it was French and for 300 years before that, Venetian. The population of the island is around 112,000, but this usually quadruples over the summer holiday season. There are an estimated 11,000 foreign residents from Europe, the majority of them from Britain.

Like Rhodes, Corfu has been on the package holiday map since the 1970s and the fact that tourism is the biggest earner for the island is widely in evidence. Stray into *Benitses, Agios Gordios, Kavos* or one of the other mass resorts and there will be chips with everything and lager louts abounding in the summer season and that's just the British. Eastern Europeans love to flock to this island too. However, Kerkyras as the locals call it, is over 30 miles long and half as wide (much wider at the top) so there is room to escape from the fomenting tourist havens and find yourself a quiet part of the island.

It is when you have found a quiet spot, that you will probably start thinking you could live there. If so, you will be delighted to discover that there is a variety of properties for sale dotted about the island and practised local professionals from agents to builders, ready to help you achieve your aim. It is also almost that your property or land will come with olive trees; there are millions of them on the island thanks to a now defunct island government custom of paying every householder for every olive tree planted. Most foreign residents tend to live away from the coast for obvious reasons, but the sea is never far away.

Corfu town, the island's capital is a bustling commercial base with all the useful facilities of a large town.

Estate Agents for Corfu

Corfu Niakas Estate: 1st Floor, G Theotoki (Sanrocco) Sq. 18, Corfu Town; ☎+30 26610 31713 or +30 26610 26348; e-mail info@corfuniakasestate.gr; www.corfu niakasestate.gr. The longest established estate agency in Corfu. Can find any kind of property or plot of land. Full range of support services for buyers provided by associated lawyers etc.

Corfu Property Agency: Kapodistriou 19, Corfu Town, Corfu 49100 Greece; ☎+30 26610 28141; fax +30 26610 46663; e-mail office@cparcorfu. In business since 1988.

Pelais Travel: Ipsos, Corfu, Greece; ☎+30 26610 97564; fax +30 2661093186; e-mail pelais@otenet.gr or info@pelaistravel.com. Properties and building plots on Corfu plus help with purchasing procedure, finding lawyer, finding best mortgage deal etc.

Kefalonia

Airport: international airport with charter flights direct to Kefalonia, or fly to Athens and take connecting flight to Kefalonia.

Ferries: drive from Athens to Patra and get ferry from Patra to Kefalonia. There are also buses from Athens to Patra.

Kelfalonia (capital *Argostoli*), is the largest Ionian island at 935 sq. km but it has about a quarter of the population of Corfu, i.e. under 40,000 inhabitants. It is as well that it is fairly empty as Kefalonia has been hit by what you could call the 'Captain Corelli effect' after the unexpected bestseller *Captain Corelli's Mandolin* and the inevitable Holywood film that followed it, has provoked an inrush of foreigners wanting to buy property on this now famous island and the present is the time to buy, as property developers are springing up to fulfil the new demand.

There are other reasons besides speculative ones, that make Cephalonia a serious consideration: it is a beautiful island with spectacular mountains including the Ainos range, forests of pine and cypress, olive groves, sheer cliffs, hidden coves and a beach (Myrtos) that has been voted one of the top 10 in the world. Rather than the strains of Captain Corelli's mandolin, you are likely to hear the clatter of hooves from Kefalonia's feral horses, descended from those turned loose after the Second World War and which are free to roam the island. Or you might watch *caretta caretta* (loggerhead turtles) or dolphins swim past from your terrace. The island has zero unemployment and claims to be crime free. Sounds too good to be true but, don't wait too long to find out as increased tourism and popularity will undoubtedly bring big changes. Property to buy and rent on the island is expensive according to agent David Watrous and is likely to be a good investment.

Useful island websites include www.kefalonia-island.co.uk and www.inkefalonia.com. The website www.kefaloniaresorts.com has a 'properties for sale section'.

Developers/Estate Agent for Kefalonia

AGDev Kefalonian Developments: Rizopaston & Doriza Street, Argostoli 28100 Kefalonia, Greece; ☎+30 26710-29312; fax +30 26710 29311; e-mail info@inkefalonia.com. Georgio Dimitropoulos. In business since 1988. Over 60 completed projects on Kefalonia. Holiday and retirement homes, luxury apartments, villas etc. Complete 'turn-key' packages from finding your plot to insuring the completed property.

David Watrous: UK ☎020-8232 9780; e-mail dew@vch.co.uk) specialises in Greek properties for investment and can put prospective buyers in touch with sellers and agents on Kefalonia.

Ermolaos Land Developers & Builders: ☎+30 2671 092907 (Andreas Delaportas); fax +30 2671 092907; www.eld-kefalonia.cm. Building 20 vacation homes of 80 sq.m. each at the village of Livadi (created in 1960) which is 5kms from Lixouri and 7 km from the coast.

Kefalonia4us: Argostoli, off Lithostroto St. (2nd Floor); ☎+30 26710 68369/28890; e-mail enquiries@kefalonia4us.com; www.kefalonia4us.com. Large selection of properties and plots of land for sale. Also short/long-term accommodation.

Kefalonia Estate Agents & Property Services: Leoforos Lixouri-Lepada 28200 Lixouri, Kefalonia, Greece; fax +30 26710-93556; e-mail info@keps.gr; www.keps.gr. Estate agents, building contractors and property maintenance services. Properties to buy, renovation properties, plots of land and build your own.

Metaxata Villas: 17 Manor Road, Caddington, Luton, LU1 4EE; ☎01582-877344; fax 01582-877344. Property Developers centred on the village of Metaxata, 5 minutes inland from the sea and 10 minutes from Argostoli airport. Traditional style new construction. Larger properties can be customised.

Papadotos Realty: ☎+30 267406 2013; fax +30 26740 61308; e-mail lalakefalonia@ hotmail.com. Specialises in the marketing and sale of affordable properties. Offers all types of property, traditional, investment, retirement, off plan, prefabricated etc. Contact Mrs. Lala Berdebes.

Unique Villas: ☎UK 01202-849165; e-mail koumoudos@aol.com. Contact Dionisios Koumoudos. Bespoke villas for those with a fairly large budget.

Vallianos Real Estate Agents & Developers: 9 K Vergoti Street, Argostoli, Kefalonia, Greece; +30-26710 23888; e-mail chris@vallianoshomes.com; www.vallianoshomes.com. Contacts: Chris and Tim Vallianos, brothers who worked in the construction business in the USA for 20 years before returning to Kefalonia.

Vinieris Real Estate Agency: 99 Antoni Tritsi Street, 28100 Argostoli, Kefalonia; e-mail vineris@kefalonianproperty.com; www.kefalonianproperty.com).

Lefkada

Nearest Airport: Preveza (a.k.a. Aktion) 20 minutes away on mainland. International airport used by charter flights.

Buses: Lefkada is connected to the mainland via a bridge and there are buses from Athens and Thessaloniki.

Ferries: ferry connections with Ithaki and Kefalonia.

Some islands are born and some are made. Lefkada (Lefkas) falls into the latter category, the Ancients having dug a canal, which sliced this former peninsula off the mainland. Nowadays, a bridge spans the gap between the two and brings you to what seems at first view an unprepossessing island of 325 square km. Persevere and you will discover some terrific, dazzling white, sandy beaches, coves and historic buildings. The interior is also beautiful and quite lush. The local population is a modest 23,000 of whom 7,500 live in the island capital also called Lefkada (or *Hora*). Many of the islanders' forbears emigrated to the cities and foreign lands leaving abandoned villages and a culture in a time warp including native costume (still worn inland in places). The largest village is Karia, which is situated in the northern part of the island.

From a property point of view, Levkas is a distinct possibility for investment and there is usually a variety of property, historic and new, on the market.

Estate Agents for Levkas

Pandev Real Estate Agency: Nidri High Street, Nidri Levkas, Greece; ☎6937 236777; fax 26450 93258; lefkas@pandev.net; www.pandev.net. All kinds of real estate: new houses and apartments ready to move into, old buildings ripe for renovation, plots of land to build on. Can help clients with all the rest of the procedures for property buying in Greece.

Villas and Apartments for Sale: Vafkeri 31100, Lefkada, Ionian Islands, Greece; ☎+30 694 782-2500; fax +30 26450 29108; e-mail info@villa-sale.ioni; www.villa-sale-ionian-greece.com. Constructs and sells all kinds private buildings, flats, maisonettes, luxury apartments and villas. On the pricey side, from €300,000.

Paxos (Paxi)

Ferries: the only way to reach Paxos is by sea (it has no airport). You can fly to Corfu and get a boat from there. There are also ferries from Igoumenitsa on the mainland to Paxos. Further information at www.paxos.web.gr/getting-there.htm.

Paxos is the smallest of the main Ionian islands at around 25 sq. km. The capital *Gaios* is a tiny, picture postcard port (population 800), which offers boat links to the nearby, and even smaller islands including Antipaxos. Most of the historic homes of the town are maintained in good order as are the buildings in the other villages *Magazia, Logos* and *Lakka* as they are nowadays unfortunately beloved of tourists. Paxos is at its worst during the high summer tourist binge when the main villages are all but overwhelmed. Out of season it is a peaceful place full of olive trees (a legacy of the Venetians who occupied the island for 500 years from the 14th century). The torrential rains of winter have long proved beneficial to the agricultural productivity of the island.

There are a few expats on the island already and there is often the occasional old property for sale. A visit to the island to stay in a rented apartment would give you time to look around. The vacation rentals company, Ask Elena (www.askelena.com) sometimes has real estate for sale; you can e-mail realestate@askelena.com for current details. Alternatively, contact David Watrous (UK ☎020-8232 9780; e-mail dew@vch.co.uk) who specialises in Greek properties for investment, and whose family connections with Paxos go back 40 years. He can put prospective buyers in touch with sellers and agents on Paxos.

For a first hand account of what it is like to live there read *The Stars Over Paxos* (Pavilion Books 1995), by John Gill.

Zakynthos

Airport: international airport with many charters from the UK from May to October. Also connecting daily flight from Athens.
Ferry: ferry connection is via Patra (drive/bus from Athens to Patra).

Zakythos (*Zante*) is the third largest of the main Ionians and the eleventh largest Greek island of 406 sq. km. Of the total population of about 45,000; 12,000 live in the capital. The island has been noted for its dense greenery from mountain pines to fertile plains, that impressed the former Venetian colonials enough for them to call it 'the flower of the Orient.' This fertility is partly due to the heavy winter rains that Zante shares with other Ionian isles. The island's main products are olives, wine and citrus fruits. If you want to avoid the touristy nightlife at its peak, stay clear of the famous beach resorts including *Laganas, Alykes, Tsilivi* and *Argasi* and move inland a little.

A couple of useful websites that tell you more about the island: www.zakynthos-greece.biz and www.zanteweb.gr.

Estate Agents for Zakynthos

KJM Properties: tel/fax 01624-677958; e-mail kjmprops@hotmail.com. New build two and three-bedroom villas with sea views in quiet location.
Wido Buller: ☎Germany ☎+49 2821 9578; fax +49 2821 98376; e-mail ueppisn@yahoo.de; widobuller@t-online.de. Sells plots and houses on Zakynthos.

Smile Tours: General Travel Agency Main Road, Lagana, Zakynthos; ☎0695 53520; fax 0695 52772; e-mail smiletours@hotmail.com. Travel agent that also offers property and land for sale.

Kythera

Airport: domestic flights from Athens all year round.
Ferries: from Piraeus it takes 10hrs. In summer there are fast ferries that take just over 4hrs.

Kythera (Cerigo) is a biggish island on its own, 20km off the southern tip of the Peloponnesus (Gulf of Laconia) and is administratively part of the mainland region of Attica (200 km northeast). It is often lumped geographically with the Ionian islands; even though it is nowhere near them, but like Zante it lies off (a different) part of the Peloponnese coast. It is also sometimes included in the Argo-Saronic group which includes Aegina.

Kythira has some lively tourist resorts including *Kapsali* but compared with other islands in its class it is much quieter than most. This might be regarded as an advantage by some property hunters although it is difficult and/or expensive to get to. For wealthy Greeks there are no such problems and there are some very upmarket summer villas dotted about the island. The island is also fairly popular with Italians.

Kythera is 284 sq. m. in area and has a population of about 3,000 having experienced a severe depopulation in the 20th century as islanders emigrated to seek their fortunes in foreign lands including Australia. Many emigrants return with zeal to their former home for summer holidays.

If Kythira sounds appealing, hurry because the tourist infrastructure is growing and property could turn out to be a reasonable investment if bought soon enough.

Finding estate agents that deal with Kythira is not easy. Hellenic Realty (www.hellenic-realty.com) may have a few properties there.

Builder and Developer

Bruel: Langebaekgaard, DK-4772 Langebaek, Denmark; ☎+45 55 39 60 10; fax +45 55 39 60 11; e-mail brueldev@post5.tele.dk. Danish company Bruelholds a number of building sites on Kythira where it constructs homes to high standards.

Typical Properties for Sale in the Ionian Islands

Location	Type	Description	Price
Corfu Island Skripero, inland on route to north of the island	Traditional village house unrenovated	50 sq. m. Two storeys. Garden. Needs extensive restoration but not a ruin	€29,500
Corfu Island Makrades (inland above Paleokastritsa)	Traditional house totally renovated	House of 85 sq. m. on 2 floors, with delightful patio garden of 70 sq.m. 2 bedrooms.	€125,000
Kefalonia Island Markata, 2km from Agia Efimia beach	Ready to move into furnished new home	45 sq.m. 2-bedrooms. Sliding doors to wrap around balcony with sea and mountain views. Plus 500 sq.m. garden with olive and fruit trees.	€80,000

Kefalonia Island Bespoke villa in self selected plot	Off-plan, some customisation possible.	4-bedrooms, 4-bathrooms. Swimming pool. All on 1 acre plot with olive grove	Plot of Land €78,000 Total cost of plot and finished house €383,000
Kythira Island Area of Potamos, 10 minutes drive to seaside	Charmingly restored, 130-year-old stone farmhouse	132 sq. m., on a plot of 183 sq.m. 2 storeys. 3 bedrooms, 3 bathrooms. Large covered balcony and terrace. Ready to move into.	€125,000
Levkas Island Evgiros	Traditional village house	100 sq.m. building on 120 sq.m. Distinctive mountain village house with great views	€110,000
Paxi Island Logos village	Traditional village house	2-storeys. Needs some renovation	€75,000
Zakynthos Island Amoudi-Amboula 15km from Zakynthos town	Beachside small house	75 sq.m. Two bedrooms. Large gardens. Private road. 60 m. from beach.	€130,000
Zakynthos Island Hillside in Meso Gerakario	Plot of land	1230 sq.m. Land includes ruined house and the property can be rebuilt to maximum size of 120 sq. m. Private road. 3km to sea. Magnificent views.	€13,000

THE NORTH EAST AEGEAN ISLANDS

Most of the north eastern Aegean islands are closer to the Turkish than the Greek coast, except for Thassos, which lies close to the coast of East Macedonia. Fewer Brits seem to holiday in the N.Aegean compared with some of the other groups of islands. The North East Aegean includes the islands of *Ag Estratios, Chios, Fouroi* and *Thimena, Ikaria, Lesvos (Lesbos), Limnos (Lemnos), Oinussai, Psara, Samos, Samothraki* and *Thassos*.

A useful website for property buying in the Aegean area is www.aegeanstyle.com/ real estate greece/.

Chios

Airport: domestic. Flight connections to Athens, Thessaloniki and Lesvos.
Ferries: Piraeus 4 hrs. Boat connections also to Lesvos, Kos, Rhodes and Thessaloniki.
As Greek islands go, Chios is a reasonably large one at 840 sq. kms. with a population of 53,500, 30,000 of whom live in the capital and port, also called Chios. The island lies between Lesvos to the north and Samos to the south. It is an interesting, wealthy and beautiful island. Its wealth is derived in large part from gum mastic (made from masticha, a white resin from the mastic tree), used as a base in pharmaceuticals and cosmetics and which grows only on Chios. The island's beauty lies in the stark contrasts between its lush valleys and the bare rocky crags of its mountains.

Chios is probably a good place for both property investment and residential tourism.

Estate Agent for Chios

George Miriagos Real Estate: 2 Agios Iakovos Street, Chios 82, 100 Greece; e-mail muriango@otenet.gr. Sells traditional mansions, villas, houses, apartments and properties with a sea view.

Ikaria

Airport: domestic. Flight connections to Athens.
Ferries: from Piraeus (8hrs. 15mins).
Ikaria, an island with a permanent population of 7,000 is characterised by mountains, especially a central ridge known as the *Atheras,* which peaks at over 3000m. Ikaria is approximately 40 km long and up to 9 km in width. It may be rocky but it is far from being barren thanks to mountain springs which create verdant landscapes, and crops that make the island mostly self-sustaining. If you buy property here it will be because you like the time warp in which Ikaria seems fixed. Properties for sale are mostly of the traditional sort. Development has barely begun and plots of land are surprisingly cheap. Ikaria could be a shrewd investment.
Useful Website: www.island-ikaria.com/local/realestate.asp – this island website has a busy property section with land and property advertised by private sellers.

Lesvos (Mytilini)

Airport: International airport with direct charter flights from many European countries. Also several domestic scheduled flights a day from Athens (50 minutes).
Ferries: from Piraeus (12hrs).There is also a service from Lavrio (south of Athens), which is near the new Athens International Airport and which takes 8.5 hours). Boat connections from Lesbos to Thessaloniki, Chios and Limnosl.
Greece's third largest island, Lesbos (1,638 sq. km.) is one of the islands closest to Turkey. It's shape is instantly recognisable as it features two large bays (called *Geras* and *Kallonis*), both with a narrow opening to the sea. The east and central part of the island is a sea of greenery – olives (over ten million of them), pine woods, oak and chestnut etc. The far northwest area is volcanic and considerably more barren. The total population of the island is approximately 110,000 and the capital of the island is *Mytilini.*

Limnos (Lemnos)

Airport: domestic. Scheduled flight connections to Athens, Thessaloniki and Lesbos.
Ferries: there are boat connections with Piraeus, Rafina, Kavala, Thessaloniki and Alexandroupolis.
Limnos, lacks the mountain springs that make some of the other Greek islands so green and fertile and regularly suffers water shortages. It has plentiful vineyards and has been famous for its honey since antiquity. Its capital is *Myrina* and the island has under 5,000 inhabitants.

Samos

Airport: domestic. Several, one hour flights a day between Athens and Samos.
Ferries: connections with Piraeus (12 hrs), also Rafina and Thessaloniki. Also connected by ferry to the Cyclades and once a week to all the N. Aegean islands.

Samos is just off the Turkish coast south east of Chios Island. Famously fertile since antiquity, Samian wines and other produce are still considered some of the best in Greece. Thanks to its fantastic beaches, the tourist industry in Samos is far more developed than most of the other N. Aegean islands and property buying by foreigners is quite popular. It is best to rent out your property during the holiday season and then come and enjoy the beauty of the island yourself, out of season. In any case, as elsewhere in Greece, summer on Samos is too hot; so hot in 2000 that a devastating forest fire swept through parts of the island and burned for a week. The island has a population of about 43,000 and the capital is Samos town.

Foreigners have been buying property on Samos for several years. A useful website is www.aegeanstyle.com/real-estate-greece/samos or e-mail samos-real@aegeanstyle.com for details of properties they have for sale there.

Construction Company/Estate Agent for Samos

Samos Properties Malagaris Construction Company: Kapetan Stamati 9, Samos Island 83100, Greece; ☎+30-273 028383; fax +30-273 022083; e-mail office@samospro perty.net. Construction company that covers all types of houses including villas, apartments, stone houses, summer homes etc.

Samothraki (Samothrace)

Nearest Airport: Alexandroupolis. Fly to Alexandroupolis from Athens (45 mins) and take ferry from there to Samothraki (2hrs).
Samothraki (population about 3,000; area 180 sq. m.) is the most north-easterly island of Greece and is the closest one to the extended tentacle of the Turkish Dardanelles, making it strategically important. It is a steep island and at its heart are the *Saros Mountains* (1,600 metres) which dominate your view of the island as you approach. As it lacks a natural inlet for a port, the capital of Samothraki lies slightly inland and is a delightful traditional town almost untouched by the tackier side of tourism. Samothraki also has waterfalls and cooler summers thanks to exposure to cooling wind, which means Samothraki does not usually run short of water as many Greek islands do. It's a difficult island to get to, so buying a property there is for those who really want to get away from it all.

Thassos (Limenas)

Nearest Airport: Kavala. Lots of charters from UK airports. Out of season Olympic Airways fly direct from UK. There are also four daily connections from Athens to Kavala and flights twice weekly from Heathrow via Düsseldorf.
Ferry. The ferry from Kavala to Thassos takes 47 minutes.
Greece's most northerly island is also one of the most beautiful. A mere 8 miles off the coastline of Evros province in East Macedonia, Thassos has long been popular with holidaying Germans who could drive down to it through former Yugoslavia. It is a verdant island with its own plentiful water supply. Even the mountains (the highest is *Mt. Ipsario* 1,204m) are verdant and there are of course olive trees seemingly everywhere. By virtue of its northerly position, Thassos mostly escapes the torrid summers of most other islands and the climate is often mild in winter. It has many beautiful sandy beaches, which have so far largely escaped the worst excesses of tourism. As a place to own a holiday or investment property, Thassos is hard to beat. There is plenty to see on the island itself and the mainland is so close you can make trips there quite easily. There are already quite a number of foreign residents and the process of purchasing property there is becoming a smoother process. One property

purchase agent who is herself a long time, intermittent, resident of Thassos is Aileen French of Thassos Property Services (UK ☎01865-766696).

More information on Thassos can be obtained at www.go-thassos.gr.

Useful websites for Thassos property include www.hellenic-realty.com, www.homes-in-greece.com/thassos and www.thassos-property.go-thassos.gr.property.htm.

Estate Agent for Thassos

Riviera Real Estate Agency: ☎+30 210 662 5621; fax +30 210 662 4927; www.greekr ivierarealestate.com.

Thassos Property Services: www.homes-in-greece.com.

Typical Properties for Sale in the N.E. Aegean Islands

Location	Type	Description	Price
Ikaria Island 5 minutes by car from Messakti beach	Plot of land	835 sq.m. (39m by 24 m) with panoramic view of Messakti beach. Ideal for summer villa	€20,000
Ikaria Island Agios Polykarpos village at 300 metres	Traditional mountain home (dilapidated)	comprising one bed single storey house 60 sq.m. and 2-storey stable 25 sq. m. each floor. Total land area and house 3,500 sq.m.	€117,000
Samos Island Pythagorion	Traditional house	900 sq. m. plot. Two level house with three bedrooms plus a basement which is a fully equipped studio guest room. Well maintained garden filled with fruit trees and decorative plants.	€235,000 negotiable
Thassos Island Glyfada resort, northern part of island	Seaside apartment (first floor)	80 sq. m. 2-bedrooms, 2 bathrooms, air con, verandas.	€160,000
Thassos Island Kazaviti village	Traditional house in formerly abandoned mountain village now revived and with protected architecture	123-year-old building on two floors. Completely restored. 20 sq. m. balcony. Terraced garden.Valley and sea views.	€90,000

THE SARONIC ISLANDS

The Saronic Islands lie within the Saronic Gulf between Athens and the Peloponnese. The proximity, especially of *Salamina, Aegina* and *Angistri* to Athens makes them popular with Greeks for, weekends and holidays and many Greeks buy or rent holiday homes there to escape from the polluted air of Athens. The remaining Saronic islands, which lie off the Peloponnese, are *Poros, Hydra* and *Spetses*.

It is difficult to find estate agents that deal with individual islands but a useful website www.greekislandsrealestate.com/argosaronic offers a range of properties from a €76,000 ruin to a €1,000,000 villa on several Saronic islands.

Aegina

Nearest Airport: Athens.
Ferry: from Piraeus takes an hour (30 minutes by hydrofoil).
Pronounced 'ayina', Aegina has an area of 85 sq km and a permanent population of 11,000, about half of whom live in the main town. Comprising mainly mountains, Aegina does however have a fertile plain in the west of the island where a variety of Mediterranean crops are grown including pistachio nuts, almonds and figs. On the eastern coast, dramatic cliffs loom above the sea, although there is a fine bay (*Aghia Marina*) which is usually packed out with tourists, many of them Greeks.

There are properties for sale on the island, particularly luxury ones but it is difficult to find estate agents. The website www.greecegreekislands.com/aegina-island.html could produce some leads and you could also try Leros Properties (e-mail lerosprope rties@yahoo.com).

Hydra

Nearest airport: Athens
Ferry: from Piraeus 3hrs.
Hydra (*Idra*), all 50 sq. km of it, has long been a very special island. In the 19th century, a number of its many rich sea captains, who bought wealth to the island through their privateering careers, beggared themselves funding the struggle for independence against the Turks. The captains' legacy to the island includes many fine mansions, which make its capital and harbour town such a pearl in an otherwise rather bleak island. In the 20th century it developed as a jet-setter haven attracting artists to its picturesque port and the trendy folk to its nightlife. The rich crowds certainly do not come for the beach life as Hydra has almost no sand. The combustion engine is banned from Hydra. For an island with so few natural attractions it has done rather well for itself and its population of 3,000.

A useful website www.hydra-island.com, a free resource directory for the island includes a selection of properties for sale there.

Poros

Nearest Airport: Athens
Ferries: several ferries and hydrofoils a day from Piraeus.
Poros is separated from the mainland Peloponnese by a 400m wide strait. It is a mere 31 sq. km making 6 km in length and 3 km at its widest. It attracts a lot of tourists.

Contact for Property on Poros: Trisha Leafe (e-mail grvillas@otenet.gr; kelsey@saronicnet.com)

Salamina (Salamis)

Salamina is only a few minutes ferry trip from the port of Piraeus 3kms away and not surprisingly such closeness to the heart of the motherland makes Salamis practically an Athenian suburb where Athenians come to chill out at weekends. Once you escape the initial industrial area (the island specialises in ship building), you can have fun getting lost there, as the island's taxing geography is bound to get the better of you. Salamina is a most peculiar shape, slightly like a scorpion with its tail curled up over its back, but with promontories and peninsulas off its underside. The southeast coast is generally considered the prettiest.

Spetses

Nearest Airport: Athens
Ferries: numerous departures from Piraeus (5-6 hrs); half that by hydrofoil. Connections also to other Saronic islands.

The small (22.5 sq. km) charming, heavily-wooded island of Spetses (population 3,500) was one of the first Greek islands to gain popularity with tourists. However, now that tourists have such a choice of cheap destinations, Spetses has lost the bulk of its package tourist trade, but still has many visitors and is a stopping place for many boats and travellers. Like Hydra it is a car-free zone, but transport is provided by island buses, or you can hire a horse-drawn carriage.

It is difficult to find estate agents for Spetses. The developer Seferiades (www.seferiades.gr) has been active there in recent years and it may be worth e-mailing to see if there are any current projects on Spetses (info@seferiades.gr).

Typical Properties for Sale in the Saronic Islands

Location	Type	Description	Price
Aegina Island Agia Marina	Luxury Villa	150 sq. m. 4 bedrooms, 2 bathrooms, 2 baths, 2 reception rooms. Entire plot approx 915 sq. m.	€450,000
Hydra Island Kamini village	Cottage	350 sq. m. on 2 floors. 2 bedrooms. Terraces, patios. Cultivated garden with fruit/nut trees.	€269,408 ready to move into incl some furnishings.
Hydra Island Kaifa, above Hydra town	Plot of land for building house	473.62 sq.m. with spectacular views.	€95,000
Poros Island Poros town centre	Traditional town house	109 sq. m. on 2 levels. 1 bedroom	€185,000
Poros Island near Galatas (6km) and 1200m from sea	Orange grove and villa	19,000 sq. m. of land with orange and lemon trees. 108 sq. m. house with 2 bedrooms	€200,000

THE SPORADES

The Sporades (which means 'scattered') group of islands reaches out in a chain east of the Pelion peninsula. The very large island of Evia (Greek name Eubaea), which lies alongside the mainland, is usually included in the Sporades although administratively it is linked with Athens. The Sporades islands include *Alonissos, Skiathos, Skopelos* and *Skyros*. Traditional architecture consists of picture book white-painted houses and Venetian style two and three-storey houses with tiled roofs and small enclosed gardens.

Alonissos

Nearest Airport: Skiathos and then hydrofoil from Skiathos to Alonissos (1hr.10mins).
Ferries: car ferries and highspeed services from Volos and Agios Constantinos (nr. Lamia) on Greek mainland.
Of all the Sporades Alonissos is the least developed and has not gone out of its way to make itself appealing to tourist masses. This backwater reputation is partly attributed the Government's not rushing in to put right the damage caused by a severe earthquake in 1965, which badly damaged the charming main town. There is very little surfaced roadway, especially down the length of the island, so that the greater part of the island is virtually inaccessible except to walkers. This means that from a property point of view it may not be the best investment. But anyone who likes the comparative calm of the island might consider this an advantage. Since the early 1970s northern Europeans have been buying up houses in the old town to renovate as holiday homes.

Useful Contact for Property on Alonissos
David Watrous: Greek Islands Club, 10-12 Upper Square, Old Isleworth, Middlesex TW7 7BJ; ☎020-8232 9760; e-mail dew@vch.co.uk.

Evia/Eubaea

Nearest Airport: Athens and then bus/train to Evia via bridge. Athens to Chalkida on Evia is 88km.
Ferries: there are various ferry and hydrofoil services from various mainland ports to various ports on Evia.
Evia, (Euboia, Evvoia) is the Greek island that never advertises itself. It is surprising that even though this is the second largest island after Crete, most Britons and Americans (except Greek Americans) have never heard of it. Evia lies parallel to the Greek mainland peninsula, that contains Athens and at weekends it is packed out with Athenians for whom it is a mere 40-minute ferry ride away.

Although it lacks a distinct identity which smaller, more remote Greek islands have, Evia has more than enough to recommend it. There are dozens of spas where you can enjoy the therapeutic qualities of the various hot springs of which there are over 70 (which is also the average age of the Athenians enjoying them). When you tire of the waters, you can enjoy beautiful countryside, undeveloped beaches and sophisticated nightlife in towns such as Amarinthos. The capital of the island is Chalkis.

A section of property for sale on Evia can be found at www.evia.greece.co.uk or e-mail enquiries about real estate to Shena at candscoops@aol.com, or telephone her in the UK on 01788-822567. Shena, who is an agent for rentals and properties for sale in Evia, says that prices range from £20,000 for a ruin in need of restoration in a non-coastal village, up to £600,000 for a house by the sea with land development potential. She says that for a two-bedroomed house in reasonable condition close to the sea, but not in a village expect to pay £120,000. Prospects for renting out are usually excellent.

Estate Agent for Evia
KEYSP Real Estate: 32 Venizelou St, 34100 Chalkis, Evia, Greece; ☎+30 22210 74080; fax +30 22210 80855; e-mail belogmar@otenet.gr.

Skiathos

Airport: served by charter flights in season, or 20 minute scheduled connecting flight from Athens.
Ferries: several ferry and hydrofoil services from Agios Konstantinos, Volos and Thessaloniki. Ferries take 3-5 hours. Tour operator clients take special buses from Athens airport to these ports to save the hassle of negotiating Athens public bus station.
The first Sporades island to embrace the god of international tourism wholeheartedly was Skiathos. The main town of Skiathos is packed to the gunnels with pleasure-seeking foreign tourists, blissfully unaware that barely a century ago, island life was anything but fun and many Greeks emigrated to escape the grinding poverty. There are direct charter flights from the UK and other European countries to Skiathos airport, and from there the tourists are disgorged onto the various beaches at the resorts via permanently crowded buses.

A useful websites for property on Skiathos include www.skiathosinfo.com/property and www.best-packageholidays.co.uk/skiathos-property.html.

Skopelos

Nearest Airport: Skiathos. Charter flight direct to Skiathos and then ferry to Skopelos which takes about an hour. Or connecting flight from Athens to Skiathos.
Ferries: go from Agios Konstantinos (2hrs by bus from Athens) and Volos.
Skopelos has a reputation for being a beautiful island, and that is down to its attractive towns including Skopelos the capital and its second town (*Glossa*), its fantastic unspoiled beaches of which there are dozens, and a serious amount of greenery that covers most of its 100 sq. kms. It is also agriculturally productive in olives, plums, pears, almonds and walnuts. Skopelos does attract its share of tourism but mostly of the variety that prefers to avoid the worst excesses of the more popular islands.

If you decide this is the island where you want to look for a property or plot of land to buy, you will find that there is a good choice of land or houses on offer. Skopelos could well turn out to be an excellent investment.

There is a growing interest in property on the island and a special website (www.greekproperties.net) details all the farms, land, houses etc for sale there.

Useful Contact for Skopelos

Yiannis Asteriadis: ☎+30 24240 22 333; +30 24240 23 955; e-mail info@greekproperties.net. Civil engineer, whose office is in the old port of Skopelos, in the National Bank of Greece and police station building. Runs Greek Properties Net and can assist with viewing properties and the property buying procedure.

Estate Agents for Skopelos

Skopelos Property: ☎+30 694771 8708; fax +30 24240 23140; e-mail info@skopelosproperty.com. Licensed real estate agent works in conjunction with Greek professionals (architects, builders, lawyers etc) to assist clients with all aspects of real estate purchase. Ask for Michael Burton-Pye.

Skopelos Real Estate: Eleftherotria Church, Skopelos Town, Skopelos Island, 37003, Greece; ☎+30 24240 22909; e-mail reals@skopelos.net; www.skopelos.net.

Skyros

Nearest Airport: Skiathos

Skyros is a rather special island that is surrounded by its own archipelago of more than a dozen little islands and islets. It is almost divided in two by its narrow waist. The southern part is mostly barren and wild and the English poet Rupert Brooke is buried there, below foraging, mini ponies (Pikermes) which are native to the island. The northern part is green and fertile. Somewhat isolated, even within the Sporades, the island does have a unique atmosphere, and pagan folklore is still much in evidence amongst its population of about 3,000. Skyros town is fascinating, its white houses stacked steeply up a hillside, crammed together, yet at the same time maintaining the privacy of their inhabitants.

Bear in mind if you are thinking of buying property there that although Skyros is different and interesting, it is rather hard to get to. There are expensive charter flights (£300+) from July to end of September, with Hellenic Travel (☎0207-267-7094).

Typical Properties for Sale in the Sporades

Location	Type	Description	Price
Island of Skiathos Skiathos town	Old town house on 3 floors.	Charming house fully renovated by French architect.1st floor at street level, second floor at another street level. 2 bedrooms. 1 bath room.	€310,000
Island of Skopelos Skopelos town	Old house	3 floors of 132 sq. m. total with car access to entrance.	€90,000
Island of Skopelos Skopelos town centre residential area 300 metres from harbour	Traditional stone house suitable for all year round occupation	3-storeys. 3 bedrooms. Needs redecoration/modernisation	€76,500
Island of Skyros	Traditional house	2-storey house of 170 sq.m. on a plot of 2,400 sq.m with trees (olive, pine etc). 150 metres from the sea. Possible to make each floor separate dwelling.	€235,000
Skyros Island Molos	Traditional style house built 1985	101 sq. m. 3-storey house on plot of 458 sq.m. and an adjacent 36 sq. m. self-contained studio apartment. 5-10 minutes walk from beach etc.	€160,000 (negotiable)

ISLANDS FOR SALE

Why stop at buying a house or plot on an island when you can buy a whole island? Well the price might stop you. When Aristotle Onassis bought the 500-acre island of Skorpios (south of Corfu) in 1963 he paid US$100,000. These days one to four million euros are needed, which is unrealistic for most individuals. Nevertheless, for the seriously moneyed, or those who can organise a consortium there are estate agents that have small islands on their books. The website www.forthnet.gr/panteris/alimia.htm advertises islands for sale.

ISLAND SNAPSHOTS

- **Evia** is nearly as big as Crete but much less well known and nearer the mainland.
- **Naxos** (Cyclades) has a wondrous unfinished statue of Apollo lying in a quarry abandoned two and a half thousand years ago.
- **Leros** (Dodecanese) is small (54sq. km) but traditional; island houses are quite cheap there.
- **Kefalonia** (Ionian) is beautiful, bigger and much less populated than Corfu. Now is the time to make a property investment on 'Captain Corelli's island'.
- **Paxos** (Ionian) is a tiny island overwhelmed by tourists in summer but out of season it is a peaceful place full of olive trees.
- **Zakynthos** (Ionian) has dense greenery, which inspired Venetian colonials to call it 'the flower of the Orient'.
- **Kythera** (Ionian) is isolated as it lies off the coast of the Peloponnese, but the tourist infrastructure is growing and property there could be a shrewd investment.
- **Chios** (N.E. Aegean) this island's beauty lies in stark contrasts between its lush valleys and bare rocky crags. It is also wealthy and a good place for property investment and residential tourism.
- **Samos** (N.E. Aegean) has been famous since antiquity. It is best to rent out your property in the holiday season and enjoy the beauty of the island yourself out of season.
- **Thassos** (N.E. Aegean), one of the most verdant islands. As a place to own a holiday or investment property, it's hard to beat.
- **Skopelos** (Sporades) could well turn out to be a good investment.

THE PURCHASING PROCEDURE

CHAPTER SUMMARY

O **UK Banks.** Banks in the UK will not lend against the purchase of property in Greece, but you can take out a loan secured against your UK home.

O **Greek Banks.** Banks in Greece will give loans in euros to intending purchasers of property in Greece secured against the Greek property.

O If you import any money into Greece you need to obtain a currency import receipt ('pink slip') from the bank as proof of importing the money for the purchase of property.

O **Tax.** It is advisable to complete a Greek tax return annually as a statement that you do not owe money to the Greek tax authorities.

O **Property for Sale.** The Greek property market is different from many in Europe in that pre-owned modern houses rarely come on the market.

O The property market for foreigners is mainly plots, apartments and old village homes needing extensive renovation. Off-plan is rare but growing.

O **Estate Agents.** It is only recently that the concept of an estate agent has evolved in Greece outside the main areas of population.

   O Your estate agent is the person to link you to the lawyer, conveyancing solicitor, tax office representative and accountant as necessary, to enable you to complete the purchase.

   O There are many unregulated house-finders in Greece who take on the responsibility of introducing buyers and sellers to each other for which they charge a fee.

O **Parking Problem.** If you are thinking of buying an apartment note that it is the exception rather than the rule that it will come with a parking space.

O **Title of Ownership.** The most common problem encountered is that the parent or grandparent of the seller purchased the land at some time in the past but never completed the paperwork necessitating lengthy and costly searches.

- ○ **The Deposit.** The purchaser pays a 10% deposit to get the purchasing process underway.
- ○ **Olive Trees.** An area of law that is strange to non-Greeks is the complicated issue of ownership of olive trees. You may have to pay a sum per olive tree growing on your land to the owner.

FINANCE

UK BANKS

UK banks will not lend against the purchase of a property in Greece. They are concerned that until Greece has proven itself as a full and reliable member of the European Union, complying with European law, there are too many uncertainties in respect of land ownership and the title being registered. However, it is very possible to borrow money from British banks and Building Societies by extending your existing mortgage on a UK property. This is far and away the cheapest and simplest way of raising finance for your overseas purchase.

It is also very possible, if the purchase cost is relatively low, just to take out a loan, possibly secured against your home, and you will find that there are many organisations happy to make a substantial loan at about 4.5 to 6% if you are prepared to secure the loan against some security in the UK.

Useful Contacts – Mortgages

The Complete Mortgage Company: (G&M Mortgages); ☎0800 08 55142; e-mail: working4u@comoco.co.uk. Broker that helps you arrange finance for properties in Greece (and elsewhere). Deals mainly with Conti (see below) at present but more companies likely in the future.

Conti Financial Services: 204 Church Road, Hove, Sussex BN3 2DJ; free phone 0800-970 0985; ☎01273-772811; fax 01273-321269; e-mail enquiries@contifs.com; www.mort gagesoverseas.com. Overseas mortgage specialist.

Domus Inc.: P.O. Box 70.878, 166 05 Voula, Greece; ☎+30 210 9635928; fax +30 210 8992069; www.domusinc.gr. Complete real estate and property brokering solutions including loan provision to European citizens for investment in Greek real estate.

Mortgages.co.uk: www.mortgages.co.uk/holiday-homes/greek-mortgages.htm. Licensed credit brokers that can help finance the purchase of a property in Greece by using the Greek property as security.

GREEK BANKS

Greece has around 10 major banks, the largest of which is National Bank of Greece, which has a branch in most large towns and islands. There is also a National Mortgage Bank of Greece, which has about 75 branches in Greece. One or two of the major banks including ETEBA (investments) and Hellenic Industrial Development Bank (commercial), operate in specialised areas. Other general banks include the Macedonia-Thrace Bank, Piraeus Bank and Bank of Athens.

Greek banks are open from 8am-2pm Monday to Friday.

Internet Banking. The larger banks offer an e-banking service with a version in English. These include The National Bank of Greece (homebanking@nbg.gr), The Bank of Piraeus (www.piraeusbank.gr) and the Hellenic Bank Association (www.hba.gr/English).

Loans from Greek Banks

Banks in Greece are happy to give loans in euros to intending purchasers of land and property in Greece. At the time of writing, the repayment rate is 5.8% (approximately), which is in line with the interest rates in Greece, which normally run at about 2% higher than repayment rates in the UK. A Greek bank, just as UK banks do, will require that the loan is secured against the property. This means that it will not be possible to borrow the cost of buying a house off plan, for a proposal to build on a plot of land or for the conversion of a ramshackle village home.

If it is your aim to borrow money from a Greek bank you will be required to provide a number of documents, which you will have to have translated from English into Greek. It is therefore advisable to prepare the papers well in advance before making your first appointment with the lending bank.

Documents Needed to Obtain a Loan from a Greek Bank

O Proof of your income, i.e. your ability to repay the loan. The last three months of pay slips will suffice.

O Proof that you do not owe either the Inland Revenue or the Social Security in your home country any money. In the UK the most recent P60 will suffice, supplemented by a letter of reference from your employer to indicate that they deduct these repayments on account of these government departments. Self employed persons need to submit the last tax coding notice and a receipt that amounts owing have been paid.

O A letter of reference from your bank indicating that you have conducted your finances responsibly over a period of at least 5 years.

O The final item is one that you will be asked to provide on a number of occasions as UK nationals do not have an identity card. You need to provide a copy of your passport, as well as any supplementary information, e.g. a marriage licence, if the data on your passport is not up to date.

After the initial meeting with the bank the approval of a loan is usually fairly straightforward. It will normally only necessitate a visit by their representative to establish that the value of the land or property, which you are borrowing the money to buy, has sufficient value to provide security to them. The bank will determine their own evaluation, which may be (or not) less than the asking price. Do not therefore expect to be able to borrow the full amount. Having a local contact who knows the bank manager would be of great benefit.

Useful Contacts – Greek Banks

Agricultural Bank of Greece: 23 Panepistoumiou Str. 10564 Athens; ☎+32 98 911; fax 32 39 611.

Bank of Piraeus: 20 Amalias & 5 K. Souri Str. 10557 Athens; ☎33 11 520; fax 32 46 481.

EFG Eurobank Ergasias SA: 8 Othonos Street, 105 57, Athens, Greece; ☎+30 210 33 37000; fax +30 210 32 33866; www.eurobank.gr. 300 branches in Greece.

General Hellenic Bank: 9 Panepistimiou Str. 10564; ☎ +32 41 289; fax +32 34 686.
Macedonia Thrace Bank SA: Ionos Dragoumi Str., 546 25 Thessaloniki; ☎ 031 54 22 135; fax 031/54 38 22.-
National Bank of Greece: 86 Aeolou Str, 10519; ☎ 33 41 000; fax 32 11 491.
National Mortgage Bank of Greece SA: 40 Panepistimiou Street, Athens 106.79, Greece; ☎ +30 1 38 48 311; fax +30 1 38 05 130.

Procedure for Importing Currency to Greece

If you import any substantial amount of currency from the UK or send it by telegraphic transfer, it is important that you declare this import. It is straightforward to ship money from any of the other EU countries. For more ways of how to do this, see the *General Introduction* at the beginning of this book. It is advisable to send money from the UK in sterling as you will always get a better rate of exchange when the receiving bank in Greece converts it to euros. If you are concerned about currency fluctuations between the value of sterling and the euro you can 'forward buy' euros at a fixed rate from a firm such as Currencies Direct. See, the *General Introduction* to this book for more details of how to do this.

Pink Slips. You need the Y9 (often called 'pink form' or 'pink slip'), from the bank as evidence that you have officially imported the currency that you are going to use to purchase land or property, or to buy your business or renovate an old home in Greece. This form is a currency import receipt, *(apodixi issagoyis Krimata).*

GREEK TAXES

Filing a Tax Return

Note that persons who are not working are not required to summit an annual tax return, but that it is *advisable* to submit a return voluntarily (assisted by one of the many tax accountants), as a statement that you do not owe money to the Greek tax authorities or Social Security. To do this, you will need a tax registration number. This is the equivalent of an English National Insurance number and entitles you to pay tax and Social Security contributions.

The Greek tax authorities will ask for your currency import receipts (see above) at the end of your first year in Greece, when you submit your first tax return, and also if you subsequently import any further currency. Tax returns have to be submitted annually and any unexplained income will be rigorously investigated. Failure to produce themt then will result in a fine.

Greek Taxes on Real Estate

There are no annual property taxes in Greece on a property worth up to €200,000. Property taxes on properties valued higher than this are about 0.25% annually. The market value of your property is assessed by the tax authorities, rather as properties are assessed in the UK for the council tax.

Tax on Large Properties. Since 1996, Greek tax authorities have imposed a tax on people who own more valuable properties. The threshold for paying this tax is raised each year and currently it is €243,600 for single people and €487,200 for a couple. There are also allowances for families with children.

The form for filing for this tax is an E-9. If you already file an income tax return (known as E-1) in Greece you will automatically be required to file an E-9. Note that even if you own no property at all in Greece you are still required to file an E-9 just to confirm this fact. If you are non-resident in Greece then you can file your return at the Tax Authority for Foreigners (18 Lycourgou Street, Athens), otherwise it should be filed with the local authority near where you are living in Greece.

If you ignore this problem, it will not affect you if you never sell or build on your property, but it will cause problems for your heirs who will be liable for a fine, back taxes and interest on unpaid tax. Apparently this does not deter some owners from using the legendary inefficiency of the tax authorities as an excuse to bury their heads in the sand.

Inheritance Tax

Inheritance tax should be taken into consideration when buying a property in Greece. The tax is not imposed on the estate of the deceased, but on each beneficiary of the estate, dependent on their share, and the proximity of their relationship to the deceased. Closest relatives paying least or nothing at all. The maximum rate is 66%.

Note that the rules on inheritance tax change are subject to frequent amendment and you should confirm the details with your conveyancing lawyer and tax accountant.

Useful Contact

Hahalis & Kounoupis PC Greek Law Group: Greek Office, 29 Voukurestiou Str., Athens 10673 Greece; ☎+30 1 360 5033; fax +30 1 360 5756; US office: 3400 Bath Pike, Suite 100, Bethlehem, PA 18017; ☎(610-865 2608; fax (610) 691 8418; e-mail georgek@fast.net; www.greeklawgroup.com. Services include estate planning and clearing up inheritance of Greek property.

Capital Gains Tax

You may have to pay capital gains on the sale of your Greek property. Capital gains is levied as a percentage of the property value and is scaled down according to how long you have owned the property. The top rate usually paid is 25%. Note that if you sell the property in order to buy another property in Greece you will not be liable for capital gains, regardless of the length of your ownership.

FINDING PROPERTIES FOR SALE

The Greek market is very different from markets in the rest of Europe in that pre-owned, modern homes rarely come onto the market. Greeks build their own homes and the market for foreign property buyers is thus mainly plots of land, apartments and old village homes needing extensive renovation and new build properties available off-plan.

ESTATE AGENTS

It is only recently that the North European concept of an estate agent has evolved in Greece outside the main centres of population. Traditionally, most property sales have been instigated by informal requests in and around the area where buyers hope to live, or by a notice pinned to a convenient olive tree on the plot of land for sale, or by a notice in a kiosk or shop window, near to the property for sale. Often this agency work will have been conducted from the agent's home, where a front room has been converted to an office. There may be some printed information available, but it is likely to be sketchy, probably only a photo and possibly an outline of the floor plan or plot of land. A surveyor will help with drawings and details of services, but the estate agent traditionally has no interest in providing these details for the buyer. Property search in Greece, mainland and islands alike, is an excursion into another land in more ways than one.

How Estate Agents Operate in Greece

You will be expected to accompany the estate agent to view all the properties he/she deems will meet your needs, but may be required to provide your own transport to them, just as in the UK. There may be a small charge made for the initial 'exploring what is available' service. Agents are becoming increasingly wary of foreigners (as well as non-local Greeks and Cypriots) who use the agent's time and transport as a means of visiting the islands or other tourist areas when in fact they have no real intention, or ability, to buy. With this consideration in mind, you may have to pay a small registration fee, usually in the region of €100, to indicate your commitment to buying a home or business. This will be refunded against any purchase made under the auspices of that agent.

You can also be reassured that agents are requesting a similar financial and contractual commitment from the vendors as they too can be unreliable in their commitment to selling. A good agent will have established all of these details before taking a property onto his books.

Equally, your estate agent is the person to link you to the lawyer, conveyancing solicitor, tax office representative and accountant as necessary, to enable you to complete the purchase. The agent may undertake to commission these services for you. You should expect to pay the agent both for obtaining the details of a suitable house for you as well as for additional services such as land registration search, purchase tax negotiation and any translation or interpretation. A good estate agent will complete all stages of the purchase on your behalf and just hand you the keys or the land deeds on completion.

Establishing the Vendor's Ownership

A good estate agent will already have established ownership before accepting a property for sale. Many agents are now refusing to handle the sale of a home or land unless the vendor can produce the papers at the time of giving the agent the instruction to sell, which prove the vendor has title to the property, as well as having the agreement of other interested parties in the family that the property be made available for sale and what the asking price is. Agents themselves are learning by experience as the market develops and they are there to protect the buyer just as much as the seller in the whole purchase process.

Finding an Estate Agent

The best means of choosing an agent is by personal recommendation, but have a check list of your own requirements that you want from an agent, and make sure that you have understood the replies to all of your questions and are happy with them. Agents in tourist areas will usually be multi-lingual but you may wish to take a trusted Greek-speaking friend with you to ensure that you have understood all the explanations and conditions. Many Greeks will gladly take on such a responsibility, but their translation and interpretation will have no legal status. Make sure that you get a translation of any documentation before you sign it – this will come at an additional cost but may save money in the long run.

THE INTERNET

The internet and the information on it is mushrooming. However, treat all information with a pinch of salt. All the main towns and cities as well as the majority of islands have a web presence. In some instances, such websites are set up by the mayor or local interest group for the promotion of tourism or other businesses. These will all have links to discussion and information pages and should all link in to estate agents' sites (under banners such as 'real estate' or 'property sales') or to individuals selling their own properties or development on line. Many of these sites are great entertainment on cold winter evenings on account of their whimsical English and flowery tone, but they should not be dismissed as a useful source of preliminary data. Collecting background information such as this can be invaluable before planning your trip, but be sure the information is up to date and as complete as possible before setting you heart on something specific.

Estate agent printed details and property newspapers and brochures, such as those which many European and North American estate agencies provide, are rare, but increasingly online details are available on estate agents' and developer's websites, as well as websites of private vendors who have built villas and wish to sell them on to other tourists or expats. These last, often set up their own web sites with fulsome details of the property and all the supporting information on the local area.

Some useful websites include *www.realtynet.gr* which is a group Greek estate agencies on the net and *www.propertygr.com* a website that advertises property by region with clear descriptions, photographs and contacts for each property. More details of useful websites can be found in the chapter *Where to Find Your Ideal Home*. Also try www.themovechannel.com/sitefinder/greece, which has a list of companies and individuals dealing in property in Greece, arranged by area, and a brief description of each.

There are many unregulated house finders in Greece:
Still much in evidence in Greece are individuals who take on the responsibility of introducing buyers and sellers to each other – at a cost, just as in the USA, to both parties, as well as the Mediterranean system of a finder's fee being paid to the person who located the property for you in the first place. (This last should be included in the purchase price.)

This is still the most common method of property search but buyers should be very wary of promises of huge plots of land with exquisite views and no planning restrictions, or of village homes needing 'just a bit of work', as well as declarations of ownership and willingness to sell. All such promises need to be treated with caution and expert advice sought at each stage.

ESTATE AGENTS' ASSOCIATIONS

Associations of agents are slowly being established. In the main towns and cities in Greece you will find membership of these agency associations proudly displayed. Membership does indicate a level of professionalism but provides no guarantees. Guarantees are obtained through the transactions of the solicitors who specialise in property conveyancing.

In towns and cities the system is much more formalised as the needs of buyers and sellers are usually very specific and time scales tighter. Agents have established their own links and networks. In the island and mainland tourist areas agents are slowly emerging, often providing a multi-lingual service to satisfy the needs of the tourist as well as the local population. They too are joining the professional associations and are often more responsive in their services as the demands of the foreign buyer have not been met in the past by the relaxed and very informal attitude so of the old style island agents.

Useful Addresses

The Hellenic Association of Realtors (HAR): Odos Kerkyyras 47, 11362, Athens, Greece; ☎+30 210 8232931; fax +30 210 8810936; e-mail info@sek.gr; www.sek.gr) was formed in 1999 and is the only professional estate agency body in Greece. Their members cover most of Greece and are listed on their website.

www.progc.co.uk – The website of Mykra Ltd – Properties in Greece, 43 Lambton Road, West Wimbledon, London SW20 OLW; (UK ☎0800 7313254 and 0208-2869511; e-mail info@progc.co.uk). Offers all kinds of property: resale, new, design and build, traditional, old. Also arranges inspection trips and legal services for buying property all over Greece.

PROPERTY EXHIBITIONS

Property exhibitions are always a good source of information on medium to larger scale developments, which are usually on the more populated islands such as Rhodes, Crete, Corfu, Kefalonia and in the tourist mainland areas of Halkidiki and the Peloponnese. The displays are usually for new development either just commenced or part built. Buyers will thus be buying off plan, where a deposit secures the plot and as building progresses the stage payments become payable by the buyer.

Exhibitions are also an excellent way to find out about styles of building and material use as well as a way of establishing which areas are under development in the immediate future. They will provide links to sources of finance for overseas purchase and development as well as details of companies providing low cost flights, holiday home insurance, removals and a range of other allied services.

Unfortunately, Greek property exhibitions are much thinner on the ground than those for Spain and France. Notices of forthcoming exhibitions may be published in magazines such as *World of Property* or may be organised by large international developers such as those advertising regularly in *Greece* magazine (see below). It is also worth checking local newspapers and free property newspapers.

Crete Property Consultants have regular exhibitions and you can check their website (www.creteproperty.co.uk) for the latest dates for these.

Note that small developers or property renovators will almost certainly not be represented at property exhibitions.

PUBLICATIONS

Greece has a modest property and residential tourism market compared to France or Spain and consequently has fewer magazines and other publications covering the subjects potential property buyers want to know about. The main one is *Greece* magazine published by Merricks Media (☎ 01225-786800; www.merrricksmedia.co.uk), a glossy with a useful selection of properties and contacts.

Property magazines and the overseas property sections of weekend newspapers will often carry small ads from individual owners or small developers and relocation agents as well as the extensive range of smart advertisements from property developers who are targeting the 200,000 Britons who retire to the sun each year. The small ads are an excellent way of establishing guide prices and availability in specific areas as well as being a source of information on the level of development in those areas of Greece.

Finding a Place for Yourself

If you haven't found what you want through an agent or developer, then by all means pay a visit to the area that interests you and ask around. However, it is advisable to seek expert help and advice before committing to any agreement, or before handing over any money. This may seem like obvious advice, but remember that when abroad, lunacy may replace usual good sense when it comes to parting with large sums of money without the protection of legally based contracts.

To Summarise

Use all possible sources of information such as those mentioned above to build up a picture in your mind of your own ideal home and location. Collect as much information as possible, from as wide a range of sources as possible before you plan your buying trip. Set your parameters down on paper, particularly about budget, location, size, type and condition and make sure you agree these with others who are to play a part in helping you find a property to purchase.

A warm spring or summer's day can seduce the hardest heart and switch off the rational part of your mind. You may see only a beautiful home instead of the pile of sun washed stones lying in the corner of a field; you may also see a group of friendly and characterful local builders, instead of two to four years of a snakes and ladders game otherwise known as restoration conducted with over-optimistic craftsmen. As Debbie Taylor puts in one of her *Heat and Dust* series of articles for the Sunday Times, when the builders came to give some estimates on her Greek ruin '*The builder swung his mallet at an outside corner, loosing an avalanche of centuries-old render. Inside the house, his son was pecking away at the plaster with a claw hammer, while an electrician ripped wires from the ceiling with demonic glee...*What are they doing to the house? *I demanded.* I told them you wanted a good quality renovation, *he (the estate agent) explained patiently.* So they are assessing what needs to be done'.

If you know your limits and capabilities where trouble and strife are concerned, then tell the agent. A good one will best match your needs and this will result in the efficient use of your and his precious time and energy, leaving you more time to plan your new home and life in the sun.

AN AGENT'S ADVICE – TAKE A YEAR OUT BEFORE YOU MOVE IN

Aileen French of Thassos Properties has been resident in Greece for nearly 30 years, speaks Greek fluently, and has been helping others buy property on the Island of Thassos for four years:

Experience has shown that the best overall approach, for those who are planning to purchase land, property or businesses in Greece, is to move to the area where you intend to live on a temporary basis in the first instance. You should rent out any accommodation you have in the UK, and then spend a year in rented accommodation in Greece and get to know the environment completely, outside the most attractive times of spring and early summer.

The year in Greece would help you to get to know how the lifestyle changes from summer, to autumn and winter: what facilities are and are not available, who the neighbours are and especially, how the weather is. Greece can be infernally hot in summer but what happens (if anything?) in the coldest and wettest months? Best of all, you have leisure to find out exactly what the property market is like. It is also probable that the market will be at its slowest in the winter and thus you should have more time and flexibility, being on the spot, to investigate alternatives and to be present when the paperwork to buy your property is being prepared. If you use this opportunity also, to learn the language and about local culture, as well as learning about the environment, you will find that the process of both finding and buying is made much easier because you will already have established yourself in the local community as a credible and serious intending purchaser, as well as having bolstered your own confidence in an environment which can still seem hostile, and certainly complex to the average naïve foreigner. Remember, the attempt to learn the language and communicate in Greek is your passport to the hearts and hearths of the local Greek community.

A trial year will also enable you to judge if you are able to live a completely different life style in an environment, which you will only ever have seen before for two or three week stretches, in brilliant sun shine, and populated by foreign tourists all in the best possible frame of mind, as they enjoy themselves and spend freely on the facilities available in the summer months.

During winter on the islands and in tourist areas, non Greek-speakers may be rare, facilities may close, there will probably be no bus or regular ferry links and you will find that many bars shops and restaurants simply drop the shutters and close as soon as the last charter flight has left. A paradise for some, but not so appealing if you are a gregarious type or need the reassurance of shops and people to keep you happy. Use this time to determine your own real needs and motivations and if you have moved with a partner, ensure that you can both enjoy the relative peace and isolation of the non-city environment for four to five months at a time.

WHAT TYPE OF PROPERTY TO BUY

Properties vary immensely across Greece. As with all of the other information already given, the situation in the cities and towns, and the majority of non-tourist areas in the mainland differs widely from the much more informal and yet tourist-friendly, approaches that are the custom in the islands and coastal tourist areas.

TOWN AND CITY HOUSES

It is rare that relatively new or modernised homes come onto the market. In towns and cities homes are normally built by families to meet their own needs, often accommodating two or even three generations and will be handed down by the parents to their children and to the children's children. However, you will occasionally find relatively new homes coming onto the market with one or more of the floors in the home incomplete. It is quite normal for a house to be sold with just one level finished and liveable in. The house then will be 'sold as seen' and it would be up to the buyer whether or not they complete the conversion of either the basement or the roof space. It is not normal for such houses to be sold piecemeal. The owners of the house own the land on which the property is built and normally only sell such properties in times of financial need or if the children no longer require the accommodation.

APARTMENTS

It is much more usual in the towns and cities, and even in tourist areas, to find apartments for sale. These might be one floor in a home, but it is more likely that they will be an apartment in a purpose-built block or even part of one floor in a two to three storey building. In such a situation, the heating will be communal and will be a fixed price per annum, as well as a service charge for the maintenance and cleaning of any common areas, such as foyers, gardens and other outside areas.

Parking problem

Note that it is an exception rather than a rule that apartments will come with parking spaces. Parking is a problem in all town and city areas in Greece and increasingly now also in villages. This is something that you will need to investigate carefully, particularly if you intend to have one or more cars when you move.

Apartments for sale are very often advertised by stickers on the door or even on lamp posts or other street signs adjacent to the property. The sticker will say the simple word *poleeté* (for sale), and a telephone number. It is then up to the buyer to telephone the number and to find out the details, such as the price and who is selling and so on. The important issue to remember when purchasing an apartment in a block such as this is to investigate what lease is available. This is exactly the same situation as with the purchase of a flat in any other area of Europe.

VILLAGE PROPERTY

It is noticeable that more and more village properties are coming onto the market. Such properties may be as minimal as a heap of bricks in the corner of a small plot of land, often on the outskirts of a village. Alternatively, the present owners and sellers of the property may have undertaken some or all of the renovation necessary to make the property liveable in. It may come as a surprise to many Europeans that seemingly derelict properties have up until recently, been inhabited by elderly people who perhaps were born there and lived there until their last days. It is essential if purchasing one of these old village properties to have a full survey undertaken to investigate the soundness of the external structure. In the majority of cases, the structure will be made out of stone without such modern necessities as damp proofing courses; or the foundations may be extremely rudimentary. Roofs too are a potential problem, they are often of local stone or slate and may just be made out of that material with no felt insulation or other water proofing underneath.

Europeans from other countries are often attracted to the idea of buying a village property, but it may well be that the costs of renovation outweigh the cost of buying another plot of land in the village elsewhere and constructing a new home to modern standards. You will also find that the local people do not value the appearance of old properties as many northern Europeans do. They invariably upgrade their own village homes with little regard to taste, so that they have a uniform look, being rendered and painted in identical fashion and with double glazed front doors and windows, and new aluminium railings on their balconies and verandas. However, there are some villages, which typify a vernacular Greek village architecture and as such are protected. Do ask what the local regulations are with respect to developing village properties, as you may find you are very limited in what you can do if you are in one of the areas designated as an official conservation area.

CONDOMINIUMS & NEW TOWN HOUSES

Increasingly developments (normally near the sea), are being undertaken by owners of plots of land adjacent to tourist areas, on both the mainland and the islands. These developments are intended as holiday accommodation. They are targeted at both Greek and other European purchasers. They tend to be relatively expensive as they have often been built with the highest quality specifications, and are luxuriously completed inside. These developments are often advertised on huge hoardings, which will monopolise your line of vision as you drive around the tourist areas. They are resplendent with architects' drawings showing the completed development in all its glory. If you are investigating the purchase of one of these properties, do ask to see one of the completed and furnished condominiums, or town houses, so that you can envisage how it will actually look with some furniture and belongings inside. Such developments often offer pools and communal areas, but make sure that it is clear, when you are investigating the purchase, whose responsibility it is to clean and maintain the communal areas and what happens in the winter when there are few or no residents in the accommodation. Such properties as these will certainly give you ideal summer accommodation, and in many instances they offer an advantage over other tourism developments in that you will be living amongst many different nationalities, including often, many Greeks. You can also rent them out if you wish during the weeks that you will not be there yourself, thus helping to recoup some of your expenses.

PLOTS OF LAND

The most popular means of purchasing property in Greece at the present time is to purchase a plot of land, apply for planning permission and have a home built to your own specification. This is done in conjunction with an architect experienced in this type of work and who will most likely be recommended by the estate agent who has negotiated the sale of the land for you.

If you are buying this type of property, it is essential that you confirm that the land you are buying is within the town plan, that is to say that it can be built upon. The presence of homes nearby does not guarantee that they are legally built. There will be local regulations as to the size of property which can be built, usually 40% of the plot size at a maximum, but that would allow a home of 120sq.metres on an average sized plot of 300sq. m. **It is absolutely essential, when purchasing land, to determine what the precise local regulations are for the size and type of home, which can be built on it.**

There is an easier variation of this option is another possibility: it is becoming increasingly acceptable to buy a piece of land and to have a pre-fabricated house constructed upon it. Specialist magazines and overseas property exhibitions in the UK will have information on such pre-fabricated constructions. They are built and constructed to a very high specification and are very acceptable in terms of accommodation, both for the medium and the long term.

LUXURY VILLAS

Villas will occasionally come onto the market and you will normally find information on these in specialist overseas property magazines. They tend to have been built to individual owners' specifications and are often very luxuriously appointed with reasonably sized plots of land and as such tend to be very expensive. They are worth a look, however, as occasionally the owner has built the villa on a plot of land perhaps he inherited, and maybe does not wish to live there any longer or finds that the children do not really wish to inherit the property. There is often room for negotiation, therefore, on the price of these properties, but don't expect to find villas and land, particularly with access to the sea or with sea views at anything resembling budget prices.

ON THE WATER'S EDGE

For some people, a house on the shores of the Mediterranean is a literal dream. There are two main types of property on the water's edge in Greece.

Marinas

With Greece's accession as a full member of the European Union, European money has been made available to a number of coastal resorts to enable them to develop marinas. In some areas, part of the development includes hotels and tourist type accommodation. These are the most expensive type of purchases, but are obviously ideally suited for those who either own or wish to own boats and need access to moorings, as accommodation of this type brings mooring rights with it, albeit at a price.

Fishermen's Cottages

As with village property described already, fishermen's cottages are often dreamt of as being the idyllic accommodation for those hoping to move to Greece. However the dream and the reality are often miles apart. These cottages, by definition, will be small and often in a very poor state of repair. They may not even have electricity or running water. However, they will be located near to the water's edge, and if the intending purchaser is a keen fisherman or yachtsman, they are often ideal in terms of location. If the basic structure is sound, and if local regulations allow the property to be renovated and even extended in line with modern requirements then it may be exactly what you want. Note however, that ceilings tend to be so low that you may find that you have to stoop when entering, and that the basement is usually nothing more than an earth floor with either earth or stone walls, because they are the places where the nets and the fishing tackle were stored and they did not need to be either dry or warm. As with village properties, these cottages require a thorough survey to be undertaken before you consider entering into any deal with the seller or the seller's family.

SHARED OWNERSHIP OR TIMESHARE

Timeshare is slowly emerging in Greece as developers understand that there is demand for holiday accommodation and that individuals who may live at some distance, do not necessarily want the responsibility of maintenance, of both a property and of land for those months of the year when they are not able to enjoy the property. However, because of the relative rarity of these properties the terms of the share agreements and the responsibility of the individual players in the shared ownership have in many cases, not been carefully thought through and any potential purchaser is advised to investigate thoroughly the terms and the conditions of shared ownership before entering into such a proposition. This topic is dealt with in more detail in the *General Introduction* of this book.

IN SUMMARY

When undertaking your property search, it is as well to have in mind a price range as well as to know the amount of work that you, yourself, or your builders are prepared to undertake in order to bring either an old or non-existent property up to scratch, so as to be habitable for you and perhaps your family and friends. It is these factors which will probably dictate the type of property that you will end up purchasing, and you will seldom find property which exactly meets your needs. Do be prepared to be flexible and imaginative in your search. A decent estate agent will give you access to architects, surveyors and builders and through speaking to them and to other people who have undertaken similar initiatives you will be able to envisage how the pile of bricks in the corner can actually one day with money, with time and with energy, be converted into your dream holiday home.

RENTING A HOME IN GREECE

It is relatively straightforward to find and to rent accommodation in Greece. It will normally be an apartment in a block of other similarly rented out apartments. Rents in all but the most exclusive tourist areas are good value. However, it is uncommon to find rented accommodation which is furnished, except in tourist areas where you will find that you are either paying a daily or weekly rate and therefore renting the accommodation as though it was a short term rental or holiday let.

Apartments

Rents in towns can be as low as 150 to 180 euros per month for a two-bedroom apartment, which is heated in the winter. The kitchen and bathroom may be somewhat basic, but you will find that these homes in apartment blocks at this price can be easily furnished and should already have some sort of heating, for example, a diesel or a Calor gas stove.

Apartments in blocks that are centrally heated, will quite often be more expensive and you will find that you have to pay the cost of the electricity or the oil on top of the agreed rental. Such apartments are easily located, as the ubiquitous stickers will be on the doors or the lamp posts nearby declaring *eneekeeazete* (to let). You will also find the same stickers at the kiosks, and again it is just a question of writing down the telephone number and telephoning to find out precisely what is available and the cost and then making contact with the person undertaking the rental.

Medium to Long-Term Renting

Furnished homes for rent are harder to find if you require a medium to long-term let. The best way of finding information is to contact estate agents in the location where you are hoping to rent, asking around in the bars and restaurants or by seeking information from the English newspapers, such as the *Athens News*, which is available in and around Athens and Attika or by looking or advertising on expat websites. But once again these homes will very rarely come furnished. It is, however, more usual to find that a family who live in a property are prepared to rent out one of the floors in their property. It will have a separate front door, and be self-contained, but it will not be furnished and you will find that in such an arrangement that the friendship, and therefore all the elements of hospitality of the owning family, are part of the package when you undertake to rent a floor in their home.

Much more common, when you are looking for rental accommodation, is to be offered the opportunity of undertaking a medium-term rental of holiday accommodation which will be furnished as though it was all ready for holiday makers. What you will find is that this accommodation has little or no heating, fairly basic storage facilities and is really only equipped for one or two-week stays. Such accommodation is usually quite expensive, particularly in the tourist areas, as the owners will calculate on the basis of letting it weekly to a tourist. Once again, ask around in the vicinity and you will be sent in the direction of those people who are hoping to let their accommodation and you may be able to negotiate a better price if they are short of clients.

Hotels

It is often advisable to find yourself a hotel room whilst you are seeking accommodation, so that you don't feel obliged to jump at the first rental opportunity that you encounter. If you are out of season in tourist areas, you will find that you can negotiate a good price in hotels, which are open in the winter months. You will also find, if you speak to the hotel owners, that they will probably be aware of other people in the vicinity who have rental accommodation.

Tenancy Agreements

Tenancy agreements are as formal or as informal as the owners themselves. You will find that you are required to pay at least a month's rent as a deposit and probably very little else in terms of a financial commitment. You may be given a one or two page contract to sign. Do speak to either a lawyer or to a trusted friend who speaks fluent Greek and English before you sign anything. You will be responsible for your own electricity and water bills unless it is written into the agreement that this service is communal to all tenants. In that case you need to be certain what your percentage of the bill will be and approximately what the monthly cost will be.

Furnishing

Furnishing rented accommodation is not difficult as the majority of stores will deliver to your home at no extra charge. It is also possible to hire a small three-wheeled vehicle, which will ship things as large as beds and wardrobes across towns and cities, very cheaply. You will also find, if you are renting accommodation in someone else's home, that they will offer all sorts of items to help you to settle in. It is advisable to accept these with the good grace that they are given, even if you just put them in a corner and perhaps return them to the owner when you leave.

Heating

Heating furnished accommodation can be more problematic. If it is a summer apartment it will not have any heating facilities and you will need to buy an efficient stove. There are several types of ceramic electric heaters which are fairly efficient to run, but the easiest, and most economical is a second-hand Calor stove. Remember that Calor stoves must be kept clean and well maintained or the fumes will sting the eyes. You will also need to give some thought to warm curtains, as well as floor covering (marble and tiles are very cold in the winter), warm bedding and probably also draught excluders for the doors.

THE PURCHASING PROCEDURE

LOCAL PROFESSIONALS

Lawyers

You should ensure that the lawyer who has drawn up the contract of sale and purchase has undertaken a thorough search, not just into the title (ownership) of the property but also into any restrictions, permissions, formal or informal, which may exist about the present and intended future use of the house and its lands or plot of land. The most common problem encountered is that the parent or grandparent of the seller purchased the land at some time in the past but never completed the paperwork at that time. This means that the present vendor has the right to sell, but before she or he can legally do this, two generations of papers and fees, taxes and land search have to be undertaken. This takes time, and while it is proceeding, the vendor will almost certainly put the price up to cover the additional expenses that they have incurred.

It is presently rare in Greece for a vendor not to be the owner, or a descendant of the original owner of the property for sale. Such scams do still exist, but your lawyer will reassure you about this.

Power of Attorney. It is common practice in Greece that if you are not going to be able to be present whilst the purchase of your land or home is completed, it will be necessary for you to appoint an agent or principal to act on your behalf. Estate agents in tourist areas will act for you in all stages of the negotiation. It is only necessary for you to go to the conveyancing solicitor and to draw up a power of attorney, authorising the agent or other trusted person to act on your behalf in legal and financial matters to do with the purchase of the agreed property.

Most solicitors will give you advice on this and offer a standard power of attorney form. (A copy of a power of attorney for various activities can be obtained from the Greek Consul in London, and an English translation is available at an extra charge.)

By granting an official power of attorney, you will be protected by law and it will mean that you are not required to attend in person, even when funds are to be drawn down to complete the purchase, unless you wish it.

Surveyors

The second item of advice to intending purchasers of existing property is to obtain the services of a qualified surveyor. Greeks do not, as a matter of course, survey properties that they intend to buy, nor does the lending organisation require a survey before making funds available. As homes are normally built to the Greeks' own specifications, the main requirement is that they will be warm, waterproof, and liveable in. Many of the construction practices would shock a fastidious British or American builder, but, providing the exterior reinforced concrete shell is sound and earthquake proof, all other faults or problems can be remedied as time passes. However, there are professional surveyors in the majority of towns. They may have qualified in the USA, UK or South Africa, and the estate agent should be able to introduce you to one. He will be able to provide an unbiased survey of the condition of the building or plot of land as well as drawing up for you, estate agent type details showing dimensions, location and availability of services, access and the approximate age of the various parts of the construction as well as their condition and the extent of work necessary to rectify any major construction problems.

FEES, CONTRACTS AND CONVEYANCING

Getting the Process Underway

Once you have found the property that you wish to purchase, the agent will confirm the selling price with the vendor if you have made an offer which is not the asking price or have requested the price be negotiated. He/she will take a 10% deposit from you to confirm your interest and the process is underway. If you decide not to proceed with the sale you forfeit your deposit. If the vendor decides not to proceed with the sale he /she is required by law to render you twice the deposit paid.

Tax Valuation of the Property

The agent will then obtain a tax valuation that is the basis of all costs and fees. This can be as little as half of the agreed purchase price on older, un-modernised properties. In towns and cities the tax valuation is not usually open to much negotiation. The tax valuation has no impact on the purchase price. It is merely a convention which has evolved in Greece, a nation with high levels of tax but which is passionate about the national pastime of trying not to pay tax whenever possible.

Before Drawing up a Contract of Sale

A lawyer who has the responsibility of checking title as well as the dimensions of the land or property will draw up the contract of sale. The lawyer must also be satisfied that there are no restrictions on the sale or future development of the land or property and if there are to clarify these in the contract. The following items should all be checked.

- It is essential, especially when buying a piece of land, to assure yourself that it comes within the town plan, that is to say that it is being sold with the right to apply for planning permission to build a house. Plots outside the town plan can also be developed but there are local restrictions on the size of the original plot, usually 4000sq. metres, and only 5% can be developed. Your lawyer will clarify this for you.
- If it is an apartment in a house or block, the shared costs and responsibilities must be detailed.
- An area of law, which seems strange to non-Greeks is the issue of the ownership of olive trees. You may find from the land search that a neighbour has a tree on your land. The most usual procedure is to buy the tree for an agreed sum, usually in the region of €50. If you decide not to do this, the neighbour will have the right to access your land to collect his olives every year and to care for and prune the tree each winter.
- Your land search should also indicate which, and how many trees may be removed if it is your intention to develop the plot.
- If others have rights of access or there are informal rights such as the right to graze sheep or collect fruit from the trees, these need to be clarified at this point. This part of the process can be undertaken very quickly if title to the land has already been established.

The agent will then direct you to a *Symvolographos,* a solicitor who specialises in conveyancing land and property.

Contract of Sale is Ready To Sign

The agent will inform you when the contract is ready to be signed. The solicitor will present the contract of sale for your (or your agent's signature) and it is at this point that the balance of the money is handed over to the vendor. The vendor should pay the agent his fee in the solicitor's presence (this is still often done in cash). The property is then yours and the agent will present his/her closing account. If they have acted as your representative they will take their fee at this point and the closing account will detail all costs and fees deducted.

The tax is normally paid by the estate agent on your behalf and is based on the tax valuation, which has been agreed. This can be deemed to be the equivalent of British stamp duty or the old purchase tax.

Legal Costs

The lawyer's fee is in the region of €20 plus 1% of the agreed taxable value. This is the charge for the search and formally establishing details of title to the land and property.

The solicitor's charge is normally 2.2% of the agreed taxable value. This includes the preparation of all of the details of the sale and purchase contracts and the actual conveyancing of the property from vendor to purchaser or purchaser's agent.

Note that up to €15,000 it is not necessary to engage a lawyer for the sale, but is not advisable to do without legal advice at any stage of the process, for all the reasons already given.

Specialist UK-Based Lawyers

Bennett & Co Solicitors: 144 Knutsford Road, Wilmslow, Cheshire SK9 6JP; ☎01625-586937; fax 01625-585362; e-mail: internationallawyers@bennett-and-co.com; www.bennett-and-co.com.

Purchase Tax

At the time of writing, purchase tax is payable on land and property up to €12,000 at a rate of 9%. From €12,001 upwards, the rate is 11 %. This varies from region to region. Your estate agent will confirm the charges for you.

Note that these percentages are payable on the agreed taxable value of the property, not on the sale price.

Agency Fees

The American system is used in Greece. That is to say, the agent works for both the vendor and the purchaser. He or she thus obtains a fee both from the seller and the buyer. Normally the agent's services fee will be 2% to both parties. The vendor's fee will be included in the selling price. The fee from the purchaser will be included in the money payable when the sales contract is completed. A good agent will negotiate with the tax representatives and save more than his or her fee to you in respect of his negotiations on the tax due.

Note that it is very important to allow for these costs of purchase, presently in the region of 13%, when you set your budget for the price range that you are hoping to buy in. The purchase price for old properties is often quoted as an inclusive price, that is to say, the advertised price includes all expenses and fees payable.

Insuring your property

It is advisable to approach a UK company such as Insurance for Holiday Homes (☎01934-424040), Copeland Insurance (020-8656 8435; www.andrewcopeland. co.uu), or Ocean Breeze Properties (www.oceanbreezeproperties.co.uk/insurance-for-homes-abroad.htm) to insure your property. In fact you will find that it is a condition of any advance from any British or Greek bank in the UK that you lodge a copy of the insurance certificate with them. You will probably find that they will not insure against the risk of damage from earthquakes. They will also restrict the use of your home to yourselves, separate insurance is needed if you intend to rent out your overseas property.

For more information on insuring property abroad, see *Security and Home Insurance* in the *General Introduction* to this book. After you have explored the various option and relative merits of different schemes, you may find that insurance with a Greek insurance company meets your needs.

WILLS

Although not part of the purchasing procedure, wills should be made immediately on completion of property purchase in Greece. Under Greek law, as in several other European countries, land and property passes to the immediate heirs – spouse and children – of the deceased. An English will is valid in Greece, but it is strongly advised that you either draw up a will (it costs about €70) and leave it with a Greek speaking executor in Greece, or leave an authorised translation of your English will, also with an executor, as the time lapse in having a will translated and all the ensuing bureaucracy is not something that heirs should have to deal with in a foreign country after the death of a parent or spouse. If a deceased person has drawn up a local will, and it does not contradict or conflict with the will(s) in other countries, then the assets can be dealt with swiftly and efficiently under local laws and procedures. There will be a charge for administering the estate in Greece but it is well worth paying it to save your heirs any problems.

WHAT HAPPENS NEXT

SERVICES

Electricity

IPPC is Greece's public power corporation, which was partly liberalised in 2001. Deregulation of the electricity market in Greece has been slower than in some EU countries and the power industry will not be completely liberalised until 2005. Most of the islands are not linked to the national grid because of the expense of laying submarine cables. Those that are, tend to be large islands closest to the mainland. Electricity consumption has been growing at the rate of about 3.4% a year and the Greek authorities were concerned about the possibility of not supplying enough power in time for this year's Olympics.

For the general consumer, Greek power cuts are fairly regular. Even though some last only a few seconds, they can be lethal to computers so it is essential to have a power back-up for your PC. Surprisingly, considering Greece's sunny climate a mere 1% of power is solar generated. New power plants are mostly gas-fired.

Getting Connected

If you buy a pre-owned property, you or your lawyer/agent should have checked that bills to that property are paid up to date otherwise you will be liable for them. If you are lucky, the agent who arranged for you to purchase your property will also have dealt with the transfer of the utilities to your name. If not, then they or their representative will accompany you to the local electricity supplier's offices to make the necessary arrangements. You will need documents that prove your identity, and property purchase or rental documents, and your tax number (see Taxes section). If you are not resident in Greece, then you will probably want to set up a direct debit with a Greek bank or the post office to make sure that your bills are paid regularly.

Voltage, Plugs and the Adaptibility of Foreign Equipment. The voltage in Greece is 220 at 50 Hz. Sockets are two-pin, with or without earth *(suku)* depending on whether they are high (e.g. washing machine) or low (e.g. table lamp) wattage. It is advisable to bring plug converters and also multi-plug extensions as Greek houses generally have far fewer sockets than is customary in the UK or US ones. Note that the electrical equipment in some other countries runs at 110 volts and for this you will need to buy or bring a voltage converter. Check first to see if the appliance has a voltage converter switch already on it. The other problem with foreign appliances is that they may (as in the USA) be designed to run at 60 Hz. It is much less trouble to buy appliances new in Greece than to fiddle about with transformers and risk having appliances designed to run at 60 Hz overheat when they are run at 50 Hz.

Water

'Water, water everywhere, nor any drop to drink'
The water supply is a perennial problem for Greece. There was such concern in the run-up to the 2004 Olympics that a multi-million pound dam project, the Evinos Water Supply Project, which includes the new 35km tunnel from the dam on the River Evinos to the Mornos reservoir, was undertaken in order to guarantee the water supply to Athens. Of

course Greece is not the only Mediterranean country with a water problem but in Greece it is particularly severe. Subsidence of the coastline has caused a drop in the water tables and the concomitant loss of vital water reserves. Areas identified as severely affected include Thessaly, and Kalohori (in the Thessaloniki prefecture). This crisis has been caused mainly by the local authorities taking a short-term view in the early 1990s, by their massive exploitation (for industry and irrigation) of the underground water resources of the Attica basin. Over exploitation and the build-up of dissolved pollutants in underground water is very marked in the central and southern parts of Attica.

The islands are also not exempt from problems, especially during the height of the holiday season when visitors flood in and water floods out. For instance Hydra would be more appropriately called Dehydra, since every drop of its fresh water supply is delivered daily and at great expense by tanker.

Water Shortages

Unless you live in a mountainous region of Greece, you are going to be affected by water shortages. Municipalities impose restrictions on the water supply and it can be turned off for days at a time particularly in rural areas; mostly in summer. Typically, water pressure drops at peak times. This is particularly noticeable on the islands when everyone returns from the beach in early evening. If you live in an upper floor apartment, this may exacerbate the problem. Note that most modern, multi-storey developments have an electric pumping system, which keeps the pressure up, but leaves you literally high and dry if there is a power cut (see above).

The water situation in Greece means that you should choose a property with care making certain that the local water supply is reliable. For this you need to research the previous years' water records and find out from other residents in the area what the water supply is like during winter and more especially, what happens in summer.

Possible Measures to Alleviate Water Shortages

Wells and Dowsers. You may be lucky enough to find a property with its own well. However if you are viewing it in winter, bear in mind that this is when it is likely to be full. You need to try to find out if it drys out in summer (many do). You can also check if there is water on the property by employing a water diviner to see if you can locate a source there. If there is water, you can have your own bore hole sunk.

Water Storage Tanks. Most detached houses will have a water tank either on the roof, or underground (with a pump), for storing rainwater. The tank can also be filled manually, when there is likliehood of an interuption in water supplies, for instance if there are engineering or plumbing works in the locality. If you are having a property built on a plot of land, you can ask for advice on installing a tank. Water can also be recycled via a tank for non-drinking uses such as irrigating the garden or for flushing WCs.

Water Potability and Quality

Water *may* be safe to drink in all urban areas; whether you would want to imbibe is another matter. Tap water is often discoloured and brownish, and/or gives off a bouquet of chemical purifiers. In some areas, the water may even be downright dangerous to drink – where agricultural chemicals such as nitrates used in fertilisers have seeped into the water supply and polluted it. Of course you may be lucky enough to get good water from a mountain spring, but these are not usual on the coast where the water supply is scarcer and more likely to be saline. Most Greeks drink bottled water and it is probably best to follow their example. Even expensive domestic water purifier plants are not the answer as they are wasteful of water.

The Cost of Water

As we see, water has a scarcity value in Greece and this is matched by the cost to the consumer, which is above the EU average.

Bills. Water is metered and charged quarterly per cubic metre on a sliding scale; the more water you use, the more it costs per cubic metre. After 100 cubic metres, the charge peaks at nearly €2 per metre. Bills can be €500-€1,000 per quarter for a villa with a pool. Note that a missed payment will not necessarily result in disconnection; however, the water company will add a penalty charge to the next quarter's bill.

Note also that the local rates are also added to the water bill and VAT on the whole is at 18%.

Telephones

The Greek telecommunications group of companies is OTE, which was founded in 1949. The Greek telecommunications market was deregulated in 2001 and there are now other telecommunications companies from all over Europe competing in Greece which means the consumer is confronted by the usual confusing array of tariffs. However, OTE remains a market leader and has offices in most towns. Among OTE's successful subsidiaries are COSMOTE and OTEnet.

Getting Connected

For many people this still means a landline. To install or transfer an existing line to your name, you will need to visit the local telephone company office with a similar dossier of documents as for the electricity office (see above). The speed of the service will normally depend on whether you are taking over an existing line or having one installed or modified, and in either case may be slow. OTE will make the connection to the nearest distribution point. It is your responsibility to complete the connection to your home.

You may want to have an ISDN line installed so that you can use the phone and the computer simultaneously. The charge for this is modest and includes the ISDN modem. It will of course cost double the standing charge of a single line.

Bills. Billing is every two months; about €20 single line rental plus calls.

Mobiles. GSM mobiles work in Greece and you can connect through OTEnet and Hellas Online via a pay-as-you-go telestet number. Ask your home mobile service provider, which provider in Greece they recommend as best value. Other Greek-based providers of various types of mobile technology include Panafon and Cosmote.

Mobile phone numbers in Greece are prefixed with 693/694 or 697.

Internet

Greece is an internet nation and there is no difficulty getting connected. The national ISP is OTEnet and others are listed below.

ADSL Broadband. ADSL was launched commercially in Greece in summer 2003.

So far the costs are very high about €290 for a modem and €150 per month for 384kbps. Providers at present are OTE and Vivodi Telecom (www.vivodi.gr); the latter is cheaper.

Useful Websites – Telecommunications & Internet in Greece
Panafonet – www.panafonet.gr
OTEnet – www.otenet.gr
ACN – www.acn.gr or www.aias.gr
Forthnet – www.forthnet.gr
Hellas Online – www.hol.gr
Telepassport – www.telepassport.gr

SECURITY

Greece has a reputation as a very low crime country and many of the islands claim to be crime free. Greeks it seems may fiddle their taxes and your bills, but they do not, on the whole, steal moveable objects in any large quantity. Athens is the exception, although even there, the crime rate is lower than in most European capital cities.

This does not mean that you should not insure your holiday home as there are external factors beyond your control such as fire, lightening, earthquake, storms, flashfloods etc. that can cause damage to and render your property unrentable or liveable in. If you have bought a village house, then there is a strong likliehood that one of the friendly locals will offer to look in on the house while you are away and keep things shipshape. If you have land with your property you can reciprocate by letting them graze their animals or grow vegetables on it and this should help forge good relationships with the community, which is about the best security you can have.

Companies that insure holiday homes in various countries on the Mediterranean can be found in the *General Introduction*. Companies that cover Greek homes include those below.

Contacts for Home Insurance for Greece
Schofields: (el 01204-365080; holidayhomes@schofields.ltd.uk).
Insurance for Holiday Homes: ☎01934-424040; info@insuranceforholidayhomes.co.uk).
Copeland Insurance: (☎020-8656 8435; www.andrewcopeland.co.uk).

REMOVALS

Before you organise the removal of your household goods and chattels to Greece you should consider how much stuff you really need to import into Greece. Some items from your home country may look out of place in a typical Greek home (old or modern), and you may need to start from scratch. Many people who buy a property in Greece use local sources to furnish it. The other problem with bringing items from your home country is that the climate in Greece may be unsuitable for them, or they may be unsuitable for the climate; heavy furnishings and some types of antiques for example.

Once you have decided what possessions you want to import into Greece you will know whether they are of sufficient quantity to require a pantechnicon or whether you will be able to hire a van and move stuff yourself in one or more stages.

Details of importing household goods from one EU country to another and a list of international removal companies can be found in the *General Introduction* to this book. Also, in the *General Introduction* is detailed information of the Pets Passport scheme which enables you take family pets abroad for short or longer periods and bring them back to the UK without quarantining.

BUILDING OR RENOVATING

Architects

The first thing to do if you are planning to build a house from scratch or renovate an old house is to locate and hire an architect *(architecton)*. A Greek architect can be a civil engineer and/or a trained architect but he (it is usually he) is still called an architect. Some have trained abroad, for instance in the USA or elsewhere in Europe. You will have to go with a local recommendation if the choice is restricted in the area where you want to buy. Often, the estate agent with whom you are dealing will put you in contact with one.

You can then discuss your proposition with the architect who will inspect the property with you and tell you whether your plans are feasible vis-á-vis the planning restrictions imposed by the local authorities. These have become fairly stringent in Greece to prevent unregulated building damaging and degrading the environment. Even fir and olive trees are protected by law.

Building Permits

Building permit regulations may vary depending on the many possible factors involved including: location, proximity to protected beaches, archaeological sites, and ecological concerns. Generally, if the plot comes within the boundaries of the town or village planning permission will be granted, usually free of restrictions. On non-urban plots or those outside village limits you can usually build on a plot of 4000 sq. m. (minimum size) if there are no other local restrictions in place.

Getting a Building Permit. Once you have agreed with your architect what is possible, you can then apply for the building permit (or the architect will do it for you), which can take several months. Foreigners do not normally have to get the permit themselves. It is nearly always done by the architect, builder, or whoever you are dealing with, who as a local, knows the right people and the shortcuts. On the whole it is not advisable to get involved at all. The permit is granted by the Ministry of Planning in the local town hall. On the mainland this may be in the nearest large town. On the islands, it is usually the prefectural capital, which may not be on the same island. For instance, a permit for Paxos island would be applied for on Corfu and so on. These are things it would take a foreigner ages to sort out. The amount you will pay for the permit is dependent on the size of the property. A permit for only a smallish plot would cost about €9,000.

Note that many plots for sale have already been checked for building permission but you should not take this for granted. Also, the Building Permit is often included in the price of the contract, but again, it is important to check this fact as otherwise you will be landed with an unexpected extra cost for which you have not budgeted.

Building Costs and Hiring Workers

There are many factors, which can influence building costs and the cost of renovation. If you are building from scratch there should be a payment plan itemising the cost of each component. This applies particularly to off plan, where the costs are already known. For bespoke building projects, the costs should be agreed between client and architect in advance. Costs depends on the state of the existing property, whether access needs to be improved, whether it is already linked to electricity and water mains, what materials are being used and the cost of individual fixtures and fittings. With renovation, costs may be more difficult to estimate as things proceed piecemeal and there may be fluctuations in the costs of materials and even wages for labour. Renovation is where buyers usually end up spending more than they ever thought possible. This may be all right if you get what you want in the end and you can grin and bear the unanticipated extra cost and extended time scale, because you feel it was worth it. Greek builders are often over optimistic and you need to try to prevent yourself being carried along with them. You should keep your feet planted firmly on the ground in your dealings with them and never, ever pay everything up front. Paying in installments is best and remember to keep some of the payment back until after completion. Debbie Taylor, whose series of *Heat & Dust* articles about her Cretan ruin ran in the *Sunday Times* stated it thus:

> Taylor's First Law of Renovations states that any renovation work always costs exactly twice as much as your first estimate. Taylor's Second Law of Renovation states that the size of the cheque paid to a builder is directly proportional to the amount of forgetting that will take place afterwards. But it's not just the nasty surprises; it's all the minor things that I never even considered, that the builders omitted to mention until it came to committing to a definite price for the job. Propping up the vine pergola while the outside of the house re-rendered. Digging a hole to put the old render and rubbish in. Digging another hole for the rubble that will be taken out of the hole for the septic tank. And what about all the rubble from all the new holes? Where will that go? What will it cost? Where, oh where will it all end?

With all the variables it is difficult to give a cost of building, but you should allow at least €700 per square metre up to a maximum of €1,600 per sq. m. For renovation it should be about 40% less.

It is unusual to do DIY on your Greek property. For one thing it might offend local sensibilities and in a small town or village you should try to avoid this. What you might do is to ask local building experts to teach you their methods and then you can do some work on your own property at a later date.

Gardens

Gardens are an individual expression of personality and come in as many different styles as the people who create them. Wherever you are in Greece everything will grow abundantly as long as watering occurs frequently; and there's the rub. If you are a permanent resident you can tend your garden and keep it irrigated. On the other hand, if you are an infrequent visitor and have no arrangements for the garden to be watered in your absence, it is probably advisable to utilise what grows naturally well with or without water. As Debbie Taylor (see above) in her *Sunday Times* articles says:

> For an organic low maintenance alternative, look at what's growing wild instead: stands of prickly pear and yucca; thickets of pink and white oleander; scrambles of jasmine and morning glory, and not a watering can in sight.

There are also citrus, walnut and almond trees, the ubiqitous olives, and of course a vine growing over the door, which is essential for a really Greek garden.

PROPERTY GLOSSARY

Accountant	*logistis*
Architect	*architectonas*
Building permit	*arthia eftisimo* (A.E. followed by a number and date).
Buyer	*agorastis*
Civil engineer	*politikos mechanicos*
Contract	*simvolio*
Conveyancing lawyer	*symvolographos*
Currency import receipt (pink slip)	*apodixi issagoyis krimate*
Deposit	*prokatavoli*
Estate agent	*ktimatomesitis*
For sale	*poleet*
Lawyer/notary	*dikigoros*
Outline plan of land	*topographico*
Power of attorney	*plirex usios*
Price	*timi*
Rooms to let	*dhomatia*
To let	*eneekeeazete*
Planning office	*graphio polivomia*
Seller	*politis*
Tax	*foros*
Taxable value	*axia foros*
Town plan/building zone	*skedia*
Town hall	*dimarchio*

MAKING MONEY FROM YOUR PROPERTY

Renting Out

The most likely way that you will earn income from your property is to rent it out to holidaymakers. Some owners contrive to live in their property and have a self-contained floor, or a converted outbuilding that they can rent out. This means that you can have your cake and eat it, but on the other hand there may be some inconveniences such as being too available to clients, (which some owners might like). In such cases, owners can probably find tenants, if not by word of mouth then through adverts on the internet on expat and regional websites.

If you rent out the entire property be it an old village house or a new villa then you will probably need an agent. If it is your intention at the outset to let out your property then it is advisable to ask the agent what contacts they have in the area. Some of the larger established agents/developers offer property management services and rentals as part of their range of services to prospective buyers. Such agents are most likely to be based on the most popular islands such as Corfu and Crete. Such agents include the ones below.

Agents Offering Property Management Services.

Alpha Estate: (info@alphaestate.gr).
Europa Real Estate Crete (www.europa-crete.com).
David Watrous: (☎020-8232 9780; e-mail dew@vch.co.uk) of the Greek Islands

Club can arrange management services and rentals for property buying clients on Crete and the Ionian islands.

Thassos Property Services: www.homes-in-greece.com. Aileen French.

The money you can make out of renting will vary widely from year to year. Larger prime location property with a garden will command the highest weekly rates (e.g. £900-£1200 for a 4-bed, 4-bath villa on Rhodes), while an old village house in a village on one of the smaller islands will rent for at least (e.g. £300 for 2-bed, 2-bath village house on Kos), with the average being about £400-£500 per week.

If you employ an agent to manage the property they will take a percentage. However, many owners prefer to pay a flat fee to a website and advertise their property there and be contacted direct. Check out www.holiday-rentals.co.uk as an example, or just type 'villa rentals greece' into your search engine to find them.

Selling On

When it comes to selling your property in Greece, you can start with the agent who sold it to you. If there was no agent involved then by the time you come to sell you will have enough contacts to help you sell.

Note that there is not usually any capital gains to pay if you use the proceeds to buy another property in Greece. Otherwise, capital gains is charged as a percentage of the value of the property, usually in the range of 10%-25%.

SPOT CHECK – GREECE & GREEK ISLANDS

Political/economic stability:	Democratic government. One of the poorest EU members and now likely to lose its massive EU subsidies which will be diverted to the new EU members. Is beggared further by the cost of staging the 2004 Olympics, and sapped by a huge public sector. The government has also singularly failed to attract foreign investment. Needs major rethink on economic front.
Sunshine:	Average 2,600 hours per year.
Cost of living/taxes:	Much cheaper than the USA or northern Europe. Approx. monthly budget for 2 people living in a property is £620. Standard VAT is 18%.
Accessibility:	Mainly relevant to the islands: lots of direct charter flights in summer. Scheduled flights to Athens and onward domestic flights or high speed ferries in winter. Not all the islands have airports.
Property availability:	Mostly old houses (ruins) and new build. New resale property rare as Greeks like to swop old for new and then stay put.
Property prices:	Cheaper land than in most Mediterranean countries but premium on choice plots; typical cost of £700 per square metre for new houses. Building permits pricey: over £6000 for a 250 sq. metres home. Ruins from about £50,000 but allow as much again to restore.
Cost of property purchase as a % of property price:	10-15%
Ease of purchase/ ease of renovation:	The purchase process for foreigners is not nearly as well oiled as in Spain and France and you need to find a team (agent + lawyer + architect/builders) who are used to dealing with foreigners. Builders may be scarce in some places and can be difficult to pin down. If you want the job finished it's best to turn a blind eye to the fact that some may be illegal workers.
Annual property taxes:	No property tax if your house is worth less than €200,000/£140,000/ $246,487.
Investment potential:	Despite Greece's problems, the main islands are a magnet for foreign property buyers. Prices have been rising at an average 20% annually but more due to inflation than demand. Demand is however picking up in the hotspots. Choose your location carefully and expect 15-20% per annum rise.
Likely problems:	(1) an EU social survey of 2003 found that Greeks are the most xenophobic Europeans. (2) Greece is in a major earthquake zone and old houses may not be earthquake resistant. (3) There are severe water shortages everywhere except in the mountains.

BUYING A HOUSE ON THE MEDITERRANEAN

THE MEDITERRANEAN

ITALY

LIVING IN ITALY

CHAPTER SUMMARY

- So familiar were the English in Italy that for generations all foreigners were termed *inglesi* by the Italians.
- **Eating Out.** Sparse or unpretentious decor is common in restaurants and does not reflect the quality of the food.
  - Young children are welcomed and fussed over in Italian restaurants.
- **Getting There.** There are non-stop flights from the UK and USA to over 30 Italian cities.
- **Crime.** The Italian state has made some headway in containing organised crime which permeates Italian life and politics to the very top.
  - Foreign visitors are not normally the target of mafia crime, and can remain blissfully unaware of its existence; unlike petty crime which is endemic in tourist places e.g. Naples.
- **Media.** The quality Italian newspapers, which include some regional ones, are excellent and informative.
  - Italian television is monopolised by trashy quiz and games shows and soaps and is frequently described as 'crap', though there are some serious news programmes.
- **Post.** The post is much slower than in the USA or UK and you have to pay extra for next day arrival (which doesn't necessarily arrive next day).
- **Social Drinking.** Drunkenness is frowned on in Italy and brawls outside bars are rare.
- However, drinking wine from a young age is an accepted part of the culture.
- **Health.** Italian state hospitals, except in the north, can be depressing places with inadequate bathing and feeding facilities; but Italy has many excellent doctors.
  - In contrast with the public sector, the private sector of the health service is amazingly well organised.
- Most Italian citizens and foreigners in Italy have private health insurance.

- **Schools.** Italian schools do not have a particularly good reputation. The exception is at primary level. 57% of Italian schools do not have a certificate of stability for their buildings.
- **Food and Consumer Goods.** Italy tempts the consumer with the best quality products in food and luxury goods the globe can offer.
- **Italy** has a dazzling array of small specialist shops.

INTRODUCTION

The English-speaking peoples have had a love affair with Italy for hundreds of years. So familiar were the English in Italy that the word *inglesi* came to mean foreigners in general. Only recently have Italians learnt to distinguish between *inglesi* (English) and *scozzesi* (Scots), between *irlandesi* (Irish) *islandesi* (Icelandic) and *olandesi* (Dutch), between *australiani* (Australians), *nuova zelandesi* (New Zealanders) and *sud africani* (South Africans). Even the blanket expression *anglosassoni* (Anglo Saxons) in the Italian mind seems to include not only native English speakers but also Dutch, Scandinavian and Germanic people in general. But the important thing is that, thanks to the input of our illustrious antecedents, the *inglesi*, or the *anglosassoni*, and now especially the *americani* are admired – or at least tolerated – by the modern inhabitants of Italy. Even the anti-American, anti-capitalist no-global protesters of Italy wear American jeans, listen to American rock music and rap; and they are motivated by the ideology of American gurus such as Noam Chomsky and Ruth Klein.

In the 1960s a small trickle of English bohemians and hippie escapists, were buying old farm houses as the rustic hinterlands of Tuscany and Liguria, some of them making their own wine and oil. For a while coastal resorts like Rimini enjoyed an influx of mass Anglo-Saxon tourism, but this was soon diverted to Spain, Portugal, Yugoslavia, Greece and Turkey. Italy's own prosperity was the cause of this mass defection. From the 1950s Italians from the towns and cities could afford to buy or rent second homes at the seaside, to send their families away to escape from the *afa* or heat of the cities in July and August, or for the duration of the long school holidays (June to September). It was their birthright and culture. The result was that the coastlines were developed by Italians themselves, for themselves. There were a few Swedish, Dutch, Swiss, German colonies – but hardly any British – who had been lured away to other shores by their entrepreneurial travel agents. Besides, the Italian coastal resorts were too crowded. The Italians had become exuberant with their wealth, and very often their developments were ugly – and you had to *pay* for your deck chair and cabin in the *stabilimento balneare*.

It is estimated that Italy has no more than 100,000 British residents. This compares with an estimated 500,000 British in France and nearly a million in Spain. So Italy has a lot of catching up to do. Central Italy might be saturated, but there are plenty of other regions, most of them with a coastline. Think of Italy as being a giant peninsula, which therefore has a very long (8,000 miles) coastline and you will get an idea of how big the possibilities are; and that is before you contemplate also the very large islands of Sicily and Sardinia.

The remoter regions of Italy, including Molise, Abruzzo, Basilicata, Apulia and Sardinia are worth considering because they have largely escaped the industrialisation, pollution and tourism of the twentieth century and perhaps more to the point, houses and land are still cheap and low fare airlines have made these remoter areas more accessible.

HISTORY

Italy is a young country and was unified only in 1861. Its present constitution dates from 1948. But it has a rich and fascinating history and not without reason or consequences is it known as *il bel paese* (the beautiful country). It was this fatal beauty which has attracted migrants from all directions from time immemorial including most of the 'tribes' and civilisations from which modern-day Italians and their culture are descended. For instance, Etruscans, who almost certainly originated from Asia Minor furnished Rome with its first kings before being driven in retreat to their heartland – roughly modern Tuscany and Umbria, where many of the current inhabitants have been proven, through DNA analysis to be their descendants. The area the Estruscans colonised, produced through history a disproportionate number of creative geniuses: Dante, Giotto, Cimabue, Michelangelo, Leonardo du Vinci, Benvenuto Cellini, Botticelli, Donatello, Masaccio, Brunelleschi, Piero della Francesca – even Napoleon Bonaparte. It is tempting to think that this pool of talent is Etruscan in origin.

From the end of the thirteenth century to the end of the sixteenth century Italy became the most advanced country in Europe economically, commercially and artistically. This was the era of the independent *Comunes* or small city states. The incredible richness and diversity of the Italian Renaissance would have been unthinkable without this multiplicity of princely courts and petty states. Here we have the origin of Italy's still flourishing regional cultures.

In 1860, Tuscany, Modena, Parma, Bologna and Romagna voted in plebiscites to join the Monarchy. Umbria and the Marches were annexed, and the Kingdom of Italy was proclaimed in 1861; this movement of independence and re-unification is known as the *Risorgimento*. After the Second World War, in 1946, Victor Emmanuel III abdicated in favour of his son Humbert, but it was not enough to save the monarchy. In a referendum on June 2 1946 Italy voted for the abolition of the monarchy and the institution of a Republic. A committee was set up to write a Constitution, which was finalised in 1948.

POLITICS

Since the foundation of the First Republic in 1946 Italy has had more than fifty different 'revolving door' governments characterised by coalitions, horsetrading and a *sottogoverno* or 'undergovernment', of bewildering complexity, of wheeler-dealers and power-brokers in Rome, offering jobs for the boys and girls. *Lottizzazione* – dividing into lots – is the name given to the system whereby a plethora of political parties has carved out shares in the various national spheres of power such as the arts, media and the trade unions. Thus the channels of the state radio and TV RAI 1,2, and 3 each belong to different parties, becoming progressively left wing according to the number. The trade unions UIL, CIGL, and CISL are the same. Even the supermarket chains have political affiliations, the Co-op being left wing and CONAD right wing. The system has been called a *partitocrazia*, or rule by political parties. Because of proportional representation each party has a chance of being represented in Parliament; official funding comes from the state according to electoral performance.

Italian politics and the Mafia are intertwined, and corruption is a way of life. Giulio

Andreotti, known as the 'divine Giulio', active in politics since 1946 and seven times prime minister for the Christian Democrats ended his career in 2002 facing a 24-year sentence for complicity with the Mafia in the murder of a journalist. The present (2003) prime minister Silvio Berlusconi (*Forza Italia*) is a defendant in lawsuits, accused of such things as false accounting and bribing judges. Even notaries – who are representatives of the state – habitually recommend the lowest declarable and not the actual price in the conveyancing of real estate. Laws are negotiable. Politicians do not go to prison.

Berlusconi is surrounded by astute lawyers, who help him block and delay prosecutors, and he is an *amicu di li amici* (a friend of friends) to the Mafia, with mafioso cronies such as Senator dell'Utri. Foreigners are horrified by Berlusconi's dictatorial instincts and breathtaking conflict of interests. In January 2003 the magistrates throughout Italy demonstrated in silent protest, each one of them brandishing a copy of the Italian constitution. The signal was: don't mess with this, it is a precious document.

THE ECONOMY

In February 2003 a Mediobanca report revealed that only 15 of the world's top 274 multinationals were Italian, the most important of which, Fiat, was in serious difficulties. Even Switzerland and the Scandinavian and Benelux countries were doing better. Only 2.4% of Italy's industrial turnover was ploughed back into research compared with 4.7% in the US and the European average of 3.7%. Further education was starved of funds – there was a brain drain, mainly to the USA sometimes via the UK. The Censis report of January 2003 gave a picture of Italy as a 'dwarf with flat batteries' Italian capital and Italian industrial plant was emigrating to central and eastern European countries where labour was cheap and welfare poor – not to the *Mezzogiorno* of Italy. Italian entrepreneurs were besotted by countries like Romania (often returning with track-suited child brides).

Economic commentators, including President Ciampi, felt that future prosperity depended on a reform of the labour market, education and research, a massive improvement in the infrastructures and the promotion of big conglomerates. From the outsider's point of view, the collapse of the Fiat motor company suggests that Italy is not good at running large conglomerates, but has a true talent for clusters of small, cutting edge, often family businesses, half in and half out of the black economy, to which the government instinctively turns a blind eye: not so much Fiat cars as Malaguti motorbikes. *L'arte di arrangiarsi* – the national art of getting round the law- is epitomised by Premier Berlusconi, of whom ex-president Francesco Cossiga said: 'It is better to be governed by a clever con-man (*un'imbroglione*) than by an incompetent nice guy'. To which the Italian people add a strong dose of civility and altruism, a surviving spirit of mutuality and an idealistic younger generation almost totally opposed to multi-nationals. Italy is still the fifth or sixth largest economy in the world: a *serie 'A'* country.

IMMIGRANTS & RACISM

In Italy, where the birthrate has been declining since 1964, immigrants are doing the jobs that Italians no longer want to do, from Senegalese fishermen in Trieste to Chinese sweatshop workers in Prato, from Cameroon tannery workers in Croce sull'Arno to Ukrainian carers in Vicenza, from Peruvian houseboys in Radda to Filipino maids in Rome. They are encouraged to pay taxes through come-clean amnesties called *sanatorie*, and according to

Antonio Fazio, the governor of the Bank of Italy, they are a 'precious resource' for Italy. But the fact remains that 62.9% of Italians are racist towards Africans, 18.5% towards eastern Europeans, 7.5% towards Asians and 3% towards South Americans (according to a recent survey by the 'National Xenophobia Observatory').

GEOGRAPHY

Mainland and Offshore Italy

Italy occupies an area of 116,000 square miles (301,278 sq km). As well as the long, peninsula, which as most schoolchildren learn, is shaped like a boot, Italy's offshore elements include the island of Sicily situated off the toe of the boot across the Strait of Messina, the islands of Pantelleria, Linosa and Lampedusa which lie between Sicily and Tunisia, the island of Elba located off Tuscany, and the rocky, barren island of Sardinia which lies west of Rome and south of Corsica. Out of a total of 20 official regions only four do not have a coastline. The Tyrrhenian Sea bounds the south west of the peninsula, with the Ionian Sea under the sole of the boot. The Adriatic Sea lies on the eastern side between Italy and former-Yugoslavia. Italy shares borders with France, Switzerland, Austria and Croatia.

Main physical features include the Alps, which form much of the northern border with Slovenia, Austria, Switzerland and France. Also in the north are Italy's main lakes: Garda, Maggiore and Como. An offshoot of the Alps curves round the Gulf of Genoa and runs spine-like down the peninsula to form the Apenines. The longest river, the Po, lies in the north and flows from west to east across the plain of Lombardy and into the Adriatic. On Sicily, the regularly active volcano, Mount Etna rises to 10,741 feet (3,274 m). Etna has been very active since 2001 and some experts are predicting more eruptions.

EARTHQUAKES & VOLCANOES

The European fault line runs right through Italy from north to south. The main risk areas for quakes are central and southern Italy (from Umbria to Calabria) where about 70% of the region is susceptible. Tremors are quite common in Umbria and the Appenines. Seismologists claim that the number, strength and frequency of quakes hitting central Italy is increasing, which has led to a drop in tourism and house buying by foreigners. Italy's last big disastrous earthquake flattened Messina in 1908, killing 84,000 people and causing the shoreline to sink by half a metre overnight. Other serious ones were Friuli (1976), Irpinia (1980), and Umbria (1997) – the most dramatic recent quake caused severe damage to the Church of Assisi in front of the television cameras. Another in Molise in 2002 caused a substandard school to collapse killing 20 children.

As if this were not excitement enough, Italy has three active volcanoes. The most infamous of these is Vesuvius near Naples, which buried 2,000 inhabitants in their hedonistic city of Pompeii in AD79. These days the volcano's rumblings are under continuous monitoring so there should be plenty of warning before it pops again. The other volcanoes are comfortingly offshore (unless you live there): Etna on Sicily and Stromboli on a small island off the western coast of southern Italy.

CLIMATE

The climate of Italy shows the kind of regional variation one would expect from a country with its head in the Alps and its toe in the Mediterranean. The Italian Riviera (Liguria) is pleasantly mild in winter, Venice is bone chillingly cold and foggy in winter, while in the south, including Sicily, winters are even milder than Liguria's and typically Mediterranean. The far south and Sicily are decidedly hot in summer.

Italy, especially its islands, is exposed to winds, which can make life very uncomfortable for people and plants depending on the season.

AVERAGE TEMPERATURES				
City & Province	Jan	Apr	July	Nov
Ancona (Marche)	42°f/6°c	56°f/14°c	77°f/25°c	55°f/13°c
Bari(Puglia)	46°f/8°c	57°f/14°f	77°f/25°f°	59°f/15°c
Cagliari (Sardinia)	53°f/11°c	60°f/15.6°c	78°f/25.4°c	69°f/20.7°c
Genova (Liguria)	46°f/8°c	56°f/14°c	77°f/25°c	55f/13°c
Naples (Campania)	48°f/9°c	56°f/14°c	77°f/25°c	59°f/15°c
Palermo(Sicily)	50°f/10°c	61°f/16°c	77°f/25°c	60°f/16°c
Rome (Lazio)	45°f/7°c	57°f/14°c	78°f/26°c	55°f/13°c
Trieste (Friuli-Venezia)	41°f/5°c	55°f/13°c	75°f/24°c	52°f/11°c
Venice (Veneto)	39°f/4°c	55°c/13°c	75°f/24°c	52°f/10°c

GETTING THERE

By Air

Non-stop flights are available from the UK to over 30 Italian cities. If you change to a domestic flight at Milan or Rome, you can reach still more. Ryanair has the largest number of Italian destinations and uses Stansted. Due to the constantly changing nature of the airline industry and the spreading network of the budget airlines, it is likely that origin and destination airports as well as airlines will change frequently.

AIRPORTS/AIRLINES: THE UK & IRELAND & ITALY							
	Aer Lingus	Alitalia	BMI	British Airways	EasyJet	My TravelLite	Ryanair
Alghero (Sardinia)				o			o
Ancona							o
Bari				o	o		
Bologna (Borgo Panigale airport)	o						
Bologna (Marconi airport)					o		
Brindisi				o			
Catania (Sicily)					o		

Florence (Peretola airport)		o						
#Forli airport (for Bologna)								o
Genova					o			o
Milan (Linate airport)	o	o	o		o			
Milan (Malpensa airport)	o	o			o			o
Naples					o	o		
Palermo								o
Pescara					o			o
Pisa (for Florence)					o	o		o
Rome (Ciampino airport)						o		o
▲Rome (Fiumicino airport)	o	o			o	o		
Treviso aiport (for Venice)								o
Trieste					o			o
Venice (Marco Polo airport)		o			o	o		

Forli is 45km from Bologna
▲Rome Fiumicino airport is also known as Leonardo da Vinci

Milan Linate is 10 km east of the city and Milan Malpensa is 46km north-west of the city. Malpensa to Milan is by Malpensa Express (train) and the Malpensa Shuttle coach.

Most of the airlines listed below allow passengers to book flights online. Other airline details can be found in *The General Introduction*.

Aer Lingus: (☎0845 084 4444; www.aerlingus.com) flies direct from Dublin.

Air Malta: www.airmalta.com has direct flights to Catania (Sicily).

Alitalia: (☎0870 5448259) flies Heathrow and Gatwick to Rome, and Gatwick to Venice and Florence.

BMI: (☎0870 6070555; www.flybmi.com) flies Heathrow to Milan (Linate).

British Airways: (☎0870 8509850; www.ba.com) uses Heathrow and Gatwick.

British European: (☎08705 676 676; www.flybe.com) flies from Southampton to Bergamo (for Milan).

MyTravelLite: (☎0870 1564 564; www.mytravellite.com) new small airline uses Birmingham.

Virgin Express: 020-7744 0004 (in the UK), 02-482 96 000 (Milan), 800-097 097 (Rome & other areas), www.virgin-express.com.

Airlines Offering Direct Flights from the USA and Canada:

NorthWest: 800-447 4747 (US – international reservations), www.nwa.com

Delta: 800-221 1212 (in USA and Canada) 800-864 114 (in Italy), www.delta.com;

Alitalia: 800-223 5730; www.alitaliausa.com.

Air Canada: www.aircanada.ca.

Travel Agents. Agents specialising in offering discount fares to Italy can be found in the Travel sections of newspapers such as *The Sunday Times, The Sunday Telegraph* and *The Mail on Sunday*. The websites of many agents and budget airlines offer special deals and discounts and special offers change frequently. It is also worth looking at the following websites:
Lupus Travel: www.lupustravel.com
Orbitz: www.orbitz.com
Holiday Choice: www.holidaychoice.co.uk

Approximate Flight Durations
London to Rome – two and a half hours
New York to Rome – ten hours
Los Angeles to Rome – Fifteen and a half hours
Sydney to Rome – just over twenty-four hours

Documents. Note that if driving to Italy it is advisable to carry all your car documents with you, i.e. driving licence, car registration document (known as *patente* and *libretto* respectively), insurance certificate, and certificate of roadworthiness.

Getting to the Islands

Ferries. There are regular ferry connections between the mainland of Italy and the islands. Large car ferries run from the ports of Genova, Civitavecchia and Naples to Sardinia and Sicily. There are also ferry connections from the mainland to the smaller Tremiti, Bay of Naples and Pontine islands. The ferries also make international trips from the mainland to Malta, Corsica, Spain, Greece, Turkey, Tunisia, Egypt and Israel. Fares are reasonable although you may have to book well in advance, especially over the holiday season in the summer months. In the winter the number of crossings is greatly reduced. In Italy the tourism office and travel agents can provide information, which can also be found on the website www.traghettionline.net or the websites of the ferry operators, some of whom are listed below.
Minoan Lines: www.minoan.gr
Agoudimos Lines: www.agoudimos-lines.com
Strintzis Line: www.strintzis.gr

COMMUNICATIONS

The Post Office

The Italian postal system, *Poste e telegrafi* (PT) is improving; mail deliveries are getting quicker, though overnight delivery can not be relied upon.

Stamps. These can be bought from the post office (*ufficio postale*) and also tobacconists (*tabaccherie)*. Post office opening times vary depending on location but they are open Monday to Friday (some open at 8am) until 2pm (some until later 6.30/7pm) and until lunchtime on Saturdays. You can get precise information on post offices' opening times from your municipal website.

Domestic Post. Items weighing under 3 kg can be sent *posta celere*, which is supposed to take one day, or priority (*posta prioritaria* – almost guaranteed next day delivery for post less than 2 kg), or ordinary (*ordinaria* – probable delivery within three or four days). For registered post (*posta raccomandata*) the post office supply a confirmation of receipt of your letter at its destination; while *Posta assuricata* insures the contents of a letter, within Italy.

Parcel Post. For parcels there is *Pacco celere1* – takes a day, less than 30 kg within Italy; *Pacco celere3* – takes 3 days, less than 30 kg within Italy.

Other Services Offered by the Post Office. In addition to the regular postal services, larger post offices in major cities are now offering financial services, as do post offices in other parts of Europe. Services offered include bank accounts *(conto bancoposta),* savings schemes, money wire transfers and bill payment services for most bills you are likely to receive (gas, electricity, telephone, rent, etc.).

Telephones

The Italian telephone giant Telecom Italia was privatised in 1997, thus bringing Italy towards liberalisation of her telecommunications market in line with EU directives. Fibre optic cables have been installed throughout the country – except in remote rural districts. Public telephones take coins, or more usually, phonecards. Note that the sign *guasto,* often posted on public telephones means 'out of order'.

CHEAP TIME

The cheapest time to make calls is from 10pm-8am Monday to Saturday and all day on Sundays. As the cheap rate for evening calls in Italy doesn't come into effect until 10pm, it is quite usual to make long distance calls late into the night.

DIALING TELEPHONE NUMBERS IN ITALY

Phone users need to dial the complete number of the person they wish to contact, including the area code, even for local calls. This system is common in Europe and possibly heralds the introduction of a seamless European phone system sometime in the future.

Expatriates (*extracomunitari*) who use international phones more than most for keeping in touch with friends around the world have long used money saving services such as call-back. Further details of cheaper ways to phone are in the *General Introduction.*

Mobiles. The mobile phone (*telefonino* or *cellulare*) has become the vital accessory without which no self-respecting Italian would dare to be seen. Tim is the mobile telephone subsidiary of *Telecom Italia* and has the widest coverage for those who travel extensively. Roaming agreements, where you can use the phone outside Italy, are another useful option for frequent travellers.

International Calls to and From Italy. To telephone the US from Italy the country code is 1 followed by the ten digit number, including the area code, e.g. 00-1 123 456 7890.

To telephone Italy from the UK dial 00 39 and then the Italian number. The first zero of the provincial code must be included. For example to ring a Rome number of 06-123456 you would actually dial 00-3906-123456. From the US it is necessary to dial the international access code of your service provider, followed by 39-06-123456.

LOCAL TELEPHONE CODES

Alassio	0182	Naples	081
Aosta	0165	Palermo	091
Bologna	051	Pesaro	0731
Bolzano	0471	Pisa	050
Cagliari	070	Riccione	054
Cattolica	0541	Rimini	0541
Como	031	Rome	06
Cortina d'Ampezzo	0436	San Remo	0184
Diano Marina	0183	Sorrento	081
Florence	055	Taormina	0942
Genoa	010	Trento	0461
Grado	0431	Trieste	040
La Spezia	0187	Turin	011
Lido di Jesolo	0421	Venice	041
Lignano	0431	Verona	05
Milan	02	Viareggio	0584

Emergency & Useful Numbers

Ambulance	118
Breakdown Services	116
Carabinieri	112 or 113
International Directory Enquiries	170
Enquiries for Europe & the Mediterranean	176
Telephone faults/engineers	182

The Internet

Italy was one of the slowest European countries to jump on the internet bandwagon, though it is now catching up – Italian municipalities (e.g. Rome) now have websites where they provide information in English for expatriates.

There are a number of free access (but you pay for the phone call) ISPs in Italy, www.jumpy.it and www.kataweb.it are two, who give away CDs in store to attract new clients.

FOOD AND DRINK

Food

Many myths surround the Italians, and their eating habits are no less liable to exaggeration or misconception than other aspects of their lives. Admittedly, whether the pasta is cooked *al dente* (just right) or *una colla* (sticky and overcooked) is an issue treated with near religious reverence. However, despite the world-famous ice creams, pizzas and pasta dishes, the Italians boast one of the lowest incidences of heart disease in Europe (and consume less ice cream than most of their European neighbours). The basis of Italian eating tends towards quality. Despite the majority of Italians finding obesity unacceptable, (unless you are as charismatic as Pavarotti), it is noticeable these days that childhood obesity has hit Italy where a recent article in *Corriera della Sera* claimed that a third of Italian children are now seriously overweight.

The three main meals of the Italian day are treated with varying degrees of importance. Breakfast (*colazione*) is usually a frugal offering of croissant (*cornetto*) or biscuits (*biscotti*), although cereals are gaining popularity in the Italian market. Italians often take breakfast (i.e. a capuccino and a croissant) in a bar. Lunch (*pranzo*) is treated as the main meal of the day in the southern regions although home-cooked food is increasingly being superseded by convenience food. Finally, dinner (*cena*), as in the majority of Mediterranean countries, is eaten late in the evening, usually between 8pm and 10pm, especially during the summer months.

The Slow Food Movement. Italy, more than France which has surrendered to Disney and Macdonalds, is still holding out as a counter culture to the Americanization of Everything. Americans are attracted in Italy by what they miss out on in America, such as fresh produce that has a taste, culinary artisans at work, life in the piazza, and slow food. The Slow Food Movement (whose symbol is a snail) is lobbying against genetically modified organisms, and is pro organic food. Also, through its publishing company (*Slow Food Editore; www.slowfood.it*) it produces a range of books which deal, in encyclopaedic fashion, with all the food traditions of Italy.

Drink

Being drunk (*ubriaco*) carries a special disapproval amongst the majority of Italians which would be thought curious by the lager-lout bravados of the British pub and club scene or the average Swedish adolescent. However, drinking wine from a young age *is* an accepted part of the culture, unlike in the USA. However, according to the Italian Statistics Institute, ISTAT, the majority of men and a significant percentage of women now choose beer above wine. This may be a result (or a cause) of the mushrooming of English-style pubs in the larger cities.

Wine. Most of Italy is wine country and there is no space to do justice to the many varieties here. Suffice it to say that some areas have gone in for professional production and export while others have kept their traditions and best wines a secret from the outside world. Probably the best known wines abroad are those from central Italy, especially the Chianti wines from the Tuscan hills between Florence and Siena. Southern Italy has the Neapolitan wines of Ischia, Capri and red and white wines from the area around Mount Vesuvius. Sicily's best-known wine is probably the sweet and treacly Marsala.

SCHOOLS AND EDUCATION

Education in Italy is a truly democratic system guaranteed by the constitution, compulsory from age 6 to 15, and controlled by the *Ministero dell'Istruzione dell'Università e della Ricerca* (acronym MIUR) the Ministry of Education, Universities and Research).

Recent changes passed through parliament in 2002 are bringing the Italian system more into line with other EU countries:

○ State schools now have local autonomy as a constitutional right.
○ They are free to organise their own timetables, curricula etc.
○ Each school must produce a plan of the education on offer (macronym *Pof*), a sort of identity card.
○ Schools – teachers and children – are to be monitored by a national evaluation institute (macronym: *Invalsi*), with assessment tests on children at 11, 14 and 16. This will be introduced gradually and only covers 25% of schools to start with.

The earthquake tragedy in Molise in 2002, in which a substandard, modern schoolbuilding collapsed and killed 20 schoolchildren, has drawn attention to the shocking physical state of many of Italy's schools. 57% of the 10,800 state schools lack a certificate of stability.

Under 10% of Italy's schools are run by religious or private bodies. Private schools have parity with the state schools and are subject to the same standards. Six regions offer vouchers to subsidise children at private schools. The *scuola statale*, the state education system, is part of the national identity, for both rich and poor. The whole nation participates in the annual drama of the state exams every summer. The aim is to keep children longer in education – up to 18 and beyond.

Implicit in the Italian state education system is the premise that school is supplementary to – and not a substitute for – the family. It is the family which must give children their main *educazione*. The word *educato* means well-brought up, well-mannered, as well as educated in the English sense. Parental back-up is vital – at home. At school – the teacher rules.

The Italian School System

The Italian school system is now organised as follows:

Scuola d'Infanzia (Infants School) otherwise known as *scuola materna* or *asilo*, lasts for three years starting from age 2½ to3 and is optional, but attended by 95% of children.
Scuola primaria (Primary School) lasts for five years starting from age 5½ to 6, and is compulsory.
Scuola secondaria (Secondary School) lasts for three years with an exam at age 13-14) to complete the first level (*ciclo*) of education. The second level (*ciclo* or cycle) offers a choice between *liceo* schools and vocational schools, with the possibility of switching courses under qualified teachers' guidance.

In Italian schools there is no streaming, no competition, no class marks, or orders. It is a contest between each student and the system: education by attrition rather than by encouragement. Unlike the American system – but more like the French system – children are not taught how to feel good about themselves. Teachers are stinting with their praise. Often this is difficult for children to cope with, and they can become depressed or even suicidal. However oral skills are encouraged. 35% of the state exam marks are *viva voce* (20% course work, 45% written). The result is that Italian educated children are notably eloquent.

International Schools

There are numerous schools in Italy that are possible options for expatriates, the majority of which are of high quality and offer a continuous style of education for transient expatriate children. They also offer easier access to UK and North American higher education and ensure that the level of English (or German, French or other language) of the expatriate child remains at native level. The organisation ECIS (www.ecis.org) can provide a list of international schools in Italy (see *General Introduction* for more information about International Schools).

Italian Universities

Italian Universities have also been reorganised in the new reforms – more autonomy and diversification and encouragement of research, and a system of credits, and scholarships.
The degrees are as follows:

O   *laurea di primo livello* or triennale after three years (general).
O   *laurea di secondo livello* or *specialistica* after five years (specialised).
O   *master*, very specialised, often tailor-made and sponsored by industry.

In a recent Censis survey the best universities in Italy, divided into five categories, were as follows:

Superlicei (up to ten thousand students): Reggio Calabria, Viterbo (Tuscia Lazio), Camerino (Le Marche).

Small Universities (between ten to twenty thousand students): Trento (Trentino/Alto Adige), Siena (Tuscany), Venice (Veneto) Cà Foscari.

Medium Universities (between twenty and forty thousand students): Calabria (Cosenza), Parma (Emilia Romagna), Pavia (Lombardy).

Mega Universities (over forty thousand students): Padua (Veneto), Bologna (Emilia Romagna), Turin (Piedmont).

Polytechnics (Universities with only two faculties: Engineering and Architecture), Turin (Piedmont), Milan (Lombardy), Bari (Apulia).

ITALIAN TAXES

There are numerous taxes in Italy and so only the main ones that expatriates will be most likely to come across will be covered below. As the tax regulations change frequently it is worth checking what the current situation is. Information is available on the internet, though self-employed expatriates earning income in Italy are well advised to employ an accountant. *The Informer*, an English language website (www.informer.it) for expatriates in Italy is a goldmine of advice on tax issues and goes into much more detail than is possible here. The taxes expatriates might incur are:

Imposta sul redditi delle persone fisiche (IRPEF). This is income tax levied in a format most people are used to, i.e. it is a progressive tax that increases with the amount you earn. US citizens in particular are likely to consider the rates very high. However, Italians get a lot in return for their taxes in the form of pensions, health care and other social security benefits and the rates are not the highest in the EU. Tax rates begin at 23% and go up to 45% for high earners. Employees have the taxes deducted at source every month by their employer based on an estimate of the year's tax – any necessary adjustment will be made early in the following year. Self-employed workers operate under a complicated system whereby some taxes are paid at source and some in arrears – expert advice from an accountant is recommended.

Imposta regionale sulle attività produttive (IRAP). This is a corporate tax that is charged to every business no matter how small. The rate is decided by the region in which the business is located. IRAP also includes health contributions. It is a tax on services and goods produced, on the difference between the value realised after specified production costs (except labour costs) have been deducted. The basic rate of IRAP is around 4.25% (reduced agricultural rate 3%).

Imposta sul redditi delle persone giuridiche (IRPEG). This is a corporate tax levied on S.r.l. and S.p.A. type companies; not generally applicable to self-employed workers.

Imposta sul valore aggiunta (IVA). This is VAT (value added tax) and is levied on all sales, whether retail, wholesale, or for services. There are three rates of 4%, 10% and 20%, the standard rate being 20%. Most foodstuffs are taxed at 10%.

Social security contributions. Whilst these are not really a tax, they amount to approximately 10% of income.

When trying to estimate your tax bill it should be borne in mind that a number of allowances are available that can be deducted from the taxable income and therefore reduce the amount of tax payable. A married employee with a dependant spouse and two children in full-time education will pay much less tax than a single, childless employee. Housing allowances, education allowances, overseas living allowances and many of the other benefits that expatriates may enjoy are all counted as part of their income and their value will be taxed and added to the tax liability.

2003 INCOME TAX RATES (IRPEF)

Income	Tax rate
up to €15.000,00	23%
€15.000,00 to €29.000.00	29%
€29.000,00 to €32.600,00	31%
€32.600,00 to €70.000,00	39%
over €70.000,00	45%
Regional and municipal IRPEF vary according to the region and city of residence.	

ALLOWANCES IN EUROS FOR DEPENDANT SPOUSE AND CHILDREN FOR 2003-2004

Spouse		
Total income up to €15.493,71	€546,18	
€15.493,71 to €30.987.41	€546,18	
€30.987,41 to €51.645,69	€496,60	
Over €51.645,69	€422,23	
Children		
General Conditions	Up to €51.645,69	Over €51.845,69
For the first child	€303,68	€285,08
For each further child	€336,73	€285,08
If single parent – for the first child same allowances as for spouse (see table above)		
Further deductions for each child under 3 years	€123,95	€123,95

Other allowances, up to a maximum of 19%, including medical expenses, life assurance, mortgage interest on property in Italy and limited university tuition fees can also be claimed in certain circumstances.

THE CODICE FISCALE

Any contract or official transaction in Italy requires, along with your identification details, an Italian tax code number (*codice fiscale*) which is made up according to a formula of letters and numbers taken from your name, date of birth, birthplace and sex. Plastic *codice fiscale* cards are issued by your local comune or tax office (Ufficio delle Imposte Dirette). They can also be obtained through Italian consulates. Numbers can be worked out for you on the internet (www.codicefiscale.com).

Owing to the complexity of taxation it is strongly recommended that you take independent, expert financial advice before moving to Italy as well as after arrival. A list of such advisors in the UK can be obtained from the Financial Services Authority (25 The North Colonnade, Canary Wharf, London E14 5HS; ☎020-7676 1000; www.fsa.gov.uk).

The estimated amount of both income and business taxes are payable in two tranches in May and November. There are big fines for non-payment and under estimation of the amount due. Late payment is also penalised with fines.

Further information and advice can be obtained from:

British Chamber of Commerce in Italy: www.britchamitaly.com.

American Chamber of Commerce in Italy: www.amcham.it.

Penta Consulting, Business & Fiscal Advisor Firm; tax-law-firm@geocities.com; www.geocities.com/WallStreet/4019/.

Invest in Italy, Investor Advisor; http://investinitaly.com.

Studio di Consulenza Aziendale:, Accountant, Largo Augusto, 3 – 20122 Milano, Italy; tel. 02 796141; fax 02 796142; info@cosver.com; www.scaonline.it.

HEALTH

Simultaneously with some of the best doctors in Europe, Italy possesses some of the scruffiest hospitals. In common with other systems under state control in Italy, the state medical system costs the government (i.e. the taxpayer) a fortune yet many hospitals are depressing places and with their lack of bathing and feeding facilities and general condition are in a far worse state than British or American ones. However, there are many excellent doctors, especially in private clinics and Italy has a clutch of world-renowned specialists. There is a pronounced north/south divide in the health service with the hospitals in the north being generally very good. However, there are usually long delays in receiving diagnostic tests, which can have severe implications when patients turn out to have serious diseases. If you use the state system you may have to wait weeks. However, the doctor treating you has the power to stamp your request for tests as most urgent, in which case you could go to the top of the list.

Many Italian residents, both nationals and expatriates, have private health insurance (see below) in case they need basic care, let alone long-term, expensive hospitalisation. Note that a list of local national health centres and hospitals is available from your local health authority (*Azienda Sanite Locale/Unita Sanitarie Locali*) in Italy; also most local embassies or consulates should be able to provide a list of English-speaking (private) doctors in your region.

When purchasing private healthcare it is essential to read the small print to ensure that the coverage is as complete as possible and covers all your possible future requirements – exclusions can be extensive. Paul Wolf of Innovative Benefits Solutions (www.ibencon.com) says, 'there are no bargains out there, you get what you pay for'.

For details of the E111 reciprocal medical treatment form and how to receive sickness and disability allowances from the home country, in Italy, see the *General Introduction*.

Using the Health Service

Anyone who makes social security payments in the EU, who receives an EU state pension, is unemployed, or under the age of 18 is entitled to the benefits of medical treatment on the Italian state health service *(Servizio Sanitario Nazionale)* free of charge. These include free hospital accommodation and medical treatment and up to 90% of the cost of prescription medicines; a contribution *(il ticket)* of 10% is required from the patient. Social security payments, which account for approximately 8% of a worker's gross income, are deducted from the employee's gross salary by the employer.

Obtaining a National Health Number. Any foreigner who has become a resident and who is eligible to receive treatment under the Italian state system is obliged to register with and obtain a national health number from the local *Unità Sanitaria Locale* (a.k.a. USL). You will need to produce your *permesso di soggiorno* (residence permit), and self-employed or freelance workers should first register with the INPS in Piazza Augusto Imperatore 32, Rome, where they will be given the necessary documentation to take to the local ASL office together with their *permesso di soggiorno*. ASL addresses can be found in the *Tuttocittà*, a supplement that comes with Italian telephone directories, or alternatively in the local newspaper.

SHOPPING

Italy tempts the consumer with the best quality products that the globe can offer. Every large town has at least one shopping centre *(centro commerciale)*, which is up to the best European or American standards of quality and design. The *Ipercoop* CO-OP chain now dominates the scene. It is a mutual co-operative society, which sells everything from white goods (made in Pordenome), to bread baked fresh on the spot in wood-fired ovens. Preference is given to local products and goods sourced in Italy under strict ecological control. *Superal, Conad, Esselunga, Upim, Standa, Despar* are names of other chains, and *Auchan* from France has partnered *La Rinascente* of Milan to carve a large niche in the north.

MEDIA

Newspapers

There is no real equivalent of the most popular British tabloids and US supermarket newspapers, and only the down market papers, e.g. *Il Messaggero* carry horoscopes, cartoons or fun features.

The most widely consumed Italian dailies are *Il Corriere della Sera* (Milan) and *La Repubblica* (Rome), both of which have circulations around the half million mark. *La Stampa* (Turin) follows with just over four hundred thousand . *Il Giornale* and *Il Messaggero* trail in with less than two hundred thousand.

The two main financial dailies – *Il Sole/24 Or* and *Italia Oggi*, are reasonably extensive in their coverage. The three sports dailies are *Corriere dello Sport, Gazzetta dello Sport* and *Tuttosport*. The regional newspapers, which focus on national news but include several pages of local news and comment, are particularly popular and widely read in Italy. These include: *Il Gazzettino* (www.gazzettino.it) Venice, *Il Mattino* (www.ilmattino.it) Naples, *La Gazzetta del Mezzogiorno* (Bari), *L'Unione Sarda* (www.unionesarda.it) Sardinia and *Il Piccolo* (www.ilpiccolo.it). Trieste.

A comprehensive listing of all Italian newspapers can be found on the website www.ciao-italy.com/categories/newspapers.htm.

English Language Publications. The English-language magazine, *Italy, Italy* (via M. Mercati 51, 00197 Rome; ☎06 322 1441, fax 06 322 3869) is for general interest and is available by subscription from the above address. Another publication, *The Informer* (www.informer.it) is published online. *The Informer* also has electronic newsletters and extensive archives of information available online to its subscribers.

The *English Yellow Pages* (via Belisario 4/B, 00187 Rome; ☎06-4740861; fax 06-4744516; www.intoitaly.it) is updated annually and contains listings for English-speaking professionals, businesses, organisations and services in Rome, Florence, Bologna, Naples, Genoa and Milan and is available to subscribers online. The online version also has listings for Palermo and Catania. Also from the same publisher is the *English White Pages*, an alphabetical directory of English-speakers living in Italy.

Television

The great majority of Italy's hundreds of channels are crammed with rubbishy quiz shows and low quality sitcoms and soaps and the general standard was described in a recent article in the London *Financial Times's, FT Weekend section* as 'My Italian TV hell.' The same article went on 'studio TV has replaced Parliament, and soft porn has replaced news.'

The three state-run channels, RAI 1, RAI 2 and RAI 3 manage to provide a higher quality programming and command higher viewing levels. RAI 3 tends to show more cultural programmes than the others.

The important independent television channels are Italia 1, Canale 5 and Rete 4: these collectively account for about 45% of Italian viewing. Although Rete 4 is thought to be more highbrow than the other two, none of them offers really serious news coverage although Canale 5 has been attempting to give greater emphasis to documentaries and news.

> In recent years there has been something of a public crusade in Italy against the probable dangers of certain types of television on the psychophysical development of children and younger viewers. The result was a watershed of 10.30pm for X-rated movies and other violent/sexually explicit programming. Italy was also a pioneer of the so-called 'violence chip', a piece of technology designed to filter out violent programmes on television when children are watching.

When shipping personal belongings to Italy it is worth remembering that Italian TV and videos operate on the PAL-BG system, which may be different to the one you are importing.

Radio

The Italian radio network was deregulated in 1976, the same year as television, with the result that the airwaves are crammed with a diverse range of obscure stations; over two and a half thousand of them. However, the three main radio channels are Radio 1, 2, and 3. The first two feature light music and entertainment while Radio 3 is similar to the UK equivalent, broadcasting serious discussion programmes and classical music. Finally there are Radio 1 and 2 rock stations which, although technically part of RAI, are on separate wavelengths.

CRIME

Organised Crime

Organised crime in Italy is a veritable state within a state. Based in the south its tentacles spread throughout Italy – and abroad. The *Mafia* or *Cosa Nostra* in Sicily is bigger, more calculating, and structured than the more chaotic and opportunistic outfits in the toe and heel and ankle of Italy. The infiltration of Albanian criminals throughout Italy has been an alarming result of the Balkan troubles of the 1990s.

Microcriminalità as the Italians call petty crime is much more of a problem but has been eliminated in central Bari for example by patrolling Carabinieri, and they are also working on central Naples. Some rural areas, however, in places like Tuscany, Abruzzo and Le Marche, Friuli and Molise, where the old local cultures prevail, are nearly crime free. To put crime into perspective, Italy is no more hazardous than, say, England. To many visitors the streets of London are more threatening than the streets of Rome. The Costas of Spain – or the South Coast of England – may well contain more criminals per square kilometre than the Rivieras of Italy.

LEARNING THE LANGUAGE

Most Italians will be flattered if you try to speak their language; and it is a beautiful language to learn.

Standard Italian evolved from Tuscan, the language of Dante. It was forged by the poets of the Middle Ages, and consolidated by writers of the nineteenth century. In 1861 only 2.5% of Italians spoke standard Italian, in 1955 the figure was 34%, in 1988 it was 86%. By 1995, 93.1% of Italians were speaking standard Italian, 48.7% were bilingual dialect Italian speakers and only 6.9% spoke in dialect alone. Nowadays a teenager from Naples and a teenager from Como, whose grandparents would not have understood each other, speak the same standard Italian. This is the language for foreigners to learn.

Learning Italian Before You Go

The BBC has a wide range of teach yourself Italian books from phrase books, to course books with cassettes. Other courses are available from Berlitz and Linguaphone. Sample self-study courses are listed below:

Buongiorno Italia! Coursebook, £10.99 (plus three cassettes at £6.99 each). This combination of texts and recordings from the BBC focuses heavily on such aspects of everyday, conversational Italian as finding the way, shopping and understanding numbers and prices. The textbook, teacher's notes and cassettes can all be purchased individually from the BBC online shop: www.bbcshop.com.

Hugo: In Three Months Italian Course Book, £5.95. 253 page book, without cassette or CD Rom; www.hugo.com.

Italianissimo, also from the BBC, has courses ranging in price from £6.99, through to a full course at £42.99. Further details on all BBC courses can be obtained online

at: www.bbcshop.com.
Italian for Dummies, US$24.99, including CD Rom. Based on the well-known Berlitz courses.

Learning Italian in Italy. The most famous Italian language schools are at Perugia and Siena universities, at the British Institute in Florence and at the Scuola Leonardo da Vinci in Florence, Rome and Siena. But all major Italian cities have schools of Italian.

A typical university course in Italian e.g. at the University of Trento, costs 400 euros (about $400), for outsiders for 50 hours of lessons in total.

ADDRESSING AND SIGNING LETTERS

The Envelope. On the envelope the polite form is : *Gentile Signore/Dottore Mario Rossi,*
which is abbreviated to: *Gent. Sig./dott. Mario Rossi.* Often abbreviated superlatives are used, such as: *Gentma dott.ssa Mario Bianchi* for *Gentilissima dottoressa Maria Bianchi*; (= very gentle) or *Preg. mo sig. Bruno Giordani* (= highly esteemed) for *Pregiatissimo signore Bruno Giordani;* or *Chiar. mo prof. Ezio Landi* for *Chiarissimo professore Ezio Landi,(Chiarissimo* = very illustrious is only used for university professors).
Then the address:
via Nazionale, 23
53031 Buonconvento (Si).

NOTE

Put the postcode before the town name (CAP = *Codice di avviamento postale*), followed by the abbreviation of the province in brackets).
If it is confidential write, *riservata-personale; c/o* or *presso* is used for 'care of'.
'For whom it may concern' is *a chi di competenza*.
The sender's address must be written on the back of the envelope: *Mittente:-* (= sender:-).
In many business and personal letters polite titles can be ignored.

SUMMARY OF HOUSING

Compared with a 27% decrease in the Italian stock market since 1999 real estate has gone up by up to 24.7%. No other form of investment has done so well.

How Property Prices are Calculated. There are many different types of property on the market including those needing renovation, completely restored, apartments and new houses and developments. The price quoted in the table (*Summary of Housing*) pertains to the area of the buildings only, for example an apartment of 80sq.m. (square metres) at €1,000 per sq.m. = €80,000. The price per square metre does not include any land, swimming pool or tennis court that may be a part of the property. The price of the land on which the property sits (this does not apply to apartments) is determined by its position, for example if you own a property on or near the coast, you can expect to pay more than you would for a property inland with very rough (rocky) terrain. You can see examples of this difference in the 'properties for sale' section in the *Where to Find Your Ideal Home* chapter.

The largest Italian estate agency, Gabetti has 500 offices nationwide (www.gabetti.it). Gabetti suggest using the following information to calculate property prices in 2004, 2005 and beyond.

- New or restored homes rise by 7.68% per annum.
- Partially restored homes rise by 7.48% per annum.
- Properties for renovation rise by 8.66% per annum.

Please note that these predictions are only a guide, subject to geopolitical fluctuations.

Sources of Information. The information/figures in the *Summary of Housing* are extracted from a twice-yearly supplement (*Osservatorio Immobilare*), part of the Milan-based financial newspaper *Il Sole 24 Ore*. Nearly all the daily Italian newspapers carry a property section at least once a week. All you need in order to buy any property magazine etc. is to say *Immobiliare* (property) to the newsagent and he will show you everything available.

There are also publications in England with Italian properties for sale, including *Italy* magazine, *UK World of Property* and *International Homes*. The equivalent publications in Italy are:- *Case e Casale* and *Ville e Casali*.

Property Exhibitions. It is a good idea to be on the lookout for property exhibitions held in different venues around the UK. At the moment these exhibitions centre on properties in France and Spain but often Italy is included with other European countries. At these exhibitions you can meet experts, financial advisors and solicitors etc. who can advise you and you have the opportunity to see what is available and the cost. For more information on exhibitions: www.tsnn.co.uk or www.internationalpropertyshow.com.

Useful Websites. If you are looking for something different and would like to purchase a property in the Venice area or on the small islands off the coast of Italy you can log on to www.vladi-private-islands.de. Other sites which list property prices include:
www.nomisna.it. This is a Bologna based research team who do real estate research.
www.real-estate-european-union.com
www.italian-realestate.com
Price per square metre e.g. 1,600 euros per sq.mt.

SUMMARY OF PRICES

Region	Province	Commune	Maximum Price (€)	minimum Price(€)
Veneto	Verona	Torri del Benaco	2,480	1,600
	Padova	Cittadella	2,841	1,550
	Vicenza	San Felice	1,750	1,100
Fruili Venezia Giulia	Pordenone	Cordenons	1,343	826
	Trieste	Rozzol	2,300	1,200
Liguria	Genova	Rapallo-Porto	2,690	1,970
	La Spezia	Cinque Terre	4,000	1,600
Emilia-Romagna	Bologna	Bazzano	2.065	1,400
	Ferrara	Porto Ganbaldi	1,850	1,500
	Forli	Savignano	1,807	930
	Ravenna	Lugo	1,650	1,050
	Rimini	Riccione-Terme	3,400	2,500
Tuscany	Florence	Scandicci	3,200	2,100
	Arezzo	Sansepolcro	2,200	1,000
	Grosseto	Massa Marittima	1,549	620
	Livorno	Cecina	3,100	1,200
	Siena	Camollia (citta) (city)	4,000	2,000
Umbria	Perugia	Citta'di Castello	2,066	878
Marche	Ancona	Senigallia	2,852	1,291
	Pesaro	Fano	2,170	1,395
Lazio	Roma	Genzano	2,000	1,260
	Rieti	Magliano Sabina	1,200	800
	Viterbo	Montalto di Castro	1,032	610
Abruzzo	L'Aquila	Roccaraso	2,580	1,700
	Pescara	Montesilvano	1,550	930
Molise	Campobasso	Tennoli	1,800	900
Campania	Naples	Forio d'Ischia	2,350	1,600
	Benevento	Telese	1,100	600
	Salerno	Vietri sul Mare	2,300	1,500
Puglia	Bari	Barletta	2,060	1,340
	Brindisi	Fasano di Brindisi	1,290	600
	Foggia	Vieste	1,800	1,000
	Lecce	Nardo	878	465
Basilicata	Potenza	Venosa	980	550
	Matera	Policoro	1,100	600
Calabria	Cosenza	Castrolibero	930	671
Sicily	Palermo	Monreale	1,446	930
	Catania	Gravina	1,446	775
	Siracusa	Augusta	1,500	550
Sardinia	Cagliari	Assemini	1,140	750
	Oristano	San Nicola	1,136	671
	Sassari	Alghero	1,549	723

Source: *Osservatorio Immobilare (Il Sole 24 Ore)* 2003

PUBLIC HOLIDAYS

Note that on Italian national holidays (*feste*) offices, shops, banks, post offices and schools are all closed. Whether museums, parks, etc, are closed will vary from region to region:

1 January	New Year's Day; *Capodanno*
6 January	Epiphany; *La Befana*
Easter Monday	*Pasquetta*
25 April	Liberation Day; *Anniversario della Liberazione*
1 May	Labour Day; *primo maggio*
15 August	Assumption; *Ferragosto*
1 November	All Saints'; *Ognissanti*
8 December	Immaculate Conception; *L'Immacolata Concezione*
25 December	Christmas Day; *Natale*
26 December	Boxing Day; *Santo Stefano*

City Festival Days. All cities. major and minor towns have a day to honour their own local patron saints. Shops and offices usually remain open on these days. Consult the tourist board in your area for information.

M.S.

RESIDENCE AND ENTRY REGULATIONS

CHAPTER SUMMARY

- Non-Italians planning to stay in Italy for over 30 days must apply for a *permesso di soggiorno* (permit to stay) even if they are from another EU country
- Those not from EU countries must apply for a *permesso di soggiorno* and a work visa before they enter Italy.

Once you have the *permesso di soggiorno* and have moved to an Italian address you should obtain a residence permit (*certificato di residenza*): this is not compulsory for EU nationals, but has several uses as proof that you have settled in Italy.

All Italian residents, whether native or foreign, must carry an identity card (*Carta d 'Identità*) with them at all times.

ENTRY REGULATIONS

Non-European Union Nationals

Italy is currently tightening its immigration laws to combat a rising flood of illegal immigrants (*clandestini*) from eastern Europe and Africa. Non-EU nationals must apply for a visitor's visa before they enter Italy. For some nationalities it is also necessary to apply for and receive the visas through the Italian embassy in their home country, though it will often be possible to apply for a visa in the area where you are permanently resident. For long-term expatriates this usually means that they can apply for their visa in the country where they are currently living, especially if they have a residence permit or other official documentation to prove they live there full-time. It is also necessary to have employment before applying for a work visa. Applications for all visas should be in person and application processing takes from 24-hours to five weeks. It is advisable to allow the maximum time, especially during the busy summer months, to ensure your visa arrives in time for your departure. The visa itself currently costs about US$30.

US Citizens can find up-to-date visa information on the website of the Italian Embassy in Washington (www.italyemb.org)

PERMESSO DI SOGGIORNO

EU Nationals: EU nationals who arrive in Italy will need to apply at the *questura*, or the police station in smaller towns, for their *Permesso di Soggiorno* (sometimes also known as a *Carta di Soggiorno*), within eight days of arrival. Reports vary as to how long it takes for the *Permesso di Soggiorno* to be issued, but three months is the official delay.

Requirements for the *permesso di soggiorno* may vary. In many cases you will be required to produce proof of financial solvency, of having some kind of income and be able to name your intended profession while in Italy, if this is relevant. The soggiorno is free of charge and issued initially for three months and then either every two years or five years. Note that failure to renew the document can result in a substantial fine. Renewals are made through the *comune*, or the *questura* in large towns and cities. The *Permesso di Soggiorno* has to be renewed every five years, no matter how long you live in Italy. All renewals must be made on special document paper, *carta bollata*, which can be purchased from most tobacconists (*tabaccherie*). Depending on your status, the *permesso di soggiorno* will have a different suffix, for example: employee, student, tourist, student, spouse, foreign spouse of an Italian, etc.

Non-EU Nationals. All non-EU nationals intending to live in the country must have received the necessary visas before arrival. Within eight days of their arrival they need to apply for their *permesso di soggiorno* to the *questura*, or the police station.

All Nationalities: When making an application for *permesso di soggiorno* it is advisable to take every document required at the time of application to make a return visit unnecessary, or worse, prevent having to repeat the entire process of waiting and aggravation. The list below is a guide to what many people have been requested to present, though the list should be checked at the office you will apply to as local requirements may vary, especially between EU and non-EU nationals.

- A valid passport. Most countries require your passport to be valid for six months or more beyond your intended stay and Italy is no exception. A photocopy of the relevant information pages, including your visa, will also be required.
- Up to four black and white passport sized photos.
- A tax stamp (*marca da bollo*) of the correct value (check what is required at the local *questura*).
- For employees, a letter of employment is necessary.
- For the self-employed, proof of registration with the Chamber of Commerce and VAT certificate (or exemption) is required.
- For students a letter from their institution is required.
- For retired/non-working people proof of financial resources is needed.
- Proof of health insurance or coverage by social security system of Italy or another country.
- Marriage/divorce certificate.
- Passports of children to be included on the *permesso di soggiorno*, if the children are not on the parents ' passport, plus the birth certificates of the children.

It is necessary to have notarised translations of certain documents and have others provided in Italian – check with the office where the application will be made for current requirements. Official translations of the marriage, divorce and birth certificates, as well as the letter of employment in Italian will probably be required. Translations should be done by an official translator and enquiries should be made at an Italian Embassy or at the *questura* where an application is to be made.

CERTIFICATO DI RESIDENZA

Once you have obtained a *permesso di soggiorno* and moved into your new Italian home, you will find it to your advantage to apply for a residence certificate, *certificato di residenza*. For non-EU citizens it is mandatory and should be applied for within 20 days of receipt of the *permesso di soggiorno*. Applications should be made at the Vital Statistics Bureau (*Anagrafe*) of the *Comune*.

The Carta d'Identità

All residents, native and foreign, are required to carry an identity card (*Carta d'Identità*) with them at all times. This is a regulation that the majority of Italians comply with, without feeling that it is any kind of infringement of their personal liberty. Outside the UK, most European countries require people to carry some form of identity at all times, as do the majority of countries around the world – the premise being that if you have nothing to hide why should you worry if the police want to know who you are. Permanent residents are issued with an identity card that includes the holder's nationality and passport number. The card should be bought from the *comune*. However, only Italian nationals can use their Italian identity card as a travel document in lieu of their passport.

Registering with the Embassy

Expatriates are advised to register with their embassy or consulate in Italy – US, Canadian and British offices are listed below. This registration enables the Embassy to keep their nationals up to date with any information they need to be aware of and also enables the Embassy to trace individuals in the event of an emergency.

Sources of Information

Before getting too far into planning any move to Italy all and every piece of information should be checked and double checked – including information in this book. Italian Embassies and Consulates in whose jurisdiction you live and your own Embassy in Italy are the best places to get information, though they might not always respond quickly.

Useful Addresses

Italian Embassies and Consulates in the United Kingdom:
Italian Embassy: 14 Three Kings Yard, Davies Street, London W1Y 2EH; ☎020-7312 2200; fax 020-7499 2283; www.embitaly.org.uk.
Italian Consulate General: 38 Eaton Place, London SW1; ☎020-7235 9371.
Italian Consulate General: Rodwell Tower, 111 Piccadilly, Manchester M1 2HY; ☎0161-236 9024. Easier to get through to than the London Consulate. For latest regulations send a request and a stamped addressed envelope to the Visa Department.
Italian Consulate General: 32 Melville Street, Edinburgh EH3 7HW; ☎0131-226 3631; 0131-220 3695.
Italian Vice Consulate: 7-9 Greyfriars, Bedford MK40 1HJ; ☎01234-356647. Operates 9.30am-12.30pm Monday to Friday.

Italian Embassies and Consulates in the United States of America:
Italian Embassy: 3000 Whitehaven Street NW, Washington DC 20008; ☎202-612-4400; fax 202-518-2154; www.italyemb.org.
Italian Consul General: 690 Park Avenue, New York, NY 10021, USA; ☎737-9100 or 439-8600; www.italyconsulnyc.org.
Italian Consul: 2590 Webster Street, angolo Broadway, San Francisco; ☎415-931

49224/5/6; visa enquiries visa@italcons-sf.org; www.italcons-sf.org.
Italian Consul: Boston ☎www.italconsboston.org.
Italian Consul: www.italconschicago.org.

Other Italian Embassies and Consulates:
Italian Embassy: 21st Floor, 275 Slater Street, Ottawa, Ontario, KIP 5H9; ☎613-232240; fax 613-233 1484; www.italyincanada.com.
Italian Consul General: 136 Beverley Street, Toronto (ON) M5T 1Y5, Canada; ☎416-977 1566; fax 416-977 1119; www.italconsulate.org.
Embassy of Italy: 12 Grey Street, Deakin A.C.T. 2600, Australia, ☎621-6273 3333; fax 612-6273 4233; www.ambitalia.org.au.
Embassy of Italy: 63 Northumberland Road, Dublin, Eire; ☎031-6601744; fax 031-6682759; http://homepage.eircom.net/italianembassy/

British Embassies and Consulates in Italy:
British Embassy: Via XX Settembre 80a (Porta Pia), 00187 Rome; ☎064-220 0001 (8am-1pm & 2-4pm); www.britain.it.
British Consulate General: via S. Paolo 7, 20121 Milano; ☎02 723001; fax 02-864 65081.
British Consulate: Viale Colombo 160, 09045 Quartu SF, Cagliari, Sardinia; ☎070-828628; fax 070-862293.
British Consulate: Palazzo Castelbarco, Lungarno Corsini 2, 50123 Firenze; ☎055-284133; fax 055-219112.
British Consulate: Piazza della Vittoria 15/16, Third Floor, Genoa; ☎10-564833; fax 10-5531516.
British Consulate-General: Via dei Mille 40, 80121 Napoli; ☎081-423 8911; fax 081-422 434.
British Consulate: via Saluzzo 60, 10125 Torino; ☎011-650 9202; fax 011-669 6982.
British Consulate: Vicolo delle Ville 16, 34124 Trieste; ☎040-764752.
British Consulate: Accademia Dorsoduro 1051, 30123 Venezia; ☎041-522 7207; fax 041-522 2617.
Other Consulates are listed on the UK Embassy website www.britain.it.

United States Embassies and Consulates in Italy:
Embassy of the United States of America: via Vittorio Venetto 119/A, 00187 Roma; ☎06-467 1; fax 06-4882 672 or 06-4674 2356; www.usembassy.it.
US Consulate General: Lungarno Vespucci, 38, 50123 Firenze; ☎055-239 8276; 055-284 088.
US Consulate General: Via Principe Amedeo, 2/10 – 20121 Milano; ☎02-290 351; fax 02-2900 1165.
US Consulate General: Piazza della Repubblica – 80122 Napoli; ☎081-5838 111; fax 081-7611 869.
American Embassy to the Holy See: via dell Terme Deciane 26, 00162 Rome; ☎06-4674 3428; fax 06-575 8346.

Canadian Embassy and Consul in Italy:
Canadian Embassy: Consular Section, Via Zara, 30, 00198 Rome; ☎06-445 981; fax 06-445 98 912; www.canada.it.
Canadian Consulate General: Consular Section, Via Vittor Pisani,19, 20124 Milan; ☎02-67581; fax 02-6758 3900.

WHERE TO FIND YOUR IDEAL HOME

CHAPTER SUMMARY

- The coastline of Italy has been relentlessly developed for over 40 years, mostly for low-rise Italian second homes.
- The apartment option for would-be buyers should be considered – it is the way most Italians live.
- Havens for retirement, not just for tourism, are in their infancy.
- **Climate.** Winds can be vicious, summers too hot, and even in Sicily winters can be longer, colder and wetter than you expect. Droughts and floods are frequent.
- The climate of Calabria, has been pronounced to be most beneficial for rheumatism and arthritis sufferers.
- The Italian property marked is buoyant rather than meteoric with prices rising about 6.5% per year.
- **Udine,** a city thirty miles inland from Trieste was recently voted, by Italians, the most 'liveable' place in Italy.
- **Le Marche.** upvalley locations seem remote and landlocked. Socialising expatriates get used to long drives on winding roads. But the coast has excellent communications.
- Apartments are inexpensive on the coast.
- **Lazio.** The massive development of the Lazio coastline over fifty years means there is an abundant supply of fairly modern apartments.
- Too much concrete inhibits recreational buyers, who prefer to head for the hills inland.
- **Abruzzo** on the Adriatic coast in the middle of the peninsula, south of Le Marche, and north of Molise, is one of the least populated regions in Italy.
- **Molise** has only 38km of coastline.
- **Campania.** Positano property increased by 23% in value in 2003. It is easier to rent than to buy, with still a big American demand.
- **Calabria** is an exciting place to visit rather than as a permanent

abode. Tourists are not usually the object of organised crime but a sinister atmosphere prevails, especially in Reggio.

○ **Sicily.** Amazing bargains are available in Sicily in stunning locations, but the summers are unbearably hot and water shortages are routine.

OVERVIEW

To the ancient Romans, who dominated it from a central position, the Mediterranean was *mare nostrum*, our sea, of which the Italian coasts were subdivided (anticlockwise) into: the Ligurian Sea, the Tyrrhenian Sea, the Ionian Sea, and the Adriatic Sea. The coastline mostly mountainous, descending into foothills, with very few coastal plains, has been relentlessly developed since the boom years of the 1950s and 60s mostly for second homes in low-rise apartment blocks. In July and August all of Italy seems to be at the seaside, even in the South, where emigrants and regulars return for their annual holidays. There are miles of *stabilimenti balneari* (bathing establishments) which are clean and well-kept, and give employment, and increasingly less wild coast remaining. In the winter many of these summer resort developments are windswept, ugly and desolate, except for favoured locations such as Rapallo, Positano, or Taormina, where affluent *pensionati* (pensioners) have retired, kept youthful by the balmy microclimates in their well-appointed *condominio* apartments or luxurious villas.

The apartment option for would-be buyers should be considered – it is the way most Italians live.

THE HINTERLAND – THE ENTROTERRA

Since AD 800, and before Italians have sought refuge inland from the slave-raids of marauding Arabs, Saracens, Turks, Barbary pirates, Moors or Corsairs. Hence the hundreds of walled medieval villages hidden in the hills inland, full of old buildings, churches, sometimes benefiting from a fertile soil and the aegis of a monastery, near enough to the sea, ideally within 10km, to enjoy a moderate maritime climate yet sheltered from winds. These are the favoured locations for a Mediterranean home, especially if a hospital and an airport are near at hand.

In the north and centre these *entroterra* villages have mostly been incorporated into the urban sprawl of the coast, whilst the abandoned farmhouses and villages in the mountains are too far uphill to enjoy the benefits of the Mediterranean climate. There are very few benign coastal plains: the Po Delta, the Tavoliere of Puglia, Catania in Sicily, Metaponto in Basilicata.

The south of Italy – Magna Graecia – Sicily and its islands and Sardinia are the most quintessentially Mediterranean – the most subject to lawlessness, but brilliant for human warmth and hospitality. Until recently the area south of Naples was perceived as being on a par with Africa; it suffered from the same problems, disease, deforestation, erosion, emigration, exploitation by Europeans institutionalised corruption and crime. Now tourism with the help of the European Union, has come to the rescue, and the age of the internet has heralded a new breed of passionate southern entrepreneur. Havens for retirement, not just for tourism, are in their infancy, which will make the gated communities of Florida and California seem bland and boring. The climate of Calabria, for instance has been pronounced to be most beneficial for rheumatism and arthritis sufferers. American timeshares are already in operation there. (www.intercomm.it/badolatomeddream/.) .

To appreciate the south it is a prerequisite that you know a bit about its history: the input of the Greeks, Phoenicians, Romans, Goths, Vandals, Arabs, Normans, Benedictines, French, Spanish, Albanians, Piedmontese and all the other components of the complex mentality, the dazzling seaside habitat and the superb food of the present day inhabitants.

But is the grass really greener on the Italian Mediterranean? Winds can be vicious, summers too hot, and even in Sicily winters can be longer, colder and wetter than you would expect. Droughts, floods and earthquakes are frequent, and domestic water often scarce. Roads and hospitals while good in the north and centre, are erratic in the south; social and health care is not up to northern European standards, (for example home help for the over 65s is 0.9% in Italy compared with 20% in the UK and 10% in Germany). As for Italian bureaucracy .... even confirmed Italophiles are baffled by it (try re-registering a foreign car in Italy). You are advised to retain your privileged tourist status if you want to avoid the bureaucratic horrors to which native Italians are inured.

Recent (2003) legislation granting amnesties for illegal building development in exchange for hefty fines (*condono edilizio*) has condemned long stretches of the Mediterranean coast (e.g. Selinunte, Naples, Bagheria) to an acceptance of third world squalor. This short-term money-raising measure, rushed through by a bankrupt government headed by a successful property developer (Silvio Berlusconi), is in collision with the strong environmental leanings of most local *comuni* (borough councils), which are admirably improving their *centri storici* (historic districts) and their infrastructures, both for the benefit of locals and to attract tourists. To judge how *green* your local council is going to be just consult the local municipal website (www.comuni.it). The strength of local governments, their *subsidiarity* within a European Union framework, is part of the policy – beneficial in this case – of the Berlusconi government – and could be identified as the potential salvation of Italy.

A recent return-to-the-country aspiration has been discerned in Italian youth: many of whom now dream of organic farming combined with *agriturismo*. For every abandoned farmhouse converted by a foreigner more have already been transformed by Italian owners into *agriturismi* for vacation rentals, to the extent that such places have become a glut on the market. There are not enough tourists to go around, and only the good agriturismos can survive. Many failed *agriturismos* are therefore for sale, at seldom less than €800,000.

In 2004 the Italian property market is buoyant with prices rising at an average of at least 6.5% a year
Bricks and mortar are regarded as a safer investment than government bonds and shares. Italian investors looking for bargains are heading for Croatia, Kenya, Romania. The grass is always greener somewhere else.

You can play safe and go to the industrialised congested north – Liguria for example – where transport systems and services are northern European, or you can eschew all the caveats, by-pass the corruption and the concrete, join hands with local patriots and settle in the south or the islands, where the Mediterranean is at its passionate best.

Or you can take the middle course and head for Abruzzo, Molise and their *entroterras* where traditional values are retained and houses are still to be found at a reasonable price.

THE NORTH WEST

LIGURIA

Capital: *Genova* (3 metres above sea level)
Climate: *Summer Max. Temp:* 27°C.*Winter Min. Temp:* 5°C. *Annual Rainfall:* 1,073mm
Airports: *Genoa, Cristoforo, Columbo International Airport:* also *Nice* in France.
Ferry Ports: *Genoa* (for Tunisia, Sicily, Sardinia, Malta), *San Remo* (for Corsica)
Liguria is a narrow strip of land, about 250km long and 30km wide, divided by the Gulf of Genoa, its capital, into the Rivieras of the rising and the setting sun- the Riviera di Levante to the east and the Riviera di Ponente to the west of Genoa. Cities rich in history such as Ventimiglia, Imperia, Albenga, Savona, Genoa itself, Rapallo, Chiavari, Camogli and La Spezia are interspersed with world famous seaside resorts such as Bordighera, San Remo, Alassio and Portovenere.

THE ITALIAN RIVIERA

This is the original *Italian Riviera*, the nearest taste of the Italian Mediterranean for generations of artistic northern tourists and settlers. In the nineteenth century it was the ultimate in wild romantic coastline, associated with poets such as Byron and Shelley, after whom the Golfo dei Poeti in Portovenere is named. In the 1890s the population of Bordighera in the winter was: 3,000 English, 2,000 locals. Alassio was a prototype Anglo-Saxon retirement colony founded by a retired Indian Army general in 1845. Thomas Hanbury started his semi-tropical gardens at La Mortola between Menton and Ventimiglia in 1867. Other names associated with Liguria are Max Beerbohm, D H Lawrence, Aldous Huxley, Cecil Roberts whose 'Portal to Paradise' is essential reading on the subject, Henry James, Virginia Woolf, Nietsche and Hemingway. These settlers were attracted as much by the climate as by the romantic shoreline – mild all year, excellent for lemons, olives, vines and floriculture. Warm damp breezes blow in from the sea, while the narrow coastal strip is protected from cold north-eastern winds by the embrace of the Alps and the Apennines. Nevertheless, the Mistral from the north west can sometimes be ferocious.

From the fertile hills of San Remo and Albenga – the centre of a huge horticultural export industry, much of it under glass, the coastline becomes increasingly craggy as you move eastwards. There are some fine sandy strands such as the ones near Celle Ligura (Savona), but most beaches are narrow and pebbly enclosed by perpendicular cliffs and often reached only by sea, such as Punta Corvo (La Spezia), or by impervious tracks and tunnels such as the ones in the *Cinque Terre* (La Spezia) – five villages of extreme beauty once inaccessible by land. There are offshore islands too, such as the Isolotto di Bergeggi (Savona) and the Isola di Polmaria (La Spezia) which are accessible by boat or dinghy, where the sea is crystal clear.
Many of these beaches have been transformed into marinas or second home havens

to cater for the booming industrial populations of the Po Valley north of the Ligurian Alps, for whom the handy Ligurian seaside has long been the mandatory resort for family holidays. From the 1950s onwards apartment blocks and the spread of concrete and tarmac have extensively defaced the Ligurian coast, especially around Genoa, Savona and La Spezia. There is a lot of heavy industry too, crammed into a confined space (shipbuilding, refineries, fish processing, metal, cement, paper etc.).

At the same time mountain villages became depopulated, where the wild Mediterranean *macchia* scrub survives, protected in several places by regional parks such as the Parco Montemarcello – Magra near La Spezia, the Parco del Beigua above Arenzano, the Parco Regionale of Portofino and several other nature reserves. Portofino and the Cinque Terre also have sea-life areas under state protection (*Aree Marine Protette*).

Genoa itself (pop. 660,000), Italy's largest port, sprawls along the coast for 25km and inland 15km up two valleys. It holds memories of a glorious past dating back to the 4th century BC. It is *'A regal city backed by an Alpine hill, superb for men and walls, whose look alone proclaims her the mistress of the sea'* according to the 14th century poet Francesco Petrarch.

In the centre the grand noble mansions give you the feeling of travelling back in time into the ancient opulence of the Genoese aristocracy, with their daring arcades, their hanging gardens and floors of flowing black and white pebble mosaics; the palazzo Reale, the Palazzo Bianco, the Palazzo Rosso and the present Town Hall, the Palazzo Doria Tursi. These contrast with the narrow purlieus, called *Caruggi*, of artisans' shops and *friggitorie* (deep-frying stalls) of the proletariat. This dualism pervades the whole Riviera. The exclusive elite of Portofino is juxtaposed with the exuberant vulgarity of Recco.

So you have a choice between the frenetic variety, ancient and modern, of the built up areas, where the climate is balmy or you can go up into the quiet villages of the steep mountainsides through narrow valleys where the climate becomes Alpine and houses are cheaper.

In the western Ligurian hinterland, in Imperia province, Dolceacqua and Dolcedo (7km from the coast) and surrounding hamlets are popular with foreign buyers (www.comunedolcedo.im.it).

Other towns have attractive hinterland villages, proceeding eastwards – Taggia and the olive growing valleys near Oneglia; Alassio; Albenga; Finale Ligure: you can explore endlessly. In the hills behind the Riviera del Levante, east of Genoa is the interesting ancient Genoese summer resort of Torriglia, on the road to the monastery of Bobbio and Piacenza.

The province of La Spezia has the glorious Cinque Terre and the corner of Liguria most favoured by the artists and intellectuals of yesteryear: Portovenere, Lerici, Tellaro, Montemarcello, which for many years now has been overcrowded and overpriced, however beautiful once.

The people of Liguria are proverbial for their parsimony, said to derive from their skills in the fishmarkets. Liguria's heroes are bold seafaring men – Columbus, Andrea Doria, John Cabot and Giuseppe Garibaldi, whose birthplace, Nice, was part of Liguria at the time.

Ligurian food excels for its exceptionally delicate olive oil, its aromatic herbs especially basil and its fresh fish. Paradoxically *stoccafisso,* dried stockfish from the North Sea, is Genoa's finest dish. *La Cucina di Ritorno* – aromatic stews awaiting the seafarer's homecoming are a tradition of the Genoese housewife. The cuisine changes from province to province from the *bujabesa* (bouillabaisse) fish stew of Imperia to the *mesciua* chick pea and bean soup of La Spezia. The wine too varies from the sciacchetrà – raisin wine of the Cinque Terre to Vermentino white and the Rossese red of the west. Wherever you are in Liguria the food and wine is delicate, varied and superb, whether in the mountains or by the sea.

Another advantage of Liguria is the excellent road and rail service. You are never far from a railway station or an *autostrada* or from an international airport, – or from a golf course. Moreover the mild climate, combined with rainfall that is much higher than that of London, is a godsend for garden lovers.

Typical properties for sale

Second homes are big business in Liguria. Due to its popularity with tourists, property prices are high. In the main centres, the ports of Genoa and La Spezia, there is a wide choice of apartments in modern buildings. Districts of Savona are undergoing restoration and properties bought there may turn out to be a good investment.

The old seaport houses are characteristically over three storeys in height – very tall, as at Camogli – colour washed in a dazzling assortment of pigments. *Entroterra* peasant houses tend to be small and hovel-like, with steep terraced land.

Location	Type	Description	Price
San Remo	apartment	Top floor of a converted villa. 3 bedrooms, 2 bathrooms, 210sq.m. Panoramic outlook over the Mediterranean	€500,000
Sestri Levante	apartment	Apartment on 3rd floor. 130sq.m. Living room, kitchen, 2 bedrooms, bathroom, cellar, central heating.	€550,000
Genoa	apartment	Apartment 3rd floor. Renovated old building in centre of Genoa 180sq.m. basement, lift.	€465,000
Casarza Ligure	house and shed	House on 2 floors 120sq.m and shed 18sq.m in need of renovation. Situated behind Sestri Levante 5km from the sea. 2,000sq.m land	€154,937
Alassio	villa	Villa stone built + small house. Total 300sq.m. Villa on 3 floors, 4 bedrooms, 2 bathrooms, shower room. Swimming pool, mature garden. Panoramic views of sea	€1,250,000

Agents for this Region: www.findaproperty.com, www.casatravella.com, www.oltre.it, www.gabettionline.it

THE NORTH EAST

VENETO

Capital: *Venice* (6 metres above sea level)
Climate: *Summer Max. Temp:* 28°C.*Winter Min. Temp:* -1°C. *Annual Rainfall:*
800mm
Airports: *Venice, Treviso, Verona*
Ferry Ports: *Venice* (for Greece, Croatia, Turkey)
The region of Veneto in the north east of Italy has Venice as its capital city – the queen
of the Adriatic – on a coastal plain with a large unique lagoon area. There is a heavily
industrialised hinterland at Mestre and several seaside resorts: Jesolo, Eraclea, Caorle
and Bibione. Bibione has extra-hot thermal springs, (51°C) and a fine marina.

The other maritime province of Veneto is Rovigo, south of Venice, which is
completely flat, its southern border being the river Po, its coastline delta country and
its northern boundary the river Adige. This area is called *Polesine*.

Veneto takes its name from the Indo-European tribe of the Veneti which
intermarried with Ligurians in the Euganean hills in about 1,000 BC. 'Ven' means
shining or noble. From the seventh century BC the town of Adria, which is now in the
province of Rovigo, was a thriving Greek seaport which gave its name to the Adriatic
sea. Although over-run by Gauls this region was never a threat to the expansion of
the Roman Empire, into which it was absorbed as the tenth province with the name
of Venetia. The barbarian invasions (Attila the Hun in AD 452 and the Lombards in
AD 569) caused an influx of refugees to the lagoon islands north of Adria, led by their
bishops. The first Doge (chief) was elected in AD 729 at Malamocco on the Lido. The
foundation of Venice itself was a spontaneous development starting in AD 810 at Rivo
Alto (Rialto).

The Venetian empire began in 1000 with the capture of Dalmatia followed by that
of Constantinople and of much of the eastern Mediterranean in 1204. Venice became
a Mediterranean superpower, eclipsing Genoa and Pisa, opening out, thanks to its
strategic position, to the lucrative spice trade of the east. By 1484 Venice had annexed
all its inland neighbours, from Bergamo to Friuli and Ravenna. Ruled by a powerful
art-loving oligarchy calling themselves the most serene republic (*La serenissima*),
Venice was a leading player in the flowering of the renaissance, producing printers,
scholars, musicians, painters and architects who made their city the most glorious
place on earth. It now receives the attention of millions upon millions of tourists. It
has sunk 23 centimetres in the last 100 years. Millions of dollars of international and
Italian money have been earmarked to 'save Venice', but the proposed tidal barrages
have yet to be built.

In the 1950s Veneto was a poor region suffering from emigration to the megacities
of Milan and Turin. This situation has been reversed for successive decades and
the region is now buzzing with small industries. The industrial area of Mestre and
Marghera is congested and polluted. Venetian families are abandoning Venice itself
to the tourists. The health service is excellent in the region. Newspaper readership,
TV viewing, and the crime rate are low. There are more church marriages and fewer
divorces than in any other region and a strong smallholding tradition.

Part-time farming by industrial workers is a relevant factor in the economy. The
sing-song local idiom, *Veneto*, has the status and prestige of a language, not a dialect,

while standard Italian is universally understood.

The diet is dominated by seafood: mussels (*peoci*), squid and its ink, often in a *risotto* of local *vialone nano* rice, and marshland game; frogs and ducks. The people are archetypal polenta eaters (*polentoni*) which has been their staple diet ever since maize was introduced in 1603; the wines of Veneto are excellent from the sparkling whites, Prosecco and Verduzzo (from Treviso) to the easy drinking reds Valpolicella and Bardolino (from Verona); and Veneto is the heartland of neat grappa drinking.

> **Apartments in Venice are sought after by foreign buyers for their romantic appeal, and the crumbling *palazzi* badly need to be renovated**.
> But if you want to escape from the tourists and enjoy all the advantages of Venice plus beaches and a golf course, you should head for the Lido (*Malamocco*), where a pied-à-terre can cost as little as €80,000. The old fishing port of Chioggia has the racy atmosphere of old Venice without the foreigners, whilst in Rovigo you will be competing with *extracomunitari* (non-EU immigrants) for the cheaper and smaller properties.

Typical properties for sale

Owning an apartment in Venice is the ultimate romantic dream. It is also an excellent investment for all-year vacation rental income. But the beautiful old buildings are cripplingly expensive to buy, renovate and maintain, so buyers are gravitating to modern Venetian developments such as those on the Giudecca, where a one bedroom ground floor 50sq.m. apartment with garden costs €225,000, or in unfashionable areas like Santa Croce.

Bargains are to be found if you avoid the international agencies and Venice itself. A good solid restored country house with an acre of garden near Rovigo, can be bought for less than a third of the price which is asked for a similar portion of an 18th century villa (with servants) near Treviso. But the aesthetic allure of Palladio is very potent on the Anglo-Saxon mind: it is part of the unique character of this region.

Location	Type	Description	Price
Isola Verde (Chioggia)	apartment	Top floor, one bedroom apartment 60sq.m. in condominium park with swimming pools near sea	€125,000
Venice (Santa Croce)	apartment	Restored, furnished, one bedroom apartment, 52sq.m. overlooking canal.	€235,000
Rovigo (Countryside)	villa	Completely restored 3 storey villa set in 5,000sq.m. of gardens	€580,000
Treviso (Countryside)	villa	Completely restored 5 bedroom, part of 18th century villa, with 2,700sq.m. garden + servants. 10km airport.	

Agents for this Region: ww.casa.it, www.venice-sales.com, www.tecnocasa.it

FRIULI-VENEZIA GIULIA

Capital: *Trieste* (20 metres above sea level)
Climate: *Summer Max. Temp:* 28°C. *Winter Min. Temp:* 3°C. *Annual Rainfall:* 1,047mm
Airports: *Trieste* (Ronchi dei Legionari)
Ferry Ports: Trieste (for Greece and Albania)

In the northeast corner of Italy – bordering Slovenia to the east, Veneto to the west and Austria to the north – this region is an extension of the *Pianura Veneta* (the plain of Veneto), with about 120km of Adriatic coastline on the Gulf of Trieste. Like Venice it consists of lagoons, causeways and salt-flats, and the island town of Grado has an analogous history, in that it was founded by refugees from Attila the Hun's invasion of AD 452. Trieste and Monfalcone are industrial cities on the coast, whilst Grado and Lignano, with their fine beaches, are elegant lagoonside resorts. Aquileia – the ancient Roman – and later ecclesiastical – capital city – is full of fascinating archaeology – a UNESCO world heritage site.

This region was Venetian until the fall of Venice to Napoleon in 1797, and subsequently part of the Austro-Hungarian empire until the end of the first world war (1919). Trieste was an imperial seaport and its surrounding coast and hot springs at Grado were the summer resort of *Mitteleuropean* nobility and bourgeoisie. In the second world war it was ruled by an Austrian *gauleiter*, after which Friuli-Venezia Giulia became one of Italy's five special status autonomous regions home to an ethnically mixed population of half a million Friulian (locally known as *furlan*) speakers, and threequarters of a million Slovenian speakers, with German speakers in the north and Veneto Italian speakers throughout – 350,000 of whom had been 'ethnically cleansed' from neighbouring Slovenia which became part of Yugoslavia after the Second World War. The current entry (2004) of Slovenia into the European Union and the consequent elimination of the border with Italy is welcomed locally as a demarginalisation of the area heralding a return to an Austro-Hungarian multi-ethnic tolerance favourable to new immigrants.

The people of the region have a reputation of being rather unmediterranean – staid, reserved and cultured. Trieste – once home to James Joyce and Italo Svevo – still retains an intellectual, highbrow flavour – with its superbly preserved cafés – a Vienna-by-the-sea. Grado, the major resort – called "the island of the sun" – is still a choice watering hole for German speaking families and over-fifties. The wilderness of its lagoons is conscientiously preserved, along with the *casuni* or thatched huts of the fishermen, as are the ancient religious rituals such as the Procession of the Virgin.

The gastronomy of the area – affected by Austrian and eastern influences – is excellently described by Fred Plotkin in his *Terra Fortunata: the Splendid Food and Wine of Friuli-Venezia Giulia.* Friuli wines – mainly from the Collio hills – especially the whites – are of sensationally high quality.

The road, rail and airport connections, – the industrialisation of the hinterland combined with a thriving and well-organised tourist industry gives this coast an air of bustling prosperity. The climate is mainly mild, marred, perhaps, by the abundant rainfall, both in summer and winter, and by the famously fierce and biting northeast wind known in Trieste as the B*ora*. Udine, however, a city thirty miles inland from Trieste was recently voted, by Italians, the most 'liveable' place in Italy.

Typical properties for sale

As befits a once prosperous outpost of the Austro-Hungarian empire
there is a large stock of period buildings, many in the *art nouveau* idiom which is called
Liberty in Italian. These are now in the process of being restored in the town centres. In
Trieste, the unrestored prices start at €800 per sq.m; restored from €1,800 to €2,600 per
sq.m. In Udine city centre, 18th century houses are still available at similar prices.

Condominium blocks of the 50s, 60s and 70s form the bulk of the property on offer.
For seekers of the modern; modular ecological, perfectly insulated detached suburban
houses are available to order, for €285,000 – €325,000, and brand new flats, with
terraces, from €148,000 for 85sq.m.

Location	Type	Description	Price
Visogliano (Trieste)	modern detached house	3-storey house, 180sq.m with integral garage and 250sq.m garden. 3 bedrooms and 3 bathrooms	€400,000
Grado	apartment	2 bedroom apartment 100sq.m, in old town, furnished. Garage.	€210,000
Lignano Riviera	modern end-of-terrace town house	3 bedrooms, 3 bathrooms 135sq.m. Garden 180sq.m. No work required.	€225,000
Duino	apartment	2 bedrooms, 2 bathrooms, 120sq.m, spacious. Terraces and sea view.	€350,000

Agents for this region: www.abitareudine.it, www.immobiliaregabbiano.com,
www.casa.it, www.tecnocasa.it

ROMAGNA

Capital: *Bologna*
Climate: *Summer Max. Temp:* 28°C. *Winter Min. Temp:* 0°C. *Annual Rainfall:*
703mm
Airports: *Bologna, Forlì, Rimini.*
Romagna is the part of the region of Emilia-Romagna which borders on the Adriatic
sea, between Veneto to the north and the Marches and San Marino to the southeast.
(San Marino is an anomalous independent republic in Italian territory). In the north of
the area is the fertile alluvial plain of the Po delta and the reclaimed wetlands and salt
flats surrounding the Comacchio lagoon (a nature reserve). The coastal plain extends
south, through the ancient pinewoods of Ravenna and Cervia, to the resort towns of
Rimini and Riccione. The population is dense, the people are energetic and active in
agribusiness, light industries and tourism. There is commercial fruit growing on a
large scale in the Lugo-Alfonsine area, ceramics etc. at Faenza, chemicals and petrol
refineries at Ravenna, and small factories and warehouses of all kinds everywhere.

Levels of pollution and traffic are very high.

At the same time Romagna's wide beaches have since the 1950s been developed for mass tourism – mostly Italian, but there are now a lot of Russian and East European visitors, especially at Rimini. Milano Marittima, Cervia, Cesenatico, Bellaria, Rimini, Riccione and the Ravenna and Ferrara beaches are packed with regimented deckchairs, umbrellas, beach bars and famed for their nightspots which offer the latest dance music as well as their own favourite Romagna style of *ballo liscio* (close dancing). In the off-season it is possible to find a strip of wild, empty beach at Cesenatico, but in July and August everywhere is overcrowded, simply because hotels and *pensioni* offer the cheapest deals in Italy here, and the food and the 'buzz' is excellent.

Fog, smog and cold winters are not normally associated with the Mediterranean, but the foreign buyer in the Romagna *entroterra* (hinterland) will have to tolerate them in exchange for the benefit of hot summers, fertile land, intellectual stimulus, accessibility, an astonishing amount of art and history, and an almost complete absence of élite expatriate cliques and 'happy valleys', (but a lot of economic immigrants). This is the real Italy. From the north southwards some places to consider are as follows:

THE REAL ITALY

O **Goro:** a small fishing and mussel-farming community on the coast, a few miles from the forest of Mesola inland (protected wildlife).

O **Codigoro:** a small town associated with the Benedictine Abbey of Pomposa, for splendid concerts and *enogastronomia* (eating and drinking).

O **Comacchio:** a 'little Venice' with its canals and historic buildings. The neighbouring wetlands and salt flats are a paradise for birdspotters. Eel is served as a gourmet speciality, and there are sentimental historic memories of Garibaldi's companion Anita who died here.

O **Ravenna:** a city of great charm and historical importance, an Etruscan foundation, the headquarters of the Roman Adriatic Fleet (at Classe, the harbour long since silted up), in its heyday the capital of the Western Roman Empire (AD 402) and the court of Theodoric (AD 493-526). Its Romanesque churches have superb mosaics. In its hinterland is:

O **Bagnacavallo:** with a castle once owned by Sir John Hawkwood, the English *condottiere*, and a convent which is the burial place of Byron's daughter, Allegra, near the peach orchards of **Lugo.**

O **Cesena:** perhaps because of its association with Cesare Borgia, is a forbidding place.

O **Forlì:** the one merit of Forlì is its international airport.

The name of Romagna came from the Roman soldiers who were granted 'viritane acquisitions' – land confiscated from the indigenous Celtic tribe (the Lingoni) in this fertile area. After the glories of the Byzantine era the region became a Papal backwater, having been donated to the Papacy by the Frankish Conquerors Pepin, and his son Charlemagne, in AD 776. Local lords, such as the Malatestas of Rimini were dominant during the flowering of the renaissance. After a Napoleonic interlude the region joined the Kingdom of Sardinia by popular vote. In the 20th century, Romagna's most infamous son, the fascist dictator Benito Mussolini, (from Predappio, near Forlì) personified the energy and impetuosity of the Romagna character. After World War II Romagna became staunchly communist. The 1950's provincial culture of Rimini was immortalised by Fellini in the films *I Vitelloni* and *Amarcord*.

Romagna lives by, off and for food, of great variety, based on butter rather than oil – rich lasagna, tortelloni and pasta everywhere, fried squid and sole at Rimini, washed down by easy drinking Sangiovese or Trebbiano wine.

Typical properties for sale

This region has beautiful villas but few come onto the market and there are very few for renovation. Ravenna, Rimini, Milano Marittima and Riccione on the Adriatic coast are popular summer resorts for young Italians and foreigners who often own apartments along the coast. Historic coastal town centres have a mixture of new buildings and period houses.

Location	Type	Description	Price
Rimini	farmhouse (casale)	House to be restored on outskirts of Rimini 190sq.m. Possibility of purchasing more land approx. 620sq.m	€290,000
Cattolica	villa	Villa situated in a park on 4 floors. 168sq.m. 3 bedrooms, 2 living rooms, 2 bathrooms, balcony, cellar and garage.	€320,000
Riccione	apartment	Apartment in pedestrian area, few metres from the sea. Cellar/store, 2 bedrooms, 2 living rooms, small room leading to balcony.	€361,519
Ravenna	villa	3 bedrooms, 2 living rooms, cellar, garage, woodstore. 130sq.m. Large terrace.	€270,000
Igea Marina	farmhouse to be restored	210sq.m 6 rooms + 1 very large. Few miles from Santarcangelo. Garden 3,500sq.m with barn 100sq.m conversion into apartments possible.	€440,000

Agents for this Region: www.casa.it, www.fiaip.it

CENTRAL ITALY – NORTHERN

TUSCANY

Capital: *Florence* (1 metre above sea level)
Climate: *Summer Max. Temp:* 29°C. *Winter Min. Temp:*   2°C. *Annual Rainfall:* 901mm
Airports: *Pisa, Florence*
Ferry Ports: *Livorno* (for Corsica, Sardinia and Sicily), *Piombino* (for Elba)
Tuscany's coastline faces west onto the Tyrrhenian sea. The Tuscan archipelago includes the islands of Elba, Capraia and Giglio. The Apuan Alps (1,945m) lie parallel to the coast between Aulla and Pisa, whilst to the south are the Colline Metallifere

(metal-bearing hills) west of Siena, and the Monte Amiata massif (1,738m) north of Grosseto.

There is a heavy concentration of population between Carrara and Livorno, stretching up the Arno valley to Florence. A new motorwary is duplicating the arterial railway line down the coast through Pisa and Grosseto, parallel with the Via Aurelia.

Tuscany acquired a distinctive culture from the Etruscans, merging with Roman, Gauls, Franks and Lombards, peaking with the city states of the Renaissance in which Pisa, Siena and Lucca were finally dominated by Florence. The abundance of artistic and architectural masterpieces the good food and wine, the ease of the language (standard Italian), the beauty of the countryside – attract more than five million foreign visitors a year (compared to a local population of three and a half million). Foreign residents love the good nature and uninquisitive civility of the people.

Tourism is the dominant industry with an emphasis on the cities rather than the coastline – which Italians find more expensive than the Adriatic riviera of Rimini.

The hill villages of the Lunigiana area around Aulla are becoming popular with British house buyers. The resorts of Forte dei Marmi and Viareggio (Versilia) still have an aristocratic cachet although they have been heavily built over for a century. The hinterland around Camaiore attracts artists and sculptors, nearby are the marble quarries of Carrara, the world centre of the marble trade.

Pisa is a thriving university town and industrial centre – a short distance from one of the most *vivibile* places in Italy, Lucca, between which cities the mild climate and rainfall favour the growth of camellias and oranges. Excellent road, rail and airport services here also give a strategic advantage to the US and NATO base (2,000 hectares) at Camp Darby, south of Pisa, a massive arsenal of military and humanitarian matériel indispensible for US operations in the Mediterranean Basin (including Iraq) and North Africa; doubling as a private beach on the 'Italian Riviera' for privileged US personnel. Known as the 'Tombolo' (sand bar) this area has never lost the louche image of the post-war era, when it was a haven for deserters, criminals and prostitutes. It stretches from Viareggio to the strip development of Tirrenia and Livorno (Leghorn), a city which has suffered much from war damage and overbuilding since its days of glory in the 18th century, when it was a free port and climatic resort; there are still grand villas overlooking the sea and a thriving untouristic and Jewish community. Cecina and the 'Riva degli Etruschi' continue the strip development down the coast, alleviated by mature windbreaks of parasol pines. Much of the Donoratico seaside is privately owned. Riparbella, Massa Marittima and Giuncarico are recommended *entroterra* locations. The seaport of Piombino, is disfigured by its derelict ironworks.

This area, known as the Alta Maremma (Upper Maremma) is famous for its Etruscan remains – at Vetulonia, Populonia, Roselle – for its history of malaria and banditry and its 'hard-headed' people.

Further down the coast are the fashionable resorts of the Punta Ala (which has a VIP marina and a golf course) and Castiglione della Pescaia, a pretty fishing port. Grosseto is an undistinguished city in a flat clayey plain, with a charming hilly hinterland (Ribolla, Scansano, Magliano Toscana, and the hot springs of Saturnia). South of Grosseto is the splendid nature reserve, at Alberese of the Parco dell'Uccellina, where wild Maremma cattle, and cowboys called *butteri*, rove, and empty beaches can be found beyond the dense cicada-loud pinewoods.

Further south is the small yachting and fishing port of Talamone, near which a coalition of Gaulish tribes was annihilated (40,000 killed) by the Roman legions in 225 AD, and which became a seaport of the ambitious republic of Siena in the 1500s. **On the south of the gulf of Talamone, via Orbetello – a one time Spanish**

Praesidium – is the peninsula of Monte Argentario, a rich and fashionable Italian resort, with fine marinas at Porto Ercole and Porto Santo Stefano. **Cosa** is the name of the ancient Etruscan and Roman port here, and Capalbio is a delightful small walled town in the smiling countryside a few miles inland.

Of the islands, Giglio is much loved (ferries from Porto Santo Stefano), and Elba (ferries from Livorno or Piombino), has crystalline seas, a mild climate and memories of Etruscan iron workers and of Napoleon's Kingdom of exile in 1812, but it is excessively populated now by summer vacationers.

In Maremma the quality of the vegetables is sensational, perhaps because of the mineral-rich soil, but the olive oil is gross and Morellino di Scansano is the only distinguished red wine. Seafood is dominated by the Livorno style; *cacciucco* is a hairy fish soup flavoured with tomatoes, garlic, olive oil and parsley. In Pisa *Ce'e* (blind things), a mass of tiny elvers, is a delicacy. Da Michele in Saturnia is the recognised Mecca of Maremma cuisine, where if you are lucky porcupine, or wild asparagus, will be on the menu.

Typical Properties for Sale

Farmhouses with a view of the sea are hard to find. Rural architecture has distinct regional characteristics from the long rectangular farms of Lucca to the square barracks with loggia structures further inland. The big house or *villa* architecture is even grander; large 15th century villas are still to be found. But most of the pretty places have long since been sold. The barns, outbuildings and remote hovels which are left are being offered at inflated prices, driving investors towards small village properties and apartments; these are far more convenient and easier to maintain.

Location	Type	Description	Price
Pomaia (Pisa)	detached one storey house	A low building in need of restoration, 110sq.m, 15km from sea, near tibetan buddhist centre 2 bedrooms, small garden.	€140,000
Rosignano Solvay (Livorno)	detached one storey house	Modern building 150sq.m, near sea and village. central heating. 9,000sq.m land, mostly olives.	€440,000
Porto Ercole (Grosseto-Monte Argentario)	luxury villa	Superbly restored farmhouse 260sq.m + 80sq.m outbuilding, well, pool, staff quarters. 2.9 hectares. sea view near harbour 350m altitude.	€2,000,000
Aulla (Massa Carrara)	Farmhouse	Restored farmhouse, 150sq.m. central heating . integral garage. 2.5 hectares.	€350,000
Capalbio	Farmhouse	Ex 'ente maremma' state-built farmhouse, restored, 2 storey, 2 bedroom. 230sq.m with garden.	€360,000

Agents for this Region: www.tecnocasa.it, www.etruscaimmobiliare.it

LE MARCHE

Capital: Ancona – (5 metres above sea level)
Climate: *Summer Max Temp:* 27°C. *Winter Min. Temp.*: 1°C. *Annual Rainfall:* 1,157mm
Airports: *Ancona Falconara* (International).
Ferry Ports: *Ancona* (to Croatia and Greece).

The 116km of the Adriatic coast is, for long stretches, a ribbon of narrow sandy beach (at Fano and Sinigallia), punctuated by the occasional rocky outcrop such as: Monte San Bartolo (Pesaro), which has steep cliffs and pebble beaches, Monte Conero (Ancona) and Grottamare (Ascoli Piceno).

Up-valley locations seem remote and landlocked. Socialising expatriates get used to long drives on winding roads. But the coast has excellent communications: the arterial Bologna-Taranto autostrada relieves the flow on the shore road along the Adriatic, which is only crowded in July and August. A projected *superstrada* linking the Adriatic with the Tyrrhenian sea (Fano – Grosseto) has reached Urbino. Ancona has direct intercity rail links with Bologna and Rome as well as an international airport.

One sixth of the population is engaged in agriculture. The people of the Marches, *Marchigiani*, are attached to their smallholdings and often conduct small craft businesses such as pottery, carpentry, wrought iron and basketwork. Important crops are: wheat, sugar beet, cauliflower and table olives. There are thousands of hectares of vineyards. Fisheries are well developed, especially mussel farming. The entrepreneurial skills of the Marchigiani have led to the creation of many successful businesses in footwear, textiles, paper, accordions and other musical instruments (Castelfidardo), mechanical engineering (Benelli motorbikes at Pesaro). There are petrochemical works at Falconara (Ancona). Levels of pollution are low, except at Macerata, which suffers badly.

The climate on the coast is dry and temperate but winds predominately from the east and north-east can be tiresome.

The Adriatic coast attracts tourists and yachtsmen with its charming seaports. Fano (population 56,000) dates back to the Roman temple (Fanum) on the Flaminian Way, which reached the coast here. The hill town of Grottamare, colonised by Picenians in the ninth century BC, by Italian aristocrats in the seventeenth century AD, and developed as a resort in the 1930s is proud of the palm and orange trees which grow on its mild seashore plain. San Benedetto del Tronto (Ascoli Piceno) is dedicated to boat building as well as tourism, and Sirolo (Ancona) is one of the most enchanting resorts in Italy with its beaches and crags in the lee of Mount Conero, where conditions are excellent for windsurfing.

Each city has its own history. Ancona for example was a Greek foundation, whilst Ascoli Piceno was founded by the Picenians. Rome conquered the area in the third century BC. In the 2nd century AD the emperor Trajan made Ancona one of the biggest naval harbours in the Mediterranean, and a thousand years later it was used for shipping crusader armies to the Holy Land. The Sienese pope Pius II died here on his abortive crusade of 1464.

The Goths, Lombards and Byzantines overran the area in the dark ages. The Franks donated it to the Papacy. For centuries the people of the Marches were employed by the Papal states as tax collectors. They are still quietly spoken, serious and hardworking, cherished as neighbours by the many expatriates who have homes in the region. A southern Italian writer, Angelo Agozzino, describes them as:

Full of polite hospitality, with a deep sense of solidarity – which spreads to all aspects of life – their respect for nature, their attachment to old traditions and culture, their constant readiness to listen and evaluate what people have to say, without preconceptions – these are civilised qualities which will greet anyone who has the good fortune to visit this region and get to know the people.

The *Marchigiani* retain a strong tradition of frugality and self-sufficiency. They still slaughter their own pigs and make their own herb flavoured sheep cheese, wine and oil. Large *Ascolana* olives stuffed and fried in batter, pigeons, rabbits, and artichokes, stuffed with *ripieni* incorporating salami, Marsala wine and other ingredients are specialities, as are stuffed squid and sole. Baked mussels, fried fish, and the local *brodetto* (fish soup) are celebrated. Given the superb pasturage of the region, the quality of the meat is so good that the meat consumption here is the highest in Italy. Mixed grills *alla brace* are unrivalled. Sweet raviolo and candied rice puddings are something offered for dessert.

Exquisite dry white *Verdicchio* wines come from this region, whilst the local reds are mostly based on the *Montepulciano* and *Sangiovese* grape.

Typical properties for sale

You can find property bargains here. Local architecture is white stucco farmhouses with external staircases. Apartments are inexpensive on the coast.

Location	Type	Description	Price
Ancona	House (Casa Colonica)	Located near centre of Ancona 400sq.m. Also small barn 40sq.m 25km from sea. House: Ground Floor, cellar, stable. 1st Floor . 5 rooms partially renovated. Land 2,000sq.m	€93,000
Fermo	Converted Farmhouse (Stucco Finished)	On hill 12km from sea. 188sq.m. 3 bedrooms, 2 bathrooms. 6,000sq.m of land including fruit trees, productive olive grove and well. (private sale) (www.casa.it)	€310,000
Petriano	2 Storey Brick Farmhouse	200sq.m + unconverted outbuilding of 50sq.m. 1,500sq.m. garden. Superb panorama. 1 km village, 19km sea, 6km Pesaro. (www.casa.it)	€80,000
S.Benedetto Del Tronto	One Bedroom Apartment	Small modernised apartment 44sq.m with 25sq.m terrace near sea.	€85,000

Agents for this Region: www.caseealsolemarche.com; www.marcheprop ertysales.com; www.italianvillasdirect.com; www.homesinitaly.co.uk

CENTRAL ITALY-SOUTHERN

LAZIO

Capital: *Rome*
Climate: *Summer Max. Temp.* 28°C; *Winter Min. Temp.* 4°C. *Annual Rainfall:* 819mm
Airports: *Rome* (Fiumicino). *Rome* (Ciampino).
Ferry Ports: *Civitavecchia*

On the Tyrrhenian Sea, the coastal strip, north to south, is called the *Maremma* – a continuation of the Tuscan Maremma, which extends as far as Tarquinia (the most famous of all Etruscan places, with its fabulous tombs and museum). After the interruption of Tolfa hills (616m) and the Linaro promontory, near the fairly unattractive seaport of Civitavecchia, the flatlands are called the Agro Romano – or the Roman Campagna – the site of Rome's international airport, Fiumicino, and of ancient Rome's silted up seaport, Ostia, at the mouth of the river Tiber. Southeast, near Latina, are the Pontine marshes, once swampy and malarial, but reclaimed over the centuries, and finally drained in the 1930s. Continuing down the coast Monte Circeo (541m) and the hills of the Circeo national park form the headland, which stands between the ancient coastal towns of Anzio and Terracina. The harbour and bay of Gaeta complete the extreme south of the region.

Except for the rocky capes of Linaro, Circeo and Gaeta, the 310km of Lazio's coastline are mostly sandy – long stretches are hideously disfigured by 20th century building. Only a few sections remain unspoilt: the nature reserve and bird sanctuary of Macchiatonda on the coast between Ladispoli and Santa Marinella south of the Tolfa hills, and the nature reserve of Tor Caldera near Anzio, the Circeo national park, and the coastal lakes of Fogliano, Sabaudia and Fondi.

THE LAZIO COAST

The best resorts for yachtsman are Tarquinia, Ponza island, San Felice Circeo, Sperlonga, and the island of Ventotene. The best beaches (north to south) are near Pescia Romana, Montalto di Castro, Ladispoli, Ostia, Tor Caldera, Nero's grotto near Anzio, Neltuno, Sperlonga and Gaeta.

The Ausonian range of mountains (1,090m) north of Terracina and Sperlonga, and the Aurunci range (1,535m) north of Gaeta shelter these seaside places from the *tramontana* winds. Because of its exceptional climate this coast has been a favourite resort since Roman times. Other towns on the Bay of Gaeta are Formia, Scauro and Minturno. Gaeta is the headquarters of the US sixth fleet. English-speaking infrastructures, schools, shops and clubs have consequently developed in this delightful region. Formia is an ancient seaport, originally Greek, with ferries to the islands of Ponza and Santo Stefano. The weather in these favoured regions of coastal Lazio is almost ideal.

Mediterranean Lazio is of course dominated by its great capital city Rome. – *caput mundi*, where all roads lead.

Rome is home not only to the Italian government but also to the Vatican, a massive multinational state within a state. It is a magnet for pilgrims and tourists, and crowded at all times of the year, its centre barred to traffic. Despite its permanent gridlock Rome has glamour and appeal for thousands of Italians and foreigners who are delighted to live there permanently, from aesthetes and intellectuals, who favour posher areas of Parioli and Piazza Navona, to the foreign workers who gravitate to the station (*Termini*) district and the seedier suburbs. Frascati and the Alban hills south of Rome, rich in myth and history, are now charming suburbs. The Lazio *entroterra* generally offers idyllic peace and order, very near to an international hub of communications, and a lively cultural capital.

Rome has always been famous for its *osterie* and *trattorie* since ancient times. "The less you spend the better you eat" is a saying there. Succulent baby lamb, tender baked artichokes, simple bacon – and – egg, or garlic – oil – and chilli flavoured spaghetti, superb charcoal grilled lobster, crayfish or sea bream from Gaeta, washed down with white Frascati wine, perhaps followed by chestnut ice cream. The food, the wine and the humour of Lazio are captivating.

Typical Properties For Sale

The expansion of Rome's population and the massive developments of the Lazio coastline over the past fifty years has led to an abundant supply of fairly modern apartments in this coastal region. Too much concrete inhibits recreational buyers, who prefer to head for the hills inland.

The medieval town centres, however, such as Sperlonga and Gaeta, offer attractive small (80sq.m) apartments in period buildings for in the region of €300,000, although more than double that price must be paid for a building that dates back to AD 1000. **The combination of modernised medieval town life, within walking distance of the sea, in this balmy climate, is very heady.**

Location	Type	Description	Price
Tarquinia	house	Ancient stone building under a pitched terracotta roof. 2 floors – completely refurbished. Mains water, electricity and gas.	€145,000
Cerveteri	house	House of stone construction 390sq.m, 5 bedrooms, 3 bathrooms – galleried drawing room. Outbuildings, vineyards Etruscan tomb. 4 hectares, swimming pool and mature gardens. 10 minutes from sea.	€670,000
Formia	apartment	2nd floor apartment in park block. 3 bedrooms, panoramic terrace overlooking the bay. 110sq.m. Cellar and garage.	€245,000
Marina Di Ardea	apartment	Seaside ground floor apartment 65sq.m. 1 bedroom, terrace, central heating. Garden.	€ 98,000
Marechiaro (Anzio)	duplex apartment	1st and top floor apartment,100sq.m, 3 bedrooms, roof terrace. Independent central heating. Splendid sea view.	€131,000

Agents for this Region: www.wcpitaly.com, www.tecnocasa.com, www.gabettionline.it, www.casa.it.

ABRUZZO

Capital: *L'Aquila*
Climate: *Summer Max. Temp:* 29°C ; *Winter Min. Temp:* 2°C; *Annual Rainfall:* 686mm
Airports: *Pescara*
Ferry Ports: *Pescara* (to Croatia)

Abruzzo on the Adriatic coast in the middle of the peninsula, south of Le Marche, and north of Molise, is one of the least populated regions in Italy – thanks to its wild mountainous interior: the Gran Sasso d'Italia is the highest peak in the Apennines (2,912m) and the centre of a huge nature reserve and national park.

On the coast, Mediterranean scrub has been largely replaced by crops, olive groves and vineyards, interspersed with ilex, ash and hornbeam.

The coastline is varied: broad sandy beaches and well tended resorts, with night life, at Alba Adriatica and Pineto ('the pearl of the Abruzzo Riviera), small rocky beaches further south at Rocca San Giovanni, and sand dunes at Punta Penna and Vasto, with areas off the beaten track rich in wildlife including the occasional sea turtle. San Giovanni in Venere is the site of an imposing Benedictine Abbey where ancient fishing contraptions called *travocchi* are still in use (at Fossacesia in the province of Chieti).

Old religious traditions, unspoilt *entroterra* villages, old fashioned people and crafts such as copper-beating are a feature of this area, which also boasts a statistical record of longevity: an excellent location for retirement – Fossacesia for example is a few minutes from the lively seaport town of Pescara, from a golf and country club (at Miglianico), from beaches, ski-resorts, autostradas, an international airport and a direct rail link with Rome and Bologna. The seaside provinces of Teramo, Pescaro and Chieti also maintain between them fourteen public hospitals for a combined population of less than a million.

Light entrepreneurial industries are developing in Abruzzo, along with fisheries and mollusc farming. Criminality is not a problem. An astonishing amount of genuine antiquity and folklore has survived the depopulation of the last century. Lookout towers on the coast still guard against the Turks and the Saracens. The climate on the coast is temperate, northeast winds predominate.

The ancient inhabitants of the region, primarily Picenians, whose most famous relic is the stone statue of the warrior at Capestrano, were brutally suppressed by the Romans. Lanciano, Vasto, Penne, Atri and Teramo are full of Roman remains. The father of the English pre-Raphaelite poet and painter Dante Gabriel Rossetti was an Abruzzo man (an exiled education minister of the Napoleonic regime). Gabriele d'Annunzio, the flamboyant poet and nationalist hero was born in Pescara in 1863; he had a strong sentimental attachment to the landscape of his childhood, and his poetry, such as *La Pioggia nel Pineto* (Rain in the Pinewood) is rich in allusions to the spirit of the place.

The food and wine here are also excellent. The quaint Adriatic village of Fara San Martino is the home of the best machine-made pasta in the world (F.lli De Cecco). Savoury *timballi*, pulses, lentils, spelt (*farro*), stuffed vegetables (ripieni), vinegar and saffron flavoured fried fish (*scapece*) are washed down by Trebbiano d'Abruzzo (white) or Montepulciano d'Abruzzo (red).

Typical Properties for Sale

Location	Type	Description	Price
Pescara	apartment new 3 storey block	Apartment by the sea. 40sq.m. 1/2 bedrooms, living room, integral garage.	€80,000
Montesilvano Riviera	apartment in old building	Facing sea. 3 floors. 150sq.m. Hall, room with fireplace, kitchen, studio. 2 bedrooms, 2 bathrooms, terrace 150sq.m, lift and garage 20sq.m.	€250,000
Torano Nuovo	town house	3 storey house. Ground floor: garage store room, front door, stairs to: kitchen/living room, bathroom. 2nd floor: 2 bedrooms fully furnished, good decorative order.	€170,000 Furnished €160,000 Unfurnished
Penne	town house with garden	3 storey house, modernised with open fireplaces and marble floors, with huge garden in town centre with views of the Adriatic.	€250,000

Agents for this Region: www.casa.it; www.abruzzoproperties.com

MOLISE

Capital: *Campobasso*
Climate: *Summer Max. Temp.* 27°C. *Winter Min. Temp.* 6°C. *Annual Rainfall:* 363mm
Airports: *Pescara* (Abruzzo)
Ferry Ports: *Termoli* (to Tremiti Islands)
Molise has 38km of Adriatic coastline bordering Abruzzo to the north and Puglia to the south east. Agriculture is a major activity, often at subsistence levels. Vineyards and olive groves flourish between the foothills and the sea. There is only one really industrialised area, near Termoli on the coast (furniture, engineering, textiles, building materials, processed foods etc.) and tourism is undeveloped. **Indeed the Italian tourist board is encouraging people to visit Molise before it becomes fashionable.** The coastal climate is mild and dry.

There are wide sandy dunes by the sea and old droving trails called *tratturi* into the *entroterra*. The coastal plain, once extensive marshland, has been drained and built on since the nineteenth century, but the original environment still survives on the banks of the river Biferno, with its tamarisk woods, canebrakes and clumps of Aleppo pine. The beach at Campomarino, where this river flows into the sea is surrounded by pinewoods and dunes covered with couch grass, heather and cistus. **Molise beaches are still wild – crowded in July and August – but delightful in the off-season.** Termoli is the only sea-port, from which ferries ply to the three Tremiti islands 25km offshore, once a Benedictine monastery, then a Bourbon prison, now a magical resort for yachtsmen and divers, in the limpid blue waters of the Adriatic.

A coast road and a railway line run along the littoral. A parallel autostrada relieves traffic but cuts off the *entroterra* from the sea. The *entroterra* villages such as Petacciato, Montenero di Bisaccia. S. Giacomo degli Schiavoni, Larino, Guglionesi, S. Martino in Pensilis, Cliternia Nuova, depopulated by massive emigration to the Americas in the twentieth century, and affected by the ferocious warfare between Allied and German troops, which was ended by the Allied landings at Termoli in 1943, are now charming well-preserved places much loved by returning emigrants and full of folklore and festivals. Guglionesi, for example, is in an ideal position between the hills and the sea, with exceptional local produce (olive oil, ricotta, pecorino) and superb restaurants.

The name Molise comes from its feudal chief High of Mulhouse, who died in 1168, by no means the last of a long line of invaders that followed the fall of the Roman empire – Molise, previously part of the Abruzzi, became a separate region in 1963.

In 2002 an earthquake killed 26 children and three adults in San Giuliano di Puglia, drawing attention to the danger of ignoring anti-seismic building codes in this area – and to the stoical character of the Molisani. Molise's most famous personality, Antonio di Pietro, the crusading Milan magistrate of the 1990's 'clean hands' (*mani pulite*) campaign, epitomises the stern integrity which lies at the heart of this old-fashioned region.

The food here, especially the seafood, is exceptionally good – and savoury – much use is made of flavourings and stuffings of ham, *ricotta, provolone, pecorino*, bacon, garlic and chilli: fried *ravioli*, thick vegetable soups. *Mucische* – sun-dried and lightly smoked mutton, thinly sliced with olive oil and chillis, is an unusual speciality. For these savoury foods you need a good Montepulciano di Molise or an Aglianico red. A Molise proverb holds that a barrel full of wine works more miracles than a church full of saints.

The Molise dialect is similar to that of northern Puglia. There are linguistic enclaves of Albanian in the province of Campobasso.

Typical properties for sale

There are many unfinished properties on the market, which can be picked up cheap. You have to be wary of cowboy developers and illegal building work that flouts the strict anti-seismic codes necessary in this area.

Location	Type	Description	Price
Petacciato	detached house	New 2 storey unfinished house with garage + 6,000sq.m land and view of the sea.	€119,000
Mafalda	town mansion	19th century Aristocratic *Palazzo*, 1,450sq.m, sea view, 1,6000sq.m garden. 20km from sea.	€1,200,000
San Giacomo	detached house	New one storey, 110sq.m. Small garden.	€110,000
Campomarino	Apartment	Modern ground floor seaside apartment, 120sq.m, with terrace.	€980,000

Agent for this Region: www.tecnocasa.it www.casa.it www.italianvillasdirect.com

SARDINIA

Capital: *Cagliari* (1 metre above sea level)
Climate: *Summer Max. Temp. 30°C. Winter Min. Temp. 6°C.*
Annual Rainfall 427mm
Airports: *Alghero, Olbia, Cagliari*
Ferry Ports: *Porto Torres, Olbia, Cagliari*

Sardinia is the second largest island in the Mediterranean after Sicily, 12km from Corsica to the north, 120km from Tuscany to the northeast and 185km from Africa in the south. It has 1,849km of coastline and very deep coastal waters, high rocky cliffs running straight for miles, often ending in promontories and surrounded by islands. Inland are ponds, marshes and extended barren hills. The northwest and northeast coastlines are jagged and impassable for long sections. The mountains inland are high (Gennargentu is 1,834m) and the valleys are deep. There is one great plain – Campidano – which extends across the south (the Gulf of Cagliari) for about 100km up to the Gulf of Oristano. Tracts of virgin forest have survived, totalling one sixth of the whole surface of the island, mostly of ilex, oak, chestnut, and carob. The forest of Gutturu Mannu in the South is the largest forest in the Mediterranean area. Sardinia is the home of the *macchia* (Mediterranean scrub): cistus, broom, heather, mastic, lentisk, arbutus, wild olive and cork oak, and the central wilderness – and old silver mines – of Iglesiente teams with wildlife: Sardinian breeds of deer, wildcat, goats, sparrows and partridges. Pink flamingoes flock to the salt marshes at the Stagno di Molentartguis near Cagliari.

The climate is mild and bright – averaging 300 days of sunshine in the year. The rain falls mainly in the autumn and winter, with occasional showers in the spring. The island is ventilated by winds from all directions. The northwest wind the *maestrale*, dominates, fresh and bracing in the winter, cooling and drying in the summer. Less frequent is the *scirocco* from the south, the *levante* on the east coast, and the *ponente* on the west coast.

Sardinia is uniquely characterised by curious stone towers called *nuraghi*, 7,000 of them scattered all over the territory, perhaps iron or bronze age forts. The island was pillaged for its mineral resources and timber by Myceneans, Cypriots, Phoenicians, occupied by Cathage (500-238 BC) and then exploited by the Romans, who slaughtered 12,000 islanders in 177 BC – and built roads, which still survive. Further invaders, Vandals, Byzantines and Arabs forced the natives to move inland; they created four autonomous *giudicati* (jurisdictions): Arborea, Cagliari, Gallura and Torres. In the thirteenth century Genoa and Pisa moved in to stake their claims. Sardinia's own warrior queen, Eleonora d'Arborea (capital Orestano), started a resistance which kept Arborea independent until the Spanish took over the whole island in 1478. Austria owned Sardinia briefly (1708 -1718) ceding it to the house of Savoy under whom a repressive feudal autonomy was maintained until 1847, followed by an unwanted unification with Italy in 1861, of which Sardinia is now an autonomous region under a special statute of 1948.

After centuries of neglect and oppression, Sardinia has retained a unique archaic culture. Traditional costumes and folk music still thrive spontaneously. The language retains archaic Latin features. In the Alghero area an ancient form of Catalan is still spoken by 15,000 people.

The Sardinian style of cookery is wild and archaic too – the roasting of myrtle-flavoured pork, lamb or kid is almost a religious ritual. Hybrid influences are apparent in cous-cous (*fregula*), crisp bread (*pane carasau*) and nougat (*torrone*). Sheep's cheese (*pecorino*) and seafoods such as lobster, are supreme. Each district has its own cuisine and wine: Vermentino white in Sassari, Connonau red in Nuovo – and vernaccia everywhere. The influx of rich Italian tourists has increased the number of refined restaurants, but the traditions are just as proudly preserved in the humble trattorias.

Sardinia still has the reputation of being a resort of the yacht-borne super rich who have a fabulous enclave on the Costa Smeralda (e.g. Porto Rotondo) in the northeast. Luxury villas, golf courses, private beaches and marinas, no pollution, a wild hinterland and an irresistible seafood cuisine, lure more than one million Italians to Sardinia every summer. Other coastal areas are sometimes marred by ugly strip development while the inner city *centri storici* are undergoing great improvements, especially Cagliari, the capital city, – and Oristano and Sassari – where the combined effect of university and hospital life are having a beneficial influence on the *liveability* of these ancient centres. But beware of water shortages.

RECOMMENDED AREAS

Of the coastal areas Gallura in the north – exposed to the *maestrale* wind – is very beautiful. The western Bosa district is claimed to be the new Tuscany and handy for the cheap flights to Alghero – whilst the country around Cagliari in the south is of great charm, sheltered from winds and convenient for city visits. Nuoro – and the 'Gulf of Oranges' on the east coast – has fine beaches and accessibility.

The natives of Sardinia give the impression of being fiercely proud, intelligent and energetic. They have furnished the '*continente*' (Italy) with a disproportionate number of intellectuals and academics (eg Antonia Gramsci, the father of Italian communism and president Pietro Nenni). Understandably rebellious, bandits have taken refuge in the Barbagia (*Barbarian country*) since Roman times; the tradition of kidnapping has probably ended with the last century, but the spirit of independence is still alive in the Sardinian Action Party (*Partito Sardo d'Azione*), who strongly resent the NATO and US presence on the island and occasionally stage violent demonstrations. (There is a US navy base at La Maddalena in the north, and an air force base at Decimomannu near Cagliari in the south). Apart from US service personnel, who are mostly made welcome, Sardinia does not attract economic immigrants. Its character remains unreconstructedly Sardinian: passionate and hospitable, if a little suspicious of foreigners.

Typical Properties for Sale

There is a good supply of modern bungalows – often in tourist *villaggi* – ideal for vacation use – and condominium apartments, but very few rustic buildings for conversion. A favourite area is Alghero in the north-west which has an airport served by Ryanair. Sassari and Bosa are full of properties to snap up and agents to sell them. A property anywhere near a beach or a village would be an extremely good investment, easy to rent in summer and delightful to live in during winter (bright sun and bracing winds).

> **When searching for your dream house do not ignore the local hazards**
> Sardinia has regular **water shortages** and 1995-2000 were emergency years; be ruthless in ensuring your own supply. Also, check for **radon gas** for which the granite substrate provides favourable conditions. You should get a surveyor *(geometra)* to do this for you.

Location	Type	Description	Price
Porto San Paolo	House	Porto San Paolo known for its pure white beaches, 10km from Olbia airport. A detached house with 3 bedrooms, 2 bathrooms. Sea-front terrace.	€140,000
Porto Cervo	Villa	2 storey large villa with 6 bedrooms, 6 bathrooms, kitchen/living room. Terrace, mature garden overlooking the bay. Private access to the sea.	€1,250,000
Sinnai (Villaggio Delle Mimose)	Bungalow	A detached modern bungalow near Cagliari. 2 bedroom 75sq.m holiday villa – with shaded terrace, large swimming pool, garden, cellar, garage, fireplace.	€143,000
Alghero	Apartment	Fifth floor, 2 bedrooms, 2 bathrooms, terrace, garage, lift, own heating. Panoramic sea view	€210,000

Agents for this region: www.fidiaimmobiliare.com, www.tecnocasa.it

THE SOUTH AND SICILY

CAMPANIA

Capital: *Naples* (72 metres above sea level)
Climate: *Summer Max. Temp: 30ºC. Winter Min. Temp: 4ºC. Annual Rainfall:* 1,007mm
Airports: *Naples Capodichino*
Ferry Ports: *Naples* (to Sardinia, Sicily)
Lying on the Tyrrhenian Coast between the Bay of Gaeta and the Gulf of Policastro, Campania is a mainly maritime region, with its capital, Naples, the hub of communication lines between the south and the centre of Italy. It has the highest density of population in Italy, a terrain mostly mountainous and hilly except for a fertile plain north of Naples, where Capua and Caserta show signs of past wealth. The Vesuvian coastline (under the volcano) southeast of Naples leads through Sorrento to the steep Amalfi coast and the city of Salerno which is the gateway eastward to Eboli and the Lucanian Apennines, and southwards to the other coastal plain of Sele, once favoured by ancient Greek settlers and still dominated by the fabulous temples of Paestum, in the lee of the Cilento mountains which extend to the Gulf of Policastro. This is the most benign area of the region, with its combination of beaches, climate

and unspoilt hill country.

The rivers Garigliano (in the north), Volturno (past Capua) and the Sele (north of Paestum) are constantly flowing down from upland forest springs. Herds of buffalo are reared extensively – particularly in the area once known as the Terra di Lavoro (capital Caserta). The local unpasteurised buffalo mozzarella is a product of great international importance. The buffalo is an ancient draught beast – originally from India – at home in the swamps and marshes of the region.

There are concentrations of factories around Naples, Sarno and Salerno, which have a pollution problem, as have the agglomerations of Pomigliano d'Arco, Casoria, Castellamare di Stabia, Pozzuoli, Torre Annunziata, San Giovanni a Taduccio, Nocera Inferiore, Pagani and Battipaglia.

The climate is extraordinarily mild along the coast, with wet winters and occasional storms in the summer. The fertile volcanic soil and the frost-free winters are perfect for citrus fruits, bouganvilleas and tropical creepers; and Paestum is famous for its roses which bloom all year.

Settlers have been attracted here since antiquity. Cumae – just north of the modern Pozzuoli – was the first Greek settlement in Magna Graecia in the eighth century BC – where Greeks and Etruscans met to trade. The Sibyl in her cave at Cumae was a real oracle. This area was known by the Romans as Campania Felix (happy Campania). Tiberius had his villa here – on the isle of Capri – and it was here that Maecenas gave the poet Virgil his rural retreat. Roman life is preserved dramatically in the ruins of Herculaneum and Pompeii – destroyed by the eruption of Vesuvius in AD 63. At Capua there was a famous school for gladiators.

Campania continued to flourish after the Romans, – thanks to its distance from the Byzantine capital – and from AD 839 the republic of Amalfi enjoyed three centuries of glory as a sea power of fabulous wealth, overcoming the Saracens, but succumbing to the Normans and the Pisans, and finally, to plague and earthquake.

In the eighteenth century the Bourbons – Charles III – took over the Kingdom of Naples – and presided over a period of enlightenment. Naples was the mandatory last stop on the Grand Tour with its splendid opera house (the Teatro San Carlo) and its colony of artists and grandees. It was the liveliest and biggest city of Italy – and the scene of Captain Horatio Nelson and Emma Hamilton's first meeting in 1793.

After a Napoleonic interlude, with Murat as King – which gave rise to the seditious movement of the Carbonari – a secret society which appealed to Byron and Shelley – the Bourbon army was defeated and the Kingdom of Naples became part of the Kingdom of Italy in 1861.

To this day Campania is full of aristocrats and monarchists. It was the favourite refuge of White Russians escaping from the Russian revolution in 1917, and a popular haven for celebrities – artists, musicians, writers. The islands of Capri and Ischia, the resorts of Ravello, Amalfi and Positano and Sorrento are associated with many famous names. A rich, aristocratic, cosmopolitan society is now thriving in these idyllic locations, often living in houses which were abandoned in despair by the impoverished inhabitants of three generations ago, who left their hillside hovels and emigrated to London and New York. Property owners in the region are now jealously hanging on to their treasured houses, which in Positano for example increased by 23% in value in 2003. It is easier to rent than to buy, with still a big American demand. Zig-zag roads past olives and carobs lead to fabulous villas with breathtaking terraces overlooking the sea amid a riot of subtropical greenery. Even the infamous back streets of Naples with their image of degradation and crime are being cleaned up and are regaining their ancient glamour. *Scugnizzi*, the traditional street urchins, still dart around, visitors are warned not to leave their cars unguarded for an instant and Neapolitan voices and mandolins still soar in heartrending melodies.

Neapolitans are proud to have resisted foreign influences and to have retained a down-to-earth gastronomical fantasy of their own – such as squid and potatoes. They have given pizza to the world – the original urban fast food – as well as mozzarella and *pommarol* tomato sauce. Pizza, pasta, seafood and salads – the Naples version of the Mediterranean Diet has become universal. Campania wine is also extremely good, with inland vineyards at Avellino and Taresi competing with coastal producers in the Cilento. The spirit of Campania is summed up by the village of Furore near Salerno, where the peasant/fishermen have "one foot in the boat and one in the vineyard".

Typical Properties for Sale

Naples, its beautiful bay, and the royal palace of Caserta, retain vestiges of grand metropolitan architecture, befitting an erstwhile capital city, but the rampant unchecked development of the last century, now continuing with the explosion of Chinese sweatshops, has pushed aesthetic immigrants to settle further south overlooking the bay of Salerno, where they can enjoy breathtaking sea views from cliffside retreats. These can be veritable feats of engineering, perched on crags, with steep flights of steps and cantilevered terraces. Lifts and air conditioning are becoming the norm.

> Positano, Amalfi and Ravello have taken over from the islands of Capri, Procida and Ischia as a magnet for world-class intellectuals – the creative elite – who compete with each other for the beauty of their villas and the refinement of their taste. Standards – and prices – are very high in this area, which is extremely popular with American visitors.

At the same time it is the teeming proletariate – including illegal immigrants which accounts for the bulk of the real estate market in Campania, with a demand mainly for one and two bedroom apartments in modern blocks. Prices are rising at an average of 15% a year in Naples and Avellino, where the vibrant and chaotic street life at sea level – contrasts with the peace and beauty of the cliff-side eyries of the super rich.

Location	Type	Description	Price
Furore	apartments	Apartments by the sea. A modern panoramic 250sq.m cliffside development overlooking the sea, on 3 levels, 4 independent apartments with large terraces, shared swimming pool.	€2,840,000
Amalfi	apartment	Recently modernised air-conditioned 2 bedroom apartment 100sq.m, all rooms with balcony overlooking the sea	€600,000
Amalfi	bedsitter	Town centre bedsitter, 22sq.m. 150m from sea	€75,000
Pogerola (Near Amalfi)	unconverted farmhouse	Hillside derelict farmhouse, 120sq.m, with 2,000sq.mof land, surrounded by magnificent Mediterranean *macchia*.	€210,000

Baia Felice (Cellole Caserta)	detached bungalow	Period bungalow, 4 bedrooms, 4 bathrooms, patio, terrace and small garden 100sq.m.	€70,000

Agents for this Region: www.tecnocasa.it; www.casa.it

PUGLIA

Capital: *Bari*
Climate: *Summer Max. Temp:* 31°C. *Winter Min. Temp:* 5°C. *Annual Rainfall:* 628mm
Airports: *Bari International, Brindisi, Foggia.*
Ferry Ports: *Brindisi, Otranto* (to Greece), *Bari.*
The heel of Italy, Puglia borders Campania and Basilicata to the west, and Molise to the north west. It has an Adriatic and an Ionian shoreline. It falls into five geographical regions, from north to south;

o   **The Gargano Promontory:** beautiful hills culminating in Monte Calvo (1055m) with the remains of a magnificent forest of massive Aleppo pines, ilexes etc. Its harbours: Rodi Garganico, Peschici, Vieste, Pugnochiuso, Mattinata and Manfredonia, on the Adriatic.
o   **The Coastal Lakes:** Lesina and Varano.
o   **The Tavoliere Plain (Foggia):** a low, sandy, dune – fringed coastline between the Candelara and Ofante rivers, backed by the Capitanata Apennines, the largest plain in Italy after the Po Valley.
o   **The Murge Plateau**, which slopes down to Bari and the coast.
o   **The Salento Peninsula**, south of the seaport of Taranto, with an amphitheatre of hills overlooking the Gulf of Taranto. Brindisi is the major port on the Adriatic side. Otranto and Gallipoli are coastal towns on either side of Cape Leuca, which is the easternmost extremity of Italy.

A characteristic of the Puglia countryside is its emptiness. Farm workers live in towns and commute to the fields. Agriculture is very important, despite a shortage of water, partly solved by government irrigation schemes. Olive oil and wine production is massive, as is the growing of tomatoes, lettuce, artichokes, fennel, eggplant (aubergines), peppers, cabbage, wheat, maize, almonds and cherries. There are bauxite quarries and natural gas deposits (at Capitanata). Marble is quarried at Trani. Taranto has a steel industry and a naval base. At Brindisi there are chemical works and other small industries and a ferry to Greece. A coastal autostrada from Bologna ends at Taranto. Lecce, in the middle of the Salento peninsula, is at the end of a railway line from Milan.

Tourism is a major industry
Visitors are attracted to the wide, sandy beaches, rocky caves, the charming ports, like Gallipoli and Otranto, and inland towns like Lucera and Alberobello, with their *trulli* (conical buildings). Busloads visit Frederick II's octagonal Castle del Monte at Canosa. There are seaside cathedrals at Bari and Molfetta and churches galore. Lecce is a gem of exuberant baroque architecture. The centre of Bari has been cleaned up and transformed into a chic nocturnal paradise with sea-front bars and restaurants. The Tremiti islands north of the Gargano are the 'pearls of the Adriatic'; packed with Italians in the summer and best visited in the off-season from Termoli in Molise (See Molise).

Puglia's fertile plains and fine harbours always made her vulnerable to invaders. In 2000 BC it was the Japygeans from the Balkans, today it is Albanians. In the eighth century Greeks from Sparta founded the cities of Taranto, Gallipoli and Otranto. In 272 BC, after the defeat of Pyrrhus, the Romans took Taranto and made Brindisi their main port for the subjugation of Greece and beyond. After Rome's fall in 410 BC Christian bishops retained power followed by the Byzantines. Arabs occupied Taranto and Bari briefly in the 840s. The Normans conquered Puglia in 1056. Splendid cathedrals and Benedictine Abbeys were built. Puglia was the favourite region of the Emperor Frederick II (as it had once been of Hannibal). But it was neglected and abused by the Angevins and Bourbons in the following centuries and entered the Monarchy of United Italy in 1860 in a state of poverty and endemic criminality which was relieved by massive emigration. Agricultural reforms were pushed through by a group of socialist intellectuals at the end of the 19th century. In the fascist era education was promoted by the foundation of the University of Bari in 1925, and trade by the inauguration of the Bari Trade Fair in 1930. During World War II Bari hosted the first anti-fascist congress in 1944 which let to the creation of the Italian Republic. In the post war years Puglia benefited from the huge subsidies earmarked for the south and built the steel yards in Taranto. Agriculture and tourism are now thriving. Alberobello, Locorotondo, Martina Franca and Cisternino in the Itria valley – 'The kingdom of the *trulli*' – have attracted scholars and artists and mystics. There is an Indian ashram and a Tibetan temple. As well as nightlife, craftsmanship thrives in Puglia. It is a creative milieu for artists.

The Salento peninsula, with Lecce, Gallipoli and Otranto is an extremely attractive area – not the end of Italy, but the beginning of Greece. There is a ferry to Greece from Otranto. Beautiful beaches, craggy on the Adriatic, wider on the Ionian. Hot, hot summers.

The food of Puglia is naturally based on fish, often raw fish, like the Japanese. Specialities are: mussel and potato stew, roasted herb-flavoured oysters, excellent thick ragù (meat sauce) with pasta. This is the home of the sun-dried tomato, and olive oil. The local wines are strong: *Terra d'Otranto, Bianco di Trani* are whites, *Castel del Monte Rosso* is a good red. For dessert there are unusual nougats and exquisite pastries.

Typical Properties for Sale

Very popular with foreigners, are the large properties with spectacular views. Coastal properties are box-shaped and whitewashed and usually built in clusters. Many villages have *trulli* – the whitewashed stone houses with a dark conical roof. The *trulli* is the emblem of the region and are usually inexpensive. The ports of Brindisi and Lecce are famous for baroque and romanesque architecture.

Location	Type	Description	Price
Gallipoli	farmhouse (masseria)	Farmhouse 5km from Gallipoli. 2 floors 25 rooms surrounded by 2,000sq.m land. Total living space 740sq.m	€250,000
Ostuni	trullo	Restored Trullo with 10,000sq.m of land with wood.	€30,000
Gallipoli	house (rustico casale)	House on 3 levels, many rooms, restored to a high specification. Balconies on most rooms, small chapel, mature garden. Land 28,000sq.m	€1,600,000
Brindisi	trullo	Trullo consisting of 3 cones with barn attached. 2 rooms, 2 alcoves, external wood burning oven. Land of 10,000sq.m. Electricity + water.	€26,000
Cisternino	villa	3 bedrooms, bathroom, living room, terraces, verandah. Plot size 1,500sq.m	€225,000

Agents for this Region: www.casa.it; www.property-abroad.com and Puglia Properties (☎020-7394 2945).

BASILICATA

Capital: *Potenza*
Climate: *Summer Max. Temp:*   24°C. *Winter Min. Temp:*   2°C. *Annual Rainfall:* 978mm
Airports: *Naples* (for Tyrrhenian coast), *Bari* (for Ionian coast), (None in Basilicata).
Ferry Ports: *Naples, Bari, Brindisi.* (None in Basilicata).
Basilicata is a poor, mainly mountainous region, situated between Calabria and Campania to the west and Puglia to the east, at the very foot of the Italian Peninsula. It has two stretches of coastline:-

Maratea – facing west on to the Tyrrhenian sea where the mountains of the Vulkture range sweep steeply down to the Gulf of Policastro to 30km of coastline – cliffs, coves and solitary narrow beaches presided over by the charming medieval town of Maratea, which has good restaurants and hotels, miles of managed beaches and consistently pure sea water. The rocky seabed is ideal for snorkelling and diving.

> As beautiful as the Amalfi coast, Maratea is unspoilt and relatively undiscovered. It has a superb climate, sheltered from the cold northern winds. The spectacular mountainside is dotted with ancient villages, castles and manors and clad with aromatic *macchia* vegetation, carobs, olives, junipers and ilex. The sea is cobalt blue, with splendid beaches of dark sand at Cala Jannita, and grottoes and stalactites at Calaficarra further south.

Metaponto – the east coast facing the Ionian sea – a flat fertile plain where you can admire the extraordinary Greek ruins of Metaponto and Policoro (Ancient Heraclea). At Terzo Cavone on the estuary of the Cavone river is a huge expanse of fine golden sand, shaded by pine forests, with excellent *agriturismo* facilities in old farmhouses and full of friendly fishermen. In the *entroterra* is the charming medieval town of

Bernarda and other villages. This Ionian coast is subject to the occasional enervating *scirocco* wind, and the rainfall is very low on the coast. The land was deforested by Piedmontese loggers after the annexation of the kingdom of the Two Sicilies, but it is easy to see how this fertile plain, dominated by mountains, was a paradise for ancient Greek colonists which included the school of Pythagoras, which retreated here from Croton c. 500 BC.

The region was previously known as Lucania – and the people here are called Lucanians – named after earlier inhabitants, the Lyki from Anatolia. In the dark ages it was a neglected outpost of successive Lombard, Saracen, Norman, Angevin and Bourbon rulers, decimated by malaria and later by emigration, At the time of annexation with Italy in 1861 it was so rife with banditry that it became the subject of a parliamentary enquiry; a public works programme (building dams, roads and railways) failed to stem the massive flow of emigration, but the criminality was stopped and organised crime is still not a problem.

Basilicata food is the ultimate in frugality: rock hard bread and a hundred different ways of flavouring pasta with chilli, strong *caciocavallo* cheese, tomatoes bursting with flavour, vegetable stews with diced pecorino and salami, fresh fish flavoured with garlic, tomato, parsley and olive oil, fried sardines with a mint and chilli sauce. *Aglianico*, white or red, is the local wine, from 'Hellenico', the original grape imported from Greece 2,700 years ago – and fried ricotto ravioli for dessert.

Typical Properties for Sale

The Tyrrhenian coast – at Maratea – is characterised by steep hillside properties – many of them cheaply built and of difficult access – whilst the Ionian coast – the fertile plans of Metaponto – is called the 'California of the south' thanks to its fruit growing and packaging industries. The city of Policoro – part of a malarial feudal estate until the 1950s – has expanded since then from a population of 800 to over 15,000, with modern infrastructures – including a golf course – well managed Greek ruins, unpolluted beaches and the last remaining coastal forest in the south (Pantano). Properties for sale are mostly modern apartments in touristic developments. Plots, on which to build *ville singole* from scratch, with fertile gardens, are on offer from €35,000. Thanks to its spacious, modern American feel of immigrant ribbon development Policoro is proudly known as the 'little US', with houses to match.

Location	Type	Description	Price
Maratea	house	Situated in old port of Maratea. 4 bedrooms, 3 bathrooms, kitchen, 2 terraces. 120sq.m floor area.	€320,000
Maratea	villa	Villa, elevated position on Maratea coast. 3 bedrooms, kitchen/diner/sitting room. 2 bathrooms. Mature garden 400sq.m swimming pool. Views over the coast out to sea.	€510,000
Bernarda (Metaponto Plain)	2 apartments together	In well-managed tourist village, 55sq.m each, with pool, restaurant etc.	€10,000 each (Timeshare)

Pisticci (Metaponto)	apartment	50 sq.m with cellar in village	€50,000
Policoro (Metaponto)	house	Detached house with garden under construction. 2/3 bedrooms, 2 bathrooms, garage, cellar, central heating and verandas.	€190,000

Agents for this Region: www.italianhome.co.uk www.casa.it www.tecnocasa.it

CALABRIA

Capital: *Catanzaro*
Climate: *Summer Max. Temp. 31°C. Winter Min. Temp. 6°C. Annual Rainfall:* 682mm
Airports: *Lamezia Terme (international) Crotone, Reggio Calabria*
Ferry Ports: *Reggio Calabria* (for Naples and Sicily)

Calabria is the toe of the Italian peninsula, bordering Basilicata. Its coastline stretches round from the Tyrrhenian sea to the Ionian sea, divided from Sicily by the straits of Messina, personified by Scylla and Charybdis, the sea monsters of ancient legend which are the modern towns of Scilla in Calabria and Carriddi in Sicily.

It is an extremely mountainous region, with the Pollino range (2,267m) in the north merging southwards into the Coastal Chain, on one side of which is the jagged coastline of the Tyrrhenian sea, on the other the inland valley of the river Crati which flows north-eastward from Carenza to the plain of Sybaris in the Bay of Taranto. To the east of Cosenza (a university town) lie the Sila mountains, south of which is the Bay of St. Eufemia and Lamezia Terme (an international airport). A mountain range called Le Serre extends down to the toe, which is crowned by the mountains of Aspromonte (1,955m) – the scene of one of Garibaldi's rare defeats in 1862. In the lee of Aspromonte is the city of Reggio di Calabria, facing east over the straits of Messina and Locri, facing the Ionian sea to the east. The region's capital, Catanzaro, is further up the coast just inland from the Gulf of Squillace. Flowing eastwards from the Sila range is the Neto river which drains into the Ionian sea north of Crotone. This estuary is a valuable, luxuriant wetlands area, still partly unexplored, a tangle of unpenetrable growth and a haunt of endangered wild fowl which have miraculously survived the annual slaughter at the hands of local *cacciatori* (hunters). The National Park of Calabria was set up here in 1968 for the protection of this magnificent environment.

The climate in Calabria is of harsh extremes with heavy rainfall in the mountains, whilst on the coastal strips it is mild, dry and frost-free – and good for arthritis sufferers.

The whole of Calabria is an area of high seismic risk. Catanzaro was wrecked several times, and Reggio di Calabria was devastated by an earthquake in 1908 and rebuilt according to the strictest ant-seismic norms.

Agriculture is widely practised, often at subsistence level, specialist crops being: citrus fruits, grapes for wine, sugar beet, potatoes, aubergines, tomatoes, onions, water melons, beans and peppers. The standard of living and the per capita income are the lowest in Italy. Industry is undeveloped despite a century of state aid.

The Tyrrhenian coast from Praia a Mare south to Paola is known as the 'Citrus Riviera' because of the perfume of citrus blossoms. Mandarins, limes and, in particular bergamots, are commercial specialities. **The best Tyrrhenian beaches are: Praia a Mare, Isola di Cerella, Citadella del Capo, Scogli di Isca – all breathtaking (*mozzafiato*). Further south is the internationally famous beach of Tropea, which was a favourite royal resort in the days of the Bourbons.**

On the Ionian coast the beach at Marina di Gioiosa Ionica is populated in the summer by aesthetes and gourmets, mostly Italian, who can buy locally made silk clothes, Attic vases, Bergamot perfume, 'grossa di Gerace' olive oil, rare 'bianco Greco' white wine, sun-dried tomatoes, sheep's cheese and eat exquisite lamb cooked in terracotta amphora. At Mammola nearby (population 3,000) there are 14 superb restaurants. In the area of Locri (the ancient Greek city of Locris) the dream of living off tourism is coming true. Emigrants are coming back. Cosenza University is a hub of youthful idealism in the forefront of youthful protest movements, and there are ski-resorts up in the mountains. The National Park of Aspromonte remembers Edward Lear, the Victorian poet and artist, with its *Sentiero dell'Inglese* (the Englishman's trail), and Norman Douglas' book *Old Calabria*, recently translated into Italian, is essential reading even for Italian visitors.

The other side of the coin in Calabria is the crime. Tourists are not affected, but a threatening atmosphere is noticeable in certain areas, especially near Reggio, which is where the *'Ndrangheta* meets the *Mafia*. There were 47 murders in broad daylight in a three and a half month period in 1997 at Villa San Giovanni – the ferry terminal town. Gioiatauro – a resort up the coast – is another place with a sinister ambience.

Historically Calabria enjoyed half a millennium of pre-Roman glory as part of Magna Graecia. Croton was the original home of Pythagoras, and its athletes excelled at the Olympic games. Sybaris was – and still is – a by-word for luxury, but was destroyed by Croton's army in 510 BC. In AD 410 Alaric, King of the Visigoths, died on his way to Sicily after sacking Rome, and is reputedly buried with his booty in the bed of the river Busento near Cosenza. Further invasions – by Byzantines, Lombards, Saracens, Normans, and settlements by Albanians and Piedmontese Protestants, left their mark on the region, which was for a long time a malarial backwater infested by brigands. Over a million Calabrians emigrated, – to Brazil, North America and Australia. The brigandry of yesteryear are the organised crime of today.

Because of its geography there are three Calabrias – each with their own dialect – Cosenza, Catanzaro and Reggio – separated by mountains. Local pride is very strong. The Byzantine-Norman hill-town of Santa Severina, near Crotone, was voted the best preserved *centro storico* of Calabria in 2001. Scilla – the ancient Scylla – is called 'the little Venice of the Tyrrhenian', has a swordfish festival in the summer – and ski-ing in the winter (on Aspromonte). Stilo – the 'city of the sun', north of Locri and Gerace – is a gem of Byzantine architecture – and the home of the sun-dried tomato.

Gastronomy, archaeology, caving, rock-climbing, skiing, trekking, hang-gliding, birdwatching, diving……. Calabria has all these in abundance; it appeals as an exciting place to visit rather than as a permanent abode.

Typical Properties for Sale

Condominium apartments from the 1970s form the bulk of property on offer in this region. Prices have remained static in Crotone, Catanzaro and Vibo Valentia, but they have risen in Cosenza, where the city centre has been revitalised thanks to EU money and the current vibrancy of the university. Modern touristic developments at the resorts of Crotone, Locri and Tropea are not particularly attractive to the foreign investor.

Location	Type	Description	Price
Catanzaro	village house	Large village house 4km from sea, with sea views for renovation would make 4/5 bedroomed house on 3 levels 237sq.m. small garden	€28,000
Cetraro West Coast	apartment	Apartment 500m from sea. Living room, kitchen, bathroom, 2 bedrooms, 3 balconies. 93sq.m.. Close to shops	€40,000
Torremezzo Di Falconara	villa	10kms south of Páola, panoramic sea views. Can accommodate 2 families. 2 apartments – each – lounge, kitchen, bathroom, 2 bedrooms, 2 bathrooms, terrace/balconies. Large mature garden – large water tank. 4km from the sea	€380,000
Capo Colonna Crotone	apartment	Top floor 65sq.m. one bedroom flat with large terrace overlooking the sea, in 3 storey block.	€92,485

Agents for this Region: www.tecnocasa.it; www.casa.it.

SICILY

Capital: *Palermo*
Climate: *Summer Max. Temp. 33°C. Winter Min. Temp. 5°C. Annual Rainfall:* 446mm
Airports: *Palermo (international), Catania, Trapani*
Ferry Ports: *Palermo, Trapani, Siracusa, Messina*
An island twice the size of Ireland (25,708ksq.m.), with a population of five million, Sicily was called *Trinacria* by the ancient Greeks because of its three corners. Each of its three coasts has a different character and climate.: The straits of Messina – Scylla and Charybdis – separate Sicily from Calabria. Sicily's eastern coast faces the Ionian sea. Messina is an uncharming ferry terminal, south of which is **Taormina, near the ancient Greek ruins of Naxos, whose fabulous hillside position, hotels, villas and citrus groves overlooking the sea, make it the finest resort in Sicily, richly patronised since Victorian times.** Southwards, past Acireale, a Roman spa town with magnificent monuments, you come to Catania, only 28km south of the spectacular volcano of Mount Etna, with its grandiose centre and associations with Bellini. The volcanic plain of Catania is the best agricultural land in Sicily, sheltered by Mount Etna to the north and the Hybla mountains to the southwest. Through Lentini, the orange-growing capital – you reach the historical parts of Augusta and Priato Gargallo which are overshadowed by petrol refineries, whilst the next city Siracusa, retains its majesty as one of the most powerful cities in the world of ancient Greece, the home of Archimedes, where plays are still produced in the splendid Greek Theatre carved into the hillside. After the baroque town of Avola, famous for its red wine and marzipan, you come to Noto another baroque city completely rebuilt after the catastrophic earthquake of 1693. Ragusa is also a baroque city with a quaint medieval quarter which survived the earthquake. There are fine sandy beaches and small fishing ports in the Gulf of Noto.

A US Naval Air base at Sigonella 16km west of Catania is known as 'Sig, the hub of the Med'. If you wish to be a landlord, rental properties suitable for American personnel can be regarded as an excellent investment here.

Sicily's south coast, facing the 'Sicilian Sea' and Africa, has shallow waters, shifting sands, lakes, lagoons and marshes with a sultry climate, exposed as it is to the *scirocco* winds. There are good orchards, olive groves and some pastures on an inland plateau about 100m above sea level. Westwards from Ragusa are Gela, Agrigento, Sciacca, Selinunte, Castelvetrano, Marsala and Trapani – all Greek foundations, of which Agrigento, with its valley of the temples is the most spectacular, the 'finest city ever inhabited by mortal men' according to the poet Pindar; and the philosopher Empedocles said of the Agrigento people that 'they built as if they were going to live for ever and they ate as if they were going to die tomorrow'.

To the *comune* of Agrigento belong the Pelagian islands, Linosa and Lampedusa, 200km from Sicily and 150km from Malta, embarcation at Porto Empedocle near Agrigento. Hotels and B & B are very sought after by Italian vacationers, but it is not often that there is a house for sale on these or any small island. Pantelleria is another recherché island even nearer Africa. The Egadi islands (Favignana) are off the coast of Trapani.

The north coast of Sicily facing the Tyrrhenian sea is steep and rocky, with deep waters, good harbours and excellent fishing, dominated by the capital city, Palermo, which rivalled Cordova and Cairo in its Arab heyday, Palermo's glory was revived by the court of Frederick II of Swabia, but it went into decline under the Bourbons; it still retains architecture from every period, including Norman. Old Palermo was planned by kings and aristocrats, but new Palermo, alas, is a concrete jungle built by *mafiosi* and bureaucrats. The gardens of aristocrats at Bagheria, their 18th century out of town summer resort, have been build over by concrete monstrosities. The seaport and resort of Cefalù retains a medieval charm, but Termini Imerese (the old Fiat works) and other places on this coast, are depressingly disfigured by rogue development. However, there is a small fertile plain near Palermo called the Conca d'Oro, and forests still cover the mountains in the northwest. The weather on the north coast tends to be harsh, sometimes windy, but it is a healthy climate.

The Æolian islands, off this coast: Lipari, Salina, Santa Maria, Panarea, Stromboli, Filicudi, Alicudi, are delightful élite resorts. Ustica is another island for yachtsmen to visit.

Sicily's history is a complicated series of invasions by Greeks, Phoenicians, Byzantines, Goths, Vandals, Arabs, Normans, Albanians, Germans, Spaniards, French, Austrians and Piedmontese and Anglo-Americans, – a variety reflected in their exotic cuisine. The Mafia was repressed by Fascism in the 1930s but revived with the American connection in World War II and is still alive and kicking, dominating urban development, local and even national government, but it represents only 1% of the population. Sicilians have a complex mentality more than usually stereotyped by class divisions, but they are emerging patriotically from the stranglehold of history, to judge by the brilliant website, www.bestofsicily.com., which is essential reading for anyone contemplating buying a house there. Increasingly standard Italian is replacing local dialects as the medium of communication, but the old fashioned way of life – colourful street markets, folk crafts, religious processions etc. remains strong. Half of all the farm labourers are immigrants, mainly from North Africa.

Typical Properties for Sale

Stunning bargains are available in Sicily in the most beautiful locations – whether the small, peasant one room cabins (known as *bassi*) or the grand modern villas built with great Mediterranean flair and style. But here, perhaps more than anywhere else in Italy, you have to be very cautious about the validity of the title and the legality of the building work. Sicilian agents and sellers can be impenetrable and manipulative. Do not be in a hurry to commit yourself and make absolutely sure there is a water supply before you buy.

Location	Type	Description	Price
Taormina	apartments	High specification in condo. residence. 3 flats in detached building: A) Basement flat 100sq.m. B) Garden flat 120sq.m. with 600sq.m. garden. C) First floor flat with large terrace.Shared pool and landscaping	€750,000 (for total 280 sq.m.) (3 together or can be sold separately)
Baia Del GamberoAugusta (Syracuse)	house	Small detached house near sea (1960's). 35sq.m. one bedroom, kitchenette, verandah. 1,400sq.m. garden including vine arbour.	€26,000
Ragusa	villa	Spacious new luxury villa in own grounds near town centre (2km). Extremely refined 800sq.m., stone built landscaped 14 bedrooms, 4 marble bathrooms. Garage, private well, computerised irrigation, wood fired oven, cellar, fireplace, 5000sq.m. (1¼ acre) garden, pergola, lawns etc.	€1,500,000
Quattropani(Lipari, Æolian Islands)	house	Detached 1970's bungalow in good condition, 125sq.m., garage, 2 terraces with garden. Sea view	€180,000
Bagheria (Palermo)	villa	Modern detached villa with large garden. 2 floors, 340sq.m., 3 bedrooms, 3 bathrooms, integral garage, central heating, built-in kitchen, wood floors, fireplace. 6,000sq.m. (1½ acre) landscaped garden.	€550,000

Agents for this Region: www.tecnocasa.it; www.casa.it

THE PURCHASING PROCEDURE

CHAPTER SUMMARY

- **Mortgages.** Recent legislation in Italy allows any bank to offer mortgages.
    - There are banks in Italy familiar with arranging mortgages for foreigners.
    - Mortgages in Italy are regulated to protect the consumer against excessive usury.
    - For dilapidated property it is easier to buy first and then get a mortgage for renovation.
- **Importing Currency:** You can save thousands of pounds by using the services of a currency dealer rather than going through a high street bank.
- **Taxes.** It is recommended that you enlist the services of a *commercialista* (accountant) as the Italian tax system is very confusing.
    - Italian property is subject to a range of taxes.
    - Italian property is taxed on a notional income, even if it is not earning a rental.
- **Insurance.** Home insurance is very expensive in Italy because the crime rate is high in the cities, so many Italians do not bother.
- **Finding Properties for Sale.** Checking adverts on websites is not always the way to find the best properties.
    - It is possible to drive around, see a ruin etc. that you like and make enquiries locally.
    - Some villages still have a *mediatore* whose function in the community is to provide a market place for property sales.
    - Estate agents that speak English are very scarce in the south and outside the most popular regions.
    - What Type of Property? There are ruins and new houses, off-plans, farmhouses, whole abandoned villages, houses in historic centres, convents, monasteries and more for sale.
    - Renting a Home Before You Buy. Renting in the region you are interested in before you buy a property is a useful way of getting to know the locality, and gives you leisure to work out

exactly what you want.

○ **Professional Assistance**. The official appointed to handle property sales is a *notaio*.

○ You will also need the services of a *geometra* (surveyor). Geometras are familiar with both the legal and technical aspects of land and buildings.

○ **Third Parties' Right to Buy**. Certain third parties have pre-emptive rights to buy (*prelazione*). To avert the possibility of a *prelazione*, you have to obtain a disclaimer (*rinuncia*) from any interested party.

FINANCE

BANKS

Foreign Banks in Italy

The major UK high street bank, Abbey, has an affiliated company in Italy, *Credit-Banca pes la casa (www.abbey.unicreditcasa.it)*. This has been operating in Italy since 1989, specialising in tailor-made insurance linked mortgages, based in Milan, with branches in Turin, Bergamo, Udine, Padua, Bologna, Genoa, Florence, Pescara, Rome, Bari and Naples. It has an English speaking call centre, *Pronto Abbey*, tel.+39 02 667 29.1, +39 02 667 29. 356 and a foreign buyers area on its website www.abbeynational.it which is well worth consulting,

The Woolwich (www.bancawoolwich.it) – a subsidiary of Barclays Bank – has been growing rapidly in Italy for the last ten years, with branches in Milan, Turin, Bergamo, Brescia, Verona, Bologna, Genoa, Rome and Naples. It offers mortgages in association with policies by the Helvetia and Vittoria insurance companies and has also formed a partnership with the leading Italian real estate franchise company Gabetti. Paradoxically it is Gabetti and not the Woolwich that offers an English language website, www.gabetti.it.

Another international bank worth considering – and inclined to be Anglophone in that it is German – is the Deutsche Bank (www.deutschebank.it), which acquired the Morgan Grenfell Group in 1989 and has branches in London, Guildford, Edinburgh, Dublin, Sydney, Melbourne, Auckland and extensively in North America. It has been growing in Italy since 1977 and with over three hundred branches, is particularly strong in Lombardy, Liguria, Campania, and Puglia. It offers a full range of financial products and services including mortgages.

To have an account in your own country with one of the above financial institutions could be advantageous for the purpose of cross-referencing and transferring funds, and also if you prefer your mortgage in your own currency. Much will depend on how conveniently their branches are located at either end.

Useful Addresses

Abbey National Mutui S.p.A: Via G.Fara 27, 20124 Milan; ☎02-6672906; fax 02-66729247.

ABN Ambro Bank N.V.: Via Principessa Clotilde 7, 00196 Rome; ☎06 321 9600; fax 06 320 4851. Via Mengoni 4, 20121 Milan; ☎02 722671.

American Express Bank:, Piazza San Babila 3, 20122 Milan; ☎02 77901; fax 02 76002308.

Banca Woolwich SpA: Via Pantano 13, 20122 Milano; 20122 Milano; ☎02-584881; fax 02-58488511.

Chase Manhattan Bank: Via M. Mercati 39, 00197 Rome; ☎06 844 361; fax 06 844 36220. Piazza Meda 1, 20121 Milan; ☎02 88951; 02 88952229.

Citibank: Via Bruxelles 61, 00198 Rome; ☎06 854 561. Foro Bonaparte 16, 20121 Milan; ☎02 85421.

Creditwest: Via Santa Margarita 7, Milan; ☎02-8813 433969; www.credem.it.

National Westminster Bank: Via Turati 18 20121 Milan; ☎02 6251; fax 02 6572869.

Italian Banks

The biggest bank is the Banca Nazionale di Lavoro which is state owned and comes fifteenth in the league table of European banks. Other major national banks include: Credito Italiano, Banco di Roma, Banco di Napoli, Banco di Sicilia and Banca Commerciale Italiana. Italian banks have become noticeably quicker and less bureaucratic in the last few years whilst retaining the element of personal contact which has disappeared in Britain. Local recognition and trust are still vitally important in Italian banking. You should therefore check out the local banks in your area and open an account with whichever is the most convenient. A vital function of a local bank is to pay your utility bills by standing order, *ordine permanente.* You simply take in your current utility bills, *bollette,* to get this set up.

Opening an Account. To open an account you need: your passport, your *codice fiscale* (an Italian tax identity number based on a formula from your passport data, and obtainable at the local tax office *ufficio delle imposte dirette,* and money.This will obtain you a *conto estero* (foreign, i.e. non-resident account), and, if required, a cheque book, *un blocchetto di assegni,* and a credit or a *Bancomat* card, *carta Bancomat.* You need to be an Italian resident to open a normal current account, *conto corrente,* but this requirement is often waived, and you are treated as a local. An advantage of the *conto estero* is that you can keep it in pounds, dollars, or Swiss francs if you prefer.

Cheques. To cash a cheque the payee has to endorse it with his or her signature on the back; especially with tradesmen, very often you will be asked to pay someone with a cheque made out to yourself, *a me stesso/a, me medesimo/a* or *mio proprio,* and endorsed by yourself. This can then be exchanged for cash at a bank, which trusts both parties. The correct figures and the signatures are important. With the euro the cents *centesimi* have to be shown as follows, even if they are zeros:

- €300,00 (in figures: note the comma, which is normally pre-printed).
- *trecento*/00 (in letters; note the forward slash).
- The wording must be in Italian. Cheques for more than €10.329,14 (corresponding to twenty million lire) must be crossed with the words *non trasferibile* (non transferable) and the payee, *beneficiario,* must be named; as required by the anti-money laundering law, *la legge antiriciclaggio.*

○   Some banks have special departments for British buyers.

As a non-resident of Italy you should have a *conto estero* (foreign account).
Italian numbers are written with the comma and full-stop in opposite positions to the UK, so ten thousand euros and 14 cents is written €10.000,14.
In Italy it is a criminal offence to issue a dud cheque.

Credit/Debit Card. The Bancomat card enables you to pay bills and tolls, and to obtain cash, by dialling a PIN number directly on to the dial supplied by the shop, hotel, restaurant, petrol station, toll booth or cash machine. Debiting is instantaneous. The Bancomat card can also be used as an ordinary credit card. It has a monthly limit, which can be renegotiated.

Useful Addresses
Banca Nazione di Lavoro: Direzione Generale, Via Vittorio Veneto 119, 00187 Rome.
Banca Nazionale dell'Agricultura (BNA): Direzione Centrale, Via Salaria 231, 00199 Rome.
Credito Romagnola: Via Zamboni 20, 40126 Bologna.
Istituto Bancario San Paolo di Torino: Via della Stamperia 64, 00187 Rome; ☎06 85751; 06 857 52400. Piazza San Carlo 156, Turin; ☎011-5551.
Istituto Monte dei Paschi di Siena: U.S.I.E. Sett. Serv. V.le Toselli 60, Siena.

UK MORTGAGES

Some people arrange loans in the UK – taking out a second mortgage on their UK property and then buying with cash in Italy. It is possible to approach UK banks and building societies for a sterling loan in this way. Note that this is different from approaching the subsidiaries of high street names such as Abbey and Woolwich which are located in Italy and are in effect no different from Italian banks when dealt with in Italy.

The method of calculation for the amount you are borrowing, if you are borrowing in the UK, is at two and a half times, or three and a half, times your primary income plus any secondary income you may have, less any capital amount already borrowed on the mortgage. Sometimes the amount that may be borrowed is calculated at two and a half times joint income, less outstanding capital.

Naturally, the mortgage will be subject to a valuation on any UK property and you can expect to borrow, subject to equity, up to a maximum of 80% of the purchase price of the overseas property, (compared with the availability of 100% mortgages for UK properties). If you are going to take out a second mortgage with your existing mortgage lender then a second charge would be taken by the mortgage company. Note that some lending institutions charge a higher rate for a loan to cover a second property.

UK and Italian Mortgages

Re-mortgaging or taking out a mortgage in the UK could have some advantages as it may be easier to arrange, and you may be able to borrow more than you would in Italy. If your income is in sterling it may make better sense to have a mortgage in the UK. Interest rates are however also an important consideration as they change frequently. The value of the euro is another variable that may affect your decision where to take out a mortgage. If it rises in value, and if you have a mortgage in Italy and you are sending money from the UK to Italy, you could be losing money every time you do this. For details of forward buying currency at a fixed rate see *Importing Currency* in the *General Introduction*.

ITALIAN MORTGAGES

A mortgage, *un mutuo*, is normally required to buy, build or renovate a property. In principle you borrow from a bank against the security of your property; if you default on your agreed repayments the bank repossesses the property. Most financial institutions such as the Abbey National, the Woolwich and the Deutsche Bank mentioned above tailor the mortgage and offer a personalised package including insurance cover. Different banks have different rules and possibilities. The smaller banks offer straightforward loans, and the insurance is up to you. Recent legislation in Italy has allowed any bank to issue mortgages, subject to strict rules against excessive usury; to protect the consumer. Non-residents are treated with more caution than Italian residents. The following arrangements are typical:

Purpose of mortgage: primary or secondary residence for purchase, renovation or completion, or for other stated purpose.
Types of repayment: fixed, variable, mixed or capped rates, or interest only. (see below)
Sum available: up to 80% of the value of the property – 60% for non-residents. NB. valuations are conservative.
Duration: normally 5, 10, 15, 20 years but up to 25 or 30 years.
Age limit: mortgage to expire at age 65, 70, 75.
Frequency of repayments: Monthly, quarterly or biennially.
Setting up expenses: typically 0.20% of the sum borrowed, but variable.
Valuation expenses: typically €300, but variable, sometimes free.
Occasional expenses: typically €1,29 for every communication or €1,00 for each repayment.
Insurance cover: insurance is compulsory, in favour of the bank, against the risk of fire, lightning, gas explosions, possibly also against the risk of impact of vehicles or aircraft, 'socio-political events', 'atmospheric events' burst pipes etc. Insurance premium to be paid in a one-off *una tantum* payment. Premium typically 0.21% of value of property for 20 year contract. A life assurance policy guaranteeing repayment in the event of your death, accident, illness or loss of job is optional.
Penalties for early redemption: typically between 0.5% and 3% of residual capital, depending on the timescale.
Evidence of income: bank guidelines require proof that your repayments are not more than 33% of your disposable income.

There is an excellent Italian website dedicated to mortgages and loans for instant competitive quotations online: www.mutuionline.it.

In order to consider your mortgage the bank will require the following documentation, which it will photocopy:

○ The preliminary sale documents, the *compromesso* or *preliminare di vendita*, between you and the vendor of the property in question, or a land registry proof of your title.
○ Your passport.
○ Your Italian fiscal code number, *codice fiscale*.

o   Your most recent tax returns (at least three).
o   Your most recent bank statements (at least three months).
o   Any other documents proving your income.

The bank will also require documentation on the property itself, which only your surveyor, *geometra,* can supply:

o   *La provenienza del bene* – The provenance of the property.
o   *Il certificato storico venternale* – a twenty year retrospective certification of the property.

Non-residents may find it difficult to obtain a mortgage to buy a dilapidated or isolated rural property, but easier to buy it first and then obtain a mortgage for renovation.

The bank will normally require at least four weeks to process your application. The next step is to get the mortgage registered officially with a notary *notaio* who will require you and the representative of the bank to sign a deed in his presence, which he will then register against the title of the property in the local Land Registry, *L'Ufficio del Registro.* You must set up the appointment with the notary well in advance, if necessary giving a power of attorney to a third party to sign on your behalf *una delega* or *procura speciale.*You, not the bank, have to pay the notary's fees which are at the notary's discretion

Banks sometimes offer cheap promotional introductory rates for a brief initial period (3-6 months).

Useful Contacts

Casa Travella: (www.casatravella.com) ☎01322-660988) is a property agent that may be able to give assistance with obtaining mortgages with some banks, for instance Banca Populari di Sondrio in Como, or Banca di Toscana depending on the region and the branches.

Conti Financial Services: 204 Church Road, Hove, Sussex BN3 2DJ; free phone 0800-970 0985; ☎01273-772811; fax 01273-321269; e-mail enquiries@contifs.com; www.mortgagesoverseas.com. Conti have many years of experience arranging finance for clients (both UK and non-UK nationals) purchasing properties overseas and is an independent mortgage broker.

Taxes on Mortgages

A single tax called an *imposta sostitutiva* of 0.25% is levied by the notary on the delivery of the mortgage. It is so called because it is a substitute for the previous stamp duties and VAT taxes in force.

Tax Concessions on Mortgages

Interest payments on a mortgage for the purchase of a first home are deductible from the IRPEF tax (see below). The deduction is at the rate of 19% on a maximum sum of 3,615 euros, subject to certain conditions, and only if the property has become your principal residence within one year of purchase. There are also tax concessions on the expenses of renovation.

IMPORTING CURRENCY

If you take more than €10,330 (about £7,200) in cash with you into Italy, you are required to declare it to customs. Taking a large amount of cash is not only risky, but you could be suspected of being a drugs dealer or terrorist by Italian customs if they find out. For the safest ways of transferring funds abroad, see *Other Ways of Transferring Funds* in the *General Introduction*.

If you are buying in euros you can guard against fluctuations in value by forward buying through a specialised company which offers better exchange rates than banks and does not charge commission. For further details, see *Importing Currency* in the *General Introduction*.

REAL ESTATE TAXES

The majority of those buying a house in Italy will have only two taxes to pay: the ICI and the IRPEF, for which you are well advised to consult a local accountant or *commercialista*. A *commercialista* is a qualified professional registered in the local *Albo dei Dottori Commercialisti* who will take care of all your taxes, for a fee. It is impossible to navigate the labyrinth of Italian taxes without the help of a *commercialista*. For details of Italian income tax and allowances see the section *Italian Taxes* in the *Italy Introduction*.

The ICI is the *Imposta Comunale sugli Immobili*, or property tax, which is levied by the local borough council *comune*, and calculated according to their own criteria within minimum and maximum limits imposed by the state, and in proportion to the *valore catastale* or rateable value of the property. It is payable in two instalments – normally at the post office – in June and December. When you buy your property you – or your *commercialista* must report it to the *comune* in a *dichiarazione* ICI. It is an unpopular new tax, which seems cheap to foreigners, averaging about €1,000 (£700/$1090) per year per property, with a reduced rate for primary residences.

The IRPEF tax is the *Imposta sul Reddito delle Persone Fisiche*, literally tax on the income of physical, as opposed to juridical, persons i.e. income tax, levied at between 23% and 45% at the time of writing. Whether you are resident or non-resident, your property is regarded by the state as having a *rendita catastale*, literally a land registry (notional) income, which is taxable, even though it is yielding no actual rent. For details of IRPEF on earned income see *Italian Taxes* in the *Introduction* section of Italy.

All habitable property must be registered in the urban building register, *catasto edilizio urbano,* which gives it a rateable value. IRPEF is payable in two instalments, June and November, the form required for it is: *modello di pagamento unificato* F.24. For more see details of IRPEF see the *Tax* section above. Both ICI and IRPEF are payable on-line. The IRPEF is under the control of the Revenue Ministry, *Ministero delle Entrate*, who have as enforcement officers not only the Tax Police, *Guardia di Finanza*, but also the National Gendarmerie *(Carabinieri)*.

Taxes Due on the Purchase and Registry of Property. Registry Tax *L'imposta del registro* of 3% of the purchase price of the property. Note that it is 7% if the property is a second home or the buyer is not resident in the municipality where the property is located which is often the case with a foreign purchaser.

1. For registering the preliminary contract of sale (optional) i.e. the *compromesso* or *contratto preliminare di compravendita*: €129,11 which is deductible from 0.5% levied on the deposit money or earnest *caparra confirmatoria* – subject to minor variations.

2. For registering the property on completion of the sale: principal residence €129,11 otherwise 1% of the declared value.

VAT on Property Bought from a Builder or Cooperative. If you buy a property from a builder or a Cooperative Housing Association you have to pay:

1. 4% VAT if the property is going to be the buyer's main residence and he/she is resident in the same municipality where the property is located; or if the buyer is going to obtain residence in that municipality within 18 months of the date of purchase.

2. 10% VAT in all other cases (e.g. second home; if the buyer is not resident in the municipality where the property is located as is often the case with foreign purchasers).

Removal of Inheritance and Capital Gains Taxes

What you lose on the swings you gain on the roundabouts: the Berlusconi government has 'suppressed' the capital gains tax, (the old INVIM), abolished the inheritance and gift tax, and there is no such thing as a wealth tax. One object of these cuts was to attract capital back to Italy, but there is no cause for rejoicing –

The capital gains tax on the sale of property might have been abolished but the IRPEF tax will still regard the profit on the property as income, *plusvalenza* if it is not the primary residence, and the abolition of inheritance tax does not affect non-Italians: Italian law regards property owned in Italy by foreigners as subject to the inheritance taxes of their home country – that is the country in which they are domiciled. Italian residence alone is not enough for them to benefit from the Italian inheritance regime.

INSURANCE

It is expensive to insure house contents in Italy and most Italians do not bother. Foreign residents from Britain will find that insurance quotes from Italian firms are at least double what they would expect to pay in the UK and North America. Italian insurance companies are also notoriously slow about settling claims.

Some English owners and permanent residents find it easier to insure their properties in Britain particularly for the provision against loss of rent and for properties left unoccupied.

For details of the required measures to make your foreign home more secure and British and American companies that will insure holiday homes abroad, see *Insurance* in the *General Introduction*.

Most mortgages include a house insurance policy, and estate agents sometimes offer house and contents insurance at competitive rates to their clients and it is worth asking them about this. It is important to note that if you are moving to the earthquake zone, most insurance policies exclude earthquake damage. Reale Mutua, (founded in 1827), is the largest mutual insurance society in Italy with 356 branches (www.realemutua.it). In some rural areas an old-fashioned tally-man or insurance agent still operates, calling on householders and issuing reminders in person, from Reale Mutua.

FINDING PROPERTIES FOR SALE

It is probably easier to find an English-speaking estate agent in the already popular areas such as Liguria and Tuscany. However, there are other parts of Italy where the aesthetic attractions are equally as good; these include Le Marche. English people have been steadily emigrating to Le Marche as their first choice (instead of Tuscany) and created a colony of English-speaking people who, in certain areas now outnumber Germans whose traditional terrain this has been. There are a few English-speaking people on the Ligurian Riviera but this part is expensive and overcrowded. Today's expatriates in search of coastal properties are looking as far afield as Abruzzo and Puglia; and Sardinia is becoming very sought after too, where the property prices are reasonable and there are a variety of places available to rival the Costas of Spain and Portugal.

When you have more or less decided what sort of property you want and where, then, the next step is to find an estate agent.

ESTATE AGENTS

A percentage of property sales in Italy are private in order to avoid paying agents' fees. However, estate agents (*agenzie immobiliari*) or other agents (*mediatori*) handle all other sales. Checking adverts on websites does not necessarily mean that you will find the best properties. There are other, possibly more fruitful methods like approaching contacts in your chosen area: *geometras,* builders' merchants, bank personnel – even the local barber hears things on the grapevine.

In old-fashioned rural communities, a tradition sometimes survives of a dealer/mediator (*mediatore*) or (*sensale*) whose function in the community is to provide a market place for houses and land. He has kept up his reputation and trust by a lifetime of discretion and honesty. The mediatore has a good memory, he seldom has written descriptions of the property which he has been entrusted with, but a vivid verbal one. In order to communicate with this archaic survivor you or a friend should have knowledge of the local dialect. Nowadays, a properly qualified younger generation, are taking over this business.

There are also amateur estate agents in the expatriate community who make it their business to seek out the desirable properties in their area in response to the ever-growing demand. You might think all the best houses have been sold but there are still occasional gems cropping up.

Finding an Estate Agent

If you want to deal with an estate agent in your area look in the local Yellow Pages (*pagine gialle*) under estate agents (*Agenzie Immobiliari*). There are also an increasing number of estate agents who have premises located in high streets of towns and cities. More and more Italian estate agents now speak English and are used to dealing with foreigners; but you might feel happier using an agent from your own country located in Italy and you can find these in the English Yellow Pages (EYP).

English estate agents specialising in Italian properties are likely to be based in Italy.

The Federation of Overseas Property Developers and Consultants – FOPDAC (3rd Floor, 95 Aldwych, London, WC2B 4JF; www.fopdac.com; e-mail info@fopdac.com) is an association of English speaking agents, lawyers and other specialists in the property field who work with people looking to buy European property; companies must meet very strict criteria for membership.

Italian estate agents have to be professionally qualified and licensed and they are required to hold an indemnity insurance. They must also be registered (law introduced in February 1989) with the local Chamber of Commerce (*camera di Commercio*) and have a certificate issued by the local *comune* as proof of registration. An agent should also be registered with the Association of Real Estate Agents (AICI, Via Nerinos, 20123 Milan), the Italian Federation of Professional Estate Agents (FIAIP, Via Monte Zebio, 30, 00195 Rome; www.fiaip.it) and The Italian Federation of Mediators and Agents (FIMAA) (www.fimaa.it).

In city environments and resort areas estate agents are becoming more commonplace and it is worth visiting them methodically with a checklist of what you are looking for. Make a note of everything and take photographs, all details and the date. Italian agents have grown wary of time wasters (*perditempo*) tourists who want a free tour of the countryside e.g. 'Dolly Duke who cruised around the country for two weeks in an obliging *mediatore's* Mercedes Benz without the remotest intention of buying; although by her appearance she was a woman of substance'. Italians have now grown wise to this practice and charge a fee for viewing properties. The fee is anything from €50 for an afternoon.

Remember, a lot of estate agents are trying to get rid of a lot of rubbish including some remote and distant hovels and you should check everything for yourself before eliminating them and that usually means looking at the property. Beware of conmen (*imbroglioni*), who may well be of your own nationality, who will take a down payment or deposit to secure a property for you and then disappear. Always bring in a trusty professional and a *geometra* to double-check on the validity of the proposed sale.

Reliable Estate Agents

The Italian Federation of Professional Estate Agents (FIAIP) have a code of practice for estate agents, which includes the following:

O He specifies in his written agency agreement the exact commission he will charge and that it will be on the actual price obtained and not on the declared price.
O He does not ask for a higher commission on selling in the event of his getting a higher price than the agreed one.
O He indicates clearly in the agency agreement whether he is to be refunded for any expenses for advertising or for any other extras.
O He refrains from inserting a tacit renewal clause in the agreement – or if there is one, he gives a reasonable short time within which to cancel the agreement.
O He never pockets for his own use any sums of money he has received as a deposit from the buyer. He puts the deposit in the vendor's name and pays the vendor the balance immediately after he has completed the searches to guarantee the absence of liens and mortgages.

Respected agencies in Italy include *Gabetti* (www.gabetti.it), *Tecnocasa* (www.tecnocasa.it) and *Grimaldi* (www.grimaldi.net). These large agencies have regional offices throughout Italy but there are many agencies, which only specialise in one area or at the most four or five. A list of all registered estate agencies in Italy can be obtained from: FAIAP (www.faiap.it).

DIY Property Search

A lot of Italians want to sell their property but want to do it discreetly as they don't want a lot of people to know. Such properties never reach estate agents, so it is worth enquiring if you see houses in need of renovation or ruins on farmland. Make discreet enquiries about the ownership and track down the owner and if you are not fluent take a local interpreter with you and impress on the owner that you are the principal and not an agent and you want to negotiate (*trattativa privata*). This could result in you getting a good property and the farmer retaining his.

On the other hand, it is possible that the landowner is so happy to know his property is sought after and therefore of a high market value, that he will not sell. However, he usually will if the price is right. If you make an agreement you must get a legal *geometra* to carry out any searches etc. before any money changes hands, see chapter on *The Purchasing Procedure*.

Estate Agents in the UK

Brian A. French and Associates: ☎0870-7301910; fax 0870-7301911; e-mail louise.talbot@brianfrench.com; www.brianfrench.com: Italian office 075-9600024 or mobile 340-341 5667 (Mr Steve Emmett). Offers one of the widest range of areas of any of the British agents including Tuscany, Umbria, Le Marche, Abruzzo and Calabria.

La Casa Emilia: 11 Westfield Avenue, Beverley, East Yorkshire HU17 7HA; ☎01482-679251; e-mail info@lacasaemilia.com; www.lacasemilia.com. Specialists in Emilia Romagna, with properties ranging from luxury villas to traditional stone farmhouses.

Casa Travella; 01322-660988; fax 01322-667206; e-mail casa@travella.f9.co.uk; www.casatravella.com; Has agents mainly in Northern and Central Italy but will help locate contacts for all other regions and will help with relocation, restoration, etc.

Hello Italy: Woodstock, Forest Road, East Horsley, Surrey KT24 5ES, England; ☎01483-284011; fax 01483-285264; www.helloit.co.uk. Letting agent for northern Tuscany (about 30 minutes from the Ligurian coast). Can provide introductions to purchasing contacts in the area, help with restoration and building and sales after care. Many clients who buy have subsequently used Hello Italy as a letting agent.

English-Speaking Estate Agents in Italy.
In addition to the estate agents' addresses listed below, there are agents' websites in *Where to Find Your Ideal Home* at the end of each individual region's description, online agencies can be found via websites such as www.findaproperty.com and www.accommodation.com.

Barga Estate Agents: Piazza Angelio 15, 55051 Barga, Liguria; tel/fax 0583-710275; e-mail info@barga-estateagents.com; www.barga-estateagents.com.

Consulenze Immobili Marche: Michael Sattler, Cascernia, 62032 Camerino; ☎+39 335 836 7630; fax +39 0737 630551; e-mail ctolkmitt@marcheproperty.com. Specialises in property in Le Marche.

House Around: Via Pesaro 16, 65121 Pescara; ☎+39 085 421 7301; e-mail enquiries@HouseAroundItaly.com. Helps non-Italian speakers buy property in Abruzzo.

THE INTERNET

Another source of property for sale is the Internet where many properties are advertised. A search using any of the major search engines such www.google.com

and www.dogpile.com will find numerous online agencies. There is also the Shop Cases section on the home page of Yahoo! Italia where property in most regions is advertised.

For information online about living in Italy you can access www.intoitaly.it. This website is especially for English-speakers.The Italian Embassy and tourist authority also supply the would-be immigrant with information on www.emit.it.

Some Property Internet Sites

www.italyhousescont.com
www.restorationitalia.com
www.turchi.it
www.ideeresidenziali.it
www.casalieville.com
www.lacasa.de
www.portocervoonline.com
www.globalmart.co.uk
www.fiaip.it
www.relocationagents.com
www.tuscandream.com
www.real-estate-europeanunion.com
www.escapeartist.com
www.italian-realestate.com
www.goitaly.com
www.casa.it
www.gabetti.it
www.grimaldi.net
www.tecnocasa.it
www.fimaa.it

ADVERTS

Italian newspapers and magazines include many homes for sale and often contain supplements dedicated to properties for sale, at least once a week. A glossary of terms that appear in such adverts is given at the end of this section.

Additionally there are magazines available for buyers in English including *World of Property* (outbound@aol.com), *International Homes* (www.international-homes.com), *Homes Overseas* (www.homesoverseas.co.uk), *Italy* (www.italymag.co.uk).

You could also look at adverts in Italian real estate magazines including *Casa per Casa* (www.casapercasa.it), *Dimore-homes* (www.dimore.com), *Cerca Casa* (www.cercasa.it) and *Ville & Casali* (villeecasali.com).

PROPERTY EXHIBITIONS

Exhibitions give prospective buyers a chance to collect details of properties that are for sale and make useful contacts. You can also talk to the expert lawyers and estate agents that take stands at these exhibitions. Sometimes there are seminars dealing with different aspects of buying a house e.g. arranging a mortgage etc. Most property exhibitions in the UK deal with France and Spain but the Homes Overseas Exhibition at Earls Court, London at the end of September has a special Italian property section with agents from many regions including Le Marche, Lazio, Puglia and Sardinia offering everything from apartments to Palazzi. Exhibitions usually last for two days; often they are at weekends. Exhibitions are advertised in magazines such as Homes Overseas and World of Property. The website www.internationalpropertyshow.com gives details of up coming property shows.

GLOSSARY FOR ITALIAN PROPERTY ADVERTS

Interior Features:
Angolo cottura – cooking corner
Bagno – bathroom
Cantina – cellar
Camera – bedroom
Cucina – kitchen
Doccia – shower
Locale – room
Ripostiglio – storeroom
Riscaldamento – heating
Servizi – kitchen, bathroom
Stanza – room
Sala – hall
Salotto – parlour
Tinello – living room/dining room

Exterior Features:
Cancello – gate
Cortile – courtyard
Campo da tennis – tennis court
Cotto – terracotta
Cemento – cement
Die pietra – of stone
Da restaurare – to be restored
Frutteto – orchard
Forno – bread oven
Giardino – garden
Infissi – collectively, doors and windows.
Legnaia – woodstore
Legno – wood
Orto – garden (vegetable plot)
Piscina – swimming pool
Pozzo – well
Restaurare – to restore
Resede di terreno – plot of land attached to property
Stufa – stove
Tetto – roof
Tettoia – canopy (tiled)

WHAT TYPE OF PROPERTY TO BUY

Unlike the old city centres in other European countries, Italy's town centres, usually the old part (*centro storico*), are still thriving residential districts. The old cities are living cities with the residents living and working in the centre. The areas outside the centre are known as *il semicentro*, where most of the purpose-built apartment blocks are located. The suburbs (*la periferia*) are where the least well off generally live, although new housing estates with detached homes and gardens are appearing – Silvio Berlusconi made a fortune in some of the first such property developments in Italy.

About 78% of Italian families are owner-occupiers, one of the highest rates in Europe after Spain. However, rich Italians looking for a second or holiday home in their own country rarely go for the type of rustic property favoured by foreigners. Italians are more likely to buy or rent a luxury seaside flat or a house in the mountains.

TYPES OF PROPERTY GLOSSARY	
Appartamento	apartment
Annesse	outbuildings
Attico	attic
Bilocale	apartment with 2 rooms
Box	garage
Casa	house or home general term
Casa canonica	priest's house, usually next to a church
Casa bifamiliare	semi-detached house
Casa padronale	landlord's mansion
Casale	farmhouse or small hamlet rustic buildings restored to high standard
Casetta	small house
Castello	castle
Capanna	barn
Cascina	farmhouse
Casa Colonica	farmhouse
Casolare	house in the country
Dependance	outhouse (granny flat)
Fienile	hay barn
Fattoria	working farm
Monolocale	studio apartment (one room), bedsitter
Masseria	huge farming estate in the south
Mansarda	loft conversion
Palazzo	palace. Used to refer to any large building including blocks of flats.
Porcilaia/porcule	pigsty
Podere	farm (smallholding)
Rustico	rustic property, usually in need of modernisation
Rudere	ruin
Stalla	stable
Terratetto	semi-detached house

Torre	tower
Trullo	stone house with conical roof (regional, Puglia)
Villetta a schiera	terraced house
Vigneto/Vigna	vineyard

APARTMENTS

Modern Apartments

Most modern *appartamenti* are constructed using a concrete frame, which is filled in with blocks. The majority of newer apartments were built in three decades from the 1950s. Buying apartments in city centres or by the coast is popular with foreigners. Internally, the walls are plastered and floors are *terrazzo* (tiled), with tiles made from marble and cement mixed, or ceramic, or marble. Some apartments come with fitted wardrobes in the bedroom and there will be bathroom porcelain plus the kitchen sink. All other furnishings and appliances have to be bought by the new owner.

Old Apartments

Nineteenth century and older apartments tend to have high ceilings which are beamed and often the walls and ceilings are elaborately decorated. The flooring can be a range of materials including terracotta tiling and wood. Sometimes the tiles have been covered with marble. The stairs, sills and window frames are made of stone, marble or travertine (a light-coloured rock). Externally, the buildings are made of brick, often with peeling stucco. The problem with older buildings is that the fixtures, fittings, plumbing etc may be old fashioned. However, this appeals to some buyers.

RURAL PROPERTIES

Farmhouses (Casali)

Farmhouses in rural settings are the most popular buy with foreigners. The typical rural farmhouse of 60 years ago or more had the living quarters on the first floor and the animals were stabled on the ground floor. It was usual to climb outside stone steps to the first floor and enter into a very large kitchen with a hooded fireplace where the cooking would be done. The hearth and fireplace were a very important focal point for the family as it provided heat, meals, and a place for them to gather and sit. The bedrooms would be off this main living room. A typical farmhouse also has very thick stone walls to keep cool in summer and the cold out in winter. In the north of Italy where temperatures drop much lower, central heating and double-glazing are essential in winter.

Property buyers should note that such farmhouses are classified as rural buildings and need to be registered for change of use to 'urban' otherwise renovation is illegal. It is as well to consider the implications of this when deciding what type of property to buy.

In planning matters the difference between a rural and an urban house is important:

○ **A Rural Building.** farmhouses, pigsties, outbuildings and the land have no value separate from the land. The property will be registered with a plan showing the land and buildings available, but there will be no interior details.

○ **An Urban Building.** An urban house (or apartment) is registered with a plan of the interior that has all the internal measurements.

○ **Change of Usage.** Any request for a change of usage from agricultural to urban (i.e. to a dwelling for people), is made through a *geometra* (surveyor) who will provide detailed drawings of any proposed improvements e.g. to convert former stables into a kitchen or the *capanna* (outbuilding) into a flat for renting out. The geometra will obtain the permission from the *comune* and then register with *il nuovo castasto* (land registry) who will ratify the permission to change from rural to urban use. Renovations can only start after permission is obtained.

Village Houses

Buying an old house in the historic centre (*centro storico*) of a small town or village can mean acquiring an architecturally and historically interesting (and possibly listed) building. The downside of living in an ancient dwelling is that it will probably need major renovation work.

The disadvantages of buying a village house are relatively few. Some people might find a village noisy or object to the regular ringing of church bells. There could also be a large influx of tourists depending on where you are. There is definitely a trend of buying houses in villages, especially amongst Americans who enjoy the social life of an Italian neighbourhood. At the moment prices for these are reasonable, even in the popular areas.

Estates and Vineyards (Ville e Vigneti)

Very large estates created by the nobility are found in the country usually within 50km of a city. They have a main house (*villa*) set in parks and gardens. Villas of this type can date from the late Renaissance or the highly ornate and extravagant baroque period of the 17th and 18th centuries. A great many estates have vineyards and olive groves attached and still in production which could be useful as a way of helping to fund the costs of running such an estate. Estates are however likely to be a minority requirement for prospective property buyers.

Ghost Towns (Paesi Abbandonati)

Ghost towns not far from the coast, abandoned by the *contadini* (country people) seeking a better or less harsh life, are found mostly in the southern regions, usually a long way from a city. Comprising a cluster of buildings they can be an interesting proposition for a buyer who likes a challenge. Abandoned villages are the ultimate restoration project and can be turned into hotels or other living accommodation that can be rented out. In Liguria, a former ghost village, Coletta di Castellano, has been turned into Italy's first cyber village. The village was purchased by a consortium that also arranged for Telecom Italia to sponsor a fibre optic link so that Coletta is a working village. The buildings have been transformed into modern apartments and the internet access for all means that those moving there can run a business from home if they wish.

Castles and Monasteries (Castelli e Conventi)

Castles and monasteries can be converted and restored into living accommodation for private individuals buying as a consortium. Some monasteries on the market come complete with frescos, cloisters and inevitably, a church or chapel within the main buildings. These properties are part of Italy's enormous architectural heritage and it can be very satisfying to bring such properties back to life.

NEW HOUSES AND VILLAS

New houses may lack the charm of older properties (or their crumbling walls and ancient plumbing), but they do have several advantages. Modern building standards ensure than new houses are very comfortable and built to a high specification. New houses are also well insulated and double-glazed; central-heating and air-conditioning are fitted as standard. New property is also covered by a ten-year guarantee (*responsibilità della ditta*), against any defects in the structure. Most services such as the central heating system, are also guaranteed for a limited period. The types of new houses available are either part of a development, usually coastal or on the outskirts of cities or towns. Such properties are normally built and sold by property developers. See also *Buying a House under Construction*.

BUYING A PLOT OF LAND

Some people dream of picking their ideal spot for a house, buying the land and having a house built from scratch just for them. If this is your intention, before you buy land you should make sure that there is planning permission for building, and check that the size of your intended building and the proposed design is legal. This is a job for a *geometra* (surveyor).

CONDOMINIUMS

Most Italians live in apartment blocks in which each apartment is privately owned but certain facilities and structures are shared – such as the foundations, the roof, the bearing walls, the stairs, the entrance, drains, sewers, wells, corridors, terraces, courtyards, porter's lodge, boiler room, heating, car park etc. This is called a *condominio* – (condominium) – a social urbanistic phenomenon which spread greatly in the second half of the twentieth century and had to be regulated by new sections in the Italian Civil Code (*Codice Civile* articles 1117-1139), and continues to be regulated by new precedents and judgements handed down by law courts throughout Italy. The *condominio*, therefore, is minutely regulated by Italian law and is not everyone's idea of the best property to live in but it does have advantages for some. Charles Butterno, a freelance writer explains how he was won over

> **Charles Butterno sees advantages in the condominium**
> *Having previously restored a Tuscan farmhouse on commission I was well aware of the unspeakable frustrations and difficulties of trying to co-ordinate the many trades necessary to brin a place back to scratch and grapple with medieval regulations.*
> *   I was also aware of the incredible and seemingly never-ending costs of maintaining a rural retreat, access roads particularly, but also land and dwellings and the invevitable enviromentally objectionable swimming pool. The four windows are the only things in my little apartment which might need attention, the rest is shared within the condominium.*

If you buy into one, and wish to fight your own corner, it is essential to have a good grasp of the language, and also to consult updated publications and guidelines on the subject such as *Condominio* by Paola Bertolotti (de Vecchi Editore) or the www.ilsole24ore/website. The best bet, however, is to delegate a *commercialista* to act on your behalf.

SHARED OWNERSHIP

Comunione

Caution is also called for when entering into co-ownership of a property – or *comunione*.

If you are married and buying a property the notary registering the deed will want to know whether you are in joint ownership with your spouse (*in regime di comunione dei beni*) or separate (*…di separazione dei beni*). This is a distinction, which English common law does not make, unless you have made a pre-nuptial agreement. Italian law assumes you are *in comunione dei beni* with your spouse unless you state otherwise.

No matter how close your friendship is, if you are friends sharing, make a written agreement covering yourselves against any conceivable eventuality.

TIMESHARE

Timesharing – *multi-proprietà* – whereby property is shared on the basis of the right to occupy it for designated times of the year has not caught on in Italy and there are relatively few compared with France and Spain. For more details of timesharing see the *Timeshare* section in the *General Introduction.*Instead of renting a room in an expensive hotel in Venice, you buy a share in a property that gives you the right to use the property for a certain number of weeks for the rest of your life. The catch is you never actually own anything, just the right to use it for a fixed period.

BUYING A HOUSE UNDER CONSTRUCTION

Buying a house under construction has all the advantages of buying a new house (see above), plus the fact that you can adapt the house/flat to your own taste and needs.

Planning Requirements

Before starting any building project planning permission has to be obtained, *le concessione edilizia*, from the *Comune,* in accordance with their *piano regolatore* or master plan. There is nothing to stop the sale of property *before* planning permission has been obtained, or while waiting for a change in the *piano regolatore*. This can take a long time and should be at the builder's risk. You should make discreet enquiries about the development company; if it is a recently created company, perhaps a S.r.l. with a capital of €5,000 (the minimum is €10,000) it is better to tread carefully.

The Specification (Capitolato)

Many developers favour rather terse specifications. Others use the technique of blinding with science. Don't hesitate to seek an explanation from the vendor of anything you do not understand in the *capitolato*. Building terminology is a jargon, which even its initiates find hard to understand. If in doubt get the help of a *geometra*, with an interpreter if necessary.

The Contract and Payments (stadi di avanzamento)

Scrutinise the contract with great care. Look out for clauses to do with revising the prices, or that are vague about delivery times. Stage payments (*stadi di avanzamento*) should be as small and frequent as possible and linked with the progress of the work.

Don't trust a developer who asks for too many, or too big, stage payments at the beginning of the job, or who asks for payment by post-dated cheque or *cambiale*, which you should never give. Always withhold a percentage (at least 10%) for payment on transfer of title (*rogito*) (not on handover of keys).

FEES, CONTRACTS AND CONVEYANCING

UK-BASED PROFESSIONAL ASSISTANCE

Lawyers

The official usually appointed to handle a property sale is a public notary (*notaio*) who in Italy acts for both the vendor and the purchaser. There are also some lawyers (*avvocati*) who are qualified to handle property transactions. Foreigners, who are generally not versed in Italian property buying procedures, may wish to appoint both a *notaio* and an *avvocato*. This way, an expatriate can have a competent professional who works for them directly explain the process to them fully and completely, and not someone who is supposed to be an impartial administrator. Italian lawyers based in the UK can represent expatriates in Italy (see names and contact sources below) when you are buying Italian property, alternatively your embassy or regional consular office should be able to supply a list of local lawyers who speak your language.

Specialist UK-Based Lawyers

Bennett & Co Solicitors: 144 Knutsford Road, Wilmslow, Cheshire SK9 6JP; ☎01625-586937; fax 01625-585362; e-mail: internationallawyers@bennett-and-co.com; www.bennett-and-co.com.

Claudio del Giudice: Rivington House, 82 Great Eastern Street, London EC2A 3JF; ☎020-7613 2788; fax 020-7613 2799; e-mail delgiudice@clara.co.uk; www.delgiudice@clara.co.uk.

Giovanni Lombardo: 020-7256-7467; g.lombardo@lombardolawfirm.co.uk.

John Howell & Co: The Old Glassworks, 22 Endell Street, Covent Garden, London WC2H 9AD; ☎020 7420 0400; fax 020 7836 3626; e-mail info@europelaw.com; www.europelaw.com.

Mr Stefano Lucatello, The International Property Law Centre, Unit 2 Waterside Park, Livingstone Road, Hessle HU13 0EG; ☎01482 350-850; fax 01482 642799; e-mail internationalproperty@maxgold.com; www.internationalpropertylaw.com.

Roberta Crivellaro: ☎020-7597 6491; r.crivellaro@studio-lea.com.

LOCAL PROFESSIONALS

The key local professionals indispensable to the purchase of a property in Italy are the surveyor (*geometra*) and the notary (*notaio*). The *geometra* performs the functions, which we associate with an architect, up to a certain level (making drawings and specifications, supervising work etc.). The difference between architects (*architetti*) and *geometri* is that an *architetto* has a more prestigious title and operates on a higher plane both financially and artistically. A *geometra* qualifies by passing the requisite high school exam, and then, following another exam after two years of apprenticeship, he is fully fledged at twenty-two. But an *architetto* has to do a five-year university course and is usually 28 before qualifying. The result is that *architetti* know a lot about the artistic and theoretical but little about the practical side of building; they charge much more, seldom visit sites – and the *geometri* get most of the work. There is a state of mutual hostility between these two branches of the same profession. *Architetti* often exploit *geometri* and *geometri* are resentful of this.

The *geometra* is now a threatened species; the system is about to change in Italy to conform with the rest of Europe: they will all become *architetti*. As it stands in 2003 you would only consult an *architetto* if you were involved in a large project or on a listed building, or if you were looking for an artistic modern treatment for the interior of an ancient building. *Architetti* are employed by the Fine Arts Commission (*la sovrintendenza delle Belle Arti*) of the Province, which is a sort of local style-police appointed by the Culture Ministry of Rome (*il Ministero dei Beni Culturali*).

The Geometra

An alert and vigilant *geometra* should pick up on any faults in a building.

The *geometra* is familiar with both the legal and technical aspects of land and buildings, and it is vital to have him carry out a site visit/technical survey and before you arrange for the legal side of your purchase, for which you will require the services of a notary or *notaio*, and more checks.

CHECKLIST FOR THE BUYER

Verbal Agreements. No verbal agreement has any value in Italian law. Handshakes in the market place belong to a past age.

Inspection of Property. Don't accept the definition of property 'as seen' (*visto e piaciuto*), and do not accept it 'in the state of fact and law in which it is at present found' (*nello stato di fatto e diritto in cui attualmente si trova*) without visiting and carefully checking everything.

Appurtenances. In particular check that all appurtenances (*pertinenze*) are specified, such as cellars, attics, garages and sheds. Attach a *geometra's* drawing of the property to the contract, signed by both parties and specify such appurtenances in writing.

Utilities and Services. Examine the utilities and services with the help of an expert. Water, gas, electricity, oil, boilers, pumps – (*impianti*). Yearly service contracts and guarantees should be obtained from the vendor.

Furniture and Fittings. Make an inventory (*elenco*) of all the items you and the vendor are agreed on for you to keep. Check that all rubbish and all the items you do not want are removed before the sale. As an extra precaution, arrange with the owner for a final check-up on the day or the day before the final contract. The same argument applies to plants, shrubs, tubs and planters etc., which you might or might not want to keep.

Mortgages. (*ipoteche*). Be aware of the fact that even if you buy a property on which the previous mortgage has been completely paid off, this does not mean it has been officially cancelled. You need to know how much the necessary formalities would cost to cancel the mortgage in the land registry (*La conservatoria dei registri immobiliari*).

PRELAZIONE – THIRD PARTIES' RIGHT TO BUY

Il diritto di prelazione – pre-emptive rights, designed to protect the small working farmer of yesteryear, are still available to people who are officially registered as *coltivatori diretti*, literally direct cultivators, who are *confinanti*, contiguous neighbours, giving them the right of first refusal on any non-urban land adjacent to their own. They are entitled to buy this at the declared price.

Sitting tenants and individuals, who are conducting a business in the property also have a right to buy.

The state – or the *comune* or other state bodies also have the right to buy, or requisition in certain cases, for example, in the case of an archaeological find, and in the case of listed buildings in the *beni culturali* category.

To avert this threat you have to obtain a disclaimer (*rinuncia*) from any interested party. For this you need the co-operation of the vendor.

Inherited or Donated Property. Beware of property acquired by donation or inheritance. A group of siblings often inherit a property, which they decide to sell, but at the last minute one of them refuses to sign. This is often used as a ruse to jack the price up, and is a frequent cause of disappointment for buyers. The only solution to this problem is for the *notaio* to assemble all the owners of the property at the early *compromesso* stage and obtain their signatures on the *compromesso*.

A *certificato di provenienza* – a certificate of provenance such as a will or a donation attests to the legal owners of such property.

Vacant Possession. Check that there are no tenants or squatters in a property supposed to be vacant, including the owner himself. It takes six to ten years to evict a tenant or squatter.

Restrictions and Limitations on the Property. Itemise all restrictions (*vincoli*) and limitations (*servitù*), rights of way (*diritti di passo*) and other burdens (*oneri*) on the property. Make the vendor responsible for any expenses required for eliminating any declared or undeclared restrictions.

Planning Regulations. The validity of a property sale contract in Italy requires documents proving that any illegal improvements have been sanctioned. The local council (*comune*) can issue a document specifying all the permissions they have granted to the property, although not many councils are aware of this. The sanctioning of illegal work is called a *condono edilizio*. Building permission is: *concessione edilizia*.

Imminent Planning Threats. If possible go with your *geometra* or an interpreter to the *Ufficio Tecnico* (planning office) of your local Council (*Comune*), which is normally open to the public two mornings a week.

Ask to see the P.R.G, the master zoning plan, (*piano regolatore generale*) to check the scenarios: housing estates (*zone edificabili*), industrial developments: (*zone industriali*), quarries, clay pits (*cave*), roads (*strade*), roundabouts (*rotatorie*), overpasses (*sopraelevate*), railways (*ferrovie*), dumps (*discariche*), composting plants (*impianti di comopostaggio*) and golf courses (*campi da golf*). There are many long term projects, such as the *Grosseto-Fano* road link, which has been long in abeyance, but is apt at any moment to bring large scale road works to the most hidden valleys of Tuscany, Umbria and the Marches.

The *ufficio tecnico* can provide you with copies of its plans, and the status of your target property, whether it is listed (*schedata*) and what the neighbours might be up to. The word *zoning* has entered the Italian language.

In the Event of any Dispute. It is wise to put into the contract an agreement to settle any eventual disputes by means of a preferably quick and cheap arbitration. A notary (*notaio*) can be appointed for this task; it is his job to be impartial. Alternatively the local *Tribunale* or law court can be named. This arrangement is called *una clausola arbitrale*.

Beware of the Vendors. Establish first that the vendor(s) have the right identity, and that they own the property. Is the vendor of sound mind? Is he under age? Is there a spouse lurking in the background with a claim to the property? Is he bankrupt?

If he goes bankrupt within two years of selling the property, the property reverts to his estate, on which you will figure as one of the creditors.

If you buy from a company it is even more imperative to check – in the local chamber of commerce – whether the company is still registered or struck off, or encumbered with debt or insolvent (*fallito*). Bankruptcies (*fallimenti*) are common. You and your professional advisers have to be extremely vigilant.

Fraud (*Truffa*). Beware of Conmen (*imbroglioni*). A single property was once sold to three different buyers on the same day at different notaries. The first notary to register the property in the *catasto* yielded the only legal owner.

In Bologna two flats were rented out to 26 different tenants at the same time, at a deposit of €43.8 per head, which the fake estate agents pocketed and then disappeared into thin air. The gang was recognised by one of the victims when its leader appeared on a TV quiz show.

That particular gang consisted of Italians and Colombians – but the con **man could** equally be British or German or American, preying on his own compatriots.

THE NOTARY

The *notaio* is a representative of the state whose duty it is to register all contracts, deeds, and titles in the appropriate registry office, and collect all appropriate taxes and duties on behalf of the state; responsible, if in default, for making good any deficit out of his or her own pocket. Women are increasingly evident in the profession. A *notaio's* office is an august and serious place and much dignity and prestige is attached to the profession. Beware of being late or casual with your appointments, and always be sure to bring all your documents and identifications. Despite this dignified appearance fees are negotiable and notaries compete for business. Many prefer to be paid in cash (*contanti*).

The buyer has the right to choose the notary. Normally the agent (*mediatore*) will supply one, your friends in the district will recommend one, or you can find one in the yellow pages. Not many notaries speak English – despite the high academic qualifications that are required for the job, so bring an interpreter if you don't speak Italian.

By law, the notary must be sure that you understand Italian, i.e. that you understand what you are signing in the contract. If he thinks you do not understand, a notarised translation of the contract must be supplied. The notary himself will arrange this for you at a cost.

Power of Attorney, Proxy (procura, delega)

If the vendor has a power of attorney, it needs careful checking by the *notaio*. Is it original? Is it a properly notarised copy? What powers does it confer? Is it of recent date?

If you require a power of attorney yourself, i.e. someone to sign for you, the two main requirements are that he should be (a) trustworthy and (b) understand what he is signing, i.e. an Italian speaker you know and trust.

The drawing up of a proxy document can be done at the *notaio's* office or in an Italian consulate anywhere. You need a valid passport or ID and if possible an Italian *codice fiscale* number.

Documents Required from the Vendor by the Notary

- Deed of provenance (*atto di provenienza*). This is normally the previous contract of sale (*rogito precedente*), but could be a will or a donation.
- Land registry details (*scheda catastale*): ground plans, plot numbers etc. These should be checked thoroughly in the inspection of the property to ensure that they correspond with the reality.
- Land registry tax certificate (*certificato catastale*). This gives details which include the rateable value (*la rendita catastale*).
- Condominium rules (*regolamento condominiale*) – if applicable.
- A photocopy of the passport or ID and *codice fiscale* – Italian tax code number of the vendor(s).
- Any planning sanctions and permissions (*condono fiscale*), if applicable.
- Marital status document (*estratto per sunto degli atti di matrimonio*) issued by the vendor's Comune. This document is necessary if the owners are in a nuptial joint ownership regime, whereby the sale is invalidated if one of them refuses to sign.
- Any rental contracts (*contratti di locazione*) or recent cancellations of same.
- The latest income tax return of the vendor, (*dichiarazione dei redditi*) proving that the property has been declared to the tax authorities.
- Further documents: certificate of habitability (*certificato di abitabilità*), heating and electrical certificates (*certificati impianti*).

Documents You Need for the Notary

- Passport or other valid ID.
- Italian Civil Code number (*codice fiscale*).
- If you have obtained an Italian residence you will also need a residence certificate (*certificato di residenza*) in order to avail yourself of certain tax reductions.

Deposits (acconto-anticipo-caparra)

The first deposit (*acconto*) you will be asked to pay is by the estate agent for his so-called 'irrevocable proposal to buy' *proposta irrevocabile d'acquisto* or *prenotazione*. This has the merit of showing that you are not a time waster (*perditempo*), it engages you to the agent and prevents you from any collusion in a private deal with the vendor, but it is no guarantee that you have secured a property. Its purpose is to give the agent a fixed amount of time, normally a month, to obtain an agreement from the owner to sell you the property. If this agreement is not forthcoming your deposit is refunded.

Agents have been known to collect several deposits from different candidates for the same property and then proceed to an auction, awarding the property to the highest bidder. To avoid falling into traps like this and to limit the risks, four precautions are recommended:

(1) Get the 'irrevocable proposal to buy' drawn up by the notary who you have engaged to handle the conveyancing. In fact this proposal must contain all the details of the definitive contract.

(2) Limit the period in which the proposal is irrevocable to 24 or 48 hours maximum, This is quite enough time for the agent to contact the owner of the property.

(3) Make this deposit minimal: a hundred odd euros. The real deposit will be paid later, at the *compromesso* (preliminary contract). No deposit should be made out to the agent, but to the vendor direct.

(4) Get the agent to specify his commission and/or expenses on a separate sheet; they are nothing to do with the deposit. The true deposit in the contract is called a *caparra*, which is governed by the civil code. It is normally 10% – 30% of the final price.

If the buyer is in default he loses his deposit. If the vendor fails to complete he has to refund the buyer double his deposit. Both parties can take the other to court to enforce the contract.

There are two kinds of *caparra*: *caparra confirmatoria* and *caparra penitenziale*. The *caparra penitenziale* allows for either party to withdraw from the deal on their own terms, jointly agreed, and the contract is not enforceable.

It is advisable to pay any deposits by banker's draft or non-transferable cheque (*assegno non trasferibile*) and to keep a photocopy of the cheque(s).

Full Declaration versus Under-declaration

Under-declaration of the price to avoid tax is common practice in Italian conveyancing deeds. The lowest you can get away with (*il minimo consigliabile*) is quantified at 100 times the figure given for the *rendita catastale* in the *Certificato catastale* (the rateable value in the land registry document). Declare any less than this and you will attract the attention of the tax assessors, who have three years in which to re-assess your declared valuation.

Completion Date

Stipulate a completion date (*data del rogito*) as soon as possible after the *compromesso*. Two or three months is the normal time. Anything could happen in between. If the time has to be longer it is all the more imperative that you have a properly notarised and registered *compromesso*. Even then the vendor might be tempted by a higher bidder *and* afford to give you back double your deposit.

The Rogito Notarile

The *Rogito* – or final contract – is the Big Day for which the *compromesso* has been a rehearsal. The time and date will have been booked well in advance. All you will need are your identity documents and the money.

It is advisable to book the *Rogito* appointment for the morning or early afternoon while the banks are open, just in case there is a hitch with the payment formalities, which a trip to the bank might immediately rectify. All parties have to be present, to sign the contract. The estate agent or *mediatore* will also probably be there (with his hand out) and it is advisable to have an interpreter to help you check all the details of the contract, which the *notaio* will read out, (unless you have previously arranged for an official English translation).

Ask the *notaio* to reassure you that he will file the contract in the Land Registry without delay – it is only then that the title officially changes hands. The Land Registry will then take about two months to furnish a certificate of your title.

SUMMARY OF ITALIAN CONVEYANCING

The sale of real estate in Italy (*La compravendita di un immobile*) is governed by the Civil Code articles 1754-1765 and also by laws (*leggi*) 39 of 3 feb 1989 and 452 of 21 dec 1990. It consists of two stages:

(1) The *Compromesso*, the preliminary contract or *preliminare di vendita*, whereby the buyer pays a deposit called a *caparra*, or earnest money, on an agreed price on a specified property, the contract to be completed by a specified date. It can be a privately signed deed between the buyer and vendor, but it is recommended that it should be done with a notary, publicly registered, and regarded as seriously as a final contract. If the buyer fails to complete he forfeits his deposit. If the vendor pulls out of the contract he must pay back the buyer double his deposit.
(2) *Il rogito* – the final contract and transfer of title, registered in the Land Registry office (*Ufficio del Registro* or *Catasto*) by the *notaio*.

Before you sign anything remember that an estate agent, however honest, is not guaranteed to be impartial. You are advised at this stage to get the help of a lawyer or a notary.

- An *avvocato civilista* is of the status of the international practitioners mentioned above.
- A *notaio:* employ a *notaio* from the very beginning, and you will get the documentation and the wording right, and avoid possible complications. A *notaio* is professionally qualified to make all the necessary checks that are required for the filing of a contract.
- The *Compromesso* is the important and binding part of this contract.

THE COMPROMESSO (SALE CONTRACT)

To explain this document in detail a translation of an Italian *compromesso* is needed. The book *Buying a House in Italy* (available at www.vacationwork.co.uk; or ☎01865-243311) has a full English translation. The full Italian text can be found on the website www.casa2 4.ilsole24ore.com (click *vendita, modulista* then *preliminare di compravendita*).

TAXES AND FEES

Taxes and duties vary on a property sale:

If the house is to be a principal residence and the vendor is a private individual (*prima casa*):
- Registry Tax – (*imposta del registro*) 3%
- Fixed mortgage tax – (*imposta ipotecaria fissa*) 129.11 euros

O   Fixed Land Registry Tax – (*imposta catastale fissa*) 129.11 euros

If the property is a second house (*seconda casa*) the total tax is 10%:

O   Registry tax – 7%
O   Mortgage tax – 2%
O   Land Registry tax – 1%

If it is a primary residence being bought by a developer the taxes are:

O   IVA (Value added tax) – 4%
O   Fixed mortgage tax – €129.11
O   Fixed Land Registry tax – €129.11

The above taxes are levied on the value declared in the deed of sale. This value cannot be less than the rateable value (*valore catastale*), which is obtained by multiplying the *rendita catastale* by 100.

Typical notary's fee (*onorario*); depending on property:

Value of property	Fee
€50,000	€1,400
€250,000	€2,000
€300,000	€2,200
€500,000	€3,000

Then increasing by €100 for each additional €25,000 of value. This is the fee on the *rogito*. The fee on the *compromesso* is 50% of the above. In addition the notary will charge for the following:

O   Accessory rights (*diritti accessori*)
O   Indemnities (*indennità*)
O   Searches (*vìsure*)
O   Authentications (*autenticazioni*)
O   Expenses (*rimborso spese*)

It is essential to ask the *notaio* for an estimate of his charges at the very start. His fees may be fixed, but with all those extras he has plenty of room to negotiate. In a typical transaction the total notarial expenses will be minimum of €8,000 (£5,600/$7,339) for a *Rogito notarile*.

POST-COMPLETION FORMALITIES

It is the duty of the notary to file and register the transfer of title and pay all taxes due, with all possible speed. Within 48 hours the local police – the *carabinieri* in a *comune* – or the *questura* in a provincial capital – must be informed of the change of ownership. The notary can do this himself or supply you with the relevant form. You will also want to transfer the utilities into your name, (electricity, water, telephone, gas, etc.) and arrange for new contracts (*volturazione delle utenze*), for which a photocopy of your contract will be useful.

WHAT HAPPENS NEXT

CHAPTER SUMMARY

- Arranging for an isolated property to be connected to mains services can be very expensive, so the purchase price should reflect this.
- Electricity. ENEL is the main supplier of electricity in Italy and bills are sent out every two months.
  - Electricity bills are estimated, and adjusted twice yearly after a meter reading.
- Plugs and Light Fittings. Most Italian plugs have either two or three round pins. All electric bulbs are screw fitting.
- Gas Tanks. Many foreign residents in remoter areas have a gas tank for central heating and there are strict regulations regarding installation.
- Bottled Gas. Bottled gas is commonly used in rural areas but also in towns and cities, especially for cooking.
- Drought. Water is plentiful in northern Italy but in central and southern parts drought is common.
  - In times of drought, water may be rationed.
  - In rural drought areas water used in the house is recycled for watering the garden.
- Wells and Bore Holes. If you have a property with an underground water supply you may need to employ a water-diviner to pinpoint the best place to sink a bore hole.
- Telephone. The Italian public utility is known as Telecom Italia.
- Security. Italian cities have a very bad reputation for petty crime but even in rural areas you should lock up your property.
  - Owners of holiday homes are often glad to have reliable people stay for free in the winter to keep the property occupied in return for maintenance, gardening etc.
- **Building & Renovating.** It is essential to have a building plan produced in conjunction with the *geometra* before you begin.
  - Under floor heating is popular and very economical.
  - Italy produces beautiful marble for bathrooms, kitchens etc.
- Making Money from Your Property – Renting Out. **Long-term rentals over a month have to be registered with the authorities.**

When contemplating a move to Italy it is preferable to buy a property connected to the main services – water, electricity, gas, sewage and telephone. If not, the further away the property is from the nearest telephone line or mains, the greater the cost of connection. If the property is not connected to mains services you should expect to pay a lower price for it.

Another important consideration is the access road to your property. Many roads to rural properties are at best a rocky path the majority of which are not suitable for any vehicles other than four-wheel drive, tractors and diggers. A good road is essential and if shared with other properties (*strada vicinale*) it is a good idea to draw up an agreement about the upkeep and the division of costs with the help of your *geometra* (surveyor) or direct consultation with the neighbours involved.

SERVICES

Electricity

The national electricity company *Ente Nazionale per l'Energia* commonly known as ENEL/Enel (www.enel.it) had the monopoly for supplying electricity before privatisation in 1998; even so there is still little competition. Estimated bills (*bollette*) arrive every two months and adjustments are made twice a year when the meters have been read. Most meters are now outside for easy access. The easiest way to pay bills is by direct debit from your bank but you can also pay at the Post Office. The cost of electricity in Italy is relatively high. The consumption charge is based on the power rating of the property, the maximum being 6KW. The charge per Kilowatt hour (*scatto*) is €0.13 on a 6KW power rating. Changing your power rating from 3KW to 6KW can be costly. Out of 22 million electrical service contracts in Italy 18 million are for 3KW, including most apartments.

Arranging a Contract with ENEL. You will have to sign a new contract (*volturazione delle utenze*) at the local ENEL office. You need to bring identification with you either your passport or residence permit, the registration number of the meter and the previous owner's paid electricity bill.

Plugs. Most Italian plugs have two or three round pins so if you are bringing electrical appliances from another country you need to purchase plug adaptors. The two-pin plug has no earth wire so large appliances using a high wattage must be plugged into earthed sockets.

Bulbs. All electric light bulbs in Italy are screw fitting. You can buy adaptors to change appliances such as lamps from bayonet to screw fittings.

Gas

Mains Gas. Most cities and large towns in Italy are supplied by the (*Societe Italiana per il GAS*) (SIG) or ITALGAS (www.italgas). If your new property has mains gas you should contact SIG in order to have your meter read and get connected. Mains gas is costly. The billing and payment system is similar to electricity (see above). It is advisable to have gas water heaters checked annually for safety reasons.

Gas Tanks. Many foreigners buy rural homes where it is quite usual to have a gas tank known in Italian as a (*bombolone*). Gas tanks can be loaned from the larger gas companies for example Agip gas, Shell gas, and Liquigas, and installation is strictly regulated. For obvious reasons, the tank must be at least 25m away from the house or road. The tank can be sited underground and pipes laid to connect it to the house. The contract with the gas company supplying liquid gas will stipulate a minimum annual purchase usually in the region of €1,200 (£840/$1,308). The size of your tank depends on your needs.

Bottled Gas. The gas bottle (*bombola*) is commonly used in rural areas but can be used in towns and cities. You pay a deposit on your first purchase of bottled gas and then you exchange your empty bottle for a full one. The bottles weigh 10 kg and 15 kg and a 10kg bottle costs €17, plus a delivery charge if necessary. A bottle used just for cooking will last an average family six weeks. If you are only using your Italian home for holidays, the *bombola* is a useful alternative to mains gas.

Water

The water supply is under the control of the local comune, eg CIGAF. As water is scarce in central and southern parts there may be only a meagre supply. For this reason it is essential if you live in a dry area to have a storage tank (*cassone*) which can be topped up when the water supply is on, or filled by tanker, though this is expensive. For flat-dwellers in the main cities a 500 litre tank may be sufficient. In remote rural areas it may be necessary to store several months of water in huge underground tanks. Water shortages are made worse whatever the region by old leaking mains water pipes. Water in your area may be rationed to a fixed number of litres per house, regardless of the number of occupants.

Recycling Water. Water restrictions in drought areas mean limited water for gardens and a ban on swimming pools. However, if you are clued-up and possess a little ingenuity there are solutions. It is possible to recycle water used for washing and bathing for the garden by draining it into a separate tank (*serbatoio*).

Another method of recycling your domestic water, is to install a water purifier (*depuratore*). This is a large tank, which is made up of sections. It is placed underground and in a position where the treated contents of the septic tank spill into it. This water passes through an aerated section. The aeration is done by means of an electric pump, programmed to work at least 16 hours a day. This pump passes oxygen into the water to feed the 'good' bacteria, which in turn eat the 'bad' bacteria. The filtered water collects in the last section and overflows into another tank which can be used for watering or irrigation. The total cost of a *depuratore* is €9,500 (about £6,650/$10,350). This includes the tanks, pipes, pump and labour.

Wells and Water Diviners. If you are told that your new property has a well (*pozzo*), you should have it confirmed by an expert. You may even wish to utilise a water-diviner (*rabdomante*) to detect where the water is and put markers down for future bore-holes. A *rabdomante* can usually determine the depth of the water, with a high degree of accuracy.

Telephone

Installing/Getting Connected. The Italian telephone service (*Telecom Italia*) was privatised in 1997. In 1998 deregulation meant competition was introduced. To get a new telephone line (*nuovo impianto*) installed in your home apply at the local Telecom Italia office where you can file an application. You need your passport (and a photocopy) for identification purposes.

For more information about using the telephone and mobiles in Italy see the section *Communications* in the chapter *Living in Italy.*

SECURITY

For information on how to make your foreign home more secure, see *Security* in the *General introduction* and for information on home insurance in Italy see *Insurance* in the chapter *Living in Italy.*

REMOVALS

Moving the Contents of Your Home to Italy.

If you live outside the EU the first step before you leave for Italy is to submit a list of the items you wish to import into Italy to the nearest Italian Consulate, who will officially stamp it. All nationalities must also apply for their *permesso di soggiorno* (permit to stay – see *Residence and Entry* chapter for addresses) from the *questura* (police station) in Italy once you have arrived. Once the permit is issued you can then import your belongings.

The removal firm will require both the list stamped by the consulate, the *permesso* and copies of documents relating to your ownership of property in Italy or proof of address. If you have not been resident in Italy long enough to have obtained the *permesso* you can obtain an attestation from the *comune* to the effect that you have purchased or leased accommodation in the area. This should allow the shipping company to import your belongings successfully.

Removals Firms

Shipping personal belongings internationally is always best done by a professional and reputable company. The companies below have specialist experience of Italy. There are dozens of large firms that deal with international removals (see *Removals* in the *General Introduction* for some contacts and addresses).

Useful Addresses – Removals to Italy
Britannia Sandersteads: Unit E3, Felnex Trading Estate, 190 London Road, Hackbridge, Wallington, Surrey SM6 7EL; ☎020-8669 6688; fax 020-8669 3366.
Inline Removals: Unit 6, Thames Road Industrial Estate, Thames Road, Silvertown, London E16 2EZ; ☎0800 092 1313; fax 020-7511 1600.

PETS

Details of exporting and importing pets from and to the UK using the Pets Passports scheme can be found in the *General Introduction.*

Regulations and Practices in Italy. Regulations now in force in most areas of Italy compel owners to have their dogs tattooed on the body as a means of checking their registration. An alternative to the tattoo is for the dog to have a tiny microchip inserted under the skin of the neck. Any loose dog without either a tattoo or microchip is liable to be destroyed. The tattoo/microchip insertion can be done by a vet, or in some areas by the *Unita Sanitaria Locale*. Dog insurance against claims for damages is advisable for those with unpredictable animals and those, whose canines have no traffic sense.

Rabies vaccinations have to be given yearly and a log-book will be provided by the vet for the purpose of recording these. Apart from rabies, which is reputedly prevalent in the far north of Italy, hazards further south are more likely to include encounters with porcupines and snakes. For animals (and human beings) it is advisable to keep a supply of venom antidote in the fridge, but make sure that it is regularly renewed before the expiry date has been reached.

CUSTOMS

Italian Customs and Your Foreign Registered Car. On arrival at customs, the owner must present the registration documents, proof of insurance and a certificate of residence. After checking the vehicle against the documents the customs will issue a customs receipt (*bolletta doganale*). The owner may then drive the car with foreign plates for up to six months before the car has to be registered in Italy. There is no duty or VAT levied on cars imported in this manner, but it is a once in a lifetime concession. If there are no customs officers present at the point of entry into Italy, it will be necessary to find a customs office and apply for your customs certificate soon after your arrival in Italy.

BUILDING OR RENOVATING

HIRING THE PROFESSIONALS

The key person for the initiation of any major building or renovation work is the *geometra* (surveyor). You need him/her to pilot your planning application (*il progetto*) through the planning office (*l'officio tecnico*) of your local borough council (*comune*).

Builders and Craftsmen

This whole process of hiring professional workmen and briefing them looks simple, but it is not. It is normally a nightmare. If anything can go wrong it will. First, before you take on any building firm or tradesmen, ask to see their work. Secondly – before a brick is lifted: think out a master plan, in conjunction with your *geometra*, of your project in such a way that you *get it right first time*. To chop and change during the course of the work is demoralising and expensive.

The building trade in Italy is now predominately manned by immigrant labour, mostly Albanian, North African, even Polish, who soon pick up the language and do the drudgery and donkey work in a brisk and workmanlike fashion, but are not over zealous in the detail. Sometimes with the connivance of their *impresario* (manager), they will skimp. Given the licence to be rustic they will be slapdash. To get the job done as you want it, constant vigilance and forethought are needed.

Local Tradesmen

Then come the decisions regarding the plumbing (*l'impianto idraulico*), heating (*il riscaldamento*), wiring (*l'impianto elettrico*) and the doors and windows (*gli infissi*).

With all your ideas clear in your head you should make an appointment with the *geometra* and the *impresario* or *muratore* (builder) for a *sopralluogo* – a tour of the site. Armed with a canister of aerosol spray paint or coloured chalk, you mark the required position of every single socket (*presa*), switch (*interruttore*), conduit (*forassite*), wall light (*applique*), sink (*lavello*), basin (*lavabo*), bidet (*bidé*), WC bowl (*vaso*) and radiator (*radiatore*). There is a standard height and position for each fixture, which a qualified tradesmen will adhere to; insist on uniformity. Ask the *geometra* to make a detailed diagram of these fixtures and fittings as a blueprint for the workers.

If you are directly employing these tradesmen it is advisable to ensure that they know each other, so that they can co-ordinate their work between themselves.

The Plumbing

The plumber's main job – connecting the water supply to the bathrooms and kitchen and fitting the central heating – is different to what you might be used to in other countries as pumps take the place of gravity. The water arrives from the mains or your own well into a water tank in the basement or garage from whence it is pumped on demand by a pump under constant pressure (*l'autoclave*). The kitchen alone must have a direct supply of drinking water from the mains, (in order to qualify for the certificate of habitability (*il certificato di abitabilità*). The pressure of the water for washing purposes therefore is powerful and constant throughout the house. The showers are power showers: no need for booster pumps. But the disadvantage of this system is that if there is no electricity, there is no water. The *autoclave* also breaks down or gets airlocked or clogged up once every three years on average, which requires professional attention. A simpler, more foolproof, water supply system must exist, but this is the way they do it in Italy.

Heating

The standard heating system is gas (rarely oil) -heated water pumped through radiators, placed under windows, or walls, in niches (*nicchie*). Aluminium radiators deliver instant heat, but cast iron ones are still manufactured and sometimes preferred for their heat retention and classic look. For buildings which are going to be used all winter under floor heating is now found to be spectacularly economical, kept on permanently from October to April at a temperature of 32°C (90F), requiring only a small wall mounted domestic boiler.

Woodwork

The longest and most craftsmanlike of all the jobs required for the renovation of an Italian house is the woodwork (*la falegnameria*), which is still done mostly in local family-run workshops, well mechanised, but with a limited rate of production, You will almost certainly prefer solid wood (*legno massello*) to plywood (*compensato*) doors, and will be given a choice of wood, in which you should favour local hard woods such as chestnut (*castagno*), larch (*larice*) or cypress (*cipresso*) for the windows (*le finestre*) and shutters. The traditional colour for doors and windows is grey, for external shutters brown, green, grey or ochre. Some local councils enforce a favoured colour or choice of colours.

Rates of Pay

As a rough indication as to the going rate for these workers, in central Italy (cheaper in the south), a *muratore* (builder) gets €23 per hour and a *manovale* (labourer) €21. Plastering (*intonaco civile*) – i.e. rendering and skimming with a lime-based plaster, excluding materials, is €14 per square metre, floor tiling is €18 per square metre, and wall tiling is €20.

The plumber and the electrician – normally quick, skilful and efficient – are not paid by the hour but will charge for the job. The standard minimum call out rate is €50. These specialists spend much of the time on the road and the advent of the mobile phone has been a godsend for them.

Il Marmista

Another specialist in Italy who deserves special praise is the marble man (*il marmista*). Marble – travertine, dressed stone – is used extensively in Italian buildings for thresholds, worktops, sills cladding, columns, paving, for shelves, tables and even sinks. Most large towns will have at least one *marmista*.

BUILDING WORKERS' OCCUPATIONS	
Costruttore	builder
Decoratore	interior decorator
Elettricista	electrician
Fabbro	locksmith or blacksmith
Falegname	carpenter
Ferramenta	hardware shop owner
Idraulico	plumber
Imbianchino	painter (whitewasher)
Ingegnere	engineer
Intonachino	plasterer
Muratore	builder or mason
Pavimentista	floor tiler
Piastrellista	tiler

Permits

La Concessione Edilizia. Finally, before any work is done, and after you have obtained the work permit (*la concessione edilizia*) you are obliged by law to put up a notice – supplied by the *comune* – specifying the type of work and the professionals involved. If you are employing direct labour and working yourself it is called *in economia*, in economy. The type of work is described as renovation (*ristrutturazione*) or ordinary or extraordinary maintenance (*mantenuzione ordinaria* or *straordinaria*). Illegal building work is rife, especially in the south where no one takes a blind bit of notice, but as a foreigner it is unwise to take such liberties.

Certificato di Abitabilità. The object of all this and the building work is to obtain a *certificato di abitabilità*, 'a certificate of habitability'. Recent law makes this certificate the responsibility of the *geometra* in charge. Without this certificate you will not get an official licence for bed and breakfast or rental operations (see the section *Making Money from Your Property*).

<hr>

Improvements without planning consent
Many house owners carry out improvements regardless of planning permission. They simply pay the fine when challenged, and get the work *condonato* (amnestied) at a later date. Be aware that Councils have been known to issue legal injunctions to stop or demolish *abusivo* work, in particular when they have received complaints from the public, and especially in the case of swimming pools. To achieve your objectives in all these cases you need the services of a *geometra* who is familiar with the planning offices involved. You will also need plenty of money (*un sacco di soldi*).

<hr>

The DIY woodworker will find local suppliers of timber cut to measure under *Legno, compensatie profilati* in the yellow pages (*Pagine Gialle* – casa). You will also find DIY outlets under *Bricolage – faidate* (do it yourself), in places like *Mister Brico City*. In the shopping malls mushrooming throughout Italy *Brico Centers* are a popular novelty. But your local hardware shop (*ferramenta*) and carpenter (*falegnameria*) should not be neglected. Through them you can find a product for ageing new wood: emulsionable oil (*olio emulsionabile*), normally used for metal lathe work, which digests the surface resins of the wood and is a godsend for house restorers. Small shopkeepers in Italy are very knowledgeable and helpful about such products.

POOLS

Swimming pools are expensive to build and run, and they require constant attention, however if you wish to rent out a country property in Italy in June, July and August, they are indispensable. But planning permission is required, and might be refused. Before buying the property you should therefore check with you surveyor (*geometra*) or directly with the planning office (*officio tecnico*) of your local council (*comune*), to ascertain their rulings on the subject. Some councils have strict aesthetic and environmentally conscious restrictions.

<hr>

Trespassers and the law
If a trespasser falls into your pool, you the owner are responsible according to Italian law. To combat this it is wise to include the pool in your insurance cover and fence it in, especially if it is out of sight and a hazard for children.

<hr>

Italian building firms are capable of building reinforced concrete swimming pools to order, but a reputable firm such as Culligan (www.culligan.it) must be employed to put in the filtration system, pool cover etc. A 50ft x 16ft (15m x 5m) pool with landscaping costs about €30,000 (£21,000/$36,634).

<hr>

Temporary pools
Should your local council refuse you permission for a pool you can install an out-of-ground 'temporary pool' which requires no permission. These can cost as little as €3,000.

<hr>

Water

You will choose according to your terrain, your pocket and your instincts but you must not forget to check on the obvious requirement: water. If you are in a drought-prone area with a hose-pipe ban and no spring, well, or rainwater tank of your own, and there are no local suppliers of water by the tankful, what do you do? Call in a water-diviner (*un rabdomante*) and a geologist (*un geologo*) and a well-digger (*un pozzaiolo*), sink a borehole, find water and put in the largest underground water tanks you can afford, one for the borehole water, the other for the rain water, which you will capture from all your roofs. After a long dry summer you can still run out of water. Pools need refilling every few years and need topping up throughout the season: Be very careful before you make the investment. The *geometra* is required by law to furnish a 'hydro-geological clearance' (*lo svincolo idrogeologico*) with the local provincial authority before permission for a pool is granted. This safeguards against environmental damage.

Useful Websites
www.culligan.it – for water purifying installations.
www.gruppoazzurro.it – 24 pool and service companies throughout Italy.
www.assopiscine.it HYPERLINK http://www.assopiscine.it – 150 associated pool industry companies.

GARDENS

A garden – or at least a terrace or courtyard – is a priority for most house hunters: a place to grow your own herbs and to enjoy the sun in winter and the shade in summer. If you have pets or children or give parties, or want to practise the healthy and creative hobby of gardening, a garden is indispensable.

There are varying hardiness zones and soil qualities in Italy, which the potential buyer should be aware of. The southern coastal and island regions where the lemon tree grows are frost-free. The central regions where the olive tree grows are mild while further north, the Po valley has extremes of heat and cold.

Most of the country is mountainous and hilly and so calcareous; heavy clay soil predominates, sometimes granite. There are fertile volcanic plains in Campania, Lazio, Sicily. Puglia has a deep productive soil. Much of the southern uplands is sheer and barren rock, and scrub macchia, as is Sardinia.

The problem of water is another decisive factor. If there is a shortage of water – and the equivalent of a hose-pipe ban on public water is universal throughout Italy you should radically reconsider your project. Why buy a house in a desert? It is no fun living through the heat of the summer without an abundance of water. Gardens in hot climates depend on it for their shadiness and charm.

But if you find yourself stuck with a shortage of water and labour – which is the normal situation for the house buyer in Italy – do not despair. The recent science of xeriscaping, pioneered in the droughts of Arizona, makes a virtue of indigenous – and exotic – plants, which thrive in arid conditions and only need watering to establish themselves in the first year. These plants include: rosemary, oleander, cypress, santolina, lemon verbena, rue, curry plant and artemisia as well as many others.

When it does rain, it usually pours. Heavy rainfall and flash floods are very common in Italy.

MAKING MONEY FROM YOUR PROPERTY

RENTING OUT YOUR PROPERTY

Once your Italian property is finished if you are not making it your permanent residence, but merely using it as a holiday home you may think about renting it out. This is usually done from spring to autumn keeping perhaps a slot for yourself in either June or July. August is very hot and the majority of businesses close down as Italians go on their holidays.

Renting is a useful way of recouping some of the cost of restoration and it is also wise not to let your property remain unoccupied for long periods for security reasons and insurance cover. The income you can expect will vary according to the degree of luxury offered, and whether the let is in the high season (July and August) mid-season (June and September) or low season (April, May and October). Rentals range from £300 for a one-bedroom apartment, to upwards of £6,000 for a luxury villa for one week in the high season.

To rent a villa in Southern Tuscany during July and August would cost £4,500 a week. For this you get:

A villa and converted barn (capanna) which sleeps 16 people.
Swimming pool – pool house with gym.
Bedrooms en suite.
Large gourmet kitchen.
Panoramic view.
A daily cleaner who also cooks, as an extra.

In the high season it is usual for people to book for two weeks. The lets are mostly to foreigners e.g. Americans and British.

You can also advertise your property and get rental customers' online bookings by having an advert on a property website such as Gecko get aways (☎0870 741 2700; www.geckogetaways.com; e-mail info@geckogetaways.com).

SELLING ON

When you buy a property in Italy – it could be that you are considering living there for the rest of your life. On the other hand you may be buying the property as a business venture and intend to restore it and then sell it on. It may be that life in Italy did not meet your expectations and you want to sell and leave. Whatever the reason you are selling, check out the current state of the property market and get more than one valuation. You can use an estate agent to do the selling, or you can arrange a private sale with the essential assistance of a notary. The price of buildings in Italy is based on the link between the cost per square metre, times the area sq.m.e.g. 300sq.m. @ 1,000 euros per sq.m. = €300,000.

If you want to arrange a private sale, a useful publication is Ville e Casali (www.villecasali.com), a national property and decoration magazine in Italian. The

classified property advertisements are listed in both Italian and English.
A 'For Sale' (vendesi) sign at the entrance to your property can be useful, if only
as a signpost indicating the location of the property. An advertisement put into
newspapers or magazines is also a must. Italy is now attracting buyers from America,
Canada, Australia and their European neighbours,

Estate Agents/Agenzie Immobiliari)

Agents' fees vary; the rate of commission can be anything from 3-8% depending on
the area and the market. The cost is usually shared between the vendor and the buyer.
It might be beneficial to use the estate agent who sold you the property as he will
be familiar with it. If this is not possible or desirable, there are lists of Italian estate
agents on the internet including www.grimaldi.net, www.arpnet.it, www.casa.it and
www.findaproperty.com. All estate agents must be registered and have a document
attesting to their legality. An estate agent must have a signed authority from the owner
and come to an agreement whereby either the estate agent has sole control over the
sale; or, seller has the right to deal with other agents and private individuals.

Tax on Plusvalenza

Although capital gains tax (INVIM), was abolished in Italy in 2002, there is
a tax which operates in a similar way on *plusvalenza* (literally 'plus value') and is levied
at 30%, less deductions for some costs (see below). It is applied to property sales that
occur within five years of purchase.
Plusvalenza (literally 'plus value') is the difference between the declared purchase
price of a property, and the declared sale price, minus deductions for renovation and
notarial fees. This means that if you expect to sell the property within five years you
should plan ahead so that you minimise the tax on the *plusvalenza*. You should ensure
that the declared price on the conveyancing documents when you buy is as high as
possible.

RUNNING A BUSINESS FROM YOUR PROPERTY

Many highly-qualified and skilled people have started up their own businesses from
home and have been extremely successful (e.g. artist, writer, website designer). A
website giving good advice and information on starting up your own business from
home is www.entrepreneur.com. 102 Lavori is an excellent publication for those
who wish to work from home using their computer; produced by the Minister of
Employment, it contains ideas for work connected to the Internet. It deals with all
aspects of business and produces a newsletter for a worldwide market.
All EU citizens have the right to work in Italy provided they apply for a libretto di
lavoro (see the Residence and Entry chapter). As an EU citizen you are free to advertise
your business on your property. Foreign professionals who have located in Italy, and
who have set up successful businesses include lawyers qualified in international law,
accountants, veterinarians, landscape gardeners and interior designers. However you
should check to see if you need any special registration for your particular profession.
You can ask at the Italian Consulate in your own country, or in Italy at the Chamber
of Commerce (camera di commercio).
The ability to communicate in Italian is imperative for anyone contemplating co-
operation with Italian ventures.

SPOT CHECK – ITALY	
Political/economic stability:	Italy is notorious for its 'revolving door' (i.e. frequently changing goverments). Italians can shrug off their politicians as if they were Armani jackets, but the Presidency is a dignified and respected office that involves a seven-year term. The economy is picking up and inflation tacks between 2% and 2.4%.
Climate:	Winds can be vicious, summers too hot, and even in Sicily winters can be longer, colder and wetter than you expect. Droughts and floods are frequent.
Cost of living/ taxes	Income tax rates are from 23% to 45% and Italians get a lot for their taxes in pensions and benefits. VAT standard rate is 20%. There are lots of irritating little taxes and the regulations change frequently.
Accessibility:	Not as many cheap flights as France and Spain but increasing year by year. Even Bari (south), Pescara (east coast) and Alghero (northern Sardinia) now have budget flights.
Property availability:	Go south. Liguria, Veneto and Tuscany are now very expensive. Marche still has modern bargains on the coast, but head for Puglia for character. Lazio has lots of modern seaside apartments, but watch out for cowboy builders and illegal developments.
Property prices:	Very few bargains left in the popular places. From about £100,000 for a small house, less for a seaside apartment. If restoration is needed add 50% to the buying price.
Costs of property purchase as a % of property price:	Varies, but on average about 15% (for registration, stamp duty, notary and lawyer fees)
Ease of purchase and ease of renovation:	Regulated estate agents operate in most areas. There may be language problems beyond the areas well-trodden by English-speaking foreigners. If possible enlist the help of an Italian – essential if you are trying to find a property without using an estate agent. A richesse of highly skilled craftsmen mean it is easy to get carried away on the restoration. Get quotes for everything and resist temptation where possible.
Annual property taxes:	High. Very unpopular annual property tax is about £1,000 on average.
Investment potential:	The Italian property market is buoyant rather than meteoric with prices rising about 6.5% a year on average. In hotspots can be 10%-20% per year.
Suitability for letting:	You may do well from letting, if you choose your location carefully. You can also let seaside apartments to the Italian market, but Italians have very high standards.

BUYING A HOUSE ON THE MEDITERRANEAN

MALTA AND GOZO

LIVING IN MALTA & GOZO

CHAPTER SUMMARY

- The Maltese archipelago has strong links with Britain and was British for over 160 years until independence in 1964.
    - There are aspects of Malta that British people find familiar such as driving on the left and red letter boxes.
- **Languages.** Maltese and English are the two official languages, and Italian is also widely spoken.
    - Maltese is a mongrel Semitic language written in the Roman alphabet.
- **Currency.** Malta joined the EU in May 2004, but will not adopt the euro for a few years.
    - The Maltese currency is the lira (pl. liri) otherwise known as the Maltese pound.
- **Taxes.** Malta has high VAT at 18%, but there are no municipal taxes or local property taxes.
    - The Maltese government encourages moderately well off foreigners to settle in Malta by offering major tax incentives for those who apply for permanent residence status.
- You can own property on Malta without becoming a permanent resident.
- Foreigners can only own one property at a time in Malta and Gozo.
- **Gozo** is 25 minutes by ferry from Malta or 15 minutes by helicopter.
    - Property on Gozo has the reputation of being cheaper than on Malta, but the differential is fast disappearing.
- **Banks.** Banks in Malta have loan products aimed at foreigners buying property in Malta.
    - It is relatively easy to open a non-resident bank account in Malta with a passport.

INTRODUCTION

The Maltese archipelago consists of only three inhabited island. The two principal islands Malta and Gozo (*Ghawdex)* and the tiny island of Comino (*Kemmuna)*, lies between them. Malta is 246 sq. kms (95 sq. miles), while Gozo is 67sq km (26 sq. miles). These islands, are situated in southern Europe, between Sicily and Tunisia, and they have hot, dry summers and mild winters.

The Maltese islands have a resident population of nearly 400,000, which is swamped by twice that number of tourists annually.

History

Malta's litany of invaders including Phoenicians, Arabs, Romans, Italians, and in later times the French and the British, have all left their cultural imprint on the islands. The stone ramparts of the famous capital Valletta were built by the Knights of St. John of Jerusalem in the 16th century. These Knights, ruled Malta until Bonaparte systematically imposed his new order across Europe and drove them from their sanctum. The balance of power in the region altered in favour of Britain after a French fleet was sunk at the Battle of the Nile (1798), when Britain took over the islands, which remained British until their independence in 1964. The links with Britain are very strong and accentuated by Maltese heroism under fire in the Second World War. English is one of the two official languages (the other being Maltese) and there are other cultural landmarks that make Britons feel familiar such as red letter boxes, and driving on the left.

Politics

Malta is a stable parliamentary democracy run broadly on the British model. The ruling party is the Nationalist Party. Eddie Fenech Adami, was formerly the leader of the ruling party and has just retired from this position to become President of Malta. The Prime Minister is Lawrence Gonzi, appointed in March 2004.

Malta and the EU. Following a national referendum in 2003, Malta officially became a member of the EU on 1 May 2004. Note that the Maltese currency is still the Maltese Lira (1 Maltese lira = 100 cents) and that Malta will not adopt the euro until at least 1997. Further currency information can be obtained at www.centralbankmalta.com/site/currency2e.html.

Geography

Population. The Maltese islands are densely populated relative to their size with many villages situated close together. There are 67 villages which are large enough to have a village council. 53 of these are on Malta and 14 on Gozo.

Getting To Malta and Gozo

The flight time from London is 3 hours. Air Malta is the national carrier operating scheduled flights. Other carriers including British Airways fly to Malta. Usually cheaper than either of these are charter flights, which go from London and most UK regional airports to Malta with prices starting from about £60. There are no bargain operator flights to Malta.

There are no direct flights to Gozo. There is a ferry connection between Malta and Gozo which takes 25 minutes between Cirkewwa (Malta) and Mgarr (Gozo), or a helicopter operated by Malta Air Charter, a subsidiary of Air Malta. The flight takes 15 minutes from Malta airport to Xewkija heliport on Gozo and costs Lm 18 (£28/$50) single or Lm 27 (£45.50/$75) return.

Those with a permanent resident status get ferry and helicopter tickets at a reduced rate.

Useful Contacts
Air Malta: Air Malta plc., Head Office, Luqa, Malta, LQA 01; ☎+356 2169 0890; fax +356 2167 3241; e-mail info@airmalta.com.mt; www.airmalta.com.
Charter Flight Centre: www.charterflights.co.uk/malta/. Specialises in Malta charter flights from all UK airports.
Malta Air Charter: ☎+356 22 999 138; fax +356 21 663195; e-mail mac@airmalta.com.mt or Gozo heliport macgozo@airmalta.com.mt. For information about helicopter flights between Malta and Gozo.

Food and Drink

Food. Traditional Maltese food is simple and rustic depending little on meat, but with a great variety of seafood and vegetables; it also follows the seasons. Vegetables that feature in Maltese food include artichokes, zucchini, giant cabbage, cauliflower, beans (fresh or dried) and tomatoes. Staples of the home kitchen include thick vegetable soups (*minestra*) and *kapunata* (ratatouille). Other typical fare includes *gbejniet* (goat or sheep's cheese), *bigilla* (paté made from broad beans and garlic) and *Aljotta* (fish soup). There is a fantastic fish market at **Marsaxlokk** every Sunday morning.

Throughout Valletta and in most villages bakers make their own special pastry

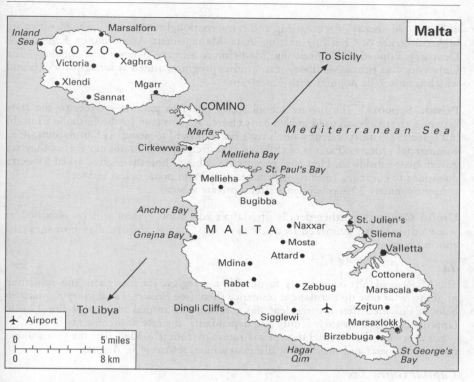

parcels filled with savoury or sweet fillings.

Drink. Malta produces a range of wines of patchy quality: reds, whites, frizzante and sparkling. Generally, the reds are better than the whites. It is difficult to tell how much Maltese wine is made from locally-grown grapes and how much from grapes imported from Italy and North Africa. The standards set by the Maltese Marsovin marque founded in 1919 (www.marsovinwinery.com), and which has its own vineyards, are high. Their products include a *méthode champenoise* (*Cassar de Malte*) fizzy white.

Schools and Education

Malta's educational system bears strong hallmarks of British influence. Education in Malta is compulsory from ages 5 to 16; about 54% of students stay on after the age of 16. Additionally, free kindergarten is provided to all three-year-olds up to school age.

Primary school phase last from ages 5 to 11. At the age of 11 all students sit an exam much like the defunct UK 11+ to stream them for the secondary phase of schooling in technical (preparation for university) or vocational schools.

Secondary School culminates in a GCSE-type exam called a Secondary Education Certificate (SEC) and after a further 2 years at a sixth-form Junior College students sit a matriculation exam at intermediate or advanced level, which, if successful allows students to move on to tertiary education.

Tertiary education is carried out mostly at Malta's only university, which has a

400-year-old history of scholarship and is internationally accredited. The faculties are in Architecture & Civil Engineering, Arts, Management, Accountancy, Economics, Dentistry, Education, Engineering, Medicine & Surgery, Science and Theology. The University also runs a Mediterranean Studies program, aimed at foreign students and which is especially popular with Americans.

Private Schools. The private school sector provides parallel services to the state system. Private schools used to be mostly church schools (run by the Catholic Church) but since 1987, independent schools have been allowed to set up as foundations, or as commercial ventures. Parents of children at church schools do not pay fees as they are government subsidised. However, parents are liable to find themselves asked for extra donations to cover the funding gaps for facilities and pedagogical services.

Approximately 30% of students attend private schools.

Useful Contact. Further details of Malta's education system can be obtained at www.education.gov.mt/edu/edu.htm or www.aboutmalta.com/grazio/education.html.

Tax

The Maltese islands have a very favourable tax regime for foreigners and returning migrants who take up permanent residence there (see *Residence and Entry Regulations* below). Provided that the resident has a minimum annual income of Lm 12,000 (approx. £18,896) for their family and dependants, the rate of income tax is 15%.

For everyone else, normal income tax rates are from 0%-35%. The tax year follows the calendar year and the date for filing an annual return is 30 August.

Capital Gains Tax

Capital gains is not normally charged on the sale of property which has been the owner's main residence for not less than three years. If the property is not a principal residence or if it is being sold after less than three years, Capital gains is payable on the sale (based on the contract price) at a provisional rate of 7%. The Maltese inland revenue then calculates the final amount due based on the variables such as how long the property has been owned and expenses of upkeep, improvements made etc. The maximum capital gains payable is 35%.

Inheritance Tax

Inheritance tax was abolished in 1992. However, in the event of property being acquired through death, the beneficiary is liable to pay a 5% property transfer tax on the value of the property. If the property is in joint-ownership then 5% is charged only on the value of half the property.

Other

Value Added Tax	18%
Stamp Duty	5%
Social Security Employer/Employee Contributions	10% and 9%
Self Employed Contributions	Lm 8-16 per week

Absent Taxes

There are no property taxes, real estate taxes, municipal or local taxes.

Useful Contacts

Dr Jean-Philippe Chetcuti: Britannia House, Melita Street, Valletta VLT12, Malta; Tel +356 2122 3767; fax +356 2122 7414; e-mail housemed@chetcuticauchi.com; www.chetcuticauchi.com/jpc. An advocate and tax consultant with a wide area of practice including tax and estate planning, company formation, property law and permanent residence permits.

Malta Financial Services Centre Attard: Part of the Malta Financial Services Authority created by act of Parliament in 1994 to regulate financial services in Malta. Its remit includes guidance on tax issues. Tel +356 441155; fax +356 249805; www.moneymalta.com/the – mfsc.htm.

Malta-Tax Consultancy Services: e-mail info@malta-tax.com; www.malta-tax.com.

Health

Malta has a comprehensive health service that is entirely free at the point of delivery to all Maltese residents and is funded through general taxation (i.e. not social security contributions, which in Malta are for pensions and welfare services). Health services are delivered through Government Health Centres and Hospitals. The main hospital is St. Luke's in Valletta, which has about 850 beds and there is a new university hospital, of similar size being built next to the university. Gozo has a general hospital with about 259 beds.

Malta has 1084 registered physicians, and over 1400 nurses and midwives. There is a high turnover of staff as they are lost to the private sector where pay and working conditions are considerably better than in the public sector. A number of residents also prefer to use private medical services that can be covered by taking out private health insurance or paid for on a per visit basis.

Further information on the health care system can be obtained at www.health.gov.mt.

Media

Much of Malta's press and other media outlets are strongly influenced by political affiliations. The press publishes in both Maltese and English and Italian television and radio are also received. The press includes *The Malta Business Weekly, The Times of Malta* and *The Malta Independent.* Television channels include the public channel *Television Malta (TVM), Super One TV* (Labour Party owned), and *Net TV* (Nationalist Party owned).

Languages

English is an official language alongside Maltese and since the majority of foreign property buyers are British this is a boon for them. English is of course the legacy of over 160 years of British colonialism.

Maltese is a mongrel of a language incorporating varying strains of Arabic from Morocco, Syria, the Lebanon and Palestine, and interestingly is the only Semitic language written in the Roman alphabet. Italian is also in fairly general use as historical usage and the all-pervasive Italian TV broadcasting accentuate its profile, especially amongst the younger Maltese.

Further information about Maltese grammar and an online dictionary can be found at www.aboutmalta.com/Language – and – Literature/index.shtml.

PUBLIC HOLIDAYS	
1 January	New Year's Day
10 February	Feast of St. Paul's Shipwreck
19 March	Feast of St. Joseph
31 March	Freedom Day
1 May	Labor Day
7 June	Sette Giugno
29 June	Feast of St. Peter & St. Paul
15 August	Assumption Day
8 September	Victory Day
21 September	Independence Day
8 December	Immaculate Conception
13 December	Republic Day
25th December	Christmas Day

RESIDENCE AND ENTRY REGULATIONS

Entry for Period Not Exceeding Three Months

Neither UK, nor US citizens require a visa to enter Malta for a visit not exceeding three months. For a list of countries that do not require entry visas for visits not exceeding three months go to www.foreign.gov.mt/London.

Permanent Residence Permit

There are advantages for foreigners who acquire permanent resident status in Malta and it is an increasingly popular option with those who buy property on Malta or Gozo. These include:

- The tax benefits already mentioned above
- No restriction on movement in and out of Malta
- No minimum stay requirements
- Imported vehicles can be registered at preferential rates
- Foreign permanent residents can rent out their properties and pay 15% income tax on the rental monies.

Who is Eligible for a Permanent Residence Permit

Any foreigner, of any nationality can apply for a permanent residence permit provided that certain conditions are met.

- The applicant has purchased a house for not less than Lm 50,000/£79,000/ $141,560 or an apartment for not less than Lm 30,000/£47,413/$85,000. Note that a purchaser may buy a ruin for less provided the cost of renovations makes up the difference.
- As an alternative to property purchase the applicant can rent a property in Malta

for not less than Lm 1,800 per annum.
- O The resident must have a minimum annual income brought into Malta of Lm 12,000 (approx. £18,896) for their family and dependants.
- O Applicants must *produce evidence* but not necessarily bring into Malta an annual income of Lm 10,000 or a capital sum of Lm 150,000 or more, which can include the property purchased in Malta.
- O No employment or engagement in business is permitted with a permanent residence permit.
- O Participation in political activities is not permitted, but involvement in local council activities is allowed.
- O Once you have been issued a permanent residence permit you should take up residence in Malta not more than one year from the date of issue.

Useful Addresses for Further Information
British High Commission in Valletta: Whitehall Mansions, Ta'Xbiex Seafront, Msida MSD 11; ☎356- 2323- 0000; www.britain.com.mt/.
Embassy of Malta in the USA: 2017 Connecticut Ave, NW Washington DC 20008; ☎202-462-3611; fax 202-387-5470.
Malta High Commission in London: Malta High Commission, Malta House, 36-38 Piccadilly, London W1V OPQ; ☎0870-005-6958; fax 020-7734 1831.
United States Embassy in Malta: Development House 3rd Floor, St. Anne Street, Floriana Valletta VLT 01; ☎356-235-960; fax 356-243-229; e-mail usismalt@vol.net.mt; www.usembassy.state.gov/malta.

WHERE TO FIND YOUR IDEAL HOME

Overview
Malta and its smaller companion Gozo, are both developing a roaring trade in real estate. Malta has long been been popular, especially with the British who represent 60% of the expatriate population there. But in the last three years there has been burst of activity in property development. This is largely due to the forward thinking Maltese government's policy of allowing Maltese citizens to repatriate their funds from hidden offshore caches at a miniscule rate of tax (as low as 3%). The total funds from this largesse came to nearly 300 million pounds, much of which has been invested in real estate causing the present modest but noticeable property boom. Prices on Malta have gone up 20-30% in the last three years, and in some swanky new developments by as much as 40%. Prices are good value rather than cheap, and they are related to the area and proximity to the sea; though as everywhere on Malta is a maximum half-hour by car from the coast, being inland is not too much of a sacrifice. On Gozo which is a mere nine-and-a-half miles by four-and-a-half miles, being inland is even less of a deprivation and prices there were traditionally cheaper than on Malta but are catching up fast.

If you are thinking of renovating an old building bear in mind that building standards on Malta are very variable as there is no standard training provided.

Malta
The 27km by 14km island of Malta is rugged and fairly dry with no rivers or lakes

or open green landscapes. Instead there are very small, cultivated parcels of land and slopes that have been terraced for agriculture. Its charm lies in its layers of history, its mixture of architectural styles, its friendly people and the ancient villages, which are peaceful but not too remote. The coastline is rocky and indented with limestone coves whose rocks are smoothed by the sea and therefore comfortable for sun worshipping and safe for swimming.

The most fashionable (and therefore most expensive) areas in which to buy property are the stylish capital Valletta and places near the capital such as Sliema and St. Julien's, the former a resort for the people of Valletta and the latter a fishing village, they have been hugely developed and now form a 3km stretch of modern town and resort with a population of about 40,000. Other fashionable spots include Tigne Point and the village of Cottonera, just south of Valletta.

The south easternmost part of Malta has become popular for property hunting because of the many attractive towns and villages where there are charming period houses to be found for sale. Popular towns include Paola, Fgura, Zeitjun and Zabbar. The seaside resort and fishing port of Marsaxlokk is not far and there is also Marsascala, a fast-developing resort. The Maltese from Valletta like this area and buy property there.

The southern central part of Malta is less developed and quieter than the southeast and the twenty-first century seems to have left some of the traditional villages there behind. Some property-buyers find this a seductive quality and properties in places such as Gudja, Zurrieq, Ghaxaq, Siggiewi and Zebbug are usually snapped up.

The central region has three large towns: Bkara, Mosta and Rabat and the ancient town of Mdina. This area has seen a lot of modern building and it has become a popular residential area, particularly for younger Maltese families.

The northern region is where the island narrows considerably and the area has many bays and inlets with beaches, that lend themselves to touristic development. In addition, the villages are full of summer residences used by the Maltese folk who live inland. There is a wide range of property available in this region, the most affordable being holiday apartments. There are also traditional farmhouses and some very up-scale villas. The most exclusive areas include the Santa Maria Estate in Mellieha and the St. Paul's Bay/Bugibba/Qawra (very lively) area.

Gozo

Gozo is a 25-minutes ferry ride from Malta (see *Getting There*). There is also a helicopter connection from Malta airport, which takes 15 minutes. The island is 14km in length and 7kms wide (nine and a half miles by four and a half miles). The commercial capital, Victoria is located inland and the population is about 27,000.

Gozo is greener than Malta and inland has a quiet rural air about it. The landscape is hilly and the villages tend to be built on hilltops, which means there are splendid panoramic views from properties situated there. Larger villages include Xaghra, Gharb, Nadur and Kercem.

The coast has its own magic seascape of rocky inlets, sandy beaches and rugged cliff faces. There is currently a spate of building of seafront apartments costing from about £130,000, which are great if you want to soak up the holiday atmosphere. Inland properties of great character and charm are also good buys on Gozo, and it has the reputation of being slightly cheaper than Malta, though this differential is fast disappearing. Gozo has had a mini-property boom, with prices in some places going up by 60% since the Millennium. Currently annual increases are more likely to be a quarter of that.

Typical Properties for Sale on Malta and Gozo

Note: as properties are traded in Maltese Liri and Malta will not be adopting the euro for a few years, prices on this chart have been converted to pounds sterling, rather than euros.

Location	Type	Description	Price
Malta: St. Julien's, not on seafront	modern apartment	2-bedrooms. Not new.	£60,000
Malta: Sliema	apartment	3-bedrooms. New marina development	£300,000
Malta: St. Paul's Bay (tourist area, NE Malta)	apartment	2-bedrooms. New development.	£55,000
Gozo: Gharb, village inland	farmhouse	large house of character being renovated to provide 3 double bedrooms. Courtyard at back.	£107,601
Gozo: Xaghra, village inland	newly built house	3-double bedrooms, one with large terrace looking out on the pool area.	£155,000
Gozo: Xaghra village inland	farmhouse	very old corner house with entrance from alley into a very large garden with swimming pool. 4 double bedrooms with en suite showers plus main bathroom and a cellar. Restored to very high standard.	£348,000

Estate Agents for Malta and Gozo

Bernards Real Estate: Locker Street, Sliema, SLM11 Malta; ☎+356 21343047; fax +356 21323560; e-mail bernard@bre.com.mt.

Cassar & Cooper: P.O. Box 36, Sliema, SLM 15 Malta; ☎+356-343730; fax +356 334374; e-mail ccprop@dream.vol.net.mt.

Dhalia: ☎+356 2149 0681; www.dhalia.com.

Christy's Gozo Properties: www.guidegozo.com/agenzija.

Frank Salt: 2 Paceville Ave, St. Julians, Malta; ☎+ 356 2133 3696; fax +356 318037; www.franksalt.com.mt.

Grands: Property Developers and Estate Agents, Grands Building, 50 Msida Road, Gzira GZR 03, Malta; ☎+356 318560; fax +356 310196; e-mail property@grands.com.mt; www.grands.com.mt.

KB Real Estate Ltd: Dingli Street, Sliema SLM 08, Malta; ☎+356 213 44541; fax +356 21343693; e-mail info@kb-malta.com.

Legends: Benrus Buildings, Triq in Naxxar, San Gwann SGN 08; ☎+356 21378932; fax +356 21378428; e-mai headoffice@legend.com.mt. Especially good selection of property on Gozo.

Owners Best: ☎+356 2149 2299; + fax +356 2149 2319; e-mail info@ownersbest.com.mt.

Perry Ltd: +356 2131 0800; www.perry.com.mt.

Propertyline Real Estate Agency: 47, St. Julians Seafront, St. Julians, Malta; ☎+356 21 38 39
    66; fax + 356 21 38 39 43; e-mail info@propertylinemalta.com; www.propertylinemalt
    a.com. Also has offices in Qawra and Gozo; see advertisement for details.
Ria Investments: 1 Rokna Apts., Qui si Sana Pl, Sliema, Malta; ☎+356 330725; fax
    +356 342920; riainvestments@vol.net.mt.
Sara Grech Ltd.: 169 Triq it-Torri, Sliema, Malta; ☎+356 21331354; fax +356
    21316357; e-mail info@saragrech.com; www.saragrech.com.mt. has three other
    offices on Malta and a letting department.
Simon Barnes: British-based agent; ☎020-7499 3434.

Useful Websites for Property Purchase Information
www.fenixmalta.com
www.maltaproperty.info
www.legal-malta.com

THE PURCHASING PROCEDURE

Banks
Loans. Loans for property purchase by a non-resident or a permanent resident in
Malta can be obtained from any local bank in Malta. Those offering favourable rates
include HSBC Bank Malta, Bank of Valletta, APS Bank and Volksbank Malta. The
amount that can be borrowed is 70% of the value of the property if buying in Maltese
Liri, and 60% if the loan is in any major foreign currency.

Opening an Account. Non-residents and permanent residents can open a bank
account at any local bank in Malta. Note that if you are transferring large sums of
money to Malta for property purchase, the best way to do this is normally through a
currency dealer such as Currencies Direct. For further details see *Importing Currency*
in the *General Introduction*.
    The Bank of Valletta is one of the largest banks, with about 70 branches in most
towns and villages across Malta and Gozo, while HSBC has about 35 branches. A list
of banks operating in Malta can be found at www.malta.co.uk/malta/bank1.htm and
www.portalino.it.banks/ – mt.htm.

Useful Addresses
APS Bank Ltd.: APS House, 24 St. Anne Square, Floriana VLT 16; ☎+356 226 644;
    +356 226 202. Central Foreign Unit 17/18 Republic Street, Valletta VLT 04, Malta;
    ☎+356 21 250 164-6; fax +356 21 232 303.
Bank of Valletta Int. Ltd: 86 South Street, Valletta; ☎+356 249 970; fax +356 222
    132; www.bov.com.
HSBC Bank Malta: Head Office: 233 Republic Street, Valletta VLT 05; ☎(personal
    banking section) +356 22933404; fax 22933699; customer helpline (in Malta) for
    home loans 8007 4444; e-mail infomalta@hsbc.com; www.hsbcmalta.com.
Volksbank Malta Ltd.: 136, St Christopher Street, Valletta VLT05; ☎+356 221 242;
    fax +356 243 219.

The Preliminary Contract
Once a property has been chosen and the price agreed a preliminary contract, the
Convenium is drawn up, which is binding on both parties to the sale. The contract is valid

BUYING A HOUSE ON THE MEDITERRANEAN

for three months, or longer if agreed by both parties. At this point the purchaser lodges a sum equal to 10% of the purchase price with the agent or notary. During this preliminary period, the notary checks the title of the property and submits applications to the various relevant government departments.

The Contract of Sale

Once the searches are satisfactorily completed and the permits issued the final deed of sale, drawn up by the notary can be signed and the purchase price and the legal expenses and stamp duty can be paid. Only when this process is completed can the purchaser obtain vacant possession of the property.

Fees and Costs

The following fees and costs are payable on the signing of the deed of sale.

- Government stamp duty on documents 5%
- Ministry of finance fee Lm 100 (£158/$280)
- Legal fees (1%-2%)
- Searches and registration Lm 75-Lm 150
- Ministry of Finance fee Lm 100

Estate Agents' Commission. Estate agents normally charge between 3.5% and 5% brokerage fees. This cost is normally borne by the vendor, but you should check that this is so.

Overseas buyers are not normally allowed to own more than one property at a time on Malta or Gozo except in areas where there are large property developments; these are Portomaso and Cottonera.

Legal Advice

Chetcuti Cauchi Advocates (contact Dr Jean-Philippe Chetcuti B.A., LL.M.(Warwick), LL.D., ACIArb – Tel. +356 79451422 or +356 21223767; e-mail housemed@chetcuti cauchi.com; website www.cc-advocates.com) are a leading Maltese law firm providing comprehensive legal and property-search assistance to foreigners seeking a residential or commercial base in Malta or to establish tax residence in Malta. Services offered include property searches and location, legal representation on purchase/rental contracts, notarial services, wills and probate, international tax planning, permanent residence permits, financial and banking services.

RENTING OUT YOUR PROPERTY

Foreigners intending to let out their property should be aware that restrictions apply on this. Properties have to be in specially designated areas, or to have swimming pools and come under Malta Tourist Authority approval for renting out.

SPOT CHECK – MALTA & GOZO

Political/economic stability:	Stable democratic government. Joined EU 2004. Has 5.2% unemployment and public deficit is triple the EU ceiling for stability and growth. Deficit makes it unlikely that Malta will adopt the euro by 1998.
Sunshine/climate:	Over 6 hours of sunshine a day in winter. Summer temperatures average 31°C/89°F. Very hot inland, coastal temperatures tempered by breezes.
Cost of living/taxes:	Flat rate tax of 15% for foreign permanent residents. Normal standard income tax is 35%. VAT 18%. There is no VAT on food. At present Malta is probably the best value place to live on the Mediterranean, but EU membership may bring prices up.
Accessibility:	Charter flights from most UK airports to Malta. Ferry (25mins) and helicopter (15 mins) between Malta and Gozo.
Property availability:	Lots of classy new developments on the coast. Older houses just inland.
Property prices:	Good value rather than cheap; apartments from £63,000 in Malta and about £50,000 in Gozo, but the price gap is narrowing.
Cost of property purchase as a % of property price:	5% duty on documents and 1% notary fees.
Ease of purchase/ease of renovation:	The government encourages moderately well off foreigners to buy property with a tax incentive of 15% flat rate income tax. There are a lot of cowboys in the contracting world. No qualifications needed to be a contractor so you can be your own and hire an architect and builders from local recommendation. Building standards poor.
Annual property taxes:	None.
Investment potential:	Excellent potential. Expect at least 15-20% in the next year. Membership of the EU will push prices up steadily. Many previous restrictions on foreigners buying more than one house or not renting out except in designated areas will cease to apply under EU legislation.
Likely problems:	Damp old houses and water shortages: old houses get damp in winter; some very damp. Malta has little fresh spring water and Gozo has none. Water comes from boreholes and desalination. Water is pumped from Malta to Gozo during summer.

BUYING A HOUSE ON THE MEDITERRANEAN

MONACO

MONACO

INTRODUCTION

Monaco is a sovereign state ruled by a Prince. Its sovereignty is limited; France runs its foreign and defence policy, and has a role in regulating the Principality's affairs. The Monegasque state started out in 1297, when Francesco Grimaldi the Spiteful from Genoa bluffed his way into the Ghibelline fortress at Monaco and took it over. The Grimaldis finally gained control of Monaco in 1308. At one time Monaco extended between Antibes and the Italian border, gaining its income from taxes on lemons and olives. In 1848 Menton and Roquebrune revolted and the principality was on the verge of bankruptcy. The ruling prince came up with the idea of opening a gambling casino in Monte Carlo, the capital, under the discreet name of the Société des Bains de Mer. This brainwave kept the principality going for a century, but the economy went into decline again after France and Italy legalised gambling in 1933. The present ruler, Prince Rainier III, was astute enough to diversify the economy, and find sources of income without having to impose income tax on the Monegasques (the state manages very well with corporation tax). He also married the Hollywood star Grace Kelly, but the ill-advised liaisons of his daughters, Caroline and Stephanie, have dimmed his image. Since the time they took up running a casino, the Grimaldis have not been invited to official functions by the British royal family.

Monaco is an ideal place to live for those who can afford it: facilities are world class, and no tax to pay. The virtual absence of crime in Monaco is one of its main selling points to rich expatriates; there is one policeman for every 100 residents (not to mention 100s of private security staff), and surveillance cameras all over the place. Litter and delinquency do not exist in such a heavily policed environment, which is why the very wealthy find this such a good place to be. In order to benefit from tax-free status, you are officially required to spend 6 months of the year here. The super-wealthy flit around the world and spend little time at home here. The French authorities have the right to inspect all bank accounts in Monaco; there are 50 'off-shore' banks here. The majority of expatriates are businesspeople rather than media stars.

GEOGRAPHY

Monaco is a tiny state covering a mere 194 hectares, wedged in between the mountains and the Mediterranean in between Nice and the Italian border. All in all, Monaco covers about half the surface area of Central Park in New York. The land area was increased by 22 hectares by reclaiming land at Fontvieille in the south for building factories. There has been a lot of new construction under Prince Rainier's regime, mostly in the form of high-rise apartment blocks. The population of Monaco is currently some 32,000, and is increasing very slowly. Only 6000 of the residents are actually true Monegasques; the remainder are tax exiles or immigrants.

Monaco's climate is the same as Nice's, virtually perfect. There are no prolonged heatwaves in summer, and virtually no frost in winter. The sea temperature never falls below 13ºC.

RESIDENCE AND ENTRY

On the face of it, it should not be that difficult to go and live in Monaco. In order to visit the Principality you only need to fulfil the same requirements as you would entering France, i.e. you can stay for up to three months if you have a valid visa to enter France, or an EU passport. In practice, gaining a *carte de séjour* is difficult: the main requirement is that you deposit a large sum of money with a Monaco-based bank – the figure of €400,000 is often mentioned – and that you buy a property in Monaco. As these come in at a minimum of €500,000, to which must be added up to 14% in transfer fees, you are looking at a cool 1 million euros to get your foot in the door. In addition to meeting the property conditions, you will have to submit a medical certificate and proof that you have no criminal record.

Monaco does not have an embassy in the UK, but does have an honorary consul. For details see www.gouv.mc.

MEDIA & INFORMATION

Monaco has little in the way of independent media, and what there is cannot be viewed on the internet. The main newspaper is *Nice Matin*, published nearby in Nice (see www.nicematin.fr). The media has some presence here with a radio station: Radio Monte Carlo, and a TV company: Télé Monte Carlo. The monthly *Riviera Times* (www.rivieratimes.com) publishes a pull-out section, *Monaco Times*. The best source of information is the internet; see the Monaco tourist office's website for links: www.monaco-congres.com. details of all kinds of property agencies and other companies are listed on www.monaco.net, and also in the French yellow pages: www.pagesjaunes.fr.

PROPERTY

There is only a limited amount of property available in Monaco, given its tiny size. The only properties on the market are apartments; the price very much depends on whether there is a view of the sea or not. The minimum rental price for a studio is €1000 per month. Real estate agents are listed on www.monaco.net, or try the following:

www.agencedesetrangers.mc
www.elite.monte-carlo.mc
www.immo2000.monte-carlo.mc
www.parkagence.monte-carlo.mc
www.royal-immobilier.com
www.westrope.monte-carlo.mc

Typical Properties for Sale

Type	Description	Price
apartment	54 sq.m. living space with 22 sq.m. terrace; 2 rooms; 1st floor of tower block; no sea view.	€950,000
apartment	105 sq.m. living space with 25 sq.m. terrace; panoramic view.	€1,400,000
studio	50 sq.m., 2 rooms, no view.	€650,000
apartment	228 sq.m.; 360 degree view over harbour; 2 parking places; cellar.	€10,000,000

MONACO – SPOT CHECK	
Political/economic stability	Monaco has been under the same ruling family for 700 years; its stability is guaranteed by the French state. There is no unemployment, and the residents have one of the highest standards of living in the world.
Sunshine/climate	Monaco has an ideal climate, with 300 days of sunshine per year and virtually no frosts.
Cost of living/taxes	The cost of living is higher than in France; accommodation is extremely expensive. On the other hand there are no taxes to pay.
Accessibility	Monaco is easily accessible from Nice Airport a mere 7 minutes away by helicopter. There is a railway station in Monte Carlo.
Property availability	Limited.
Property prices	There is no cheap property; studios start at €500,000.
Cost of property purchase as % of value	Total costs are 14%.
Ease of purchase and ease of renovation	The purchasing process is complicated and expensive. There is little scope for renovation.
Annual property taxes	There are no property taxes.
Investment potential	Prices are so high that it would be optimistic to expect them to rise further.
Suitability for letting	While there is potential for letting, rentals will not cover your initial outlay.

BUYING A HOUSE ON THE MEDITERRANEAN

SPAIN

LIVING IN SPAIN

CHAPTER SUMMARY

- Every year Spain hosts a staggering 50 million plus visitors; greater than than the total indigenous population.
- **Cost of living.** About 30% less than the UK.
- **Economy.** The highest GDP growth in the EU in 2003.
- A fifth of Spain is affected by desertification and soil degradation.
- The Mediterranean coasts are in the area of Spain affected by drought.
- Malaga is the fastest growing city on the Mediterranean.
- The postal service is slow and unreliable and you have to use more costly express delivery for time sensitive mail.
- **Education.** More than 70% of young people stay on at school until eighteen, while 40% receive professional training.
- **Health.** Preventable diseases such as TB, tetanus and diphtheria are still around in Spain because there are not enough health facilities in poor areas.
  - Spanish private health insurance policies tend to be limited to specific local hospitals.
- **Shopping.** Some of the best local produce is found in the *ventas* – local daily municipal markets and in weekly outdoor markets.
- **Media.** Spain has one of the lowest newspaper readerships in Europe.
- **Crime.** Spain has a hard drugs epidemic and many drug barons launder their cash through real estate on the costas, particularly the Costa del Sol.
- **Languages.** The lingua franca of Spain is Castilian Spanish, but if you live in the province of Catalunya and send your children to school they may be taught in Catalá (Catalan).
- **Property.** Prices for property are rising on average 17.5% a year.

INTRODUCTION

Spain has been popular as a holiday destination since the first charter flights of the 1950s opened up the Mediterranean Costas (from south to north) these are: Costa del Sol, Costa Tropical, Costa de Almería, Costa Càlida, Costa Blanca, Costa del Azahar, Costa Dorada and Costa Brava. The costas are situated within the provinces (south to north) of Andalucia, Murcia, Comunidad Valenciana and Catalunya. Spain plays host to a staggering number of visitors (51.7 million in 2002) annually, which numerically exceeds the total indigenous population of nearly 40 million; 14 million visitors to Spain are British. The onset of mass tourism inevitably led to an expatriate property boom estimated to total half a million to 700,000 British owners alone Far fewer are registered as residents, but this is probably because many do not bother to do so, especially since residence permits have recently become non-obligatory. The total number of second homes based on the costas is about three million and Spain has about one million European non-Spanish residents.

There is a lot more to Spain than just the Spanish Costas and it is worth doing some background reading to acquaint yourself with its rich and varied history. For those interested a *Concise History of Spain* (Cassell) by Melveena McKendrick outlines the main events from early times until just before General Franco's demise. During the Franco era Spain was isolated and trapped in its own time warp by a repressive dictatorship. In three decades Spain has crammed the cultural development of a century leaving a huge generation gap between the Franco era and the current twenty-somethings. As in Italy, the family is more important than the individual and grandparents, who grew up under Franco still dominate the scene, albeit from the background. Similar to Italy also, is the grown-up aged 30 or so who still lives with his or her parents. Unlike the British and the Americans who spend long hours at work and are obsessed with it, many Spaniards have adopted the attitude that work is just something you have to do during the day and real life takes place after work going out with friends and having fun.

Excellent backround information on the regions can be obtained by calling the Spanish Tourist Office brochure line (☎09063 640 630) for some brochures on your destination or region, and its history.

The Cost of Living. Spain is no longer the cheap haven that it was in the 1970s and 80s when land and houses were cheap and food and drink were ridiculously cheap. The cost of living has now caught up with other parts of Europe. When the euro was adopted in 2002, most peseta prices were rounded up when converting to the euro equivalent, causing a mini cost of living rise all round overnight. It is true that alcohol and tobacco cost much less than in other European countries and most staple fresh foods including meat and fish are generally less expensive. Eating out can be excellent value. There is a plentiful supply of good, reasonably priced restaurants, which offer a menu of the day with three courses and wine for €6 ($6) a head. A glass of beer or wine costs €1 and a *tapa* (snack), €2. Electrical goods, clothing and footwear are alarmingly expensive, even with home-produced goods undercutting imported ones. Petrol is however cheap and Spain has no road tax.

It is difficult to predict the weekly budget in euros that you need to live in Spain because there are so many variables. However, basic living is going to cost about a third less than in the UK.

HISTORY & POLITICS

Important events that have shaped Spain's past (and present) include the fascist dictatorship of General Franco; its imperial expansion during the sixteenth and seventeenth centuries; as well as the earlier domination by Islamic invaders for over 500 years from AD 718, which left it a legacy unique in Western Europe of Moslem art and architecture and has influenced also its musical traditions and literature.

It took the Christians 36 years to complete a military reconquest of Spain in the 13th century, although the Arabs retained their final stronghold of Granada until the 15th century; there was a period of colonial expansion and the colonising of vast territories in Latin America and Asia; more recently, a bitterly fought Civil War and the right wing military dictatorship of General Franco coloured the Spanish experience of the last century. It is nearly 30 years since Franco's death in 1975.

Government. Only since 1996 with the election of the government of a centre-right (the Partido Popular formerly under José Maria Aznar who served two terms and handed over to his deputy Mariano Rajoy in early 2004) can Spain be said to have entered a period of true democracy, with an elected government and a main opposition party both with experience of democratic government. In March 2004, after a surprise election result following the Madrid rail bombings the Spanish Socialist Workers' Party romped into power. The current prime minister is José Luis Rodriguez Zapatero. The national legislature (the Cortes) consists of two chambers: a senate of 257 members, 208 of whom are elected and 49 appointed as regional representatives (with little influence). The second chamber is a Congress of Deputies comprising 350 members elected by individual constituencies. In addition, each autonomous region has its own regional parliament.

The Economy. In the latter years of Franco's dictatorship there were some signs of economic progress; between 1961 and 1973 the economy was growing at the rate of 7% annually, second only to Japan, and helped in no small way by the arrival of multinational companies and a boom in tourism. An estimated 1.7 million Spaniards left Spain to work abroad and sent their earnings back to swell their home bank accounts. Today, five of the seventeen provinces of Spain including the Mediterranean ones of Valencia, and Barcelona, between them produce nearly half the country's industrial output. The structure of the Spanish economy is based primarily on the services sector followed by industry, which together produce 90% of GDP. GDP growth is at 2.3% and consumer price inflation is 2.8%. In 2001 and 2002 economic growth in Spain was greater than the EU Zone as a whole making Spain a fairly dynamic force in the EU monetary scene. The billions of euros (37 billion in 2002) Spain earns annually from tourism helps to offset the country's considerable trade deficit. Unemployment, which has been a continuing problem, and is one of the highest in the EU, dropped from 13% to under 10% for the first time in 2002; it is currently 9.4%.

GEOGRAPHY AND CLIMATE

Climatic and topographical conditions are very dry along most parts of the Mediterranean coasts, particularly Valencia. Despite this the Spanish Mediterranean littoral is very active agriculturally because it has irrigation systems, developed over the generations which have made the coastal belt one of the most productive areas of Spain. Almería is one of the driest provinces in Spain, yet is known for its production of vegetables. Nonetheless, water, or the lack of it, is one of Spain's most critical issues. A fifth of the country is affected by desertification and drought and as much as half of it could be subject to problems of soil degradation in the foreseeable future.

The Mediterranean coast avoids the extreme temperatures found elsewhere in Spain but the costas in the north and east may be subject to cold winds which bring snow to the Pyrenees and to the meseta (central plain) in winter. To some degree, the mountainous ranges of the hinterland protect the costas from extremes of climate and funnel warm air to the costas throughout the summer. The Balearics have their own weather patterns, usually warm, comfortable summers, tempestuous autumns and chilly winters.

Population. The population figures for the biggest cities on the Mediterranean are: Barcelona 1,454,581; Valencia 739,412; Málaga 542,079; Almeria 170,000. Palma de Mallorca in the Balearics 302,000.

AVERAGE MAXIMUM TEMPERATURES				
Area	Jan	Apr	Aug	Nov
Málaga	17°C	21°C	30°C	20°C
Murcia	12°C	19°C	29°C	20°C
Alicante	16°C	22°C	32°C	21°C
Valencia	15°C	20°C	29°C	19°C
Barcelona	13°C	18°C	28°C	16°C
Mallorca	14°C	19°C	29°C	18°C

CULTURE SHOCK

Traditionally southern Spaniards are known for self-reliance and self-centredness for being smouldering and quarrelsome by turns, for being macho, petulant for women; and on occasions capricious. Much of this is changing, or has already changed, as Spaniards have become better educated, particularly the women, and democratised and with a wider outlook than their forbears. Towards foreigners, Spaniards tend to be warm and genuinely helpful. They usually show less formality than the Italians or Portuguese.

GETTING THERE

About a third of the millions of international passengers who visit Spain each year travel by air; and of these more than 70% use charter flights. The UK and Spain are the only two countries in the world to have such a high percentage of charter flights; and relatively cheap air tickets are one of the reasons so many Britons decide to live there. There has also been a huge increase in low-cost scheduled services to most of the cities on the costas and also to Mallorca; a trend which is increasing with the proliferation of budget airlines and their scramble for routes.

Low Cost Airlines

Alicante: **Bmibaby** from Cardiff/East Mids/Manchester/Teeside; **british european** (flybe.com) from Southampton/Exeter; **EasyJet** from Bristol/East Mids/L'pool/ Gatw/Lut/Stansted/Newcastle; **GB Airways** from Gatw & **Monarch** from Luton/ Gatw/Manchester; **MyTravelLite** from B'ham.

Barcelona: **Bmibaby** from East Mids/Manchester; **EasyJet** from Luton/Gatw/ Stansted/East Mids; **Monarch** from Manchester.

Almería: **GB Airways** from Gatw; **MyTravelLite** from B'ham.

Gibraltar: **GB Airways** from Gatw; **Monarch** from Luton/Manchester.

Girona: **Ryanair** from Stansted.

Ibiza: **Bmibaby** from East Mids; **EasyJet** from Stansted.

Málaga: **Bmibaby** from Cardiff/East Mids/Manchester, Teeside; **british european** (flybe.com) from Southampton/Exeter; **EasyJet** from Bristol/East Mids/L'pool/ Gatw/Lut/Stansted; **GB Airways** from H'Row; **Monarch** from Luton/Gatw/ Manchester; **MyTravelLite** from B'ham.

Menorca: **GB Airways** from Gatw; **Monarch** from Luton.

Murcia: **Bmibaby** from East Mids/Manchester; **british european (flybe.com)** from Exeter/Southampton; **GB Airways** from Gatw; **MyTravelLite** from B'ham/Gatw; **Ryanair** from Stansted.

Palma de Mallorca: **Bmibaby** from East Mids/Cardiff/Manchester; **E a s y J e t** from Bristol/L'Pool/Gatw/Lut/Stansted; **GB Airways** from Gatw; & **Monarch** from Manchester; **MyTravelLite** from B'ham.

Valencia: **GB Airways** from Gatw.

Full details of the budget airlines above are given in the *General Introduction* of this book.

Useful Contacts – Charter Flights etc.

Avro plc: www.avro-flights.co.uk; ☎0870 458 2841. Charter airline flies from most UK airports to Alicante, Almeria, Gerona, Ibiza, Mahon (Menorca), Murcia, Palma and Valencia.

Charter Flight Centre: www.charterflights.co.uk/spain. Useful website with Charter Flights to Spain covering Alicante, Almeria, Gerona, Ibiza, Mahon (Menorca), Málaga, Murcia, Palma and Reus (nr Barcelona).

Excel Airways: www.excelairways.com; ☎08709 98 98 98; Flights from Gatwick, Manchester and Glasgow to Alicante, Almeria, Ibiza and Malaga. Low cost airline.

Flybe (British European): Exeter International Airport, Clyst Honiton, Devon, Exeter, Devon EX5 2BP (☎0870 567 6676; www.flybe.com). Tiny fares. Flies mainly from Southampton and Exeter to the Spanish Costas.

Globespan: www.flyglobespan.com. Charter airline that flies from Scotland (Glasgow & Edinburgh) to Palma, Malaga and Barcelona from April to November.

Iberia Airlines: Iberia House, 10 Hammersmith Broadway, London W6 7AL; ☎0845 8509000. National carrier of Spain.

Loco Flights: www.locoflights.com. Sells low cost flights from Bimingham, Gatwick, Glasow, Manchester, Nantes, Newcastle to Málaga and Alicante.

Monarch Airlines: London Luton Airport, Luton, Bedfordshire LU2 9NU; ☎01582-400000; 08700 406300; www.monarch-airlines.com & www.flymonarch.com. Specialises in scheduled flights to the Spanish costas and Gibraltar. Uses Luton, Gatwick and Manchester airports. Very competitive fares from about £29 one-way. Carries pets (in the cargo hold under the DEFRA scheme) on scheduled flights from all UK airports. Inbound pets can go only to Gatwick .

COMMUNICATIONS

Post. Mail deliveries can be somewhat slow and unreliable in Spain. Parcels and registered mail have to be collected from the post office (*el correos*). Stamps can be bought in *estancos* (tobacco shops) as well as post offices. It is unwise to rely on the standard Spanish postal service if you have urgent mail. Important and time sensitive mail can be sent by the post office Express delivery service (*Postal Exprés*) which guarantees delivery between 24 hours and three days depending on the destination. Courier services operating in Spain include domestic companies such as Seur as well as the international ones, DHL and UPS.

Opening times at the main post offices are from 9am-9pm, Monday to Friday and 9am-2pm Saturdays. Times may be more limited in smaller, local post offices and longer hours may be kept in the bigger towns and cities.

Telephone. Telecommunications were deregulated in Spain in 1998, but the government still maintains a 40% stake in the former national telecommunications company Telefónica (www.telefonica.es), which has now spawned fully or partially-owned subsidiaries like Teleline and Terra. Telefónica, retains a powerful hold on the telephone service and if you want a landline installed you will have to sign a contract with with them. To get a line installed in a new house you go to your local Telefónica office with your passport or *residencia* and the *escritura*. If you are renting take the rental agreement and some form of proof of address.

If you want to reduce expenditure on calls abroad, this can be done through a 're-seller' service, i.e. a company such as Aló or Tele2 that buys bandwidth from the network in bulk at wholesale prices and then undercuts their telephone call prices by up to 75%. Another hugely cheaper alternative is to subscribe to a callback company.

Useful Websites

The following companies offer lower prices on long distance and international calls than Telefónica:

Retevisión: www.retervision.es
Jazztel: www.jazztel.com
Telforce: www.usewho.com/telforce
Aló: www.alo.es
Uni2: www.uni2.es

FOOD & DRINK

Food in Spain is taken very seriously. Dining is an important ingredient in the country's social lifestyle. A light breakfast may be taken at 8am followed by a mid-morning snack at 11am and tapas at 1pm. Lunch (*la comida*) is the big meal of the day and is generally served between 2pm and 4pm. A snack may follow at 6pm; then an evening tapas at 8pm. Dinner (*la cena*) is traditionally served late, between 9pm and 11pm. Restaurants are rated by vertical forks (from one to five), on a plaque outside the entrance. Prices must be listed both outside and inside the establishment.

Few people would dispute that food and drink are one of the big attractions of Spain. The Mediterranean is heaven for fish and seafood lovers, but sadly they are not cheap. The bases of cheaper fish dishes are likely to be *bacalao* (salted cod), *merluza* (hake), or *calamares* (squid). Paella is to Spain what pizza is to Italy, it originated in one place, in Spain's case Valencia, and then spread throughout the country to become almost the national dish. It can be made with meat (often chicken or rabbit) and/or seafood e.g. prawns.

Meat and fish are often grilled, rather than fried, which is good news for those who are health conscious. Vegetarians will fare less well as vegetables are usually a minor accompaniment to a meal, although salads and vegetable soups are commonly served as starters. The Spaniards are not big on desserts and often prefer fresh fruit. The two most common desserts are flans and crème caramel; both come in regional variations.

Restaurants can be very cheap or very expensive and it will probably be obvious which is which. Note that *marisquerías* serve only seafood. The best value restaurants, which have a *menú del dia* for about €6 are *comedores* which means dining room or canteen. *Comedores* are unpretentious, working men's eating places that serve mainly substantial lunches and are usually family-run. You will often find them tacked on to a bar or pension. The roadside equivalent of comedores are *ventas* where you can get wholesome regional cooking at low prices. Specials are usually a good bet as they should be freshly made and *menú de degustacion* is more upscale than the menu of the day and about twice the price.

The next best-known Spanish foods are *tapas* (snacks and tasters) served in bars, They can be anything from snails to kidneys and from chickpeas to tripe. They are smaller portions than a meal, maybe three or four bitesworth and they usually cost €1 to €3 a portion. Clubbing together with a group of friends and having a mixture of tapas can be almost a meal in itself.

Drink. Spain used to be synonymous with plonk and sangria. Vast quantities of low quality wine, as well as some notable ones were produced. However the huge national investment in wine-making and vineyards has raised the standards. Nowadays if you drink the house or local wine it will be drinkable and cheap at less than 50p per glass. Galicia in the north is famed for its whites and Rioja for its reds. Mediterranean drinks include Cava which is marketed as Spain's champagne, and is made principally in Catalunya, while Valencia has a reputation for brandy and fortified wines like sherry (named from the town of Jerez de la Frontera) and Manzanilla; the latter made at vineyards which reach the seaside.

Beers are more expensive than wine and Spanish ones are not usually top of any connoisseur's list. Spirits are much cheaper if you buy the Spanish brands of gin etc. and the measures are generous and have been the downfall of many a bibulous expat. Even coffee is often drunk mixed with a dash of whisky or brandy.

In the Balearics it is difficult to escape restaurants geared to the tourist trade. Try to avoid the main tourist areas and you will find places where the Spaniards eat. Prices tend to be higher in Balearics; about twice as expensive as on the mainland for a full course meal. Maó on Menorca claims to be the birthplace of *mahonesa* (mayonnaise) which dates from the time of the French occupation in the eighteenth century. Balearic food is otherwise aimed at the new invaders i.e. the tourists.

SCHOOLS AND EDUCATION

The spectacular growth of the Spanish educational system over the past few years has resulted in many changes, but there are still the four basic levels of education in Spain: pre-school; primary (*Educación General Básica*) known as *EGB*; secondary; and university.

Background

More than 70% of young people stay on at school until the age of eighteen while 40% receive professional training. Today there is a body of over one million students in Spanish universities. Interestingly, the high rate of higher education is principally a result of the number of female students at university, who exceed the number of males in both secondary education and in the first years of university. The ration of males to females is only less on the professional training courses, where they constitute 45% of the student body.

More details of the Spanish education system (state and private) can be obtained from the *Spanish Embassy Education Office* in London (20 Peel Street, London W8 7PD; ☎020-7727 2462; fax 020-7229 4965) or the *Ministerio de Educación, Cultura y Deporte* in Madrid (c/Alcalá 34, 28071 Madrid; ☎915 321 300; www.mec.es). At present, a large part of all non-university education is private, and Catholic education represents a small minority (about 20%) of the whole educational system. However, it is more prevalent in school than university education.

The Structure of the Education System

Pre-School. This is divided into two categories: playschool (under 3 years of age); and kindergartens (3-6 years); both age groups attend voluntarily and for free at infant schools (*escuela infantiles*). Private schools charge a fee, which tends to be most expensive in the non-subsidised. Facilities tend to vary greatly from region to region.

Primary. Catering for children from the age of six, primary education is both compulsory by law and free in Spain in the state sector. Those who have completed the last year of primary school receive the *Título de Graduado Escolar* – a prerequisite for secondary education and university. Those who do not receive the *Título* are given the *Certificado de Escolaridad,* which can be used for entrance to technical training courses.

Secondary. The *BUP* (see above) provides students with a three-year academic training as a preparation for university. The first and second years are divided equally between the natural sciences, mathematics, languages and the humanities, while a specialisation is made in the third year. The *Título de Bachiller* is awarded at the end of the course if no more than two subjects have been failed in the final examinations, and this certificate may be used to enter the second stage of the technical training course or to attend a one year pre-university course, the *Curso de Orientación Universitaria* (COU). Students who enter for this level must pass all subjects, as COU is an essential preliminary to university. Some students go on to technical training centres rather than entering the COU course.

University. The Spanish university system, like many of its European counterparts, dates back to the Middle Ages. Salamanca University, founded in 1218, is the oldest in Spain. Over the last twenty years, the university system has experienced its greatest growth in history, while at the same time advancing towards a self-governing and decentralised system. There are presently 50 or so state universities in Spain and 20 private ones. Most, if not all, of the private universities are tied to the Catholic Church, one of which, the Opus Dei University in Navarre, carries far more influence than its size would warrant – the majority of its intake comprising the sons and daughters of the powerful, wealthy and aristocratic. The Complutense in Madrid, and the Central in Barcelona, are by far the largest Spanish universities – the former comprising nearly 100,000 undergraduates, the latter nearly 80,000. Despite their size, these two universities are generally regarded as being the best in Spain.

International Schools

Spanish law requires all foreign schools to be supported by their embassies and the *National Association of British* Schools *in Spain* (NABSS, C/Comercio 4, Escalera 2a, Bajo A, 28007 Madrid; ☎915 520 516; www.nabss.org) works with the British Council to ensure that all its member schools are visited regularly by British inspectors, who then report to the Spanish Ministry of Education.

A list of international schools in Spain which teach the British or American curriculum, or a combination of Spanish and international systems (such as the French and German curricula) is available from the *European Council of Schools (ECIS)*; www.ecis.org. The *ECIS Iberian Office* can be contacted at: *ECIS,* C/Augusto Figueroa 32-34/1°G, 28004 Madrid; ☎915 626 722; fax 917 451 310. For further details of ECIS see *International Schools* in the *General Introduction*.

There is a multitude of British and American schools in Spain. Other schools offer a dual system of Spanish- and English-language teaching and curricula which provide the opportunity for children to be equally well qualified to live and work in Spain or in the UK in future life. Such schools are required to allocate at least 20% of the total number of places available to Spanish students. Another option for parents is to enrol children in a school that teaches the UK curriculum but also includes some Spanish studies (taught in English) in the same curriculum.

TAXES

Income Tax

Income Tax is *Impuesto Sobre la Renta de las Personas Físicas*. Non-residents must make an annual tax declaration to the Spanish Tax Agency who will be interested in any income received in Spain deriving from such things as interest on accounts held with a Spanish bank or monies from renting out property, and of course any employment undertaken. Any such income will be taxed at a flat rate of 25% and will also need to be declared to the tax authorities at home. If your income comes to less than €7,800 a year you do not need to file a tax return.

Income tax is generally assessed on the household. If you are married then the joint income of husband and wife will be assessed. The income of dependent children in the household will also be included in the tax assessment. If you are a cohabiting common-law couple then the sole income of the individuals will be assessed.

There are a number of allowances, deductions and tax credits available on income tax. Your accountant or tax adviser will be able to give you the latest rates of these.

DEDUCTIONS ALLOWABLE FROM GROSS INCOME	
*Vital Minimum**	approx. 3,305 euros (under 65s)
Vital Minimum	approx. 3,907 euros (over 65s)
Vital Minimum	approx. 6,611 euros (married couple
Disability Allowance	approx. 6,912 euros
*Vital Minimum is the Tax Threshold.	

Up to date information about the minimum earnings before tax is liable can be obtained on the Spanish Tax Office website www.aeat.es. Local provincial tax offices (*oficina de información al contribuyente*) in areas where there are many expatriates may be able to deal with your questions in English. Further information about tax or any changes in rates can be found in a leaflet entitled *Taxation Regulations for Foreigners*, available from any *hacienda* in Spain.

VAT (Impuesto sobre el Valor Añadido (IVA)

The rate of VAT in Spain is normally 16%, though food for human and animal consumption and a range of items used for agricultural production including seeds, carry a rate of 7%. There is a super-reduced IVA of 4% on standard bread. flours and cereals used for the production of bread, milk, cheese, eggs, fruit and vegetables, books, periodicals, pharmaceutical products and items specifically designed for handicapped people. Health, education, insurance and financial services are all exempt from VAT as is the transfer of any business, providing the buyer continues the existing business concern, rental of private property etc.

Who Can Help With Tax?

Unlike in Britain where accountants, solicitors and bank officials all have some knowledge of tax matters, in Spain the *aesor fiscal* deals with all tax business. For those with complex tax returns or those for whom the word 'tax' succeeds only in producing blind panic, the *aesor fiscal* offers invaluable assistance. For fees beginning at around £50 for relatively straightforward tax returns, this official godsend will complete the form on your behalf, and even save you a lot of money by virtue of his or her wisdom and general expertise. For further details contact the *Asociatión Española de Asesores Fiscales – AEDAF – (C/*Montalbán, 3, 6°, 28014 Madrid; ☎915 325 154; fax 915 323 794; www.aedad.es) in Spain.

HEALTH INSURANCE AND HOSPITALS

The Spanish National Health Service

The Spanish health service combines both public and private healthcare and anyone who makes social security payments or receives a state pension, is unemployed or under the age of 18, is entitled to free medical treatment. Today 98% of the population is covered by the state health system; however, free treatment is only available in certain hospitals, where waiting lists tend to be long. The shortcomings of the healthcare system are evinced by the fact that preventable diseases such as TB, tetanus and diphtheria are still around in Spain. There are not enough hospitals – especially in the poorer areas – and the emphasis of treatment still lies with curative rather than preventative medicine. Social security resources are inefficiently distributed and administered, and it is primarily because of this that various attempts to reform the health service in recent years have failed. Many Spanish residents, nationals and foreigners, take out private health insurance. Spain has a number of resident English-speaking doctors and it is sometimes possible to join local schemes where for a fixed premium (£100 or so) a certain number of free consultations can be taken. These can be very worthwhile.

One serious drawback from a retired person's point of view of the medical treatment provided by Spanish social security (*Seguridad Social*) is that although it provides financial cover for surgery and hospital treatment, it does not include funding for general medical treatment such as trips to the dentist or a GP. Moreover, the Spanish social security system caters particularly poorly for outpatient and after-care treatment and facilities. Social security will only cover about 75% of a patient's treatment costs; thus the patient has to meet 25% of the costs incurred (or budget for payments for private health insurance to cover this). Those who have worked in Spain and paid into a private top-up scheme – as most Spanish nationals and residents do – will have the bulk of this contribution covered.

Using the British/Spanish NHS if You are Living in Spain

It is essential that all British nationals intending to move to Spain register their change of address with the Overseas Division (Medical Benefits) of the Department for Work and Pensions Benefits Agency before leaving the UK. Paperwork will then need to be completed in order to receive the Spanish national health card (*cartilla*) from the Spanish social services. This card (or a photocopy of it) must be produced whenever medical treatment is needed; and will cover the holder for 100% of medical treatment and 90% of prescription charges. The *cartilla* will also entitle the holder to full benefits in any other EU country. The two systems of National Insurance in the

UK and Social Security (*Seguridad Social*) in Spain are transferable insofar as if you return to Britain at any future time payments towards one count towards the other, and vice versa. What happens is explained in detail in various leaflets available from the Pensions and Benefits Overseas Directorate in Newcastle (☎0191-218 7777). The 'Euroadviser' in your local Jobcentre in the UK may also be able to advise. In Spain, further information about social security can be obtained from the *Instituto Nacional de la Seguridad Social (INSS)*, Servicios Centrales, c/Padre Damián, 4-6, 28036 Madrid; ☎915 688 300; www.seg-social.es.

For further information on using health services in the EU, see *Health* in the *General Introduction*.

Private Medical Insurance

Although the level of convenience, comfort and attention offered through private insurance schemes is superior to that received by National Health patients, the treatment itself will not necessarily be of a higher quality. However, a growing number of foreign residents in Spain are opting to remove themselves from the long waiting lists and sometimes chaotic conditions of the Spanish National Health Service to take out private health insurance. Those who only spend a few weeks or months a year in Spain will anyhow require private medical insurance to cover the balance of the cost not covered by the E111 (see *General Introducion*). One of the advantages of UK health insurance schemes is that their policies cover the claimants for treatment incurred anywhere in Europe, not just in Spain itself. With an increasing number of insurance companies offering this kind of cover, it is worth shopping around as cover and costs vary. For a list of worldwide health insurance providers see *Private Health Insurance* in the *General Introduction* to this book.

Private Medical Insurance – Spanish Providers. Spanish insurance policies are widely available and have a distinct advantage over those offered in the UK or USA in that payment for medical treatment is made in the form of vouchers. This means that you can use them to pay for services at the time of treatment, rather than having to pay for treatment up front and then claim back costs from an insurance company after the event. However, although the premiums on Spanish insurance policies may appear cheaper and more attractive than those offered by British or American companies you may well find that a policy is limited to specific local hospitals – not too helpful if you are in urgent need of treatment but nowhere near a hospital on the policy list. Additionally, the small print needs to be read very carefully (perhaps treatment is only refunded if surgery is performed, or outpatient treatment i.e. visits to the local GP and the dentist, is not included in the policy). Other policies may offer limited cover on surgery, medicines and hospital accommodation. If you do decide to get a Spanish policy make sure that you have read the small print and policy in an English translation.

Sanitas (Avda. Ramon y Cajal 4, 29600 Marbella; ☎952 774 450; fax 952 775 912; www.isanitas.com) is the leading private healthcare provider in Spain with more than 1.2 million members and 50 years experience in the healthcare sector. Their Sanitas Health Plan is specifically aimed at foreigners living in Spain. The cost of private health insurance varies according to age. For example someone aged 62 is likely to pay the equivalent of £49 per month for a policy, which will include dental treatment and insurance when travelling outside Spain. Sanitas has an English-speaking agent.

Other private health insurance companies in Spain include Asisa, DKV Seguros and Mapfre.

SHOPPING

Every region of Spain has its locally produced goods: Catalonian textiles are famous around the world; handmade wooden furniture is one of the traditional products of Valencia; all Spanish leather goods are of a high quality and fine rugs and carpets can be found in the markets and shops of the south.

Food Shopping. Spain's thriving import market means that many international brands of canned and frozen foods and drinks are available in Spain. All large towns have modern supermarkets that as well as food, stock a wide variety of goods as diverse as tableware, clothes, toiletries and hardware.

For those determined to integrate more fully into the Spanish way of life there are municipal markets (*ventas*) – controlled by the local governments, which offer the best prices and often the highest quality fresh produce. The *ventas* can provide a whole new world of gastronomic discovery. For example, handmade (as opposed to industrially produced) sausages can still be found, offering a staggering variety of textures and tastes. The red *chorizo* sausage is the best-known Spanish sausage, consisting of ground pork and fat, paprika or peppers and garlic, pepper, oregano and nutmeg. *Longaniza* is the long, thin version of the chorizo, and the chorizo de Pamplona is a smoked variety. The *sobrasada, salchichón, morcilla* and *butifarra* sausages are but a few of the others available.

Most towns and all cities have a *venta*, usually open from 9am to 2pm daily where you can buy fresh produce (fish, meat, fruit and vegetables), and often other products such as dried fruits, spices, cut flowers and hardware may also be on sale. These markets are very popular and first thing in the morning you will see flocks of Spanish housewives out with their shopping baskets at the stalls. Prices at these indoor markets tend to be fixed.

Weekly outdoor markets are also very popular in Spain and most towns have at least one held in the main square, or some wide-open space. The large markets draw stall-holders from all over selling anything from fresh fruit to cameras, shoes, fake perfumes, tools etc.

Hypermarkets are very popular in Spain and most large towns and cities have at least one, usually situated on the outskirts. The main hypermarkets in Spain are Alcampo and Carrefour (both French owned), as well as Eroski and Hipercor (part of the El Corte Inglés giant). Hypermarkets tend to be huge and sell everything. Prices are generally reasonable. Discount stores such as Lidl, Día and Plus have sprung up in towns and cities all over Spain and are popular for basic foodstuffs and hardware.

Non-food Shopping

Department Stores. The most important department store in Spain is El Corte Inglés, one of the country's most successful and profitable enterprises. There's an El Corte Inglés store in practically every city, stocking as much and more than the *hypermercados*. El Corte Inglés offers customer services such as in-store cards, home delivery and free parking for cardholders. Prices, however, are on the high side. Other chain stores include the clothes shops such as Zara, Bershka, Pull & Bear and Massimo Dutti, DIY stores such as Leroy Merlin and Aki, and the ubiquitous furniture store, Ikea. Many of these stores can be found in shopping centres, which increasingly feature as huge retail parks on the outskirts of towns and cities. The sales (*rebajas*) are particularly good for electrical and home appliances and clothes.

English Language Bookshops. English-language bookshops are scattered along the *costas* and in the big cities (try Julian's Library, Calle España 11, Fuengirola), or the Turner English Bookshop, Calle de Genova 3 in Barcelona.

Shop Opening Hours

Opening hours are strictly regulated in Spain and vary depending on the area, type of shop and the time of year. Most general stores are open Monday to Friday from 10am to 1.30-2pm and then again from 4.30-5pm to 7.30-8pm and on Saturday mornings. In the larger towns and cities many shops also stay open on Saturday afternoons. In the south of Spain during the height of summer, some shops may not open up again in the afternoon until 6pm – staying open until 9pm or later. In some places, particularly in small towns and villages, there's often one day or afternoon a week when all shops are closed.

Most shopping centres and department stores are open continually (without closing) from 9.30am until 9.30pm or later Monday to Saturday. Some may also open on Sundays and public holidays, although this depends on the region and time of year. **Sundays.** Nearly all shops stay closed on Sundays although bakeries are often open on Sunday mornings and may sell basics other than bread and cakes. If you are stuck for food on a Sunday the larger petrol stations often have a mini-market attached to the premises. And there are always bars open that will sell you tapas.

Shops are allowed by law, generally, to open on a maximum of twelve Sundays and public holidays a year, usually coinciding with the Christmas period and over the summer. In tourist areas, shops are generally allowed to open on Sunday mornings during the high season.

MEDIA

Newspapers

The circulation of the daily press in Spain is far lower than in most other European countries. Only eight newspapers in Spain sell more than 100,000 copies a day and it is estimated that only one Spaniard in every ten buys a daily newspaper. Freedom of the press was not established in Spain until 1978, but the removal of the censorship laws have not lessened a certain apathy in the Spaniard towards newspapers, and journalism in general. Spain has no real equivalent of the British tabloid newspapers.

The most popular daily newspaper in Spain is *El País* (Miguel Yuste 40, 28017 Madrid; www.elpais.es) with a daily circulation of about 450,000. Other leading national newspapers include, *La Vanguardia Española* (Pelayo 28, Barcelona; www.lavanguardia.es), *El Mundo* (Pradillo 42, E-28002 Madrid; www.elmundo.es), *El Periódico* (published in Barcelona and with a mostly Catalonian readership), and the sports papers *AS* and *Marca*.

English-Language Media in Spain

The Spanish costas and the Balearics are well served for English-language publications:

Costa Blanca News: weekly newspaper, established 1971. Large classified section. E-mail cbnews@ctv.es.

Ibiza Now: fortnightly newspaper, established 1984. E-mail ibizanow@ctv.es.

Lookout: quarterly, established 1963. E-mail lookout@jet.es.

Majorca Daily Bulletin: daily, established 1962. E-mail master@majorcadailybulleti n.es.
Marbella Life: monthly glossy magazine, established 1983. E-mail hotelmag@vnet.es.
Sur in English: free weekly newspaper. Has the largest circulation of all English-language media. Aimed at southern residents. 30+ pages of classifieds. E-mail sureng@surinenglish.com.

Television

The Spanish, like the British and the Americans, are a nation of telly addicts. They watch more television than any other country in Europe, except Britain, and nearly every Spanish household contains at least one television set.

Radio

The most popular radio networks include *SER*, which has five different stations, *Los 40 principales*, directed mainly at young people, *Cadena Dial*, which alternates Spanish music and news, and *Cadena M80*, which is aimed primarily at an older audience; *Radio Olé* broadcasts Spanish music; *Sinfo Radio* which is ten years old in 2004 is a mixture of specialised music with news.

English-Language Radio in Spain. There are a score of small, English-language radio stations broadcasting in Spain, mainly for the benefit of tourists. Their particulars can be found on the website www.typicallyspanish, click on TV & Radio in Spain.

CRIME AND THE POLICE

Crime

One factor that has contributed to the increase of crime in Spain is a growing drug problem. The Socialists in 1983 effectively decriminalised the use of cannabis for a time. The law was then revoked and now all non-prescribed drug use is illegal, but possession of a small amount of cannabis for personal use is unlikely to lead to a fine or prison sentence.

The core of the drugs epidemic, however, lies in the spread of hard drugs such as cocaine and heroin. Madrid's Barajas airport is a particularly popular entrance point for drugs from Latin America destined for the European marketplace. Across the Strait of Gibraltar in Morocco there are large farms producing the lucrative cash crops of cannabis and hashish, much of which gets smuggled into Europe via Spain. Spain also has increasing problems with crime syndicates from Morocco, Colombia, Italy and Eastern Europe. Dirty money is being laundered through real estate companies based on the Costa del Sol, which is in danger of being taken over by organised gangs involved in the construction businesses there.

Tourists are unsurprisingly a target for criminals, with much petty theft located along the costas. Crimes against tourists range from purse snatching and car break-ins or theft of belongings on beaches to armed burglary (a favourite with Spain's teenagers apparently). Live away from the popular and tourist-saturated coastal areas and you are likely to enjoy a blissfully crime-free existence. Everybody tends to know everybody else's business in the more rural areas and so a thief will have a hard time remaining incognito.

Police

The roles and responsibility of the three main police forces in Spain:

Policía Municipal (blue and white uniforms) are based in police stations called *comisarías*. They deal with crime in urban areas as well as issuing residence permits, identity cards, etc.

The Guardia Civil (green uniforms) patrol the rural areas of Spain – also acting as border patrol and frontier guards – and have responsibility for roads and prisons. The *Guardia Civil* is a predominantly military force called out to combat riots or strikes and mass peaceful demonstrations.

Policía Nacional (brown uniformed). The *Policía Nacional* – and their machine-guns – can be found mounting zealous vigil over embassies, stations, post offices and barracks in most cities. Serious crime such as theft, rape or mugging is dealt with by them.

The Basques and Catalans both have their own police forces.

THE LANGUAGES OF SPAIN

Learning the language

Castilian (i.e. standard Spanish) is the language all Spaniards understand and it is spoken nationally. Few outside their communities can communicate in the regional languages such as Catalan, Galician and Basque. If you choose to live in the great Catalan city of Barcelona or in Valencia, Castilian Spanish will usually be understood. If you have children who will be going to local schools, be aware that it will be compulsory for them to learn the regional language, possibly to the exclusion of Castilian.

Stuart Anderson visited Catalunya in 1999 and bought an isolated property there. He started learning Spanish and visiting Spain for holidays prior to moving there.

Stuart Anderson says learning the language is top of his advice list to newcomers
Firstly, and most important: learn Spanish to a reasonable degree of fluency before even venturing on the housing front. Otherwise you will be beholden to other people who have the linguistic skills – and perhaps forever dependent. Being able to converse with the local people pays great dividends and establishes new friends.

Self-Study Courses. The BBC produces some excellent workbooks and cassettes at various levels. Further information is available from BBC Customer Services (☎0870-2415 490), via the website www.bbcshop.com or from BBC Education (www.bbc.co.uk/education/languages/spanish). The BBC now also offers an online beginners' course called 'Spanish Steps' as well as the self-study course *España Viva*. Public libraries lend out these and other courses.

Open University (OU), Central Enquiry Service, PO Box 724, Walton Hall, Milton Keynes MK7 6ZS; ☎01908-653 231; www.open.ac.uk offers courses leading to an undergraduate degree in Spanish. For example 'A Fresh Start in Spanish' is a level 1 course aimed at people who already have a grounding in the language. It runs from

February to October and costs £325.

Language Courses in the UK. Evening language classes offered by local authorities and colleges of further education usually follow the academic year and are aimed at hobby learners or those wishing to obtain a GCSE or A level. Intensive Spanish courses offered privately are much more expensive.

Conversation Exchanges. A more enjoyable way of learning a language (and normally a more successful one) is to link up with a native speaker of Spanish living in your local area, possibly by putting an advertisement in a local paper or making contact through a local English language school.

Spanish Societies. There might be an Anglo-Spanish society in your area: check with the Hispanic and Luso Brazilian Council (Canning House, 2 Belgrave Square, London SW1X 8PJ; ☎020-7235 2303; www.canninghouse.com). Also ask about its cultural and educational programmes. The Society also has a library of 50,000 books on Spain.

Instituto Cervantes. This is now the largest worldwide Spanish teaching organisation, with headquarters in Madrid (C/ Libreros 23, 28801 Alcalá de Henares, Madrid; ☎918 856 100; www.cervantes.es).
The Cervantes Institute in London, sometimes referred to as the Spanish Institute is at (102 Eaton Square, London SW1W 9AN; ☎020-7235-0353).,

Language Courses in Spain

An annotated list of Spanish schools and universities offering Spanish language courses is available from the *Hispanic and Luso Brazilian Council* (for address see *Spanish Societies* above) for £4 and includes the current prices and details of the courses.

Serious language schools usually offer the possibility of preparing for one of the internationally recognised exams. In Spain the qualification for aspiring language learners is the DELE (*Diploma de Español como Lengua Extranjera*) which is recognised by employers, universities, officialdom, etc. The DELE is split into three levels. Most schools say that even the Basic Diploma requires at least eight or nine months of study in Spain.

Language Schools in Spain. There are thousands of language schools offering Spanish courses for foreigners. Look for relevant adverts in the press, for example in the Málaga-based *Lookout* magazine (lookout@jet.es).

SUMMARY OF HOUSING

The price of property along the Spanish costas has been rising steadily over the years. However in the last few years Spain's economy has come up from behind to outperform all others in Europe. One of the results of this has been a huge rise in property prices, which doubled between 1998 and 2002, and are currently increasing on average at the rate of 17.5% a year. The rise is higher in some areas; in the capital Madrid it is 30% and in Barcelona 20%.

Some economic pundits consider that the housing bubble might burst, as it did in 1972, and send prices crashing. The likely cause will be that many more Spaniards have become home owners; up from about 70% in the 1980s to a current estimate of over 80%; the highest rate of home ownership in Europe. The type of mortgage favoured by Spaniards is very long-term with variable rates, so if there are any adjustments to the interest rates, many Spaniards currently overstretched financially, will find themselves in financial difficulties and many will be bankrupted by mortgage payments of up to a third of their income.

Most of the housing for foreign residents is being built on the Costa del Sol at the rate of 47,000 houses a year, and it is being bought, if the newspapers are to be believed by drug lords laundering their cash through real estate companies. Still, the Costa del Sol has long had the soubriquet Costa del Crime and this merely reinforces it.

While property prices have increased enormously in the most popular areas, there are still affordable properties by the sea as the table below shows.

Inland, up to one hour from the sea is also popular and it is getting harder to find properties suitable for renovation as building and extensions are not normally allowed. This means there is a finite number of properties for sale. You have to be prepared for a thorough and time consuming search; possible spread over several months or longer. Patience should get you what you want in the end.

According to the *Sociedad de Tasación*/Society of Valuation (C/Conde Aranda 15, 288001 Madrid; ☎ +34 914 360 206; info@st-tasacion.es) , buying prices per square metre are approximately €2100 (Barcelona), €2000 (Madrid), €1400 (provincial capitals) and €900 (small towns).

PUBLIC HOLIDAYS AND FESTIVALS

The total number of national holidays per year, including the many regional ones, is fourteen. In addition, the various regions and localities have their own festivals and carnivals (often commemorating local saints, with dates liable to change from year to year) when very little apart from bars and hotels will be open for business. As in France, August is the month when all those who can, take their annual holiday and at the end of the month up to 20 million Spaniards take to roads to get home as fast as possible – the majority heading from the coasts to the major cities. Many local amenities, especially in the larger cities, close for all or part of August and this should be noted when dealing with bureaucracy etc.

PUBLIC HOLIDAYS		
1 January	Año Nuevo	New Year's Day
6 January	Epifanía	Epiphany
March/April	Viernes Santo	Good Friday
March/April	Domingo de la Resurrección	Easter Sunday
April	Lunes de Pascua	Easter Monday
1 May	Fiesta del Trabajo	Labour Day
15 August	La Asunción	Feast of the Assumption
12 October	Día de la Hispanidad	National Day
1 November	Todos los Santos	All Saints' Day
6 December	Día de la Constitución	Constitution Day
8 December	Fiesta de la Hispanidad	Feast of the Immaculate Conception
25 December	Navidad	Christmas Day

RESIDENCE & ENTRY REGULATIONS

CHAPTER SUMMARY

O **Residence Permits.** Since March 2003, Residence Permits are no longer obligatory for EU citizens staying longer than 90 days.

   O Although not obligatory, residence permits can be applied for voluntarily and are essential for opening bank accounts, buying cars, voting etc.

O **Non-residents.** If you spend less than 6 months in Spain each year, you are deemed to be non-resident.

   O Non-residents are still obliged to pay the council tax on their property and income tax on all income arising in Spain.

O **Non-EU Nationals.** Non-EU nationals have to apply in advance for a visa (but not for visits) and this may have to be accompanied by an application for a work permit.

O **Gestors.** Many bureaucratic matters can be dealt with by gestors, who are a kind of fixer who deals with all the paperwork and are well worth te extra expense.

REGULATIONS FOR CITIZENS OF THE EU

Abolition of Residence Permits. Spain is a member of the European Union and immigration procedures for citizens of other EU countries follow a similar pattern. However, since March 2003 British and other EU citizens intending to stay in Spain continuously for longer than 90 days have not needed a Residence Card. The categories covered by this edict include: employees, self-employed, students and EU dependants of an EU or Spanish national. Dependants who are non-EU nationals still need a residence permit applied for in advance of entry to Spain.

Exceptions to the Abolition of Residence Permits for EU Citizens. The relaxed regulations do not extend (in most cases) to EU citizens who have retired to Spain and those of independent means. There are some applicants who fall into these two categories who may be exempted and advice must be sought on this from the Spanish authorities.

Voluntary: Residence Cards and Other Certificates. There are however advantages to having a Residence Card and if you wish to apply for a residence card or a certificate confirming non-residence or residence status you should do this direct to the local Comisaria de Policia or Oficina de Extranjeros (Foreigners Office) in the larger cities. **Documents for a Residence Card Application.** Unfortunately, the list of required documents can vary from office to office and region to region but the process is relatively straightforward. The advantage of having a Residence Card is that you can get a *Número de Identidad de Extranjero (NIE)* which you need for opening a bank account, filing tax returns and most other documents and for voting in local elections. Residence Visas may have to be renewed periodically. If you move out of Spain or back to your country of origin, then once the residence permit has been handed in at the police station, your right to residency in Spain automatically ceases. Further advice can be obtained on all the above from the Ministry of the Interior's website: www.mir.es.

WORK AND RESIDENCE PERMITS FOR NON-EU AND EEA NATIONALS

Non-EU or EEA nationals applying to take up residence in Spain have much more red tape to cope with. However, the volume and variety of the bureaucracy will vary according to nationality (and if there are reciprocal health and tax agreements for example). All non-EU nationals should first of all apply for a visa and work permit through the Spanish Consulate in their own country if they are intending to live or work in Spain.

TAX AND RESIDENCY

If you own homes in Spain and in your native country you will be deemed to be resident in the country where your centre of interests lie, i.e. the country where your personal and economic relations are stronger, or in the country where you live most of the time. If you sell your home in your native country and move to Spain permanently you will be deemed to be a Spanish resident. If you spend less than six months a year in Spain you will be classed a non-resident but will be required to carry out certain obligations:

O   Pay local rates.
O   Pay utility bills.
O   Pay income tax on any earnings through business activities in Spain.
O   Declare all capital assets in Spain and where necessary pay wealth tax on these.

Spanish Embassies and Consulates in the UK

Spanish Embassy: 39 Chesham Place, London SW1X 8SB; ☎020-7235 5555; fax 020-7259 5392.
Spanish Consulate General: 20 Draycott Place, London SW3 2RZ; ☎020-7589 8989; fax 020-7581 7888.
Spanish Consulate General: Suite 1A, Brooke House, 70 Spring Gardens, Manchester M2 2BQ; ☎0161-236 1262; fax 0161-228 7467.
Spanish Consulate General: 63 North Castle Street, Edinburgh EH2 3LJ; ☎0131-220

1843; fax 0131-226 4568.

Spanish Residency – Registering with Your Embassy

Once resident in Spain, as anywhere in the world, it is also advisable to register with your embassy or consulate a list of these is provided below.

British Embassies and Consulates in Spain

British Embassy: C/ Fernando el Santo 16, 28010 Madrid; ☎917 008 200; fax 917 008 272; www.ukinspain.com.

British Consulate-General: Paseo de Recoletos 7/9, 28004 Madrid; ☎915 249 700; fax 915 249 730.

British Consulate: Plaza Calvo Sotelo 1/2, 03001 Alicante; ☎965 216 022/216/190; fax 965 140 528.

British Consulate-General: Edificio Torre de Barcelona, Avenida Diagonal 477-13, 08036 Barcelona; ☎933 666 200; fax 933 666 221.

British Honorary Vice-Consul Benidorm: to be contacted through Alicante.

British Consulate-General: Alameda de Urquijo 2-8, 48008 Bilbao; ☎944 157 600; fax 944 167 632.

Honorary Consular Agent: Plaza San Cristóbal 3, 18010 Granada; ☎669 895 053; fax 958 274 724.

British Vice-Consulate: Avenida de Isidoro Macabich 45-1°, 07800 Ibiza; ☎971 301 818/303 816; fax 971 301 972.

British Consulate: Edificio Eurocom, Bloque Sur, C/ Mauricio Moro Pareto, 2, 2°, 29006 Málaga; ☎952 352 300; fax 952 359 211 (Postal address: Apartado Correos 360, 29080 Málaga).

British Consulate: Plaza Mayor 3D, 07002 Palma de Mallorca; ☎971 712 445; fax 971 717 520.

British Vice-Consulate: Sa Casa Nova, Cami de Biniatap 30, Es Castell, 07720 Menorca; ☎971 363 373.

British Consulate: Edificio Cataluña, c/ Luis Morote 6-3°, 35007 Las Palmas de Gran Canaria; ☎928 262 508; fax 928 267 774.

British Vice-Consulate: Plaza Weyler 8-1°, 38003 Santa Cruz de Tenerife; ☎922 286 863; fax 922 289 903.

Honorary British Consulate: Paseo de Pereda 27, 39004 Santander; ☎942 220 000; fax 942 222 941.

Honorary British Consulate: Apartado de Correos/PO. Box 143, 41940 Tomares (Sevilla); fax 954 155 018.

Honorary British Consulate: ☎986 437 133; fax 986 112 678; email vigoconsulate@ ukinspain.com.

Spanish Education, Labour and Social Affairs Office: 20 Peel Street, London W8 7PD; ☎020- 7727 2462; fax 020- 7229 4965; www.sgci.mec.es/uk/. For advice on work and social security in Spain; and publishes *Regulations for British Nationals Wishing to Work or Reside in Spain.*

Other Embassies and Consulates

United States

Spanish Embassy: 2375 Pennsylvania Avenue, NW, Washington DC 20037; ☎202-728-2330; fax 202-728-2302. There are Consulates in Boston, Chicago, Houston, Los Angeles, Miami, New Orleans, New York (☎212-355-4090), Puerto Rico and San Franciso.

United States Embassy: Serrano 75, 28006 Madrid; ☎915 872 200; fax 915 872 303; www.embusa.es.

Canada
Spanish Embassy: 74, Stanley Avenue, Ottawa, Ontario K1M 1P4, Canada; ☎613-747-2252/7293; fax 613-744-1224. Consulates in Edmonton, Halifax, Montréal, Québec, Toronto, Vancouver and Winnipeg.
Canadian Embassy: Edificio Goya, Calle Núñez de Balboa 35, 28001 Madrid; ☎914 233 250; fax 914 233 251; www.canada-es.org.

VISAS AND PERMITS FOR NON-EU CITIZENS

For non-EU citizens, the process outlined below covers both the residence and work visas required. Non-EU citizens are supposed to complete the process legalising their work and/or residence status in Spain before starting work/residence. With regard to work permits Americans and others from outside the EU will also have to know which permit to apply for. Note that Class F only concerns you if you do not actually live in Spain but close enough to the Spanish frontier to commute to work in Spain. Excellent detailed information on the legal processes can be seen on the website of *The Broadsheet*, an English-language monthly magazine in Madrid (www.thebroadsheet.com).

WORK PERMITS

As in other EU and EEA (European Economic Area) countries, nationals of EU member states do not require a work permit should they find employment in Spain.

EU nationals entering Spain to set up a business or who are already in some form of self-employment do not require a work permit, but do have to register with the local police after their arrival.

Non-EU citizens will require a visa to *live* in Spain (although not necessarily to visit the country) and both a residence and a work permit. Work permits can cost up to €300 and are normally issued for 1-5 years, and there are different classes of permit.

A Spanish embassy or consulate can advise on the strict rules of residing in Spain, (i.e. foreigners are normally prevented from doing work that could be done by the Spanish, or undercutting wages and conditions which apply locally) and advise on the documents you will need and the forms to be filled in. You may need to present evidence of qualifications or diplomas held; photocopies of your passport and visa application; a certificate declaring you have no criminal record (or details if you have) and a medical certificate. If you can show evidence that your work is needed to 'organise and start up a foreign enterprise moving entirely or partly to Spain' or other documents that might favour your application so much the better. Unfortunately, the list of required documents can vary and will also depend (for non-EU citizens) on whether a work permit is being renewed at the same time.

Using a Gestor for Bureaucratic Procedures. Many administrative matters may be more conveniently tackled by a *gestor*. A gestor is basically a 'fixer' who can deal with all kinds of bureaucracy for you, and can prove to be a godsend when it comes to dealing with paperwork, permits and bureaucrats. Their offices (*gestorias*) are listed in the yellow pages (*las páginas amarillas*). The simplification of procedures for EU citizens does not mean you will be able to do without the services of a gestor. Often the only way for you to find out precisely what is required in many administrative matters is to queue at the counter of a gestoria along with your fellow foreigners.

Get a good *gestor* advises Stuart Anderson

To try and cope with all the bureaucracy on one's own in a foreign country is never worth it. With the purchase of the house, which was a private deal with the previous owners (i.e. no estate agents involved), we sought out an English-speaking abogada (using the helpful services of the local Collegio de Abogadas). Her work was thorough and she made all the necessary arrangements right through to the completion of signing in the presence of the notario and the processing of the escrituras (which duly arrived some three months later). For other purposes we have used a gestor, again extremely valuable and well worth a little extra expense. He led us through the steps required for arranging car insurance; private health insurance; property and contents insurance; and kindly reminding me before my 62nd birthday that I needed to arrange a medical test for myself in order to update my driving licence. A good gestor is worth his weight in gold and we found ours by recommendation.

WHERE TO FIND YOUR IDEAL HOME

CHAPTER SUMMARY

○ Property prices on the coast of Spain are constantly rising, but those who know where to look are still able to find some fantastic bargains.

  ○ The Costa Cálida, the Costa de Almería and the Costa del Azahar are the least developed of the Mediterranean coasts and offer undiscovered retreats at much lower prices.

  ○ Many buyers are looking slightly inland for idyllic rural dwellings only a stone's throw from the coast.

○ **Costa del Sol Property Hotpots:** Luxury developments near to the sovereign territory of Gibraltar and inland from Malaga around Lake Iznajar.

○ **Costa Tropical Property Hotspot:** Inland from the Costa Tropical, the Alpujarras region offers cheap ramshackle houses for renovation in an area of outstanding natural beauty.

○ **Costa Cálida:** The area is booming and with a new international airport due in 2006, demand in this region, which was restricted by poor infrastructure, should rise dramatically.

○ **Costa Blanca:** The Costa Blanca has a sizeable north/south divide. Cheap apartments are the most popular buy in the south, whereas in the north private villas are highly sought after.

○ **Costa del Azahar Property Hotspot:** Valencia has undergone extensive regeneration and is being hailed as the next big thing, although prices are still much lower than in Barcelona and Madrid.

○ **The Balearic Islands:** Mallorca, Menorca and Ibiza offer some of the most expensive properties in Spain, but their natural beauty and individual charms make them amongst the most popular for foreign property buyers.

OVERVIEW

It would be foolish to think of the Spanish Mediterranean coast as a single destination.

Spain has around 1,400 miles of Mediterranean coastline, incorporating four different autonomous communities, eleven different provinces, three different languages, eight different costas, not to mention over a hundred different golf courses. Then of course there are the Balearic islands, lying off the coasts of Valencia and Catalonia. Each of these areas retains a distinctive culture, cuisine, landscape and degree of independence from the Spanish state. They also offer a wealth of distinct opportunities for buying property.

For many years Spain has been the property buyer's paradise. Traditionally cheap property, the availability of timeshares, as well as offshore banking and a welcoming atmosphere for expats, have all contributed to its attraction for second-home buyers and potential residents. Many have bought property that they would never have been able to afford at home. However, the downside of the Spanish economy consistently outperforming all other large European countries is that house prices are going up and up, surging an average of 15% per year since 1998. The biggest price increases have occurred in the coastal areas due to a flood of foreign buyers looking for property close to Spain's swathes of stunning beaches. All of this does not signify that Spain is no longer a buyers market. The bargains are still out there, they have just become a little trickier to find, which is why it has become increasingly important to know where to look.

Brits still overwhelmingly opt to buy property along the Costa del Sol and the Costa Blanca because of the ease of access by air, the vast array of available properties, some of the best beaches in Spain and good leisure facilities, particularly for golfers. The Costa Cálida and the Costa del Azahar are less developed, and have traditionally attracted more Spanish buyers than foreigners, however this is changing as prices on the other *costas* have risen. Less development means a greater slice of the 'real Spain' as the agents describe it, and a more peaceful way of life. To enjoy these benefits it is necessary to buy now as both of these *costas* have new airport developments on the way, which will bring thousands more visitors into the area, and push up demand and of course prices.

Another way of avoiding the overly developed areas and finding much cheaper prices, is to look slightly inland. The idea of an idyllic rural dwelling in an unspoilt environment, away from the hustle and bustle of modern life is clearly appealing. Even more appealing are the prices. Property with real character can be bought for prices, which have not been seen on the coast for a long time.

The average price of a second home in Spain is around €200,000; the most sought after properties being newly built complexes. Prices obviously vary depending on the size of a property and the location. For example the average cost of a property in Alicante is €111,705, while on the Costa del Sol average properties sell for €251,349.

Information Facilities

A good starting point when looking for information on Spain in your home country is the Spanish National Tourist Office (www.tourspain.es), who can provide national maps, railway guides and brochures for all the main Spanish towns and regions. In Spain itself you will find an SNTO in every large town and from these you can obtain specific local guidebooks and information on hotels, car hire, the principal sights, and so on. In addition, there are tourist information bureaux run by individual municipalities. Generally speaking, the tourist offices and bureaux only carry information on their own particular region. The *Mapa de Comunicaciónes España*, which can be supplied by the SNTO, lists details of each of the local tourist information offices, with information on customs posts, driving in Spain and speed

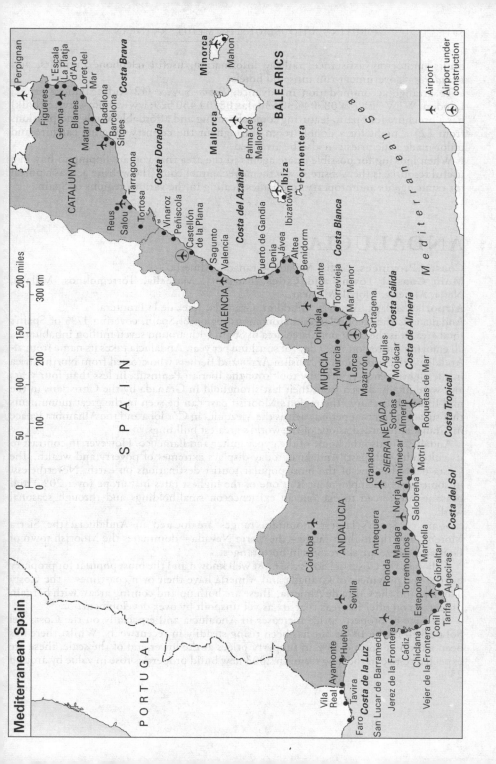

Mediterranean Spain

Airport
Airport under construction

PORTUGAL

SPAIN

CATALUNYA

Costa Brava
Perpignan
L'Escala
La Platja
d'Aro
Loret del
Mar
Figueres
Gerona
Blanes
Mataro
Badalona
Barcelona
Sitges
Tarragona

Costa Dorada
Reus
Salou
Tortosa
Vinaroz
Peñiscola
Castellón
de la Plana
Sagunto
Valencia

Costa del Azahar
VALENCIA
Puerto de Gandia
Denia
Jávea
Altea
Benidorm

Costa Blanca
Alicante
Torrevieja
Mar Menor
Orihuela

MURCIA
Murcia
Lorca
Mazarrón
Aguilas
Cartagena

Costa Cálida

Costa de Almería
Mojácar
Sorbas
Almería
Roquetas de Mar

Costa Tropical
Motril
Salobreña
Almuñecar
Nerja

SIERRA NEVADA
Granada

ANDALUCIA
Córdoba
Sevilla
Antequera
Ronda
Malaga
Torremolinos
Marbella
Estepona
Gibraltar
Algeciras
Tarifa
Conil
Vejer de la Frontera
Chiclana
Cádiz
Jerez de la Frontera
San Lucar de Barrameda
Huelva
Ayamonte

Costa del Sol

Costa de la Luz
Vila
Real
Tavira
Faro

BALEARICS
Minorca
Mahon
Mallorca
Palma de
Mallorca
Ibiza
Ibiza town
Formentera

Mediterranean Sea

200 miles
300 km

limits, motorway assistance, railway information, useful telephone numbers, and *paradores* – government-run inns and hotels.

To arrange accommodation in advance, *Room Service* (42 Riding House Street, London, W1W 7EU; ☎08704 430 530; fax 08704 430 529; www.room-service.co.uk) has a brochure for Spain, featuring some charming and affordable hotels and pensions from £25 a night for a double room throughout the country. Flights, car hire and tailor-made itineraries can also be arranged.

When looking for possible estate agents in the area that you are hoping to buy in a useful resource is the website, www.themovechannel.com. The website acts as a portal for estate agents and property companies dealing in the various regions of Spain.

ANDALUCIA

Coastal Provinces. Cádiz, Málaga, Granada, Almeria.
Main Coastal Towns and Cities. Estepona, Marbella, Torremolinos, Málaga, Nerja, Almería, Motril, Mojácar.
Airports. Málaga, Almería, Gibraltar, Granada, Jerez de la Frontera.
Andalucía is the second largest autonomous region of Spain, covering 17% of Spain's total area. It is the most populated area of Spain with around seven million inhabitants, all enjoying the region's 300 days of sunshine per year. Andalucia takes its name from al-Andaluz – the stronghold of Muslim Arabs and Berbers who crossed from North Africa in the eighth century, virtually took over the Iberian Peninsula in less than four years and were finally driven from their last stronghold in Granada by the Christians in the mid-fifteenth century. The region's Moorish past can be seen in the great monuments that survive from that period such as the Mezquita in Córdoba and the Alhambra Palace in Granada, regarded as one of the world's greatest buildings.

Andalucía is also the home of the gypsy guitar and flamenco. However, in contrast to its culturally rich past, Andalucía today displays extremes of poverty and wealth. The Costa del Sol is one of the most popular tourist destinations on earth. Nevertheless, in some areas unemployment is at one of the highest rates in Europe (over 20%) and peasants are forced to eke out an existence on smallholdings and through seasonal work.

Some of Spain's largest mountain ranges are located in Andalucia: the Sierra Morena, and the highest range – the Sierra Nevada – dominates the Moorish town of Granada. There are ski resorts in both ranges.

Although the Costa del Sol is the most well known and the most popular for property buyers, the provinces of Granada and Almería have their own coastlines – the Costa Tropical and the Costa de Almería. These are both up and coming areas, with bargain properties on offer in areas that are as yet unspoilt by over-development.

The pace of property price increases in Andalucía and especially on the Costa del Sol peaked in the 1970s but has been rising steadily in recent years. Whilst there has been a drop of around 15% in property prices at the lower end of the scale, these are expected to rise in the long term. In 2003 new build properties rose in value by around 25%.

THE COSTA DEL SOL

UK residents account for 200,000 of the permanent population of the Costa del Sol and more than 60% of British people looking to buy property in Spain choose to join them. Most of the development so far has taken place west of Málaga, with perpendicular concrete running virtually all the way to Marbella. The western reaches of the Costa del Sol – between Málaga and Cádiz – has one of the most developed coastlines in Europe. The notorious tourist centres of Fuengirola, Torremolinos and Calahonda are along this stretch, as well as the more upmarket towns such as Marbella, Estepona and Puerto Banús. Property for sale along this stretch is either new or fairly new re-sale buildings. The highest prices will be asked for property lying between the N340 and the sea and in the environs of Marbella. Inland there are still some bargains to be had, but the more beautiful the setting (e.g. towns such as Ronda and Mijas), the higher the price of property.

At the most westerly point of the Costa del Sol lies Gibraltar, still British and a banking and money moving centre. Luxury housing developments are beginning to sprout in the vicinity, notably at Sotogrande and La Duquesa, and many people are choosing to live not too far from English-speaking Gibraltar where they can shop at Marks and Spencer and Mothercare and visit the local Safeway supermarket. Now that the final stretch of motorway linking Estepona to Sotogrande has been completed, it is possible to travel to the western part of the Costa del Sol from Malaga airport within an hour.

East of Malaga, development has been a little less rampant but concrete does proliferate, especially around the resort of Nerja. The eastern Costa del Sol does not have the same long swathes of beaches as the west, but the area has managed to hold onto its roots and prices here are generally cheaper.

A top end villa with pool located a few miles from the sea will fetch around half a million pounds. A villa on a smaller scale on the coast will sell for around €380,000 depending on location. Smaller houses in good condition away from the sea can go for €234,000, while it is possible to buy one-bedroom flats in golf complexes for about £110,000. In general you will find that prices are lower inland (although a property in the white villages will not be cheap).

The Costa del Sol and the Birth of Mass Tourism

The history of tourism on this coast goes right back to the eighteenth and nineteenth centuries when the famous wines of Málaga and the superb climate began to attract the romantic travellers. By the late nineteenth century large numbers of these travellers would arrive every year for the winter season and to celebrate *Semana Santa* (Easter).

In the first half of the twentieth century, there were several pioneers of mass tourism, including the philanthropist George Langworthy, known locally as *El Ingles*. He purchased a property called *Castillo de Santa Clara* in Torremolinos, and in 1930 turned the residence into the first hotel establishment on the Costa del Sol. Others followed his example, opening their residences to tourists in the 1930s and 40s and the area became well known for leisure and relaxation. In the 1950s, the first charter flights to the region began and the first luxury hotel, 'Pez Espada' opened its doors in 1959. The early 1960s saw the area popularised by famous faces such as Frank Sinatra, Orson Wells and Julio Iglesias and by 1969 the district of Malaga had 32 hotels and over 10,000 vacancies for tourists.

Suddenly the Costa del Sol was the place to be and the tourists flooded in. Very soon people started to buy second homes, especially around Mijas. Marbella became inundated with the rich and famous, many buying summer residences. The developers moved in up and down the coast and the rest is history. Today over eight million people visit the Costa del Sol every year, and the demand for property here is huge. According to a recent report by Hamptons International, the Costa del Sol is the fastest growth area of population in Europe.

Sotogrande. As well as having some of the most expensive and exclusive properties on the Costa del Sol it also has some of the best sporting amenities. Since the 1960s when the western end of the Costa del Sol still consisted of little more than windswept dunes and small Andalucían villages, Sotogrande has stood as an exclusive getaway for the wealthy. The original resort, designed to attract the well-heeled, spreads among the broad beachfronts near Gibraltar and has since grown into a fully-fledged community with numerous residential developments. Malaga airport can be reached by car in an hour. Gibraltar airport is only minutes away but has fewer flights to choose from than Málaga. Sotogrande remains an exclusive location offering some of the highest quality property, along with the highest prices, on the Costa del Sol. In addition to the villas of Sotogrande proper there are more recent apartments available in the port. The range of the development is so extensive that it is almost a small town. Sotogrande has the finest golf courses on the Costa del Sol with the Valderrama, Almenara, La Cañada, San Roque Club and Real Club de Sotogrande courses close by. Sotogrande also has a large marina, polo and horse riding facilities, commercial services and an excellent international school.

La Duquesa. A prestigious and well-managed development, the port of La Duquesa offers full marina services for boating enthusiasts as well as the promenades encircling the port offering a variety of restaurants, bars and cafés. Two nights a week the port hosts a unique Crafts Market, popular with the local residents as well as visitors. La Duquesa Golf and Country Club boasts an 18-hole course. In addition to golf the club offers many facilities including tennis, squash, and a fully equipped gym. Close by are the Alcaidesa Links course overlooking Gibraltar; Valderrama, host of the Ryder Cup and World Championship; Sotogrande, a parkland course; and La Cañada. San Roque, host to the qualifying schools, is also only a few minutes away. There are another 40 or so courses within an hour's drive or under construction. Winter and spring skiing are only two hours away in Granada.

Casares, fifteen minutes drive from La Duquesa, is the quintessential Andalucían hilltop village. Its incredible setting, perched on the edge of a cliff topped by a medieval castle, has made Casares the most photographed town in Spain. Ronda (45 minutes away) is an historical city with its famed and spectacular bridge straddling both sides of the huge gorge bisecting the town. Ronda has beautiful churches and monuments which serve to highlight the incredible scenery surrounding the city. The drive to Ronda is an event in itself as it passes through ancient hilltop villages along rugged mountain ridges.

Estepona is a modest jewel of the Costa del Sol, the whitewashed old buildings of its historic town centre sandwiched between a wide, glistening beachfront and a dramatic mountain backdrop. It is a town large enough for major shopping and entertainment but small enough to cover in a comfortable walk and to offer an intimate ambiance. Located just beyond the areas of mass tourism, Estepona retains an authentic flavour of small-town Andalucía.

The old town centre has winding narrow lanes with white townhouses and plazas. Estepona port has numerous bars and restaurants and plans are afoot for the expansion of its marina into a major port with berthing for cruise liners. Other draws are the renovated beach promenades and seafront, the Estepona Equestrian Centre and riding school, the Estepona and nearby Duquesa golf courses, plus a dozen or so others dotted around Marbella and Sotogrande. Nearby attractions include the gigantic wildlife park, Selwo, and the white villages such as Casares and Gaucin. The British enclave of Gibraltar and flash Marbella lie less than half an hour to either side. Estepona is a long-time favourite of many foreign residents, but property prices, especially for villas and townhouses, have risen dramatically over the last few years. A villa in Estepona costs around €385,000.

San Pedro de Alcántara, just 10km west of Marbella and 20km east of Estepona is also just a few minutes drive away from the Sierra de Ronda mountain range. In the second week in October San Pedro also has the last summer fair (feria) in Andalucía. There is an ancient basilica and necropolis in woods next to the Bora Bora Beach Club on the town's sea front. Nueva Alcántara is the beach side area by San Pedro, home to a great deal of new development with thriving shops, restaurants and hotels.

Marbella. This small but cosmopolitan city has long been associated with decadent discos and nightclubs, chic boutiques and palaces built for rich Arabs and the jet-set. The pretty town is conveniently located half an hour's drive from Málaga airport and the old town, dating from the Middle Ages, has been carefully restored. Nearby is Puerto Banús harbour with its floating gin palaces, and behind the town is the spectacular Juanar mountain reserve. Marbella boasts 27km of coastline with 24 beaches within its city limits, as well as mountains topped by the unmistakeable La Concha peak. Some of the world's finest golf courses are situated nearby.

When searching for property be aware that some have been developed on rustic and greenfield sites – planning permission may have been given illegally and banks will refuse mortgages on such properties. Cash buyers should also be cautious and get everything thoroughly checked by their lawyers.

Prices of property in and around Marbella are some of the most expensive in Spain and the renowned 'Golden Mile' along the coast contains some of the most expensive property in Europe! Whereas a penthouse apartment in Estepona, just down the road, would cost around €200,000, the same apartment on the Golden Mile would set you back more than a million euros. Villas, especially at the top end of the market, are highly sought after and there appears to be no limit on their price. As many as twenty per cent of new developments in Marbella are sold before a single brick has been laid. Nevertheless, if you are buying property in Marbella as an investment you will find that the region is very popular for rentals and you should have no problem finding tenants who are prepared to pay handsomely for your property. Rental income for a villa can be as high as €1500 - €1900 per week during peak periods.

Fuengirola is a very family oriented resort with over five miles of beaches, that has long been popular with holiday-makers and property buyers alike. The area has been extensively developed (although less so than Torremolinos) and there are plans for new residential developments along the river to the north. There are numerous cheap apartments to be found in Fuengirola, but those looking for something bigger should try the new residential developments of Torreblanca and Las Lagunas on the outskirts of the town.
Mijas is located on a mountainside 8km inland of Fuengirola and apart from being

billed as a typical Andalucían white village with Moorish origins, it also has a fair amount of holiday and second home developments. The walled town is picturesque with winding lanes and little squares filled with restaurants and shops and a miniature bullring. Mijas is the place of choice for many permanent, expat residents. The many hilltops surrounding the town and along the descent to the coast are natural attractions for a dream villa with magnificent views. Nearby attractions include the new horseracing venue, the Mijas Hipódromo, the first of its kind on the Costa del Sol, and the Tivoli amusement park. While enjoying the tranquillity of the mountain setting, the coast is only minutes away at Fuengirola and Benalmádena. Marbella is about 15 minutes drive to the west while Málaga airport – to the east – is closer still.

Below Mijas proper is Mijas Costa, a series of residential developments which are home to a huge number of German, British and Scandinavian expatriates. Property here is cheaper than in the village itself, but doen't have the same charm.

Benalmádena is located to the west of Málaga and Torremolinos, although due to the expansion of both Benalmádena and Torremolinos it is difficult to say where one resort ends and the other begins. Benalmádena's tourist explosion occurred later than Torremolinos' and so has managed to avoid some of the uglier 1970s developments that make up the latter. The new Puerto Marina has an 'international' feel to it and the area is crammed with a variety of nightclubs and bars playing the latest music and staying open until sunrise (or later). The town boasts a sea-life centre and the Tivoli theme park and Benalmádena Costa has aimed for a more family-based clientele than the 'young, fun-in-the-sun' image associated with Torremolinos. The municipality of Benalmádena is divided into three areas: Benalmádena Pueblo, Benalmádena Costa and Arroyo de la Miel. Benalmádena Pueblo, the original village, remains largely a typical Andalucían village 280 metres above sea level in the foothills of the mountains sweeping down to the sea. This is the quietest area of the three. Arroyo de la Miel, the area between the old town and the costa, is far more commercialised and this is where the railway station, and many shops and businesses can be found.

Benalmádena has a fair amount of affordable property away from the marina and a new residential area is planned north of Benalmádena. Remember that if you are intending to rent your property out, the closer you are to the beach, the more consistent your rental income will be. This area gets very hot in the summer and potential holiday-makers will want to be as near to the sea as possible.

Torremolinos was the pioneer in tourism in the Costa del Sol and is still the busiest resort on the Costa del Sol. It is a gaudy seaside resort complete with sweeping beaches, Irish pubs, numerous shopping arcades and an enormous expatriate population.
Property here is characterised by high-rise apartment blocks, although villas can be found to the west of the resort. The cheaper properties (often under €90,000) are to be found in the apartment blocks that were part of the first waves of development in the sixties and seventies.

Inland Costa del Sol

Although the Costa del Sol is still proving incredibly popular with foreign buyers, agents are registering an increased interest in properties inland. As prices on the *costa* have doubled over the last five years and are set to double again over the next five years, for many they have become prohibitively expensive. Inland properties are cheaper and often offer far more character than a beachfront apartment.

The town of Antequera, one of the largest in the province in terms of area, is surrounded by plains devoted to olive and cereal production, 542 metres above sea level and backed by the El Torcal and El Arco Calizo Central Sierras. Beyond Antequera there are numerous other red-roofed, white walled unspoilt villages where an undisturbed and unhurried way of life continues much as it has done for centuries.

The crops which provide the livelihood of most of the villagers in this area are irrigated by water from Lake Iznajar nearby. This breathtaking feature is actually a valley that was purposely flooded in the late sixties, but it has become a valued attraction for those who could not bear to be away from water during Andalucia's baking hot summers. Properties around the lake command slightly higher prices, but not much. Village houses which need a little bit of work often go on the market for less than €75,000 and it is possible to find an out of town, slightly run down property for as little as €45,000.

Nerja, some 55km east of Málaga on the N340 coastal highway, marks the eastern end of the Costa del Sol. Once a quiet fishing village the town now has a population of over 12,000 but development has seen more villas than concrete tower blocks being erected. Nerja boasts 16km of beaches and is flanked by the dramatic Sierra Almijara. All major water sports are available here, including water skiing, scuba diving and sailing. The towns' old quarter has narrow, winding streets and whitewashed houses with wrought iron terraces. The spectacular Balcón de Europa has a magnificent promenade along the edge of a towering cliff, giving panoramic views of the Mediterranean and the small coves and beaches below. A few km from Nerja are enormous natural caverns containing paintings over 20,000 years old and other prehistoric remains. One of them has been transformed into a concert hall, where many performances are staged during the summer.

Nerja does not suffer from the excess of hotel complexes and high-rises that plagues other resorts, and it has an altogether more Spanish feel. Although property here is slightly more expensive than in other parts of the eastern Costa del Sol, prices are still reasonable. A small apartment in the town can be found for under €130,000.

THE COSTA DE LA LUZ

Those looking for a bargain may be disappointed by the steep price rises on the Costa del Sol. However, it may be worth looking in the neighbouring Costa de la Luz where prices are considerably lower. Although not on the Mediterranean, The Costa de la Luz (Coast of Light) is rapidly gaining in popularity. Once a very poor part of Spain where property could be found at bargain basement prices, the Costa de la Luz is now benefiting from increasing numbers of tourists. As a result property prices have gone up, but the region still offers fantastic value for money, especially considering its fine golden beaches and traditional whitewashed villages. Temperatures are slightly milder in the winter than on the Costa del Sol and the beaches are more spread-out, and often backed by sand dunes and pine trees. This part of the coast has not yet seen the high-rise hotel development of other areas and inland there are still plenty of cheap properties for renovation.

Property Hotspots

Tarifa. The southernmost point in Europe is situated at the point where the Mediterranean Sea and the Atlantic Ocean meet. Tarifa is only 14km away from Africa and has nearly 38 kilometres of beaches in the municipal area, which are a considerable draw for surfers from around the world.

Conil de la Frontera is a small town with a traditional Spanish atmosphere. Although becoming an increasingly popular tourist resort, it is still a typical Andalucían town with narrow cobbled streets, tapas bars and an open-air market at weekends.

Chiclana de la Frontera. Situated at the south of Cádiz Bay. To the east is the river, Cano de Sancti Petri, separating Chiclana from San Fernando and Cádiz. At the mouth of this river on the Atlantic coast lies the beautiful island of Sancti Petri, and very fine sandy beaches. The ideal coastline and hotels and sports complexes make Chiclana a high quality destination.

Sanlúcar de Barrameda. Situated on the mouth of the Guadalquivir River next to the Parque Nacional Doñana, Sanlúcar de Barrameda has a typical fisherman's quarter 'Bajo de Guia' and bodegas where the Manzanilla wine is produced. The town has good sports facilities, a yacht club and a bullring. Horse racing is held on the fine beaches here in the month of August.

Arcos de la Frontera. The starting point of the White Villages Route, this village is one of the most atmospheric in Spain, surrounded by olive and orange trees, and fertile farmland. Since 1962 the old quarter has been declared an area of historical artistic interest for its natural beauty.

Typical Properties for Sale on the Costa Del Sol

Location	Type	Description	Price
Marbella – 'Golden Mile'	Townhouse	3 bedrooms, spacious accommodation, private garden with patio, roof terrace, communal swimming pool.	€399,000
Fifteen minutes drive west of Marbella	Golf course Apartment	2-bedrooms, with views over the golf course.	€120,000
Mijas	Apartment	2 bedrooms, views of the coast and mountains from terrace, sauna.	€341,250
Estepona	Townhouse	2 bedroom, 2 bathroom townhouse, central Estepona, views of town centre.	€145,000
Torremolinos	Apartment	Studio apartment in high-rise block, town centre.	€59,000
Fuengirola	Apartment	Brand new two bedroom apartment, near beach with sea views. Communal pool and gardens.	€185,000
Antequera (inland)	Townhouse	4 bedrooms, central town location with patio terrace and garage.	€225,000
Lake Iznajar (inland)	Farmhouse	8 bedroom farmhouse overlooking the lake, with 1.5 acres, pool, tennis court.	€350,000

Estate Agents for the Costa del Sol

Andalucian Dream Homes S.L.: Centro Comercial La Alzambra Oficina 3.3, Nueva Andalucia E29660; ☎952-813303; freephone from UK 0800-107 0003; fax 952-815786; e-mail info@andaluciandreamhomes.com; www.andaluciandreamhomes.com.

Images of Andalucia: Tara, Cortijo del Roble, Carboneras, Villanueva del Rosario, 29312 Malaga; tel/fax 952-111178; e-mail propertysales@imagesofandalucia.com; www.imagesofandalucia.com.

Marbella Prime Estates S.L: Centro Comercial La Colonia 22 & 10, Avenida Virgen del Rocio, San Pedro, Marbella 29670, Malaga; ☎952-853390; freephone from UK 0800-1982 081; fax 952-787675; e-mail info@prime-spain.com; www.prime-spain.com.

Millar Homes: C/ del Puerto 24, Puerto Paraiso, 29680 Estepona, Malaga; tel/fax 952-808047; e-mail mark@millarhomes.com; www.millarhomes.com.

Utopian Properties: 23a Castle Street, Cirencester, Gloucestershire GL7 1QD; ☎01285-644247; fax 01285-644201; e-mail info@utopian-properties.com; www.utopian-properties.com.

THE COSTA TROPICAL

The Costa Tropical is a sixty kilometre stretch of coastline running from just east of Nerja to Adra. It takes its name from the sub-tropical climate which allows the cultivation of exotic fruits and crops such as avocadoes, mangoes and bananas. Until a few years ago it was lumped in with the Costa del Sol but it has now been re-branded in an attempt to highlight the region's distinct character.

Whilst there are similarities with the Costa del Sol, Tropical has managed to avoid mass tourism and some of the uglier high-rises. The warm micro-climate found on this coast is created by the shelter of the Lujar and Chaparral mountains near the coast, and the Sierra Nevada behind, with some of the highest peaks in Europe. The warm winds coming across from North Africa give this sheltered *costa* mild temperatures all year round. As a result the coast is filled with dense orchards, which are guarded by Moorish watchtowers and fortresses nestling on the cliffs.

The coast is a mere forty-five minutes from Granada and it takes just over an hour to get to the Sierra Nevada. This leads to the fairly bizarre situation between October and April, when you can, if so inclined, ski in the Sierra Nevada in the morning and sunbathe on the coast in the afternoon. The ski fields are approximately an hour away by car.

Diving has become a very popular pastime on the Costa Tropical and the 320 days of sunshine a year make it a year round activity. The area is regarded as so important that is has recently been designated as a National Marine Park. Around the *Penon*, a massive rock jutting out into the sea which acted as a prison in the first and second centuries, an artificial reef has been built to shelter and encourage sealife. There is also superb cave diving in the area.

The area is still far less developed than the Costa del Sol to the west and environmental concerns from the town councils suggest that this will continue. From Salobreña to Motril the coastline remains entirely undeveloped, although there are plans to extend Motril's golf course and there are even discussions to build a yacht marina. One factor which has traditionally put people off buying on this coast is the abundance of plastic greenhouses along the coast. Not only has this restricted development (farmers believe they can make far more money from the greenhouses than from selling off land to developers) but the ugly abundance of plastic has put people off the area and adversely affected the value of property. This situation will more than likely change in the near future due to the massive development of greenhouse farming just across the water in Morocco, where exotic fruits can be grown and harvested far more cheaply.

Almuñecar is the most established tourist centre on the Costa Tropical and is becoming increasingly popular among foreign residents. The town is considered one of the prettiest and most picturesque spots on the Costa Tropical, although it is marred by the fairly horrendous developments along the front. Nevertheless the town is very popular in the summer months with Spanish holiday-makers and it is easy to see why. The old town, with its steep winding streets, geranium studded balconies and sunlit plazas is very attractive and has the feeling of an Arab medina. The tiny streets and squares are crammed with fascinating little shops and open air bars. The Phoenicians, Romans and Moors have all laid claim to Almuñecar and their diverse influences are still reflected in the town's architecture.

Almuñecar is full of surprises. Ten minutes walk back from the beach, where most coastal towns are swamped with holiday apartments, is a vast orchard of custard apples, enveloping a Phoenician necropolis right in the centre. Towards the Moorish castle there is also the Cueva de Siete Palacios, a vaulted structure that was built into the side of the hill in the first century. It now houses the archaeological museum.

Central town houses in Almuñecar cost around €200,000, whereas a three bedroom apartment, centrally located goes for around €125,000.

La Herradura. Named after the distinctive horseshoe shape of the bay, La Herradura is a picturesque fishing village suburb of Almuñecar, with narrow streets, whitewashed houses and floral plazas. The daily market provides locals not only with locally grown exotic produce but also with an abundance of locally caught fish and seafood. The bay itself is a haven for many watersports as it is sheltered from the coastal winds and there are numerous scuba diving centres at the nearby Marina del Este.

Salobreña. Located 2km inland from the coast, Salobreña is set high on a crag surrounded by a tropical plain. Originally the town was surrounded by the sea, but over the centuries the water receded to leave a fertile plain which now produces exotic fruit and sugar cane.

Salobreña has been far less developed than many other coastal towns. The old town is a maze of narrow streets leading up to a Moorish castle from which there are breathtaking views of the mountains and the plain. Salobreña town hall is very conscious of preserving the town's traditional image and in recent years has invested in freshly cobbling the streets. Development in the area is therefore restricted.

Salobreña Castle

Salobreña has a long and intricate history. One of its most important historical sites is the tenth century Moorish castle which looks down upon the town. Once the summer residence of the Kingdom of Granada, the castle housed extensive dungeons where any misbehaving sultans were incarcerated. One such reprobate, Yusuf, was sentenced to death by his brother. However, he cunningly avoided this fate by demanding, as his last request, one last game of chess with a fellow captor. Legend has it that he managed to prolong the game for several weeks, just long enough for his personal army to come to the rescue.

The castle is very well preserved, although the dungeons have long since disappeared.

At the bottom of the town is Salobreña's modern development of low-rise attractive apartments, bars and restaurants, and the commercial centre where you will find shops, supermarkets, banks and the town hall. The long black sandy beach below the town stretches all the way to the port of Motril and is far more relaxed than the beaches at Almuñecar. The seafront is lined with *chiringuitos*, simple beach bars.

Salobreña offers residents a lively cultural scene with concerts, films and plays all year round. In the summer outdoor shows are held in the castle and there are also colourful annual fiestas and ferias.

The amount of construction currently underway along the front means that there are plenty of off-plan opportunities for the home-buyer. Unfortunately it also means that the sugar cane plantations which have been the villagers' bread and butter for so long may also soon disappear.

Castell de Ferro. Further along the coast, east of Motril, the Costa Tropical's centre for trade, culture and commerce, is the small, sheltered fishing village, Castell de Ferro. Although the small town beach is fairly uninspiring, there are pretty, wide beaches to the east and west. The village benefits from being remarkably unspoilt; there are no noisy nightclubs or 'English/Irish Pubs', although there are ample attractive Spanish bars and restaurants. This is a charming, well-preserved village in tranquil surroundings.

New build apartments here have wonderful views of the sea and the mountains. For a three bedroom, two bathroom apartment expect to pay around €250,000.

Inland from the Costa Tropical – Alpujarras

Only fifty kilometres in from the coast, the Alpujarras region is a beautiful and unspoilt area of mountain villages and deep valleys tucked away in the foothills of the Sierra Nevada. The area boasts spectacular scenery of laden orchards, deep gorges, lush green valleys and pine forests. Hidden amongst this dramatic landscape is a string of seventy or so villages, some of the most picturesque to be found anywhere is Spain. Whitewashed houses built haphazardly on top of one another tumble down steep slopes. Each balcony is strewn with geraniums, carnations and wild roses, and red peppers and corn are hung up to dry against the thick stone walls.

After centuries of isolation, newly constructed roads are opening the region up and the peaceful, slow pace of life that Chris Stewart describes in his bestseller *Driving over Lemons* has become a real draw for foreigners looking to move to Spain. In the villages many ramshackle houses have been bought up by foreigners and those who live there describe the area as a microcosm of traditional Spanish life.

A property with a little land, which needs renovation in this region may well be on the market for just €50,000. If it is the peaceful life that you are looking for, in an area of outstanding natural beauty, then you are likely to find your ideal home in Alpujarras.

Typical Properties for Sale on the Costa Tropical

Location	Type	Description	Price
Almuñecar	Townhouse	Three bedroom house, central location, sea and mountain views.	€210,000
La Herradura	Apartment	Frontline beach apartment. 2 bedrooms, 2 bathrooms, big terrace, sea views.	€283,000
Salobreña	Villa	3 bedroom, brand new villa with swimming pool and sea views.	€450,000
Castell de Ferro	Apartment	3 bedroom, 2 bathroom brand new apartment with sea/ mountain views.	€250,000
Alpujarras	Cortijo (farmhouse)	5 bedroom traditional farmhouse with views of Sierra Nevada.	€130,000

Estate Agents for the Costa Tropical

Costa Tropical Properties C.B: Edificio Aqua 122, 40 La Mamola, 18750 Granada; ☎958-829944; mob 636-795749; e-mail costatropical@arraki.es; www.costatrop icalproperties.com.

Granada Costa Real Estate: Calle Acera del Pilar 4, 18967, La herradura, Granada; ☎958-618138; fax 958-640910; e-mail info@granadacosta.com; www.granadacosta.com.

Inmobiliaria Costasol S.L.: Plaza Madrid no. 4, 184690 Almuñecar, Granada; tel/fax 958-881988; e-mail jomacostasol@telefonica.net; www.costa-sol.info/.

Inmobiliaria Lingwood: Monte de los Almendros, 18680 Salobreña, Costa Tropical de Granada; ☎958-611128; fax 958-617007; e-mail mlingwood@salobrenavillas.com; www.salobrenavillas.com.

Mengel & Partners Internationa:, Marina del Este S/N, Apto. De Correos 603, 18690 Almuñecar; tel/fax 958-640883; e-mail info@mengel-partners.com; www.mengel-partners.com.

THE COSTA DE ALMERIA

Almería is now one of the wealthiest regions of Spain, largely because of its thriving agricultural industry. Would be second home-owners are attracted to the hottest corner of Europe because of its unspoilt and dramatic coastline; 190km of clean, sandy beaches. The Costa de Almería is not yet as overcrowded as most other Spanish tourist resorts. Made up of bays, inlets and cliffs, it is an ideal place for those who want to get away from it all and live in a more traditional Spanish environment. The climate in Almería is subtropical, with an average winter temperature of 16° Celsius. It has the most sunshine hours of the whole of Spain, 3,000 per year. The area is great for water sports and there are a number of golf courses, such as the 18-hole golf course Marina Golf at Almería's main resort, Mojácar Playa. The subterranean caves at Sorbas are of great interest and include the most important gypsum karst in Europe. There is also the Mini Hollywood theme park in the desert near Tabernas where a few fistfuls of Spaghetti Westerns were filmed. There is an international airport 8km from Almería city (which also has a train station), and other airports at San Javier in Murcia and Alicante serve the area.

This coast missed out on the seventies boom and with so much untamed rural hinterland, properties in this region are still among the cheapest you will find. As a result the province as a whole is now booming. Estate agents are billing what was once considered the poor relation to the Costa del Sol as the number one investment area. Annual growth for 2002 and 2003 was around 25% and forecasts for the future suggest further significant growth. Particularly poignant is the fact that this is the area where the Spanish are choosing to buy investment properties and many are finding that by buying off-plan properties they are able to double their money in as little as eighteen months.

If you are looking for bargains there are many to be found just a bit inland. Many home-buyers have realised that for the price of a two bedroom apartment on the coast, they could buy their own house inland. In the Altas/Albox region, fifteen minutes from the coast, plots of land amongst orange and almond groves are currently being sold off by developers, with planning permission for villas of varying specifications ranging from 2 bedroom villas at €165,000 to six-bedroom villas at €425,000. **Albox**, a charming white town of narrow streets and picturesque squares is one of the fastest growing towns in the region, yet country properties here can be found for as little as €60,000.

Almerimar was purpose built to provide facilities for holiday-makers and those who wish to retire from the irritations of modern life. The beach is wide and sandy, with crystal clear waters, and the marina, which was built around the original harbour houses boats from all over Europe. Golfing fans may be attracted by the resort's 18-hole course around which there are numerous villas and apartments for sale.

The only problem with buying in Almerimar is that there are hardly any resale properties available. However, there is a selection of high quality, attractive new-build apartments under construction near to the marina.

Roquetas de Mar. One of the largest resorts on the Costa de Almería is Roquetas de Mar. Once a typical fishing village, the area has been developed into a thriving centre for package holidays, popular for its wide sandy beaches, golf courses and water sports activities. However, the old coastal town, made up of a maze of narrow, Moorish streets, still retains some of its traditional charm.

As the fastest growing town in the region, Roquetas de Mar offers the opportunity to see high returns on your investment as despite the building of thousands of new homes in the area, prices are continuing to rise. The government has invested heavily in the resort and plans to continue doing so until at least 2007. The whole resort will be extended east towards the neighbouring resort of Aguadulce and new developments will include a shopping centre, casino and sports pavillion. The planning of the new developments in this area has been quite tastefully done and is a far cry from the concrete jungle further up the coast at Vera.

Almería has recently become a popular area for foreigners to buy property and around

3,000 Brits have chosen to settle there. The city is located at the foot of a mountain, which is crowned by the impressive Alcazaba, one of the best surviving examples of Moorish military fortification. The city itself is fairly modern and is constantly expanding. In 2005 the city is due to host the Mediterranean Games, a competition held every four years for all of the countries within the Mediterranean basin. As a result the city is currently benefiting from a wave of inward investment, which is not just focusing on sports grounds but also on general facilities. Although prices are currently much lower than those on the Costa del Sol, they are likely to rise in the next few years, so those thinking of buying here should move fast.

Almería is a fairly industrial city and not particularly attractive. It is also a fairly wealthy area and therefore the cost of living is high. However, if you are relocating to Spain and need to be in a city, this is still a bargain area for property.

Mojácar. The upper Moorish fortress town of Mojácar Pueblo stands on a towering crag overlooking the modern beach resort of Mojácar Playa – a strip of beach 7km long. In the 1960s Mojácar had become a ghost town after most of its inhabitants went north to find work in the factories of the Barcelona region. To attract new residents the town's mayor gave land away to anyone who promised to build within a year. Mojácar started to grow and in the following decades tourist developments started to spring up.

The upper village is an attractive whitewashed tangle of cobbled streets spilling down the hillside. The streets are filled with arts and crafts shops and in the centre is the Fuente Mora, the Moorish fountain which was the site of the surrender to the Catholic Kings in the fifteenth century. Mojacar has a long and varied history and its inhabitants are fairly traditional in their outlook. Down at the Playa area however, the atmosphere is quite different. Here you will find the beach bars and the *discotecas* which are very popular throughout the summer months. The beach itself is excellent and as with all of this coast, the water is warm and clear.

A two bedroom apartment with sea views in Mojácar costs around €170,000 and a similar apartment slightly further back from the sea goes for around €140,000.

Directly south of Mojácar is the Cabo de Gata nature reserve. Around the area of Mojácar and Vera there are seven golf courses. Road access is excellent in this area, and the airport at Almería is approximately 45 minutes away by car.

San Juan de los Terreros. Twenty-five minutes east of Mojácar on the border of Costas Cálida and Almería is the small coastal town of San Juan de los Terreros, the most easterly village of Andalucia. The village is made up of coves, almost all with sandy beaches. Fishing boats continue to run in and out of the bay and the view from the rocky headlands is spectacular.

San Juan de los Terreros has become an important new destination for home buyers. Despite its small size, investment in the town's development is quite high and the beaches, restaurants and tranquillity of the area are attracting buyers in their droves. Fortunately most of the development has been tastefully done and the town retains its traditional seaside charm.

Prices here are very reasonable. Detached three bedroom villas in the area can sell for as little as €170,000.

Typical Properties for Sale on the Costa de Almería

Location	Type	Description	Price
Almerimar	Apartment	2 bedrooms, overlooking golf course, views of the beach and Sierra Nevada.	€130,000
Mojacar Playa	Villa	3 bedrooms, beachfront. Brand new. Communal pool.	€132,323
Roquetas de Mar	Townhouse	4 bedrooms, 2 bathrooms, 200m from beach, central location.	€183,600
San Juan de los Terreros	Apartment	2 bedrooms, walking distance from beach, communal pool and garden.	€115,000
Tabernas (inland) – Oasis de Tabernas development	Villa (off-plan)	3 bedrooms, 2 bathrooms, private swimming pool.	€165,000

Estate Agents for the Costa de Almería

Almerisol Properties S.L: Av. Mediterraneo 99, 04740 Roquetas de Mar, Almería; tel/fax 950-333680; mob 620-075596; e-mail sales@almerisol-info.com; www.almerisol-info.com; UK office: ☎0871-7110632.

CGM Inmuebles: Residencial Roquemar, 04740 Roquetas de Mar, Almería; ☎950-329212; fax 950-338147; e-mail frank@cgm-inmuebles.com; www.cgm-inmuebles.com.

Español Homes: Units 6-12 The Parade, Exmouth, Devon, EX8 1RL; ☎01395-260311; fax 01395-271089; e-mail info@espanolhomes.com; www.espanolhomes.com.

*Inmobiliaria Zurimar:*Las Garzas, Local 2 Avda. Playa Serena 04740, Roquetas de Mar, Costa de Almería; tel/fax 950-333878; e-mail info@zurimar.com; www.zurimar.com.

Prime Properties: Local 46, Parque Comercial, 04638 Mojacar, Almería; ☎950-475289; fax 950-473007; e-mail office@prime-properties.biz; www.prime-properties.biz.

MURCIA AND THE COSTA CALIDA

Main Towns and Cities. Murcia, Aguilas, Mazarrón, Cartagena

Airports. San Javier Airport (47km from the city of Murcia on the northern shore of Mar Menor) offers internal and international flights. Alicante airport (El Altet) is only 68km from Murcia. There are also plans for a new regional airport at Corvera (open in 2007).

The Costa Cálida, which runs from Aguilas to La Manga, boasts white sandy beaches and crystal clear water, deserted coves, more than three thousand hours of sun a year and a yearly average temperature of 18°C. One of the picturesque fishing villages along the 'warm coast' may just be the place to buy a year round sunny retreat.

The Costa Cálida, despite having missed out on the tourist boom which hit the Costa del Sol, has a lot to offer. For nature lovers there is the stunning Sierra Espuña National Park within a half hour drive, and even closer is the Sierra de Carrascoy mountain range. Many consider the Costa Cálida to be the last coast to offer a slice of the 'real Spain'. It is still a very agricultural region, with crops as diverse as tomatoes, citrus fruits and cotton grown here. As yet there is no heavy industry in the region.

For those interested in sport, the region offers excellent facilities. At La Manga Club there are international golf courses and tennis centres and the Mar Menor, Europe's largest salt water lagoon offers sailing, windsurfing, diving and jetskiing.

Although not on the coast, the region's capital, Murcia is a real draw to the area. Despite being the commercial centre of the region, very few tourists visit the city and as a result it has a peaceful, unspoilt air and a very traditional slow pace of life. The city is also renowned for its Baroque cathedral, museums and beautiful 19th century architecture.

The Costa Cálida is currently being billed as an up and coming area. The Spanish themselves have been buying holiday homes here for generations, so pie and chips and all-night karaoke are blissfully absent from the region, but foreigners are beginning to catch up. The coast still has reasonably priced property; there are a lot of new developments springing up, and more and more budget airlines are flying into San Javier airport from all over the UK. Growth in the region is huge and is expected to be as high as 25%-30% over the next five years. In the past, development in the Costa Cálida was restricted by poor infrastructure. However, improved roads and the evolution of San Javier from an ex-military airport with one flight a week, to an international airport delivering 600,000 visitors a year to the region have improved accessibility and hence demand for housing. Demand is set to continue, especially considering the plans to open a custom built international airport in 2007 in the region, with the capacity for twenty-two planes an hour.

These developments all suggest that you should move fast if you are considering buying in the area. Property prices rose dramatically in 2003 as increasing numbers of people, deterred by the prices of the Costa Blanca just next door, began looking further afield. In the Club La Manga resort, a two-bedroom apartment which would have set you back €147,000 two and a half years ago, is now selling for over €340,000 and there is more demand than ever for affordable holiday homes. Developers are realising the potential of the region and there are plans to build an entire new town near to Murcia, with 18,000 properties!

The down side of all of this development is that the region's major attraction, the fact that it remains unspoilt by mass tourism and holiday home developments, cannot last for too much longer. Some of the best bargains in this region are to be found a bit inland where the landscape is dominated by vineyards, rivers, mountains and apricot trees.

Aguilas. Those in the know suggest that Aguilas is the up-and-coming place to buy property. The town has remained unspoilt. It was first settled as a seaport in Roman times and remains a trading centre for fish. There is still an evening fish auction every day at 5pm in the port's warehouse. The town's beautiful beaches and 15th century castle with ruined watchtowers are all a draw for tourists and residents alike and the town is famed for having a particularly riotous carnival for three days and nights in February.

A comprehensive guide to buying property in Aguilas is available from Casa del Sol (see address below). Currently there are quite a lot of off-plan opportunities to be found in this area. Notably, properties that will take around eighteen months to build are available at the Almanazora Country Club development just fifteen kilometres outside the town. These range from two-bedroom apartments from €150,000 to small semi-detached and detached villas with roof-top terraces.

Mazarrón. Mazarrón is actually two towns in one, the port and the main town. The main town is 5km inland and contains all the usual amenities such as the town hall, indoor market, banks, medical facilities and shops etc. Puerto de Mazarrón on the other hand is set in a wide sweeping bay, with 35 km of coastline and a backdrop of the high mountain ranges of the Sierra Espuña. The area's superb sandy beaches and secluded coves have attracted Spaniards to buy holiday homes here for generations. The current lack of hotels makes this area not so much a resort as a typical Spanish town.

Estate agents dealing with Mazarrón are currently reporting a surge of interest in property in the area. Property prices here are rising, with land prices increasing by 400% in recent years. However, this is not as alarming as it sounds as land prices here were much cheaper than in similar locations on some of the other costas. Quite large houses can still be found in this area for under €150,000, and there are bargains to be found, such as two bedroom bungalows for as little as €100,000.

Developers are certainly beginning to see the potential of this area, and new urbanizations are rapidly appearing. For example, in La Cumbre, a smart residential area of Puerto de Mazarrón the stylish new development *Residencial Mare Nostrum* has new 1, 2, or 3 bedroom apartments with large terraces, private solariums and garage space and a communal pool and garden starting at €140,000.

Mar Menor and La Manga. To the north of the Costa Cálida, La Manga ('the sleeve') sits on a narrow strip of land that stretches 22km out into the Mediterranean Sea, creating the largest saltwater lagoon in Europe – el Mar Menor. With a maximum depth of only eight metres, the water in the Mar Menor remains at a constant 18°C throughout the year and is calm all year round making it ideal for children. There are all types of water sports available here with no less than thirteen scuba schools and 19 sailing clubs.

Curative properties of the Mar Menor

One of the more bewildering sights to be found on the shores of the Mar Menor is that of people wallowing in the mud. The climactic conditions of the area have created deposits of mud and clay in certain areas and these muddy deposits are said to have healing properties, curing everything from arthritis and rheumatism to skin complaints.

The warm waters of the calm sea have been recognised as having health benefits ever since the time of the Romans who built a number of baths in the area, but until recently the sea's healing properties were considered nothing more than local legend. However, in 1995 Murcia University made a study of the sediment and found it to contain unusually high levels of chlorine and sulphate as well as calcium, magnesium and potassium. The presence of so many minerals in the mud provided scientific evidence for long-established local beliefs.

The best place to experience the Mar Menor mud therapy is at the thermal baths in Los Alcazares.

There are many new complexes being developed around the Mar Menor to cater for the surge of interest in the area. One example is the Polaris World development, a complex made up of large detached villas. The development has been designed in a 'Florida' style, with tree-lined boulevards. Each property comes with a lawn, with its own sprinkler system, fitted kitchens and air conditioning. Optional extras are also available, such as swimming pools, built-in barbecues, jacuzzis and interior design services. A three-bedroom villa with two private sun terraces, garage and a 400 sq.m. plot of land starts at €353,400.

La Manga is a modern resort with a cosmopolitan atmosphere. With 40 km of beaches and the possibility of choosing between two different seas, the 'sleeve' is popular with Spaniards and foreigners alike and it gets very busy. Access to La Manga is now fairly good, with the San Javier airport just 20 minutes away providing daily flights to the UK.

Property in La Manga strip is sought after and is more expensive than in the rest of the Costa Cálida. New developments and urbanizations are being built but there are obvious restrictions to the amount of space that can be developed further. A property in La Manga is likely to see high returns.

In the vicinity of the 'sleeve' is Club La Manga, a huge sports resort with world class sporting facilities including golf courses and ten tennis clubs. There is a common confusion between La Manga strip and La Manga club, which is not actually on 'the sleeve' itself. The purpose built La Manga Club resort is a golfers' paradise, featuring three golf courses, which play host to many international tournaments. Around this complex, the luxury villas and apartments are clustered together in small villages, all with international restaurants, bars and entertainment. The resort has property available to suit almost all budgets, although property is much more expensive here than on the strip itself. The cheapest options here start at €120,000. For further details visit www.lamangaspain.com.

Lorca. A half hour drive inland from Aguilas, just before you reach the Parque Natural de Espuña is the region's third city, Lorca. The city has a distinct aura of the past, fusing Baroque and Renaissance architecture and surrounded by stunning countryside. Lorca was an important frontier town from Roman times to the end of the Reconquest, prospering again in the 17th century. As a result it is filled with impressive buildings such as the town hall which is built in two blocks and connected by an arch that spans the street. Lorca really comes alive on Good Friday when it puts on an extravagant spectacle of horseback processions and lavish costumes, at a time when much of Spain is engrossed in solemn ritual.

Typical Properties for Sale on the Costa Cálida

Location	Type	Description	Price
Aguilas	Penthouse apartment	2 bedrooms, roof terrace. Part of a development with communal tennis courts, swimming pool, gardens and a lake.	€136,000
Puerto Mazarrón	Duplex	2 bedrooms, brand new, 200m from beach. Built around communal pool and gardens	€114,200
La Manga	Apartment	2 bedrooms, fully furnished, sea views.	€120,000
Club La Manga	Luxury villa	5 bedrooms, private pool and grounds, full access to facilities at Club La Manga	€1.5 million
Lorca	Farmhouse	4 bedrooms, 2 bathrooms, located on outskirts of Lorca with 200 olive trees in grounds.	€359,404

Estate Agents for the Costa Cálida

Casa del Sol: 51 High Street, Emsworth, Hants PO10 7AN; ☎0800-7313893; www.casadelsol.co.uk.

Casas & Houses: Hotel Los Delfine Local Comercial #9, 30380 La Manga del Mar Menor, Murcia; ☎968-145656; fax 968-564997.

Chicano Agencia Inmobiliaria: Jaime El Conquistador, 11 – Entlo., 30008 Murcia; ☎968-247810; fax 968-246589.

Mar Menor Properties: contact Andrew Millard, 1ˢᵗ Floor, 32 Market Place, Wetherby, West Yorkshire, LS22 6NE; ☎08700-503500; fax 08700-503501; e-mail sales@m armenorproperties.com; www.marmenorproperties.com.

Promociones Tesy S.A.: C/ Alameda San Antón, 20-bajo, 30205 Cartagena, Murcia; ☎968-527433/527563; fax 968-124914.

VALENCIA

Provinces: Valencia, Alicante, Castellón.

Main Towns and Cities: Torrevieja, Alicante, Benidorm, Jávea, Puerto de Gandía, Valencia, Sagunto, Castellón de la Plana, Vinaroz.

Airports: Alicante, Valencia. New airport due to open at Castellón de la Plana in late 2006.

The Valencia region has strong historical associations with the Catalonian/Aragonese partnership which conquered it in the twelfth century, and shares a linguistic heritage with Catalonia, although arguments still rage as to whether Valencian is in fact a language in its own right or a dialect of Catalan.

In the province of Alicante is the Costa Blanca ('White Coast') which has a thriving community of expatriates and the highest number of British expats of any area of Spain. The beaches and resorts of the Costa Blanca: Denia, Jávea, Calpe, Altea, Benidorm and Villajoyosa to name but a few; are incredibly popular with both tourists and property buyers. Access to the Costa Blanca is easy from Alicante airport.

The White Coast gets its name from Greek traders who founded *Akra Leuka* or the blank foothill there around 2,500 years ago, but it was only really in the 1960s, when the picturesque village of Benidorm began attracting package tourists that the area started to take shape as the holiday haven it has become today. The Costa Blanca may have been overdeveloped in places but this does not detract from its natural beauty and serenity. Indeed, the World Health Organisation cites this stretch of coastline as one of the healthiest places on earth due to its climate, recreational facilities and relaxed way of life. Environmental issues are therefore now at the forefront of local politics in the region and as a result further development has been restricted in many areas and construction companies are being forced to show a commitment to a sustainable environment.

There is quite a large north/south divide on the Costa Blanca. Property prices are far cheaper in the south and as a rule, the north attracts a more refined crowd searching for a villa with private swimming pool, whereas in the south property-buyers are usually young families or couples looking for an apartment. On the Costa Blanca as a whole, property prices are currently increasing by around seventeen to twenty-two per cent per annum, so it is still a good place to invest. Those buying off plan can expect an investment return as high as forty per cent.

In the provinces of Valencia and Castellón is the Costa del Azahar, which runs from just north of Denia to the town of Vinaroz. It offers some breath-taking scenery, mild winters and real value for money when it comes to buying property. In the centre of this coast lies Valencia, Spain's third city which provides an enticing blend of the traditional and the contemporary avant-garde. It is a vibrant and exciting city offering history, culture and fantastic cuisine, mixed with an abundance of nightlife.

COSTA BLANCA SOUTH

The southern region of the Costa Blanca, running from the border with Murcia up to Alicante, is generally cheaper to buy property in than the northern reaches and offers far better value for money. There are some excellent, blue-flag winning beaches here and some of the resorts are developing excellent sporting facilities, hotels and nightclubs. Although the up and coming regions are considered to be Almería and Murcia, this area offers some strong competition and is an ideal choice for those with families.

Heading inland from the southern Costa Blanca there are many comparatively unexplored areas where fincas can be bought for as little as €70,000.

Torrevieja is overdeveloped and is one of the fastest growing resorts on the Costa Blanca (the town has swelled by 100% since 1998), but that fact doesn't mean that one has to write off the whole area. With a superb climate, great beaches, first class sport, recreation and health facilities and the low cost of living, as well as being just 35km south of the airports at San Javier and Alicante, there are a few reasons to look for property here. Apart from its beaches, Torrevieja offers stunning cliff walks, many natural beauty spots, a well-served marina and the two attractive lagoons of Las Salinas.

Torrevieja, is at present one of the growth areas for property with many new *urbanizaciónes*, villas and flats being built by development companies. Because of the glut of new properties, prices around Torrevieja are among the cheapest on the Costa Blanca, though many are used as holiday homes only, and during the tourist season the town and the beaches are packed to capacity. Two-bedroom apartments in the area start at around €100,000. For those looking for a strong investment, Torrevieja has a consistently high rental demand throughout the year and property prices are expected to rise in the next few years. This leaves investors in the enviable position of being able to pay for the property from its rental income and then sell it off at a profit.

South of Torrevieja there are excellent golf courses (the area is fast becoming a Mecca for golf enthusiasts of all handicaps), a dozen varied beaches, two good marinas and plenty of restaurants and bars. This ten mile stretch of coastline is often known as the Orihuela Costa and has gained popularity with both Spanish and foreign homebuyers. Property prices here are currently very cheap but experts forecast a dramatic rise in the next ten years.

Santa Pola. The port town of Santa Pola boasts several miles of superb beaches and is home to the Mediterranean's largest deep sea and coastal fishing fleet. The town is also famous for its salt flats – miles of protected wetlands, which combined with the continuing commercial salt production, are important sources of both revenue and natural beauty for this popular town. Santa Pola is the main embarkation point for Isla de Tabarca – a little island in the bay once used as a prison and now home to a small fishing community.

Cabo Roig. One of the most exclusive developments along the Costa Blanca situated 8km from Torrevieja, Cabo Roig is characterised by broad palm lined avenues and landscaped gardens and is just a few minutes drive from the superb Villamartin golf complex. There are excellent restaurants at the Cabo Roig marina and a maritime walk follows the coastline of the peninsula.

ALICANTE AND THE COSTA BLANCA NORTH

Alicante was called 'Lucentum' – City of Light – by the Romans. Close by is the maritime town of El Campello, with a modern marina and fine blue-flag beach. Alicante has good medical care facilities and an infrastructure that supports the large number of retirees who have decided to move into the area. South of Alicante property is relatively cheap, and there is plenty of it, though over the last three years prices have increased by 20% a year. The area running from Denia to Murcia is a favourite place to buy in Spain at present, along with the Canary and Balearic Islands.

As the main city of the Costa Blanca, Alicante has much to offer with the architecture, arts, crafts and cuisine a wonderful fusion of styles, together with miles of coastline. While tourism has replaced port activity as the main source of revenue in the region, Alicante still has a bustling and vibrant harbour. The San Juan de Alicante beach is to the east of the city and is over 7km long. Gran Alacant, at the southernmost reach of Alicante's influence, is located just south of the regional capital and close to the airport. It is also convenient for Benidorm, Terra Mítica and the North Costa Blanca, making it a very popular resort town. The town has benefited from continuing massive investment, creating high quality residential and business developments. There are plans for further redevelopment of the area, including a high-speed train line from Valencia and an expansion of green areas in the city.

Property prices in central Alicante are fairly high, so you would be well-advised to explore the residential areas surrounding the city. Living in the centre has its advantages, but these are marred by pollution, traffic congestion and a rising crime rate.

North of Alicante, the coastline can be quite spectacular and except for the blot of Benidorm, the northern reaches of the Costa Blanca have had restricted development, which has led to a rather exclusive and expensive area of property acquisition. The 'golden triangle' of Denia, Javea and Calpe are sought after and property prices are high compared to those south of Alicante.

Denia, named after the Roman Goddess Diana, is an old town sitting at the foot of the Montgó Mountain, which shelters the town from the hot winds of the meseta offering a microclimate with an annual average temperature of 19°C. A short distance inland is the La Sella golf club. The Montgó Nature Park offers walks, trails and horse riding and is a haven for the region's flora and fauna.

Extending from Denia to the north, there are twenty miles of blue flag beaches.

Brand new developments in the Denia area are currently offering off-plan properties with private pool, surrounded by orange groves for around €240,000.

Inland from Denia is the Orba Valley, one of the most beautiful locations on the Costa Blanca. Those with the time and inclination to restore an old finca should certainly have a look in this area, where there are several available at bargain prices. The stunning views over the valley make this an idyllic rural area and perfect for hiking enthusiasts. The easier option is to investigate some of the new developments in this area. For example, at Porta D'Orba overlooking the valley there are new two bedroom villas with pools from just €225,000.

Jávea (Xábia). Jávea is an attractive village, known locally as 'Amanecer de España', or the Dawn of Spain as its location, jutting into the Mediterranean, makes it one of the first places to catch the morning sunlight. The area is a favoured venue for naturalists, scuba divers and water sports enthusiasts due to its many submerged caves and rock formations creating diverse marine life. The town consists of three parts with the pretty and laid-back old town lying inland, and the port and marina 3km away. Nearby is the main beach resort of El Arenal, the beginning of 25km of coastline.

Villas here start at around €300,000, so it is not a cheap place to invest. However, the area has for many years been popular with foreign property buyers and 20% of the town's population are British expatriates, making their presence felt with an enthusiastic cricket, bowls and bridge scene. It is easy to see why people are drawn here. Jávea is relatively quiet for most of the year and only the resort of El Arenal endures the excesses of the tourist season in July and August.

Inland from Jávea is the Jalón Valley, which has long been a retreat for British buyers seeking peace and quiet. Brand new, two-bedroom villas just five minutes from the market town of Jalón are available here for around €240,000 and there are some bargain older properties with stunning views to be found.

Moraira. One of the most charming towns along this stretch of coastline is Moraira. Once a small fishing village, it has developed into a holiday and retirement resort with a marina and several good sandy beaches. Moraira stands out because it has managed to retain so much of its original character. The local planning authorities have exerted strong control over development in the area and managed to avoid high-rise monstrosities. As a result, the only developments are detached villas spread out over quite a large area.

Understandably this has become a popular area for foreign home-buyers, but it is still possible to find a detached, two bedroom villa in the Moraira area for as little as €100,000.

Calpe is overlooked by Peñón de Ifach – a stunning rocky peak resembling the rock of Gibraltar, which rises 332 metres above the town. Once used as a watchtower to forewarn of Barbary Coast corsairs, it is now a national park with a trail leading to its summit. Below the Peñón de Ifach are two large bays where a harbour and the town itself are situated. The town was once famed for its artistic appeal, and Ernest Hemingway spent his summers here in the 1930s.

Calpe was originally a fishing village and retains its character, due to the fact that there are few hotel developments, although the town now contains a number of attractive bars and restaurants near to the harbour. Two bedroom apartments can be bought here for around €120,000.

Altea has preserved its charm and the town's whitewashed old quarter features winding cobbled streets which lead you to the main square by a magnificent church with its cupola roof inlaid with deep blue and white tiling. From here the views over the town to the sea are stunning. The beaches are pebble, rock and sand around Altea and there are secluded coves here.

As one of the prettiest towns on the Costa Blanca, demand for property is high, as are the prices. Development here has been restrained and new properties are mainly located on the seafront, but an increasingly diverse range of properties is being made available here. Property in Altea itself is expensive, but in the surrounding area it is possible to purchase a two-bedroom detached villa for around €150,000.

Near to Altea and next to the slopes of Morro de Toix is a new residential complex called *Oasis Beach*, offering superb views of the sea. When finished, Oasis Beach will comprise four apartment blocks of one, two and three bedroom apartments each with a jacuzzi on the terrace and access to a communal swimming pool. The apartments start at €260,000.

Benidorm, for those seeking noise, has it all – great beaches, water sports, restaurants, cafés and bars and heaps of nightlife. However, Benidorm stands as a cautionary tale to town-planners everywhere. The old part of the town has been completely enveloped by concrete tower blocks as a result of over-development and package tourism gone mad. If you are looking for a resort with vast numbers of tourists, 'English' pubs on every corner and the opportunity to eat 'full English breakfasts' at any time of day and on any given street, then Benidorm is for you.

Millions visit Benidorm every year, attracted by the two kilometres of golden sand, and beautiful weather. Many have decided to buy property here and the local authorities are trying to promote Benidorm as a pleasant family-oriented town, increasing its popularity for buyers. There are over three thousand British residents here alone. Inland is Terra Mítica, a theme park on the scale of Euro Disney, designed (allegedly) to reflect Mediterranean history. It attracts many thousands of visitors every year and there are plans to develop it further, with a number of hotel and residential complexes to be built in the surrounding area.

Because of the vast amount of real estate that has transformed Benidorm from the tiny agricultural village it once was, property prices here are still reasonable. If you are buying a holiday home to let out for the rest of the year, then you will find that the demand for rental properties is fairly high and the season runs all year round. An apartment located near the beach would certainly provide a consistent income.

Typical Properties for Sale on the Costa Blanca

Location	Type	Description	Price
Torrevieja	Apartment	3 bedrooms, first floor. Close to amenities and the sea.	€81,268
Santa Pola	Apartment	2 bedrooms, located on beachfront, situated on ground floor of small block of flatlets. Communal roof terrace.	€276,400
Jávea	Villa	4 bedrooms, 3 bathrooms. Sea view, lawned garden with fruit trees. Private pool.	€472,775
Moraira	Bungalow	2 bedrooms, panoramic views, next to beach, communal pool.	€220,000
Calpe	Villa	3 bedrooms, 3 bathrooms. Located on hillside with stunning views over Calpe and the Med. Private pool and garden.	€480,847
Benidorm	Apartment	1 bedroom, sea view and large terrace. Located in development with pool, tennis and gym.	€145,145

Estate agents for the Costa Blanca

Gran Sol Properties: Edificio Apolo 1, Calle Corbeta, 03710 Calpe, Alicante; tel/fax 965-835468; e-mail info@gransolproperties.com.

IPC Property Consultants Ltd: 38 Church Street, Seaford, East Sussex, BN25 1LD; ☎01323-899204; fax 01323-899210; info@ipc-homes.com; www.ipc-homes.com.

Keysol Properties: 173 Silverdale Road, Tunbridge Wells, Kent, TN49HT; ☎0845-601 8306; e-mail admin@ocioazul.com; www.propertieskeysol.com.

Lambourne Properties: Calle Ronda Colon 1b, 03730 Javea; tel/fax 965-795916.

Sucasita S.L.: 32 Clifford Road, North Shore, Blackpool, Lancashire FY1 2PU; tel/fax 01253-628513; www.sucasita.co.uk.

THE COSTA DEL AZAHAR

The coastline along the provinces of Valencia and Castellón is lined with magnificent orange plantations amidst lush green vegetation giving it the name – the Costa del Azahar or the Orange Blossom Coast. The strong smell of pines drifting down from the mountains mixed with the intoxicating smells of orange trees in blossom and the almond groves really brings this 112km stretch of coast to life. Surrounded by the extensive, spectacular La Safar mountain ranges and excellent white sandy beaches, the Costa Del Azahar offers views of stunning and contrasting landscapes.

Dotted along the shoreline are small summer resorts, perhaps the best known of which is the ancient fortified town of Peñiscola. The coast here boasts miles of sandy beaches and very calm waters, particularly safe for bathing and for practising all kinds of water-sports.

Properties along this lesser-known coastline are bought mainly by Spaniards, but appeal to foreigners as prices remain reasonably low and access is relatively quick and direct from Valencia airport. This Costa is still very much a developing area, overlooked by the millions of second home buyers heading north to the Costa Brava or south to the Costa del Sol. The new airport at Castellón de la Plana is due to open in 2006 and will make the area far more accessible to foreign home-buyers, almost certainly creating a huge surge of demand. New developments and attractions are already springing up as a result. For example a huge theme park, *Mundo Ilusion* is currently being built near to Torreblanca and aims to cater for two to three million visitors annually.

Prices have gone up dramatically in recent years. If your interest lies in this stunning, peaceful stretch of coast, branded 'the garden of Spain' by estate agents, then snap up a property at bargain prices while you still can.

Oliva and Gandía. At the southern most tip of the Costa del Azahar, just before it turns into the Costa Blanca around Denia are the two traditional market towns of Oliva and Gandia. The two towns are surrounded by a sweeping bay with mountains to the west and eighteen kilometres of magnificent white sandy beaches to the east. Property prices are generally lower here than in the international tourist areas and the cost of living is certainly cheaper.

Oliva is set back from the coast and retains its traditional charm. It is possible to find fairly large townhouses in the sleepy town for as little as €110,000. If you are looking for a beach-front property, Playa de Oliva has a large number of villas and apartments for sale and this area is surprisingly free of ugly concrete developments. The marina and golf complex are also down on the shores of the Mediterranean.

Gandia is also set back from the coast, but most people look to buy property in the Gandia Playa coastal resort, with over four miles of palm-lined beaches. Property here is not cheap, two bedroom apartments start at around €210,000, but the area has a much more relaxed attitude than you would expect from a coastal resort due to the fact that tourists do not visit this area in large numbers. It is a clean, pretty and relaxed stretch of coastline.

Valencia is Spain's third largest city and is a truly exciting and vibrant place, accurately labelled by many 'the City of Contrasts'. Founded by Roman legionaries in 138 BC, Valencia has a traditional atmosphere with an impressive array of architecture going back to the Middle Ages. However, in recent years Valencia has seen a huge amount of investment and modern development and the brand new area, the City of Arts and Sciences has been praised for having brought ultramodern urbanism right into the heart of its traditional town. The modern-day city of Valencia has sprawling suburbs of high-rise blocks and its fair share of beggars and gypsies; however, the city is forever linked with the romantic figure of El Cid.

El Cid

Otherwise known as Ruy Diaz de Bivar, El Cid was a soldier of fortune in the dark days of the Moorish occupation. Tradition and legend have cast a deep shadow over the history of this brave knight, to such an extent that his very existence has been questioned. Through his chivalric exploits, El Cid became the hero of one of Spain's earliest epic poems the *Cantar de mío Cid,* as well as the subject of folk legends and ballads. The reality was probably more prosaic; he fell out with his monarch, fought for the Moors, then became reconciled with his ruler by changing sides once again and was rewarded with the governorship of Valencia.

Valencia may not have the same diversity and vitality as Madrid and Barcelona, but it is a city which thrives on festivities, colour and noise. Some of the best nightlife in mainland Spain can be found here and the *Las Fallas* festival, which takes place in March is one of the most important festivities in Spain. During the week of *Las Fallas de San Jose,* there are endless processions, bullfights and firework displays, terminating in the *Nit de Foc* when the entire city lights up with bonfires in every street, burning enormous caricatures of popular satirical figures.

Those relocating to Spain for business reasons will discover that Valencia is commercially speaking, the most important city on the Spanish Mediterranean coast. It has a thriving business district and over forty international trade fairs are staged in the city every year, offering professionals from a variety of economic sectors the ideal platform for launching and distributing their products. The city is pushing hard to meet the demands of the twenty-first century and despite the fact that the locals speak Valenciano, the use of English is higher in Valencia than in most other Spanish cities.

Cheap housing is available around the outskirts of the city, but for those who wish to live fairly centrally, prices are still at least thirty per cent lower than in Barcelona or Madrid, although this is unlikely to last. Valencia has enjoyed such a remarkable regeneration in recent years that it is now being hailed as the next big thing. Valencians are enthusiastically buying up run-down properties and transforming them into elegant residences. The Swiss winners of the America's Cup have chosen to host the 2007 competition in Valencia and the huge area around the port will be completely redeveloped, causing prices to soar in that area and possibly in the city as a whole.

Benicássim was caught up in the mass tourism explosion which took place in the

1960s and as a result developed into one of the most important tourist centres on the Costa del Azahar, attracting mainly Spanish visitors. The resort enjoys ten kilometres of beaches boasting fine golden sands and the prestigious Blue Flag.

Not far from Bencicássim is the Desierto de las Palmas nature reserve, 2,000 hectares of oak and pine forests, and not a desert at all. Housed within the reserve are the remains of a Carmelite convent which was closed to the outside world for centuries.

> **Benicássim is famed for its Moscatel wine**
> It was once well-known as a wine producing region, although over the years the vineyards have dwindled in numbers. The vine only thrives in the humid conditions of countries bathed by the Mediterranean. As well as producing sweet white wines, the Moscatel grape is used in the new convent in Desierto las Palmas to create Carmelite liqueur, which has been made there since the late nineteenth century. Free wine tasting visits are on offer from *Bodegas Carmelito*.

Those thinking of buying property in Benicássim should be aware that in the last ten years the town has become host to an enormous annual music festival. The festival runs during the first weekend of August and attracts some of the world's biggest names in alternative music. During this time the whole town is swamped with young revellers and the surrounding areas turn into an overflow campsite.

Oropesa. One of the more developed tourist resorts on the Costa del Azahar, Oropesa's beaches spread from Torre La Sal at Ribera de Cabanes as far as Benicássim. There are property developments all around these beaches and on the nearby hilltops and a recently built marina. This area is really booming now, partly as a result of massive investment at the new Marina D'or resort boasting one of the largest health spas in Europe

Peñiscola is perched on the Rock of Peñiscola, rising majestically out to sea, and fortified by large solid sections of wall dating back to the twelfth century. The town is very attractive and is a favourite tourist destination for both Spanish and foreign tourists. The old town of Peñiscola has been preserved practically in its entirety. Tourist development hasn't destroyed the monuments within the town nor those buildings that line the beach on the road between Peñiscola and Benicarló.

> **Impressive castle and fortifications at Peñiscola**
> Built by the Knights Templar, the impregnable walls create a spectacular fortress that has in its time stood up to the assault of both Barbary pirates and British troops during the War of Spanish Succession. In 1411, the castle became the home of Pope Benedict XIII (Papa Luna) after he had been deposed from the papacy during the fifteenth century Church schisms. Having escaped from Avignon, Papa Luna set up his court here for six years. More recently the castle and its ramparts were used as the set to film part of *El Cid*, starring Charlton Heston.

Peñiscola is developing rapidly and plans are currently going through for a new marina and golf course in the area. A beachside, three-bedroom apartment in Peñiscola currently sells for around €200,000, and non front-line villas can be found for around the same price.

There are several new housing developments in this area. For example, just outside the town is a new urbanisation called Les Moles, which is made up of several two bedroom semi-detached houses with living/dining room, bathroom, fitted kitchen and terraces with access to a communal pool. These houses start from as little as €126,300.

Benicarló. South of Tortosa, Benicarló has a fishing port as well as excellent beaches, which stretch as far as Peñiscola. A coast road links both towns. The resort area between Benicarló and Peñiscola is so built up that it is difficult to know where one town ends and the other begins.

If golf is your thing then head inland just a few kilometres from Benicarló where a new development has been built on the fairways of an eighteen-hole championship golf course. Two and three bedroom apartments are available on the Panorámica Golf and Thermal Resort from around €140,000.

Typical Properties for Sale on the Costa del Azahar

Location	Type	Description	Price
Oliva Beach	Semi-detached house	5 bedrooms, 2 sun terraces, large garage. Only a 2-minute stroll from the beach.	€216,000
Valencia	Apartment	2 bedrooms, central location.	€102,200
Peñiscola	Apartment	3 bedrooms, beach front, fabulous sea views.	€209,080
Oropesa	Apartment	3 bedrooms, 2 bathrooms. Located in high rise apartment block with communal pool. Sea views.	€175,000
Benicarló	Villa	4 bedrooms, 2 bathrooms. Private pool and gardens. Quiet area 3km from beach.	€264,300

Estate Agents for the Costa del Azahar

Almond Grove Properties: ☎+44 (0)1327-350099; e-mail sales@almond-grove.org; www.almond-grove.org.

Costa Spanish Eyes: Calle Joanot Martorell 21 bajo, Oliva 46780, Valencia; ☎962-838215; 962-855610; e-mail info@costaspanisheyes.com; www.costaspanisheyes.com.

Cúspide: Avenida República Argentina no. 48, Gandia; ☎962-961757; www.cuspide.es.

Procoim Inmobiliaria: Plaza de la Constitución, s/n, 12598 Peñiscola, Castellón de la Plana; ☎964-480626; cheap rate line from UK 0871-4254302; fax 964-467546.

Oranges and Lemons: Calle Alcalde Francisco Llorca 15, 1°C, Oliva, 46780 Valencia; ☎962-853112; fax 962-855096; e-mail orangesandlemons@wanadoo.es; www.orangesandlemons.com.

CATALONIA (CATALUNYA)

Coastal Provinces. Tarragona, Barcelona, Gerona.
Main Coastal Towns and Cities. Reus, Salou, Tarragona, Sitges, Barcelona, Blanes, Lloret de Mar, La Platja d'Aro, Girona, L'Escala, Figueres, Roses.
Airports. Barcelona, Gerona, Reus.
Catalonia, whose first ruler was the hirsutely-named Guifré el Pelós ('Wilfred the Hairy'), is one of the regions of Spain which has its own distinct historical, and some would say national, identity, with its own Catalan culture and language. Although covering less than 7% of the total area of Spain, Catalonia is home to over six million inhabitants; about 16% of the total population of Spain. This has long been one of the most exciting and cosmopolitan parts of Spain, and Barcelona a fascinating centre of politics, fashion, commerce and culture.

In the twelfth century, Catalonia was an autonomous part of the kingdom of Aragon, an alliance that enhanced its political influence and brought far ranging cultural influences to Aragon from Provence and Roussillon in France by way of Catalonia. The Catalan language is closely related to the Langue d'Oc, still spoken in some parts of southern France that once formed part of a united kingdom with Catalonia. Catalonia was one of the Mediterranean powers in the Middle Ages and today there is still a Catalan-speaking outpost on the Italian island of Sardinia.

The decline of Catalonian wealth and power in the fourteenth century weakened Aragon to the extent that Castile became the dominant regional power. For the next five centuries the Catalonians attempted to consolidate their autonomy while successive Spanish dynasties tried to stake a claim to it. Towards the end of the nineteenth century, the broad-based nationalist movement of Catalanism began to gather momentum and attracted the attention of Madrid, which offered a limited autonomy to the region. This was subsequently repressed by the dictator, Primo de Rivera, and any further thoughts of autonomy were interrupted by the Civil War, during which Barcelona became the final refuge of republicanism and anarchism and held out against Franco's armies until the bitter end in 1939.

Franco's retribution against the Catalan language and culture took the form of book-burning and the changing of street and place names. However, in the decades following the end of the Civil War, Catalan nationalism mellowed and Catalanism became characterised more by bravura than violence and extremism. Perhaps one of the reasons for this change is that during most of this century the Catalonian region has been settled by many migrant workers from poorer parts of Spain, attracted by the industry and wealth of the area. The result is that about half of the people of Catalonia are descended from immigrants, which has led to a bilingualism similar to that of Wales, with Spanish universally spoken, but Catalan favoured in schools and universities. This immigration has also contributed to the dilution of some of the strong nationalist feelings in the region.

The province of Barcelona includes part of the Pyrenees. It is also home to one of the national symbols of Catalonia, the monastery of Montserrat built around the legend of the Black Virgin, an icon reputedly hidden on the site by St. Peter and rediscovered in the ninth century amidst the sort of miraculous happenings usually associated with such shrines. During the Franco era the monastery clandestinely published the Montserrat Bible in Catalan and became a centre of nationalist gatherings.

The northern costas, the Costa Brava and the Costa Dorada were the first to be invaded in the 1950s by tourism and property development. There is a large Spanish presence among the property owners in this region so it has remained pretty culturally intact, unlike the Costa del Sol. Because of Catalonia's proximity to the French border overland travel between UK and Spain is pretty fast. A motorway running along the east coast connects southern France to the South of Spain.

Low cost flights from UK airports have made Spain's northern costas even more accessible and this has made the area increasingly attractive for second-home buyers, with Ryanair offering services to Girona on the Costa Brava and Reus on the Costa Dorada.

THE COSTA BRAVA

For many the Costa Brava ('the rugged coast') is the only place in which they would consider buying property. The beauty of this coastline, with its cliffs and coves led to the beginnings of mass tourism in Spain, which in turn has led to the over-development of the area. Between Blanes and Sant Feliu de Guixols some of the worst aspects of mass tourism can be seen, but the further north toward the French border you travel the less sprawling the development. Property is still being developed along the coast but there is increasing demand due to the recent decision of Catalonia's new government to clamp down on coastal building. Property remains comparatively expensive in the Costa Brava, partly due to the Spanish and French love affair with the region, and this ban will undoubtedly push prices even higher.

There is also a great demand inland, especially for the large country houses (*masias*) with land. Prices for such properties, even if they are in need of restoration, go for about £350,000 due to the demand for a sparse supply.

At the northern end of the Costa Brava are the small and unspoilt resorts of Calelle de Palafrugel, Figueres and Cadaques. This area is still relatively unknown to many British holiday-makers and there are almost no noisy nightclubs and lager louts, only beautiful scenery and peaceful, sandy bays and coves. For those interested in watersports, this area has excellent wind surfing at the resorts of Roses, Estartit and Platja d'Aro and snorkelling at Aigua Blava. Proximity to the Pyrenees offers the possibilities of hiking in the summer and skiing in the winter.

The main airports serving this coastline are at Barcelona and Girona. Demand for property in the area is driven by Spanish buyers and property inland will be cheaper than that on the coast, especially if you are prepared to renovate.

L'Escala was once the most important fishing port in the region. The promontory on which the town is built juts out into the sea to form a sheltered bay ideal for mooring a traditional Mediterranean fishing fleet. Running to the west and east of the town are several kilometres of beach as well as rocky coves. L'Escala is a relatively small resort offering a gentle pace of life to its residents along with good access to the northern Costa Brava – the Golf de Roses, the town of Figueres – home of the Salvador Dalí museum, and Cadaques, the pretty fishing village where Dalí lived for many years.

Pals. Eight kilometres north of Pallafrugel is the medieval village of Pals with its many excellent seafood restaurants and a peaceful hilltop setting. Much of Pals' recent popularity can be attributed to the stunning views, three local golf courses and the huge variety of water sports available nearby at Platja de Pals – a popular and small beach surrounded by dense pine forest which leads inland almost as far as Pals.

Aigua Blava, which means blue water in Catalan, has a beauty and serenity that has been undisturbed for centuries and locals are still intent on protecting the area from all attempts to commercialise or over-develop the area. The bay is made up of pine-tree covered cliffs sloping down to form promontories into the sea. Around the pretty coves and beaches are restaurants dishing up freshly caught seafood.

Buying a property in the Aigua Blava bay is really for those seeking peace and quiet away from the strains of modern life. The nearest shops are a ten-minute drive, so a car is essential. Nevertheless, the area has superb golfing facilities. Because of the local restrictions on development there are not many properties for sale, but should you find one, not only would it be a wise investment, but also a wonderful area to own a holiday home.

St. Feliu de Guixols is one of the most attractive resort towns on the Costa Brava with its small streets, yacht harbour and medieval architecture to explore. The town is built alongside a horseshoe-shaped sandy bay and is set against the backdrop of Sant Elm – a mountain topped by a ruined Benedictine monastery offering wonderful views. St Feliu is a busy, clean, welcoming resort with beaches, cafés, bars and restaurants.

Tossa de Mar is one of the highlights of the Costa Brava. Although it is a very built up and developed resort, it is still very attractive and has a far more Spanish feel than Lloret de Mar 13 km to the south. The town dates from Palaeolithic times and retains evidence of the occupation of the Romans and the Moors. The Vila Vella (old town) is divided from the rest of the town by a well-preserved 12th century wall. Tossa has a narrow natural harbour formed by the surrounding cliffs, and four beaches. It is renowned for its charm, superb seafood restaurants and excellent nightlife.

Lloret de Mar is a resort that most people have heard of due to its popularity with British package tourists. Lloret is a holiday resort and does not pretend to be anything else. It has sprawling high rise tower blocks, five sand/shingle beaches and rows of uninspiring cafés, restaurants and bars. The town does however, have some attractive coves and lookout points within walking distance and a new palm-lined promenade has just been added in an attempt to make the area more aesthetically pleasing.

If it is a beach holiday home that you are after, Lloret de Mar may well be the answer. It is perfect for the first-time buyer because property here is so cheap. You can find a one-bedroom property for as little as €50,000 and you will find that rental yields are very high.

Blanes is about an hour's drive north of Barcelona and situated at the southern end of the Costa Brava, Blanes is a colourful resort town. The long sandy beach is one of the longest on this stretch of coast and the town is popular with Spaniards due to its proximity to Barcelona.

The international airports at Girona and Barcelona are half an hour and just over an hour away respectively. Local road and rail links are excellent. There is a marina, a port, an aquarium and two botanical gardens. Rather unusually this resort manages to combine modern facilities with the traditional feel of a Mediterranean fishing town. For golf aficionados there is the Club de Golf l'Angel; other courses in the area include Santa Cristina d'Aro, Caldes de Malavella and Playa d'Aro. There are two water parks and in Andorra, two hours away by car, there is excellent skiing.

Property here is fairly cheap, as is the cost of living. Two bedroom apartments sell for as little as €90,000. Recently though there has been an increase in the number of foreign purchasers, so prices are likely to rise.

Platja d'Aro is a lively beach resort set at the mouth of a river valley. There are many good shops and several excellent seafood restaurants in this busy resort, all of which offer great value. Platja d'Aro has a 3km long stretch of well-serviced sandy beach and the town is also ideally located for day tripping – Barcelona can be reached in less than two hours. Inland from Platja d'Aro begin the foothills of the Gavarres range, ideal for hiking, walking and horse-riding.

Typical Properties For Sale on the Costa Brava

Location	Type	Description	Price
L'Escala	House	3 bedrooms, 2 bathrooms, 2 garages. Roof terrace, sea views. 200m from the beach.	€249,000
St. Feliu de Guixols	New apartment development	4 bedrooms, 5 minute walk to beach, communal pool.	€211,872
Tossa de Mar	Semi-detached villa	3 bedrooms. Panoramic sea views.	€299,000
Lloret de Mar	Apartment	3 bedrooms, balcony. Quiet area with few neighbours.	€110,182
Blanes	Spanish style villa	3 bedrooms, 2 terraces. Superb views of the Pyrenees. Beach and 2 international golf courses nearby. Large private pool.	€360,000
Platja d'Aro	New development	4 bedrooms. Own rooftop pool.	€719,293

Estate Agents for the Costa Brava

B&H-Casas CostaBrava-Inmo S.L.: Ptg. Tarragona 51 No 4, Apt. 119, E17130 La Escala; ☎666-760227; fax 972-775409; e-mail info@costabrava-immo.com; www.costabrava-immo.com.
Brava Casa Real Estate Internacional S.L.: Pani 83b (avda. Juan Carlos I), 17487 Empruriabrava; ☎972-456185; fax 972-456029; www.bci-immobilien.de.
Delfin Inmo S.L.: Av. Rhode 253, E-17480 Roses; ☎972-257664; fax 972-257691; e-mail delfin@ventamatic.com; www.delfininmo.com.
Porfinca: Avinguda Catalunya 19 (C252), Sant Antoni de Calonge, Girona; ☎972-661492; fax 972-660027; e-mail porfinca@porfinca.net; www.porfinca.net.
Real Estate Costa Brava S.L.: Plaça del Mercat 29-30; Sant Feliu de Guixols, Girona; ☎972-322410; fax 972-326971; sales@immospain.com; www.immospain.com.

BARCELONA

Barcelona city, much to the chagrin of the capital Madrid, is held by many to be the most lively and interesting city in Spain. Not only is it a huge industrial centre and port (with a population of three million), and the spiritual home of individuals of such startling originality as the architect Gaudí and Pablo Picasso, it is also the most liberal (or decadent, depending on your viewpoint) city in Spain and currently one of the most fashionable in Europe. The notorious red light district, the *barrio chino*, is now used as the term for similar districts elsewhere in the country. The sheer energy and sophistication of the place is a great attraction, especially for European nightclub goers, and the city is near enough to the Costa Brava (where many foreign residents are based) to make it regular port of call for those who want a change of pace.

Work on the famous Gaudí cathedral, La Sagrada Familia, started in 1882 and left unfinished after the architect was killed by a tram in 1926, has continued (controversially) and the cathedral is likely to be completed in the next twenty years or so. For years it remained open to the skies and many Barcelonans would have preferred to see it left that way, as a monument to its creator. The facilities left behind by the Olympic Games in 1992 are another attraction, as is the Picasso Museum on the Carrer de Montcada.

Barcelona airport, Prat, is 14km from the city centre and although the airports of Gerona and Reus are further away, the low cost fares available to these airports may make the extra journey worthwhile.

Property in the city itself is fairly expensive. Property prices soared by nearly 20% in 2003. In the city centre it is very rare to find anything other than apartments. For those looking to buy townhouses and villas, these are mainly located in the north (Pedralbes, Tres Torres and Sarria) and west (Les Corts) of the city.

Period two-bedroom apartments in the Ciutat Vella fetch around €140,000-€240,000, while large three bedroom apartments in Eixample can fetch between €220,000 and €780,000. In top notch central areas expect to pay around €5,890 per square metre of apartment. The price drops the further away from the centre of the city a property is. Cheaper, more outlying areas such as Gracia, west of Eixample, has real estate selling at around €900 per square metre. A very desirable area for modern apartments is Vila Olimpica down by the port.

Prices in Barcelona are rising so rapidly at the moment that capital gain on your investment should be substantial. Also those looking to let out property will find that Barcelona's status as the conference capital of the Mediterranean creates high demand for short-term lets.

Typical Properties for Sale in Barcelona

Location	Type	Description	Price
Pedralbes (north Barcelona)	Townhouse	3 bedrooms, spacious living area, quiet location.	€375,000
Gracia (half a mile north of central Barcelona)	Apartment	3 bedrooms, 3 balconies, large terrace with Jacuzzi. Lively area.	€250,000
Bario Gótico (central Barcelona)	Apartment	1 bedroom, beautiful area, small balcony.	€433,000

Estate Agents in Barcelona

Grupassa: Rambla de Catalunya, 123, 08008 Barcelona; ☎932-179508/965555; fa: 932-373945.

Mundo Agencia: C/ San Hermenegildo, N° 24 Local, Barcelona; ☎934-174079; fa: 934-1722937; e-mail david.deboet@grupomundoagencia.com; www.grupomund agencia.com.

Standing Inmobiliario S.A.: Passeig de Gracia, 61 (1° - 2ª), 08007 Barcelona; ☎934-871487/872625; fax 932-157080.

THE COSTA DORADA

The Costa Dorada (the Golden Coast), running south of Barcelona to the Delta de l'Ebre, is less wild than the Costa Brava and the closer you are to Barcelona the higher the cost of property. There are fewer coastal centres of population along this coast, with most development around Vilanova in la Geltrú and Torredembarra, and the terrain becomes less attractive and flat as you head south toward Tarragona. Sitges, a fashionable resort since the late 19th century, is the star of this stretch of coast but because of its status property here is more expensive than elsewhere and apartments in town especially can be very hard to find.

The Costa Dorada is less of a draw to holidaymakers than the Costa Brava or Costa del Sol and for this reason property is somewhat cheaper than on those coastlines. Against this is the fact that many of the resorts along the Costa Dorada become ghost towns during the winter, and both the busy main coastal road (the N-340), and the Barcelona-Valencia railway line run parallel to the beaches.

Calafell, Cubelles, Altafulla, Cambrils and Tarragona are all places worth looking for property due to their proximity to the beaches. Salou is one of the oldest and most famous resorts on the Costa Dorada and remains popular with northern European tourists as well as with the Spanish. There are several marinas along this coast and four golf courses. There are waterparks and Port Adventura, the largest theme park in Spain, is situated 7km west of Tarragona.

Although the Costa Dorada does not have the density of foreign residents of other places in Spain, the number of foreign visitors to the area means that there is access to English-language newspapers and magazines as well as the supermarkets stocking certain foods from 'back home' and pubs and restaurants catering for those after non-Spanish cuisine.

Most visitors to the Costa Dorada fly in to Barcelona Airport, which is about an hour's drive from Salou. The small airport at Reus – north-west of Tarragona – handles an increasing number of charter flights. If you will be working anywhere along the Costa Dorada, the Barcelona-Valencia railway line serves the main towns and resorts as it runs all the way along the coast.

Sitges. Few resorts can boast the prime location of Sitges – fifteen minutes from Barcelona airport, twenty minutes from Barcelona city centre, seventeen beaches stretching along four km of coastline, and a full cultural life and busy festive calendar. The intense cultural life and the organisation of mass events like film, theatre, music, jazz and tango festivals make Sitges today a cultural capital of prestige. Sitges has three pleasure ports: Aiguadolc, Garraf and Port Ginesta, a golf course, horse riding, tennis, swimming, bicycle promenade, bowling, the Natural Park Garraf (10,000 hectares of green), etc. The nightlife in Sitges is unbeatable. Discos, bars, pubs and cafés make Sitges one of the most fun, vibrant places on the Mediterranean.

Up until the 1950s the resort was filled with the weekend residences of Barcelona's wealthy, but their impressive city villas have now been joined by modern apartment blocks. Because of the popularity of Sitges property prices here are high.

Tarragona is the southernmost provincial capital of Catalonia. Two airports, Reus just 7km away, and Barcelona's International airport just 90km away, provide easy access. Its seaport is one of the most bustling on the Mediterranean. Motorways link Tarragona with Alicante and the French border and the rest of Europe and with Madrid and the Basque Country.

Tarragona is a city open to the sea, with an important seaport as well as a large fishing port. Its 15km of coastline boasts long beaches with fine sand, coves sheltered by rocky outcrops and dotted by green Mediterranean pines groves. Water sports: sailing, windsurfing, rowing, water skiing, scuba-diving are all served by the facilities and equipment at the city's Nautical Club and Maritime Club. Tarragona has become an important commercial centre, with good shopping in its pedestrian-only shopping districts.

Salou is the liveliest resort on the Costa Dorada. Summer visitors are attracted by the sandy beaches, which run virtually all along the seafront and also Universal Studios Port Adventura theme park just outside the resort. Many of Salou's beaches are long and wide, others nestle in small, secluded coves, along the foot of the rocky Cape Salou.

The area has recently undergone a major regeneration programme, so the popularity of the area is likely to increase, as are property prices. Several residential areas are currently being built and British buyers are first in line to snap these properties up.

Cambrils has more than 9km of beaches and more than 4km of illuminated seafront promenade. Home to the fishing fleet, Cambrils port is also home to the yachting marina; the place to come for sailing and all other sports related to the sea. The historic centre of Cambrils still has a distinct medieval air within its fortified walls and watchtowers. The most popular Cambrils dishes include the different types of romesco sauce, fish suquets, rice and noodle rosejats, grilled or fried mixed fish platters, seafood, paellas and sarsuelas.

Miami Platja is a resort situated on the coast 6km from Cambrils, 15km from Salou and 110km from Barcelona. Its gift are the 12km of beaches, a mixture of rock and sand, some of which have merited the Blue Flag of the EU for their quality and services. Miami Platja is close to the golf club of Bonmont Terres Noves.

The resort has a huge number of developments and is very popular with foreign homebuyers, largely because it offers good opportunities for capital growth. A well-positioned two bedroom apartment in Miami Platja costs around €150,000.

Typical Properties for Sale on the Costa Dorada

Location	Type	Description	Price
Sitges (15 minutes from central Barcelona)	Luxury villa	4 bedrooms. Panoramic sea views. Near Terramar golf course. Very large terrace. Large private pool. Beautiful garden. Attached guest house with bedroom, en suite bathroom and kitchen.	€1.9 million
Tarragona	Studio apartment	2 bedrooms, near to Tarragona port. Spacious living area.	€121,401

5 minute drive inland from Reus airport	Traditional stone farmhouse	2 bedrooms. Set in 9.8 acres of land. Fairly ramshackle house, but plenty of land to develop.	€370,620
Salou	Apartment	3 bedrooms. Beachfront with panoramic sea views. Large terrace.	€294,496
Miami Platja	Studio apartment	Beachfront property. Large terrace with sea views	€82,939

Estate Agents for the Costa Dorada

Dorfman Immobilien: Lista de Correos E-43300; Mont Roig del Camp; ☎977-179661; fax 977-172557; info@dorfmann.com; www.costa-dorada-casa-finca.com.

Finques Ebre Mont: Generalitat 81, 43500 Tortosa; ☎977-448778; fax 977-448348; e-mail ebro.costadorada@telefonica.net; www.ebro-costadorada.com.

Micasa Agencia Inmobiliaria: C/ Barcelona 16, 1° 1ª, 43840 Salou, Tarragona; ☎977-351227; fax 977-388054; e-mail salou@micasa-inmo.com; www.micasa-inmo.com.

Real Estate Tortosa: Rambla Catalunya 76, 3-4-3, 43500 Tortosa; ☎977-580610; e-mail 977580610@telefonica.net; www.gerhardtomann.com.

Rustic Catalunya: Rambla Democracia 8, 43780 Gandesa; ☎977-420548; e-mail properties@rusticcatalunya.com; www.rusticcatalunya.com.

THE BALEARIC ISLANDS (LAS ISLAS BALEARES)

Main Towns and Cities: Palma (Mallorca); Mahon (Minorca), Ibiza Town, Sant Francesc Xavier (Formentera).
Airports: *Palma, Mahon (Maó in Catalan), Ibiza Town.*
The Balearic Islands lying off the Valencian and Catalonian coasts have been under Spanish sovereignty since the Romans incorporated them into their province of Hispania (which comprised the whole of the Iberian Peninsular). Together, the four main islands of Mallorca, Menorca, Ibiza and Formentera make up less than 1% of the area of Spain, with a total population of around 750,000.

Because of government restrictions on development and limited land availability, prices on the islands are higher than on the mainland and it is difficult to find a well located property for less than €150,000. The islands are therefore the number one choice for buyers looking for luxurious properties, glamorous surroundings and the best weather. Homes on the islands are coveted by the rich and famous and Formula One's Schumacher brothers are among the many owners of multi-million pound villas.

The largest island of the group is Mallorca, which attracts an estimated three million tourists a year. Tourist development is mainly concentrated in small areas of the coast, notably around Palma and in the northeast around Pollensa. A three bedroom beachside apartment at Pollensa sells for around €320,000.

The other islands are mainly summer resorts and are fairly quiet out of season. The liveliest and most up-market is certainly Ibiza, which gained its reputation for tolerance towards foreign visitors in the sixties when it became popular with hippies and several rock stars bought properties there. More recently aficionados of house music and rave culture have made it a popular destination among the young. Menorca is more sedate and family-orientated.

Access to the Balearic islands from the UK is easy as there are numerous charter flights all year round. There are ferry connections to Ibiza from Denia and Barcelona and from Valencia to Ibiza and Palma. It is also possible to reach Mahon in Menorca by ferry from Barcelona.

Mallorca

Mallorca has become an extremely desirable place to live. The rich and famous, including Michael Douglas, Claudia Schiffer and Richard Branson have all made a home on the island and are helping to dispel the unfair myth that the island offers little more than high-rise hotels and cheap package holidays. It is certainly true that there are areas of the island that were ravaged by developers in the sixties and seventies, but these are more or less confined to the Bay of Palma and a few enormous resorts. Most of the island retains its staggeringly diverse natural beauty, with the striking cove beaches of the northwest coast, the rugged peaks of the Serra de Tramuntana, and an array of charming old towns. The island's capital Palma has also been much maligned in the past, and those who visit more often than not have their preconceptions shattered by a lively, vibrant city steeped in history and culture.

It is estimated that there are 15,000 British residents on the largest of the four islands, although Mallorca lags behind the Costa Blanca and the Costa del Sol in terms of popularity. The largest number of foreign home-buyers on the island has always been the Germans, followed by Scandinavians and Dutch. However, the slump in the German economy has led to many Germans selling up and it is the British who are snapping up these re-sale properties.

Property prices in Mallorca do not compare favourably with the other Balearic Islands, or even much of mainland Spain. Demand on the island has pushed prices up.

The greatest number of foreign buyers are attracted to the southwest corner of Mallorca which has better weather, a popular coastline and exclusive residential areas. However, more and more buyers are considering inland villages, due to the lower prices and the lack of tourist activity. Those who live in the main tourist areas, particularly the east coast of the island, point out that the end of season exodus and the subsequent closing of businesses can be quite depressing.

Even on a relatively small island such as Mallorca, climate variations occur and the areas west and north of Palma enjoy the most favourable winters. The availability of leisure as well as the opportunities for mixing socially will also vary and buying in one of the more beautiful but remote areas of the island will necessitate a certain amount of travelling about.

Property prices in Mallorca are currently rising by around 25% a year and as long as development restrictions on the island remain, demand will continue to increase. Mallorca is therefore a safe place to invest if you can afford the initial outlay.

Palma. Around half of the island's population live in the bay of Palma and the city itself is beautiful and impressive, with bustling streets, grand architecture and a cosmopolitan outlook. Unlike most of the other coastal towns in Mallorca, Palma really is a Spanish city and is as vibrant and elegant as the cities on the mainland, with an extensive cultural life that includes theatre, opera and fine cuisine.

Cost of living is comparatively high in Palma, but job prospects are good because unemployment rates are very low. If you are thinking of relocating permanently to Palma, you will find opportunities in the services sector, and there is also a demand for professionals amongst the international companies that have chosen to relocate there.

If you are looking to buy property as a buy-to-let investment, currently Palma is the place to look. Demand for rental properties is very high even out of season and a two bedroom apartment in the city could command rent as high as €1500 per week.

Magaluf epitomises the damage that can be done by over-zealous and poorly planned development. Although the beaches are still undeniably attractive, the resort of Magaluf is filled with ugly concrete high-rise hotels and apartments, spilling into the neighbouring resort of Palma Nova. Not only that but Magaluf has for a long time been popular with the 18-30 crowd and is described as a twenty-four hour party capital, filled with nightclubs, bars and fast-food chains. There is very little of Spain to be found in this resort, but if it is Blackpool in the sun that you are looking for, Magaluf will certainly impress.

Buying property here as an investment may be a shrewd financial move. As with the rest of Mallorca, property prices are high but there is a high demand for lettings all year round and during peak times you can expect to collect around €1000 per week. However, your tenants will probably be groups of young people, which increases the likelihood of high maintenance costs.

Puerto Pollensa (Port de Pollença). The Badia de Pollença is a sweeping, horseshoe shaped bay, with sheltered waters that are ideal for swimming. The focus of the bay is Port de Pollença. Once a small fishing village, the town has retained its intrinsic character and charm and offers a relaxed and fairly traditional way of life, there are none of the noisy nightclubs and high-rise buildings of other resorts. Pollença is a place for relaxation.

Set in an area of natural beauty, Pollença offers long, sandy, blue flag beaches and a attractive backdrop of the Boquer mountain range. Many bars and cafes are centred around the marina which offers superb views across the wide bay.

Menorca

Menorca is the Balearics' second largest island, but unlike parts of Mallorca, it has remained relatively untouched by tourism. It has also avoided the twenty-four hour club culture that plagues Ibiza. Menorca's charms lie in its relaxed atmosphere, picturesque towns, stunning scenery and deserted beaches with crystal clear waters. There are more than a hundred idyllic beaches on Menorca and although the government here has been trying to improve access to the more remote ones, there are still beaches that can only be reached by foot. There is nothing more satisfying than a scenic hike to your own private beach.

Demand is increasing on Menorca as more and more people are attracted to the island's beauty and tranquility. Expatriates cite such aspects of island life as the minimal crime index, peace and quiet and the friendly familiarity of the locals as the main reasons for choosing Menorca as the location for their second home or full time residence.

The entire island was designated a biosphere reserve in 1993, and it is largely a rural green paradise, filled with ancient relics and monuments. Romans, Arabs, Catalans, British and French rulers have all at some point made their mark on Menorca. The British and the French occupied Menorca for most of the eighteenth century, making it the last part of Spain to be controlled by a foreign ruler. However, the islands most interesting history comes from the Talaiotic people who inhabited the island in around 2000BC. There are numerous undisturbed Talaiotic watchtowers, altars and burial chambers scattered around the island.

As demand increases, so unfortunately do property prices, which are in general slightly higher than in Mallorca, but still lower than on Ibiza. This rise, around 17% in 2003, has been exacerbated by new restrictions on further development. Currently no new building work is permitted at all, although rumours abound that this decision may be reconsidered in 2005. However, one of Menorca's main attractions is that it remains fairly undeveloped and on the coast, some of the Balearics' best beaches and secluded coves are virtually untouched.

Around 70-75% of property buyers in Menorca are British.

Holidays are not enough

According to Drew Galloway of Vil-la Inmobiliari whereas previously most people were looking for a holiday home, these days people are seeing the long-term advantages of living on the island and are looking to either retire there or split their time equally between a home in Menorca and a home elsewhere.

Potential buyers should be aware that from October to April the island is hounded by a strong northerly mistral-like wind known as *Tramuntana.*

Maó (Mahon). The island's capital, situated on the east coast of the island is a fairly quiet little town but it has always been popular with the British who have traditionally been the main foreign home-buyers here. This may be something to do with the Georgian influence in the town's architecture, the sash windowed town houses which dominate the town. There are only a few high-rise buildings. Maó is set in a natural harbour and is a popular destination for cruise ships. Despite the fact that it is a port, it doesn't have a squalid side. In fact the harbour is very attractive, with numerous cafés and restaurants.

Buying property in Maó is very popular with families who see it as an attractive, bustling city that is also safe for children. A townhouse in the centre costs around €250,000.

Ciutadella is a far more Catalan city. It was the capital for most of the island's history, until the British moved the capital to Maó in 1722. However, the bulk of the Menorcan aristocracy kept their palaces in Ciutadella and there is little of the British and French architecture that dominates Maó. Instead there are baroque and gothic churches, narrow cobbled streets and fine old palaces. There are a number of untouched little cove beaches near to Ciutadella, the best of which is Cala Turqueta – a lovely cove surrounded by wooded limestone cliffs.

Ibiza

Ibiza offers something to please everyone, from the culture, fashion and superb cuisine in Ibiza town and the stunning coves and beaches on Ibiza's coastline to the wild twenty-four hour clubbing in San Antonio and hippy chic in Santa Eulalia. Those worried about Ibiza's culture of excess will find that the clubbers and revellers are concentrated in Ibiza Town, San Antonio and Santa Eulalia. Away from the resort areas is a stunningly beautiful island with dense pine forests (the Greeks named the island Pituisa or 'Pinery') and towering cliffs and some of the best beaches in the

Balearics. The over-development which plagued Mallorca in the 1960s is far less visible in Ibiza and most of the island has an unspoilt rural air. Ibiza also offers a climate of almost perpetual sunshine.

Property on Ibiza is expensive and the island is home to numerous millionaires. The restrictions on development in the Balearics have caused prices in Ibiza to soar even more than on the other islands. Nevertheless it is a fairly safe place to invest as there will probably always be a ready rental and re-sale market for your property.

Ibiza Town (Ciutat d'Eivissa). Most of the residents of Ibiza live in Ibiza Town and it is easy to see why. The medieval part of the town (Dalt Vila) is a maze of narrow cobblestone streets, whitewashed houses and Gothic buildings, topped by the cathedral with its 10th century Gothic tower and illuminated clock which shines out across the harbour.

Property prices are high but you can make a great deal of money from renting your property out. During peak periods it is possible to make around €3000 a week from a property in Ibiza Town.

Platja d'en Bossa. Just south of Ibiza Town is the purpose built resort of Platja d'en Bossa. The resort was created to take advantage of Ibiza's longest blue-flag beach, which offers clear waters, safe swimming and numerous beach bars and cafés. This is a beautiful area to have a holiday apartment, but it is certainly not somewhere to consider moving to full-time. During the winter the temperature drops significantly and the area becomes fairly deserted.

Property here compares favourably with the rest of the island, although it is still expensive. A two bedroom apartment will set you back at least €220,000.

San Antonio (Sant Antoni de Portmany). Situated on the opposite coast from Ibiza Town, but in fact only ten miles away, San Antonio is the biggest and liveliest resort on the island and is swamped every summer by thousands of British clubbers, invariably on cheap package holidays. There is little to attract older visitors to the area as nearly all of the bars, restaurants and apartment blocks are designed solely to appeal to the swarms of British thrill-seekers, who are unconcerned by the sprawling, concrete, high-rise skyline. However, there are a few small sandy beaches at the resort and out of season, families and couples are able to take advantage of these. The spectacular beaches of Cala Conta, Cala Bassa and Cala Tarida are only a short ferry ride away.

San Antonio is trying to shake off its image as a haven for sun, sex, booze, and general depravity, but much of the damage has already been done. However, property is considerably cheaper here than on the rest of the island and offers far better value. In peak season there is a very high demand for rentals and those who want to avoid the all-night revellers could consider buying a holiday apartment here and renting it out in July and August.

Formentera

The tiny island of Formentera is the smallest of the inhabited Balearics. It can only be reached by ferry from Ibiza town (approx. 11 nautical miles), although there is a regular service every two hours. The island is only 35 square miles and is home to only 5,000 people, but for those looking to really get away from it all, Formentera feels like a new world waiting to be discovered. The island is yet to be spoiled by tourism development and there are only a handful of hotels and hostels, all of which close for the winter. The beaches are long, sandy and flanked by palms and pines, and they are never overcrowded.

Property on Formentera is not easy to come by, but those who are willing to persevere will find that there are a few small apartment developments and some villas and converted farmhouses.

> **Hippy heaven on Earth**
>
> Seven hundred hippies arrived in Formentera in 1968 and by the summer of '69 there were around 1,300 – more than a third of the population of the island again. Both Ibiza and Formentera became known at this time as 'heaven on earth' amongst the hippy communities and they would swarm to the islands for the summer months every year. But the summer of love was the hippy peak because in 1970 Franco, outraged that the hippies were bringing the islands into disrepute, had three thousand hippies forceably ejected from Ibiza and Formentera.
>
> The hippies' legacy can still be found in Formentera's second city, Sant Ferran at the notorious hippy haunt, Fonda Pepe's bar, which looks much the same now as it did forty years ago.

Typical Properties for Sale on the Balearic Islands

Location	Type	Description	Price
Magaluf (Mallorca)	Apartment	2 bedrooms. Part of high-rise block. 5 minute walk from the beach.	€150,000
Puerto Pollensa (Mallorca)	Magnificent country house	4 bedrooms – each with private terrace, 4 bathrooms. Built in 2001. 14,000 sq.m. of land. Private swimming pool and garden. 5 minutes from golf course.	€1.3 million
Maó (Menorca)	19th century Casa senorial	15 bedrooms, 1 bathroom. Needs modernisation.	€802,955
Ibiza Town (Ibiza)	Apartment	2 bedrooms, 2 bathrooms. Sea views. Communal pool. Quiet location.	€185,000
San Antonio (Ibiza)	Studio Apartment	Beach front apartment block. Sea views from balcony. Communal pool	€84,300

Estate Agents for the Balearic Islands

Balearic Properties: Cecili Metel 36, 07460 Pollença; ☎971-532221; fax 971-534506 e-mail info@balearic-properties.com; www.balearic-properties.com.

Fincas Eivissa S.L.: Carretera Ibiza – San José, Kilometro 1.5, Can Bellotera, Apartado 460, 07817 – San Jordi, Ibiza; ☎971-398185; fax 971-306771; e-mail fincaseivissa @interbook.net; www.fincaseivissa.com.

Mallorca-Residence S.L.: C/ Tous y Maroto, 6a Desp. B, E-07001, Palma de Mallorca; ☎971-214740; fax 971-214741; e-mail info@mallorca-residence.net www.mallorca-residence.net.

Menorca Homes: Beechwood House, No. 2a Wych Lane, Adlington, Chesh ire SK10 4NB; tel/fax 01625-828801; e-mail sales@menorcahomes.com; www.menorcahomes.com.

Terra de Sol: Puerto Portals, Local 44, 07181 Calvia, Mallorca; ☎971-676963; fax 971-677035; e-mail terradesol@wmega.es.

Vil-la Inmobiliari: Plaza del Carmen 3, 07701 Mahon, Menorca; ☎971-367852; fax 971-368566; e-mail vil-la@vil-la.com; www.vil-la.com.

VIS Inmobiliaria S.L., Paseo Vara de Rey 3, 07800 Ibiza; ☎971-300912/300738; fax 971-306952; e-mail info@vis-ibiza.com; www.vis-ibiza.com.

THE PURCHASING PROCEDURE

CHAPTER SUMMARY

- **Banking.** There are different current account requirements for residents and non-residents.
  - Spanish banks charge for everything and current account maintenance charges are consequently high.
- **Spanish Mortgages.** Usually a larger deposit (30% or more) is required and a smaller loan (only 50% for non-residents) is granted, than for UK mortgages.
- **Converting Currency.** To avoid losing on currency fluctuations when converting to euros, you can 'forward buy' at a fixed rate through a specialised company.
- **Spanish Wills.** You need a Spanish will for your Spanish property foreign wills are not usually recognised in Spain.
- **Estate Agents.** Use only API or GIPE registered agents as these are licensed and bonded and use accredited lawyers.
- **Types of Property.** It is usually much easier to buy new rather than old property. Old property requires a mountain of paperwork if you want to rebuild or modify it and it may be difficult to establish who owns it.
  - Buying property 'off plan' is very popular even though you may see only an architect's model or plan before you buy.
  - Some housing developments away from towns and villages can feel deserted and desolate in the winter.
  - Timeshare is hardly ever a good investment.
- **Conveyancing.** The total cost of conveyancing is about 10% of the purchase price.
- **Lawyers.** It is important to employ an independent lawyer who will protect your interests throughout the purchasing procedure.
  - Lawyers' fees are likely to start at about £1,000 or 1% of the purchase price.

FINANCE

BANKS

All banking activity in Spain is controlled by the Banco de España, which has its headquarters in Madrid and branches in all provincial capitals. Banks in Spain are divided into clearing banks and savings banks and there are also a number of foreign banks operating throughout the country.

To open an account in Spain you will be required to present your passport or some other means of proof of identification, proof of address, and an NIE number (tax identification number). It is advisable to open an account in person rather than rely on a *gestor* to do it for you. It is also advisable to open an account with one of the major banks as they are likely to have far more branches.

The two banking giants in Spain at present are the BSCH (*Banco de Santander Central Hispano*), which resulted from the merger of the Santander, Central and Hispano banks, and the BBVA (*Banco Bilbao Vizcaya Argentaria*). Other banks in Spain include the *Banco Atlántico, Banco de Andalucía* and *Banco Zaragozano*. Most large towns will have at least one branch of these banks and in the cities there will often be several branches, offering all the usual banking facilities, including mortgages and internet and telephone banking facilities. Standard bank opening times are from 9am to 2pm on weekdays and from 9am to 1pm on Saturdays, although these may vary from bank to bank. Internet banking has become popular in recent years in Spain and internet-only banks operating in Spain such as *ING, Patagon* and *EvolveBank* offer preferential rates of interest on savings accounts. Internet banking is obviously very useful for checking on your account and carrying out banking transactions while abroad.

It is best to open a bank account in Spain immediately on arrival – or even before leaving home. This can easily be arranged through the major UK banks – which all have branches in Spain – or through a branch of the larger Spanish banks that have branches in the UK. The banks which will provide such a service include Banco De Santander Central Hispano (Santander House, 100 Ludgate Hill, London EC4M 7NJ; ☎020-7332 7451; www.bsch.es); Banco Bilbao Vizcaya Argentaria (100 Cannon Street, London EC4N 6EH; ☎020-7623 3060).

If you use your property in Spain only as a holiday home you can have all correspondence from your bank in Spain sent to your main home address abroad.

ATMs

There are ATMs (automated teller machines) all over Spain and you can usually find them in the larger of the villages. Three ATM networks operate in Spain – 4B (the most common), ServiRed and 6000 and you can generally use any ATM to draw money from your account, although there may be a fee charged. As well as cash withdrawals, paying cash into your account and consulting your balance, some ATMs now allow you to carry out other transactions such as renewing your mobile phone card or making theatre seat reservations. Spanish ATMs offer you a choice of language of instruction.

BANK ACCOUNTS

Those who are resident in Spain for tax purposes may open the type of current account *(cuenta corriente)* and savings account available to all Spanish citizens. Non-residents may only open the current and savings accounts available to foreigners, which will still allow you to set up direct debits to pay utility bills while you are away from your property and keep a steady amount of money in the country.

The *Cajas de Ahorro* savings banks have branches throughout Spain which, apart from the Catalan La Caixa and Caja Madrid, tend to be regional. Many of the savings banks actually started out as agricultural co-operatives and many still act as charitable institutions – investing part of their profits each year in social and cultural causes. The savings banks all issue a bank card enabling the holder to withdraw money from the ATMs that they operate.

Spanish banks charge for just about every banking transaction imaginable and costs are notoriously high. Particularly high are charges made for the payment of cheques into your account and for transferring money between accounts and/or banks. Before opening an account be sure to ask for a breakdown of any charges that may be forthcoming, including annual fees. If you plan to make a lot of transfers between banks and accounts you may be able to negotiate more favourable terms.

UK MORTGAGES

You should ensure that if a loan is arranged in the UK then all of the details of this are included in the Spanish property contract deeds *(escritura)*.

The Norwich and Peterborough Building Society (www.npbs.co.uk) lends a minimum of £40,000 to people wanting to use a sterling-dominated mortgage to buy on the Costa del Sol – along the stretch of land from Gibraltar in the west to Motril in the East. *Norwich and Peterborough* has reduced the rate on its Spanish two-year fixed rate mortgage from 5.04% to 4.49% and it also offers a base rate tracker mortgage. The *Society* can lend up to 75% for a new property on the stretch of the Costa del Sol mentioned above but will only lend 65% for an old house in the mountains. Barclays also provides local mortgages in Spain and has 160 branches in Spain covering almost all the holiday areas including Costa del Sol, Costa Blanca and the Balearics. However, Barclays will only lend on property worth over €130,000 (about £91,000) and up to a maximum of 70%. Further information on the website www.mortgagefornonresidents.barclays.es.

Hove-based *Conti Financial Services* (www.mortgagesoverseas.com). also deals with overseas property mortgages and offers repayment and interest-only mortgages in euros. The *Abbey's* offshore mortgage service (www.anoffshore.com) offers a variable rate deal. The rate is slightly higher for a sterling loan than for a euro mortgage. To those who would rather pay the extra to have the choice of being able to repay in sterling the difference in rates of 0.75% may not seem much, but it will cream off a tidy sum from a house costing £250,000 or so.

SPANISH MORTGAGES

Many Spanish banks offer euro mortgages both within Spain and through branches in the UK. Spanish mortgage companies peg their rates to a number of different indices, offering an index-linked rate plus the company's percentage. You will need to provide the mortgage company with an identification card, a fiscal identification number, evidence of income and details of your financial situation and, if married, your spouse's consent may be required.

In Spain the method used to assess your mortgage is also a little different from that in the UK. You will have to put all your UK and, if you have any, your Spanish earnings and income forward, and get references from your UK bank. Any other borrowing you have will also be assessed. Although repayment mortgages still predominate, there are endowment and pension-linked options as well. The self-employed must have held such status for a minimum of three years and be able to show fully audited accounts of earnings.

Spanish mortgages generally offer fixed or variable interest rate mortgages, mixed interest rate mortgages and fixed repayment instalment mortgages. There will be additional costs incurred, related to the registering charge on property in Spain. Acquisition, construction and renovation mortgages are available.

Remember that if you take out a Spanish mortgage you will need to have the currency available in your Spanish bank account to meet the monthly mortgage repayments. There are likely to be tax implications and you will need to ensure that your lawyer explains the legalities in both countries to you.

Mortgage lenders deciding how much to advance a potential buyer, both in the UK and in Spain, will not take into consideration any possible income derived from renting out the property. However, in truth it may be possible to offset the cost of the mortgage against the income received from renting out a property and so reducing tax demands. And in effect the rental value on a property should repay the mortgage if problems occur.

Barclays offers euro mortgages through its Spanish subsidiary and other overseas mortgage companies include *Banco Banesto; Banco Halifax; Citibank Espana, Deutsche Bank, Caja Madrid* and *Banco Atlantico*. Spanish banks are not interested whether you have an existing mortgage in the UK.

OFFSHORE MORTGAGES

Offshore companies which own property in Spain are subject to an annual 3% tax on the property's rateable value (approximately 70% of its market value) unless the owners are prepared to submit the name of the ultimate beneficial owner and proof as to the source of the money used to buy the property. Once this information has been established and the tax levied – or so it is intended – the owners will then not find it so worthwhile to avoid capital gains and inheritance taxes; and the transfer of ownership of property through sale or death will become obvious. This is a highly complex issue and must be dealt with by an expert.

Offshore property mortgages are available through many building societies and banks. One such is *Abbey,* which has offices in Gibraltar (237 Main Street, PO Box 824, Gibraltar; ☎76090; fax 72028) and can provide a free booklet *Buying your home in Spain or Portugal,* and Jersey (PO Box 545, Abbey House, 41 The Parade, St Helier, Jersey JE4 8XG; ☎01534-885 100). Also the Newcastle Building Society (www.newcastle.gi) and the Norwich and Peterborough BS (www.npbs-gibraltar.co.uk) both organise mortgages in Spain from their Gibraltar offices.

Another organisation specialising in Spain is *Conti Financial Services* (www.mortgagesoverseas.com). *Cornish & Co,* solicitors, can help you set up an offshore mortgage or overseas trust in Spain. Their address is: Lex House, 1/7 Hainault Street, Ilford, Essex IG1 4EL; ☎020-8478 3300; fax 020-8553 3418/3422; www.cornishco.com). In addition Cornish have offices in Spain (Urb. 'La Carolina', Edificio Comercial, Ctra. Cádiz km 178.5, 296000, Marbella) and Gibraltar (Hadfield House, Library Street); and associate offices in Portugal and the USA. They also publish a short *Guide to Buying Property in Spain.*

Useful addresses

Banco Halifax Hispania: ☎01422-332 466 (UK); 902 310 100 (Spain); www.Halifax.es.

Conti Financial Services: 204 Church Road, Hove, Sussex BN3 2DJ; free phone 0800-970 0985; ☎01273-772811; fax 01273-321269; e-mail enquiries@contifs.com; www.mortgagesoverseas.com. Overseas mortgage specialist.

Kevin Sewell Mortgages & Investments: 37A Market Place, Devizes, Wilts. SN10 1JD; ☎01380 739 198; fax 01380 723 249; email ksewell@netcomuk.co.uk. Independent mortgage broker.

Mortgages in Spain: PO Box 146 , Ilkley, West Yorkshire LS29 8UL; ☎0800 027 7057; fax 0845 345 6586; www.mortgages-in-spain.com. Mortgage brokers dealing with Skipton Building Society and Caja Duero – a Spanish mutual savings bank.

Norwich and Peterborough Spanish Home Loans: Peterborough Business Park, Lynch Wood, Peterborough, Cambs. PE2 6WZ; ☎0845 300 2522; www.npbs.co.uk. Also a branch in Gibraltar at 198-200 Main Street; www.npbs-gibraltar.co.uk

Solbank ☎020-7321 0020 or in Spain 902 343 888; www.solbank.com. A Spanish bank offering various mortgage and banking services.

TRANSFERRING FUNDS & IMPORTING CURRENCY

Importing money into Spain can take time and there are various ways of going about transferring funds including using a currency exchange broker such as Currencies Direct. Some solicitors can transfer money between accounts held at home and in Spain and for many potential buyers this may be the quickest and easiest way of doing things. For more details on this subject, see *Importing Currency* in the *General Introduction*.

Pensions. If you are having a pension paid into your bank account in Spain make sure that it is converted to euros before being sent, otherwise you will have to pay commission on the exchange. Also be aware that money left sitting in a Spanish bank account attracts little interest and it is therefore advisable to only take into Spain the money that you need and leave the rest offshore or, if you live on or near the Costa del Sol, perhaps open a non-resident account in Gibraltar.

Remember that if the vendors of the property are non-resident in Spain they are likely to want the purchase price paid in the currency of their home country.

Exchange Control. Spain abolished all its laws on exchange control in 1992 and at present there is no limit on the amount of foreign currency or euros which can be brought into Spain and no limit on the amount of currency and euros which anyone is allowed to take out of the country. However, any amounts over €6,010.12 are required to be declared to customs within 30 days.

TAX

There is no special tax relief for foreigners residing in Spain; capital gains and disposable assets are included as part of income and are taxed accordingly; residents are liable to pay Spanish tax on their worldwide income. This means that all income is taxable, be it from a pension, private investments, dividends, or interest.

Tax Reference Number
Property-owning non-residents as well as residents of Spain need a tax reference number – *Número de Identificacion Extranjero (NIE)*. You can obtain an NIE from the foreigners' department of a Spanish police station. You will need to fill out a form and present your passport and passport-size photographs. The NIE is the equivalent of the *Número de Identificacion Fiscal,* which is issued to all native Spaniards.

Most taxes are based on self-assessment. Although you are not required by law to employ a fiscal representative (*Representante Fiscal*) choosing to use the services of one is an important consideration when strict deadlines are laid down by the Tax Agency and where penalties are imposed for late payments. A fiscal representative could be a lawyer or a *gestor* and will need to be registered with the Tax Agency as acting on your behalf.

The Spanish Tax Agency (*Agencia Estatal de Administración Tributari* commonly referred to as the *Hacienda*) has a website at www.aeat.es with information on Spanish taxes in general and some pages translated into English. For more information on the Spanish tax system, contact your nearest Spanish embassy or consulate, or the *Ministerio de Hacienda*, C/Alcalá 9, 28014 Madrid; ☎901 335 533. More detailed advice may be forthcoming from the *Direccion General de Tributos*, C/Alcalá 5, 28014 Madrid; ☎915 221 000 or your local tax office.

In 1998 the *Ley del Impuesto Sobre la Renta de No Residentes* (Non-residents Income Tax Act) was passed by the Spanish government to tackle the problem of wresting some taxable income from the one million or more non-resident property owners in Spain. Under this ruling, anyone not resident in Spain, i.e. who spends less than 183 days in the country each year, is still liable for Spanish tax on income *arising* in Spain, e.g. from renting out property. In this case, the recipient of the income will be taxed in Spain and will have to apply for tax relief when they pay income tax in their own country. Additionally, there is a possibility for EU citizens who are non-resident property owners in Spain to pay Spanish taxes under the Spanish Resident Income Tax Act (*Impuesto Sobre la Renta de las Personals Físicas*). Non-residents must declare any investments in property over €3,005,060.52 to the Tax Agency. This is mainly for statistical purposes.

Taxes on Real Estate

Tax on Rateable Value. Between 1.1% and 2% of the value of the property, based on the *Valor Catastral* (the rateable value of the property). The percentage will vary depending on the town council where the property is located, and a 25% tax rate will be levied on that percentage. There are no deductions or allowances on this tax against expenses.

A non-resident company will be taxed at 3% of the *Valor Catastral* of the property that it owns in Spain. This tax is not levied if the company and shareholders are resident in a country that has a double taxation agreement with Spain.

If you own two properties in Spain you will be charged a property tax on the second (non-principal) residence.

Tax on Rental Income. If you are buying a property to let, the taxes applicable on income received will vary depending on circumstances and whether you are resident or non-resident.

CAPITAL GAINS TAX (*IMPUESTO SOBRE EL PATRIMO-NIO*)

Every time a property changes hands in Spain, taxes and fees are incurred. Capital Gains Tax is calculated on the net gain in the declared (as shown in the *escritura*) purchase price of a property when bought, and the price that it fetches when it is subsequently sold. There are certain allowances available on this tax for the cost of conveyancing and any improvements to the property. Those resident for tax purposes in Spain will need to include the Capital Gains in the tax return of the year in which the gain occurred. Capital Gains Tax for non-residents on the sale of a property is 35%. Capital Gains Tax is calculated at a maximum of 18% for residents.

If you own a property through a company and the property has not risen in value when you come to sell it is possible to change the ownership structure without incurring a large Capital Gains Tax bill.

There are several circumstances where the vendor of a property in Spain is exempt from paying Capital Gains Tax:

o   Those aged 65 years or over, who are resident in Spain and whose property has been the principal residence of the individual for at least three years.
o   If a resident of Spain sells his or her principal residence in Spain of at least three years and reinvests all of the proceeds of the sale into another property that will become his or her principal residence.
o   Residents and non-residents who bought the property which they are selling before 31 December 1986 will not have to pay Capital Gains Tax.
o   If a resident is 65 years old or over and sells his or her principal residence to a company in exchange for the right to reside in the property till death and a monthly payment.

There are several circumstances where the vendor of a property in Spain has partial exemption from paying Capital Gains Tax. For details of these you should ask your fiscal advisor. They are to do with the year of purchase and whether or not part of the proceeds of the sale are invested in another property that is is your principal residence.

INHERITANCE TAX (*IMPUESTO SOBRE SUCESIONES Y DONACIONES*)

Gifts on the death of an individual can bring high rates of taxation in Spain – sometimes at a rate of well over 70% on inherited wealth. The Spanish Inheritance Tax is paid by the persons inheriting, and not on the value of the estate of the deceased. If the deceased was resident in Spain for tax purposes then all his or her assets worldwide will be subject to Spanish Inheritance Tax; if the deceased was a non-tax resident then only the property in Spain will be subject to tax – the rest of the assets being subject to the tax in the country of residence. If the beneficiary is a resident of a country that has a double taxation agreement with Spain then he or she will not be taxed twice.

Property is valued by the Tax Agency at the market rate, or the *valor catastral* depending on which is the higher. Furnishings etc. are usually valued at 3% of the value of the property. Outstanding debts are deducted from the value of the assets, and stocks and shares and bank balances are valued at the date of death. Another point to recognise is that under Spanish law life insurance policies written in trust in the

UK are not binding should the policyholder die while a resident of Spain. The policy proceeds will be taxable.

SPANISH WILLS

After buying any property in Spain, the purchaser needs to draw up a Spanish will with a Spanish lawyer witnessed by a notary. This is essential, as under Spanish law if the foreign resident dies intestate (leaving no will) or without having made a Spanish will, the estate may end up being claimed by the Spanish state, as it is a difficult and lengthy process for a British will to be recognised in Spain. You should not include any property held outside Spain as this could lead to further complications. In other words, British and Spanish assets should be kept entirely separate in a British and Spanish will respectively. To validate a Spanish will you need to obtain a certificate of law (*certificado de ley*) from your consulate which states that the will is being made under the terms of UK national law, which includes a provision for the free disposition of property. Any lawyer will be able to organise this for you.

As a foreign national the Spanish civil code allows you to leave your Spanish assets in accordance with the national law of your country of origin. Once a will has been made you should ask for a copy, known as a *copia simple* from the *notario* who will keep the original. A further copy will be sent to the Central Wills Registry in Madrid.

One company which works with 'Property transactions and wills.' in Spain is *Bennett & Co. Solicitors*, (144 Knutsford Road, Wilmslow, Cheshire SK9 6JP; ☎01625-586 937; fax 01625-585 362; www.bennett-and-co.com). Other firms in the UK include *Cornish & Co.* (Lex House, 1/7 Hainault House, Ilford, Essex IG1 4EL; ☎020-8478 3300; www.cornishco.com), *Mr Stefano Lucatello, The International Property Law Centre,* Unit 2 Waterside Park, Livingstone Road, Hessle HU13 0EG (☎01482 350-850; fax 01482 642799; e-mail internationalproperty@maxgold.com ; www.internationalpropertylaw.com), *John Howell & Co:* The Old Glassworks, 22 Endell Street, Covent Garden, London WC2H 9AD; ☎020 7420 0400; fax 020 7836 3626; e-mail info@europelaw.com; www.europelaw.com, *Fernando Scornik Gerstein* (32 St. James's Street, London SW1A 1HD; email cedillo@fscornik.co.uk), and *Florez Valcarvel* (130 King Street, London W6 0QU; ☎020-8741 4867).

If you are a part-time resident in Spain it is a good idea to appoint a fiscal representative – who will need to be resident in Spain and through whom the tax authorities in Spain can deal with your tax liabilities. A fiscal representative can be a lawyer, a bank, accountant or a *gestor*. The Institute of Foreign Property Owners (*Fundación Instituto de Propietarios Extranjeros – FIPE*) is a membership organisation providing a support service and newsletter for a small yearly subscription. FIPE can be contacted at Apartado 418, 03590 Altea, Alicante, Spain (☎965 842 312; fax 965 841 589; www.fipe.org).

FINDING PROPERTIES FOR SALE

SPANISH ESTATE AGENTS – *INMOBILIARIA*

In Spain dealing with a registered estate agent means using an agency belonging to either the Agente de Propiedad Inmobiliaria (API) or the Gestor Intermediario de Promociones y Edificaciones (GIPE). These agencies display their certificate of registration and identification number on the premises and seeing these should give you some confidence in moving forward with that agency. Any API registered estate agency employs an API accredited lawyer and has paid a bond. They are then bound to act in accordance with regulations of the API and can be sued if they don't.

Estate agents in Spain tend to concentrate on the area around where their office is based and have a good knowledge of the possible problems or otherwise associated with planning regulations, utility provision etc., in their locality. Estate agents dealing with properties on the costas are very likely to speak English or be English. Agencies may be one-office outfits, or part of a large chain, or only deal specifically with the selling of their own developments and properties.

Spanish estate agents in general provide far less detailed descriptions of property than that which we are used to at home. Photographs of properties and details will be of varying quality, though in general the more expensive the property the better the marketing will be.

When dealing with Spanish estate agents, because of the sometimes 'cash in hand' nature of things in Spain, you may be asked to sign a *nota de encargo* before being shown a property or properties. This document protects the agent's interests, and ensures that he will be paid the commission should you go ahead and buy one of the properties on his books. This is because a property may be placed with several agents all of whom are after their commission from the sale.

Commission

The commission rate charged by estate agencies can vary from 5% to 15%, with property deposits averaging 10%. A higher commission is payable on cheap properties than on more expensive ones, and the rate will also vary from region to region – higher rates being charged in more popular resort areas, though the commission recommended by the API is, in most regions, 3%.

BUYER BEWARE

In 2000 a new law was passed in Spain, which relaxed the need for Spanish estate agents to be qualified and members of a professional body of estate agents. This has led to an unrestricted market and any potential buyer of property in Spain should be careful about with whom they deal. Make sure that *all* staff, or at least those representatives that you are dealing with, are API members – not just the owner of the business.

Some but not all estate agents carry professional indemnity insurance. It is also worth asking whether the estate agent has a bonded client bank account where any monies can be put until the sale of a property has gone through with the *escritura* signed in front of the notary. This will guard against paying a deposit straight to the vendor who, in theory could take the deposit and then sell to another buyer.

Once a deal has gone through, any issues that arise over the property will have nothing to do with the agents. It is therefore imperative to get a lawyer (an independent lawyer, rather than one recommended by the estate agency or the vendor) to check all contracts thoroughly before buying a property.

Useful Contacts

There are hundreds of estate agents dealing in property in Spain, too many to list more than a few here. You can get the names of about fifteen member agents dealing with property in Spain from the *National Association of Estate Agents*, Arbon House, 21 Jury Street, Warwick CV34 4EH; ☎01926-496 800; www.naea.co.uk (select the international section). They can send or e-mail a list of members specialising in Spain. Or contact the *Royal Institute of Chartered Surveyors*, 12 Great George Street, Parliament Square, London SW1 3AD; ☎020-7222 7000; www.rics.org.

Estate Agents

Eden Villas, Springfield,tranent Grove, Dundee DD4 OXP; ☎0800-781 0821; fax 01382-502082; e-mail info@edenvillas.co.uk; www.edenvillas.co.uk. Eden Villas are an experienced, professional, family run company specialising in quality service for clients looking for property to buy in Spain. With offices servicing the Mediterranean coast from the Valencia region right through to Costa del Sol, Eden offer advice to meet individual client needs, be that for investment, holidays or permanent residence.

Luna Alta Properties, Avenida Marina Alta (N332), Gata de Gorgos 03740, Alicante, Spain; ☎96-645 4040; fax 96-645 4160; e-mail info@lunaaltaproperties.com; www. lunaaltaproperties.com. Luna Alta Properties are an established Real Estate Company based in Gata de Gorgos, Alicante. With 30 years' experience they offer properties for sale, from Calpe to Gandia, & inland to Jalon, Alcalali, Lliber, Castells. Luna Alta can guide from start to finish in property search/purchase/sale.

Mercers Limited, St Marys Court, 39 Market Place, Henley on Thames, Oxon RG9 2AA (☎01491-574807; fax 01491-637699; e-mail sales@spanishproperty.co.uk; www.spanishproperty.co.uk. An agency with over 21 years' experience of selling freehold Spanish properties, with offices on both the Costa Calida and the Costa de la Luz. All types of properties are handled, from townhouses near the beach to detached villas on a golf course, whether for investment, holiday properties or for those planning to move to Spain.

The Spanish One-Stop Shop, Acacia Hall, High Street, Dartford, DA1 1DJ; ☎01322-391040; fax 01322-286630; e-mail mail@spanishone.freeserve.co.uk; www.spanishonestopshop.co.uk. An agency with an extensive selection of new and re-sale properties in southern Spain including the Costa del Sol, the Costa Tropical, Almeria, Mazarron, the Costa Calida and the north and south of the Costa Blanca. A complete purchase and after-sales service is offered.

ADVERTS

When you begin looking into the possibilities of buying a property in Spain you will very quickly become aware of the vast number of companies out there who are keen for you to do business with them. Take out a subscription to one of the property or lifestyle magazines such as *Living Spain* or *Destination Spain* and you will find the back pages crammed with advertisements placed by property developers, estate agents, removals firms, lawyers and insurers and accountants. The property pages of the weekend national newspapers almost always have articles on buying property abroad and these pieces will include sample prices of properties and details of the companies interviewed. Note that many property advertisements will include the size of the property (and/or land) in square metres, which allows you to compare prices regionally.

Magazines. There is a rising number of glossy magazines published both in the UK and in Spain. These are some of the magazines dealing with Spain and Spanish property:

Destination Spain: launched November 2003. Monthly. C/Sandunga 52, 03700 Denia (Alicante), Spain; ☎+34 902 454 557; e-mail destinationspain@marina-alta.com.

Everything Spain: launched December 2003. 6 issues a year. Tel 01342-828700; fax 01342-828701; e-mail esmag@brooklandsgroup.com; www.everythingspainmag .co.uk; subcriptions: Everything Spain, P.O. Box 306, Sittingbourne, Kent ME9 8BR.

Living Spain: 6 issues a year. Year's subscription £17.85.Subscriptions 01283-742970.

Spain: monthly. www.spainmagazine.info; ☎0131-226 7766.

Spanish Magazine: launched November 2003. Merricks Media, Cambridge House South, Henry Street, Bath BA1 1JT; ☎01483-211222; subscriptions 01225-786844; leanne.newton@merrickmedia.co.uk.

The Internet. There is an internet 'forum' website (www.spanishforum.org/spain) which has features and advice on buying property and living in Spain. Some other useful websites are: www.spanishpropertysearch.co.uk, www.which-spanish-property.com which covers an area from Alicante to La Manga, while www.overseaspr operty.shop.com covers the Costas Calida and Blanca, Alicante city and province; also try www.spanishproperty.uk.com, which deals with all types of property on Costas Blanca, del Sol, Calida and Almeria.

UK & English-Language Newspapers. Daily and weekend national UK newspapers all carry adverts for property abroad – mostly in the property sections, but also sometimes at the back of the travel pages.

You may want to take out a subscription to some of the English-language newspapers published in Spain – many of which are regional rather than national in scope. There are also a number of free sheets available from establishments such as bars, estate agents and tourist offices, which carry property advertisements. A full list of all English-language press in Spain can be found on the UK government run official website, www.ukinspain.com.

Property Exhibitions

There is no shortage of property exhibitions, which you can visit around the UK. On the whole, it is better to go to one of the larger ones such as the annual Viva España exhibition held at Olympia, London every January, which is not only a general exhibition about Spain, but also houses probably the largest number of property and estate agents, lawyers etc that deal with Spanish property, at any UK Spanish property exhibition.

Large international estate agents such as Hamptons International and Knight Frank have regular Spanish property exhibitions in London and Birmingham. The Spanish specialist estate agent Town & Country have a permanent Spanish property exhibition at their premises in Trowbridge, Wiltshire (☎01225-755811).

Besides the larger exhibitions, there are many events described as 'exhibitions', held in hotels, usually at weekends and they are advertised locally. These are usually just selling operations where the object is to get you to buy a property rather than educate you about Spanish property and deal with your questions in detail. Many of the sellers will not have even visited the properties they are selling.

WHAT TYPE OF PROPERTY TO BUY

OLD HOUSES

The British especially love old houses they can do up, but there are usually hoops of paperwork to go through to own and rebuild them. Old properties can be found in towns, cities, villages and in the middle of nowhere, but those on the coast or near it are the most difficult to locate and you may find you have to go exploring to find them. Before buying an old property, you should arrange to have it surveyed before signing any contract. Make sure that boundaries are clearly marked on both the property deeds and (more importantly) on the *escritura*. There are other points to consider including water and harvest rights, rights of way, future building plans for roads, factories etc.and whether there are any debts on the property. These are discussed in greater detail later in this chapter (see *Lawyers* section of *Fees, Contracts and Conveyancing*. You may also need to etablish who the legal owner is if there is no *escritura* (title deed).

FINCAS

Finca is a generic term used in Spain to describe a large estate or plot of land. Included on this land may be a farmhouse, orchards, olive groves, outbuildings, or a modern or derelict detached house. In Catalonia there are large grand farmhouses called *masiás*; in Andalucía such farmhouses are called *cortijos*. Due to their relative isolation fincas are highly sought after, especially those situated along or near the coast. Most fincas have been found and renovated. If you can find one, rebuilding it, apart from the expense entailed, will need the go ahead from the local council (see *Building or Renovating*). The *masiás* around Barcelona are particularly in heavy demand by both Spaniards and foreigners.

NEW HOUSES

There are several options when it comes to purchasing a new property, each with their own set of rules and pros and cons.

Buying Off-Plan (sobre plan)

This saves developers from going to the expense of building villas or apartments and then waiting for customers. They sell homes before they are built, or before they have finished building them. Clients will be shown the design and plans of a property with specifications, municipal permissions, a model of the development to be built, and perhaps the interior of a show house. Interested clients will be flown out to view the location of the proposed property and, if happy, will be asked to sign a contract. The contract will contain a clear description of the property, the schedule for completion and the dates when down payments on the property will be due. Note that:

○ The buyer pays for the house or flat in instalments and will pay an initial – often hefty – deposit, and the final payment once the home is completed (usually a year to 18 months later, if on schedule).

○ If a property has been partially completed on the signing of the contract, a higher initial payment may be required.

○ Pitfalls: delays can occur in the building process, and clients may not be given information on any further development planned on the *urbanización* (housing estate), or the surrounding land. It is therefore essential to know the development company's track record, and to have an independent lawyer check the contract before it is signed.

○ Landscaping of the property, access, utility provision, and additional maintenance charges are all matters that should be clarified in the contract. If not, they may come as a nasty shock after paying the final instalment.

○ It is vital to get a termination agreement backed up by insurance guaranteeing that every aspect of the property will be professionally finished before you move in.

○ You must confirm that any payments made before the completion of the property are paid into an escrow account – money paid into such accounts cannot be touched by the developer until the property is completed. An extra charge will be made for the use of such an option but the bank will then guarantee your money should the developer go bust etc.

○ It is a legal requirement that property developers have a bank guarantee to ensure that, should they become bankrupt before the completion of a project, the buyer who has paid instalments will not lose their money.

Self-build

If your dream is to find a plot of land in an ideal location and then have a house built on it, there are a number of bureaucratic hoops to be jumped through before this can happen. Potential builders can spend a year or more waiting for the necessary licences to be granted before being given the nod to start building. Finding a site can also be very difficult, and finding land to buy is practically impossible in the Balearic Islands since an embargo on new building has come into force.

The ratio of build (the size of the house to be built) to plot is determined by local planning authorities and it therefore makes sense to ascertain what this is before going ahead and buying a plot. Before buying a plot you should run checks on the general status of the land:

○ Is it in a conservation area where there will be tight regulations on planning permission?

○ Are there public rights of way over it?, or by-laws pertaining to water, hunting, grazing, harvesting rights?

○ Are there likely to be objections to the building schemes that you may have?

○ How costly will it be to install services such as sewerage, a telephone, electricity, or a water supply?

○ Are the ground/resources suitable should you want to put in a swimming pool or tennis court?

You will want to consult the town plan *(plan general de ordenación urbana)* at the local town hall, which outlines the areas that have already been given over to development where planning permission should be relatively easy and straightforward to obtain. Furthermore, the town plan will tell you at a glance whether the piece of land you are interested in, has major restrictions imposed on the size or height of proposed building projects. Also check the details of the separate plots around the one that you are interested in. Are they set for further development? Find out what types of regulations pertain to the surrounding land? These will give you a good idea of what regulations will pertain to your piece of land.

The vendor must be in possession of an escritura or other officially recognised deed of title. Get boundaries sorted out and marked on the escritura if they aren't already. It is likely to take at least two months for plans of the building project to be ready for submission to the authorities. To get a plan for your house you will need to get in touch with a firm of builders or an architect.

If you find an architect, you can work together to come up with an original design that will answer your needs and pass the building regulations. An architect's fee is typically 6% but may run to as much as 9% of the total cost of the building. Once you and the architect have finalised the plans building specifications *(memoria)* are prepared. These include such things as the type of materials to be used, the specification of window- and door-frames, guttering, tiles etc., and are submitted to the Town Hall. Once approved, a building licence will be issued and a fee will be due (around 3-4% of the total cost of the project, depending on the region).

The process of buying a plot of land will involve obtaining one escritura, while the building of a property on that land will necessitate obtaining a second.

Because so many foreigners are interested in self-builds there are a lot more clued up agents and developers than previously buying up plots of land, often with services and *permiso de obra* already obtained, to sell on to clients. Property developers also sell plots on their housing schemes *(parcelas)* for buyers to build their own house on. For example, in 2003 there were plots ranging from 1,500 square metres to 4,600 square metres for sale at £75-£160 per square metre available in Sotogrande on the Costa del Sol.

Be aware that IVA (Spain's equivalent to VAT) will need to be paid on building land at 16%; IVA at a rate of 7% will be added on to building costs.

Useful Contacts

Househam Henderson Architects: 3 Charlecote Mews, Staple Gardens, Winchester SO23 8SR; ☎01962 835 500, or in Madrid – Fernando el Santo 25, 1-D, 28010 Madrid; ☎913 081 555 (Spain); www.hharchitects.co.uk. UK architectural practice with a Spanish office.

Punta de Lanza: C/ Compañá, 30, 1°, 29008 Málaga; ☎619 641 635; fax 952 603 629; www.puntadelanza.com. One stop shop architectural service in Andalucía.

APARTMENTS

City flats *(pisos)* in Spain tend to be large and airy. There are a also a great many holiday flats from the 1960s and 70s around the coastal areas frequented by summer visitors and they come onto the market at reasonable prices. However, they tend to be smaller and less soundproof than more recent apartments, because they were built for short-let holidays and not designed to be lived in on a full-time basis. Older apartments may well be in need of some repair, either cosmetic or structural. Flats are generally easy to sell on, and are cheap to maintain. In the cities almost all property available will be apartments.

VILLAS

There are plenty of villas, purpose-built for holiday use, along the Spanish coastline. A detached villa will sell for more than an equivalent-sized ordinary house in town but will give more privacy as villas tend to be set in their own grounds. Most villas are relatively modern and you are unlikely to have a problem with access to water, electricity and telephone connections and drainage.

HOUSES

Houses in towns and villages are the best way to get absorbed into Spanish life, even though you will always be a foreigner. Houses in villages and towns tend to have shady, rather dark rooms with small patio areas at the back of the property. Properties in the centre of villages are generally in terraces and may come with roof terraces – typical in the south of Spain. Get a surveyor to check this type of house as they are usually aged and may need rewiring, or re-plumbing, or to have some structural work done. Such houses in the villages and towns can have a great deal of character, far more than the modern developments and bring the added bonus of placing you right in the heart of Spanish life.

URBANIZACIÓNES

Visit any property exhibition and you will see a variety of *urbanizaciónes* (property on housing estates) on offer – from studio and duplex apartments to semi-detached houses and detached villas on huge landscaped estates. You will also come across a number of different purchasing options available to the prospective buyer – timeshare, leaseback and outright sale. Because beach frontage property is now at a premium in Spain it may well be worth investing in an *urbanización* further inland. If you decide to buy into an *urbanización* away from the beaches or without a sea view you are going to get more for your money in terms of the size of the property and the amount of surrounding land.

DESOLATE IN WINTER?

Some *urbanizaciónes* are part of towns and villages while others may have been developed around a marina or golf course (which may mean that they are away from communication centres and correspondingly may become rather desolate places out of season – beware). You may find developments that appear to be entirely populated by one nationality, or are very insular, or where everyone clusters around the communal swimming pool and makes for the local bar every evening – giving a feeling of homely community where you will meet and become life-long friends with people like yourself. Owners of properties on *urbanizaciónes* may be mainly retirees, or the majority may only visit for a few weeks a year leaving the place a bit of a ghost-town for much of the rest of the time.

The advantages of *urbanizaciónes* is that they can make for a readymade social circle, security will be less of a problem if there are friendly neighbours always around, and cheaper properties can be found in otherwise expensive areas. It is also likely to be easier to sell on such properties. The disadvantages of *urbanizaciónes* are the possibility of higher community charges for maintenance of the estate (you will be part of a *comunidad de propietorios* – see below), a lack of privacy and space, and the worry of difficult, noisy, nosey or boring neighbours.

La Comunidad de Propietarios (Community of Owners)

Buying an apartment in a block, or a villa in an *urbanización* will involve you joining a *comunidad de propietarios* whereby you will be involved in the running of the apartment block or estate. This involves attending meetings to discuss the communal aspects of such matters as provision of garbage collection, the lighting of communal areas (including street lighting), and general maintenance. This system of co-operative maintenance is similar to the condominiums in America, though there is nothing analogous in the UK.

CUOTAS

The community charges (*cuotas*) payable by the individual owners will vary depending in the services used, amenities taken advantage of, together with the size of the individual's apartment or villa. It may be as little as €50 a month but is likely to be more. The community fees are not affected by whether an owner is a full-time or part-time resident in Spain. Failure to pay community fees by one or more of the owners can lead to all sorts of problems within the *comunidad*, such as being unable to pay its debts or provide some services. The actions of such debtors led to a law being passed in 1999 whereby action can be taken against debtors and, in extreme cases, the debtor's property may be auctioned off to reclaim fees due on it.

TIME SHARE & OTHER FORMS OF MULTIPLE OWNERSHIP

Timeshare

Despite having a bad name from some of the selling practices involved, timeshare is increasing in popularity in Europe, particularly Spain, as a low cost option, but it is hardly ever a good investment.

Sale and Leaseback

Leaseback is popular in Spain and is a certain type of contract whereby you can buy a property from a developer at a reduced price, which may be as much as a third off the cost price of a similar property. In return for this saving the property is leased back to the developer for a set number of years. The developer then takes up the cost of furnishing, managing and the maintenance of the property over the lease period and rents out the property to holidaymakers as self-catering accommodation. The purchaser retains the right to use the property over a certain number of weeks during the year, and is the registered owner of the property – named as such on the escritura.

This scheme is more likely to be found in upmarket, rather than bargain basement properties and is an option worth considering should you only want the use of a holiday home, without the complications of maintenance or having to find tenants when the property is empty. Leaseback makes sense if you have the initial capital to put into a property and are not in a rush to become a full-time resident of Spain.

CO-OWNERSHIP

Buying a property between several people can be beneficial to all those involved as long as everyone is happy with the contract, and periods of use of the property are settled well in advance as there will be times, such as at the height of the high season, over the Christmas or Easter holidays, when everyone will want to use the property.

BEWARE OF CO-OWNERSHIP DEALS

Some property developers offer schemes whereby four co-owners buy a property with the right for each owner to use it for three months a year, with the developer continuing to manage the property. However, such schemes are invariably more expensive that buying privately and the total cost of the 'package' will benefit the developer rather than the buyers, who will be charged a higher price for the property than would a single buyer.

RETIREMENT VILLAGES

The over-55s make up over 50% of the total number of foreign owners of property in Spain. However, this is not reflected in the number of retirement homes being built in the country. This gap in the market has led some developers to build top-end retirement homes and sheltered housing with 24-hour medical facilities on site, particularly along the Costa del Sol around Marbella, and along the Costa Blanca. These properties usually have swimming pools, restaurants, medical block, shopping centre, gym etc., and as with *urbanizaciónes,* additional service charges are payable (around €30-€180 per month) on top of the purchase price of the flat. The number of such places is growing especially along the Costa del Sol, Valencia, Huelva and Alicante. A one bedroom flat costs around £58,250, while a two-bedroom apartment starts at £78,700.

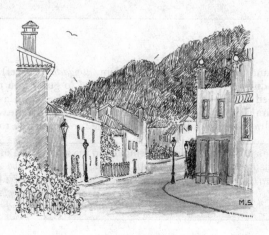

FEES, CONTRACTS AND CONVEYANCING

FEES

Total inclusive costs (lawyers, land registry, *notario*, taxes, bank charges, associates fees etc.) bring the overall costs of conveyancing to around 10% of the cost price of a resale property in Spain. Tax on new property is 7%, to which must be added 4% additional fees. The cheaper the property the more the likelihood of that percentage rising due to the minimum charges imposed by lawyers and others involved in the conveyancing.

TYPICAL FEES & COSTS ON BUYING A €125,000 (£87,500/$147,280) PROPERTY		
Notary Fees	Preparation of *escritura*, registering of ownership, stamp duty	€1,950 (£1,365/$2,294)
Legal Fees	Making searches on registries, preparation of escritura, translation of contracts, etc	€1,250 (£875/$1,471)
Plus Valia	Capital Gains Tax levied by the Town Hall on increased value of land since last sold	€120 (£84/$141)
VAT (IVA) 7%	Payable on the declared value of the property	€8,750 (£6,125/$10,302)
Connection Charges	Water, electricity, gas, drainage, telephone	€425 (£297/$500)
	TOTAL	€12,495 (£8,746/$14,711)
		Fees exclusive of VAT

LAWYERS

It is very important to employ an independent *abogado* (lawyer) to protect your personal interests during the purchase procedure and to guide you through the legal processes concerned with purchase. It is also vital to engage a lawyer who knows his way around rural laws as Bill Walsh found out with hindsight when he bought a manor house in Almería with outbuildings suitable for conversion to a hostel.

Bill Walsh explains the repercussions of employing the wrong type of lawyer
We used an abogadgo *for the purchase, but it was still fairly traumatic as he was a city lawyer (there weren't any local, english-speaking gestors) and didn't know much about laws affecting property such as ours and what licences we needed. For example we got reported by a neighbour for having a well dug without their permission. We'd already got four licences*

for it but he didn't know that within half a mile of a dried up river bed you need another permit too. He got the hunting laws wrong and he didn't bother to find out about the Andalucian tourist laws, which affected us greatly. For nearly ten years our business was illegal without our realising it and I am still unable to develop certain aspects that we had planned and he had told me would be 'no problem'.

A solicitor should check that the vendor is the legal (and sole) owner of the property and whether there are any outstanding charges or bills on it. The lawyer should be able to check that the property has, or is being built with, proper planning permission and has all the necessary licences. Once given the go ahead, the solicitor can then arrange for currency to be transferred to Spain, the title deeds (*escritura*) to be transferred into the buyer's name and registered with the Land Registry and for due fees and taxes to be paid.

Your lawyer should be either a specialist lawyer from home or an English-speaking Spanish *abogado*. Be wary of using the services of a lawyer recommended by the vendor or their estate agent, as their impartiality could be questionable.

The lawyer will also be able to:

O   Advise a client whose name should be registered as the owner of a property as ownership will have knock-on effects as regards taxation.
O   Advise on how to pay for the property – whether through a mortgage, re-mortgaging, forming a company, cash, etc., and how to minimise costs.
O   Arrange for Power of Attorney should it be necessary (see below).
O   Draw up the contract for the sale of the property or between a builder, architect and client.
O   Obtain an NIE number on behalf of the client (this number is needed for the payment of taxes and the purchase of property in Spain).
O   Recommend local tradesmen, surveyors, agents, mortgage brokers and banks that will suit a clients needs.

Finding a Lawyer. In the major Spanish coastal resorts local lawyers used to dealing with foreigners advertise their services in local free sheets and the English-language press.

Other Conveyancing

If you are hoping to buy property with land attached in a rural part of Spain then your lawyer will be useful for finding out about what the planning restrictions are in the area and if there are local bylaws in force for water, grazing or hunting and access rights on the land. You will also want your lawyer to check out where property boundaries end and begin as these may differ from what has been written in the *escritura*, what the owners of the property believe, and what is registered in the Land Registry. If you are buying into an *urbanización* or an apartment block where you will be part of the *comunidad de propietarios* you will also want the rules and regulations checked by a lawyer.

You should get your lawyer to check everything that is put on the table by the agents before signing anything. Don't rely on a notary to do the work that a lawyer would normally do.

Lawyers' Charges. The fees charged by a lawyer for their work buying a new or resale property are likely to be about 1% of the price of the property, although there may be a minimum charge (around £1,000). You will need to be aware that apart from the basic fee, should additional negotiations need to be undertaken on your behalf you will be charged.

Consulates and embassies in Spain will hold lists of English-speaking lawyers in their locality. In the UK the *Law Society* (113 Chancery Lane, London WC2A 1PL; ☎020-7242 1222; www.lawsoc.org.uk) also holds lists of registered English-speaking lawyers in Spain. The Consejo General de la Abogacia Española have their headquarters at C/Paseo de Recoletos 13, Madrid 28004; ☎915 232 593; fax 915 327 836; www.cgae.es. An exhaustive list of English-speaking Spanish lawyers throughout Spain can be obtained from the US Embassy website www.embusa.es/cons/attorney.html. From this last you can select the lawyers that handle real estate matters.

Useful Addresses
UK-Based Spanish and English Lawyers
Baily Gibson Solicitors: 5 Station Parade, Beaconsfield, Bucks. HP9 2PG; ☎01494-672661; www.bailygibson.co.uk. Susana Diez, head of Spanish Law Dept. is a Spanish lawyer and member of the Bar Assoc. of Bilbao.
Bennett & Co. Solicitors: 144 Knutsford Road, Wilmslow, Cheshire SK9 6JP; ☎01625-586937; fax 01625-585362; e-mail internationallawyers@bennett-and-co.com; www.Bennett-and-co.com. Associated offices throughout Spain.
Cornish & Co: Lex House, 1/7 Hainault Street, Ilford, Essex IG1 4EL; ☎020-8478 3300; fax 020-8552 3418; www.cornishco.com. Spanish office: ☎952 866 830; email cornish@mercuryin.es. Gibraltar office: ☎41800; email cornish@gibnet.gi.
John Howell & Co: The Old Glassworks, 22 Endell Street, Covent Garden, London WC2H 9AD; ☎020 7420 0400; fax 020 7836 3626; e-mail info@europelaw.com; www.europelaw.com.
De Pinna Notaries: 35 Piccadilly, London W1J 0LJ; ☎020-7208 2900; fax 020-7208 0066; www.depinna.co.uk.
Hector Diaz: 14 Old Square, Lincoln's Inn, London WC2A 3UB; ☎020-7404 9349; fax 020-7404 9348; www.hectordiaz.co.uk; e-mail hdiaz@hectordiaz.co.uk. The majority of this firm's work is property-related.
Javier de Juan: 36 Greyhound Road, London W6 8NX; ☎020-7381 0470; fax 020-7381-4155; www.spanishlaw.org.uk. All procedures to do with property purchase: conveyancing, wills, mortgages and insurance.
Mr Stefano Lucatello,The International Property Law Centre, Unit 2 Waterside Park, Liv-

ingstone Road, Hessle HU13 0EG; ☎01482 350-850; fax 01482 642799; e-mail internationalproperty@maxgold.com; www.internationalpropertylaw.com.
M Florez Valcarcel: 130 King Street, London W6 0QU; tel/fax 020-8741 4867. Property lawyer.

English-Speaking Spanish-Based Lawyers

Anderson & Asociados Abogados: Centro Dona Pepa Local 1-2 Urb Reserva de Marbella, Ctra. Nac. 340, km. 193,6 Marbella 29600; ☎952 932 997; fax 952 934 902; www.andersonabogados.com specialist in property conveyancing, based on the Costa del Sol.
Buño Leon: Pintor Lorenzo Casanova, 66, 1ºA, 03003 Alicante; ☎+34 965 92 18 53; fax +34 965 92 14 50; www.cbleon-abogados.com/ingles; e-mail bufeteba@terra.es. General lawyer, based in central Alicante. Has a foreigners real estate transaction department.
De Cotta McKenna y Santafé Abogado: Centro Commercial Valdepinos 1 y 3A, Urbanización Calypsoi, 2964 Mijas-Costa; ☎+34 952 931 781; fax +34 952 933 547; e-mail cottalaw@cybonline.com, and another office at C/. Diputación, 6-2º A Nerja, 29780 Malaga; tel+34 952 527 014; fax +34 952 523 428. Deals with rural and inland properties, rentals and all conveyancing matters. Has international clients including Dutch and French.

INSPECTIONS AND SURVEYS

Spaniards, in common with some other European countries' nationals, tend not to bother with a survey when buying property. However, if you are buying a property on a mortgage, the lenders often require a survey, even if it is only to provide an appraisal of the purchase price.

For new properties, and property that is less than ten years old, all builders must guarantee their work against major structural defects for a decade. However, should you be buying an older resale property, or even a derelict building that you are hoping to renovate, you would be wise to get a survey done.

Inspections. When viewing a property that you are interested in, look for signs of subsidence, bowing walls, damp patches or strange smells. Check for dry rot (stick a knife into windowsills and other likely areas where damp may have struck), a leaking roof (stains on the ceilings), cracks or fractures in the walls. You should also check the state of all the plumbing, electrics, and water heating systems, as well as the drainage and water provision. If there is a well on the land ask the vendor if it has been tested recently. Take your time and get a feel of the place – you will usually be able to tell if there are any structural problems.

If you are still not sure, a local builder may be able to give their opinion of the structural soundness or otherwise of the property. In any case, you may want a quote from a few builders as to the likely cost of renovation.

Surveys. A trained surveyor on the other hand will be able to give you a full and detailed report. Such a survey might cost £1,000-£1,500 depending on the surveyor, scope of the survey and the size of property). Spanish surveyors tend to concentrate on different aspects to their British equivalents, although those who are used to dealing with foreigners are likely to provide you with a report similar to what you would expect to get back home. Be sure to get any report that is presented to you in Spanish translated into English. Alternatively, you will find British RICS qualified surveyors such as Andrew Tuckett, (☎649 961 630; email atuckett@terra.es.) or *Gibsons* (urb Bahia Azul 75, Estepona, Málaga; ☎952 794 628; www.gibsons-spain.com) who may have moved to Spain and are able to carry out professional surveys and valuations. These surveyors will often advertise their services in the local English-language newspapers and property magazines. Although they will be able to give you a sound structural analysis of the property, unless they have the equivalent Spanish chartered surveying training they will be unable to advise on certain aspects such as building regulations.

Check List after a Survey
- Has there been a completion of a survey to your satisfaction?
- Has there been any alteration done to the property that has not been registered with the authorities?
- How much are the local taxes and charges?
- Is there adequate water, drainage, electricity and telecommunication provision?
- Is the vendor the legal registered owner of the property?

Additional Checks for Off-plan and New Build Property
- A full break-down of the materials, fixtures and fittings used in the building of the property.
- Be clear what you are paying for. What are the finishings? Will the surrounding land be landscaped? What will the property look like (have you seen a show home to gauge this)?
- Make sure that all completion licences (*certificado de fin de obra*, *licencia de primera ocupación*, and the *boletin de instalación*) have been obtained.
- Make sure that the developers or builders have obtained the necessary planning permissions to build upon the land.
- Make sure that the payment schedule and completion date are clear.
- Make sure the developers or builders are the legal owners of the land they are developing.
- Protect yourself and insure against the possibility of the developer or builders going bankrupt before completing the property.
- Check that the property has been registered with the local authorities for real estate taxes.

Additional Checks for Self-build Plots
- Will you be given a permit to build (*permiso de obra*) from the town hall.
- How much will it cost to build on the land and can you afford the costs – get quotes from architects and builders.

CONVEYANCING

If, for some reason, there is such a pressing time limit that you may lose a property that you are interested in unless you sign NOW, then at least try to fax over a copy of the contract to your legal representatives. Contracts are often short, containing the details of the vendor and purchaser, the purchase price, a legal description of the property, the date set for completion and possession of the property and the type of payment involved in the sale.

Whichever type of contract (see below) is offered to you, make sure it is in your mother tongue as well as in Spanish, and make sure that you have your lawyer check it before you sign. There may well be clauses that either you or the vendor will not accept and these will need to be negotiated, as will the purchase price and the amount of deposit payable.

Deposits

There are strict conditions relating to the repayment of deposits, so you must make sure that you are informed of these by your lawyer. When paying a deposit ensure that the money is kept by the estate agent or legal representative of the vendor in a bonded account until the sale has gone through. This will guard against a crooked vendor, or estate agent, taking your deposit and then deciding to sell the property to another instead.

Purchase Contracts for Resale/New Properties

When you are satisfied that the property won't be falling down in the near future, or you have decided, 'to hell with the expense, it's what I've always wanted...' then you will be ready to sign contracts with the vendor.

Note that there may be potential tax advantages as well as other savings at a later stage by registering the property in the joint names of a wife and husband or partner, or in the name of your child or children, or in the name of the person who will stand to inherit the property, or in the name of a limited company.

There are three differing types of contract that you may be asked to sign at this stage:

Offer to Buy. A formal offer to buy the property at a fixed price – the contract being valid for a set period of time. Should the vendor accept your offer then a non-returnable, negotiable, deposit will be payable and the contract will become binding between the two parties.

Reservation Contract. An agreement between the potential buyer of a property and the vendor or estate agent. This type of contract dictates that the property is taken off the market for a set period of time. A reservation fee is paid by the potential buyer, which, if a full contract to buy is signed within the set period, will count toward the full price of the property to be paid. If problems concerning the property are unearthed during the reservation period (such as the vendor not being the named owner on the *escritura*) and the potential buyer decides to pull out then the reservation fee will be lost. The clauses in this type of contract, therefore, need to be carefully checked.

Private Purchase Contract. A full and binding contract to buy. You will pay a negotiable deposit of around 10% of the purchase price, the balance to be paid on the signing of the *escritura*. Obviously, before signing such a contract you will want to get your lawyer to check it.

The contract will be prepared by either an estate agent or developer or, if you decide to buy privately from an individual, by the vendor's lawyer.

Purchase Contracts for Off-Plan Properties

For properties that are still under construction at the time of purchase, stage payments will be required during the construction period. It may be possible to arrange the payment schedule to suit the purchaser's individual needs and a typical payment schedule could be as follows:

- ○ On the signing of the contract: A deposit of 20% payable by bankers draft, personal cheque, cash, traveller's cheques or credit card.
- ○ After a set period, or on completion of a certain phase in the building work (e.g. completion of the exterior walls and roof): 25% of the agreed purchase price.
- ○ After a set period, or on completion of another phase in the building work (e.g. completion of interior, fitting of interior furniture and windows and doors: Another 25% of the agreed purchase price – the timing of this payment may vary and is generally dependent upon the building project completion date.
- ○ On completion or signing of the *escritura*: Outstanding balance payable.

With such contracts it is advisable to negotiate a clause in the contract that allows you to withhold a certain percentage of the cost price – say 10% – for a certain period after you have moved into the property as a guarantee against possible defects. This will ensure that the builders will come back to rectify any problems that crop up, and a good firm should be happy to provide this type of insurance. You may also want to alter the specifications of fixtures and fittings, type and style of tiles, faucets, etc., that have been specified by the builders/developers. If you do alter specifications there will be changes to the price structure and also to the completion date.

Make sure that the developer is the legal owner of the land, has obtained the required building regulations and that the required payments are held in a bonded account until completion and your taking possession of the property.

Registries

The Land Registry (*Catastro*) contains details of the physical and topographical details of a property as well as a valuation, while the Property Registry (*Registro de la Propiedad*) only holds the details of ownership and title. These two registries may have differing details of the same property and a potential buyer should check that the description of a property in the contract tallies with that in both the Property *and* Land Registries. It may take a month or so for the Land Registry to provide a *certificado catastral* outlining the boundaries and measurements of a property so you should ask for it as soon as you have found the property of your choice.

The Notary

The Spanish Notary Public – the *notario* – although a lawyer, does not give legal advice to either the vendor or the purchaser of a property. The job of the *notario* is to witness the signing of the title deeds (*escritura*) in his or her office located in the area where the property is being purchased and to deal with other administrative matters. Once the *escritura* has been signed, the purchase price of the property is then handed over to the vendor, or the vendor confirms that payment has already been received. Proof of payment is then noted down in the *escritura* which is then registered in the local Property Register. Before preparing the *escritura* a *notario* will ensure that the purchaser has received the property as stated on the contract and that the vendor has received the correct purchase price. The *notario* will also advise on taxes that are due on the property.

Notarial Fees. Notaries collect their fees from the vendor and the purchaser and these fees are charged in accordance with a sliding scale of charges set by the Spanish government. These will vary depending on the price of a property and the amount of work the *notario* has done on behalf of the two parties in preparing documents. Note that not all notaries will speak English and you may therefore need to be accompanied to meetings by a Spanish speaker.

Power of Attorney

The person buying or selling a property does not necessarily have to be present when the title deeds are signed in front of the *notario* and, for a fee, a Power of Attorney can be granted which will allow another person to attend on the vendor's behalf instead. If a Power of Attorney has been arranged outside Spain, it will need to be witnessed and stamped by a *notario* in Spain.

SIGNING THE ESCRITURA

The signing date of the *escritura* will have been fixed in the contract to buy, but the date may slip a little depending on the status of the checks on the property made by your lawyer. It should normally take place two to three months after signing the contract to buy a resale or new property but will take longer if you are buying off-plan. If there are problems such as sorting out ownership of the property or outstanding taxes on the property then this can obviously hold matters up.

When the *notario* has received all the documentation he or she needs to complete the *escritura* you should receive a draft copy. Though a notary is a trained lawyer who has taken further exams to qualify for the post of notary, it is not a requirement of the job to do the work of a lawyer and you should have your own independent lawyer check the draft.

Once everything has been settled the vendor and the purchaser (or someone acting on their behalf who has been granted Powers of Attorney) meet at the notary's office. The notary will read through the *escritura,* after which the two parties will sign the document.

Completing Payment. For properties that are ready for immediate occupation, full payment is made before signing the escritura and taking possession of the property. It may be that the money paid for a property is to be transferred to wherever in the world the vendor wishes to receive it. However, if the purchase price is paid into a Spanish account, then the importation of currency will need to be registered with the Spanish authorities and your solicitor should deal with this for you. Many people hand over a banker's draft at this point as it can be witnessed by the *notario* there and then, but other methods of payment are available (see *Importing Currency* and *Transferring Funds* in the *General Introduction*). At the same time the notary will collect his fee and inform the purchaser of any taxes payable on the transfer of property. Remember that if the vendor is a non-resident there will be 5% withheld from the purchase price, which will be paid to the Spanish Tax Agency on the vendor's behalf due to Capital Gains Tax liabilities.

After the signing of the *escritura*, the payment of the purchase price and all fees, the notary will give the purchaser a copy (*copia simple*) of the *escritura* and the keys to the property. The original (*primera copia*) will be sent to the Property Register and the new owner's name registered. It can take several months for the process of registering the change of title deeds as all taxes and fees must be paid before a property can be registered in the new owner's name. Once a certificate has been issued stating that the name of the owner of the property has been registered, the purchaser's lawyer should collect it and forward it on to the new owner.

WHAT HAPPENS NEXT

CHAPTER SUMMARY

- **Utilities.** Water shortages are frequent along the Mediterranean and in the Balearics during summer.
  - Always check that the previous owner has paid their utilities bills up to date or you may have to pay them yourself.
- **Moving Your Possessions to Spain.** If you have a second residence or holiday home in Spain you will not have to pay import duty on your possessions, though you might have to pay a deposit (refundable after two years).
- **Building & Renovating.** If you are buying a plot of land, check with the town hall to find out whether planning permissions and building permits will be granted and to find out what developments are in the pipeline for their area.
  - Building permits cost around 4% of the build.
  - If possible try to hold back say 10% of the builder's fee until the house has 'settled' in case any flaws reveal themselves shortly after completion.
  - Even very small alterations to a property must be approved by the town hall. If you do not bother with this the house may have to be altered back to its original state before you can sell it.
- **Making Money from Your Property.** The renting season on the Mediterranean extends from spring to autumn and even winter.
  - VAT at 16% is charged on short-term lettings.
  - Long-term tenancies can give the tenant the right to remain for at least five years, even if the contract states the rental is for one year.
  - If you are running a business from your home you will need a business licence.
- **Selling On.** There is a thriving market for resale properties.
  - A villa bought for £200,000 on the Costa del Sol in 1997 would now be worth £450,000.

SERVICES

Utilities

Electricity. The domestic electricity supply in Spain is mostly 220v or 225v AC, 50Hz and, less commonly in the more remote country areas, 110v or 125v AC. UK appliances should perform quite adequately, if a little more slowly, using an adaptor, while US appliances will need an adaptor plus a 220-110v transformer. Make sure you choose the right socket – flat pins for 220v or 110v. Light bulbs are usually 110v and are of the continental screw-in type. Buy the necessary adaptors in your home country as they will be harder to find, and more expensive, in Spain.

Organise meter installation or reconnection through your regional branch of the electricity company well in advance, as the waiting lists for both services can be very long. New owners of a previously occupied property will need to present to the electricity company the deeds of the property (*escritura*), a Spanish bank account number to pay by standing order, and some form of identification document. The electricity company will inspect the electrics in case they need updating – you will need to have this done before you can transfer the contract for electricity to your name. Billing is every two months and VAT (IVA) at the standard rate is added.

Gas. Mains gas is available only in larger cities and some large housing developments. Bottled gas (supplied in cylinders known as *bombonas*) is cheap (a large 12.5kg cylinder will cost approximately £5), and commonly used for cooking and heating in most homes.

Because gas is generally a cheaper form of energy than electricity many properties run as many household appliances as possible on it. There are safety issues when using gas, make sure that the property has adequate ventilation, that pipes are checked regularly to ensure that they haven't perished and regulator valves are in good order.

Water. Mains water is heavily treated and safe to drink but can have an unpleasant taste so most Spaniards drink bottled mineral waters.

Although there is surplus rainfall in the north, providing an adequate natural water supply, water shortages often occur over the summer months along the Mediterranean coast and in the Balearic Islands.

The mains water piped to private premises is metered, with charges calculated either per cubic metre used, or at a flat rate. To have a water meter installed, you will need to apply to the local water company office with the same documents as for the electricity company (see above).

Air Conditioning. Many modern air-conditioning units will also incorporate warm air heating systems. If you can't afford air conditioning then installing either fans on the ceilings or portable fans is a good idea, especially in the hotter parts of Spain such as Almeriá.

Registering with the Town Hall
You will need to notify the local Town Hall (*ayuntamiento*) that you own property within their jurisdiction, and register with the municipality for local rates (*Impuestos sobre los Bienes Inmuebles (IBI)*). Make sure, before you move into a property, that the previous owner has paid all the utilities companies' bills and the rates up to date as otherwise you will have to pay them.

Insurance

It is always a good idea to shop around to see what options and premiums are available. Ask neighbours in Spain for recommendations and remember to always, *always*, read the small print on any contract before signing. Do not underinsure property and remember that insurance will also be needed if a property is being built to order by a developer or builder.

The head office addresses of several major British insurance companies that have operations in Spain are given below; these may be worth contacting on arrival. For more information about insurance of property abroad see *Security and Insurance* in the *General Introduction* of this book.

Useful Addresses

Axa Aurora: Paseo de La Castellana 79, 28046, Madrid; ☎915 551 700. Mortgages and insurance.

Commercial Union Assurance Co: Via Augusta 281-283, 08017 Barcelona; ☎932 534 700. Mortgages and insurance.

Direct Seguros: Ronda de Poniente 14, 28760, Tres Cantos, Madrid; ☎902 404 025. Insurance.

Eagle Star Insurance Company: Via Augusta 200, 08017 Barcelona; ☎934 140 070.

Knight Insurance: Ed. Lance del Sol, Pta.I, 1ª, Avda. Jesus Santos Rein s/n., Los Boliches, Apartado 113, 29640 Fuengirola, Málaga; ☎952 660 535; fax 952 660 202; www.knight-insurance.com.

Ocaso Insurance Services Ltd: 3rd Floor, 110 Middlesex Street, London E1 7HY; ☎020-7377 6465; www.ocaso.co.uk. Spanish company specialising in holiday home insurance.

Plus Ultra Compaña Anonima de Seguras y Resuguras: Plaza de Cortes 8, 28014, Madrid; ☎915 899 292; www.plusaltra.es.

La Unión Española de Entidades Aseguradoras y Reaseguradoras (Spanish Union of Insurance and Reinsurance Companies): Calle Núñez de Balboa 101, 28006 Madrid; ☎917 451 530; www.unespa.es.

Sagatel: 020-8282 0330/0800-015 0751; www.saga.co.uk/finance/holidayhome/

Employing Local Staff

The minimum wage in Spain is €451 per month and if an employee works less than 40 hours per week, payment will be in direct proportion to the hours worked. For general information about employing local staff, see the *General Introduction*.

MAKING THE MOVE

Whether you are moving to your property in Spain for a trial period in order to see whether you wish (and can afford) to live there full-time, or whether you are moving some of your belongings there in order to set up a business, it is advisable to make a trip out to your property first, unencumbered with belongings. Check that all services are connected and that all papers and permits are in order. While you are in Spain you could look into the costs involved in hiring removals men or hire cars or a van from the Spanish end. Organise your financial affairs in Spain, set up direct debits to pay the utility companies, and organise the transferral of funds from your bank account at home to your account in Spain. Then go home, let your house, either privately or through a management company, or sell it, and begin your journey into a new life.

Union Jack's advice for moving to Spain

People whose job it is to know these things, say that moving house is a traumatic experience that registers right up there with bereavement and divorce. It seems that, no matter how much we may be looking forward to living in our new home, the business of packing up the old one can be very stressful - with so much to organise its often difficult to know where to begin. However, a little advice on how to organise your move can be a great help, so here are a few tips to help you plan your move.

Whether you're moving a three bedroom, house, a few boxes, or a car, the procedure is basically the same. The first thing that you need to do is think carefully about the items you wish to take with you and compile a room-by-room list. This will be very helpful when you start calling removal companies for quotes. If you are taking most of your belongings you should ask if they will send someone to do a free onsite estimate for you – if you have a large number of items most removal companies will be happy to do this. They will then be able to take all necessary measurements required and use their experience to accurately estimate how many boxes you will need for your breakables, clothes and personal belongings.

When you receive your quotes it is worth checking what each service actually includes, as prices will vary depending on whether the service, is door to door, includes wrapping and packing, storage charges, and insurance. You should also remember that if you decide to take extra items to the ones on your quote, or even leave some items behind, you should let your removal company know as soon as possible as this may well alter the final cost of your move.

Check that your quote includes an export wrapping and packing service, this will ensure that your goods are wrapped to the highest standard by professionals, which keeps your belongings safer, incurring less breakages, and improves the chances of a successful insurance claim in the unfortunate event that anything does get damaged. However, if you really want to pack any personal belongings yourself, ask to have boxes sent to you well in advance. As Union Jack specialises in removals to and from Spain we know the value of good export wrapping and packing and offer the service as standard with all our quotes.

When your belongings are delivered to your new home, try to check breakable items as they are unloaded – even with the best packing in the world accidents can happen. If you discover any damage check your insurance policy, and contact your removers. Most reputable companies will be happy to sort out legitimate claims sympathetically. Remember that photographic evidence is usually required by insurance companies, and this aids all concerned.

You may also want to inquire about storage. From our experience we know that people often have to wait to move into their new home and recognise that there can often be a period when you have nowhere to keep your belongings It is for this reason that we include a limited period of storage, free of charge, as standard.

The above is just a sample of the advice we regularly provide to people who move with Union Jack Removals – with over twenty years experience in moving people to and from Spain we've pretty much seen it all and are happy to pass on the benefit of that experience when you call.

For further advice, or a free quote, call Union Jack on 01395-233486 or visit their informative web site at www.unionjackremovals.com.

General Conditions of Import

EU Nationals. If you are moving to Spain permanently you will need to have proof of intended permanent residence in Spain such as a residence permit, which though no longer compulsory, is useful for bureaucratic procedures; if you haven't received this before leaving home the initial *visado de residencia* will suffice, but a deposit may have to be paid. This deposit exempts the holder from customs duties and will be returned once the permit has been produced.

You need an application form (*Cambio de Residencia*) requesting the Head of Customs to allow the goods free entry into Spain (obtainable from the Consulate) as well as an itemised list of the contents in duplicate, written in Spanish, which shows the estimated value in euros. These should accompany the goods or shipment and should have been legalised (stamped) at the Spanish Consulate. If you are sending the goods with a removals company, they will also need a photocopy of your passport, which has been similarly legalised.

Non EU Nationals. It may be possible to gain exemption of duties payable on importing effects:

- If the individual has not been resident in Spain during the two years prior to the importation of the goods.
- If the goods enter Spain within three months of the individual's arrival.
- If the goods are for personal use, are at least six months old and will not be sold in Spain for at least two years.

However, if the individual decides to leave Spain within two years of arrival, he or she will have to export the goods again (a relatively simple process within the EU) or pay duty on them.

Importing Goods for a Second Residence/Holiday Home. Another form of concession on import duties is available for those who wish to import furniture for a second residence or holiday home; this is known as the *vivienda secundaria*. Entitlement to this exemption does not involve taking Spanish residency but you have to pay a deposit (around 50% of the value of the goods), which will be returned on the expiry of a two-year period.

It is quite common for second home-owners to move belongings to Spain over several years.

You can obtain information concerning the export of household goods and personal effects from the Spanish Embassy or Consulate by sending an sae with your request. Spain constantly amends and alters its regulations regarding the importation of personal and household effects and the most up-to-date information will probably come from a removal company specialising in exports to the Iberian Peninsula. These can provide quotes, and should also be able to give information on Spanish import procedures on request.

Charges. The approximate charge from the UK to Spain is £120 to £150 per cubic metre plus a fixed fee for administration and paperwork. The amount will vary greatly on either side of this estimate however, depending on where in Spain the shipment is going and where it is coming from in the UK. The price per cubic metre should decrease with the volume of goods you are transporting. Some contacts for International Removers can be found in the *General Introduction*. The following companies specialise in UK/Spain moves.

Useful Addresses

Ambassador UK Ltd: www.ambuk@aol.com; ☎0800 0281 216. Specialists in UK/ Spain and Portugal.

David Dale Removals: Dale House, Unit 3, Langby Industrial Estate, Borough-bridge, North Yorks Y051 9BW; ☎01423-324948; Spain ☎+34 966 7847 13; www.daviddale.co.uk. Storage facilities in Alicante and Malaga.

The Old House: ☎020-8947 1817; fax 01323-894474; www.amsmoving.co.uk. Total UK/Spain coverage.-

Union Jack Removals: e-mail mail@unionjackremovals.com; ☎01395 233486; Spanish office: ☎+34 966 788 017; e-mail tommy.unionjack@terra.es. Two decades of moving people between the UK and Spain.

IMPORTING PETS INTO SPAIN

Before deciding to take your pet to Spain think carefully about the implications for both yourself and the animal. Local authorities in the regions of Spain have different regulations and it is a good idea to check what these are before importing your pet.

In 2000, 'Passports' for pets were introduced. These allow people from the UK to take their animals abroad and to return with them without enduring the compulsory six-month quarantine that was formerly in force. For full details of this scheme see *Removals and Pets* in the *General Introduction*.

Note that in some cities in Spain dogs have to be registered and insured, a dog licence required or a tax levied. Information on the registration formalities once in Spain will be found at the local town hall (*ayuntamiento*).

There have been no cases of rabies in terrestrial animals in Spain since 1977. However, several bats have been found to be carrying rabies virus in Andalucia, Murcia, Valencia and the Balearics; the most recent incidence was in 2000.

BUILDING AND RENOVATING

Once you have found a property you will want your lawyer to run checks on it to find out if you will be permitted to carry out such building work as you have planned. There are several local authorities you are obliged to consult.

The Town Hall (Ayuntamiento)

In Spain there are occasionally unexpected changes made to the categorisation of the different 'zones' under a town hall's jurisdiction. If this happens while you are in the middle of building on your plot of land you may find that you have built in the middle of a 'green zone' where building is prohibited, or in a rural area where no new construction is allowed. It may even be the case that building is only allowed on plots that are several times larger than the one you intend to buy. You or your lawyer will need to find out from the town hall about such things.

Depending on the authority, a property could theoretically be pulled down if it has been erected without planning permission; or a horrendous fine imposed. The local town hall is the place to go for information on whether planning permissions and building permits will be granted. The town hall also houses the PGOU (*Plan General de Ordenación Urbana*) – the Town Plan. The Town Plan will tell you if the land is located on an existing and approved urbanisatión (in which case planning permission should not be a problem), and the nature of the restrictions on the land. For example, if the land or property is on land zoned as *rustico* you will not be allowed to build. Also check the plots of land surrounding the one that you are hoping to buy. See what developments are in the pipeline if any – these could be possible housing developments or planned roads commercial enterprises.

The Land Registry (Catastro)

The land registry is where you will find a property's topographical description. The land registry holds details of a property's boundaries, its exact location, and a description of a property which will be invaluable when it comes to deciding whether all you have been told about a property or plot of land by the vendor is in fact true. The *Catastro* will also give the assessed value *(valor catastral)* of the plot or property, which is used to value the property for tax purposes.

The Property Registry (Registro de la Propiedad)

If you discover at the town hall that you will be allowed to go ahead and build/renovate, and are clear on the exact borders and boundaries of your land, you will also need to find out if the vendor is in fact the owner, and indeed is the sole owner, of the land or property. The Property Registry holds the title deeds *(escritura)* of any land or property and you will want to be sure that the developers are the registered owners of the land. Your lawyer will be able to obtain a *nota simple* from the Registry. The Registry can also check if there are any debts on the land or property, which you are liable for if the owner has not paid them. All these checks are the same as those applying to any property purchase in Spain.

Permits

If you are going to be carrying out major building work, either erecting a new building or renovating an existing property you will need to get a building permit *(licencia de obra)* from the town hall. Before buying a property in need of renovation or a building plot make sure that the vendor, and *notario* are aware that you will only buy subject to the planning permission and building licence being granted. Building permits cost around 4% of the cost of the build.

WHO CAN HELP WITH BUILDING AND RENOVATING

If you are thinking about building your own home, during the planning stages you will need to take into account all the associated costs that will crop up during the building – e.g. the cost of extending services such as water, electricity and telecommunications lines to the property, road access and drainage, etc., and remember that most quotes can only really be estimates. The true cost of a building project will escalate due to modifications that may need to be made to overcome unforeseen hurdles, or the changing of minds about what is wanted in the way of interior fitted furniture, tiling, bathroom appliances etc.

It is always advisable to discuss your ideas with your lawyer, a builder and an architect or surveyor before going ahead and buying a plot of land or a property in need of renovation.

Build or Renovate?

If you are looking to renovate rather than build from scratch, then ask yourself whether you have the know-how yourself to renovate a tumbledown property or whether you have the necessary funds to hire builders who do. Depending on the amount of work involved in renovating a property, new build often tends to work out cheaper, by up to a third, than renovation. Shop around and get several quotes as these will vary a lot, and will depend on the size of the property, or the planned building work, and perhaps on how *au fait* you are with Spain and your ability to negotiate in Spanish.

Architects

Employing an architect to design and oversee the building of a small villa may come to between £800-£1,600 for a small house, much more for a large villa. A registered architect, like a builder, must guarantee their plans and the instructions given to the builder for a period of ten years. Even though it may seem easier to deal with an architect from home, or someone who's mother tongue is English, a Spanish architect familiar with local building rules and regulations, and the local climate, is likely to more helpful to you in the long run.

An architect's fees will include plans (make sure that you are completely satisfied with them) and the supervision of the building project. The fee will also include the copies of the plans necessary for approval by the College of Architects before you can obtain the building permit and should also include the cost of preparing the *memoria*, or building specification. This states such things as the quantity and sizes of tiles, bricks, pipes etc, that are needed for the project, the type of concrete and cement needed, and the rest of the building materials to be used. It is likely that you will want to be involved in deciding on the type of electrical and bathroom fixtures and fittings, the colour and type of the tiles for the kitchen and bathroom, etc. Windows and doors and the kitchen units can all be discussed with the architect or builder while the *memoria* is being compiled.

Builders

Once the *memoria* is complete it is then given to the builder/s in order to get a quote for the cost of the building work involved. This quote will obviously be given after having taken into consideration all the materials listed in the *memoria*, and though it may change a bit as work proceeds, any alterations that you make to it later on will cost you extra – and you will need to amend the contract that you have with your builder accordingly.

When you sign a contract with the builder get your lawyer to check it to see whether there are any clauses included that may work to your detriment. The contract should include the *memoria*, the total price for the job with payment schedule and work to be carried out. The cost of the job, will need to be negotiated with the builder. Builders will often ask to be paid 50% before they start work with the balance payable in stages as the work progresses. Try and negotiate with them and if possible include a clause in the contract whereby you hold back say 10% of the total for a period to insure against possible building flaws or defects. Such things may not be evident until the house has managed to 'settle'.

Bill Walsh lives in Almería, where he bought a manor and estate buildings ripe for conversion and he has a lot of experience with builders.

Bill Walsh has dealt with many local builders and tradesmen

Our first builder was excellent. He retired before we'd finished phase one. Our second builder was good himself, but most of his team were poor. I've had a problem with a drain for nine years because it was put in wrongly. My third builder was a criminal and took my 25% deposit and vanished. My fourth builder was a very poor builder with a team to match. My fifth builder is excellent and totally reliable. Most other Spanish artisans (electricians,

> *plumbers, carpenters) seem very reliable in their standard of workmanship and in turning up for work when they should. There are also British tradesman in this area; many I gather are working illegally.*

Any builder you employ should be covered by an insurance policy so that if they go bankrupt while in the middle of working on your house you will be able to claim compensation. By law, a builder in Spain must guarantee any work carried out for a period of ten years.

It is also advisable to remain, if possible, on site or nearby, while the builders are at your property. Also being aware of what is going on will ensure that the architect's original plans are being adhered to and that the fixtures and fittings are those that were originally agreed on. If you are unable to be on site yourself try to find someone reliable to stand in for you.

SWIMMING POOLS

With the amount of sunshine the costas enjoy, owning a home with a pool seems a must. Unfortunately, swimming pools aren't cheap – either to install or to maintain. The cost of installing an average sized pool of, say, 8 x 4 metres, is likely to total around €15,000. This price excludes the cost of heating. Even if you buy a property with an existing pool you will need to consider the costs involved in its upkeep and maintenance.

> A regular, rectangular pool is far easier to maintain than a freeform pool in the shape of a kidney or whatever, will be cheaper to build, and depending on the size will be better for actually swimming rather than 'lounging'. It will also be easier to find a pool cover to fit a rectangular pool.

The depth of pools in Spain is mostly around 1.4 metres – around shoulder height – and they are usually finished with either blue or green tiles, or the cheaper cement-based 'Grecite'. Filters, chlorine and heat pumps are expensive.

Because electricity in Spain is relatively expensive (and about three times the price of gas or oil) it may be an option – should you want to heat your swimming pool – to go for a heater that is fired by gas or oil or, even better, use solar panelling. If you do decide on solar panelling you will need to consider stainless steel for most of the installation, as swimming pool water and copper don't react too well.

Your pool should have at least a five-year guarantee.

MAKING MONEY FROM YOUR PROPERTY

RENTING OUT PROPERTY

Owing to the sunny climate in the south the renting season can extend into spring and autumn – and even through the winter – so potentially, income you could earn from property there is much higher than it is in more northerly countries. If your property is in a major tourist area – the Costa del Sol, the Balearic Islands, the Costa Blanca, etc., then demand is likely to be high. Demand is likely to be much lower for properties in some of the lesser known resorts, or tucked away inland. Grouped houses or apartments in low-rise complexes also tend to do better than individual villas; and there are very high occupancy rates in places like Alicante during the summer where there is a rising demand for long-term leases and quality residences to rent.

Many golf courses in Spain are surrounded by residential developments, which, although villas or apartments on these are expensive to buy, can provide a healthy return on your investment. Golfers flock to Spain to improve their handicap on these courses, especially during the northern European winter. In addition, the golfing fraternity tend to be fairly well off and will pay a good price for the convenience of staying in course-side properties. For those intending to rent out as an investment only, and not expecting to make use of the property themselves, buying an apartment in one of the larger cities, especially Barcelona, though expensive, will guarantee a regular flow of tenants.

Some estate agents dealing in Spanish property will arrange lets for Spanish property in the areas in which they specialise (and advertise in expatriate newspapers and elsewhere).

Note that VAT (at 16%) for short-term lets, and income tax, will have to be paid on earnings from rental.

It is a legal requirement for those letting out property on short-term lets to be registered with the tourist authorities. Subject to the property being deemed suitable for letting by the tourist authorities you will be issued with a permit. Although many owners are not registered there are fines imposed for non-registration.

Rental Contracts

In Spain there are two types of rental contract: short-term, known as *alquiler de temporada*; and long-term known as *alquiler de vivienda*. A short-term contract covers any period under a year, long-term covers tenancies of least five years.

Short-Term Rentals

Rental returns on short-term holiday lets are high and this kind of contract is probably the best option for foreign property owners since your property can be available for personal use during the year and you can avoid the possibility of not being able to evict problem tenants. However, it may also mean that during the low season your property will remain empty and you are receiving no income from it.

Short-term lets require a lot of management time, as tenants may be coming and going every week or fortnight, especially during the high season. Obviously, if you are resident in Spain and live near the property then this may not cause much of a problem and the cheapest option will be to manage the property yourself. You will need to be on hand to clean the property before new visitors arrive, welcome the visitors and hand over the keys, troubleshoot and provide information about the area. If you also have other work or run other businesses then managing your own rental business on top of this may become onerous.

Bear in mind that short-term rentals usually mean a lot of wear and tear on fittings and furnishings, and items will have to be replaced on a regular basis. Short-term tenants on holiday will probably take less care of the property than a long-term tenant would. However, this statement may be qualified if you are looking to attract very wealthy tenants.

Long-Term Rentals

Long-term rentals, regardless of what the contract may state, are for a minimum period of five years. Even if the contract states that the rental period is for one year, a tenant is well within their rights to renew the tenancy annually for up to five years under Spanish legislation..

Recovering a property before the five-year term is up can be problematical. In practice, it is fairly unusual for a landlord to recover a property from a long-term tenant before the five-year period is up unless, of course the tenant doesn't pay the rent. Seek legal advice before committing yourself.

Tenants' Legal Rights

- A tenant has the right to pass on the tenancy to a spouse or child.
- If a landlord puts a property up for sale and does not offer the tenant the opportunity to buy then the tenant has the right to annul the sale of the property.
- Should the landlord decided to sell the property a tenant has the right to buy the property if he or she can match (or improve upon) the offer of another interested party. There will be no obligation to sell to a tenant if they offer a lower bid than another party.

TAXES

Non-residents renting out property are liable for income tax at the rate of 25% from the very first euro of rental income. Even if a tenant pays you rent in a non-euro currency in a bank account outside Spain, legally this income arises in Spain because the property itself is situated there. Although many owners undoubtedly do let their property out on the quiet taking this risk is not recommended; and it is advisable to keep records of all income generated through renting.

Running a Business from Your Property

Anyone intending to make letting property a full-time business, or who provides hotel-type services such as Bed & Breakfast, or deals with a lot of visitors on a short-term basis will find such activities will be deemed to be a business; and therefore all income received will need to be declared, with 25% of the rent set aside as a witholding tax paid to the Spanish government; and an extra 16% VAT (IVA) added to the rent, which must be paid to the Spanish Finance Ministry. This tax is declared on Form 210, available from *haciendas*. The positive side of declaring new business status is that maintenance expenses can be deducted from rental income before tax is calculated.

SETTING UP A BUSINESS

Anyone intending to set up their own business must first of all follow a few basic but essential procedures. Depending on your level of fluency in Spanish you may find the services of a *gestor* invaluable when going about the bureaucratic procedures involved. You will need to apply to the local town hall for a business licence (*licencia de apertura*), which will be granted once the authorities are sure that the premises is suitable for the proposed business, that they comply with planning permission and that it is safe and hygienic. This can take up to six months. Detailed information on starting or buying a business in Spain can be found in the book *Starting a Business in Spain* (£12.95, Vacation Work Publications; www.vacationwork.co.uk; ☎01865-243311.

Employing Staff. If you are going to take on staff you will be required by law to employ at least one Spaniard, and comply with Spanish labour laws in connection with minimum wages, social security payments etc. It is possible to register as a self-employed person (*autonomo*) if running a one-person operation. In this case, it is necessary to pay a monthly contribution to the social security system (health plus pension). You will have to register with the Spanish Social Security Service for income tax and IVA (VAT) and you will require an NIE (tax identification number). You should also register with the Spanish National Health Service.

Useful Contacts – Professional Bodies in Spain
Architects: Consejo Superior de los Colegios de Arquitectos de España, Paseo de la Castellana 12, 28046 Madrid; ☎914 352 200; www.cscae.com.
Commercial Agents: Consejo General de Colegios de Agentes Comerciales de España, Goya 55, 28001 Madrid; ☎914 363 650; fax 915 770 084; www.cgac.es.
Estate Agents: Consejo General de los Colegios Oficiales de Agentes de la Propiedad Inmobiliaria, Gran Vía 66, 2a Planta, 28013 Madrid; ☎915 470 741; www.consejocoapis.org.
Lawyers: Consejo General de la Abogacía España, C/Paseo de Recoletos, 13, 28004 Madrid; ☎915 232 593; www.cgae.es.
Pharmacists: Consejo General de Colegios Oficiales de Farmacéuticos de España, Villanueva 11, Planta 6, 28001 Madrid; ☎914 312 560; www.cof.es.

PROPERTY MANAGEMENT COMPANIES

If you are not going to manage your property rentals yourself you will need a property management agency to find and vet tenants for you, but there may be an extra charge for this. Monthly statements are often forwarded on to non-resident owners detailing the income and expenditure pertaining to a property. Rental income may be deposited in the owner's Spanish bank account, sent to owners wherever they may be, or held for collection.

If you are buying solely to let, rather than buying for your own holiday or permanent use then it is a good idea to sound out property management companies to see where there is most need for holiday properties. Obviously, the costas and the Balearics require rental properties but within these large areas there will be some parts more heavily touristed than others.

Agents' Commission varies but most charge around 15% of the gross rental. Any repairs, cleaning and maintenance costs incurred by the agent will be billed to you and listed on your monthly statement. Management companies are likely to have contacts with the local council, banks and other offices and know about Spanish bureaucracy, which will be to your advantage.

You can also advertise your property and get rental customers' online bookings by having an advert on a property website such as Gecko get aways (☎0870 741 2700; www.geckogetaways.com; e-mail info@geckogetaways.com).

Useful Addresses

AWS Real Estate Services: Urb. Carolina Park, Edificio Aries No 37, Crta. de Cádiz, km 178,5 Marbella, 29600, Malaga; ☎952 827 705; www.aws-realty.com; info@theawsgroup.com. Rental and maintenance management, bill paying services on the Costa del Sol.

Ocean Star Services: Commercial 15, Avenida Rio Nalon, Los Alcazares, 30710 Murcia; ☎ +34 968 171512; fax +34 968 170003; e-mail stan@oceanstarservices.com. Sales and property management.

Home Iberia: Unit 1, St. Peter's Road, Maidenhead, Berks S16 7QU; ☎01628 631 999; fax 01628 638 666; www.homeiberia.com.English property management company dealing with properties on the Costa Blanca and the Costa del Sol.

Menorca Home Care: Apartado 524, 07700 Mahón, Menorca; tel/fax 971 377 090; www.menorcahomecare.com.

SELLING ON

There is a thriving market for resale properties in Spain. Resales may be carried out privately or by engaging the services of a registered property agent who deals with all matters including advertising the property, accompanying prospective buyers and dealing with the legal technicalities of the sale (contracts, signing before the notary, paying necessary taxes on the property etc.). The vendor (you in this case) does not necessarily need to hire a lawyer. Make sure that if you have paid the *plus valia* tax on the property when you bought it, it is paid by the purchaser when you come to sell, otherwise you will have paid the tax twice.

Capital Gains. Note that Capital Gains Tax is charged on the profit from the sale of property, and depending on how long you have owned a property before selling on, this tax could be as high as 35% for non-residents and 18% for residents, though there are exceptions to the rules (see *The Purchasing Procedure*). The longer you own a property, the less capital gains you pay and the more the value of the property will appreciate; rent it out, rather than go for a quick sale. A villa bought on the Costa del Sol for £200,000 in 1997 would now be worth around £450,000, which is far above rates of inflation.

There are a number of documents that you will need to gather together when it comes to selling on your property. These are:

- The *escritura*: this details any charges, mortgages etc. that there are listed as being against the property.
- Receipt of payment – of the *Impuesto sobre Bienes Inmeubles – IBI*: This indicates that the Real Estate Tax has been paid on the property to date. The IBI receipt will also show the *valor catastral* – the value of the property as assessed by the local authorities (though this may well be lower than the market rate).
- The *Referencia Catastral*: file number of the property as kept by the *Catastro* (Land Registry). The Catastro has a record of the physical characteristics of the property – boundaries etc.
- Copies of all utility bills – preferably going back a while to give the purchaser an idea of what to expect.
- Copies of any community charges imposed by the *comunidad de propietarios* should your property be part of an *urbanizacón* or apartment block.
- Copies of the transfer tax, stamp duty and *plus valia* tax that you paid on the

property when you originally bought it.

○ Declaration of income tax: Depending on whether you are resident or non-resident in Spain your tax liabilities through the sale of property will differ. If you are a non-resident the purchaser will retain a 5% tax deposit from the purchase price and pay it on your behalf to the tax authorities. If you are a resident you will want to make sure that your tax status is known by the notary and purchaser.

SPOT CHECK – SPAIN

Political/economic stability:	Democracy and liberal economy since Franco's death in 1975. Surprise displacement of right wing PP by socialist party in March 2004 due to M-11 terrorist attacks in Madrid. Spain is currently Europe's fastest growing economy. Investment in infrastructure is very high and unemployment has been reduced massively over the last twenty years, although it is still fairly high at approx. 10%.
Sunshine/climate:	It is possible to enjoy sunshine all year round – especially on the Southern Med coast and in the Balearics. Costa del Sol offers 3000 hours of sun each year.
Cost of living/taxes:	Prices in Spain are approximately 26% lower than in the UK, although the average household income is fairly low. VAT standard rate is 16% but there is a reduced rate of 7% for a number of goods and a super-reduced rate of 4% for basic foodstuffs and other essential items.
Accessibility:	50 million people fly into Spain every year. There are a huge number of flights and these are constantly increasing. Budget airlines have made it cheaper to fly than to travel by bus or train and it takes around 2½ hours from London to Madrid or Barcelona. New airports are planned in 2006 in Murcia and Castellón.
Property availability:	The market is very geared to developments for foreigners. New developments are being built relentlessly and it is possible to buy off-plan. Because foreigners have been buying property here since the 1960s there is also a huge market for resale properties.
Property prices:	Prices have gone up and up over recent years. Despite these rises, the average cost of a house is still at least €80,000 less than the average house price in the UK and it is still possible to find well positioned ruins, slightly inland for as little as €50,000. However, on the Costa del Sol average properties sell for around €251,349.
Costs of property purchase as a % of property price:	Around 10% on a resale property (includes lawyers, land registry, *notario*, taxes, bank charges, associates fees etc.). VAT on new properties is 7% and 4% must be added for additional fees.
Ease of purchase and ease of renovation:	There are well-established procedures for foreigners to buy property in Spain. Involves signing of the deeds (*escritura*) before a public notary, at which point full payment is made and the keys to the property handed over. For properties that are still under construction at the time of purchase, stage payments will be required during the construction period. Any renovation requires a licence, costing around 4% of the total building costs. Restoring an old building should be approached with caution and certainly discussed with a lawyer to ensure there are no issues over planning permission. Builders work to a high standard, but it is a good idea to get references before allowing them to start work.

Buying a House on the Mediterranean

TURKEY

LIVING IN TURKEY

CHAPTER SUMMARY

- Turkey hosts around 13 million tourists a year, less than one million of them from the UK.
- **The cost of living** is about 40% less than in the UK.
- **The economy** is starting to recover after a catastrophic collapse in 2001. Prospects remain uncertain.
- **Education.** Wealthier people usually send their children to private schools.
- **Health.** Turkey is a healthy country although smoking continues to be ubiquitous. Standards of healthcare in state-run hospitals are often poor, those in private hospitals much higher.
- **Shopping.** Choice is very limited compared with Western Europe.
- **Media.** Despite the wide range of newspapers, magazines, and television and radio channels, self-censorship continues to prevent the full range of opinions being heard.
- **Crime.** Turkey has a very low crime rate, especially away from the cities.
- **Languages.** The official language of the country is Turkish. In tourist areas English is widely spoken.
- **Property.** Property prices in desirable areas may be rising at more than 50% a year. However, in less desirable areas they are static. It's still possible to find bargains, albeit in need of extensive restoration.

INTRODUCTION

Turkey was slower than other Mediterranean countries to stake its claim to a place in the tourism market but by the late 1980s word was out about a country that boasted many of the same attractions as Greece – azure seas, sandy beaches, stunning archaeological sites – but which had, at the same time, a much lower cost of living. The fact that it was also an Islamic country where modern mosques rubbed shoulders with all-but-forgotten Byzantine churches added a whiff of the exotic to the mix although most holidaymakers were relieved to discover that they could still visit Turkey without having to adjust their behaviour too much. Since then the pace of modernisation/westernisation has hotted up especially in İstanbul and along the coast. Turkey wants to join the European Union, but so far the EU, for various reasons, has not shown itself amenable and no date has been set. Obviously, membership of the EU would fast forward Turkey's rate of development.

The inevitable result has been that an increasing number of foreigners are deciding to settle in the country. Many of them are Shirley Valentines that have fallen for Turkish men; others are couples retiring to live by the sea. However, a significant number are settlers who have decided to buy and restore one of the country's innumerable crumbling wood or stone houses. Relatively low prices continue to act as a strong draw although in the most popular areas they are rising just as fast as elsewhere in the Mediterranean.

By the standards of Western Europe Turkey is still a cheap place to live, with prices of many items roughly half what they would cost in the UK. Throughout the 1990s Turkey suffered from hyperinflation which made it difficult to plan ahead. However, since 2001 the price of many household requirements seems to have stabilised. Even so, it is safe to assume that if the country ever achieves its goal of EU membership the cost of living will rise as rapidly as it did in Spain, Greece and Portugal. In 2005 the government hopes to lop six zeros off the current cumbersome currency denominations. In theory that means that something which costs ten million Turkish lira would 'reduce' in price to ten Turkish lira. However, if the euro experience is anything to go by it is more likely that it will 'reduce' to TL11 or TL12.

It is also true to say that house prices are an exception to the general rule about prices stabilising. The cost of properties along the coast continues to soar, as does that of desirable properties in İstanbul or Cappadocia.

It is hard to make firm comparisons between prices in Turkey and the USA, and those in the UK because there are so many variables. On the up side, eating out usually costs a fraction of what it would in the UK. Petrol is cheaper as is car insurance. However, buying a second-hand car is roughly three times as expensive as it is in Britain or America. If you heat your home in Turkish style with a coal and wood-burning stove fuel will seem cheap by British standards. If, however, you install oil or gas-fired central heating a Turkish winter may cost you twice as much as an English one.

Anyone thinking of moving to Turkey also needs to bear in mind that the price of Western 'luxuries' can be many times what it is at home. A tin of cat food, for example, costs three times what it would in the UK or the USA. Coffee, cornflakes, Cheddar cheese, fruit yoghurts and anything similarly 'foreign' costs significantly more in Turkey.

HISTORY & CURRENT POLITICS

History

Turkey's crossroads position at the point where Europe meets the Middle East and the Caucasus has guaranteed it a turbulent and varied history. It can sometimes seem as if all the world's great powers have trekked through at some point, with the Turks themselves relatively late arrivals on the scene.

The Hittites, the Phrygians, the Lycians and the Lydians all left their mark on the landscape but it was the Greek colonists and the Romans who followed them who were most successful in stamping Asia Minor in their own image. When the Roman Empire finally imploded under its own internal strains and split into two parts, 'Turkey' became part of the Eastern, Byzantine Empire with its capital at

Constantinople (later İstanbul).

The Byzantine emperors fought a losing battle against invaders both from the Arab world and from Central Asia, and eventually the Seljuk Turks settled large parts of the country with their capital at Konya. Ultimately the Ottoman Turks got the upper hand, ringing İstanbul and forcing their way through its sturdy walls in 1453. The last Byzantine emperor, Constantine XI Dragases, died trying to defend the city.

The Ottomans quickly secured not just the whole of geographic Turkey but also much of the surrounding area, establishing an empire that, in its heyday, stretched as far as the walls of Vienna. But, like all great empires, the Ottoman one steadily sowed the seeds of its own destruction, growing weaker and weaker until eventually it lined up on the wrong side in the First World War and imploded. It was during the famous campaign at Gallipoli that Mustafa Kemal (later Atatürk) came to prominence and it was not long after the war ended when he began to lay the ground plans for a Turkish republic. The victors in the war eased his path by attempting to share Turkey out amongst their allies. When the Greeks invaded Smyrna in 1922, Atatürk took his chance to drive them out of the country; the end result of the Turkish War of Independence was that all the Turks still living in Greece and all the Greeks still living in Turkey were forced to change places, which is why in some parts of the country there are many fine old Greek houses standing empty. In 1923 Atatürk proclaimed the new Turkish Republic in what had been the heartlands of the Ottoman Empire and promptly moved its capital from 'Greek' Constantinople to Ankara in central Anatolia.

Politics

Since then the 80-year-old republic has had its ups and downs. Atatürk himself was a strong and unusually forward-thinking leader who pushed through a ban on the wearing of fezes, enforced a switch from the use of Arabic to the modern Turkish script and insisted on female emancipation, advising women to throw away their headscarves. Unfortunately the leaders who followed him were rarely strong enough to capitalise on this good start. Military coups took place in 1960, 1970 and 1980. In the early 1990s Prime Minister Turgut Özal did his best to introduce Turkey to capitalism and the free market. Unfortunately his premature death left his plans incomplete and the politics of the last ten years have been hogtied by internal contradictions that a series of weak coalition governments were unable to resolve.

In 2002, an 'Islamic' party swept to power in a landslide victory comparable with the Blair victory of 1997. Prime Minister Recep Tayyip Erdoğan had a history of Islamic activism which made him an unpopular choice of leader with the İstanbul intelligentsia. However, in his first year in office he moved fast to try and negotiate Turkey's admission to the European Union, pushing through controversial changes such as a ban on the death penalty that were seen as prerequisites for admission.

In 2003 Turkey suffered first from its proximity to Iraq and then from a series of bombs which exploded in İstanbul towards the end of the year. The result was a disastrous year for tourism, one of the mainstays of the Turkish economy. In spite of that the weak Turkish lira started to strengthen as the government brought inflation under control.

Turkey is a democracy governed by a prime minister and cabinet along familiar European lines. However, behind the scenes the army continues to hold significant influence and the only 'Islamic' government that had been elected before 2002 was 'persuaded' to stand down by army shenanigans. However, the nature of the 2002 election in which all the old political parties were seen off and their places taken by people the establishment had tried to marginalise suggests that the Turkish democracy is finally coming of age. Certainly it is hard to see the army removing Erdoğan from power, especially after his great popularity was confirmed by local elections in 2004 which saw his AK Party win power in town halls countrywide.

Parliament sits in Ankara where 550 MPs represent Turkey's different constituencies. Until 2002 they also represented political parties from all sides of the political spectrum but by the time of the 2002 elections most of the old parties had been so discredited that the overwhelming majority of MPs now belong to just two parties the AKP (Justice and Development Party) and the CHP (Republican People's Party).

GEOGRAPHY & CLIMATE

Although Turkey lies at the point where Europe meets Asia, only one per cent of the country is actually in Europe. İstanbul is unique in that it straddles two continents, the Bosphorus river marking the division between them. The country's north coast skirts the southern shore of the Black Sea which divides it from Russia; at the north-east end it soars into the Kaçkar Mountains as they rub up against Georgia. The western side of the country runs down the eastern side of the Aegean; many of the Greek islands are so close that they are visible from the Turkish coast. The southern side of the country is framed by the Mediterranean Sea, with the soaring Taurus Mountains, just inland, hemming in coastal development. Turkey's eastern side has potentially troublesome borders with Azerbaijan and Iran, its southern side with Iraq and Syria. Inland, the country consists of the vast Anatolian plateau with, at its heart, the extraordinary, volcano-generated landscape of Cappadocia, a maze of valleys and gorges with crazily-shaped 'fairy chimneys' jutting up from the ground.

A country as vast as Turkey (788,695sq. km) inevitably experiences a wide variety of climates. In İstanbul and along the Aegean and Mediterranean coastlines temperatures can rise as high as 40° C in July and August but rarely fall below freezing in winter. In contrast most of the east of the country is blanketed with snow from December through to April and temperatures in the south-east soar to unbearable levels in summer. The Black Sea has a more temperate, rainy climate although the north-eastern hinterland is snowbound and barely accessible for most of the winter. The interior of the country experiences great extremes of temperature, with snow on the ground from December through to March and then stifling heat in July and August. Except in the far east of the country almost everywhere in Turkey is at its most pleasant in May and June, and September and October.

AVERAGE MAXIMUM TEMPERATURES				
Area	**Jan**	**Apr**	**Aug**	**Nov**
Istanbul	8°C	13°C	29°C	10°C
Izmir	11°C	21°C	32°C	20°C
Antalya	13°C	21°C	32°C	20°C

CULTURE SHOCK

Given that 98% of Turks are Muslims it is inevitable that visitors will experience some culture shock. On the other hand, Turkey has had 80 years of secular government and a long history of intermingling with the western world so that of all the Islamic countries it is the most moderate and easy for an outsider to handle. Indeed there are parts of İstanbul and the Aegean and Mediterranean coasts where it would be possible to forget the reality of an eastern outlook altogether. On the other hand, no visitor to the east of the country (or even to parts of İstanbul, İzmir and Ankara) could fail to realise that they were venturing into places where people live life by a completely different set of rules.

Alcohol. Although Islam forbids the consumption of alcohol the Greeks who lived in Turkey before the arrival of the Ottomans were keen cultivators of the vine and even today many Turks turn a blind eye to this particular restriction. Once again the most relaxed attitudes will be found along the coast, although visitors to İstanbul and Cappadocia will have no trouble tracking down their favourite tipple. The one time when even foreigners need to be careful about public consumption of alcohol is during Ramadan, the Islamic month of fasting. At that time no good Muslim will touch alcohol and it is regarded as very impolite to imbibe in front of them.

Sex and Gender Relationships. In traditional Islamic society men and women never mixed with each other outside their families and in the more conservative parts of the country this is still the case even today. However, this traditional sexual segregation is falling apart not just along the coast but also in big towns like İstanbul and İzmir, and visitors will see young Turkish men and women holding hands in the street just as they would in England. The problem for outsiders is that Turkish society is held together by many unspoken social rules that it is difficult for them to 'read'. If you want to win the respect of Turks it makes sense to dress conservatively and tone down the public necking; while nothing is usually said directly to those who offend against local mores, you can be sure that plenty is said behind their backs.

Homosexuality is still taboo (although not illegal) in much of the country. However, there are pockets of İstanbul, İzmir and Bodrum where openly gay bars and clubs operate with impunity. Some Turkish baths are known meeting places for gay men.

Nightlife. Along the coast and in İstanbul, İzmir and Ankara it's possible to find a nightlife every bit as wild as at home. Head out east, however, and you might as well forget it. There are the male-only tea-houses and a few sleazy *gazinos* (bars) and that's about it.

Turkish Baths. One distinctive feature of Turkey is the *hammam*, or Turkish bath, a communal bathing facility which may or may not have separate sections for men and women. Visiting a *hammam* for a scrub and a massage is one of the great pleasures of a trip to Turkey. The *hammams* also come in handy if a rental property has inadequate washing facilities.

GETTING THERE

By Land. It is possible, if expensive, to get to Turkey by train via Budapest or Bucharest. There are also bus companies that operate to Turkey although the journey is long and boring.

By Air. Unfortunately none of the cheap airlines currently operating out of the UK flies to Turkey with the exception of Bosphorus European Airlines which flies every Sunday to Northern Cyprus, stopping in İstanbul on the way; tickets cost around

£100 one way plus tax. Most of Europe's scheduled airlines fly to İstanbul but to get a cheap fare you normally have to take an indirect service with a delay of one or more hours along the way.

From May through to October it is sometimes possible to buy a ticket on a charter airline that has booked more seats than it has secured package holiday bookings. Normally these are return tickets for stays of no more than one month. However, there is nothing to stop you throwing away the return portion if you want to stay for longer. Charter airlines fly from the UK to Bodrum, Dalaman and Antalya.

Another option is to buy a ticket with one of the low-cost airlines to, for example, Paris or Frankfurt and then pick up a flight to İstanbul with Onur Air for around €100. Virgin Airways also flies to Athens whence it is possible to take the creaky old train or faster bus to İstanbul.

To get to Cappadocia people usually fly to İstanbul and then catch an overnight bus to Nevşehir which increases the cost by about £25. A better option is to fly to Kayseri airport with THY or Onur Air (around £40 one way) and then take a shuttle bus to Cappadocia for about £5 (one hour).

Useful Contacts – Airlines
Bosphorus European Airlines: IKB, IKB House, 230 Edgware Rd, London W2 1DW; ☎020-7724 8455; fax 020-7724 8655; Cumhuriyet Caddesi, 135/5, Elmadağ İstanbul; ☎0212-230 4701.
Onur Air: Şenlikköy Mahallesi, Çatal Sokak 3, 34153 Florya, İstanbul; ☎0212-663 2300, www.onurair.com.tr.
Turkish Airlines (THY): 125 Pall Mall, London SW1Y 5EA; ☎020-7766 9300; www.thy.com; Cumhuriyet Caddesi 199-201/3, Taksim, Istanbul; ☎0212-225 0556.

COMMUNICATIONS

Post. The Turkish postal service is reasonably efficient, bar the occasional lost letter. In towns mail is delivered to houses and to mailboxes in apartment blocks. In rural areas you may have to call at the *postane* (post office) for your mail; arrangements vary according to individual postmen.

Urgent items can be sent by *APS (Acele Posta Servis)* from big towns. TNT, UPS and FedEx all operate in İstanbul, İzmir and Ankara. Otherwise you may have to rely on whichever courier firm serves your area.

Most post offices open from 9am-5pm Monday to Friday, closing at 1.30pm on Saturdays and all day on Sunday.

Telephone. Despite efforts to sell Türk Telekom, so far the government-owned company maintains its monopoly which means that the cost of phone calls is higher than you might expect.

Turks love *cep telefonlar* (mobile phones); services are provided by Türkcell and Telsim. If you can't get a landline installed in your house it's possible to manage with just a mobile, especially one which operates with prepaid counters (*Hazır Kart*). All calls to mobile phones used to be very expensive but nowadays it is sometimes cheaper to call from one mobile to another rather than to a landline. Calling from a landline to a mobile remains frighteningly expensive.

FOOD AND DRINK

Turkish cuisine is regarded as one of the world's finest and certainly the quality of the ingredients ensures that even the poorest families eat fairly well, albeit on a diet low in meat and fish. The mainstay of restaurant fare is the kebab which comes in a wide variety of forms, from the familiar revolving *döner* to the spicy chunks of an Adana kebab. Kebabs are usually preceded by soup, commonly *mercimek* (lentil) or *domates* (tomato), more traditionally *işkembe* (tripe) or *kelle paça* (sheep's foot). Alternatively the restaurant may wheel out a tray of *mezes* - hot and cold titbits like *cacık* (cucumber dip), *börek* (cigar-shaped rolls of pastry with savoury fillings) and *yaprak sarma* (stuffed vine leaves). Along the coast and in İstanbul restaurants also serve fresh fish, although prices reflect their increasing scarcity. Dessert is frequently a plate of fruit although Turks also love *sütlaç* (rice pudding) and other milk puddings.

Vegetarians can survive perfectly well in Turkey because of the excellent fruit and vegetables. Non-vegans will also find a wide range of goat and sheep cheeses to choose from. However, they do have to take care in restaurants since even a seemingly innocuous lentil soup may turn out to have been made using meat stock.

Turkish society would cease to exist if there was an interruption in the tea (*çay*) supply. Every social transaction is oiled with copious glasses of tea served in tiny tulip-shaped glasses with equally copious quantities of sugar. In contrast tiny cups of thick, sweet Turkish coffee are served relatively infrequently; Nescafé is a far more common beverage while cappuccino is the drink of choice for Istanbul's young professionals.

Despite the Islamic prohibition on alcohol Turkey has a thriving wine industry. Both reds and whites are produced although quality is variable. The Turkish tipple of most men's choice is *raki*, a locally-made aniseed drink similar to the Greek *ouzo*; most people cut it with water. The local beer, Efes Pilsen, also attracts a devoted following.

SCHOOLS AND EDUCATION

All children must attend school from age seven to age 15, after which many choose to go on to study at a *lise* (high school). All state schooling is free of charge and follows a centrally-devised curriculum. Teachers must have a degree and foreigners are forbidden to teach in state schools although they can teach in private ones. Much teaching, at all levels of the education system, relies heavily on rote learning.

Opinions vary as to the standard of Turkish education. In big towns the schools may be perfectly adequate although, a lot depends on which district you are living in. On the other hand many expatriates prefer to send their children to school at private *kolejs* where the standard of language teaching in particular is likely to be higher and the range of extra-curricular activities wider. Fees usually cost in the region of £1000 per year.

The Structure of the Education System

There is no state provision for pre-school children but many expatriates pay for their children to attend private *anaokul* (kindergarten) between the ages of four and six. Sometimes kindergartens are similar to prep schools, readying children for the first year of school, but often they are more like playgroups.

İlkokul (primary school) starts at age seven and ends at age 11 after which children go to *ortaokul* (middle school) until age 15. After eight years of compulsory education Turkish children can go on to high school (*lise*) until they are 17. *Fen Lises* concentrate on science subjects, while *Anadolu Lises* concentrate on languages and *Meslek Lises* on vocational training.

Turkey has many universities but competition for places at the best of them is fierce. University entrance is decided by means of an annual exam which consists of a set of multiple choice questions; a student's score dictates where and what they can study. To improve their chances of passing many students take extra classes at *dershanes* (private classes) or employ private tutors.

International Schools

There are several international schools in İstanbul and Ankara. Two of the most popular are:

İstanbul International Community School, Karaağac Köyü, Hadımköy, İstanbul; ☎0212-857 8264.

Bilkent International School, East Campus, Ankara; www.bupsbis.bilkent.edu.tr.

TURKISH TAXES

Income Tax

Not everyone in Turkey has to pay *gelir vergisi* (income tax) since employers pay it on behalf of their employees. The self-employed do have to pay tax at a rate of 15-40%, although they can offset the expenses of running the business as in the UK. Every year the Ministry of Finance announces what it regards as the minimum cost of living which acts as a kind of personal tax allowance.

Traditionally few people have paid tax in Turkey. However, as the government pursues its goal of European Union membership it is starting to clamp down on tax evasion, starting with rigorous enquiries into rental income in certain parts of İstanbul. It must be assumed that this is a process that will become more intrusive, so anyone working in Turkey would be well-advised to seek the advice of a *muhasebeci* (accountant).

Sources of Information

For detailed information about the Turkish tax system log onto www.deik.org.tr or www.geocities.com . Alternatively www.tapo.co.uk gives you access to Turkish Attorneys and Paralegals Online.

KDV (Katma Değer Vergisi)

Value-added tax at a variable rate is included in the price of most goods and services. Tourists can ask to have it refunded on big-ticket items and some people who are working in Turkey without work permits manage to reclaim the VAT paid on purchases when they are going in and out of the country to renew their visas.

HEALTH

On the whole Turkey is a healthy place to live in although smoking remains commonplace. However, standards of health care are not high unless you can afford to pay for treatment.

The Turkish National Health Service

Turkey has no system of general practitioners. Instead doctors specialising in different branches of medicine set up surgeries near the local hospital. Since people may not know what is wrong with them many end up going to hospital when in the UK or the USA they would visit their doctor first. Social security (*SSK*) and state (*Devlet*) hospitals are open to everyone. They are free to everyone who is working legally and whose employer is paying their state health insurance premiums (*Bağ-Kur*). Otherwise users must pay for treatment and medication. In most cases the cost is less than for private medical treatment in the UK. However, conditions inside many of the hospitals, especially in rural areas, are depressing. Turkish medics also regularly over-prescribe drugs, even when they have failed to come up with a diagnosis.

Private Medicine

The best doctors and nurses often end up working in private hospitals where pay and conditions are much better. In İstanbul and Ankara some private hospitals have an excellent reputation. Prices are high by Turkish standards although not by UK standards (around £50 for an initial consultation). However, away from the big cities even private hospitals can be disappointingly inefficient.

Useful Addresses – Turkish International Hospitals
German Hospital: Sıraselviler Caddesi 119, Taksim, İstanbul; ☎0212-293 2150.
American Hospital: Güzelbahçe Sokak 20, Nişantaşı, İstanbul; ☎0212-311 2000; fax 0212-234 1432.
European Hospital: Fulya Sağlık Tesisleri,Cahit Yalçım Sokak 1, Mecidiyeköy, İstanbul; ☎0212-212 8811.
Florence Nightingale Hospital: Abide Hürriyet Caddesi 290, Çağlayan, Şişli, İstanbul; ☎0212-231 2021.
International Hospital: İstanbul Caddesi 82, Yeşilyurt, İstanbul; ☎0212-663 3000.

Private Medical Insurance

Because of the poor standards in state hospitals many foreigners take out private health insurance so that they can go straight to a private hospital. Unfortunately not all policies cover all hospitals, so you need to make sure you know which ones you will be able to use. Some policies don't become effective until you have been paying premiums for three or even nine months. Many companies also offer several levels of cover and will be keenest to tell you about the most expensive. One solution is to visit the nearest private hospital and check which insurer they recommend.

Reputable general Turkish insurance companies include *Yapı Kredi Sigorta, İsviçre Sigorta, Anadolu Sigorta, Koç Allianz* and *Güneş Sigorta*.

SHOPPING

Anyone living in Turkey quickly learns to live with a far more limited range of goods than what they were used to at home, and one of the pleasures of ex-pat life is tuning into the grape-vine to learn which hard-to-find item has put in an appearance at the local supermarket.

Turkey is a great country for buying good quality fresh fruit and vegetables, as well as rather pricier meat, fish and regional cheeses. The best place to shop for fresh produce is the nearest *pazar* (street market). In towns the *pazars* supplement the normal range of shops but in rural areas there may only be one or two small general stores (*dukkans, markets*) selling tins and tubes of tomato paste, packets of pasta and rice, bread, eggs, packet soups, cakes, biscuits, sweets and dairy products.

For the big monthly shop for household goods and toiletries most people head for the nearest supermarket. Several chains, including Migros, Gida, Yimpaş, Tansaş, Beğendik and Carrefour, operate in Turkey; Tesco is also rumoured to be on its way. The supermarkets are the most likely sources of such ex-pat necessities as breakfast cereals, soy sauce and fruit-flavoured yoghurts.

The large supermarket chains often sell household goods and clothing as well as food. Otherwise, big furniture stores include the Kelebek, İstikbal and Bellona chains. The best places to shop for electrical goods are branches of Arçelik and Beko.

It is hard to buy English-language books outside İstanbul, İzmir and Ankara and the coastal resorts. In other areas with a big tourist market (Cappadocia, for example) the gap is usually filled by book-exchange schemes. In İstanbul many of the English-language bookshops selling new books at reasonable prices are around İstiklal Caddesi in Beyoğlu.

Shop Opening Hours

Shops tend to stay open whenever there is the slightest chance of a customer. That means that you can usually find somewhere to do your food shopping from 9am until at least 10pm from April to October. In winter shops will still stay open late in İstanbul, although along the coast they may close altogether as their tourist clientele evaporates.

Shops sometimes close briefly while their owners attend the mosque for the five-times-daily prayer ritual. Even shopkeepers who don't usually go to the mosque may well close around Friday lunch-time when the week's most important prayers are held.

MEDIA

Newspapers

Turkey has a flourishing newspaper readership and newsstands around the country boast a wide range of titles. For those who expect conservatism in Islamic countries some of the titles will come as a surprise. *Bulvar*, for example, makes the *Sunday Sport* look tame.

Most censorship in Turkey is not overt. However, newspaper editors know what topics will trigger unwelcome attention (the Kurdish 'problem', the Armenian genocide, support for Communist ideas) and usually opt for the easy path of self-censorship.

The most popular daily papers in Turkey are the middle-of-the-road *Hürriyet* and *Sabah*. *Cumhuriyet* is the broadsheet favourite of the left-leaning intelligentsia while *Radikal* is its easier-to-read equivalent. *Akşam* and *Zaman* push the party line of the religious groups.

English-Language Newspapers in Turkey

The only English-language newspaper is the *Turkish Daily News* but with its microscopic inspection of Turkish politics and repetitive presentation it's a very dull read. It's available not just in İstanbul and the coastal resorts but also in most big towns.

Television

Gone are the days when the imams thundered that the angels would not visit the homes of those wicked enough to own a television set; these days the imams themselves have televisions as does the poorest household in the most out-of-the-way community.

Until 1991 the only channels available were provided by *TRT,* the state broadcasting authority. These days, however, many people have access to cable or satellite services which beam in endless game shows, sit-coms and films dating back to the 1970s.

English-Language Television in Turkey

The *Cine-5* satellite channel has been screening English-language movies for many years but recently it has been upstaged by *Digiturk* which offers a huge range of programmes in Turkish, English, French, German and Dutch. For a subscription of around £13 a month viewers can receive *BBC World, BBC Prime, CNN, Fox News, Euro News, CNBC-e, Hallmark Turkey, National Geographic, the History Channel* and *Animal Planet* as well as numerous other channels.

Radio

The main radio broadcaster, *TRT,* offers everything from news and chat to world music and jazz. *TRT3* broadcasts short foreign-language news bulletins throughout the day.

CRIME

Compared with most Western European countries Turkey is blissfully free of crime. In most parts of the country you can walk the streets late at night without the slightest worry. However, as with every other aspect of life, the pace of change is such that cracks are starting to occur in this general picture, and foreigners, especially tourists, make easy targets for those with ill intentions. Most of what happens is the usual pickpocketing on crowded trams and in crowded markets. People using bank ATMs (cash machines) have also found apparent 'helpers' actually robbing them; alternatively they have been followed and robbed. More seriously lone male foreigners in Istanbul are lured into bars, only to find themselves forced to foot outrageous bar bills for everyone present. Worse still, some have been drugged by so-called friends who then rob and abandon them. Women must expect some degree of sexual harassment, whether in İstanbul and the resorts or further east. Most of it is light-hearted and unthreatening but inevitably there have been incidents of more serious assault, and even rape. Dressing and behaving modestly should act as some sort of protection.

Police

Turkey has several different police forces but you are unlikely to become involved with any of them. In case of trouble you should look for the nearest *karakol* (police station) and report what has happened. In a rural area the *jandarma* function in much the same way as the normal police force. If stopped by the *trafik polisi* or *trafik jandarma* there is rarely any need to worry although you may be obliged to pay an on-the-spot fine for speeding or whatever else they have pulled you over for.

LEARNING THE LANGUAGE

Turkish is understood by almost everybody except in pockets of the east where some women in particular may not speak it.

Many Turks are great linguists, readily mastering not just English, French or German but also Japanese, Russian and any other remotely useful language. Indeed, in the coastal resorts and the tourist heart of Istanbul a foreigner need rarely speak a word of Turkish although if they do it will always go down well.

The best of the 'teach yourself' books is *Teach Yourself Turkish* by Asuman Celen and David Pollard; you can buy just the book or a combined book and cassette package. Hugo publishes *Turkish in Three Months*, an unrealistic target for all but the most linguistically gifted.

British local authorities sometimes offer evening classes aimed at people intending to holiday in Turkey. Details should be available at your local library.

If you're more serious about learning Turkish, the best way is to enrol at a language school in Turkey, the majority of them are located in İstanbul.

Useful Addresses – Language Schools

Taksim Dilmer: İnönü Caddesi, Prof. Dr. Tarık Zafer Tunaya Sokak 18, Taksim, İstanbul; ☎0212-292 9696; www.dilmer.com .

Tömer, Halaskargazi Caddesi 330, Şişli, İstanbul; ☎0212-232 5632; www.tomer.com.tr.

International House, Nispetiye Caddesi, Güvercin Durağı, Erdolen İşhanı 38/1, 1. Levent, İstanbul; ☎0212-282 9064.

SUMMARY OF HOUSING

The average Turk usually aspires to live in an apartment block, preferably one in which other family members can live on separate floors. Increasingly Turkish towns consist of canyons and housing estates of six and seven-storey apartment blocks, many of them with shops on the ground floor. These are mass produced to meet all levels of demand, whether for cheapness and simplicity or great luxury. However, in the earthquakes of 1999 housing like this was thought to have contributed to the terrible mortality rate.

It is only in the last ten years that Turks themselves have taken an interest in restoring old buildings. Until then most people who did well aimed to move as fast as they could into a brand-new apartment. But for those who are interested in restoration Turkey still has a lot of offer. In most towns a handful of crumbling Ottoman houses await buyers with the money and patience to bring them back to life. Inland there are villages that have been virtually abandoned as young people move into towns in search of a better life. Along the coast and in Cappadocia there are also many properties that were abandoned during the Graeco-Turkish population exchange of 1923 when more Greeks were forced to leave Turkey than Turks returned. Only along the coast is it becoming harder to find a dream property as the value of land suitable for hotels soars.

Who Can Buy Properties

Property ownership laws in Turkey are based on reciprocity which means that a foreigner can only buy in Turkey if a Turk can buy in their country. Most Western countries do allow Turks to buy, so this is not normally a problem. However, it seems to take longer for a *tapu* (title deed) to be transferred into the name of an American than that of someone from Britain or Germany.

How Property Prices are Calculated

The good news is that most Turkish property prices are still fairly low by British or American standards, the bad news is that the way they are calculated bears no resemblance to how it is done in the UK. Until ten years ago the rough value of a property would have been clear to everyone. However, as a housing market has developed over the last few years, so many people have lost sight of reality when it comes to working out what their house is worth. Commonly, a family will decide what they want to do with their lives (buy two flats and a car in another town, for example), decide how much that will cost them and then say that their property is for sale for that sum. The fact that no one has bought a similar property in a similar location for anything like that price will be shrugged off as irrelevant. Nor does it always follow that a more realistic offer backed up with hard cash will be accepted.

To that problem must be added the difficulties caused by Turkish inheritance law. This decrees that when someone dies their property will be divided between all their children; so overnight a house with one owner may acquire five of them. If the property is not immediately sold and then one of the five owners dies, their share may have to be divided again between all their children. In next to no time the property can wind up with 20 owners, all of whom have to agree to any sale. When you add into the equation that some of the owners will have moved to İstanbul or Ankara or even to Europe and that they may have inflated ideas about property prices, it's easy to see why some potentially promising properties end up unsold.

In theory if only one person is holding up a sale it is possible to go to court and force them to sell. However, such are the potential risks and costs involved that houses in dispute are more often left to fall down.

> **Anne Humphreys tells how she was held up by Turkish inheritance laws`**
> The house had originally been offered to me rent-free if I would install a bathroom and toilet, but since it had a crack running down the façade I turned it down. Then one day I heard the 'owner' say that he was going to do it up and sell it, whereupon I asked if he would consider selling it as it was. He said that he would, I said that I was interested, we agreed a price – and then I discovered that there were actually four owners, only three of whom wanted to sell. It took eight months to come to an agreement with all of them and of course the price rose by £1000 in that time. Göreme.

It is clear that house prices in Turkey are rising. However, where one flat in İstanbul may have risen £56,000/$100,000 in value over a ten-year period, another in a less desirable location may actually have fallen in value. All of which means firstly that it's imperative that people do their homework before buying and secondly that they should take all promises that their property is a guaranteed investment with a shovel full of salt.

Sources of Information

In big towns *emlakçılar* (estate agents) operate more or less as they would in the UK. Most of them sell properties in a specific area so that you need to work our where you want to buy and then visit the agents working in that area. *Turkish Daily News* carries ads from estate agents who speak English.

In rural areas there may be no official estate agents in which case you will be dependent on word-of-mouth information with all its potential pitfalls. Although the internet has helped by providing a way for would-be agents to market properties, it would be a mistake to buy solely on the basis of information provided over the web.

PUBLIC HOLIDAYS

Because Turkey is a Muslim country its calendar follows a different rhythm to that of Western Europe. What is more, the major Islamic festivals follow the lunar calendar, which means that, like Easter, they fall on different dates every year. As well as these religious festivals there are several public holidays linked to the history of the Turkish Republic. These fall on fixed dates every year.

PUBLIC HOLIDAYS	
1 January	NewYear's Day
21 March	Kurdish New Year
23 April	Turkish National Sovereignty and Children's Day
1 May	Labour Day
19 May	Youth and Sports Day
30 August	Victory Day
29 October	Turkish Republic Day
10 November	Anniversary of Ataturk's Death

RESIDENCE & ENTRY REGULATIONS

CHAPTER SUMMARY

- European citizens can stay in Turkey for three months on payment of a variable visa fee at the border
- Visas can be extended once within the country. After that all foreigners must leave the country and come back in again on a new visa.
- Many foreigners leave Turkey every three months to avoid the bureaucracy of visa renewal.
- Owning a house in Turkey speeds up approval of a resident's permit.
- Obtaining a work permit is so difficult that most people work illegally and renew their visa every three months like tourists.
- Turkish citizens carry a *kimlik* (identity) card but it is not easy for foreigners to obtain this.

VISA INFORMATION

Citizens of the European Union can enter Turkey for a period of up to three months on payment of a visa fee at the border or arrival airport. This visa allows for multiple entries within the three-month period. The charge depends on their country of origin and tends to be reciprocal; if the country concerned makes life difficult for Turks, then Turkey will charge their nationals a higher visa fee. For some years British citizens have been charged £10 for a three-month multiple-entry visa.

Since Turkey is not yet part of the EU, procedures for residents of most Western countries are exactly the same as for EU citizens; only the cost of the visa, visa extension and residency permit will vary depending on the country. US and Australian citizens currently pay $20, while Canadians pay $45.

Visa Renewals. Visas can be renewed for a further period of three months through the *Yabancı Bürosu* (Foreigners Office) of the *Emniyet Müdürlüğü* (Security Police) in the nearest big town. This long-winded procedure usually involves visits to innumerable departments to collect all sorts of meaningless signatures, and the price charged can be exorbitant in comparison with the cost of a visa at the border. Normally you will have to leave your passport for up to a week before the process is

602 BUYING A HOUSE ON THE MEDITERRANEAN

completed. Most people (especially if they don't speak Turkish) find it easier to travel
to Greece, Bulgaria or Northern Cyprus overnight and then come back in again on a
new visa. Visa extensions are stamped into a pink or blue booklet which goes inside
your passport.

Residence Permits

Applying for an *ikamet tezkeresi* (residency permit) is basically the same as applying
for a visa extension and involves the same bureaucracy. You can apply for residency
either in your country of origin or in Turkey, although things may proceed faster if
you make the initial approach abroad. The Turkish Embassy in the country where
you make your application will expect you to bring an application form printed from
their website together with your passport, photographs and proof of funds to support
yourself without working. In theory the procedure can take up to two months. In
practise if you own a house in Turkey and can show the *tapu* (title deed), it may well be
processed in a week. You will then have up to a month to present yourself at a branch
of the *Emniyet Müdürlüğü* and embark on the paperchase required for extending a
visa. Since you have to pay both at home and in Turkey the total cost of obtaining a
year's residency can run to several hundred pounds – which means that it may still be
worth going back and forth between Turkey and Greece instead.

Residency is usually granted for one year initially but when you renew it (which can
be done without leaving Turkey again) you will usually be given permission to stay for
two, three or five years. It is worth checking the price carefully with a Turkish speaker
since it has sometimes been the case that one person pays the same for one year as
someone else paid for three. Prices go up every January.

A resident's permit does not allow you to work legally in Turkey. However, it does
mean that you will be allowed to import your belongings from the UK without having
to pay duty on them.

Work Permits

If you have arranged work before coming to Turkey your employer should organise a
çalışma vizesi (work permit) for you. Once they have done that they are also expected to
pay your health insurance. However, most foreigners who are working in Turkey do so
without an official work permit and leave the country for a day or so every three months in
order to obtain a new visa. This is the case even with many of the people teaching English
for private schools in Turkey and it's certainly the case with most of the people working
as nannies for the İstanbul elite or freelancing as translators, journalists etc. The official
at the Greek border crossings are used to these arrangements and rarely make difficulties.
The lucky few persuade their employer to apply for a work permit for them after they have
started work in which case they have to leave the country to pick it up.

Having a residency permit doesn't automatically give you the right to work. Nor
surprisingly, does being married to a Turk. Some professions (for example, doctors
and dentists) are reserved for Turks. However, people working for themselves and able
to prove that they are investing in Turkey can usually obtain a work permit with the
help of a good lawyer.

Kimlik

Every Turkish citizen has a *kimlik* (identity card) which they must carry with them all
the time. A foreigner who takes on Turkish citizenship will eventually be issued with a
kimlik card at which point they will be able to apply for a telephone line in their own
name, obtain a Turkish credit card, register to vote and generally become an upright

citizen (*vatandaş*). However, becoming a citizen seems to be getting harder. Until 2003 a woman who married a Turk could claim citizenship on the spot. Now a British woman who marries a Turk has to wait five years before she can apply for citizenship.

Sources of Information

Getting hold of information in Turkey is not easy so some foreigners employ lawyers to steer them through the paperwork. One useful source of help is www.mymerhaba.tr, which has lots of information for expatriates, as well as a chatroom where you can ask others how they achieved something.

Another useful source of advice is the International Women of İstanbul group. Contact them via Posta Kutusu 80, 34330 Levent, İstanbul; ☎0532-412 4240; karen@iwi-tr.org.

Useful Addresses

Turkish Embassy in the UK

Turkish Embassy: 43 Belgrave Square, London SW1X 8PA; ☎020-7393 0202; fax 020-7393 0066.

British Embassies & Consulates in Turkey

British Embassy: Şehit Ersan Caddesi 46/A, Çankaya, Ankara; ☎0312-468 6230; fax 0312-468 3214.

British Consulate: Mesrutiyet Caddesi 34, Tepebaşı, 80072 Beyoğlu, İstanbul; ☎0212-293 7546; fax 0212-245 4989.

British Consulate: Yeşil Marmaris Travel Agency & Yacht Management Building, Barbaros Caddesi 249, Marmaris; ☎0412-6486; fax 0412-412 5077.

USA

Turkish Embassy: 1714 Massachusetts Ave, NW Washington, DC 20036; ☎0202-659 8200; fax 0202-659 0744.

United States Embassy: Atatürk Bulvarıı 110, Kavaklıdere, Ankara; ☎0312-455 5555; fax 0312-467 0019.

United States Consulate: Şehit Halil İbrahim Caddesi 23, İstinye, İstanbul; ☎0212-229 0075; fax 0212-323 2037.

Canada

Turkish Embassy: 197 Wurtemburg St, Ottawa, Ontario KIN 8L9; ☎0613-789 4044; fax 0613-789 3442.

Canadian Embassy: Nenehatun Caddesi 75, Gaziosmanpaşa, Ankara; ☎0312-436 1275; fax 0312-446 4437.

Canadian Honorary Consulate: Büyükdere Caddesi 107/3, Bengun Han, 3rd Floor, Gayrettepe, İstanbul; ☎0212-272 5174; fax 0212-272 3437.

Australia

Turkish Embassy: 60 Mugga Way, Red Hill, ACT 2603; ☎02-6296 0227; fax 02-6239 6592.

Australian Embassy: Nenehatun Caddesi 83, Gaziosmanpaşa, Ankara; ☎0312-459 9500; fax 0312-446 1188.

Australian Consulate: Tepecik Yolu 58, 80630 Etiler, İstanbul; ☎0212-257 7050; fax 0212-257 7054.

New Zealand
Turkish Embassy: 15-17 Murphy St, Level 8, Wellington; ☎04-472 1290, fax 04-472 1277.
New Zealand Embassy: Level 4, İran Caddesi 13/4, Kavaklıdere, Ankara; ☎0312-467 9056; fax 0312-467 9013.
New Zealand Consulate: İnönü Caddesi 92/3, İstanbul; ☎0212-244 0272; fax 0212-251 4004.

WHERE TO FIND YOUR IDEAL HOME

CHAPTER SUMMARY

- Most foreigners buy properties in İstanbul, along the Aegean and Mediterranean coasts or in Cappadocia.
- For city-lovers **İstanbul** provides the most exciting lifestyle.
- Most British settlers have bought houses along the coast between **Kuşadası** and **Antalya**
- Along the North Aegean coast **Assos** and **Ayvalık** are good places to buy.
- **İzmir** is of little interest to foreign settlers.
- **Kuşadası** and **Marmaris** are popular places to settle along the South Aegean coast.
- **Dalyan** in the Western Mediterranean is very pretty but more British people are buying in **Hisaronu/Ovacık** near Fethiye.
- **Antalya** has everything going for it – shops, beaches, restaurants, a great bookshop and a wide range of properties.
- East of Antalya most visitors and settlers tend to be German.
- East of Kızkalesi the coast is heavily industrialised and few foreigners have bought houses.
- **Şanlıurfa, Mardin** and **Midiat** in the south-east boast beautiful old stone houses, should the political situation ever make buying in the east seem viable.

OVERVIEW

While tourists can be found all over Turkey, foreign settlers still stick to a few tried and tested places, primarily along the Aegean and Mediterranean coasts, in Cappadocia and in the big cities of western Turkey. Resort towns such as Kuşadası have such large foreign populations that almost one in three marriages is now between a Turk and a foreigner (usually between a Turkish man and a foreign woman). The coast is interestingly segregated along national lines, with most British people visiting and settling south of İzmir and as far along the Mediterranean coast as Antalya, while east of Antalya most of the tourists and settlers are German.

In İstanbul, İzmir and Ankara most of the foreigners who come to stay have professional jobs for large international companies or work at the embassies and consulates, although there is a fair smattering of nannies and private English teachers, often working illegally. As you would expect of big cities, there is a wide mixture of foreigners, with representatives of most nationalities and big contingents from the English-speaking world.

Cappadocia has attracted a more mixed bag of settlers; a village such as Göreme has one or two representatives from a dozen different countries even though its overall population is only 2,000. These days almost all the Cappadocian villages have at least one foreign resident, usually from Europe.

Despite the cultural differences the foreign settlers and their Turkish neighbours rub along quite nicely and there is no reason to imagine that that will change in the foreseeable future. It has probably helped that most people have bought houses in areas which already have such large tourist populations that they go almost unnoticed in the crush. In places such as Göreme there are occasional mutterings about foreigners 'swamping' the village and all the houses being sold to foreigners but so far these antipathetic voices are few and far between. However, if too many foreigners settle in small communities they will inevitably change its character, something that most of the settlers view with as much regret as the locals. Rising house prices are also making it harder for locals to buy in their own communities. However, it is probable that house prices would have risen anyway as more Turks grew affluent. In any case many of the houses which foreigners have bought were derelict and few locals have the money or inclination to restore them.

It is probably easiest for foreigners to fit in along the coast where there are already flourishing and supportive expatriate communities. A few lucky individuals may land jobs as English teachers but most people work in the tourism industry: as reps for the overseas tour operators, as hotel and pension operators or in the many restaurants, travel agencies and dive shops. Because the coast is the most westernised part of Turkey and most people are already familiar with the ways of tourists, most foreigners find they can live there without having to adapt much to fit in.

So far few foreigners have bought houses in the east of Turkey where life is much harder, with a harsh climate, greater poverty and an on-going struggle for Kurdish rights. Anyone choosing to move out east would probably find houses there going for a song. On the other hand they would have to learn to speak Turkish and be prepared to make more adjustments to their lifestyle to fit in with their neighbours.

Estate Agents and Developers

As Turkey has fewer estate agents than most Mediterranean countries some of them are listed below rather than under each region. As the property market expands so will the number of agents. The Turkish Tourist Office in London can provide a list of estate agents and websites (☎0207-629 7771; www.gototurkey.co.uk.).

Useful Contacts – Estate Agents and Developers

ABC Real Estate: ☎+90 256 612 88 66; e-mail info@kusadasihomes.com or jane@kusadasihomes.com; www.kusadasihomes.com. Based in Kusadasi on the south Aegean coast.

A Life in Turkey: A Life in Turkey, P.O. Box 303, Hull, HU4 7WY; ☎01482 355114; e-mail advice@alifeinturkey.com; www.alifeinturkey.com. Contact Caroline Hales. In Turkey contact Mike Shields (☎+90 537 825 8933). Properties on the

Aegean coast (Marmaris, Fethiye etc) of Turkey.

Avatar International: Suite 208, Boundary House, Boston Road, Hanwell, London W7 2QE; ☎08707-282827; www.avatar-turkey.com. Specialises in emerging markets and alternative areas including Turkey. Resale and new development properties. Works with partners in Turkey.

Aymet Homes in Turkey: Yalı Caddesi (above Summer Garden Restaurant), Altınkum, Didim Aydin, Turkey; ☎ +90 256 813 11 10; fax +90 256 813 11 18; e-mail info@aymethomesinturnkey.com. Offers all kinds of property on the coast.

Black Lion Property Services: Yalıboyu Mah. 3, Nolu. Sok 7, 07960 Kalkan, Antalya; ☎ +90 242 8441345; fax +90 242 844 2789; e-mail info@2blacklions.com; www.2blacklions.com. All types of modern properties and land for sale. Also offers construction services and property management.

Kalkan Estates: Suite 208, Boundary House, Boston Road, Hanwell, London W7 2QE; ☎08707-282827; e-mail uk@kalkanestates.co.uk; www.kalkanestates.co.uk. Properties in Kalkan (50 miles south of Fethiye), and the Kaş Peninsula, both on the Mediterranean coast of Turkey.

Kaunos Tours: PTT. Karşisi, 48840 Dalyan/Mügla, Turkey; ☎+90 252 2842816; fax +90 252 2843157; UK contact: ☎017879-441467; e-mail property@kaunostours.com; www.kaunostours.com. Has been selling and managing property in Dalyan area for over ten years.

Kent Real Estate Property Services: Kemal Seyfettin Elgin Bul., No 14/14 Kat:2, 48700 Marmaris, Mügla, Turkey; ☎+90 252 4122247; www.kentestateagency.com. Several years' selling in the Mamaris area.

Mavi Real Estate and Property Services: Yalıboyu Mah, Kalkan 07960, Kalkan/ Antalya, Turkey; e-mail info@kalkanproperty.com; www.kalkanproperty.com. Also provides support those want to let their property once they have bought it and/or property management.

RealEstate Turkey: ☎01227-771300; e-mail enquiries@realestateturkey.co.uk; www.realestateturkey.co.uk. UK-based agent that deals in new and resale properties in Bodrum and nearby. Contact Wendy Wilson.

Returk Construction & Real Estate Company: fax +90 312 285 6921; e-mail dvarli@return.com; www.turkeypropertyforsale.com. Contact Dogăn Nadi Varli. Coastal real estate around Fethiye (Aegean) and elsewhere in Turkey.

Sun Resort Estates Ltd: 67-71 Oxford Street, London W1D 2EN; ☎0207-494-4770; fax 0207-734 2321; e-mail info@sunresortestates.com; www.sunresortestates.com. Contact Nancy Sokmen.

İSTANBUL

Population: approx. 12 million
Airport: *Atatürk International*

İstanbul is Turkey's most vibrant and cosmopolitan city. It is also its most crowded, with much of the population growth having taken place over the last 15 years as the problems in the east persuaded many families to move to the city in search of a better life. The result is that the historic core of the city on the European side is now completely surrounded by sprawling modern development, much of it unplanned. Even along the shores of the Bosphorus demand for housing has been so great that many of the beautiful old wooden *yalıs* (the summer homes of the wealthy) have burnt down in mysterious accidents, their place taken by far less attractive modern housing.

The consequence of the huge influx of people from the conservative east is that İstanbul is being pulled in two directions at once. In wealthier parts of the city many people lead a live not much different from that in Western Europe. However, in many of the poorer outlying suburbs, women still cover their heads and people lead a life not so different from that of cities like Van in the east.

In İstanbul it is still possible to find reasonably cheap and historically interesting houses for sale in areas like Fener and Balat along the shores of the Golden Horn. However, many foreigners are keen to buy houses or apartments with Bosphorus views and even the cheapest of these will have a sizeable mark-up. Some of the most interesting historic buildings can't be sold to foreigners anyway.

It's important to remember that İstanbul lies on an active earthquake fault line and that a devastating earthquake is expected in the foreseeable future. Since the massive quakes of 1999 that killed an estimated 20,000 people in north-eastern Turkey, the price of houses in parts of İstanbul thought to be especially vulnerable have slumped in value, so it's essential to be wary of unexpectedly cheap apartments.

Heather Dixon tells how it is important to see potential, even when things look unpromising at first sight
I saw my flat in Istanbul advertised in an estate agent's window at the same time as someone

> told my husband about it. We came to have a look and found it in a poor state of repair. The ceiling was blackened with soot from the stove, the wooden panels dividing the rooms from the central hall were caked in paint and there was dingy lino covering the wooden floorboards.

İstanbul offers a variety of job openings for foreigners. The best paid work for women is usually nannying for the city's elite; otherwise, some of the language schools offer reasonable wages, sometimes with accommodation thrown in. There is also plentiful private work tutoring individuals in English. Many of the men working in İstanbul have been sent there by their firms and this is one part of the country where there are as many foreign men married to Turkish women as vice versa. There is a flourishing expatriate community operating at all sorts of levels and it's in İstanbul that a foreigner can live a life that is most like that at home, with a wide range of foreign goods readily available in the shops, cinemas showing the latest movies in their original languages and bookshops selling English-language titles. However, İstanbul is also crowded, noisy and time-consuming to move about in (although public transport is excellent) and prices in the most popular areas are only marginally cheaper than in the UK.

Desirable areas to live in include Kadıköy, Moda and Suadiye on the Asian side of the Bosphorus and Taksim, Cihangir, Şişli, Nişantaşı, Etiler, Levent, Bebek, Beşiktaş and Ortaköy on the European side.

İstanbul property prices are in a state of flux. In Beyoğlu a 200-square-metre apartment that just four years ago would have cost $45,000 might now be worth more than $120,000. Elsewhere, however, an apartment in an area seen as particularly vulnerable to an earthquake might actually be worth less than five years ago.

THE NORTH AEGEAN

Centres of population: *Çanaçale, Ayvalık, Bergama, Foça, İzmir*
Airport: *Adnan Menderes International, İzmir*
The North Aegean coast stretches from the Straits of Gallipoli in the north as far as İzmir in the south. With its fine sandy beaches and historic monuments, it's a popular area with holiday-makers but has not attracted as many settlers as the South Aegean or Mediterranean, perhaps because it lacks the huge resorts that have drawn so many people further south.

Heading south from İstanbul you pass through the uninviting town of Tekirdağ and then drive out onto the Gelibolu Peninsula where the Gallipoli campaign took place. The town of **Gelibolu** itself sits invitingly around a harbour ringed with fish restaurants. However, it is primarily a crossing point for ferries and has not attracted much attention from foreign buyers.

The main crossing point for the Straits of Gallipoli runs between **Eceabat** on the north bank and **Çanaçale** on the south. Eceabat is a small, sleepy waterside settlement which more or less lives for battlefield tours and the hard-drinking antics of visiting Australians and New Zealanders. Çanaçale, on the other hand, is a pleasant small town facing out over the straits, with a good choice of restaurants and bars, waterfront promenades and tea gardens and a reasonable selection of shops and cinemas. The whole town springs to life for the ceremonies associated with ANZAC Day (25 April) and then slumps back down again afterwards. Although a disproportionate number of tourists visit for ANZAC Day there is a steady throughput of tourists all summer. Most of them come to visit the Gallipoli battlefields and the nearby ruins of Troy although a daring few come to emulate Hero's feat in swimming across the Straits.

Unfortunately Çanaçale is strategically important and it is difficult for foreigners to get permission to buy there as a result of the Military Prohibited Areas and Secure Areas law which also restricts foreign home ownership in other places near military bases.

Accessible by boat from Çanaçale are Turkey's two Aegean islands, **Gökceada** and **Bozcaada**. In theory Bozcaada, with its lovely sandy beaches and gorgeous old stone houses, would make a great place to buy a house. Unfortunately, foreigners are currently forbidden to buy on either island as a result of the military restrictions law.

South from Çanakkale one of the most desirable places to live in all of Turkey might be **Assos** (aka Behramkale). Assos proper consists of a series of old stone houses fronting onto a tiny harbour, all of them now hotels and restaurants. Uphill however, in the village of **Behramkale** some foreigners have bought ruined stone houses and restored them as hotels or pensions. However, Assos' relative proximity both to İstanbul and parts of the coast popular with Turkish holidaymakers means that bargains are likely to be increasingly hard to find.

Yet further south from Assos is the small town of **Ayvalık** which had a far bigger Greek population before 1923. Its back streets are still full of fine old stone houses many of them unoccupied. Increasingly these are being snapped up by Europeans who have been paying around $20,000 for sizeable terraced houses. While many of them need modernisation and repair, they are not ruinous and could be lived in while the work was being carried out. Similar houses on nearby **Cunda** island are more expensive than those on the mainland because their potential for tourism is higher.

South again from Ayvalık is Bergama, an important town in Graeco-Roman times which has subsided into a backwater, overlooked even by most tourists unless they are bused in for a quick whip around the sites. Consequently few foreigners have settled here. Most of the housing is in high-rise apartment blocks although there is one quarter to the north of the Galinos river where more old Greek houses stand waiting for restoration.

Within easy reach of İzmir are several small resorts which might make pleasant homes. Quietest and most backwaterish is **Çandarlı** which would only really suit somebody very self-sufficient. But just a bit further south are the two Foças. **Eski Foça** is a well-established, classy holiday resort, popular with weekenders from İzmir. Some of its waterfront hotels have the feel of Victorian seafront hotels but tucked down the back streets are a few old houses that might be turned into pleasant modern homes. **Yeni Foça** is much smaller and more cut-off. On the other hand it is like an Ayvalık in miniature, its back streets lined with old Greek houses in reasonable condition and begging to be restored.

İZMİR

Until 1923 İzmir (then Smyrna) was one of Turkey's liveliest cities with a large Greek and Armenian community. However, while Atatürk's forces were driving out the mainland Greeks who had invaded in 1922 much of the old town burnt down. Consequently the modern city has little to show for its illustrious past, and although it has a relatively laidback ambience and a calmer lifestyle than Ankara, it has not generally found favour either with tourists or settlers. It has a population of about 2.5 million.

Most foreigners who settle in İzmir do so because their work has taken them there. There are plenty of apartments for sale or rent, although not much else that is more interesting. The one exception is the Alsancak area to the north of the city where streets of old Chios-style Greek houses have not only survived but are being turned into bars and restaurants faster than they can be advertised. The government plans to move into the Balçova and Karşıyaka neighbourhoods and start similar restoration work which means that prices in both areas are likely to rise in the foreseeable future.

SOUTHERN AEGEAN

Centres of population: *Kuşadası, Milas, Güllük, Bodrum, Muğla, Marmaris*
Airports: *Adnan Menderes International, İzmir; Bodrum International*

Just south of İzmir is **Kuşadası**, a seaside resort which has always attracted lots of British, Irish, German and Dutch holidaymakers. It's a big, brash place, especially at the height of summer, where restaurants cater unashamedly to British tastes and the nightlife, especially along the notorious Bar Street, can be wild. Kuşadası wouldn't suit anyone in search of the 'real' Turkey. On the other hand its thriving tourism industry ensures there are plenty of seasonal jobs, albeit not necessarily well-paid ones.

Most of the foreign women who have married Turkish men in Kuşadası live in comfortable modern apartments or in the pensions that they run together. However, in the old part of town, at the top of a very steep hill, there are a lot of old stone houses which have the potential to become comfortable homes or small tourism businesses. Prices are likely to be as steep as the approach roads and the competition means that it would be tough carving out a profitable niche for a business. Still, there is more to Kuşadası than is sometimes apparent from a fleeting visit.

Nearby **Selcuk** is the antithesis of Kuşadası; small, relatively quiet and nowhere near as overdeveloped. As a result it has attracted its fair share of foreign settlers, some of whom have also bought houses in the surrounding countryside. Selcuk has also proved attractive to Turks retiring from well-paid jobs in the cities and looking to start small, upmarket hotels.

Selcuk is the nearest town to Ephesus, one of Turkey's honeypot tourist attractions, which means that in summer it is heaving with tourists. However, whereas Kuşadası tends to appeal to people on package holidays, Selcuk has always appealed to independent travellers, particularly from Australia and New Zealand. It is therefore full of small, family-run pensions and restaurants that cater to that particular market. As usual there are plenty of apartments for sale or rent, although to buy anything bigger would require a big outlay of cash.

Heading south from Selcuk you come eventually to **Bodrum**, another of Turkey's hyper-resorts but one which has managed to retain some of its original character, at least in the centre of town which is packed with little white houses and tiny, winding alleys. The snag with Bodrum is the scale and type of tourism that it attracts. While it might make a great place to live in the winter and spring, in summer it is almost impossible to move along the streets, and the nightlife which kicks off at 11 pm thunders on into the early hours. Consequently most foreigners who buy houses in this part of the country do so not right in the heart of Bodrum or in neighbouring Gümbet (a modern version of Bodrum with the bars but without the historic character) but out on the Bodrum peninsula where prices are rising stratospherically as word gets out.

The trouble is that the peninsula is not very big and the demand for places intense. When considering where to buy it's important to bear in mind exactly what could be built right beside you at a later date. Pretty little Gümüşlük, for example, has a protection order on it which means that nobody can dump a high-rise hotel on the waterfront. However, the protection only extends to the actual village which means that serried ranks of holiday homes are now visible marching over the hillside and damaging the view.

Not far south from Bodrum is **Marmaris**, the third of the Aegean's mega-resorts. Wrapped around a natural harbour backed with rocky islands, Marmaris must once have been very beautiful, but these days you have to poke pretty hard to see what once made it a magnet for the rich and famous. Like Kuşadası, Marmaris has courted the bottom end of the British package-holiday market very successfully but the price that it has paid is pell-mell, unplanned development and a town that more or less lives for tourism for half the year. There are plenty of job opportunities for English-speakers in bars, hotels, restaurants and travel agencies and no shortage of new apartments to buy.

Overlooked by most foreigners is nearby **Müğla**, the administrative and transport centre for the region. With no major tourist attractions and a location inland from the sea, Müğla has not so far attracted foreign settlers. However, the whitewashed houses in its back streets are so pretty that it can only be a matter of time until the buyers move in.

Beyond Marmaris itself stretches a strip of land made up of the Datça and Hisaronu peninsulas. This is a beautiful part of the country where pine forests smile down on bright blue waters and development has been blissfully limited – so far. The reason for this unusual state of affairs is that the access road through the peninsula is winding and slow. Should a new road be built it is hard to imagine how such serenity could survive. **Datça** itself, at the far end of the peninsula, is like a Marmaris in miniature. However, most other settlements on the peninsula are very small and some of the foreigners who have settled here have bought old stone houses, restored them and turned them into boutique hotels or classy restaurants catering for the passing *gület* (yacht) trade.

Typical Properties for Sale in the Southern Aegean
(Prices are in pounds sterling)

Location	Type	Description	Price
Bodrum	Duplex	130 sq. m. Four bedrooms	£75,152
Bodrum	Apartment	90 sq. m.	£14,000
Marmaris	Villa	140 sq. m. Three bedrooms	£64,000 to £74,000
Bodrum/Bitez	villa	80 sq. m. semi-detached in a development of 20.	£36,000
Mamaris centre	Apartment	110 sq. m. 3 bedrooms. 3rd floor. Lift and small communal garden.	£60,000

WESTERN MEDITERRANEAN

Centres of population: *Ortaca, Dalaman, Hisaronu, Fethiye, Kaş, Kalkan, Finike, Kemer*

Airports: *Dalaman International, Antalya International*

East of Marmaris the coastline becomes more and more beautiful, with mountains soaring up above the road and pine trees gently inclining towards the sea. Not surprisingly this is a part of the coast that is extremely popular with foreign settlers.

The small resort of **Dalyan** is particularly idyllic, set as it is on the banks of a river which runs straight down to the beach in one direction and up to mud baths in the other. The river is also overlooked by a series of Lycian rock-cut tombs which provide a backdrop for most views. Access to Dalyan is made easy by the fact that the airport at nearby Dalaman is served by charter flights from the UK. A duplex property in a courtyard complex in Dalyan will fetch around £40,000.

Heading east from Dalyan you come to **Fethiye**, a big and popular resort if not quite on the Marmaris scale. Fethiye has a gorgeous location and many of its hotels and pensions boast panoramic views over a bay dotted with rocky inlets. The older part of town makes up an increasingly small percentage of Fethiye, but it does have an old *hamam* and a number of historic monuments, mainly dating from the Lycian period. A two-bedroomed, 80-square-metre apartment there goes for about £79,000 while a four-bedroomed, 220-square-metre villa is on sale for £106,000.

However, Fethiye has always lived in the shadow of its prettier neighbour, **Ölüdeniz,** which boasts a fine sandy beach and a perfectly preserved lagoon. Developers quickly homed in on Ölüdeniz and in a bid to protect it, the government banned further development near the beach and instead allowed a settlement called **Hisaronu** to be built in the hills above it. This wholly artificial village became extremely popular with British holidaymakers and now Hisaronu and neighbouring **Ovacık** are at the epicentre of British settlement in Turkey. If you want to be able to eat, drink and entertain in the same way that you would do at home but with the added benefits of constant sun in summer, a lovely beach nearby and pine forests all around you, then the appeal of Hisaronu will be obvious. If, on the other hand, you want something old or authentically Turkish, then don't even bother to drop by.

Currently Hisaronu and Ovacık are a developer's dream, with villas and duplexes going up at an astonishing speed. Unfortunately few of them are built with an eye to their neighbours so that the end result is a mish-mash of jarring architectural styles. Estate agents in the area have been luring buyers with promises that their villa will soar in value when Turkey enters the European Union. Such claims should be taken with a large pinch of salt since Turkey may never get into the EU. Even if it does there is so much land available for new building that it is unlikely that buyers will want to invest in properties whose price includes a mark-up to benefit the previous owner.

East of Fethiye are two small, relatively upmarket towns which offer complimentary attractions. **Kaş** has a pretty location facing onto a harbour and is sprinkled with ancient monuments including a Graeco-Roman theatre and several Lycian tombs. For visitors it has an enticing array of bars and restaurants serving up a mixture of Turkish and European cuisine. It also has some wonderful shops, many of them lining a street of exquisite restored wooden houses which drip bougainvillea in summer. **Kalkan,** in contrast, has a wonderful choice of small boutique hotels and pensions in restored wood and stone houses but a less alluring array of restaurants and shops. These days buying anything other than a modern apartment in either Kaş or Kalkan is likely to require major investment. However, there is nothing to stop people buying in the surrounding villages, many of them virtually abandoned by a population who see life in the town as far more inviting. In theory ruinous stone houses in villages like **Bezirgan** should be going for a song. In reality their owners may have inflated ideas of their worth or there may be so many owners that getting them all to agree to sell may be tricky.

Almost every visitor to Kaş winds up taking the boat trip to Kekova which also takes in the gorgeous village of **Kaleköy** or Simena. The fact that one of Turkey's super-rich Koç family has a holiday home here should offer some indication of how wonderful a place this is; views of the sea littered with huge Lycian sarcophagi, a scattering of stone and wood houses, bougainvillea everywhere and absolutely nothing to do - that's Simena. Until recently prices have remained surprisingly reasonable because access to the village is so tricky. However, it is unlikely that that situation can continue for much longer. Anyone wanting to buy in Simena would need to check very carefully what plans there may be to improve access and think hard about the likely implications of that.

Continuing along the coast the main road skirts the idyllic settlement of **Olimpos/ Çıralı** which lies in a conservation area ensuring that it is one of the few parts of the coast where high-rise hotels don't loom over the beach. It would be very difficult to buy in Olimpos itself which is really just a row of ramshackle pensions. However, some foreigners have bought land in Çıralı with a view to building a house there.

Beyond Olimpos most settlements are part of the greater Antalya conurbation. **Kemer** is a popular resort for British package holidaymakers but lacks any real Turkish character.

ANTALYA

Antalya is an interesting place which manages to be both a mega-resort with great beaches and alive-and-kicking Turkish town at the same time. What's more it manages to cope with the demands both of the package tourists who stay in high-rise hotels near the beach and of the independent travellers who patronise the smaller hotels and pensions in restored or copied old Ottoman buildings in the **Kaleiçi** part of town inside the old walls.

Probably because of this ideal mixture, lots of foreigners have bought homes in and around Antalya. Some have bought apartments to live in, some have bought apartments to let to other foreigners and a few have bought old buildings and restored them either as homes or as small hotels. It probably helps that there is a wider range of work available in Antalya too. Most foreigners probably work in tourism or as teachers. However, there are other possibilities as well and the chance to live a fairly normal life, with good shops, restaurants and cinemas and a mixture of expatriates and Turks all rubbing along nicely together.

Typical Properties for Sale – Western Mediterranean

Location	Type	Description	Price
Fethiye	Apartment	80 sq. m. Two bedrooms	£79,000
Fethiye	Villa	220 sq. m. 4 bedrooms.	£106,000

Dalyan	Villa	860 sq.m. 4 bedrooms. balconies. Near beach.	£68,000
4km inland from Dalyan	Detached house	80 sq. m. floorspace, plus 470 sq.m. garden. Surrounded by trees and olive grove. Built 2001.	£50,000
Kalkan	Duplex	semi-detached. 2 bedrooms plus attic bedroom, 2 bathrooms, swimming pool and roof terrace.	£93,000
Dalyan	House	Detached. 4 bedrooms. Total floor space 84 sq m. Large garden 1320 sq. m. All mod cons.	£100,000
Antalya	Apartment	two bedrooms	£57,500

EASTERN MEDITERRANEAN

Centres of population: *Side, Alanya, Anamur, Silifke, Tarsus, Mersin, Adana, İskenderun, Antakya*
Airports: *Antalya International; Adana*

East of Antalya most people will address you in German rather than English. Even so, British tourists visit Alanya and Side in particular and both places have their contingent of foreign residents.

Alanya is a biggish town wending its way inland from a pleasant fishing harbour overlooked by the remains of a Seljuk castle and walls. Unlike Antalya, though, modern Alanya has little life beyond tourism which means that in winter it effectively closes down. The nightlife is good, if not especially trendy, and there's a good choice of places to eat. Shopping prospects, however, are grim since the town lives for tourists rather than for its long-term residents. Fortunately Antalya is only a short bus hop away.

There is no shortage of modern apartments to buy in Alanya, the most pricey of them offering sea views. This is also a good area to try if you want to buy a villa or duplex.

Side, just to the west of Alanya, started life as a fishing village which didn't leave it much scope for growing to cope with the influx of tourists in the 1980s and 1990s. Although the old part of the town, with its Graeco-Roman ruins, still has some character, almost all the old houses have long since given way to shops and restaurants wholly focussed on the tourist market. Side has great beaches, so this might be a good place to buy a sea-facing apartment or villa but most people will probably find it rather soulless.

Beyond Alanya the coast road becomes more winding and slower and there are fewer tourists let alone foreign settlers. That is not because of lack of development because Turks have built second-home complexes facing every bay big enough to take them, but from Taşuçu eastwards much of the coast is heavily industrialised. There are only two sizeable resorts in this area but neither **Anamur** nor **Kızkalesi** currently has much to offer foreign buyers.

CAPPADOCIA

Although not on the Mediterranean, Cappodocia warrants a mention because of the unique character of the beautiful landscape, the amazing 'fairy chimneys' and the availability of cave dwellings for conversion or restoration.

Centres of population: *Aksaray, Nevşehir, Kayseri, Niğde*
Airport: *Kayseri*

Cappadocia differs from other parts of Turkey in that the foreigners who have bought properties here have mostly bought crumbling stone houses in the villages. Some of these were abandoned after the 1923 Graeco-Turkish population exchange, others when their owners moved in search of work or a better life; a few (*afet evleri*) were abandoned when they were judged unsafe after landslides in an area of constantly shifting soil. Most of these houses need major work to install lighting, water and sewerage as well as to make them habitable. What is more many of them lie in conservation areas or within the Göreme National Park where what can and cannot be done to a property is strictly controlled, especially when the purchaser is a foreigner.

Cappadocia was quick to adapt to tourism with the result that most locals are used to the ways of foreigners. Even so, settlers need to be more prepared to adapt to local customs than those opting to live by the sea; women, in particular, will fare much better if they are prepared to cover themselves up (no one expects Westerners to wear headscarves but they do appreciate them covering their legs, arms and chests). So many people in the area work in tourism that foreigners can get by perfectly well with hardly any Turkish. However, to integrate with neighbours who don't work in tourism they will need to learn some of the language. There are very few job opportunities for foreigners that pay more than subsistence wages so most people who have settled in the area for reasons other than romance tend to be self-employed in vaguely arty occupations (writers, artists, photographers, crafts workers).

***

Anne Humphreys on why she chose to buy in Göreme

I wanted to take a year out and live somewhere that was both historically interesting and naturally beautiful – Cappadocia fitted the bill perfectly and I chose Göreme because I already knew people there. It suited me to live in a village that had a mixture of Turks living a traditional lifestyle, Turks working in tourism and speaking good English, expatriates from a variety of countries and tourists. That way I figured that I was unlikely to get bored.

***

The provincial capital is **Nevşehir**, a dreary place with little going for it except its usefulness for shopping. When Nevşehir doesn't stock it, Kayseri is the next best choice. Kayseri is also the most convenient airport for the area since the mothballing of the brand-new Tüzköy airport.

The backpacker heart of Cappadocia, **Göreme** is where most people come on their holidays and then make the decision to stay. It's an interesting village where almost every old house has been at least partly hacked out of the rockface and where rock cones – called fairy chimneys – lurk down back alleys. It's an inviting place to live although with its limitations – most of the shops cater for tourists, for example. But Göreme is very small which means that there is little saleable property. What there is is usually completely ruined and it can be a minefield negotiating with multiple owners, not all of them living in the village. Five years ago it was possible to pick up a big cave property in Göreme for around £2,000 but those days are long gone and now you are more likely to be asked for more than ten times that sum. Given that it will cost at least £10,000 to modernise any of the houses, you would need to allow for spending at least £40,000 to buy and restore a house there now.

> **Anne Humphreys tells how she managed to fit in to her Turkish community, despite being older than many foreign settlers**
> *It wasn't as hard as I had expected to adjust to living in a village. It helps that Göreme has a long history of welcoming foreign tourists so that I didn't seem as strange as I might once have done. But I was lucky in my neighbours who were very welcoming once they understood that I was ready to learn the language and didn't mind adapting to their ways. I think it helps that I was older and didn't mind not being able to hang out in bars or bring men home with me.*

Uçhisar is rapidly following down the same path as Göreme. Like Göreme it's very pretty, with even better views, but like Göreme it's also very small, with limited opportunities for buying. Prices have been pushed up recently as not just foreigners but also Turks from other parts of the country have moved in to snap up properties suitable to turn into hotels and pensions. Traditionally Uçhisar has been most popular with French speakers.

Ürgüp is bigger than Göreme and Uçhisar, which means that it has a better range of shops and feels more like a real town. The nicest part is the Esbelli Mahallesi where hoteliers and private house-owners have done a fine job of restoring the old stone houses. A few properties are still available although they are unlikely to come cheap. Elsewhere in town it's possible to buy apartments, condos or even stand-alone houses although these lack historic character. A three-storey house in a modern part of town was recently on the market for around £100,000, while a huge old Greek house with spectacular views is for sale for closer to £180,000.

Avanos also feels more like a real town and has the benefit of the Kızılırmak river running through it. Like Uçhisar it has long been popular with French visitors and as you walk along the high street you are likely to be greeted with 'bon jours' rather than 'hellos'. Like Ürgüp, Avanos offers a mixture of old properties in need of extensive restoration but with bags of character and brand-new apartments with all mod cons and no character.

Ortahisar is an interesting village because unlike the places mentioned above it receives relatively few tourists and yet has become increasingly popular with foreign settlers; arguably it is now the place of choice for foreign buyers. This is because the houses there – mainly old Greek stone-built houses backed onto caves – are still great bargains, offering loads of space and character for little money. Unfortunately Ortahisar is a conservative town with little life going on there. The expatriate community is also fairly fissiparous, with one or two representatives from all sorts of countries and far less of the sense of community that holds Göreme together.

Elsewhere in Cappadocia there is at least one foreign settler in most of the villages; İbrahimpaşa is an increasingly popular choice.

THE PURCHASING PROCEDURE

CHAPTER SUMMARY

○ **Turkish banks** have proved unreliable in the past although the situation seems to be improving.

○ **Mortgages** don't exist in Turkey. Most people pay cash for their houses.

○ **Purchase tax** of one and a half per cent of the value must be paid on all property transactions.

○ **Local property taxes** are very low.

○ **Household insurance** is inexpensive. In rural areas few people bother with it.

○ In towns most people use estate agents. In rural areas most transactions still take place directly between buyer and seller.

○ The most popular types of property are **apartments** in towns and **villas** by the sea. Some people buy old stone or Ottoman wooden houses in need of restoration.

○ **Rental properties** are easy to find in big towns but thin on the ground in the country. You may have to meet the cost of improvements yourself.

○ You should expect to pay small **backhanders** to speed up the purchase procedure.

FINANCE

BANKS

The only foreign bank with a big (and growing) presence in Turkey is HSBC which therefore makes a good bet for currency transfers etc. Failings in the Turkish banking system led to several economic crises in the late 1990s, including the economic meltdown of 2001. However, the situation is stabilising and reliable banks to choose from include Türkiye İş Bankası, Akbank, Yapı Kredi, Garanti and Vakıf. Most have branches in all major towns. Garanti (www.garanti.com) advertises that it employs English-speaking staff.

Opening a Turkish bank account is usually straightforward. You need to show your passport as proof of identity; otherwise formalities are minimal. Most banks want you to have a Turkish tax number before they will open an interest-bearing account for you; however, if you look doubtful this requirement sometimes evaporates. You can open an account in sterling, dollars or euros, or in Turkish lira although normally only Turkish lira accounts pay interest. Once you have a Turkish lira account you will be able to apply for an ATM card that will let you draw money from any hole-in-the-wall outlets free of charge. Acquiring a Turkish credit card is far trickier.

Sandra Brown describes how she bought her house in İstanbul without using either a bank or a lawyer

I didn't find the İstanbul bureaucracy particularly hard to deal with. I didn't even use a lawyer. I brought the money from the UK in cash and went to the tapu office in the Hippodrome with it wrapped up in newspaper. All six owners came along as well as a translator and we all drank tea together. Then I handed the cash over in an anteroom and the family divided it up and counted it on the spot. I didn't even have a surveyor – I just walked around the house and sniffed for mildew, although the builder did tell me that he thought the structure was fairly strong. Because it was an old wooden house I had to visit the Koruma Müdürlüğü *(Conservation Management) and get a* proje, *and because the walls of the park belonged to the army I also had to get permission to buy from the army. We wrote a* dilekçe *to the general and visited the military base to get the paperwork signed. Luckily I didn't have to deal with the* Kültür Bakanlığı *(Department of Culture) as well which might have been possible since they have control over anything that could be said to be an archaeological site.*

UK MORTGAGES

A British or American bank is unlikely to lend money for the purchase of a Turkish property, although they may let you remortgage a British or USA property to buy a second home in Turkey. Other people opt to sell their current house to release the cash to buy in Turkey.

MORTGAGES WITH TURKISH BANKS

You will not be able to take out a mortgage in Turkey. Interest rates on loans are cripplingly high so no such system has developed yet.

IMPORTING CURRENCY

Although the Turkish lira is convertible and there are no restrictions on its import or export, it is not much in demand so buying and selling it overseas usually requires advance planning and goes along with poor exchange rates. There are no restrictions on how much money you can bring into Turkey.

Provided you are in the UK to make the arrangements, most British banks can arrange a transfer of funds for a house purchase within a week. On the other hand if you are already overseas and want to arrange the transfer from your new base you may find the bureaucracy cumbersome and slow even if you have already set up a Turkish bank account and know all the necessary codes for inter-bank transactions. Normally you transfer your money from the UK into a foreign-currency account in your own or the seller's name.

Nearly always cheaper than banks and recommended by experts and users is to transfer money through a currency broker such as Currencies Direct. For further details see *Importing Currency* in the *General Introduction* to this book.

REAL ESTATE TAXES

Property Purchase Tax

Everyone who buys a property must pay 1.5% of the purchase price as *emlak vergisi* (property tax). However, as Turkey has no up-to-date land-price register most people get away with understating what they paid to reduce the amount of tax due. Until now this has not caused problems but as Turkey tidies up its bureaucracy to impress the European Union this may not continue to be the case.

Environment and Cleaning Tax

All property owners pay an environment and cleaning tax *(Çevre ve Temizlik Vergisi)* in May and November. The money is usually collected with the water rates and covers the cost of rubbish collection and other local services. The sums involved are absurdly small by Western Europe standards: typically, £20 a year.

MOVING TO TURKEY

If you are moving to Turkey permanently you should inform the Inspector of Taxes at your local branch of the Inland Revenue and provide them with proof of your departure (ie proof that you have sold your UK home along with the title deed of a property abroad or evidence that you are renting overseas). If you keep a house in the UK you may be able to prove that you are no longer resident but you will still have to pay tax on any rental income from the property.

If you are going to work for a Turkish company, show the Inland Revenue the P45 from the last English firm you worked for and enquire about any tax rebate if you have worked in the UK for only part of the tax year.

If you are only going to be working abroad temporarily you will have to be careful that you don't spend more than 183 days in the year in the country (or 91 days a year averaged over a four-year period) to avoid becoming liable to UK tax.

Anyone thinking of moving to Turkey should first seek advice from *The Centre for Non-Residents (CNR):* St John's House, Merton Rd, Bootle, Merseyside L69 9BB: ☎0151-472 6196; fax 0151-472 6392; www.inlandrevenue.gov.uk/cnr.

INSURANCE

Compared to most of Western Europe Turkey is enviably free of the sort of crime that bothers house-owners. Consequently few people insure their homes against burglary etc. In rural areas a dog in the courtyard is still seen as the best form of crime prevention. If you want to take out house and contents insurance, a well-known company is Koç Allianz Sigorta A.S. (H.Q. Bağlarbaşı Kısıklı Cad. 9, Altunizade 81180; +90 216 310 12 50; fax +90 216 310 02 22) which typically charges £250-£500 a year for a two/three bedroom villa.

Since the disastrous earthquakes of 1999 everyone buying a house is required to take out *deprem sigortası* (earthquake insurance) also known as DASK. This applies even if the 'house' is little more than a pile of stones. However, most people assume that if the worst comes to the worst and İstanbul is destroyed by an earthquake, their insurance will turn out to be worthless. You can get earthquake insurance policies from general insurance companies like Güneş and others listed in the section *Private Medical Insurance.*

FINDING PROPERTIES FOR SALE

It cannot be emphasised too strongly that there is no substitute for on-the-ground research, preferably on your own or with a foreigner who has already bought in the area, before approaching anyone for professional assistance. Although most estate agents are reliable and most advertisers genuine, so many naïve foreigners have been stung that caution must be the byword at all times.

ESTATE AGENTS

In big towns and along the coast there are plenty of estate agents who speak English and are used to dealing with foreign buyers. However, in rural areas house purchases still have to be negotiated directly between the seller(s) and the buyer. Even in towns you may be able to find out what is for sale by talking to people in local tea-houses. Even if you use an estate agent you should be aware that they sometimes hold back information on cheap properties or particularly good deals; you will have to be very determined to ensure you are told about everything available.

Although you will obviously save the agent's fee by buying privately, you need to be very sure of what you are doing before you start down this road. Without an estate agent, an owner can ask any price, however unreasonable, for their property, especially as most Turks assume that *yabancılar* (foreigners) are all millionaires.

Some useful websites are below.

Useful Websites – Estate Agents

Avatar (www.avatar-turkey.com)
Demos (www.demos-ltd.com.tr/)
İstanbul Real Estate (www.istanbulrealestate.com)
Home in Turkey (www.homeinturkey.com)
Kuşadası Homes (www.kusadasihomes.com)
Lameta (www.lameta.com)
Property-Turkey (www.property-turkey.co.uk)
Real Estate Turkey (www.realestateturkey.co.uk)
Turkey Real Estate (www.turkeyrealestate.com)

Specialist UK-Based Lawyers

Bennett & Co Solicitors: 144 Knutsford Road, Wilmslow, Cheshire SK9 6JP; ☎01625-586937; fax 01625-585362; e-mail: internationallawyers@bennett-and-co.com;

www.bennett-and-co.com.

John Howell & Co: The Old Glassworks, 22 Endell Street, Covent Garden, London WC2H 9AD; ☎020 7420 0400; fax 020 7836 3626; e-mail info@europelaw.com; www.europelaw.com.

ADVERTS

Some properties are advertised in newspapers either privately or through estate agents; look in the *Turkish Daily News* as a starting point.

Several websites also offer Turkish houses for sale and some of them are perfectly trustworthy. However, some of them show pictures of houses that are not even for sale or that haven't been built yet. You may also spot *Satılık Ev* (House for Sale) signs and phone numbers scrawled on walls.

Do not neglect also to check the property pages of UK newspapers Turkey is beginning to feature increasingly in articles, and adverts from developers in Turkey occasionally appear in them.

PROPERTY EXHIBITIONS

Until recently Turkish properties rarely featured at UK property exhibitions. However, as the market grows, it is more likely that at least the more expensive options will be advertised overseas. To find out when and where the next property exhibition will be taking place check out www.tsn.co.uk or www.internationalpropertyshow.com.

INTERNET

The internet is not widely used in Turkey yet to sell property, but it is still worth using a search engine to look for property in a named, popular area such as Dalaman or Alanya, to find agents' and property developers' properties as well as sites on which owners sell direct. Some estate agents contact details including websites are listed at the beginning of *Where to Find Your Ideal Property*.

WHAT TYPE OF PROPERTY TO BUY

APARTMENTS

Turks commonly live in apartments and buying an apartment certainly offers several advantages, especially if you choose a newly-built block. Firstly, you shouldn't have to do much work before you can move into it. Then there are plenty of apartment blocks all over Turkey and prices are usually fairly reasonable. If you don't plan to stay in Turkey all the time an apartment offers less of a security risk than a house. And because Turks themselves love apartments you will probably be able to sell your apartment if you decide to move.

Most apartment blocks in Turkey consist of a series of individually-owned flats sharing some common services, most notably those of a *kapıcı* (concierge) who looks after the cleaning of the common areas. Some *kapıcıs* also fetch bread and newspapers or pay the fuel bills for you. Normally all residents pay the *kapıcı* a small monthly fee.

In general Turkish building standards are poor and some newly-built apartment blocks have collapsed even without the stresses of an earthquake so it's worth paying a structural engineer to check the building before you buy into it.

Many of the older apartment blocks in Istanbul look fairly sturdy. However, maintenance standards are rarely high and you should assume that you will probably have to pay for rewiring and other structural repairs before moving in.

CO-OPERATIVE HOUSING

Because of the lack of a mortgage system, many Turks buy their homes through co-operative housing schemes. Every month they pay money to the co-operative developers so that they can proceed with the next phase of building. In general, this is an option only likely to appeal to people married to Turks since it is a slow way of buying with obvious potential for coming unstuck: some developers go bankrupt before work on the complex is complete; others have been known to make off with the money entrusted to them. However, theoretically buying into a high-quality co-operative housing scheme could make a good long-term investment.

SHARED OWNERSHIP

Some foreigners buy with Turkish friends or partners. In theory there is nothing wrong with this provided that both buyers are in a position to make an equal investment. However, all too often it is the foreigner who provides most of the capital and all too often the end result is argument over who owns what. In such disputes a Turk will usually come out on top simply because they understand the language and the legal system better than the foreigner.

No one should buy with a Turk without taking legal advice first. They should also have known the person with whom they plan to buy for a long time. Certainly they should never agree to a situation in which the *tapu* (title deed) is only in the Turk's name since this means that legally they are the sole owner.

VILLAS

Along the coast there are many villas or duplexes – two-storey buildings in their own plots of land. These are very popular with foreigners, especially the British. However, the value of new villas is sometimes inflated by estate agents who assure foreign buyers that they will rise in value when Turkey joins the European Union. Of course Turkey's future EU membership is not yet certain. Nor is it certain that people will buy second-hand properties whose price has been marked up to allow a profit for the owner when they could buy a brand-new villa more cheaply.

TOWN HOUSES

It is still sometimes possible to buy a house instead of an apartment and some of the most desirable properties will be old wooden houses dating back to Ottoman times or old stone houses dating back to before 1923 and owned in the past by Greeks. In most cases such properties are in need of extensive renovation; it is advisable to get a structural survey done before agreeing to buy and to talk to other people who have bought recently to find out much the bill is likely to come to.

CAVE HOUSES

In Cappadocia, in Central Anatolia, many foreigners buy and restore ruined cave houses. People in this region traditionally hollowed houses out of the soft tuff soil and the rock cones ('fairy chimneys') created by volcanic eruptions in prehistory. In the 1980s hoteliers cottoned on to the potential appeal of these homes as hotels, most of them now consisting of stone houses built in front of and incorporating cave networks with intriguing internal fittings which used to serve as ovens, mangers, wineries and cupboards. At the same time some foreigners started to appreciate the potential for turning such properties into homes with character. From a slow start the number of foreigners settling in Cappadocia speeded up in the late 1990s.

While it is possible to find cave houses that are just about habitable in Mustafapaşa, Ürgüp and Ortahisar, most foreigners have been buying ruins in Göreme, Uçhisar, Avanos and İbrahimpaşa and then restoring them. The initial outlay can seem very reasonable. However, in most cases at least as much again will be needed for the restoration. Even the houses that are still habitable need rewiring, modern plumbing and other major investments like the installation of central heating.

In all these cave settlements zoning restrictions apply. These are enforced by the planning officers of the *Koruma Müdürlüğü* (Conservation Management) in Nevşehir, although the local *Belediye* or *Kaymakamlık* (local authorities) will have a map of the village which indicates which zone a property falls into. In Göreme, for example, the easiest properties to buy and restore are those regarded as simple village homes whose exterior may not be changed but whose interior is not of such consequence. Houses with fairy chimneys are more problematic. Technically these continue to be the property of the government with the 'owners' having to pay an annual rent. Before permission is given for properties incorporating chimneys to be restored, would-be purchasers have to get an architect to draw up a *proje* (project) indicating what will be done. Then they have to pay for a geological survey to ensure that there is no danger of slippage. Other properties usually significant historic monuments, cannot be sold to foreigners at all.

Anne Humphreys explains the restrictions on restoring a bit of Turkey's heritage
Before finalising the contract I brought someone from the Koruma Müdürlüğü in Nevşehir to look at the property. He took pictures of the outside and wrote a list of what I could and couldn't do – basically I could change the interior but not the exterior. Fortunately although the house mainly consisted of caves they were not in a fairy chimney; if they had been I would have had to have a geological report and would have had to pay an architect to draw up a plan for the restoration. I was particularly lucky in having a friend in the village who is very interested in architecture and who supervised the building work for me.

RENTING A HOME

If you think you would like to move to Turkey it makes sense to find a rentable property in the area that you like and to live in it for some time before committing yourself to buying. This will give you a chance to find out the difference between holidaying somewhere and settling there before making the big financial outlay of buying. It will also allow you to inspect all available properties at your leisure. In rural areas where you will almost certainly end up buying directly from a property owner it will also give you a chance to tune into the local grapevine and assess the going price for properties and any potential snags.

RENTAL AGENCIES

In the cities *emlakçılar* (estate agents) deal with rentable properties too. Most are based in the area where they let properties, so if you know where you want to live it should be easy to find a local agent. The notices in their windows rarely give any more information than where the property is, its size, the number of rooms and the monthly rent, so you may have to inspect several places before finding something with a bathroom, kitchen and décor you can live with. In general top-floor flats tend to be the most expensive except in blocks which lack lifts when the reverse is true.

The agent usually charges the equivalent of one month's rent for his services (on top of perhaps two months' rent which has to be paid in advance).

English-speaking agents advertise in *Turkish Daily News* or you can ask other ex-pats for recommendations. You can also look out for signs saying *Kiralık Ev* (House for Rent) or *Kiralık Daire* (Apartment for Rent). Alternatively, it's worth checking the noticeboards at local language schools, Internet cafés with a large foreign clientele (the Yağmur Internet Café in İstanbul has a useful notice-board for anyone wanting to rent in the popular Galata or Cihangir districts) or at your embassy where foreigners looking for flatmates and people hoping to let to foreigners advertise. These are also good places to find adverts for second-hand furniture belonging to ex-pats who are on their way home.

In rural areas you will have to ask around to find rentable accommodation, but there may not be much available and you may have to stay in a pension for weeks while you look. Even when you do find something you should be prepared to do some work to make it habitable: rented accommodation often has very poor bathroom and kitchen facilities; in some cases it may even be dangerous – you should look in particular at gas water heaters in bathrooms and kitchens and if in doubt get a plumber to check their installation. Sometimes landlords will let you offset the cost of repairs and improvements against your rent. Rarely will they pay for or organise the work themselves.

Anne Humphreys rented in Göreme
It was difficult to find anywhere that didn't need to be virtually rebuilt but eventually I found what I was looking for. I had one very big room set up in Ottoman style with bench seating round the walls and a wood and coal-burning stove. The water heater was so dangerous it had to be moved before I could move in and I had to repaint everywhere and buy most of the furniture. But the rent was only about £50 a month and the views were spectacular.

TENANCY AGREEMENTS

If you rent through an estate agent you should get a tenancy agreement which sets out how much notice each side must give before vacating/reoccupying the property. The agreement normally lasts for one year during which the rent cannot be increased. It is very rare for any property inventory to be taken and you may find that everything in a flat, right down to the shower fittings, has been removed by the previous tenant.

In rural areas, tenancy agreements are unheard of and landlords think nothing of demanding their property back at a few days' notice.

In İstanbul it would be hard to find a decent rental property for less than £170/$300 per calendar month; apartments in the more popular Bosphorus suburbs can cost as much as £4,450/$8,000. Coastal rents are usually around £175 to £200 per month but in a village £50 a month might seem expensive.

Useful Contacts – Rental Agents

Evren Real Estate Agency: Küçükbebek Caddesi 3/1, Bebek, İstanbul; ☎0212-257 7284; fax 0212-265 7160; www.evreninternational.com.

Golden Key International: Francalacı Sokak 27/3, Arnavutköy, İstanbul; ☎0532-575 0808; kevenk@tnn.net

Premier Real Estate Agency: Cevdetpaşa Caddesi 33/A, Bebek, İstanbul; ☎0212-287 2797; fex 0212-263 4264; www.premieremlak.com.

FEES, CONTRACTS AND CONVEYANCING

If you are buying a town property through an estate agent you will probably need to use a lawyer, and the purchasing procedure may not seem all that different from the UK. In rural areas, however, it is common to do without a survey or a lawyer. Unless you are buying a very expensive property you will probably find conveyancing fees surprisingly reasonable; although some backhanders may be needed to speed things up, they are unlikely to be for large sums.

SURVEYS

If you are using an *avukat* (lawyer) to help you buy your property, they should organise a survey for you. If not, before buying a property you should go to the town planning office (often in the Belediye building) and find out the number of the *tapu* (title deed) for the land. If you take this to the local *tapu* office you should be able to see the deed which will tell you how much land it covers and who owns it. Armed with this information you should go back to the town planning office and check whether there are any outstanding *dilekçeler* (petitions) that are likely to affect the property: for a playground, for example. The town planner should be able to tell you about access to mains water, sewerage etc.

THE DİLEKÇE
The *dilekçe* (petition) is a very Turkish phenomenon and one that is hard for foreigners to understand. Whenever you want anything to happen, be it applying for residence or opening a new electricity account, you will have to have one of these slips of paper, written in very formal Turkish, which petitions the official to do something for you. Unless you are fluent in Turkish you will not be able to write your own *dilekçe*. Sometimes photo shops near the Belediye will prepare one for you; sometimes someone in the actual office will do it.

CONVEYANCING

Once you have agreed to buy you go to the *tapu* office with the sellers. There you will hand over the payment for the property and the officials will give you the *tapu*. When a foreigner is buying they are required to bring a *tercume* (translator) to translate the deed of sale. In practise the *tercume* usually does little more than ask you to clarify anything ambiguous about the sale.

Fees

You will need to agree a fee in advance with the estate agent since some charge considerably more than UK agents. If you use a lawyer they are likely to charge about £250 for conveyancing. The translator will charge around £25.

Heather Dixon shows how marrying a Turk makes conveyancing easy

My brother-in-law took care of the conveyancing. He carried out a search and discovered that we would have to pay five year's outstanding emlak vergisi *(property tax), an insignificant sum of money. When we were ready to exchange contracts we deposited the purchase price with a third party - a dentist. Then we all went to the* tapu *office where the dentist released the funds to the owners in a mix of sterling, marks and lira. We didn't need a translator because I was married to a Turk. Of course we understated the purchase price to reduce our tax liability.*

WHAT HAPPENS NEXT

CHAPTER SUMMARY

○ **Power cuts, water shortages** and **limited access to natural gas** are facts of life in many parts of Turkey.

○ Non-Turkish citizens can rarely get a **phone** line in their name but mobile phones are ubiquitous.

○ New owners have to pay **outstanding electricity or water bills** before they can open an account.

○ Since **burglary** is rare few people bother with security beyond a guard-dog.

○ Good **cleaners** are easy to come by, other workers more tricky.

○ People with Turkish residency can move their belongings from the UK without having to pay duty. **Importing a car** is prohibitively expensive.

○ To find **reliable builders** you will need the help of a Turkish-speaker and will need to keep watch over their work.

○ The likeliest way to make money out of a Turkish property is as **holiday accommodation**.

SERVICES

The utilities rarely function as smoothly as they do in the UK or the USA. Even in the big cities, power cuts are a fact of life, especially in winter, and when the power comes back on again it often does so erratically and damagingly. Summer water shortages are another constant, especially in the Anatolian heartlands. Nor is every part of the country connected to *doğal gaz* (natural gas).

Electricity

Provided the property you are buying already has an electricity supply, you should be able to take it over without difficulty. To open a new *abonelik* (account) you will need to visit the nearest office of TEDAŞ, the monopoly electricity supplier. You may have to bring the existing *elektrik saatı* (electricity meter) with you; any outstanding bill will have to be paid before a new account can be opened. In rural locations TEDAŞ may operate out of the Belediye (town hall).

If you are restoring an old building without an existing electricity supply you may have to pay TEDAŞ to draw up a *proje* (plan) before an electrician can start work.

Meter-readers print your electricity bill on the spot. It will show a period of 10 days within which the bill can be paid. In rural locations you may be able to pay the bill at the Belediye. Elsewhere you will have to pay the money into one of the banks indicated on the bill. Late payment incurs a fine that will be added to the next bill.

Gas

Although natural gas pipelines have been laid in most of the big cities, few rural areas have access to natural gas. Nor is this likely to change in the foreseeable future.

In big towns the gas bottle suppliers (Aygaz, İpragaz and Likidgaz) send delivery lorries around town, using recorded jingles to alert users; if you hear your supplier you call out to them to stop. In rural areas you telephone the local supplier and they deliver and connect the bottle.

In rural areas bottled propane gas is used to power everything from cookers to central heating systems. *Tüpler* (bottles) in assorted sizes are readily available; the small ones are reasonably cheap unlike the giant industrial bottles required for central heating which are both expensive (around £35 a time) and unwieldy.

If you have a *şofben* (water heater) that runs on gas it is vital to ensure that it is correctly installed. Gas water heaters should never be put in bathrooms and only in well-vented positions in kitchens. Every year people die from inhaling gas in poorly ventilated rooms.

> **Helen Dixon explains how she got natural gas installed**
> *We went to the gas company office and got an engineer to draw up a* proje. *Once that was done we could get the builders to install the pipes. The gas company sent engineers to check their work. Once that was done we paid around £50 for a new* abonelik *(account). The first person in a block who wants to connect to the natural gas supply pays for the pipes to be laid. Then if other tenants want to be connected they pay the first person a percentage of the original cost.*

Wood and Coal-Burning Stoves

In rural areas the cheapest way to heat homes is with a stove fuelled by *odun* (wood) and *kömür* (coal). There are a few year-round coal merchants; however, from August onwards lots of shops open up to sell fuel – the earlier in the year you buy, the cheaper the price. Although you can buy wood and coal by the sack, most people buy supplies for the whole winter.

The quality of coal varies considerably. The most expensive and effective is *ithal* (imported) coal. Cheaper coal is high in sulphur and doesn't always burn well.

To get a stove going you will also need kindling wood. In the country most people collect their own kindling from their fields so it is not easy for individuals to buy it. Supermarkets sometimes sell commercial firelighters or you can resort to pouring bottled cologne over your wood.

Water

If you are taking over a property with an existing *su* (water) supply, you just have to visit the Belediye (town hall) and find the water office. For a nominal fee they will change the *abonelik* (account) into your name.

Even if you are installing a new water supply the bureaucracy is minimal. You still go to the Belediye and pay a small sum to open a new account. Water-meter readers come round with machines that calculate the bill. However, you will have to go to the Belediye and pick up your bill which can be paid on the spot. You pay any environmental taxes due at the same time.

Solar Power

Increasingly Turks use solar panels to heat their water. These may look ugly (and can freeze in winter) but they usually repay the initial installation cost very quickly. A solar panel alone will not be enough to heat the water all year round, since it needs the high sun of summer to keep the supply replenished. However, with a solar panel on the roof and a wood-and-coal-burning stove in the lounge household fuel bills can be kept to a minimum.

Telephone

It is difficult for a foreigner to get a phone line installed in their own name without paying a hefty deposit and you certainly need to have established residency before you visit Türk Telekom – the sole supplier - to request a new *hat* (line). Phone bills can be paid at Türk Telekom offices or at local post offices. Although many services we take for granted (eg callback) are still unavailable you can get an itemised phone bill.

If getting a land line proves impossible, it doesn't matter since *cepler* (mobile phones) are ubiquitous. There are two mobile-phone providers: Türkcell and Telsim. To sign up for an account with one of them you will need a residency permit. You will also need to take along a subscriber with the same company who is prepared to act as your guarantor. Failing that you can buy a *Hazır Kart* which provides a set number of call units. The units can be replaced at any store displaying the *Hazır Kartı* logo.

If all else fails you can use a British mobile phone provided you have arranged a roaming facility. American mobile phones cannot be used in Turkey.

Security

Since the crime rate is low, security is not a big issue. In İstanbul and Ankara the homes of the rich and famous are ringed with barbed wire, closed off behind metal gates and staffed by security guards. However, this is the exception – elsewhere installing a burglar alarm would be seen as extraordinary although some people keep guard dogs chained in their yards,

Staff/Cleaners

To find someone to clean your house you just need to ask around; many women will happily take on the work for minimal payment. Finding other staff to work for you is not necessarily so easy. The biggest problem will be dependability, followed by an infuriating reluctance to take the initiative.

MAKING THE MOVE

Customs

Once you have a residency permit you are entitled to bring your household goods into Turkey free of customs duties. If you need to approach Customs for advice you may need the help of a Turkish friend since it is unlikely that anyone there will speak English.

Foreigners are only allowed to import a car for six months at a time. Normally its import is written into a passport to prevent it from being sold within the country. It will not, then, be possible for you to leave the country within that six-month period without taking the car with you. If you need to keep the car in the country for longer than that you should apply well in advance to the Turkish Touring and Automobile

Club for advice.

Useful Contacts – Customs and Motoring Organistions
Gümrükler (Customs) Genel Müdürlüğü: Ulus, Ankara (☎0312-310 3880).
Türkiye Türing ve Otomobil Kurumu: Birinci Oto Sanayi Sitesi Yanı. Seyrantepe, 4
    Levent, İstanbul; ☎0212-282 8140).

Removals
 Most people opt to use an international removals firm although other people have
found more ingenious ways of moving their belongings. Problems are unlikely to
occur until your belongings reach İstanbul where the port authorities are notoriously
corrupt. You will probably need assistance from a Turkish friend to get your belongings
released from the Customs warehouses there.
    Within Turkey there is a very effective domestic cargo system; just find a local office
of Aras Kargo and tell them what it is that you want to move. They deliver all over the
country although they may leave your belongings in the nearest town rather than trek
out to a village. The company takes charge of packing whatever you want to deliver
but will not carry anything fragile or valuable unless it is insured.
    Some professional removal services operate in the big cities. They are not usually
very expensive but will charge separately for hiring the removal vehicle and the men
needed to do the work. In rural areas most removals are done by tractor and trailer.
You ask around until you find someone whose tractor is not otherwise engaged and ask
the owner to find men to help him move your belongings.

Useful Addresses – Removers
Dolphin Movers: 2 Haslemere Business Centre, Lincoln Way, Enfield EN1 1TE;
    ☎020-8804 7700; www.dolphinmovers.com
Cargomonde: ☎0212-249 6479; fax 0212-249 6480; www.cargomonde.com
For more removal companies see the *Removals and Pets* section of the *General
Introduction.*

Importing Pets
You can import one dog, one cat, one bird and ten fish into Turkey. A dog or cat
must have a **Certificate of Origin** and a **Certificate of Health** which is less than 15
days old and confirms that it has had an anti-rabies vaccination (rabies is endemic in
Turkey).
    In general Turks rarely keep pets other than birds and fish so most vets outside the
big cities are only used to treating farm animals and charge a lot for vaccinations,
neutering, anti-flea treatment etc. In İstanbul more people keep cats and dogs but
most vet's surgeries are in the wealthier parts of town.
    Tinned cat and dog food is hard to find especially outside İstanbul, Ankara and
İzmir. It is also expensive (over £1 a tin). Sacks of dry food are just as expensive. Cat
litter is also hard to find outside the big cities.

BUILDING OR RENOVATING
Finding reliable builders and decorators can be tricky. Given the number of cowboys
at work, it is essential to take advice from locals and then to go and check the work to
see how competent it was. To ensure it is carried out properly you need to be on the site
most of the time; you could employ a supervisor but would need to be sure that their

taste coincided closely with yours. Turkish workers are rarely good at finishing things off well; electricity sockets will be installed any old how, with holes bashed through tiles to fit them in; tiles are stuck up at any angle; rawl-plugs are optional extras; and paint is sprayed on without using dust covers.

Turkish building practice is also very idiosyncratic. For example, if you order a window from a *marangoz* (carpenter) the glass isn't automatically installed; usually you have to contact and pay a *camcı* (glazier) separately. Likewise, if you have cupboards made you will have to remember to add the price of painting and varnishing onto the carpenter's quote.

The quality of building materials is improving: ten years ago it was hard to find attractive bathroom tiles; now they are everywhere. If you buy in bulk you usually qualify for a discount, especially if you pay in cash (you can usually pay in instalments as well).

Hiring Workers

Unless your Turkish is fluent you will need to find a Turk – and preferably someone you know and trust - to hire the workers for you. There are different rates of pay for different tasks and most will seem low by Western Europe standards (typically around £20 a day). Oddly enough, they can be even cheaper in a big city like İstanbul where there is a lot of competition. The *sanayi sitesi* (industrial estate) on the outskirts of town is a good place to find carpenters, upholsterers, ironmongers and other workers.

Builders often work in teams under an *usta* (master craftsman) who oversees what is done and makes all the decisions; you discuss your requirements with the *usta* who relays them on to his team. The *usta* commands a higher rate of pay than his workers. Usually you pay the *usta* and he divides it up amongst his team.

> **Sandra Brown on backhanders and plumbing**
> *Some of my builders turned out to be moonlighting shepherds so I wouldn't recommend accepting the cheapest quote offered. I also suspected the usta of adding his own cut to the backhanders he paid along the way. The biggest problem was the plumbing, but that seems to be a common experience in Turkey.*

DIY

Those who are good at DIY are at a considerable advantage when it comes to renovating a property. Not only will they know what needs to be done but they may well be able to do it at least as well as the so-called professionals. Increasingly in the big towns there are big DIY warehouses (İstanbul has a big branch of Bauhaus across the road from the Esenler bus station), which stock everything you need.

> **Heather Dixon on her renovation discoveries and DIY restoration**
> *When we removed the lino we found beautiful floorboards underneath which had to be stripped and polished. We removed all the peeling wallpaper and ten layers of paint from the wooden wall panels which now match the floorboards. Best of all as soon as the painter started work on the ceiling he told us that the soot concealed lovely 19th-century frescoes. I was able to restore these myself and now only the bathroom (where the ceiling fell down) is without frescoes.*

Swimming Pools

The best villa complexes in coastal areas come with pools included. Elsewhere you need to bear in mind that water shortages can be a problem at exactly the time of year that a pool seems most desirable; for that reason it may be difficult to get planning permission to build a pool in areas such as Cappadocia.

If you decide to install a private pool you will need to ask around for reliable workmen. The best and most economical swimming pools are those that fill right to the top and have an overflow which carries off scum and leaves. Excess water is then passed through a sand filter which cleans it ready for recycling into the pool. However, installing a pool like this can cost up to £20,000. Cheaper pools without filters quickly go green and have to have their water changed every year.

Gardens

In the big towns and along the coast garden centres sell plants, trees and garden furniture. Elsewhere, your best option may be to visit the local market in spring when plants and soil are usually on sale. Finding a professional gardener is likely to be difficult although finding labourers to do the heavy work will not be.

MAKING MONEY FROM YOUR PROPERTY

The most obvious way to make money out of a property in Turkey is to run it as a pension or hotel or let it out on a self-catering basis. In theory it is possible to buy a property, restore and modernise it, and sell it on at a profit but it would take a fairly canny buyer to work the Turkish property market effectively without years of experience and a good grasp of the language. Certainly it would be a mistake to assume you could make the sort of windfall fortunes associated with property development in the UK or Spain.

Hotel and Pensions

Many foreigners have proved adept at running hotels and pensions in Turkey, especially when they are married to or in partnership with a Turk. Because Turkish and Western culture is so different, foreigners can bring an understanding to the business that is difficult for all but the most worldly Turks. Foreign tourists often show a preference for staying in hotels and pensions with foreign owners if only because they know they will be able to communicate with them in their own language.

However, competition in most of the resorts is fierce and growing fiercer and tourism to Turkey was badly affected by external politics in the early 2000s. It will probably pick up again but the combination of growing competition and falling visitor numbers has left many hotels and pension-owners struggling to keep going.

If you do decide to open a pension the bureaucracy may initially sound quite daunting. However, provided you speak Turkish or are going into business with a Turk much of it is routine. You will not be allowed to open a pension right beside a mosque, a school or a Belediye building and you will need a licence from the local police and from the Belediye. Before granting a licence the police will want to see, among other documents:

O   planning permission for the building
O   a health certificate showing that you don't have any infectious diseases
O   a fire certificate for the building

- a photo-copy of the *tapu*
- a note from the *muhtar* (neighbourhood official) confirming your identity and residency status
- proof that you have a clean police record

In most areas prices are set by the local authority annually; you can charge less than they say but not more. Would-be hoteliers also need to be aware that there are much higher tariffs for water and electricity and that they will have to undergo medical check-ups every year in order to keep their licence.

Running a Business from Your Property

There is nothing to stop people running simple businesses from their home. For example, some Turkish expatriates are writers, artists and photographers who can just as readily work from their homes in Turkey as from their homes in the UK or the USA, albeit on the margins of legality. To do anything more overt without a work permit would be to court the unwelcome attentions of the authorities.

Renting Out

Some types of property lend themselves to being rented out more readily than others. For example, some owners of historic houses in Istanbul have been able to lease them to the embassies to house their staff for worthwhile rents. Elsewhere, however, rents are often so low that letting a property would barely cover the cost of the inevitable wear and tear.

Foreigners who have bought homes in the resorts do have the option, however, of renting out their houses as holiday homes. This can be much more lucrative since tourists will not be familiar with the low level of local rents – besides which they will almost certainly be looking for higher standards of equipment and décor and for a sea view. Technically this is not legal without a work permit. However, the chances of being found out are small.

Heather Dixon in Istanbul rented out her flat there
We contacted the British Consulate and asked if they would like our flat for members of their staff and that worked very well. Eventually I was able to save enough from the rental income to buy out my (now ex) husband's share in the flat and move back into it myself.

Selling On

The market for second-hand homes is still in its infancy which makes it hard to assess the potential for reselling at a profit but there are few signs as yet to suggest that anyone can make a quick buck this way, particularly if they have had to pay a lot to modernise a property. Probably the easiest properties to resell would be the apartments in city-centre locations which are most popular with Turks. However, foreigners are rarely interested in buying these.

People moving into areas like Cappadocia usually want to pick their own ruin and mould it to their own image rather than buying a property that has already been restored to someone else's requirements. However, for those prepared to bide their time, it could well be that a resale market will develop. Certainly when one couple in Cappadocia were forced to sell their beautifully-restored house, it was widely believed that the new owner had bought it as an investment rather than because he wanted to live in it.

TURKISH GLOSSARY

Account with a utilities company	*abonelik*
Accountant	*muhasebeci*
Carpenter	*marangoz*
Conservation Management	*Koruma Müdürlüğü*
Environment and cleaning tax	*çevre ve temizlik vergisi*
Estate agent	*emlakçı*
Foreman of building team	*usta*
Identity card	*kimlik*
Income tax	*gelir vergisi*
Lawyer	*avukat*
Local official	*muhtar*
Mobile phone	*cep telefon*
Mobile phone prepaid cards	*hazir kart*
Natural gas	*doğal gaz*
Petition (asking permission from officials)	*dileçke*
Plan (e.g. for building project)	*proje*
Post office	*postane*
Property tax paid on property purchase	*emlak vergisi*
Residency permit	*ikamet tezkeresi*
Security Police (for visa renewal)	*Emniyet Müdürlüğü*
Title deed	*tapu*
Town hall	*belediye*
VAT	*katma değer vergisi (KDV)*
Work permit	*çalışma vizesi*

SPOT CHECK – TURKEY	
Political/ economic stability:	Neither the 'democratic' government, nor the economy is very stable. The army still uses its power to influence political events. Until recently inflation was running at over 50%. Turkey wants to join the EU but some pundits say it will take her ten years to achieve the necessary criteria.
Climate:	In İstanbul and along the Aegean and Mediterranean coasts temperatures can reach 40C in July and August and rarely go below freezing in winter.
Cost of living/ taxes	Considerably cheaper to live in than any other Mediterranean hot property spot. Income tax is paid by the self-employed at 15-40% but is commonly dodged. VAT is paid at variable rates.
Accessibility:	No low cost operators but plenty of charter flights May to October to Bodrum, İzmir and Dalaman. Not cheap; £179 return to Dalaman in June 2004.
Property availability:	Mostly new build. Very little resale yet. Rural or village properties may have buying restrictions for foreigners – they must not be in a military zone. In practice, permission can be sought in military areas.
Property prices:	Cheap, cheap, cheap. Some estate agents advertising apartments from £14,000. But prices in a state of flux; some going up and others, especially in parts of Istanbul where earthquake expectancy is strong going down.
Costs of property purchase:	Some people have bought rural property without a lawyer or an estate agent and paid only the 1.5% property tax. Otherwise, total is usually 4.5% including 3% agent's commission.
Ease of purchase/ease of renovation:	Can be very bureaucratic if buying a rural or heritage property. New build easier. Lots of builders to do restoration but standards very variable and mostly slipshod finishing.
Annual property taxes:	Negligible. £20-£30 a year. New build exempt for five years
Investment potential:	Anything possible in the next ten years especially if Turkey joins the EU. Prices going up so plan your purchase carefully to maximise potential.
Suitability for letting:	The best bet is to have a property near a resort. Technically, this is not legal without a work permit, but being discovered is rare. Although renting in Turkey is very cheap, you can justify charging holiday-makers more for higher standards.
Other:	The threat of earthquake hangs like the sword of Damocles over Istanbul. Rabies is endemic throughout Turkey.

Complete guides to life abroad from Vacation Work

Live & Work Abroad

Live & Work in Australia & New Zealand..£10.99
Live & Work in Belgium, The Netherlands & Luxembourg.........................£10.99
Live & Work in China £11.95
Live & Work in France...£10.99
Live & Work in Germany £10.99
Live & Work in Ireland £10.99
Live & Work in Italy...£10.99
Live & Work in Japan...£10.99
Live & Work in Russia & Eastern Europe £10.99
Live & Work in Saudi & the Gulf...£10.99
Live & Work in Scandinavia..£10.99
Live & Work in Scotland..£10.99
Live & Work in Spain & Portugal £10.99
Live & Work in the USA & Canada £10.99

Buying a House Abroad

Buying a House in France...£11.95
Buying a House in Italy..£11.95
Buying a House in Portugal...£11.95
Buying a House in Spain..£11.95
Buying a House on the Mediterranean £13.95

Starting a Business Abroad

Starting a Business in France £12.95
Starting a Business in Spain £12.95

Available from good bookshops or direct from the publishers
Vacation Work, 9 Park End Street, Oxford OX1 1HJ
Tel 01865-241978 * Fax 01865-790885 * www.vacationwork.co.uk

In the US: available at bookstores everywhere
or from The Globe Pequot Press (www.GlobePequot.com)